Microsoft® Specialist Guide to Microsoft® Windows 10 (Exam 70-697, Configuring Windows Devices)

Byron Wright
Leon Plesniarski

CENGAGE
Learning·

Australia • Brazil • Mexico • Singapore • United Kingdom • United States

Microsoft® Specialist Guide to Microsoft® Windows 10 (Exam 70-697, Configuring Windows Devices)
Byron Wright, Leon Plesniarski

SVP, GM Science, Technology & Math: Balraj S. Kalsi

Senior Product Director: Kathleen McMahon

Product Team Manager: Kristin McNary

Associate Product Manager: Amy Savino

Senior Director, Development: Julia Caballero

Content Development Manager: Leigh Hefferon

Senior Content Developer: Michelle Ruelos Cannistraci

Product Assistant: Abigail Pufpaff

Marketing Director: Michelle McTighe

Production Director: Patty Stephan

Senior Content Project Manager: Brooke Greenhouse

Art Director: Jack Pendleton

Cover image: iStockPhoto.com/monsitj

For product information and technology assistance, contact us at
Cengage Learning Customer & Sales Support, 1-800-354-9706.

For permission to use material from this text or product,
submit all requests online at **www.cengage.com/permissions.**
Further permissions questions can be e-mailed to
permissionrequest@cengage.com.

Library of Congress Control Number: 2016944367

Student Edition:
ISBN-13: 978-1-285-86857-8

Losse-leaf Edition:
ISBN-13: 978-1-337-68341-8

Cengage Learning
20 Channel Center Street
Boston, MA 02210
USA

Cengage Learning is a leading provider of customized learning solutions with employees residing in nearly 40 different countries and sales in more than 125 countries around the world. Find your local representative at **www.cengage.com.**

Cengage Learning products are represented in Canada by Nelson Education, Ltd.

To learn more about Cengage Learning, visit **www.cengage.com**

Purchase any of our products at your local college store or at our preferred online store **www.cengagebrain.com**

Printed in the United States of America
Print Number: 02   Print Year: 2017

Brief Contents

Contents

CHAPTER 5
User Management

CHAPTER 6
Windows 10 Security Features

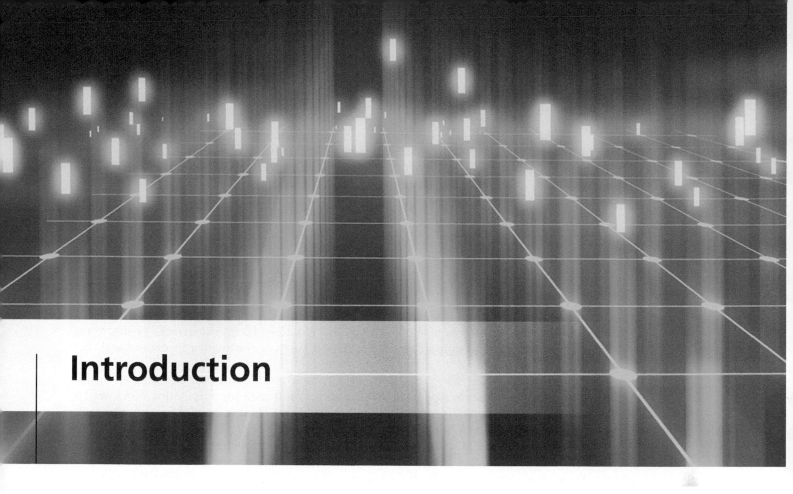

Introduction

Welcome to *Microsoft® Specialist Guide to Microsoft® Windows 10*. This book offers you real-world examples, interactive activities, and many hands-on activities that reinforce key concepts and prepare you for a career in network administration using Microsoft Windows 10. This book also features troubleshooting tips for solutions to common problems that you will encounter in the realm of Windows 10 administration.

This book offers in-depth study of all the functions and features of installing, configuring, and maintaining Windows 10 as a client operating system. Throughout the book, we provide detailed hands-on activities that let you experience firsthand the processes involved in Windows 10 configuration and management. We then provide pointed Review Questions to reinforce the concepts introduced in each chapter and help you prepare for the Microsoft certification exam. Finally, to put a real-world slant on the concepts introduced in each chapter, we provide Case Projects to prepare you for situations that must be managed in a live networking environment.

Certification

Microsoft Specialist Guide to Microsoft Windows 10 is intended for people getting started in computer networking as well as experienced network administrators new to Windows 10. To best understand the material in this book, you should have a background in basic computer concepts and have worked with applications in a Windows environment. The Microsoft Specialist certification allows technology professionals to prove their expertise in working with specific Microsoft technologies. This book prepares you to take exam 70-697: Configuring Windows Devices, which leads to the Microsoft Specialist certification in Windows 10. In addition, if you have a Microsoft Certified Solutions Associate (MCSA) certification in Windows 8, you can upgrade this certification to an MCSA in Windows 10 by completing exam 70-697. After completing this book, you will not only be prepared to take the certification exam, but will also be prepared to implement and maintain Windows 10 in a business environment.

New to This Edition

The entire book has been updated from Windows 7 to Windows 10, covering the functions and features of installing, configuring, and maintaining Windows 10 as a client operating system. New activities, review questions, and case projects have been created to reinforce the concepts and techniques presented in each chapter and to help you apply these concepts to real-world scenarios. A new, full-color interior design brings the material to life and full-color screenshots provide a more detailed look at the Microsoft Windows 10 interface.

Chapter Outline

The topics covered in the 14 chapters of this book are comprehensive and organized as described in the following descriptions.

Chapter 1, Introduction to Windows 10, outlines the versions of Windows 10 and discusses the new and enhanced features in Windows 10. The Windows 10 user interface, hardware requirements, and application support are also covered. Finally, connectivity applications and networking models are discussed.

In **Chapter 2,** Installing Windows 10, we discuss the considerations for choosing an installation method and installation type. We also explore the tools used for automating Windows 10 deployment in the Windows 10 Assessment and Deployment Toolkit. Installation options such as imaging, provisioning, and Windows To Go are discussed.

Chapter 3, Using the System Utilities, examines the tools used to manage Windows 10. These include Administrative Tools and settings. These are used to configure hardware components, power management, and display settings, and to schedule tasks. Windows PowerShell is also introduced.

In **Chapter 4,** Managing Disks and File Systems, we explore disk technologies and partition styles. Basic disks, dynamic disks, and virtual hard disks are discussed, including the tools to manage them. The new Storage Spaces disk management feature is discussed in depth, along with file permissions.

Chapter 5, User Management, covers the creation and management of user accounts for Windows 10. The new Windows 10 authentication methods are discussed. In addition, user profiles and integration with Windows-based networks are explained.

Chapter 6, Windows 10 Security Features, explores a wide variety of security settings in Windows 10, including the local security policy, auditing, User Account Control, and malware. Data security features such as Encrypting File System and BitLocker are also covered. Finally, managing Windows Updates is covered.

Chapter 7, Networking, has comprehensive coverage of networking connectivity in Windows 10. There is a discussion of IP version 4 and IP version 6. Data sharing with file shares and homegroups is explored. There is also coverage of Internet connectivity, wireless networking, and Windows Firewall.

In **Chapter 8,** User Productivity Tools, we identify features to manage files and printing. File management with File Explorer and OneDrive are both covered. Installation and management of printers by using various methods is explored. Finally, features in Microsoft Edge and Internet Explorer are covered.

Chapter 9, Windows 10 Application Support, examines the application types that can run in Windows 10, the installation types for each, and app compatibility solutions. We also cover the registry, virtual desktops, and RemoteApp.

Chapter 10, Performance Tuning and System Recovery, details how to use tools such as Performance Monitor, Resource Monitor, and Task Manager to identify and resolve performance problems. Tools for data backup and recovery are also discussed. Finally, the various tools for system recovery such as Windows Recovery, device driver rollback, and System Refresh are explained.

In **Chapter 11,** Microsoft Intune Device Management, we describe how you can use Microsoft Intune to manage mobile devices and non-domain-joined computers. Processes for controlling app deployment and Windows updates are covered. Mobile device management functions such as remote wipe are also explained.

Chapter **12**, Client Hyper-V, explains how to install and use Hyper-V in Windows 10. Concepts related to virtual machines, virtual memory, virtual processors, virtual hard disks, and virtual network adapters are explained. Management options for virtual machines are also covered.

Chapter **13**, Enterprise Computing, describes and demonstrates management features that are required in larger organizations. There is an overview of Active Directory concepts, followed by an explanation of how Group Policy can be used to manage many computers. Enterprise deployment and management tools, including Windows Deployment Services, Windows Server Update Services, and Microsoft BitLocker Administration and Monitoring, are discussed. Finally, we describe Distributed File System and BranchCache.

In **Chapter 14**, Remote Access and Client Support, we describe how you can implement remote data access and data synchronization for mobile and remote clients. For remote access, virtual private networks and DirectAccess are explained. Remote Desktop and Remote Assistance for computer support are configured. Data synchronizations using offline files and Work Folders are discussed.

Appendix **A**, Microsoft Windows Exam 70-697 Objectives, maps each exam objective to the chapter and section where you can find information on that objective.

Appendix **B**, Preparing for Certification Exams, provides strategies and additional resources for studying for the 70-697 exam.

Features and Approach

Microsoft Specialist Guide to Microsoft Windows 10 differs from other networking books in its unique hands-on approach and its orientation to real-world situations and problem solving. To help you see how Microsoft Windows 10 concepts and techniques are applied in real-world organizations, this book incorporates the following features:

Chapter Objectives—Each chapter begins with a detailed list of the concepts to be mastered. This list gives you a quick reference to the chapter's contents and is a useful study aid.

Activities—Activities are incorporated throughout the text, giving you practice in setting up, managing, and troubleshooting a network system. The activities give you a strong foundation for carrying out network administration tasks in the real world. Because of the book's progressive nature, completing the activities in each chapter is essential before moving on to the end-of-chapter materials and subsequent chapters.

Chapter Summaries—Each chapter's text is followed by a summary of the concepts introduced in that chapter. These summaries provide a helpful way to recap and revisit the ideas covered in each chapter.

Key Terms—All terms introduced with boldfaced text are gathered together in the Key Terms list at the end of the chapter. This provides you with a method of checking your understanding of all the terms introduced.

Review Questions—The end-of-chapter assessment begins with a set of Review Questions that reinforce the ideas introduced in each chapter. Answering these questions correctly will ensure that you have mastered the important concepts.

Case Projects—Finally, each chapter closes with a section that proposes certain situations. You are asked to evaluate the situations and decide upon the course of action to be taken to remedy the problems described. This valuable tool will help you sharpen your decision-making and troubleshooting skills, which are important aspects of network administration.

Text and Graphic Conventions

Additional information and exercises have been added to this book to help you better understand what's being discussed in the chapter. Icons throughout the text alert you to these additional materials. The icons used in this book are described as follows:

Tips offer extra information on resources, how to attack problems, and time-saving shortcuts.

Notes present additional helpful material related to the subject being discussed.

The Caution icon identifies important information about potential mistakes or hazards.

Each hands-on activity in this book is preceded by the Activity icon.

Case Project icons mark the end-of-chapter case projects, which are scenario-based assignments that ask you to independently apply what you have learned in the chapter.

Instructor Companion Site

Everything you need for your course is in one place! This collection of book-specific lecture and class tools is available online via *www.cengage.com/login*. Access and download PowerPoint presentations, images, the Instructor's Manual, Solutions Manual, Test creation tools, Syllabus, and more.

- *Electronic Instructor's Manual*—The Instructor's Manual that accompanies this book includes additional instructional material to assist in class preparation, including suggestions for classroom activities, discussion topics, and additional quiz questions.

- *Solutions Manual*—The instructor's resources include solutions to all end-of-chapter material, including review questions and case projects.

- *Cengage Learning Testing Powered by Cognero*—This flexible, online system allows you to do the following:

  ○ Author, edit, and manage test bank content from multiple Cengage Learning solutions.

  ○ Create multiple test versions in an instant.

  ○ Deliver tests from your LMS, your classroom, or wherever you want.

- *PowerPoint presentations*—This book comes with Microsoft PowerPoint slides for each chapter. They're included as a teaching aid for classroom presentation, to make available to students on the network for chapter review, or to be printed for classroom distribution. Instructors, please feel free to add your own slides for additional topics you introduce to the class.

- *Figure files*—All the figures and tables in the book are reproduced in bitmap format. Similar to the PowerPoint presentations, they're included as a teaching aid for classroom presentation, to make available to students for review, or to be printed for classroom distribution.

MindTap for *Microsoft Specialist Guide to Microsoft Windows 10 (Exam 70-697, Configuring Windows Devices)*

MindTap is an online learning solution designed to help students master the skills they need in today's workforce. Research shows employers need critical thinkers, troubleshooters, and creative problem solvers to stay relevant in our fast-paced, technology-driven world. MindTap helps you achieve this with assignments and activities that provide hands-on practice, real-life relevance, and certification test prep. Students are guided through assignments that help them master basic knowledge and understanding before moving on to more challenging problems.

MindTap activities and assignments are tied to Microsoft certification exam 70-697 objectives. The hands-on labs provide real-life application and practice. The IQ certification test prep engine allows students to quiz themselves on specific exam domains, and the pre- and post-course assessments are mock exams that measure exactly how much they have learned. Readings, labs, and whiteboard videos support the lecture, while "In The News" assignments encourage students to stay current. MindTap is designed around learning objectives and provides the analytics and reporting to easily see where the class stands in terms of progress, engagement, and completion rates. Use the content and learning path as is or pick and choose how our materials will wrap around yours. You control what the students see and when they see it. Learn more at *http://www.cengage.com/mindtap/*.

Instant Access Code: (ISBN: 9781337282222)

Printed Access Code: (ISBN: 9781337282239)

CourseNotes

This laminated quick reference card introduces critical knowledge for the Microsoft Windows 10, Exam 70-697 in a visual and user-friendly format. CourseNotes serve as a useful study aid to the textbook, or as a quick reference tool during the course and afterward.
ISBN: 9781305072459

Before You Begin

Almost all of the activities in this book can be completed by using a single computer running Windows 10. For the computer running Windows 10, you can use a physical computer or a virtual machine, whichever is the most convenient. However, there are some special considerations:

- Chapter 12, Client Hyper-V, requires a physical computer. The hardware requirements to implement Client Hyper-V are met by most modern computers and are listed in Chapter 12. A minimum of 4 GB of RAM and a processor that supports hardware virtualization are required.

- Chapter 13, Enterprise Computing, requires a second computer to act as a server to complete activities. This server is running Windows Server 2016 and instructions for installation are provided in Chapter 13.

Software

All activities that require specific software to be downloaded provide links within the lab. However, it is beneficial to download some of the larger pieces of software ahead of time and make them available for students. Installation steps for the software are provided in the appropriate activities. The software recommended for download ahead of time is:

- Windows 10 Enterprise Edition (Trial)—*https://www.microsoft.com/en-us/evalcenter/evaluate-windows-10-enterprise*

- Windows 10 Assessment and Deployment Toolkit—*https://msdn.microsoft.com/en-us/windows/hardware/dn913721.aspx*

- Windows Server 2016 Evaluation—*https://www.microsoft.com/en-us/evalcenter/evaluate-windows-server-technical-preview*

Classroom Setup: Notes for Instructors

Although this course can be performed on physical computers, it is significantly easier to manage if you use virtual machines. Some activities performed in the course are destructive to the local operating system configuration or applications. This makes it undesirable for students to use a physical computer. Students could use Client Hyper-V to create and manage their own virtual machines. Or, virtual machines could be hosted on a server.

Activities from Chapter 12, Client Hyper-V, can only be performed on a physical computer. If it is not possible for students to use a physical computer to complete these activities, consider demonstrating them in the classroom by using a single computer.

 If you are using server virtualization, VMware ESX and Hyper-V in Windows Server 2016 support nested virtualization. In such a scenario, Client Hyper-V could be enabled in a Windows 10 virtual machine to complete the activities in Chapter 13.

Activities from Chapter 13, Enterprise Computing, require Windows Server in a separate virtual machine. The ideal scenario is for students to each have their own virtual machine for running Windows Server 2016 and joining their own domain. To avoid naming conflicts, you will need to provide students with a unique naming system for domains and unique IP addresses for the servers. These requirements are noted in the appropriate activities.

It is assumed that the client computers are using a dynamic IP address and that there is connectivity to the Internet. Some Activities require students to access the Internet. This is a requirement when accessing cloud-based resources, such as a Microsoft account, OneDrive, and Microsoft Intune.

Acknowledgments

We would like to thank the entire team that we have worked with at Cengage Learning. As on previous projects, you help us take what we know and turn it into an excellent book that can help people improve within the IT industry.

In particular, we would like to thank Deb Kaufmann and Karen Annett, whose suggestions invariably led to improved readability and clarity. We would also like to thank Danielle Shaw, who painstakingly reviewed every step in every activity to verify the accuracy of the steps. A special thanks to Tony Chen (College of DuPage), David Parker (Arizona Western College), and Paul Weisinger (Wisconsin Indianhead Technical College), the peer reviewers who evaluated the first draft of our chapters and provided feedback on them. Your insights were a valuable contribution to the book.

Byron would like to thank his family Tracey, Samantha, and Michelle for tolerating cranky Daddy on a deadline every once in a while. He'd also like to thank every student from his classes who helped him learn to explain technical concepts in a way that people understand.

Leon would like to thank his loving wife, Angela, and his boys, Tyler, Terry, Andrew, Nathaniel, and Matthew, for sharing their family time with all the people who will use this book as part of their greater education. Always learn, always improve yourself.

About the Authors

Byron Wright (@ByronWrightGeek) is the owner of BTW Technology Solutions, which provides Exchange Server and Office 365 implementation and migration services. Byron is a Microsoft MVP for Exchange Server since 2012. He has a broad range of knowledge about Microsoft operating systems, Active Directory, networking, security, and cloud services.

As a Microsoft Certified Trainer (MCT), Byron provides practical advice and exam-relevant content to a wide variety of organizations. He has authored and co-authored a number of books for Cengage Learning on Windows Server 2003, Exchange Server 2003, Windows Vista, and

Windows 7. Byron also occasionally teaches information systems course for the Asper School of Business at the University of Manitoba. You can view Byron's blog with technology content at *http://byronwright.blogspot.com*.

Leon Plesniarski is a Senior Solutions Architect who has been building with Microsoft Products since 1984. Leon's formal training was in Computer and Electrical Engineering, but he has since applied his skills primarily in computer networking. Leon has worked as a network administrator and technical instructor. He currently works as a consultant for Broadview Networks to analyze client requirements and provide practical solutions for their needs. In recent years, he has had a strong focus on Microsoft cloud services, such as Windows Azure, Office 365, and Microsoft Intune.

Leon leverages his teaching skills and experience as a Microsoft Certified Trainer (MCT) to create learning materials that are technically accurate and easy to understand. He has previously created course materials for A+ certification. For Cengage Learning, he has authored books on Windows Vista and Windows 7.

chapter 1

Introduction to Windows 10

After reading this chapter and completing the exercises, you will be able to:

- Describe the versions of Windows 10
- Discuss the new and enhanced features in Windows 10
- Understand the Windows 10 user interface
- Define the hardware requirements and understand the hardware support of Windows 10
- Describe the application support built in to Windows 10
- Identify essential connectivity applications used in Windows 10
- Understand the networking models supported by different versions of Windows 10

Microsoft is moving Windows away from its heritage of enabling a single device like a personal computer to a world that is more intuitive for users, enables mobility, and has a core foundation of trust. Windows 10 features a universal application platform that provides a consistent experience across a variety of devices, not just personal computers.

With its latest client operating system, Windows 10, Microsoft safely and reliably connects users with the information they need in the digital cloud-enabled world, providing enhanced user interface and operating system features. Applications, services, and content can potentially move seamlessly across multiple devices, which enables people to stay productive and connected on the move.

Windows 10 is the successor to the previous Microsoft client operating system, Windows 8.1. The computing community was slow to adopt Windows 8 and Windows 8.1 largely due to the perception that the user interfaces and upgrade costs over Windows 7 were not popular. Many businesses had just completed an upgrade from Windows XP to Windows 7 and they were challenged to endure another round of upgrades and new equipment purchases.

Windows 10 maximizes performance on today's hardware, which is very important as new computers and processors no longer fully support older versions of Windows. Hardware manufacturers have started to produce devices that have no compatibility with older Windows operating systems and must be used with Windows 10. This allows a new and wide range of innovative and even revolutionary devices to operate with Windows 10, streamlined to operate with agility because of longer battery life, faster boot times, improved responsiveness, and thinner and lighter hardware designs. Using Windows 10 is meant to be more enjoyable and productive for users. The user has many device choices with a variety of price points, feature sets, and performance levels for desktops, laptops, tablets, and phones that can all run Windows 10.

This chapter outlines the versions of Windows 10 and the features available in each. This information enables users to determine which version is appropriate for their specific needs. The chapter also introduces new and improved features in Windows 10, including the updated user interface, hardware requirements, and system hardware support. Updated features for application support, connectivity applications, and enhanced networking models are also covered in the chapter.

Windows 10 Versions

Windows 10 is available in different versions to meet different consumer requirements. In most cases, a consumer can upgrade from one version of Windows 10 to another to get the extra features found in enhanced versions. Retail versions support a feature called **Easy Upgrade**. A new product key can be obtained or an upgrade can be purchased directly from the online Microsoft Store. The upgrades will trigger small downloads from Microsoft after they are purchased, unlocking an upgraded edition of Windows 10 on the computer in as little as 20 minutes.

If Windows 10 is preinstalled from the factory by the original equipment manufacturer (OEM) of the computer, the Windows 10 license is tied to that computer hardware. This limits the operating system upgrade and downgrade rights to the terms specified by the OEM Windows 10 license. OEM licenses of Windows 10 are not transferable to new computer hardware. The hardware itself can be upgraded (except for the motherboard of the system) to add new or upgraded devices to the computer.

In corporate and education environments, Windows 10 licenses may be purchased in bulk by purchasing a volume license (VL) that entitles upgrades of computers with an existing operating system to a volume-licensed version of Windows 10.

The four mainstream versions of Windows 10 are:

- Windows 10 Home
- Windows 10 Professional
- Windows 10 Enterprise
- Windows 10 Education

Additional specialized versions of Windows 10 are:
- Windows 10 Mobile
- Windows 10 N & K Editions

General descriptions of each product and new Windows 10 features are provided in the following sections. More specific descriptions of these features follow these sections.

Windows 10 Home

Windows 10 Home concentrates on enabling the home user to enjoy a rich and productive personal experience. Business enhancements such as encrypted files, joining a domain, and processing Group Policy settings are not available unless the operating system is upgraded to a business-grade edition. This version includes the following:

- Fast startup with Hiberboot and InstantGo
- 32-bit and 64-bit versions
- Battery saver
- Customizable Start menu
- Side loading of applications
- Windows Defender and Firewall
- Cortana
- Windows Hello
- Continuum
- Microsoft Edge
- Mobile device management
- Microsoft Passport
- Device encryption
- Windows Update
- Easy Upgrade from Home to Professional edition

Windows 10 Professional

In a corporate environment, the enhanced manageability of Windows 10 Professional allows a business to simplify its operations and concentrate on doing business. This version includes the features of Window 10 Home plus the following:

- 64-bit version supports up to 2048 GB of RAM
- Domain join
- Group Policy management
- Remote Desktop
- Client Hyper-V
- Enterprise Mode Internet Explorer (EMIE)
- Assigned Access
- Azure Active Directory join with single sign-on to cloud-hosted apps
- Windows Store for Business
- BitLocker drive encryption
- Enterprise Data Protection
- Windows Update for Business

- Current Branch for Business
- Easy Upgrade from Professional to Enterprise edition

Windows 10 Enterprise

Windows 10 Enterprise is available only to customers who purchase **Software Assurance (SA)** from Microsoft. Software Assurance, an option that provides for automatically receiving the latest version of a product, is available to medium- and large-scale customers who purchase Microsoft products at a volume level, on a per-user or per-device licensing basis.

This version includes the features found in Windows 10 Professional and adds:

- *Direct Access*—Provides seamless remote access when a mobile computer is outside the office and has access to the Internet
- *AppLocker*—Reduces malware by using rules to identify applications that are allowed to run
- *BranchCache*—Speeds up access to documents across a WAN by caching them at a branch office
- *Windows To Go Creator*—Creates a mobile installation of Windows 10 on a USB drive that can be used on multiple computers
- *Granular UX Control*—Locks down Windows 10 so that only a single application can be run
- *Credential Guard*—Isolates credentials stored in memory to enhance security
- *Device Guard*—Restricts a device to only running trusted applications for protection from malware and tampering
- *Long Term Servicing Branch*—Avoids the requirement to update Windows 10 when it is used in secure environments and for running specialized equipment

Windows 10 Education

Windows 10 Education provides the same feature set as Windows 10 Enterprise with the exception of the Long Term Servicing Branch feature. It supports educators and students as new curriculum changes to ebooks, apps, and online content. Similar to Windows 10 Enterprise, licensing is negotiated between the educational institution and Microsoft as part of a volume purchase.

Windows 10 Mobile

The Windows 10 Mobile edition is designed for mobile phones to provide a user experience that is uniform across desktops, tablets, and the phone itself. Applications can adapt to different phone form factors and screen sizes to give users a high-fidelity representation of their data that keeps the look and feel of their other Windows 10 devices.

Not all desktop applications run on Windows 10 Mobile because applications that have similar experience across different devices must be written to a common standard. Microsoft publishes a **Universal Windows Platform (UWP)** that allows developers to code applications that target device families, not a single operating system. A device family can be generic (that is, universal) or specific to a device family such as desktop, mobile, Xbox, or embedded. If an application is designed to support multiple device families, including the mobile device family, the user interface will adapt to different forms of input, screen sizes, and controls. UWP helps the developer maximize the reach of the application by creating **universal apps.**

Windows 10 Mobile includes:

- Preinstalled Microsoft Office with universal apps, including Word, Excel, PowerPoint, and OneNote
- Continuum for phones
- Microsoft Passport

- Always-on VPN
- Hardware-based protection with UEFI Secure Boot, trusted platform model (TPM) processor, and Device Guard
- Enterprise Data Protection
- Mobile Device Management
- Windows Store and Windows Store for Business

Windows 10 N & K Editions

The N releases are sold in countries that do not allow Microsoft to bundle in Windows Media Player and other media software as part of the operating system. This is required by court rulings to allow fair competition for vendors who write similar software. Windows Media Player can still be freely downloaded and installed as part of a "Media Feature Pack" on this Windows edition by the user if desired.

The K releases are only sold in South Korea and also have some features, like Windows Media Player, removed as well.

New and Enhanced Features of Windows 10

Microsoft has added several new and improved features to Windows 10 that make it more secure, reliable, and easier to use than earlier Windows operating systems. Not all features are available in all versions of Windows 10. The customer can buy the minimum version of Windows 10 that has the desired features. If the customers' needs expand, they can upgrade to a different version to obtain the extra features. Several of these important features are:

- 32- and 64-bit computing support
- Microsoft Passport
- Windows Store
- Microsoft Edge
- Cortana
- Windows Update
- Easy Upgrade
- Continuum

To help introduce some of these features and prepare for later chapters, you will now install Windows 10.

Activity 1-1: Installing Windows 10

Time Required: 30 to 60 minutes
Objective: Install Windows 10

Description: You have just received a new copy of Windows 10. You are considering deploying Windows 10 for your organization. To sell the management team on implementing Windows 10, you need to install the system and provide a demonstration of the new features. In this activity, you install Windows 10 (a new install, not an upgrade) on your computer.

Your instructor may give you some additional steps to perform if the Windows 10 installation requires additional configuration for your student environment. This activity assumes you are starting the computer from a DVD or a virtual equivalent.

1. Ensure that your computer is configured to boot from DVD. The boot configuration of your computer is configured in the BIOS of your computer. Refer to the BIOS documentation specific to the computer to determine the steps to complete this requirement. Many newer computers will boot from the DVD drive automatically if there is no operating system installed on the system's hard disk.

2. Place your Windows 10 DVD in the DVD drive of your computer.

3. Restart your computer.

4. If directed by the startup screen, press any key to boot from DVD. This message may only appear if the hard drive has an existing bootable partition or if the computer's boot sequence is configured to allow it.

5. The system will proceed to load the first part of the installation program. When the Install Windows screen appears, confirm the installation language, time and currency format, and keyboard layout are correct, and then click **Next**.

6. Click **Install now**.

7. Select the **I accept the license terms** check box, and click **Next**.

8. Click **Custom: Install Windows only (advanced)**. This is required to perform a new installation. (Upgrades are covered in Chapter 2, Installing Windows 10.)

9. On the Where do you want to install Windows screen, if necessary, install additional disk drivers as described by your instructor.

10. If there are any existing partitions, delete each partition using the following steps:

    a. Click the partition to select it.

    b. Click **Delete**.

    c. Click **OK** to confirm that you understand that all data on the partition will be deleted.

11. Examine the number in the **Free space** column. Exercises in Chapter 4, Managing Disks and File Systems, will require at least 8 GB of space to remain unallocated.

12. Click **Drive 0 Unallocated Space** and click **New**.

13. In the **Size** text box, enter a value that is no less than **50000** and that leaves at least 30 GB of disk space unallocated, and then click **Apply**.

14. In the warning window, click **OK** to acknowledge that additional partitions may be created. Windows 10 automatically creates several partitions to support recovery and advanced boot options.

15. Click **Drive 0 Partition 4** to select it, and then click **Format**.

16. Click **OK** to confirm that all data on the partition will be lost when it is formatted. There is no data on this partition at this time.

17. If necessary, click **Drive 0 Partition 4** to select it, and click **Next**. Windows now copies system files to the hard drive, reboots, performs additional configuration tasks, reboots one or more times, and then asks for user input again. This portion of the installation can take up to 30 minutes but may be faster depending on your hardware. When your computer reboots, do not press a key to start from the DVD.

18. On the Get going fast screen, click **Use express settings**. As the operating system prepares itself, greeting messages will display on the screen. The background color will cycle between black and a color to indicate that the computer is busy and a warning will display notifying you not to turn off the computer. It may take several minutes to complete background activities.

19. On the Choose how you'll connect screen, click **Join a domain**, and then click **Next**.

20. Under Who's going to use this PC, type **User***x,* where *x* is a number assigned to you by your instructor.

21. In the Enter password and Re-enter password boxes, type **password**.

22. In the Password hint box, type **Refer to Activity 1-1** and then click **Next**. As the operating system prepares itself, greeting messages will display. The background color will cycle between black and a color to indicate that the computer is busy in the background.

23. Windows 10 will attempt to enable network connections to establish connectivity to the Internet. Click **Yes** to allow your PC to be discoverable by other PCs and devices on the network. This secures your network connection.

24. Right-click the Start button and select **Command Prompt (Admin)** from the shortcut menu. If you are prompted by User Account Control to allow this application to make changes to your computer, click **Yes**.

25. At the command prompt, type the command **hostname** and press **Enter** on the keyboard. Note that the name of the computer is listed as the output of the command, and that the name has been automatically generated during the operating system's installation.

26. At the command prompt, type the command **shutdown /s /t 5** and press **Enter** on the keyboard. This will cause the computer to close all running applications and shut down the computer in 5 seconds. Note that the computer can be shut down from the Start menu, but this command-line technique is commonly used by administrators who are remotely managing a user's computer.

32- and 64-Bit Computing Support

Windows 10 comes in both 32-bit and 64-bit processor versions. The 32-bit version is limited to addressing 4 GB of RAM. If a computer has more RAM than 4 GB, the extra RAM will be unavailable to the 32-bit edition. The 64-bit version is becoming popular as users are running applications that demand more RAM than the 32-bit version can use. Most new computers, with the exception of some tablets and low-cost computers, are 64-bit devices.

Depending on the version of Windows 10, the 64-bit editions can support up to 2048 GB of RAM. The practical limit to how much RAM can be installed in a computer is usually a limit of the computer hardware design. Server class computers may support adding more RAM than desktop computers, but they will likely not support the installation of Windows 10 as an operating system. A better choice for server class computers is a server-class operating system such as Windows Server 2016.

The 64-bit version of Windows 10 has a greater theoretical limit for processing data, which may allow it to complete calculations faster than a 32-bit version, even on the same computer hardware.

If users determine that their computer hardware cannot use the 64-bit edition, they can upgrade their hardware or they can use a 32-bit edition of Windows 10 instead.

Microsoft Passport

Traditional passwords are a simple mechanism to secure access to data and services, but the protection they provide is limited. A password is only one form of protection, and attackers who obtain that password have the same access as the user. Efforts by administrators to increase password complexity, password length, frequency of password changes, and password history to limit password reuse are valuable but can give the user even more incentive to simplify password management and unwittingly increase the risk of being compromised. Users tend to simplify their password management by reusing one password on multiple systems, making only small changes to a complex password they took time to memorize, keeping notes about the password in insecure locations, and other behavior that undermines security.

Attackers have better tools and strategies today, which also makes a password alone a weak mechanism for protecting a user's identity. The trend to prove users are who they say they are is moving to authentication based on **multifactor authentication (MFA)**. Each authentication factor is a different form of evidence confirming the user's identity. Instead of authenticating with one factor, like a password, the user must be able to prove at least two, a challenge known as two-factor authentication. Common factors the user can be tested on include something they know (such as a password), something they have (such as a smart card), and something they are (a fingerprint or retina scan).

Microsoft Passport is an MFA mechanism built in to Windows 10. It is designed to securely track multiple authentication factors for a user's identity on the device running Windows 10. Those factors can be used and managed on one device running Windows 10 for multiple sign-in identities representing the same user on different systems. For example, one user could store an identity to sign in to the local machine, another for a corporate domain connected to over a network, and another identity based in an Azure Active Directory environment connected to over the Internet.

The details tracked by Microsoft Passport for authentication are stored securely as individually protected and encrypted elements so that even if one identity is compromised on a device running Windows 10, the other authentication factors are not easily accessible to an attacker. Data encryption is applied to each authentication element and stored locally in the device's software or within a local hardware-based **trusted platform module** (**TPM**) if the Windows 10 device has one present.

Mechanisms to authenticate the user for individual biometric factors in Microsoft Passport have been standardized into a system called **Windows Hello.** The initial mechanisms supported by Windows Hello include a **PIN** (personal identification number) code, facial recognition, and fingerprints. If the computer's hardware doesn't support facial or fingerprint recognition, it can potentially be added with external expansion hardware available in stores. As new hardware becomes available (e.g., retina scanners), other methods can be added to Windows Hello that test other biometric data to validate a user's identity.

The PIN component is specific to the computer or device running Windows 10. It is stored and used locally only on that computer or device. On the surface, a PIN can be as simple as a four-digit numeric code, which appears similar to a password because it is something that the user must type. The difference is that an attacker would need to have two things for the PIN to be a threat—knowledge of the user's PIN and the specific Windows 10 device it was created on. The PIN method is primarily required in case something happens to limit the other Windows Hello test methods, for example, a personal injury to the user or a biosensor hardware failure.

Similar to the PIN, Windows Hello can test other biometric authentication factors against data that is stored securely on the local Windows 10 device. If the user has two computers running Windows 10, the tests for facial recognition, fingerprints, and PINs will be Windows 10 device specific. If one computer is stolen, there is less risk of an attacker using that device's data to compromise the remaining device.

A simple tactic such as keeping the PIN different on each device makes it even more challenging for the attacker. Multiple factors can be combined in a Microsoft Passport identity so that a user must pass all tests to successfully authenticate and gain access. To avoid brute force attacks where an attacker tries to guess or hack authentication, incorrect attempts can be limited to a failure threshold that could trigger a device lock.

Microsoft Passport is Windows 10 device specific to protect an individual's identity and is built in to every version of Windows 10. To add central management for user authentication and device registration in the enterprise, corporate administrators must deploy a different solution called Microsoft Passport for Work. This allows administrators to control security settings such as PIN complexity and biometric options through Active Directory group policies and Azure AD mechanisms. An enterprise implementation that deploys Microsoft Passport for Work can be complex and require many components; however, this is Microsoft's preferred solution for integrating Windows 10 device identity management with current and future enterprise directory infrastructures.

Windows Store

Windows 10 comes with many productivity and other applications, but more are available online from the Windows Store, an application store available to all users. A user must have an Internet connection and a Microsoft account to obtain applications from the Windows Store. Some applications are free and some are available at extra charge. Because Windows 10 can run on so many different types of devices, the Store offers applications that are also specific to desktops, laptops, phones, and Xbox units.

The Windows Store can be launched from within Windows 10 to install new applications and update installed applications. Individuals can select applications from the Windows Store to personalize their Windows 10 device to better service their needs. Corporate administrators have the option of using the Windows Store for Business, which gives them advanced controls to organize, customize, and manage deployment of applications relevant for the organization's users and their business needs.

Microsoft Edge

Windows 10 includes a web browser called **Microsoft Edge**. This browser is new and is the default browser for Windows 10. The older Internet Explorer web browser is still included with Windows 10, but it is not available directly from the application menus. Microsoft Edge represents a fresh start with a browsing engine designed for all devices running Windows 10, not just the typical desktop or laptop computer.

Microsoft Edge is designed to perform much faster than Internet Explorer and many competing third-party browsers. Much of the speed increase was made possible by not including legacy features and functions that were built in to Internet Explorer. Microsoft Edge presents a new way to surf and interact with the web. Microsoft Edge is still under development, with new features promised as updates to Windows 10.

Microsoft Edge has some notable new features. When a user signs in to a device running Windows 10 using a Microsoft account, data such as favorite sites and stored web content can be synchronized between all of the user's Windows 10 devices. The stored web content is known as a reading list, and can be viewed without a live Internet connection at the user's convenience. Web content can be cluttered with links, ads, and other formatting that make it hard to read some web text. Microsoft Edge allows the user to enable a reading view that can remove that visual clutter, improving the user's ability to focus on key content. To enrich the browsing experience, Microsoft Edge also allows the user to add notes, highlights, and free-form writing on a webpage. The annotated webpage can be saved for future reference or shared with others. Browsing the web has become a richer experience with Microsoft Edge, and finding information has been enhanced with a new feature that helps to research browser content called Cortana.

Cortana

The methods and amount of data a user can connect to with Windows 10 is greater than ever. Microsoft knows people need help to search, organize, and manage information in their lives. Windows 10 includes a personalized virtual assistant application called **Cortana** to assist with these tasks.

Cortana is more than a search utility, but it does have powerful features for searching the device running Windows 10 and the web. Depending on the countries and languages for which Windows 10 is configured, Cortana can speak and listen while interacting with the user. Cortana is designed to customize what it knows about the user by tracking the user's interaction with it and the computer as a whole in a local database called the notebook.

Cortana can optionally link into external accounts that the user has on services such as Office 365, Xbox Live, and some non-Microsoft accounts as well. Cortana can search data and be more aware of your interaction with those external accounts to get a better picture of you and your needs. That data helps Cortana provide recommendations plus personalize and customize the experience on the Windows 10 device.

When the user signs in with a connection to a Microsoft account, the personalized data in the notebook can be synchronized to the cloud. This information can then be synchronized to other devices running Windows 10 where the user is connected with that same account. Multiple devices running Windows 10 can collectively learn and continuously customize the user's interaction with calendars, contacts, locations, reminders, and the overall digital life enabled by Windows 10. Security and privacy settings allow the user to decide if that data is collected at all, stored in the cloud, or cleared at the discretion of the user.

Windows Update

Windows 10 uses an update philosophy that is different from Windows 7 and Windows 8. In the past, each major version of Windows was released on a three-year schedule. Incremental fixes and security patches were distributed through the Windows Update service between major version releases. Starting with Windows 10, the operating system features and core applications are updated on a regular basis, which potentially removes the need for a major version update. Because major feature updates are distributed together with fixes and security patches, Windows 10 is continuously improved as if it were a service the user has subscribed to. This operating system update strategy is commonly referred to as **Windows as a Service (WaaS)**.

Windows Update is integral to the continuous evolution of Windows 10. Users need to remain connected to data and services on the Internet, with standards and practices that must remain current and consistent for all users and applications working on devices running Windows 10. As data sources, services, standards, and practices evolve at a rapid pace, so too must the Windows 10 operating system.

Windows 10 Home edition has a very aggressive update schedule that is fully automatic by default. Updates in that edition are downloaded and installed automatically with little notice to the end user. Update delays are limited and it is not possible to control which updates are implemented. As stated in the typical end user license agreement for the Windows 10 Home edition, the user agrees to this assertive update policy by installing the operating system. The advantage to users is that they stay current and enabled with new features that help them use Windows 10 every day.

Business users need more control over the upgrade cycle, so there are more options to time and select updates for the Windows 10 Professional, Enterprise, and Education editions. Enterprise customers who do not want feature updates can also optionally deploy a version of Windows 10 Enterprise that is on the Long Term Servicing Branch (LTSB), which does not update itself with new features automatically. Special-purpose computers used to control manufacturing machinery, government operations, and military controls are examples of prime candidates for the LTSB version of Windows 10 Enterprise. In general, most enterprise computers can benefit from the periodic installation of new features that are made available by Microsoft. Those updates and patches can be managed with update controls and services available to network administrators in a managed business environment.

Easy Upgrade

If users are running Windows 10 Home edition, they can upgrade to a more advanced edition of Windows 10 such as Professional or Enterprise. The upgrade to Windows 10 Professional can be purchased online through the Windows Store as a one-time purchase for any Windows 10 Home user. The upgrade to Windows 10 Enterprise is a special upgrade that is activated by changing a product key identifying the Windows 10 system. The product key for Enterprise editions is obtained when a company purchases licenses for Windows 10 Enterprise in bulk as part of a contract negotiated with Microsoft. This volume licensing grants the users of that company the ability to use Windows 10 Enterprise at work and at home, even on their personal devices, limited by the terms of the contract.

When Windows 10 is installed on a computer, the device is typically registered with Microsoft device registration servers on the Internet. The installation process takes a snapshot of the computer's hardware and calculates a digital signature to identify that computer and match the operating system edition and license key assigned to it. In most cases, if Windows 10 is reinstalled, the license key assigned to that system is remembered and can be reapplied automatically. As long as the system hardware doesn't change too much, the hardware's digital signature will still match the old license record. The Easy Upgrade process can update the license matched to that hardware's digital signature, allowing the operating system to download new functional features and complete the upgrade process within an hour or less.

Continuum

When Windows 10 is installed on a computer with a touch screen, it can be used in desktop mode or tablet mode. **Desktop mode** is designed for a traditional computer with a mouse and keyboard. **Tablet mode** is optimized to make touch easier by making icons larger. Also, when in tablet mode, there is no desktop. Instead, the Start screen with live tiles is maximized to make finding and selecting applications easier.

Many new mobile devices, such as Microsoft Surface, have multiple form factors. They can convert between a laptop form factor and a tablet. Some devices fold the keyboard away to change to a tablet, while others have a detachable keyboard. Windows 10 automatically adjusts the display and input methods depending on the form factor being used. When a keyboard is detached or folded away, the device automatically switches to tablet mode. This automatic switching between modes is called **Continuum**.

On mobile phones running Windows 10, **Continuum for phone** allows you to use your phone like a desktop computer when appropriate peripherals are connected. You can attach a mouse, keyboard, monitor, or projector. Continuum for phone requires specific hardware support in the phone and you need to identify support before purchasing the phone.

User Interface

The user interface of Windows 10 has been updated to present a fresh new look for tools used to interact with the operating system. Several new or improved features in this area include:

- Lock screen
- Start menu
- Search interface
- Taskbar
- Notification area
- Advanced window management

Lock Screen

The Windows 10 lock screen is displayed when the computer first starts, as shown in Figure 1-1. The lock screen is a security and display layer that initiates access to the local device running Windows 10. Previous versions of Windows presented a screen asking the user to press Ctrl+Alt+Delete to initiate the sign-in process. Given that Windows 10 is used with a larger range of devices, the lock screen was changed to a format that is similar to what you would see on a smartphone. Useful information can be displayed on the lock screen, such as weather, battery charge indicator, date and time, Windows Store information, Cortana, and other customizable details that would be safe for anyone to see.

Figure 1-1   Windows 10 lock screen

When the user triggers the lock screen to remove itself by performing an action like clicking the mouse, pressing a key, or touching a touch-sensitive screen, the sign-in screen replaces it and allows the user to select an account from a list of known accounts at the lower-left corner of the screen and sign in, as shown in Figure 1-2.

Figure 1-2   The Windows 10 sign-in screen

Start Menu

Many users were disappointed when the Start menu was removed in Windows 8. The same Start menu that was popular in Windows 7 returns to Windows 10 with an updated look, as shown in Figure 1-3. Clicking the Start button opens the Start menu. Right-clicking the Start button opens a shortcut menu that lists frequently accessed computer administration functions, as shown in Figure 1-4.

Figure 1-3   The Start menu

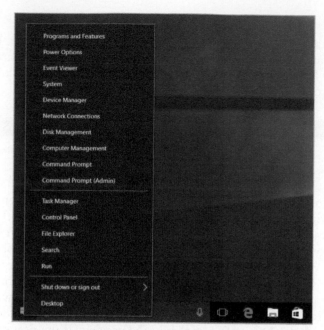

Figure 1-4 Shortcut menu for administrative tasks

When browsing the Start menu, as shown in Figure 1-3, three columns of information are displayed. The left-hand column displays small icons to identify the currently signed-in user and access File Explorer, system settings, and power controls. A description of each small icon can be seen by hovering the mouse over the icon. If desired, this column can be expanded by clicking the menu icon at the top of the column. The middle column lists a series of links, with the user's most used applications at the top, and a sorted list of installed applications below that. The right-hand column includes application live tiles that display up-to-date information from applications and allow the user to fully launch those applications. The application live tile feature was made popular by Windows 8; however, Windows 8 did not offer the blended experience of a Start menu together with application live tiles. Windows 10 offers the best of both worlds in its Start menu.

Jump lists are reintroduced with Windows 10 to identify what content was recently opened by an application, or what content is automatically linked to the menu item. The left-hand column of the Start menu displays an arrow next to the Start menu item if the item has a jump list associated with it. Clicking the arrow will open the jump list for that item. If a user clicks an item on the jump list, the content or listed application is opened. If nothing is selected and the user clicks elsewhere, the jump list disappears.

Search Interface

A search tool is available next to the Start button, as shown in Figure 1-5. The search tool is able to browse the local computer and the web for information requested by the user. This is also a primary place to connect with Cortana, the virtual private assistant.

Figure 1-5 Search interface

Taskbar

The taskbar is a horizontal bar located at the bottom of the screen by default. It contains the Start button, search tool, and Task View button to the left and the notification area to the right. In the middle is an area to keep track of open windows (see Figure 1-6). The Task View feature is discussed in the section, Advanced Window Management.

Start button   Search tool   Task View   Taskbar   Notification area

Figure 1-6   Windows taskbar

When multiple windows are open, the screen can get cluttered and screens overlap each other. To organize what windows are open, a button is placed on the taskbar with an icon representing the running application. Note that there is no text included with the icon on the taskbar.

Hovering the mouse over an icon for an open program (indicated by a colored bar beneath the icon) displays a preview of each window the application has open above the taskbar button. Hovering the mouse over a preview window previews only that window on the desktop. This is known as the Peek feature, where a user can conveniently peek at an active window without having to fully switch to it. If the mouse is moved away from the preview window without selecting it, the desktop reverts to the way it was before the preview. If the user clicks a preview window, that window becomes the active window.

Taskbar buttons can represent a shortcut to an application, even if the application isn't actively running. Application icons can be pinned to the taskbar and Start menu to make it easy to launch popular applications. When an application icon is pinned to the taskbar, the icon remains on the taskbar even after the app is closed. If an application is not pinned to the taskbar, the taskbar button for that application disappears when all of that application's windows are closed.

Notification Area

The notification area is located on the right side of the taskbar (see Figure 1-6). In previous versions of Windows, this area was called the system tray. Many users complained that the area could easily get cluttered with notifications and icons from multiple applications and the operating system. The notification area has been simplified by default to display the clock and icons for volume, network connectivity, and Action Center notifications. Additional icons may be displayed for touch screen controls, battery power, and stylus utilities, depending on the hardware capabilities of the device running Windows 10.

The Action Center lists important notifications from the operating system to the user in one place. The user should periodically check this area to see if there are new notifications of problems or solutions that Windows 10 has discovered.

Other applications can add icons to the notification area, but they are not displayed automatically. The extra icons are viewed by clicking the up-arrow icon at the left-hand side of the notification area, which pops up a window displaying other notification icons that may be active. Administrative settings can be used to change what icons are displayed in the notification area.

Advanced Window Management

It can be difficult to organize many open windows on the screen, so Windows 10 enables advanced window management features called Snap, Shake, and Task View.

Snap allows windows to quickly be resized by clicking the title bar of the window and dragging it to the top, sides, or middle of the screen. If the window is dragged to the top of the screen, an outline is drawn showing that the window will be resized to fill the screen. If the window is dragged to the right or left sides of the screen, an outline is drawn showing that the window will be resized to fill half the screen on that side. If the window is left inside the borders of the screen, it resumes the last size and shape it had before being docked to a side or top of the screen. Note that it is not until the user lets go of the mouse button that the screen will actually resize and lock itself into position.

Shake helps to minimize all other windows except for one the user is interested in. If a user clicks the title bar of a window and moves (shakes) the mouse from side to side, all other windows automatically minimize. Repeating the shake restores all other windows to their original size and location.

Task View has a dedicated taskbar icon next to the search field at the lower-left side of the screen, as shown in Figure 1-6. Clicking Task View changes the display to show an ordered preview of all application windows that are currently open. Clicking a window's preview image brings that window forward to become the active window. Clicking the Task View icon also allows the user to access a new feature called Virtual Desktop. **Virtual Desktop** allows the user to create multiple desktops that can host different open windows. The windows on a desktop are specific to that virtual desktop. The user could decide to have one virtual desktop to show only business-related applications, and perhaps another to show only personal applications. Using the Task View control, users can toggle between virtual desktops as required and avoid a confusing mix of windows on a single desktop.

Hardware Requirements and System Hardware Support

Windows 10 is designed to provide a similar look and feel across systems with different device hardware and device capabilities. A user or company can purchase hardware that best fits operational requirements such as portability, environment sensors, connectors to external devices, display features, security, processing power, RAM, and storage. If desired, the operating system can be upgraded from one version to another if the need for enhanced operating system features arises.

The degree to which a computer's hardware can be upgraded is determined by the manufacturer and its consideration for expandability and upgradability. It is the consumers' responsibility to make sure the features of their computer or device they buy can be changed or expanded, or to determine that a nonupgradable system will suit their needs.

Consumers have many computers and components to choose from. How do they know what will work with Windows 10? Newer systems are advertised as being Windows 10 compatible. For older hardware running Windows 7 or Windows 8.1, Microsoft distributed hundreds of millions of free Windows 10 upgrades to consumers during the first year of Windows 10's release. Microsoft has tried to simplify the choice by creating a testing program for computer hardware called the Get Windows 10 app. It will do a compatibility check and notify the user if there are any applications, devices, or other compatibility issues that will stop an upgrade. If there are no upgrade issues found, the app will offer a free upgrade to Windows 10.

If you have a Windows 7 SP1 or Windows 8.1 computer, you can install the Get Windows 10 app to verify hardware and software compatibility. This app is downloadable from *https://support.microsoft.com/en-us/kb/3035583*. After installing the app, right-click the Get Windows 10 icon in the notification area and click *Check your upgrade status* and then click *Check your PC*. Your computer is then analyzed and any known compatibility issues are displayed.

As of this writing, the free upgrade is being offered to consumers who have an edition of Windows 7 with Service Pack 1 or Windows 8.1 that are eligible for the upgrade. The offer is targeted at mainstream consumers, so it is not available to computers running the Enterprise edition of Windows, running an edition of Windows RT, or those that are joined to a domain. Consumer computers may also not be eligible because they are missing required updates or are not running with a valid license. The most common problem found with older hardware is device driver compatibility with Windows 10. The basic hardware requirements for Windows 10 should be easy for legacy systems to meet in most cases as the minimum hardware requirements for Windows 10 match those originally set for Windows 7.

Table 1-1 lists minimum hardware requirements for Windows 10.

Table 1-1   Minimum hardware requirements for Windows 10

System component	Recommendation
CPU	32- or 64-bit processor, 1 GHz or faster
System RAM	1 GB (2 GB for a computer with a 64-bit CPU)
Disk space	16 GB for 32-bit editions, 20 GB for 64-bit editions
Video card drivers	DirectX 9 graphical processor and WDDM 1.0 (or higher)

Processor Support

Windows 10 is designed for modern 32- and 64-bit processors. To enhance Windows 10's performance, Microsoft has built-in support for several enhanced processor configurations. The processor in a device is responsible for executing the operating system code and the user's applications. The **central processing unit (CPU)** is the most common legacy term used to describe the processor, but a newer term is being used in computer marketing materials, **System on a Chip (SoC)**. The SoC combines a CPU together with other supporting hardware on one silicon chip. The supporting hardware built in to the SoC can include graphics processors, memory management, and power management as typical examples.

Some newer computers built on a SoC platform may require Windows 10 to fully unlock the hardware experience built in to that one chip. Microsoft has notified enterprise customers that after July 2017 they will not guarantee compatibility for Windows 7 or Windows 8.1 installed and running on newer SoC-based devices. As newer hardware is released, the expectation is that Windows 10 may be required as the minimum operating system for that hardware to operate correctly. The CPU processor at the core of a SoC is still responsible for executing application instructions.

The actions performed by a CPU are defined by the instructions it is given. Programmers compile a list of instructions to build their applications. These instructions are typically grouped into units of code called **threads**. A thread is spawned, or started, by a process. The process itself is created by the applications and the operating system as they run. Threads and processes are common terms used to describe what the CPU is working on. To visualize what a thread and process represent, consider the following breakdown of an application.

A single application can be described by the tasks it must accomplish. For instance, you can describe the tasks a user is experiencing with a word-processing application. The user opens a new document and types in text at the keyboard. The user wants the application to format a visual representation of the document, perform a spell check and grammar check, highlight errors it finds, and periodically save a copy of the text to disk. The word-processing application in this case is the process. Formatting, spell check, and saving to disk are each executed by a different thread, or unit of code.

With the introduction of Windows, the idea of multitasking became popular. **Multitasking** gives the appearance that the computer is running multiple applications or processes at the same time. The operating system is switching from one thread to another very quickly, giving the illusion that all processes and their threads are running concurrently. In the word-processing example, users can see all those tasks happen at the same time while they type.

Applications designed to run in Windows run as one or more processes. A single **process** in Windows represents a collection of data, files, and instructions with a specific purpose while it is running. One or more application tasks can be assigned to a single process. In the example, the spelling and grammar check with suggested fixes can be part of one process; the auto-save to disk can be part of another.

Processes are typically described in Windows by the application they service, the user who launched them, and other attributes. The operating system uses its own processes to perform system actions such as managing files and network connections.

When a process executes a single task, it runs a small block of code, a thread, for that task alone. The programmer decides what a single thread should do. Windows assigns that single thread to the CPU for execution.

Preemptive multitasking allows a single process to be interrupted by another process, even if the first process has not completed. To control the interruptions, Windows uses a system of priority levels and time windows to control scheduling of the processes and threads.

Each thread is given a window of time to execute in before the operating system checks to see if the CPU should switch to another thread. If the thread has not finished its task, it must wait for its next turn. The time window a thread is allowed to run in is known as a **quantum**. The thread can be preempted by another thread before its quantum is over—even before it has started processing.

To help determine which thread gets to go next, and which threads are allowed to preempt others, the threads and processes are assigned a priority level. The higher the priority level, the greater the chance that the process will preempt the current thread or get the next quantum.

If there are no threads that are ready to run, there is an operating system process (the System Idle Process) always ready to run.

If a thread is not finished running, perhaps because it had to wait or it was preempted, it is typically restarted on the same processor that previously ran it. This is known as **processor affinity**, where the thread is restricted to which CPU can run it.

When multiple processes and threads are running, it doesn't make sense for a programmer to write all of the instructions for an application into a single file. Windows programs are usually written in a modular nature, with different files holding different pieces of the application. Code modules are saved in **Dynamic Link Library (DLL) files**. Code modules in the DLLs can be shared between applications. Updates to applications can replace individual DLLs instead of the entire application.

Activity 1-2: Switching Between Applications

Time Required: 5 minutes

Objective: Observe how to switch between running applications

Description: In this activity, you start multiple applications and use the application switcher feature of Windows 10 to quickly change which application is in the foreground.

1. If necessary, start your computer and sign in as **User***x*, where *x* is the student number assigned by your instructor. If you are presented with the lock screen, click anywhere on the screen to dismiss it and reveal the sign-in screen. The user name you are signing in as should already be selected and on the screen. Enter the password for that account in the password field, and then press **Enter**. Note that the password must match the password used for the operating system installation in Activity 1-1.

2. Click the **Start** button and start typing the word **notepad**. Note that the search window automatically appears and suggests a highlighted best match to the search term, Notepad, Desktop app. Press **Enter** to launch the Notepad application and enter some random text into the Notepad editor window.

3. Click the **Start** button and start typing the phrase **Internet Explorer**. Note that Microsoft Edge is the default browser and Internet Explorer is available on the system as an alternate browser for compatibility sake but is not visible on the Start menu. Press **Enter** to launch Internet Explorer; if you are prompted, select **Use recommended security and compatibility settings**, and then click **OK**. Leave Internet Explorer at the starting page.

4. Hold down the **Alt** key and press **Tab** once. Do not release the **Alt** key.

5. Notice that each running application has its active content displayed in a miniature preview window.

6. Press the **Tab** key repeatedly to cycle the highlighted box from one application to the next.

7. Press the **Tab** key until Notepad is highlighted. Release the **Alt** key.

8. Notice that the **Notepad** application becomes the foreground application.

9. Hold down the **Windows** key on the keyboard and press **Tab** once. Release the **Windows** key.

10. Notice that each running application is displayed in a slightly different preview window. This is called Task View. Click the Internet Explorer preview window. Note that Task View closes and Internet Explorer becomes the foreground application.

11. On the taskbar, at the lower-left side of the screen, click the Task View button that is just to the right of the search field. Note that Task View reopens, making the Task View feature available to mouse input or touch screen controls. Click the Notepad preview window. Note that Task View closes and Notepad becomes the foreground application.

12. Close all applications without saving any changes.

13. Right-click the Start button, and then click **Shut down or sign out** to open its jump list. Click **Sign out** from the pop-up menu to sign out from the local computer.

Activity 1-3: Working with Task Manager

Time Required: 20 minutes
Objective: Observe how to start and stop applications with Task Manager

Description: The operating system is constantly starting and terminating processes as required. The Task Manager tool enables users to monitor and manage this activity. In this activity, you start Task Manager and use it to start and stop applications and processes. You see how Task Manager can filter which processes are shown to the user and how to sort the list of running processes.

1. If necessary, start your computer and sign in.

2. Start **Notepad** and enter some random text.

3. Start **Internet Explorer** and leave it at the starting page.

4. Right-click the system clock at the lower right of the screen.

5. Click **Task Manager** from the shortcut menu.

6. Notice that if this is the first time Task Manager is opened, a basic application/task view is selected. Click the **More details** option at the lower left of the Task Manager window to open an expanded view of Task Manager details.

7. Click to highlight the **Notepad** application and then click the **End Task** button at the lower-right corner of the Task Manager window. Note that you were not prompted by Notepad to save your work.

8. Notice that Notepad is no longer running in the taskbar.

9. In the Task Manager window, click **File** to open the File menu, and then click **Run new task** from that menu.

10. In the Open field, type **notepad** and click **OK**.

11. Notice that Notepad has started in the background and is now listed on the Processes tab. By default, the Task Manager window is always displayed on top of all running application windows.

12. Click the **Processes** tab in Task Manager to make sure it is selected.

13. Click the **Name** column header to sort the list of processes by name. Note that the processes are grouped into major categories: Apps, Background processes, and Windows processes. Each category has a number next to it indicating the number of processes active in that category.

14. Find and highlight the App process with the name Notepad. Right-click the Notepad process and select the **Go to details** menu item from the shortcut menu. Note that this changes the active tab to the Details tab and highlights the application's detailed process entry.

15. Notice the shortcut menu items to Set Priority and Set Affinity.

16. Click the **Set Priority** menu item and notice the options in the shortcut menu. *Do not change* the default setting of Normal. The Set Priority option allows you to increase or reduce how often the multitasking system pays attention to that process. When you move the mouse to another menu item, the shortcut menu closes automatically.

17. Click the **Set affinity** menu item and notice the Processor affinity window opens. The Set Affinity option allows you to limit which processors can run the selected process. Click **OK** to close the Processor affinity window without making any changes.

18. Right-click the **notepad.exe** process and select **End task** from the shortcut menu. Note that there is more than one location within Task Manager to accomplish a common task such as ending a running task.

19. Notice that you are prompted with a warning when you try to terminate the program from the Details list of processes. An application can spawn multiple processes, and terminating just one might leave the others in an unstable state. At this detailed view of processes, the

system will warn you that ending one process could cause instability. This view of running processes must be used carefully for advanced troubleshooting and servicing by the IT administrator. Click the **End process** button in the Task Manager warning window and notice that Notepad has closed.

20. Click the **CPU** column header to sort the list of processes by CPU utilization. Notice that the number in this column is indicating how much of the CPU's time is spent on that process.

21. Notice that the System Idle Process is periodically listed as taking the most CPU time. The Name column may not be wide enough to display the full process name. The column can be made wider by clicking on and moving the column divider.

22. Close the Task Manager window.

23. Close all applications without saving any changes and sign out of Windows.

If your computer only has a single processor and it does not support hyperthreading or multiple cores, the Set Affinity option may not be available.

Multiple Processor Support

Windows 10 includes support for multiprocessor systems. **Multiprocessor** systems have more than one physical CPU. Each additional CPU allows the computer to process instructions in parallel, at the same time. Windows 10 Professional, Enterprise, and Educational editions support a maximum of two physical processors. The Windows 10 Home edition supports only one physical processor.

Hyperthreading Support

Some processors produced by Intel include a technology called **hyperthreading**. These CPUs have extra hardware built in to allow more than one thread to be processed at the same time on a single CPU.

When a single thread is running, it may have to pause and wait for an external event, such as fetching a value from memory. During that pause, another thread can receive attention from the CPU to maximize the amount of work done by the CPU. Each thread processed by the hyperthreading environment runs in its own virtual space, keeping the threads independent.

Threads are created by the operating system and the applications the user runs. The operating system and the applications have to be aware of hyperthreading to maximize the flow of processing between threads. Windows 10 is designed to support hyperthreading.

Multicore Support

A CPU feature such as hyperthreading can boost performance if the operating system and its application processes are written to be aware of it. Unfortunately, that is not always the case.

Threads created by applications can limit themselves so that only one thread can execute and the CPU cannot use its extra hardware to work on another thread in parallel. Any performance benefits while running those tasks are lost. The threads would have to be redesigned by the programmer to remove the bottleneck.

Rather than redesign how the threads share a CPU and work together in those applications, a performance boost can be obtained by introducing multicore CPUs. The CPU package physically looks like one CPU, but internally contains multiple CPU cores.

Each CPU core is capable of running its own thread, even if the thread is not aware of the other cores. This is similar to having multiple CPUs in the computer, but each core is part of a single CPU package.

The cores share some connections to the rest of the computer, so performance will occasionally suffer as shared resources are managed. Compared with a single-core CPU, performance for running parallel threads can be greatly enhanced on a multicore CPU.

Plug and Play

Windows 10 monitors its total environment—what hardware components it is using, when they are available, and what types of programs are running to use that hardware. Newer computing devices that have large-scale device integration, like SoC systems, require more dynamic hardware management than previous Windows editions.

The hardware components (devices) are defined by the type of service or resource they represent. They interact with the operating system through a software module called a device driver. The **device driver** is made up of programming code written by a joint effort between Microsoft and the hardware's developer and supplied as one or more files.

Like Windows 7 and Windows 8, Windows 10 is designed to support plug and play technology. Hardware devices are not always available to the operating system: Components can be powered down to save power, others are unplugged, and some are wireless and are out of range.

Plug and Play technology assumes that hardware components can be connected or activated at any time while the operating system is running. The device driver is automatically loaded by the plug and play system and, after a brief initialization period, the hardware is available for use.

Plug and Play technology is not new, but Windows 10 attempts to be more aware of what the user is doing with this hardware and what the operating system can do to maximize the user's experience. The goal is to make the hardware work for the user, not the other way around.

Power Management

Windows 10 is designed to work in a diverse range of physical environments. Many of those environments impose limits on how much power is available. Computers powered by Windows 10 and meeting the latest hardware power standards can consume less power than ever before. This power economy can translate into laptops that can run longer on battery power and buildings full of computers that will reduce companies' energy bills significantly.

Much of this power savings is realized by exposing more power management features to device drivers and allowing those drivers to better integrate with the operating system. For example, the Fast Startup feature of Windows 10 captures the state of the computer's operating system and drivers, saving them to a file on the local hard drive before the computer enters a low-power hibernation mode. When the computer is woken up, the hibernation image is loaded faster than starting the operating system from scratch. If a device running Windows 10 supports hibernation, this feature can be enabled primarily as a software feature. In Windows 8, this feature was referred to as Hiberboot.

Some manufacturers are building hardware that can enter a very low-power sleep mode where some functionality remains active, including access to the network. If the hardware supports it, the Windows 10 Modern Standby feature allows a device to sleep but continue to perform basic tasks like downloading Windows updates, checking for new email for the user, or notifying users when someone is trying to reach them through an online chat request. This feature is specific to computer hardware that supports Modern Standby and would be used as a shopping criterion during the device acquisition stage. In Windows 8.1, this feature was referred to as InstantGo.

Tablet Hardware

Windows 10 Home, Professional, Enterprise, and Education editions include support for tablet computers as a standard feature. A tablet computer is similar to a laptop in its portability, but it does not rely on a traditional keyboard for data entry. Instead, it typically uses a specially designed pen known as a stylus and a touch sensitive screen for input.

A **multitouch** compatible tablet or monitor does not require a stylus to use the tablet enhancements. Multitouch supports the use of one or more fingers, touching the screen at the same time to recognize gestures such as zoom in, zoom out, scroll, rotate, and right-click.

Some new computers can behave like a laptop or a tablet depending on how they are configured. If the screen is detached from a docking station or a laptop is convertible into a tablet, Windows 10 can detect the change and switch to tablet mode. In tablet mode, Windows 10 assumes that the traditional keyboard and mouse are not available and the user will interact using touch or stylus inputs on the screen. When the computer is changed back to desktop mode by being docked or reconfigured physically, the input controls change back to using the keyboard and mouse as the primary input mechanism.

Media Support

Windows Media Center for Windows 7 and Windows 8 allowed the computer to become part of a full at-home entertainment system. This can include music devices, TV, game consoles such as the Xbox, and online entertainment such as Internet TV. Windows 10 no longer supports Windows Media Center and if a computer has it installed, it will be removed during an upgrade to Windows 10.

Windows Media Center is an example of a solution that enabled intelligent entertainment hardware that was connected locally at home. At the time of Windows 7, most advanced entertainment systems still revolved around local devices and a local network. Windows 10 supports new media features that "cut the cord" and extend entertainment to Internet streaming and subscription-based online multimedia services. If users still rely on Windows Media Center to power a home entertainment system, they should consider keeping their legacy system and not upgrading it to Windows 10.

Disk Technology

Physical disk storage can be connected to a computer internally or externally, using connection technology such as SATA, SCSI, or USB. In addition to physical disks, virtual hard disks are supported by Windows 10. To the user and the operating system, the virtual disk appears as just another physical disk attached to the computer; however, it is not. A virtual disk's contents are stored inside a single file on a real physical disk. As long as there is space, one physical disk can contain many active virtual disks.

Disk technology supported by Windows 10 is fully covered in Chapter 4, Managing Disks and File Systems.

Disk Partition Styles

When a computer is first started, firmware, which is built-in code to initialize the hardware and load an operating system, starts first. That code looks to an attached device, typically the hard drive, to locate and load an operating system. The oldest style of firmware, BIOS, recognizes the MBR partition style. A newer and alternate type of firmware, UEFI, recognizes the GPT partition style. The partition style tells the firmware where to look next on the device to access valid data and, ultimately, load the operating system.

Disk partition styles supported by Windows 10 are fully covered in Chapter 4, Managing Disks and File Systems.

File Systems

Windows 10 supports several file systems to organize files and directories within a disk partition. FAT32 and NTFS are the most common file systems encountered by a computer's administrator. NTFS is the preferred file system for storing files within folders for Windows 10. There are other specialized file systems that are also supported by Windows 10 but used in specialized circumstances, such as exFAT and ReFS.

File systems supported by Windows 10 are fully covered in Chapter 4, Managing Disks and File Systems.

FAT32 Windows10 offers support for the FAT32 file system, which was introduced as an enhanced version of FAT with Windows 95 OSR2.

The FAT32 file system uses a 32-bit numbering system to increase the number of data blocks that can be managed and organized as part of a single partition. The FAT32 theoretical partition size limit is 2048 GB.

Unfortunately, the method used to organize the clusters in such a large partition is inefficient and not necessary, as better alternatives exist. The maximum partition size supported for FAT32 in Windows 10 is 32 GB. For larger partitions, the NTFS file system is commonly used.

NTFS   A new version of **NT File System (NTFS)** is supported in Windows 10. NTFS was introduced originally with Windows NT and has been revised with each successive Windows operating system.

NTFS has support for organization and management features that do not exist in FAT-based file systems. Files and folders are represented in a more virtual and expandable format using metadata to represent their data and attributes. The metadata is the detailed information that the operating system uses to display and organize the files and folders.

NTFS partitions are theoretically limited to 256 terabytes (TB, 1 TB = 1024 GB), but the practical limit is lower simply because physical disks available to the average consumer are much smaller than that.

NTFS file systems offer several enhancements over FAT technology:

- *Secured storage*—Access to folders and files can be limited based on permissions and rights that can be individually configured for each file and folder.

- *File names stored in Unicode format*—The names of files and folders can be stored in many different languages following the Unicode character standard. This is an improvement over the limitation of using the traditional ASCII English character set.

- *File and folder compression*—Any file or folders can be compressed or decompressed automatically using built-in compression technology to conserve disk space. This feature has been greatly enhanced with Windows 10 to reduce the amount of disk space consumed by the operating system itself. This allows inexpensive tablets and similar devices with limited storage to run Windows 10.

- *Disk space quotas by user*—The administrator can set space limits for individuals allowed to store files on the NTFS partition.

- *Alternate data streams*—A single file can contain more than one stream of data. The main stream is used to store the actual file data, and optional alternate data streams can be created to store extra information with the main data stream. For example, this can be used by an application to store a thumbnail for a larger image.

- *File encryption*—The contents of a file can be encrypted using the **Encrypting File System (EFS)** as an additional safeguard.

- *Volume mount point*—A folder can be created in an NTFS partition to act as a gateway to another partition accessible to the operating system. The space on that partition then becomes available as part of the original NTFS partition.

- *Fault tolerance*—The NTFS file system uses a log-based system to track changes that are made to the file system. When a low-level error occurs, or the system crashes, NTFS has the ability to repair incomplete transactions by rolling the changes back to the last known good point. If a part of the disk goes bad, NTFS has the ability to try and move any valid data from that part of the disk to another spot on the disk, and to automatically map the defective area as bad to avoid using it in the future. Depending on the number of disks available, NTFS supports storing file data redundantly across multiple disks to increase the chance that data will still be available in the event of a disk failure.

- *Transactional NTFS*—Transactional NTFS allows applications to monitor the sequence of events used to save data to NTFS files and folders. If an application decides not to finish writing changes to a file, it can use Transactional NTFS to roll back the changes made to that file.

Legacy Application Support

The core of Windows 10 has been redesigned by Microsoft to provide application features that could not be achieved in earlier versions of Windows. Windows 10 achieves many of these new features by implementing features in ways that are not compatible with older applications. Those older applications have a few options to try to run successfully under Windows 10.

For more information about application support, see Chapter 9, Windows 10 Application Support.

Compatibility Settings

Compatibility settings are available as a property of an application after it is installed. Windows 10 is directed by the compatibility settings to emulate an environment for that application that is based on an older operating system. The older operating systems to simulate include:

- Windows 95
- Windows 98/ME
- Windows XP Service Pack 2
- Windows XP Service Pack 3
- Windows Vista
- Windows Vista Service Pack 1
- Windows Vista Service Pack 2
- Windows 7
- Windows 8

Some legacy applications were written with the assumption that the user running them has administrator privileges to the entire computer. For this reason, the compatibility settings allow the option of granting administrator privileges to a legacy application while it runs. This must be used with caution for applications that are not truly trusted.

Compatibility Troubleshooter

If users are not comfortable selecting compatibility settings, a wizard is available to assist them. The Compatibility Troubleshooter has the ability to guide the user through different compatibility settings and, if that doesn't work, report the results to Microsoft.

Client Hyper-V

It is possible that, even with compatibility settings, an application will not run on Windows 10. In this case, there are a few options that chiefly apply to the larger corporate environment. A virtual computer running an older operating system can be hosted by a Windows 10 computer with Client Hyper-V. Those virtual computers can run other operating systems and their own applications. The virtual computers do not even have to be running a Windows operating system. This is important to Enterprise customers who are looking for ways to simplify their environment.

The Windows 10 Client Hyper-V virtualization technology allows the creation of a virtual computer system that can be hosted on Windows 10 Professional and Enterprise editions. The virtual computer shares the computer's hardware with Windows 10; therefore, the computer's hardware must fully support virtualization and that feature must be enabled in BIOS settings. The computer running Client Hyper-V will need more RAM than the minimum recommended specifications for Windows 10. The minimum operating system that can be a guest is Windows Vista with Service Pack 2 and the newest is Windows 10. All licensing and updates are managed separately for any virtual machines running in the Client Hyper-V environment.

Connectivity Applications

Instead of fortifying the idea that users work only on their own computers, Windows 10 provides several tools to help connect users to other computers and resources that they can leverage. Several of these connectivity applications are:

- Remote Desktop
- Remote Assistance
- Homegroups

Remote Desktop

Remote Desktop is included with Windows 10 Professional, Enterprise, and Education editions. Remote Desktop allows users to remotely connect to their computers using the Remote Desktop client over TCP/IP. Once connected, the user can sign in and begin running applications.

Remote Desktop is covered in Chapter 14, Remote Access and Client Support.

Remote Assistance

Remote Assistance is a stand-alone application included with all versions of Windows 10. A user can ask for help from a trusted professional over the network using email, file transfer, or the Easy Connect service. Easy Connect allows a computer to be discovered over the Internet using a generated password and the IPv6 network protocol. This is accomplished by establishing a live connection between the computer and public servers configured to support this service. The password uniquely identifies your computer on the public server. The professional service provider can connect to chat, transfer files, run diagnostics, and reconnect across reboots.

Remote Assistance is covered in Chapter 14, Remote Access and Client Support.

Homegroups

Homegroups provide a mechanism to easily share printers, pictures, music, videos, and documents with other Windows 7 or newer computers using homegroups. Each computer that joins the homegroup system must present a valid homegroup password to communicate with other members. Each computer can be configured with limits on what content, or type of content, is shared with other homegroup members.

Homegroup networking is covered in Chapter 7, Networking.

Networking Models

Networks connect multiple computers to share data and resources over a network. A network model details a logical framework for sharing, securing, and managing data and resources across that network. Just as there are different versions of Windows 10 to meet the differing needs of customers, there are also different network models available to connect computers. Some networking models support more computers and offer greater administrative control. Other models try to simplify the framework for simpler and smaller environments. The specific networking features of Windows 10 are covered in Chapter 7, Networking. The networking models supported by Windows 10 and covered here include:

- Workgroup model
- Domain model
- Windows Peer-to-Peer Networking

Workgroup Model

When a computer is first connected to a network, it typically is configured as a member of a workgroup. A workgroup is a loosely knit collection of peer computers on a network where no computer has control or superior role to any other computer. The peers share resources with each other over the network. This can be useful for a small number of computers in a typical home or small business network.

Each computer is identified by its name and address on the network. The workgroup itself is identified by an assigned name. The default workgroup name is typically WORKGROUP.

Workgroup membership rules are simple; a computer can be a member of only one workgroup at a time. More than one workgroup can coexist on the same network. Being a member of a workgroup helps a computer find shared resources such as files and printers on its peers, but it does not restrict it from accessing resources located outside its own workgroup.

The workgroup design is traditionally known as a peer-to-peer networking model; however, Microsoft introduced Windows Peer-to-Peer Networking technology with Windows XP SP2 to extend the boundaries of the traditional workgroup. These enhancements will be covered later in the chapter.

The workgroup design has strong advantages in informal environments. Its simple design and function allow easy sharing of files and printers. Even in the small office setting, the workgroup model can be effective at sharing information quickly among members. The factors for business to determine if the workgroup model is appropriate are the degree of computer management required and the need to centralize data into a central location.

Managing a workgroup can be difficult because each computer is in control of its own resources, its own users, and the permissions and actions assigned to them. A new user who needs to access shared files and printers on multiple machines on the network will need an account created on each workgroup machine to which that user requires access. Each of those machines will then need permissions configured to allow that user to access the required resources.

This can become a management nightmare, especially when changes or removal of access are required. Because separate users control each computer, each user must receive training on the care and control of their computer. When changes are required in security settings, each user must be monitored to ensure the changes are made throughout the workgroup.

The computers in a workgroup are usually part of a single local area network operating with direct access between each computer. Network routers typically act as physical boundaries of the workgroup. Network addressing is a logical boundary, as all workgroup members typically have the same network address. It is not typical to see a workgroup span outside a single local area network. This is altered with the introduction of the Windows Peer-to-Peer Networking technology.

Microsoft recommends that workgroups should not be used for more than 10 to 20 computers. There is a practical limit to sharing resources from workstation class computers. All Windows 10 editions are limited to support a maximum of 20 simultaneous connections.

Note that this does not limit the number of members in the workgroup, only the number of computers accessing a shared resource simultaneously. If the shared resource needs to be accessed by more users at the same time, the domain model becomes a better solution.

Domain Model

The domain model is a client/server strategy that allows central administrative management of its members. A domain is a collection of computers and users that are identified by a common security database. The database is stored on one or more dedicated servers called **domain controllers (DCs)**. Computers that are part of the domain can reference the domain database and read the user and computer accounts contained within. Member computers can access shared resources on other computers from the same domain, using the security information referenced by the DC to restrict access.

The domain model is also covered in Chapter 13, Enterprise Computing.

Each member of the domain can take on a client or server role. Servers host centralized resources and the clients access those shared resources.

The major differences between the workgroup and domain models are how the members are managed and the limits to sharing resources. A Windows 10 computer can be used as a server in a domain, but the connection limits mentioned in the workgroup model still apply. Server-class operating systems, such as Windows Server 2016, can theoretically have an unlimited number of clients access a shared resource simultaneously. The practical limit with centralized servers becomes overall performance and licensing.

Domain networking is typically employed in business environments, so not all editions of Windows 10 have support for it. Windows 10 Professional, Education, and Enterprise editions support joining a domain networking system.

When a server shares a resource, it can define permissions to access the resource based on the domain user and computer names stored on the DC. If a new user is added to the domain, each domain computer can directly reference the new domain user name by verifying it with the domain controller. Likewise, if a domain user account needs to be removed, it only has to be removed from the domain database on the domain controller and not each domain member computer.

A computer can be a member of a workgroup or a domain, but not both at the same time. A computer cannot be a member of more than one domain at the same time. The computer and the domain must be identified by unique names.

Access to shared resources in other domains and workgroups is still allowed, but the user has to authenticate to those resources. The user would be prompted to provide a user ID and password for the foreign system.

More than one domain can coexist on a network, with the domain defining a security boundary. Changes made to the security or configuration of a domain usually only impact domain members. However, it is possible for different domains to trust each other to allow shared access between domains. The limits of how domains trust each other depend on the type of domain in use.

Active Directory Domains   With the introduction of Windows Server 2000, Microsoft introduced a domain model generally referred to as **Active Directory (AD)**. The Active Directory model has a central database of user and computer accounts and centralized tools to manage them. The domain database is stored on dedicated DC servers. All DCs are capable of updating the database and replicating those changes to the other DCs in the domain. This is commonly referred to as **multimaster replication**.

Active Directory systems use a different naming strategy based on TCP/IP-based **Domain Name System (DNS)** technology, using names that appear similar to common Internet names, such as *microsoft.com*. This was done to better support the TCP/IP network protocols that link networks around the globe today.

From an administrator's perspective, another advantage to Active Directory is the ability to manage the user and computer environment of its members. The administrator can use Active Directory Group Policy to define items such as installed applications, security settings, environment settings, and limits. The Group Policy settings are stored as part of the Active Directory database and are visible to all members of the Active Directory forest. The Active Directory administrator can define specific criteria that control to what computers or user the settings apply.

Computers that understand what Group Policy is can read those settings and update themselves accordingly. Native support for processing Group Policy was introduced with Windows 2000.

Each new operating system enhances the administrator's flexibility with Group Policy by introducing support for new settings and controls that did not exist before. Windows 10 introduces several hundred new Group Policy settings. The client operating system must understand what a single Group Policy setting is before it can apply it.

Windows 10 can be a client of a domain, but it can never be a DC. To create an Active Directory domain, you are required to purchase and install a Windows Server operating system that supports Active Directory on a dedicated computer (which can be a physical or virtual system). Likewise, domain Group Policy settings only apply if the Windows 10 computer is a member of the domain.

Azure AD Join   Azure Active Directory is a directory service hosted by Microsoft as a cloud-based service over the Internet. In corporate environments, a company can register itself in Azure AD, which is made widely accessible by Microsoft's cloud services.

A Windows 10 device can register with Azure AD to enable centralized management of that device by the company's administrators. This allows employees and students to be connected though that enterprise cloud experience. The act of registration can enable access to organizational applications and resources whether the Windows 10 device is owned by the corporation or the individual.

The traditional AD domain model is still used with corporate computers, on-premises, with limited domain management functionality outside the corporate private network from the Internet. The traditional domain join can still provide the best on-premises managed experience for devices that are capable of domain joining.

Azure AD join is suitable for devices that cannot join a domain and in environments where users can best be managed from the cloud with **Mobile Device Management (MDM)** solutions such as Microsoft Intune instead of traditional domain management tools like Group Policy. As organizations move their business to the cloud and reduce on-premises infrastructure, Azure AD becomes key in several areas. Users can use their own identity in Azure AD to sign in to the Windows 10 computer and other cloud-based services using a same or single sign-on experience. Access to corporate applications and resources can be managed with subscription licenses linked to Azure AD accounts, which enables a dynamic management experience even as users and devices come and go. To enhance the corporate appeal of Azure AD join, end users can provision a brand-new device out of the box without a corporate administrator's involvement, enabled by a self-provisioning experience powered by Azure AD.

Windows Peer-to-Peer Networking

Microsoft introduced **Windows Peer-to-Peer Networking** as a client operating system enhancement for Windows Vista and later operating systems. This technology is similar in concept to the traditional workgroup model, but the technical details about how it operates are unique. The traditional workgroup is usually limited by the physical and logical boundaries of a basic network—respectively, the routers and network addresses assigned to computers. The traditional workgroup requires computers to share a common network addressing scheme and the same physical local area network (LAN).

This places a limit on sharing content across larger networks. Companies and individuals are forced to implement centralized servers to enable sharing technologies in these environments. This restricts ad hoc collaboration between users and companies because some type of preplanning and infrastructure deployment in advance is required.

Windows Peer-to-Peer Networking technology tries to remove these limits and make peer-to-peer infrastructure scalable from the LAN to the Internet. It does this by first removing the old restrictions of router and network addressing by basing communications on the TCP/IP IPv6 protocol.

The IPv4 standard defines traditional TCP/IP communication between computers. IPv6 is a newer standard for TCP/IP communication that resets the limits as they apply to peer-to-peer computing. Windows Peer-to-Peer Networking clients anywhere on the Internet can communicate with each other and form a peer-to-peer network, as long as they are using IPv6.

Once Windows Peer-to-Peer Networking clients establish communication with each other, they can interact to securely share resources—without a central server.

There is no reliance on central server technologies such as DNS, Active Directory, or Certificate Authorities; Windows Peer-to-Peer Network clients manage themselves with technologies and techniques specific to Windows Peer-to-Peer Networks. For example, Peer Name Resolution Protocol (PNRP) is used by Windows Peer-to-Peer Networking clients to discover each other.

Applications take advantage of this new peer-to-peer infrastructure to allow users to find each other, exchange data, and share data processing in real time. Note that the scope of allowed connectivity depends on the application, not the peer-to-peer protocol itself. For example, Windows 10 uses this mechanism to download and share Windows updates among Windows 10 computers as part of a feature called Windows Update Delivery Optimization. The update sharing can be configured to support distribution of Windows updates to peers on the local network or even to peers on the Internet. Microsoft includes controls to customize or restrict this behavior, and to be sensitive to expensive data connections as part of the update settings. The peer-to-peer networking technology is simply the mechanism for enabling this powerful sharing feature.

Chapter Summary

- Windows 10 is available in several editions: Windows 10 Home, Windows 10 Professional, Windows 10 Enterprise, and Windows 10 Education. There are also several special versions: Windows 10 N & K editions and Windows 10 Mobile.

- This chapter introduced the new and enhanced features of Windows 10 and how they help you organize and access information across different devices running Windows 10. Users can securely interact with Windows 10 using new authentication mechanisms enabled by Microsoft Passport and Windows Hello. Interacting with the web has been enhanced for cloud-based applications, including a new web browser called Microsoft Edge. Windows 10 comes in 32- and 64-bit versions.

- Windows 10 offers a streamlined user interface that combines a Start menu similar to that from Windows 7 and live tiles similar to those of the Windows 8 Start screen. Searching has been enhanced with Cortana, a virtual personal assistant. The application environment supports multitasking, multithreading, multiple processors, application compatibility emulation, and virtual computing.

- Minimum hardware requirements must be met with Windows 10, but those minimum hardware requirements have not changed since Windows 7. Hardware designed specifically for Windows 10 can have additional features unlocked by installing Windows 10 on the device. New features are frequently updated by Windows Update as part of a continuous update process in which Windows is treated as a service. Home and business users can have a slightly different update frequency, with consumers treated to the most frequent updates and corporate administrators having more control over what updates are installed and when. Windows 10 includes support for faster processors, System on a Chip, Plug and Play technology, efficient power management, and portable tablet and phone hardware that connects through advanced network connections to provide a rich user experience. Data is stored locally using backward-compatible file systems such as FAT32 while still providing newer file systems such as NTFS and ReFS.

- Application support in Windows 10 is designed to work on more than one level, for legacy applications or newer universal apps. A program can take advantage of basic compatibility settings, or the Compatibility Wizard can guide the user through choices. If an application cannot be made to work with Windows 10, Client Hyper-V may provide a legacy virtual operating system environment hosted on Windows 10 Enterprise if the underlying hardware supports that feature.

- Networks enable data sharing between computers, but Windows 10 also enables the user to share computers and resources through tools such as Remote Desktop, Remote Assistance, and homegroups. The emphasis is on connecting users to the tools they need, across devices, even if they are not local to the resource they are accessing.

- Windows 10 can participate in the workgroup or domain networking models. The workgroup model has been enhanced with the addition of TCP/IP IPv6 and Windows Peer-to-Peer Networking technology to extend the boundaries of the workgroup beyond the traditional local area network. The domain model has been enhanced with Azure AD join to allow computers to access corporate information from outside the private corporate network while still giving corporate IT the ability to securely manage the users' devices and interaction with corporate resources.

Key Terms

Active Directory (AD)   A domain security database of user and computer information that is stored on domain controllers and referenced by domain member computers. This database is stored on multimaster replicating domain controllers running a server-class operating system such as Windows Server 2008 or Windows Server 2012. The older Windows NT domain controllers cannot hold Active Directory security databases.

Azure AD join   Feature that connects Windows 10 computers with a domain hosted in Windows Azure AD instead of an on-premises domain.

central processing unit (CPU)   A device responsible for the actual execution of instructions stored in applications and operating system code. Windows 10 supports 32- and 64-bit CPUs.

Continuum   The Windows 10 feature that automatically adjusts Windows 10 between desktop mode and tablet mode as the device state changes.

Continuum for phone   The feature for Windows 10 phones that allows external peripherals, such as a mouse, keyboard, monitor, or projectors, to be used.

Cortana   A personalized virtual search assistant. Cortana can use voice recognition to accept commands from the user.

desktop mode   The traditional configuration for a Windows 10 computer that is optimized for use with a mouse and keyboard.

device driver   Software written by the developer of a hardware component that tells the operating system how to talk to and control the hardware.

domain controller (DC)   A server responsible for holding a domain security database that contains a list of user and computer account security data.

Domain Name System (DNS)   A standard service in the TCP/IP protocol used to define how computer names are translated into IP addresses.

Dynamic Link Library (DLL)   A file that holds application code modules. These modules are shared among applications, so the file is also called a library. DLL files can be replaced to update an application without having to replace the entire application.

Easy Upgrade   A simple upgrade process that can be used to upgrade Windows 10 Home to Windows 10 Professional. An Easy Upgrade is purchased through the Windows Store.

Encrypting File System (EFS)   A component of the NTFS file system that is responsible for encrypting individual files. Those files are not readable without the correct digital identification.

hyperthreading   A technique used in certain Intel processors to improve their overall performance by working on more than one thread at a time.

Microsoft Edge   The new web browser in Windows 10 that replaces Internet Explorer. It is completely redesigned to avoid the legacy support issues encountered with Internet Explorer.

Microsoft Passport   An MFA (multifactor authentication) system in Windows 10 that enhances security by avoiding the use of a user name and password. Biometric authentication on the client allows access to the remote system.

Mobile Device Management (MDM)   An administrative system that allows corporate administrators to deploy, secure, monitor, and integrate mobile devices such as laptops, tablets, and smartphones into the corporate ecosystem.

multifactor authentication (MFA)   A security system that requires more than one method of proving someone or something is who or what it is declared to be. Different methods are used to independently verify the user's identity for a transaction or sign-in attempt, such as a password plus a fingerprint. Each layer increases the difficulty an attacker faces trying to breach the security of a target.

multimaster replication   The replication of changes to the security domain database among multiple domain controllers. When a domain has multiple domain controllers, all domain controllers are capable of making changes to the security domain database they share.

multiprocessor   A term used to refer to a computer with more than one CPU.

multitasking   A term used to describe the appearance of more than one application sharing the CPU of the computer. To the user, the applications all seem to be running at the same time.

multitouch   A method of input on a touch screen or a touch pad that allows two or more points of contact on a high-precision touch device. This enables precision gestures to interact with the Windows 10 environment.

NT File System (NTFS)   A standard for organizing files and folders on a hard disk partition. This standard is more complex than FAT but adds more management features. This is the preferred standard for storing files on a hard disk.

PIN   A personal identification number that allows users to identify themselves during the authentication or sign-in process.

Plug and Play technology   A general term used to describe hardware that can be plugged in to the computer system and removed at any time. The computer will recognize the hardware dynamically, load a device driver for it, and make it available to the user in a short period of time.

preemptive multitasking   A method for applications to share a CPU and appear that they are all running at the same time. This method adds time limits and priority levels to determine how long an application can use the processor and which application gets to go next. An application can also be preempted by another application if it has a higher priority level.

process   A term used to describe the files, memory, and application code that combine together to form a single running application. Each application running on a multitasking system is referenced by a single process.

processor affinity   A standard in which a process that starts in a computer with more than one CPU is usually assigned to that CPU again the next time it runs.

quantum   The amount of time allocated to a program running in a preemptive multitasking environment. Once a program's quantum has expired, it must wait for the next available quantum.

Software Assurance (SA)   An option when purchasing Microsoft software that allows you to automatically receive the latest version of a product. For example, if you purchased Windows 8 with Software Assurance, you would automatically be able to upgrade to Windows 10.

System on a Chip (SoC)   A hardware platform that combines multiple devices that would normally be found as discrete components inside a computer, but instead are combined into a single silicon chip. The SoC design allows for the creation of computers with a small physical form factor, power savings, and simplified device construction.

tablet mode   The configuration for Windows 10 that is optimized for use with a touch screen.

thread   A piece of code that performs a specific single task. An application is written as one or more threads, each of which performs a specific task within the application. The thread is typically seen as a unit of work for the CPU to perform.

trusted platform module (TPM)   A third-party standard to define a method of trusting the computer environment before an operating system is started. This helps to prevent the theft of a hard disk and placement of the disk in a foreign system to steal data.

universal apps   A developer platform strategy to enable the development of applications that can run on every Windows device, such as phones, tablets, laptops, desktops, and Xbox gaming centers.

Universal Windows Platform (UWP)   A common application platform available on every device that runs Windows 10. The UWP provides a guaranteed core programming interface across devices. The developer can create a single application package that can be installed onto a wide range of devices and unlock the unique capabilities of each device.

Virtual Desktop   A new feature in Windows 10 that allows users to create multiple desktops with different applications and switch between them on a single monitor.

Windows as a Service (WaaS)   An update process for Windows 10 in which new features are continuously published and installed to existing Windows 10 installations.

Windows Hello   Biometric authentication functionality in Windows 10. At release, Windows Hello supports fingerprints, facial recognition, and iris scanning.

Windows Peer-to-Peer Networking   A networking technology included in Windows Vista and later operating systems that allows clients to use IPv6 to communicate with each other over LANs or the Internet.

Review Questions

1. A friend has asked you which version of Windows 10 should be purchased to start a new home-based business. Your friend needs only one computer for now, and requires support for Windows Store applications needed to manage the business. Your friend is not very experienced with computers and has asked for easy-to-use features. Which version of Windows 10 do you recommend?

    a. Windows 10 Education

    b. Windows 10 Home

    c. Windows 10 Professional

    d. Windows 10 Enterprise

2. The minimum specifications for Windows 10 require greater CPU and RAM resources than Windows 7. True or False?

3. _____ on a Chip is a hardware component capable of reducing the overall size of a computer.

4. The new web browser included with Windows 10 is called _____.

    a. Charlie

    b. Virtual Desktop

    c. Cortana

    d. Microsoft Edge

    e. Windows Hello

5. You are adding a new 500 GB hard drive to your computer. The hard drive must be formatted with a file system to organize files into folders on that drive. The recommended file system to use is _____.

    a. exFAT

    b. NTFS

    c. ReFS

    d. FAT

6. You are considering purchasing an inexpensive computer from a friend that has a 32-bit CPU and 8 GB of RAM. You install Windows 10 Home, 32-bit edition, but you can't see the full amount of RAM. What is wrong?

    a. The CPU does not support hyperthreading.

    b. You need to install a 64-bit version of Windows 10.

    c. The CPU does not support multiple cores.

    d. You must install Windows 10 Professional.

    e. Windows 10, 32-bit editions cannot support more than 4 GB of RAM.

7. Your workstation is running Windows 10 Professional and you decide to share a folder on your computer. Twenty-two people in your office are trying to connect to that folder at the same time over the network. The first 20 people can connect, but the other two cannot. To fix this, you could _____.

   a. buy a computer, software, and licenses to run Windows Server 2016

   b. restart your computer

   c. make sure the network card is using WDF device drivers

   d. none of the above

8. Computers that belong to the same domain can access a common security database of user and computer account information. This type of database on Windows Server 2016 domain controller servers is also known as a(n) _____ database.

   a. primary

   b. workgroup

   c. jet

   d. Active Directory

   e. backup

9. Which of the following is an advantage of domain networking?

   a. no central security database

   b. built in to every version of Windows 10

   c. centralized security management

   d. support for up to 25 simultaneous shared connections

10. A new company will have 40 workstations in one building sharing a single network. All users must be able to share files and printers with each other. Access to shared information must be secure and simple to administer. The best technology for this system is _____.

    a. workgroups

    b. Windows Peer-to-Peer Networking

    c. people to people

    d. domain networking

11. The new virtual personal assistant built in to Windows 10 can search multiple places for information that relates to your needs, including which of the following? (Select three.)

    a. the local computer

    b. Microsoft Passport

    c. the web

    d. external accounts

12. In tablet mode, Windows 10 will assume that _____ is (are) not generally available.

    a. multitouch

    b. a keyboard and mouse

    c. Microsoft Passport

    d. multifactor authentication

13. The main network protocol used to communicate between Windows 10 computers is
    _____.
    a. TCP/IP
    b. X.25
    c. SLIP
    d. Peer-to-Peer
    e. Teredo

14. The Window 10 version of TCP/IP supports the newer communication protocol called
    _____.
    a. IPv5
    b. IPv6
    c. IPv4
    d. WDDM
    e. IPv8

15. A user has a computer running Windows 7 but cannot seem to activate the free upgrade
    offer to Windows 10. The computer is a 32-bit CPU model with 4 GB of RAM and a 500 GB
    hard drive with 200 GB of free space. The free upgrade is likely unavailable because
    _____.
    a. the system does not meet minimum hardware specifications
    b. there is not enough free space on the hard drive
    c. the system is missing prerequisite Windows Updates
    d. the system is running Windows 7 Extreme
    e. the offer is only available to users of Windows 8 or 8.1

16. Application windows can be docked to the sides and corners of the screen using a feature
    called _____.
    a. Snap
    b. Shake
    c. Virtual Desktop
    d. Peek
    e. Docker

17. An administrator of a manufacturing company would like to manage corporate computers
    with Group Policy. The administrator is reviewing a purchase request for 20 new computers
    from the business owners. Which version of Windows 10 should the administrator consider
    for installation on the new computers? (Select two.)
    a. Windows 10 Home
    b. Windows 10 Professional
    c. Windows 10 Education
    d. Windows 10 Enterprise
    e. Windows 10 Ultimate

18. Windows Hello supports multiple biometric authentication methods, including facial recognition. The failsafe method to authenticate in case the facial recognition method is unavailable is _____.

    a. fingerprint sensor

    b. retina scanner

    c. PIN

    d. Microsoft Passport

19. Some hardware can be added to the computer without having to restart or power down the computer. After a short period of time, the device driver automatically loads and the hardware is available to applications and the user. This type of hardware is considered compatible with what type of technology?

    a. Plug and Go

    b. InstantGo

    c. Plug and Play

    d. Legacy

20. Windows 10 takes up less room on storage devices when the operating system is installed. One reason for this could be the enhanced _____ feature of the newer edition NTFS file system.

    a. self-healing

    b. compression

    c. alternate data stream

    d. hard linked

21. Software Assurance customers can take advantage of extra applications provided with Windows 10 Enterprise edition. What feature included with this edition will allow a virtual computer to be hosted by the computer running Windows 10?

    a. SoC

    b. NTFS

    c. UNIX native application support

    d. Client Hyper-V

    e. Terminal Services

22. Which of the following is an advantage of homegroup computing?

    a. requires one or more expensive servers

    b. supports 20 workstations

    c. no security enforced

    d. simple to set up initially

23. A thread represents the files, data, and instructions that make up a single running task or application. True or False?

24. You are installing a computer to run a nuclear reactor management system. The software lists Windows 10 as a requirement. To ensure that future feature updates do not impact the stability of the software, you should consider what type of Windows 10 installation?

    a. WaaS

    b. Any version

    c. Core

    d. LTSB

25. Which of the following is a disadvantage of workgroup computing?

    a. requires one or more expensive servers

    b. supports an unlimited number of workstations

    c. no centralized security management

    d. simple to set up initially

Case Projects

Case Project 1-1: Selecting a Windows 10 Version for a Small Organization

Master Motors has 18 computers. They are replaced only as necessary due to hardware failure or new software requirements. No server is in place to centrally manage resources or security and no plan exists to add one in the next 3 months. Master Motors may expand to two new locations in the next 12 months. Two computers have recently failed and require replacement. The owner would like to also purchase three extra computers as spares and for possible expansion. Which version of Windows 10 should be purchased with the new computers?

Case Project 1-2: Dealing with Users Who Bring Their Own Devices to Work

Gigantic Life Insurance has 4000 users spread over five locations in North America. They have called you as a consultant to discuss different options for deploying Windows 10 to the desktops in their organization. They are concerned that users will be bringing their own mobile devices such as tablets and laptops to connect to their work data. This will improve productivity, but they are concerned with what control they have over the users' access to corporate data. How will Windows 10 help the company manage users who bring their own devices?

chapter 2

Installing Windows 10

After reading this chapter and completing the exercises, you will be able to:

- Choose a method for installation
- Choose a type of installation
- Perform an attended installation of Windows 10
- Describe tools in the Windows 10 Assessment and Deployment Kit
- Perform an unattended installation of Windows 10
- Understand and perform image-based installation
- Use provisioning to customize Windows 10 installations
- Implement Windows To Go

For end users, operating system deployment is a rare event that doesn't need to be optimized. For professionals in the computer industry, optimizing deployment is a critical process that can save many hours of work and reduce support calls. You need to be aware of the various installation methods so that you can choose one that is appropriate for your organization.

Most organizations have developed some variety of automated deployment process. In this chapter, you will see how to use Windows System Image Manager to perform an unattended installation by using answer files. You will also learn how to use Sysprep and the Deployment Imaging Servicing and Management (DISM) tool to perform image-based installations. To configure already deployed instances of Windows 10, you will learn how to use Windows Imaging and Configuration Designer to create and apply provisioning packages. Finally, you will learn about using Windows To Go for users who need to take a standardized workspace on the road.

Windows 10 Installation Methods

Windows 10 supports a number of different installation methods. Which method you choose varies depending on the number of computers in your organization, the speed of your network, and the level of customization that is required.

The three most common installation methods for Windows 10 are:

- DVD boot installation
- Distribution share installation
- Image-based installation

DVD Boot Installation

The **DVD boot installation** method is the least suitable method for a large volume of computers. It requires you to visit each computer with a DVD and to leave the DVD in the computer during the installation process. This method is suitable for small organizations that only occasionally install Windows 10.

The degree of customization performed with a DVD boot installation is low because it includes only the drivers and components included on the Windows 10 installation DVD. It does not include additional applications or updates. However, you can add drivers during installation by using a USB drive or other removable storage media.

To speed up a DVD boot installation, you can put the installation files on faster media, such as USB storage. The USB interface on modern computers is typically much faster than a DVD drive. You performed a DVD boot installation in Activity 1-1 in Chapter 1, Introduction to Windows 10.

Distribution Share Installation

A **distribution share installation** requires computers to be booted into Windows Preinstallation Environment (Windows PE) from removable storage and then run the Windows 10 installation from a distribution share on a server. Windows PE is a limited version of Windows that is loaded from removable storage during the Windows 10 Setup process. The removable storage you boot from could be a CD-ROM or flash drive. The installation files on the distribution share are created by Windows System Image Manager (SIM).

The speed of a distribution share installation varies because all of the files must be transferred across the network. An installation over a 100 Mbps network is typically slower than a DVD boot installation. However, over a 1 Gbps network, a distribution share installation is typically faster than a DVD boot installation.

The level of customization for a distribution share installation is higher than a DVD boot installation because you can include additional files such as updates or drivers as part of the installation process.

Image-Based Installation

An **image** is a copy of a previously prepared operating system that has been copied to a file. **Image-based installation** requires you to create a customized image that you apply to each computer. After the customized image is created, it is placed on a distribution share by using Windows SIM. This installation type requires computers to be booted into Windows PE from removable storage and then copying the customized image onto the computer.

An image-based installation is the fastest type of installation because all configuration is already complete. However, you may need several images for different types of users. In larger organizations, it is reasonable to put forth the effort required to develop multiple images.

The highest level of customization is achieved by using image-based installations. Image-based installations can include service packs, updates, additional drivers, and even installed applications.

Windows 10 Installation Types

When an organization moves to a new desktop operating system, the network administrators must decide whether to upgrade existing systems or perform clean installations. A **clean installation** is an installation of Windows 10 performed on a computer that does not have existing data or applications. If you are deploying to existing computers, a clean installation requires you to wipe the hard drive first. If clean installations are performed, there must be a plan for migrating user settings and files from the old operating system to the new operating system.

In the past, most organizations chose to perform clean installations when deploying a new operating system because the computers tended to be more stable afterward. However, Microsoft now recommends in-place upgrades instead. This is because in-place upgrades to Windows 10 perform a clean installation in the background and then migrate settings.

A new option in Windows 10 is provisioning a previously installed operating system. With provisioning, you modify an existing installation to match organizational requirements rather than reinstalling the operating system. This is faster than reinstalling an operating system.

Upgrade Installations

An **upgrade installation** is also referred to as an in-place upgrade. Upgrade installations automatically migrate the user settings, files, and applications that exist in the previous operating system to the new operating system on the same computer. For example, when you perform an upgrade from Windows 7 to Windows 10, the user settings and files are retained. All of the applications are retained as well.

To upgrade to Windows 10, a computer must be running Windows 7 with Service Pack 1 or Windows 8.1. Also, upgrades must be to an equivalent version. For example, Windows 8.1 Pro can be upgraded to Windows 10 Pro. For a list of allowed upgrade paths, see the Upgrade editions section of Specifications at *https://www.microsoft.com/en-us/windows/windows-10-specifications#upgrade* on the Microsoft website.

Upgrades to Windows 10 are automatically advertised to computers running Windows 7 Service Pack 1 and Windows 8.1. The installation files for Windows 10 are cached on the hard drive before the upgrade is advertised to users. Users can then choose to perform the upgrade. In many business environments, this behavior is blocked because upgrades need to be performed in a more organized way. You can obtain the installation media to perform Windows 10 upgrades from the Software Download page for Windows 10 at *https://www.microsoft.com/en-us/software-download/windows10*. The media creation tool on this page creates a bootable DVD or USB drive.

You cannot use image-based installation when you perform an upgrade to Windows 10. You must run Setup.exe to properly upgrade an existing computer. Only DVD boot installations and distribution share installations use Setup.exe.

Because the Windows 10 installation is image-based, the upgrade process captures settings from the previous operating system and applies them after Windows 10 is installed. You can see this during the upgrade process. A potential downside to this process is that the upgrade may not migrate all settings and applications because settings stored in a nonstandard way might be missed.

Most computer hardware and software are compatible with Windows 10. However, in a business environment, you should verify that all important applications are compatible with Windows 10 before upgrading. Check with the application vendor for compatibility information.

Clean Installations

Most Windows 10 installations are clean installations. Home users typically get Windows 10 when they buy a new computer. A new computer always has a clean installation. Even in corporate environments, new operating systems are often implemented when new computers are purchased. Using new computers ensures that they are powerful enough to run the new operating system and new applications are often introduced at the same time.

When a clean installation is performed on an existing computer, the hard drive of the computer is wiped and reformatted to erase the contents before installation. This raises concerns about losing files stored on the local hard drive of the computer.

Clean installations can be performed by any installation method. This includes the DVD boot, distribution share, or image-based installation methods.

In most corporate environments, computer usage rules dictate that users cannot store any files on their local hard drive. However, in practice, many users store important files on the local hard drive despite the usage rules. Network administrators are, therefore, always concerned about locally stored data as part of performing a clean installation on an existing computer.

Even when a clean installation is performed on a new computer, there are concerns with data migration. When a new computer is obtained, users often want to retain files and settings from the old computer.

Migrating User Settings and Files

Deploying Windows 10 should not affect the ability of your users to perform their jobs. To provide a consistent experience when Windows 10 is implemented, Windows 10 should have all of the same user settings as the previous operating system.

Windows 10 stores user settings in user profiles. Each user profile is stored as a folder in the C:\Users\ directory. For example, the user profile for the user Joe is stored in C:\Users\Joe. In this folder are a number of subfolders that hold information such as Start button configuration, Desktop icons, Documents, and the Microsoft Edge cache. In addition, this folder contains a registry file named Ntuser.dat that holds user-specific registry information related to application configuration and some Windows configuration settings for that specific user.

During an upgrade to Windows 10, profiles are automatically upgraded and settings within the profile are retained. When a clean installation is performed, there must be a process in place to migrate user profiles to the new computer.

 Windows 7 and Windows 8.1 included Windows Easy Transfer to migrate user profiles to a new computer. Windows 10 does not include Windows Easy Transfer. Microsoft has partnered with LapLink to provide PCmover Express free for noncommercial use. You can obtain PCmover Express at *http://pcmoverfree.azurewebsites.net/*.

Microsoft provides the User State Migration Tool (USMT) for migrating user profiles to Windows 10. USMT is a set of command-line tools that are part of the Windows 10 Assessment and Deployment Kit (ADK). Larger organizations create scripts to capture user profile data before operating system deployment and apply user profile data after operating system deployment.

Most small organizations do not use tools for migrating user profile data. Instead, administrators manually copy important profile information such as favorites and documents. If these folders have been redirected to shared folders on the network, then no migration is required.

Attended Installation

An **attended installation** requires you to manually start and perform the installation by running Setup.exe. You perform a DVD-based installation by running Setup.exe from the Windows 10 DVD or perform a distribution share installation by running Setup.exe from a network share. For a single computer in a nonstandardized environment, the simplest method is to boot from the Windows 10 DVD, which automatically runs Setup.exe for you.

Windows 10 minimizes user involvement during installation. You enter information only at the very beginning and very end of the installation. The middle portion of the installation requires no intervention by you. This installation process allows you to spend a few minutes starting an installation, leave to perform other tasks, and then spend a few minutes finishing the installation.

In Activity 1-1, you performed a clean installation of Windows 10 by booting from the Windows 10 DVD. Please refer back to that activity for the steps that were performed.

An attended installation does not ask for any network configuration information. A new attended installation installs TCP/IP for networking and uses DHCP to obtain its IP address and configuration. Any additional network configuration, such as joining a domain or setting a static IP address, must be performed after installation is complete.

Product Activation

Product activation is a process put in place by Microsoft to reduce piracy. If an installation of Windows 10 is not activated, some operating system features are disabled. At minimum, some personalization features are disabled. At this writing, no other functionality is impaired, but older Microsoft operating systems have also forced a shutdown every 60 minutes for a nonactivated system.

Product activation requires very little additional work on the part of a computer user and significantly reduces piracy. It is now designed to inform a user that an unscrupulous retailer is selling illegitimate copies of Windows 10 rather than to punish the user.

You can activate Windows 10 from the Activation tab in Update & security. Figure 2-1 shows the Activation tab for a computer that has already been activated. You can also view the edition of Windows 10 and change the product key.

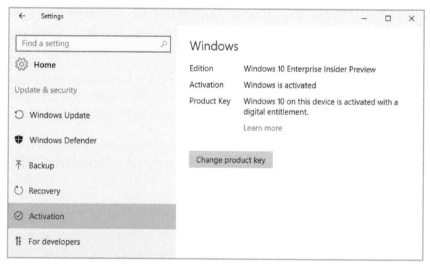

Figure 2-1   Windows 10 activation status

When Windows 10 is activated, the product key used during installation is associated with the specific computer that is performing the activation. Information about the hardware in the computer is used to generate a unique identifier that is sent as part of the activation process. No personal information is sent as part of the activation process. If another attempt is made to activate a different computer using the same product key, the attempt is denied.

If you perform significant hardware changes to your computer, you may be forced to reactivate Windows 10, because Windows 10 calculates that it is installed on a new computer. Reactivation is not forced for simple upgrades such as an additional hard drive or additional RAM. However, installing a new motherboard typically requires reactivation.

In practice, at the time of this writing, Microsoft has been allowing two automatic product activations before requiring users to phone the Activation Center. This is useful when moving your copy of Windows 10 to a new computer. If you do need to phone the Activation Center, Microsoft confirms your license information and the reason for an additional installation before giving you an activation code.

For more information about activation, see the Activation in Windows 10 page at *http://windows.microsoft.com/en-us/windows-10/activation-in-windows-10*.

Smaller organizations typically obtain Windows 10 when they purchase a new computer (OEM) or at a retail store. Both OEM and retail software activate over the Internet or by phone as described previously. Larger organizations typically purchase Windows 10 through a volume license agreement. A volume license agreement allows for three types of activation:

- *Multiple Activation Key (MAK)*—This type of product key functions the same as an OEM or retail product key that can be activated over the Internet or by phone. However, a MAK can be used on a specific number of computers rather than just once. This simplifies key management for midsized organizations.

- *Key Management Service (KMS)*—This type of product key requires you to install KMS on a computer to act as a central point for product registration on your internal network. Product keys are installed on the KMS server and activated by having the KMS server communicate with the Internet. Computers activate by communicating with the KMS server on the internal network. This scenario simplifies key management in very large organizations. It also allows activation to occur in scenarios where the client computer is not able to directly perform activation due to firewalls.

- *Active Directory–based activation*—If computers will contact an Active Directory domain at least every 180 days, you can implement Active Directory–based activation. Computers activate by communicating with Active Directory rather than a specific server. This option for activation was introduced for Windows 8 or newer operating systems. This is an improvement over KMS because there is no need to communicate with a specific server.

For more information about volume activation, see the Volume Activation for Windows 10 page at *https://technet.microsoft.com/en-us/itpro/windows/deploy/volume-activation-windows-10*.

Activity 2-1: Viewing Activation Information for Windows 10

Time Required: 5 minutes
Objective: View activation information for Windows 10

Description: You know that Windows 10 automatically activates after installation if it has Internet connectivity. In this activity, you verify that your installation of Windows 10 activated properly.

1. Click the **Start** button and click **Settings**.
2. Click **Update & security**.
3. Click **Activation**.
4. Read the activation information for your computer. Notice that your product ID is listed here. You can also change your product key here if necessary.
5. Close the Settings window.

Windows 10 Assessment and Deployment Kit

Home users are typically not concerned with how an operating system is deployed or the tools used for deployment. Many home users buy a computer preconfigured with an operating system and never need to install the operating system themselves. Other home users who do like to install the operating system are not greatly inconvenienced by an inefficient deployment process because they perform installations only occasionally.

Conversely, network administrators are much more concerned than home users with how operating systems are deployed. Network administrators are responsible for deploying operating systems to many computers; inefficiencies in the deployment process can extend the length of deployment projects and cost their companies additional staff time. Long projects and additional staff time result in higher costs.

To help network administrators deploy Windows 10, Microsoft provides the **Windows 10 Assessment and Deployment Kit (ADK)**. Windows ADK contains a number of tools to prepare for deployments and automate the deployment process. Figure 2-2 shows the features available in the Windows 10 ADK.

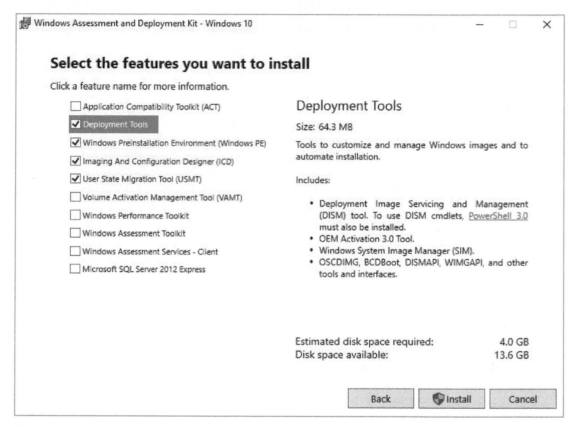

Figure 2-2   Windows 10 ADK features

Application Compatibility Toolkit

Computer hardware and operating systems do not add value to an organization; applications are the tools that bring value to organizations. It is essential that the applications that ran on an older operating system still run properly on a new operating system. The **Application Compatibility Toolkit (ACT)** helps organizations identify which applications are compatible with Windows 10 and which applications are not.

ACT can scan computers on the network to gather an inventory of applications that are installed. If ACT identifies applications that are not compatible with Windows 10, it also sometimes identifies mitigations that allow noncompliant applications to run, such as running the application as administrator. Microsoft SQL Server is required to install ACT. You can choose to install Microsoft SQL Server 2012 if required.

Deployment Image Servicing and Management (DISM) Tool

The **Deployment Image Servicing and Management (DISM)** tool is used to perform imaging and offline servicing of **Windows Imaging Format (WIM)** images. WIM is a file-based image format that stores multiple images in a single file. In Windows 7, you could use ImageX to perform imaging operations. The functionality provided by ImageX has now been included in DISM for Windows 10.

Offline servicing is typically used by large organizations that want to apply Windows updates or drivers to an image. However, it can also be used to update Windows PE images. DISM can use answer files created by the Windows System Image Manager (see the next section) to define which updates should be applied. Only the offline servicing section of the answer file is used.

Windows System Image Manager

Windows System Image Manager (SIM) is a graphical tool for configuring unattended installs creating distribution shares. Windows SIM is also included in the Windows Automated Installation Kit (WAIK), discussed later in the chapter.

You can use Windows SIM to:

- Create answer files for unattended installations.
- Add device drivers and applications to an answer file.
- Create and add files to a distribution share.

Windows PE

Windows PE is a limited and non-GUI version of Windows 10 that can be used for installing, troubleshooting, and repairing Windows 10. In the past, an MS-DOS boot disk would be used for many of these tasks. Configuring MS-DOS boot disks for network connectivity was particularly cumbersome. Windows PE includes networking components and allows you to use current Windows drivers for network connectivity rather than searching for older MS-DOS drivers.

When you boot from the Windows 10 installation DVD, Windows PE is the operating system that controls the installation process. Windows PE provides more flexibility during the installation process than the boot environment used in older operating systems such as Windows XP. Without the feature-rich installation environment provided by Windows PE, the installation process could not use WIM.

Windows Imaging and Configuration Designer (ICD)

The **Windows Imaging and Configuration Designer (ICD)** is a new tool in the Windows 10 ADK that helps to create provisioning packages and create image media. A provisioning package is used to configure an existing deployment of Windows 10 in a specific way. The option to create image media simplifies the image deployment process by removing the need to manually run imaging commands by using DISM. Certain portions of deployment can be automated by Windows ICD, but you cannot create a completely automated deployment of Windows 10 by using only Windows ICD.

User State Migration Tool

The **User State Migration Tool (USMT)** moves desktop settings and applications from one computer to another. Some features of USMT include the ability to:

- Capture user configuration state.
- Apply user configuration state.
- Migrate Encrypting File System (EFS) certificates with the /copyraw option.
- Create a configuration file by using the /genconfig option.
- Use hard links to simplify data migration on the same computer.

Volume Activation Management Tool

Volume Activation Management Tool (VAMT) is used to provide activation services for Windows operating systems and Microsoft Office. In Windows Server 2012 R2 or Windows Server 2016, you can install the Volume Activation Services server role, which is equivalent to VAMT.

VAMT is useful for installing management tools for volume activation on computers other than a server where Volume Activation Services is installed. Also, you can install VAMT on Windows Server 2008 R2 or Windows Server 2012 if you do not have Windows Server 2012

R2 or Windows Server 2016 in your environment. VAMT can also be used to configure proxy activation where a local computer at a remote site forwards activation information to the central Key Management Service (KMS).

Performance and Assessment Tools

The Windows 10 ADK includes several tools for collecting performance information and assessing client performance. The idea behind these tools is to help you identify the source of any performance problems when you are testing Windows 10 deployment. For example, after an upgrade, a specific application may be performing poorly. You can use the performance and assessment tools to help identify the source of the issue. These tools are more likely to be used by application developers or those supporting custom applications than network or desktop administrators.

Windows 10 ADK includes:

- *Windows Performance Toolkit*—This option includes Windows Performance Recorder and Windows Performance Analyzer. Windows Performance Recorder collects performance information and stores it in Event Tracing for Windows (ETW) recordings. Windows Performance Analyzer is used to analyze the ETW logs.

- *Windows Assessment Toolkit*—This option is a tool for triggering a specific workload on computers so that the results can be analyzed. You can use this tool to compare performance of Windows 7 computers and upgraded Windows 10 computers to confirm that there has been no performance degradation.

Activity 2-2: Downloading Windows 10 ADK for Offline Use

Time Required: 30–90 minutes
Objective: Download the Windows 10 ADK for offline use

Description: The default installation of the Windows 10 ADK downloads and installs only the components that you select. However, you anticipate using the Windows 10 ADK on several different computers. In this activity, you download the files for offline installation. After the files are downloaded, you can copy the directory to any location and install the features that you select.

To save time, your instructor may already have downloaded these files to make them available on a network file share or external storage. Verify with your instructor.

1. If necessary, start your computer and sign in.

2. On the taskbar, click **Microsoft Edge**.

3. In the Where to next box, type **https://msdn.microsoft.com/en-us/windows/hardware/ dn913721.aspx** and press **Enter**.

4. On the Download the Windows ADK page, scroll down, and under Windows ADK for Windows 10, Version 1511, click **Get Windows ADK for Windows 10**. (If you are using a newer version of Windows 10, your Version number may differ.)

5. In the pop-up box with 'adksetup.exe finished downloading', click **Run**.

6. In the Windows Assessment and Deployment Kit –Windows 10 window, click **Download the Windows Assessment and Deployment Kit – Windows 10 for installation on a separate computer**.

7. In the Download Path box, type **C:\ADK** and click **Next**.

8. On the Windows Kits Privacy page, click **Yes** and click **Next**.

9. On the License Agreement page, click **Accept**.

10. Wait while the files are downloaded. Because the download is approximately 4 GB, it can take 30 minutes or more for the download to complete.

11. When the download is complete, click **Close**.

12. Close Microsoft Edge.

Activity 2-3: Installing the Windows 10 ADK

Time Required: 10 minutes

Objective: Install the Windows 10 ADK

Description: To begin testing automated deployment for Windows 10, you need to install the Windows 10 ADK. To minimize the disk space used, you will install only the required tools.

This activity assumes that the ADK files have been downloaded to C:\ADK. If your files are in another location, run adksetup.exe from that location instead.

1. If necessary, start your computer and sign in.

2. On the taskbar, click **File Explorer**.

3. In the navigation pane, click **This PC**, double-click **Local Disk (C:)**, and double-click **ADK**.

4. Double-click **adksetup**.

5. In the Windows Assessment and Deployment Kit – Windows 10 window, click **Next** to accept the default installation location.

6. On the Windows Kits Privacy page, click **Yes**, and click **Next**.

7. On the License Agreement page, click **Accept**.

8. On the Select the features you want to install page, select only the following features and then click **Install**:

    • Deployment Tools

    • Windows Preinstallation Environment (Windows PE)

    • Imaging and Configuration Designer (ICD)

    • User State Migration Tool (USMT)

9. In the User Account Control dialog box, click **Yes**.

10. On the Welcome to the Windows Assessment and Deployment Kit – Windows 10 page, click **Close**.

11. Close File Explorer.

12. Click the **Start** menu, click **All apps**, scroll down, and click **Windows Kits**. You can see that the new tools are located here.

13. Close the Start menu.

Unattended Installation

Unattended installations do not require administrator intervention. The entire process can be automated using an answer file. An **answer file** is an XML file that contains settings used during the Windows installation process. Installation settings are read from the answer file instead of requiring administrator input during installation. Unattended installations are faster than attended installations and can be more consistent when the same answer file is used each time.

Using an unattended installation gives you a wider range of configuration options than can be performed during an attended installation. For example, an attended installation does not allow you to configure network settings. An unattended installation allows you to configure network settings and many other settings by putting the necessary information in the answer file.

To perform unattended installations of Windows 10, you must understand:

• Answer file names

• Configuration passes

• Windows System Image Manager

Answer File Names

When you perform a basic unattended installation, you can specify the name of the answer file or allow Setup to find the answer file automatically. You specify the name of the answer file by using the /unattend switch when you run Setup. The /unattend switch allows you to specify the path and name of the answer file.

If you do not specify the name of an answer file, Setup will search for an answer file. This allows you to perform unattended installations by putting an answer file on removable media and then booting from DVD. Removable media includes floppy disks, USB drives, CD-ROMs, and DVDs.

The name of the answer file searched for varies depending on the configuration pass being performed. When performing a full setup without using Sysprep, you need to use an **autounattend.xml** file. Configuration passes and the required answer file name are listed in Table 2-1. If an autounattend.xml file is used, it is cached to disk as **unattend.xml** for use by later configuration passes.

Table 2-1   Configuration passes and answer file names

Configuration pass	Answer file name
windowsPE	Autounattend.xml
offlineServicing	Autounattend.xml
Specialize	Unattend.xml
Generalize	Unattend.xml
AuditSystem	Unattend.xml
AuditUser	Unattend.xml
oobeSystem	Unattend.xml

Setup also looks in multiple locations for an answer file. The most common locations used are removable storage or the \sources folder in the Windows 10 distribution directory. Table 2-2 shows the order in which locations are searched for answer files.

Table 2-2   Answer file search locations in order

Location	Notes
Registry key HKLM\System\UnattendFile	The registry key points to the location of the answer file. This is suitable for upgrade installations or when using Sysprep. You specify the name of the answer file.
%WINDIR%\panther\unattend	This location is not searched when Windows PE is used to perform the installation.
%WINDIR%\panther	Answer files are cached here during installation for use during multiple configuration passes.
Removable read/write media in order of drive letter	The answer file must be located in the root of the drive. Subfolders are not searched.
Removable read-only media	The answer file must be located in the root of the drive. Subfolders are not searched.
\sources directory in a Windows distribution folder	Valid only for the Windows PE and offlineServicing passes. The file must be named autounattend.xml.
%WINDIR%\system32\sysprep	Valid for all configuration passes except the windowsPE and offlineServicing passes. The answer file must be named unattend.xml.
%SYSTEMDRIVE%	Typically not used.

It is important to realize that answer files are cached in the %WINDIR%\panther directory and are reused during later actions that look for an answer file. For example, if an answer file is specified during the initial Windows 10 installation, it is cached to %WINDIR%\panther. Later, if Sysprep is run, the cached unattend.xml is reused before searching removable media or the sysprep folder. To resolve this problem, you can specify a specific answer file when running Sysprep, remove the unwanted unattend.xml file from %WINDIR%\panther, or place the new unattend.xml file in a location that is higher in the search order. The variable %WINDIR% represents the installation directory for Windows 10, which is C:\Windows.

Configuration Passes for a Basic Installation

Windows 10 has multiple phases of setup, but a single answer file is used for all configuration passes. Different portions of the answer file are used for different configuration passes. Some settings can be configured in multiple configuration passes. However, only the last applied setting is effective.

The overall process for a simple unattended installation, booting from DVD, uses configuration passes in the following steps:

1. Windows PE starts.

2. Setup.exe starts and reads the answer file (autounattend.xml).

3. The windowsPE configuration pass is performed.

4. The specified Windows image is copied to the local hard drive.

5. The offlineServicing configuration pass is performed.

6. The computer reboots.

7. Windows 10 starts.

8. Basic system configuration is performed.

9. Specific configuration is performed, including security ID (SID) generation and plug and play components.

10. The specialize configuration pass is performed.

11. The computer reboots.

12. Windows 10 starts.

13. The oobeSystem configuration pass is performed.

14. Windows Welcome is displayed.

 Additional configuration passes are triggered when Sysprep is used to configure Windows 10.

The windowsPE Configuration Pass   Most network administrators expect to perform tasks like partitioning before running an automated install. However, with Windows PE you can automate this early portion of the installation process, just as you can automate the installation and configuration of Windows 10 components.

The **windowsPE configuration pass** is used at the start of the installation to:

- Partition and format the hard disk before installing Windows 10. Including this information ensures that you do not need to manually partition and format the hard disk before installing Windows 10.

- Specify a specific Windows image to install.

- Specify credentials for accessing the Windows image. This is useful when accessing the Windows image from a network share.

- Specify the local partition to install Windows 10 on.

- Specify a product key, computer name, and administrator account name.

- Run specific commands during Windows Setup.

The offlineServicing Configuration Pass   The offlineServicing configuration pass is used to apply packages to a Windows 10 image after it is copied to the computer hard drive, but before it is running. The packages can include language packs, device drivers, and security updates.

The benefits of applying packages to a Windows image offline are:

- *Faster installation*—It is faster to install multiple packages offline than after installation is complete. This is particularly true if some packages require system reboots when performed online.

- *Enhanced security*—Applying security updates after the system is up and running leaves the system vulnerable until the updates are applied. Applying security updates offline ensures that the system is never vulnerable to the exploits fixed by the update.

 When you are applying an image rather than installing from DVD or distribution share, you can use DISM to apply offline updates to the image before deployment.

The specialize Configuration Pass   A wide variety of settings related to the Windows interface, network configuration, and other Windows components can be applied during the specialize configuration pass. This is the most common configuration pass to implement settings. The settings in the **specialize configuration pass** are applied after the SID (security ID) is generated for the local computer and hardware is detected by using plug and play.

The oobeSystem Configuration Pass   The **oobeSystem configuration pass** is applied during the user out-of-box experience (OOBE). The user out-of-box experience is the portion of the installation where users are asked for information after the second reboot. Information requested includes time zone, administrator name, and the administrator password.

Many of the settings you can apply during the oobeSystem configuration pass are the same as the settings you can apply during the specialize configuration pass. Therefore, it makes no difference whether you configure a component during the specialize configuration pass or during the oobeSystem configuration pass for a basic unattended installation.

 The distinction between using the oobeSystem configuration pass and the specialize configuration pass is relevant when using Sysprep to prepare workstations. This is discussed in the Sysprep Configuration Passes section.

Sysprep Configuration Passes   The **Sysprep** utility is used to manage Windows 10 installations that are imaged. Depending on the use scenario, additional configuration passes are triggered by Sysprep.

The configuration passes that can be triggered by Sysprep are:

- The **generalize configuration pass**, used only when Sysprep is used to generalize an installation of Windows 10 by removing specific information such as the computer name and SID. This is done before imaging to allow the image to be used on multiple computers.

- The **auditSystem configuration pass** and **auditUser configuration pass**, used only when Sysprep is used to manage or audit an installation of Windows 10 that has just been imaged. The auditSystem settings apply before user sign-in, and the auditUser settings apply after user sign-in.

- The oobeSystem configuration pass, used when Sysprep is used to trigger the Windows Welcome after reboot. This may be done just before a new machine is delivered to a client.

The configuration passes triggered by Sysprep integrate with the configuration passes used by a basic installation. Figure 2-3 shows how the configuration passes triggered by Sysprep relate to the configuration passes triggered by Setup.exe

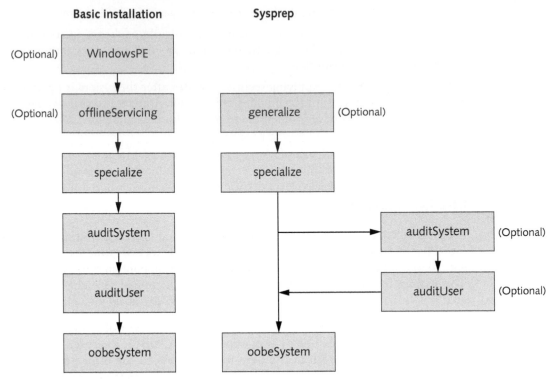

Figure 2-3   Configuration passes

Windows System Image Manager

The Windows System Image Manager (SIM) is the utility that allows you to create and modify answer files that are used for unattended installations. You can also perform a variety of other installation-related tasks. Common tasks you can perform with Windows SIM include:

- Creating or updating an answer file
- Adding device drivers or applications to an answer file
- Creating a configuration set
- Applying offline updates to a Windows image

Creating or Updating an Answer File   Windows SIM allows you to create an answer file to control the installation of Windows. The installation can be from a distribution share, the Windows 10 installation media, or an image you have created. Windows SIM reads the configurable settings for an image either directly from the image or from a catalog file.

A **catalog file** lists all settings and packages included in an image. The states of all the settings are also included in the catalog file. For example, if the image has configured the screen saver to lock the system after 10 minutes, this will be reflected in the catalog file created by scanning that image. Using a catalog file is faster than scanning the image directly. However, catalog files are not updated automatically. You must manually update the catalog file for an image after you update the image. The Windows 10 installation DVD includes catalog files for the versions of Windows 10 included on the DVD.

After an answer file is created, you can easily update it by opening the existing answer file with Windows SIM and modifying it. When you modify the existing answer file, Windows SIM ensures that all of the settings are still valid based on the catalog file or the image. Some of the answer file settings you may want to include for an unattended installation are listed in Table 2-3.

Table 2-3 Answer file settings

Configuration pass	Setting	Description
windowsPE	Microsoft-Windows-International-Core-WinPE | UILanguage	The default language used for the installed operating system.
windowsPE	Microsoft-Windows-International-Core-WinPE | SetupUILanguage | UILanguage	The default language used during Windows setup.
windowsPE	Microsoft-Windows-Setup | UserData | AcceptEula	The option to accept the license agreement.
windowsPE	Microsoft-Windows-Setup | UserData | ProductKey | Key	The Windows 10 product key used to identify the edition of Windows 10 in the WIM file.
windowsPE	Microsoft-Windows-Setup | ImageInstall | OSImage | InstallToAvailablePartition	The option to specify that Windows is installed to the first available partition. Alternatively, you can specify the disk and partition to install by using other settings.
specialize	Microsoft-Windows-Shell-Setup | ProductKey	The product key used for activation.
specialize	Microsoft-Windows-Shell-Setup | ComputerName	The computer name for the Windows installation. To generate a random name, use *.
oobeSystem	Microsoft-Windows-International-Core | InputLocale	The default input locale for the Windows installation.
oobeSystem	Microsoft-Windows-International-Core | SystemLocale	The default system locale for the Windows installation.
oobeSystem	Microsoft-Windows-International-Core | UILanguage	The default UI language for the Windows installation.
oobeSystem	Microsoft-Windows-International-Core | UserLocale	The default user locale for the Windows installation.
oobeSystem	Microsoft-Windows-Shell-Setup | OOBE | HideEULAPage	The option to avoid displaying the license agreement.
oobeSystem	Microsoft-Windows-Shell-Setup | UserAccounts	The user accounts that are created during installation.
oobeSystem	Microsoft-Windows-Shell-Setup | UserAccounts | AdministratorPassword	The password for the local Administrator account.
oobeSystem	Microsoft-Windows-Shell-Setup | TimeZone	The time zone of the Windows installation.

Adding Device Drivers or Applications Windows 10 ships with a large number of device drivers that support most hardware available at the time of release. However, as new types of hardware are released, there is a need to install additional drivers or updated versions of drivers. You must create a **distribution share** to hold a copy of device drivers you are installing.

A distribution share contains two folders for updating drivers:

- *OEM*—The drivers located in this folder are used during the initial setup of Windows 10 when Setup.exe is run from installation DVD or a distribution share. These drivers will be available for Windows when plug and play hardware is detected.

- *Out-of-Box Drivers*—The drivers located in this folder can be used either during the windowsPE configuration pass or the auditSystem configuration pass. The windowsPE configuration pass is performed for all unattended installations where Windows PE is used to run Setup.exe. The auditSystem configuration pass is only performed when the Sysprep utility is used to prepare images. Adding drivers during the auditSystem configuration pass allows you to add drivers to an existing Windows image without running Setup.exe from the installation DVD or a distribution share.

Windows SIM allows you to create a distribution share and then specify applications and device drivers from the distribution share that are to be installed during an unattended installation. The path to the distribution share should always be referred to by the **Universal Naming Convention** (UNC) path to ensure that it can be accessed over the network during unattended installations. For example, a distribution share on a server should always be referred to by a path such as \\servername\sharename.

Creating a Configuration Set   A distribution share typically has device drivers and packages that are used by multiple answer files. For example, a company might have only a single distribution share for all of its Windows 10 installations, but the various answer files are used to build workstations for different user types. Each answer file uses only some of the files on the distribution share.

A **configuration set** is the subset of files in a distribution share that are required for a particular answer file. For example, a retail store might have an answer file that includes a special scanner driver for the computers running the cash registers. A configuration set for that answer file would include the special scanner driver, but not any of the other drivers and packages in the distribution share that are not referenced by the answer file.

It is best to use a configuration set when workstations cannot access the distribution share. A configuration set allows you to minimize the amount of data that is placed on DVD or copied to a remote location. The answer file created when you create a configuration set uses relative paths so that the configuration set can be moved without introducing errors in the answer file.

Applying Offline Updates to a Windows Image   Offline updates are software packages containing device drivers or security updates that are applied to an image during the offlineServicing configuration pass of the installation. If offline updates are included as part of the installation process, they are installed before Windows is functional.

Installing software updates before Windows 10 is running ensures that problems are fixed before the system is functional. This is particularly important for security updates that could be exploited between the time of system installation and installing the security updates.

Packages used for offline updates are included in a configuration set, as are other software packages required during an unattended installation.

You can also apply offline updates to a Windows image by using Deployment Image Servicing and Management (DISM). This applies the update once to the image file, rather than each time during installation.

Activity 2-4: Creating an Answer File

Time Required: 30 minutes

Objective: Create an answer file that can be used for an unattended installation

Description: You would like to streamline the process you use for installing new Windows 10 workstations. The biggest problem you run into when deploying new installations of Windows 10 is finding the proper product key. In this activity, you create an answer file that automatically enters in the product key for you during configuration.

This activity assumes that you are using a 64-bit evaluation copy of Windows 10 Enterprise edition. There may be slight variations in these steps if you are using another edition of Windows 10.

1. If necessary, place the Windows 10 DVD in your computer.

2. Click the **Start** button, type **command**, and click **Command Prompt**.

3. Type **md c:\wininstall** and press **Enter**.

4. Type **xcopy d:*.* c:\wininstall\ /s** and press **Enter**. This command assumes that the DVD drive on your computer is assigned the drive letter D:. If the DVD drive letter is different, replace **d:** with the appropriate letter. This copies the contents of the Windows 10 DVD to your hard drive. This step will take some time to complete.

5. When copying is complete, close the command prompt.

6. Click the **Start** button, type **windows system**, and click **Windows System Image Manager**.

7. In the Windows Image pane, right-click **Select a Windows image or catalog file**, and click **Select Windows Image**.

8. Browse to **C:\wininstall\sources**, click **install.wim**, and click **Open**.

9. In the Windows System Image Manager dialog box, click **Yes** to create a catalog file.

10. In the User Account Control dialog box, click **Yes**. This process takes 10–15 minutes.

11. Click the **File** menu, and click **New Answer File**. A new untitled answer file has been created in the Answer File pane. Notice that it lists the configuration passes in the components, and also lists packages.

12. In the Windows Image pane, if necessary, expand **Windows 10 Enterprise Evaluation Technical Preview**, and expand **Components**. This lists the categories of settings that you can configure in the answer file.

13. Expand **amd64_Microsoft-Windows-Setup_10.0.xxxx.xxxxx_neutral** (**.xxxx.xxxxx** represents a subversion number that changes depending on the revision version of Windows 10), and expand **UserData**.

14. Click **ProductKey**. Notice that the upper-right pane is now labeled ProductKey Properties and shows information about the ProductKey setting. You can see that the only configuration pass that this setting can be used in is the windowsPE configuration pass.

15. In the Windows Image pane, right-click **ProductKey**, and click **Add Setting to Pass 1 windowsPE**. This adds the setting to the currently opened answer file, and selects it in the Answer File pane.

16. In the ProductKey Properties pane, double-click **Key**. This allows you to edit the product key.

17. Type the product key for Windows 10 Enterprise, including the dashes(-), and press **Enter**. If you do not have a product key for Windows 10 Enterprise, type **NPPR9-FWDCX-D2C8J-H872K-2YT43** (a generic key provided by Microsoft for trial installations).

18. Click **WillShowUI**, click the drop-down arrow, and click **OnError**, as shown in Figure 2-4. This configures the product key entry screen to be displayed only if an error is encountered with the product key in the answer file.

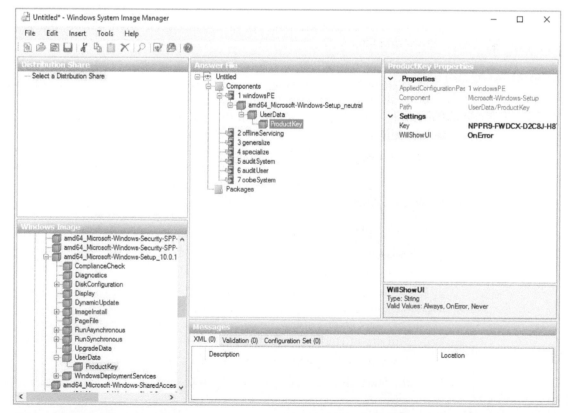

Figure 2-4   Windows SIM settings

19. Browse through some of the other settings available in the Windows Image pane. Take note of which configuration passes the different settings can be configured in.

20. Click the **File** menu, and click **Save Answer File As**.

21. In the File name text box, type **autounattend** and click **Save**. This file can be copied to removable storage or another appropriate location for use during an unattended installation.

22. Close Windows System Image Manager.

23. Click **Microsoft Edge** on the taskbar.

24. In the Where to next box, type **C:\wininstall\sources\autounattend.xml**, and press **Enter**.

25. You can now see the structure of the XML file you created with Windows System Image Manager. It shows the product key you entered and the OnError choice for showing the user interface.

26. Close Microsoft Edge.

Activity 2-5: Creating a Distribution Share

Time Required: 5 minutes
Objective: Create a distribution share that can be used for installing Windows 10

Description: After receiving some new computers, you find that they are only able to display a resolution of 800 × 600 with 256 colors when Windows 10 is installed from DVD. After doing some research, you realize that Windows 10 does not include the correct video driver for the new computers. To avoid manually updating the video driver after installation, you decide to create a distribution share that you can place the appropriate video drivers in. In this activity, you create a distribution share.

This activity creates a distribution share on the local C drive due to hardware restrictions. The distribution share would normally be located on a server and accessible over the network.

1. Click the **Start** button, type **windows system**, and click **Windows System Image Manager**.

2. In the Distribution Share pane, right-click **Select a Distribution Share**, and click **Create Distribution Share**.

3. Select the **C:\wininstall\sources** folder and click **Open**.

4. In the Distribution Share pane, expand **C:\wininstall\sources**. Notice that three folders are listed, as shown in Figure 2-5. These folders are used to store device drivers and packages that can be added to the Windows 10 installation. You must copy any device drivers and packages into these folders to make them available.

5. Close Windows System Image Manager.

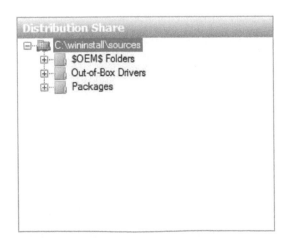

Figure 2-5 Distribution share folders

Image-Based Installation

In a corporate environment, you need a quick and easy way to deploy workstations. Attended installations take too much time to be practical. Unattended installations are better suited to a multi-workstation environment, but after installation, you still need to install additional applications and customize them to meet corporate standards. An image-based installation allows you to quickly deploy Windows 10 to workstations, complete with applications and customizations.

Corporate environments have been using imaging for many years as a method to quickly deploy workstation operating systems and applications. Sysprep has long been included as a deployment utility to support third-party imaging software. However, Microsoft also includes multiple tools for imaging. Windows 10 includes the DISM utility, which can capture, modify, and apply images. ICD can also be used to prepare and deploy images.

The overall imaging process is as follows:

1. Install and configure Windows 10 and applications on a source workstation.
2. Use Sysprep to generalize the source workstation for imaging.
3. Boot the source workstation using Windows PE.
4. Use DISM to capture the image from the source workstation and store it in a distribution share or external storage.
5. On the destination workstation, use Windows PE to connect to the distribution share or external storage.
6. Use DISM to apply the image to the destination workstation.

Sysprep

In a corporate environment, the most common use for Sysprep is preparing workstations to capture an image. This process is known as **generalization**. Generalization removes system-specific data from Windows. System-specific data includes the computer name, computer SID, and hardware information. After generalization is complete, the workstation image is captured and placed on a distribution share.

You can specify an answer file to use during generalization. If you do not specify an answer file, Sysprep will search for unattend.xml to use as an answer file. If an unattend.xml file was used during the initial Windows 10 setup, it is cached to the local hard drive and will be found when Sysprep is run.

 The generalize configuration pass is performed only when Sysprep is used to generalize an installation.

When a generalized image is applied to a workstation, that workstation creates all of the system-specific data that is required, including the computer name and computer SID. It also detects the plug and play hardware and loads drivers for the detected hardware. After the system-specific information is generated, the computer is either put into audit mode or Windows Welcome is run.

In order to properly use Sysprep, you need to understand the following:

• System cleanup actions
• Sysprep limitations
• Sysprep command-line options

System Cleanup Actions When you run Sysprep to generalize an image, you must also select a system cleanup action, as shown in Figure 2-6. The system cleanup action determines the behavior of Windows 10 after configuration. The two available system cleanup actions are:

• Enter System Out-of-Box Experience (OOBE)
• Enter System Audit Mode

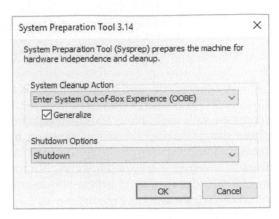

Figure 2-6   Sysprep cleanup actions

Out-of-Box Experience   In most cases, you will choose the **System Out-of-Box Experience cleanup action** when generalizing an image. This configures the image so that on first boot, Windows Welcome is launched to collect any necessary information from the user before the configuration is finalized.

The oobeSystem configuration pass is performed when Windows Welcome is launched and will use an unattend.xml answer file if one is available. If the answer file is properly configured, the entire Windows Welcome can be automated.

Audit Mode   Audit mode is used by organizations that want to perform additional modifications to an image before distributing it to users. In audit mode, you can install additional drivers or applications for users, then use Sysprep to trigger Windows Welcome on the next boot. You can also use audit mode to verify that the workstation is properly configured before delivery to the end user. To enter audit mode, select the **System Audit Mode cleanup action**.

Using audit mode is helpful when you want to continue using the same base image for many different varieties of hardware and end users. A single base image is applied to the computers, and then audit mode is used to add any specific drivers required by that model of computer and any specific applications required by the end user. Using audit mode prevents the OOBE from running. The process for using audit mode has the following steps:

1. Perform initial installation and configuration of the operating system.

2. Run Sysprep and select audit mode.

3. Take an image of the prepared operating system. This is the base image.

4. Apply the base image to a computer and sign in to add drivers or applications.

5. Run Sysprep and select OOBE.

6. Take an image of the updated operating system.

7. Deploy the updated operating system to computers.

8. Have the users start the system and run OOBE.

The ability to continue using the same base image is particularly important for organizations that must perform significant testing on workstations to ensure quality. When a consistent base image is used, the testing for the functionality in the base image needs to be performed only once. Only the additional modifications need to be tested.

The auditSystem and auditUser configuration passes for unattended installations are performed only when audit mode is used. The auditSystem configuration pass runs before user sign-in. The auditUser configuration pass runs after user sign-in. Both configuration passes can be used to automate customizations performed in audit mode, rather than requiring manual intervention. Automating tasks performed in audit mode reduces testing requirements, as the automated process only needs to be tested once, rather than on each computer.

Sysprep Limitations   Sysprep is a very useful tool and is a requirement for deploying Windows 10 by imaging. However, like any tool, Sysprep has a few limitations you should be aware of, particularly those restrictions related to hardware.

Sysprep limitations include the following:

- Drivers must be available to support Plug and Play hardware of the destination computer. However, the hardware does not need to be identical.

- Sysprep generalization resets the activation clock a maximum of three times (rearms). This limits the number of times Sysprep can be used on derivative images before activation is forced. For example, a computer manufacturer may make multiple modifications to an image and run Sysprep after each modification to prepare the workstation for imaging. Activation is only cleared from the computer three times. On the fourth time, an error is generated.

- If a computer is a member of a domain, running Sysprep removes the computer from the domain.

- Sysprep will not run on upgraded computers.

- After running Sysprep, encrypted files and folders are unreadable because the encryption certificates are lost when user profiles are removed.

When you generalize an image, it performs a rearm each time. You can prevent a rearm from being performed by using the SkipRearm setting in an answer file. This lets you generalize an image more than three times. For 64-bit installations, this setting is found in the amd64_Microsoft-Windows-Security-SPP_10.0.xxxx.xxxx_neutral component. Use a value of 1 to enable SkipRearm.

Sysprep Command-Line Options   Sysprep has both a command-line interface and a graphical interface. In most cases, network administrators prefer to use the graphical interface because it is more intuitive. To run Sysprep in graphical mode, run C:\Windows\System32\Sysprep\Sysprep.exe without specifying any options. In high-volume situations, you may prefer to use Sysprep in batch files. Running Sysprep in batch files requires you to use command-line options. The command-line options for Sysprep are listed in Table 2-4.

Table 2-4   Command-line options for Sysprep

Option	Description
/audit	Starts the computer in audit mode on reboot. Cannot be used with /oobe.
/generalize	Removes system-specific information from the computer, such as computer SID.
/mode:vm	Optimizes the functionality of /generalize for virtualized environments. Hardware settings are not generalized and redetected. Must be used with /generalize and /oobe.
/oobe	Starts Windows Welcome on reboot. Cannot be used with /audit.
/reboot	Reboots the computer after Sysprep completes. This is useful for immediately testing the post boot experience. Cannot be used with /shutdown or /quit.
/shutdown	Shuts down the computer after Sysprep completes. This is useful to prepare for imaging. Cannot be used with /reboot or /quit.
/quiet	Prevents Sysprep from displaying dialog boxes. This is useful when Sysprep is used in batch files.
/quit	Allows the computer to continue running when Sysprep completes. Cannot be used with /reboot or /shutdown.
/unattend:answerfile	Specifies an answer file to use for unattended setup.

Activity 2-6: Generalizing Windows 10 by Using Sysprep

Time Required: 30 minutes
Objective: Use Sysprep to generalize Windows 10 for imaging

Description: After using unattended installations for a period of time, you decide that you would like to include applications automatically as part of the Windows 10 installation to new workstations. You have not used Sysprep before, and you want to see what the user experience is like after Sysprep is performed to ready a workstation for image capture. In this activity, you use Sysprep to generalize Windows 10 for imaging, then you restart Windows 10 to see the user interface that is presented when the image is applied to new workstations.

1. Click **File Explorer** on the taskbar.

2. In the Address bar, type **C:\Windows\System32\sysprep** and press **Enter**.

3. Double-click **sysprep**.

4. In the System Cleanup Action box, select **Enter System Out-of-Box Experience (OOBE)**. This option is used to prepare a computer for delivery to an end user.

5. Check the **Generalize** check box. This option removes computer-specific information, such as SID and computer name.

6. In the Shutdown Options box, select **Shutdown**. This turns off the computer after Sysprep is complete, so that an image can be captured from it.

7. Click **OK**. Sysprep looks for an unattend.xml file to process during the generalize configuration pass, generalizes Windows 10, and shuts down Windows 10. After Windows 10 is shut down, it is ready for an image to be captured. To capture an operating system image, you would boot Windows PE from removable storage and run DISM to place the image on external storage or a network share.

8. If you get the error 'Sysprep was not able to validate your Windows installation,' use the following steps to resolve the error:

    a. Click **OK** to close the error dialog box.

    b. In File Explorer, double-click **Panther** and double-click **setupact**.

    c. In Notepad, scroll down to the bottom of the file and a line stating that 'Package *PackageName* was installed for a user, but not provisioned for all users. This package will not function properly in the sysprep image.' Make note of the package name.

    d. Click the **Start** button, type **powershell**, right-click **Windows PowerShell**, and click **Run as administrator**.

    e. In the User Account Control dialog box, click **Yes**.

    f. In the Windows PowerShell window, type **Get-AppxPackage *PackageName* | Remove-AppxPackage** and press **Enter**. You can use wildcards in the package name.

    g. After this is complete, run Sysprep again. If the error is generated again, review **setupact** for additional packages that are blocking Sysprep and repeat these steps until Sysprep runs successfully.

9. Start your computer. Notice that the startup screen is the same as that seen during installation. Windows 10 now detects plug and play hardware, reboots, and then starts the out-of-box experience. If an unattend.xml file is found, the settings for the oobeSystem configuration pass are applied.

10. Click **Next** to accept the default settings for country/region, app language, keyboard layout, and time zone.

11. Click **Accept** on the page with the license agreement.

12. Click **Use Express settings**.

13. Click **Join a domain** and click **Next**.

14. In the Who's going to use this PC box, type **User***x*.

15. In the Enter password and Re-enter password boxes, type **password**.

16. In the Password hint box, type **From Activity 1-1** and then click **Next**. Notice that you cannot reuse the same local user name because Sysprep did not remove the existing user account. You need to enter a new user account to continue. You can avoid being forced to create a new user account by using an answer file.

17. In the Who's going to use this PC box, type **NewUser***x* and click **Next**.

18. Click the **Start** button. Notice that you are automatically signed in as NewUser*x*.

19. Sign out and then sign in as **User***x*.

20. Click **Start** and then click **Settings**.

21. In Settings, click **Accounts** and then click **Family & other users**.

22. Under Other users, click **NewUser***x* and click **Remove**.

23. In the Delete account and data window, click **Delete account and data**.

24. Close the Settings window.

DISM

Most corporations are already using imaging tools to deploy operating systems and applications to desktop computers. DISM is included as part of the Windows 10 ADK to create, modify, and apply workstation images. This tool is unique and offers advantages over third-party imaging tools.

Features and Benefits   The DISM tool includes a number of features and benefits:

- A single **image file** (.wim) can hold multiple images. Within each image file, single instance storage is used. That is, if multiple images in the same image file have the same file, it is stored only once. This means that for each image added to an image file, the size increase is minimized.

- File-based imaging lets you capture images from one partition type and restore them on another. It also eliminates problems with mass storage controllers and matching **Hardware Abstraction Layer (HAL)** layers.

- Images can be taken of an entire partition or just a particular folder. This means you can use images to capture information for backup, such as databases. This can be useful when you are moving applications to a new computer.

- Images can be applied to an existing hard drive without destroying the existing data. However, this method cannot be used to apply operating system updates or application updates.

- Images can be compressed with either fast compression or maximum compression. This allows you to optimize images for speed or size depending on your environment. When multiple images are stored in the same file, they must use the same compression type.

- Images can be mounted to a folder in an NTFS partition for modification.

- When DISM is combined with Windows Deployment Services (WDS), you can completely automate the deployment process to include partitioning and formatting hard drives. DISM does not perform partitioning or format hard drives.

 DISM is capable of working only with .wim files. It cannot interact with images created by third-party imaging applications.

Image Capture   After a workstation is prepared for image capture, you must shut down the computer before imaging. Shutting down the computer ensures that there are no open files when imaging is performed. You can boot the computer using Windows PE to perform the imaging operation.

The syntax for capturing an image is:

DISM /Capture-Image /ImageFile:*imagefile.wim* /CaptureDir:*path* /Name:*imagename*

The /Capture-Image option specifies that an image is being copied from disk to an image file. This option assumes that no image file already exists. To add an image to an existing image file, use the /Append-Image option instead.

The /ImageFile:*imagefile.wim* option defines the .wim file that will hold the image. If you do not specify the full path to the .wim file, it will be created in the current directory.

The /CaptureDir:*path* option defines the source files that are to be captured as part of the image. To capture an entire partition, specify the root of the partition. For example, specifying C:\ would capture the entire C drive.

When multiple images are stored in a single image file, you should include a name for each image with the /Name:*imagename* option. Each image in an image file is uniquely identified by a number. The name is used as an easy way to identify the contents of each image, and can be used in place of the image number when accessing the image. Table 2-5 lists other options that can be used when capturing images.

Table 2-5   DISM options for capturing images

Option	Description
/Bootable	Marks a volume image as bootable. This is applicable only to Windows PE images that can be booted directly from the image file.
/CheckIntegrity	Checks the integrity of the image file as operations are being performed on it.
/Compress:[max|fast|none]	Specifies the level of compression used when capturing to a new image file. This option is not available when capturing to an existing image file. Compression speed primarily affects image creation, not application. Fast is the default compression type used if a level is not specified.
/ConfigFile:configfile.ini	Allows you to specify files to be excluded during image capture. You can also specify files that should not be compressed.
/NoRpFix	Prevents files with reparse points outside the specified path from being captured.
/Verify	Identifies errors and file duplication.
/WIMboot	Allows you to create a runnable operating system in an image file. The computer must be using UEFI instead of BIOS.

Activity 2-7: Capturing an Image

Time Required: 10 minutes
Objective: Create an image using DISM

Description: After confirming how Sysprep is used to generalize Windows 10 for imaging, you want to try capturing an image. To keep your test manageable in scope, you are only imaging part of the file system rather than the entire C drive. In this activity, you image the C:\Program Files\Windows Kits\10 folder.

When imaging the entire C drive including the operating system, you must boot from Windows PE to ensure that all files are closed. When imaging data files, DISM can be run from Windows 10. This activity allows you to perform the basics of imaging without using Windows PE.

1. Click the **Start** button, type **deploy**, right-click **Deployment and Imaging Tools Environment**, and then click **Run as administrator**. DISM must be run using administrator privileges and does not automatically elevate privileges by using UAC.

2. In the User Account Control dialog box, click **Yes**.

3. Type **md \images** and press **Enter**. In a production environment, you would typically store images on a network server rather than a client computer.

4. Type **dism /capture-image /capturedir:"C:\Program Files (x86)\Windows Kits\10"** /imagefile **C:\images\Win10ADK.wim /name:Win10ADK** and press **Enter**. This takes an image of

the Windows 10 ADK folder and creates the Win10ADK.wim image file. The image is given the description Win10ADK. Any options with spaces must have quotes around them.

5. Type **dir \images** and press **Enter**. The file WIN10ADK.wim is approximately 1.8 GB.

6. Type **dism /append-image /capturedir:"C:\Program Files (x86)\Windows Kits\10\ Assessment and Deployment Kit\Windows Preinstallation Environment" /imagefile C: \images\Win10ADK.wim /name:WinPE** and press **Enter**, as shown in Figure 2-7. This command images the Windows Preinstallation Environment folder and places it in the same Win10ADK.wim image file. The image is given the description WinPE.

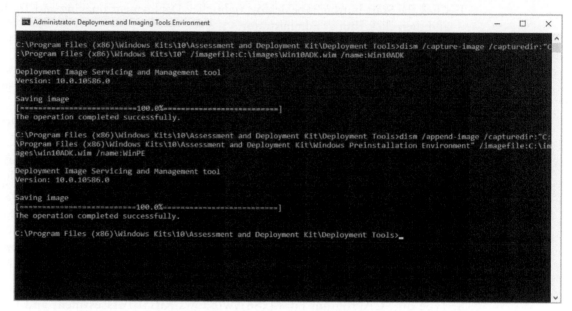

Figure 2-7   Using DISM to append an image

7. Type **dir \images** and press **Enter**. Notice that the file Win10ADK.wim is still approximately 1.8 GB because of the single-instance file storage used by WIM files. The Windows Preinstallation Environment folder contains about 1.7 GB of data.

8. Close the Deployment and Imaging Tools Environment window.

Image Application   When you are using DISM to deploy images with operating systems and applications, you must boot using Windows PE and connect to the distribution share holding the image file. After you are connected to the share, you can use DISM to apply an image to the local workstation.

 It is important to remember that DISM cannot create or format partitions. Partition management must be performed manually or scripted within Windows PE.

The syntax for applying an image file is:

DISM /Apply-Image /ImageFile:*imagefile.wim* [/Index:*imageindex* | /Name:*imagename*] / ApplyDir:*destinationpath*

The /Apply-Image option indicates that an image is going to be placed on a local hard drive from the *imagefile.wim*. The *imageindex* or *imagename* is used to specify which image from *imagefile.wim* is applied. The /ApplyDir option specifies the location on the local drive where the image will be placed. For example, C:\ indicates that the image will be placed at the root of the C drive.

If the image has been split into multiple files, you must include the /SWMFile option. The / SWMFile option is used to specify the name and location of additional .swm files. For example, if the first of three split image files is BaseImage.swm, /SWMFile:BaseImage*.swm ensures that DISM finds BaseImage2.swm and BaseImage3.swm also.

Activity 2-8: Applying an Image

Time Required: 10 minutes

Objective: Apply a WIM image to a computer

Description: One of the unique benefits of the WIM format is the ability to add files to an existing computer when an image is applied. Applying an image does not remove the existing files on a partition. You want to test this functionality. In this activity, you apply the WinPE image to restore missing files.

1. Click the **Start** button, type **deploy**, right-click **Deployment Imaging and Tools Environment**, and then click **Run as administrator**.

2. In the User Account Control dialog box, click **Yes**.

3. Type **dism /get-imageinfo C:\images\Win10ADK.wim** and press **Enter**. This displays information about the images included in Win10ADK.wim. Notice that image number 2 is named WinPE. You can refer to images by their name or index number.

4. Type **rd "C:\Program Files (x86)\Windows Kits\10\Assessment and Deployment Kit\ Windows Preinstallation Environment" /s /q** and press **Enter**.

5. Type **dir "C:\Program Files (x86)\Windows Kits\10\Assessment and Deployment Kit"** and press **Enter**. You can see that the Windows Preinstallation Environment folder is not there.

6. Type **md "\Program Files (x86)\Windows Kits\10\Assessment and Deployment Kit\ Windows Preinstallation Environment"** and press **Enter**. This re-creates the Windows Preinstallation Environment folder so that the WinPE image can be placed in it.

7. Type **dism /apply-image /imagefile:C:\images\Win10ADK.wim /name:WinPE /applydir:"C:\ Program Files (x86)\Windows Kits\10\Assessment and Deployment Kit\Windows Preinstallation Environment"** and press **Enter**.

8. Type **dir "C:\Program Files (x86)\Windows Kits\10\Assessment and Deployment Kit\ Windows Preinstallation Environment"** and press **Enter**. You can see that the files have been restored to the Windows Preinstallation Environment folder.

9. Close the command prompt.

Other Image Management Tasks   DISM is capable of performing additional image management tasks. Table 2-6 describes the additional options for DISM that can be used to manage images.

Table 2-6   DISM image management options

Option	Description
/Delete-Image	Deletes a specified image in an image file. However, only metadata information and XML about the image are removed. The image file is not optimized and may contain unneeded information.
/Cleanup-Mountpoints	Frees all resources associated with a mounted image that becomes corrupted. Mounted images are not unmounted.
/Commit-Image	Commits changes to a mounted image. If you do not commit changes, they are never written back into the .wim file.
/Export-Image	Exports a specified image from an image file into a new image file. Exporting all images to a new image file optimizes the image file.
/List-Image	Lists the files and folders contained in an image.
/Mount-Image	Mounts an image in a .wim file to an empty folder for viewing or modification. You can use the /ReadOnly option to prevent accidental modification.
/Split-Image	Splits a .wim file into smaller .swm files. This is useful when storing image files on media with limited capacity.
/Unmount-Image	Unmounts an image from an empty folder. Use the /Commit option to commit changes at the same time.

Image Maintenance

When you use images to deploy Windows 10, you can include a preconfigured installation of Windows 10 and applications. When you build the image, you include any necessary applications and updates that are available at that time. Maintaining images requires you to apply software updates to those images and possibly modify Windows 10 features that are enabled in the image. You can maintain an image by using DISM or Sysprep with audit mode.

DISM allows you to perform a wide variety of maintenance tasks on a Windows 10 image while it is offline. An offline image is still stored in a .wim file and not applied to a computer. Maintaining an image offline simplifies maintenance, but you are limited in the tasks you can perform. DISM can also modify an operating system that is running as an alternative to graphical tools. Windows 10 includes DISM as a utility.

Some common scenarios for using DISM for offline maintenance include:

- *Add device drivers*—As your organization purchases new computers that require new drivers, you can add those drivers to an existing image. This ensures that all hardware is properly detected when the image is applied.

- *Apply Windows updates*—Over time, additional updates for Windows 10 are released that are not included in the image. Deploying Windows 10 without the latest updates is a security risk because some malware takes advantage of computers without security updates. Applying updates before an image is applied reduces the security risk. Windows updates must have an .msu or .cab extension. Service packs cannot be applied by using DISM.

- *Enable Windows features*—After initial development of an image, you may find that a specific feature that is needed for users has not been enabled. Rather than modifying the configuration of each computer after an image is applied, you can use DISM to enable the feature.

- *Identify the need for application updates*—To determine whether applications in an image need to be updated with a specific application update, you can use DISM to query whether a specific .msp file is applicable. However, application updates cannot be applied by using DISM. Application updates must be delivered after the image is applied.

If you are using DISM to add multiple device drivers and install multiple Windows updates, performing the maintenance at a command line can be quite time consuming. Each driver and Windows update requires a command to be entered separately. As an alternative, you can use an answer file with DISM. First, you build an answer file by using Windows SIM that includes the necessary drivers and Windows updates in the offlineServicing portion of the answer file. Then run DISM and specify the answer file. DISM uses only the offlineServicing portion of the answer file.

For detailed information about the capabilities and syntax for using DISM, see DISM Reference (Deployment Image Servicing and Management) at *https://technet.microsoft.com/en-us/library/hh824915.aspx*.

The only way to have complete control over the update of an image is to apply that image to a computer, make any necessary modifications, and then capture the image again. This is time consuming, but it allows you to apply any type of software updates, including applications and service packs.

Typically, you run Sysprep to generalize an image just before capturing it. However, each time you run Sysprep to generalize an image, it requires reactivation. Windows 10 can be reactivated only three times and then Sysprep will cease to function. You must carefully consider this as you update images. Using SkipRearm in answer files helps to mitigate this concern.

Windows PE Boot Media Creation

An operating system on a hard drive cannot be running while an image is being taken or applied. You need an alternative way to get access to the data on the hard drive and run DISM. Windows PE, a small version of Windows that can be installed on a CD or a USB drive, can be used as part of the imaging process. Windows PE is included as part of the Windows 10 ADK.

To create a Windows PE boot media that you can use for imaging, complete the following steps:

1. Run **copype.cmd** to create the folder structure with the necessary files.
2. Mount ISO\Sources\boot.wim.
3. Copy any desired files into boot.wim.
4. Commit the changes to boot.wim
5. Use MakeWinPEMedia.cmd to create a bootable USB drive or .iso file.

For detailed information about creating bootable Windows PE media, see Windows PE (WinPE) at *https://msdn.microsoft.com/en-us/library/windows/hardware/dn938389%28v=vs.85%29.aspx*.

If you need to customize Windows PE for your hardware, you can use DISM to add any necessary drivers. For example, new hardware may require you to add a new network driver to the Windows PE image.

Activity 2-9: Creating Windows PE Boot Media

Time Required: 10 minutes
Objective: Create Windows PE boot media

Description: To enable imaging, you need to have a portable operating system with the ability to run DISM. In this activity, you create an .iso file that can be burned to a CD and used for imaging operations.

1. Click the **Start** button, type **deploy**, right-click **Deployment and Imaging Tools Environment**, and click **Run as administrator**.
2. Type **cd ..\Windows Preinstallation Environment** and press **Enter**.
3. Type **copype.cmd amd64 C:\bootcd** and press **Enter**. This command creates the necessary folder structure for the 64-bit version of Windows PE in the C:\bootcd folder. For a 32-bit version of Windows PE, use the option x86 instead of amd64.
4. Type **dism /mount-image /imagefile:C:\bootcd\media\sources\boot.wim /mountdir:c:\bootcd\mount /index:1** and press **Enter**. This command mounts boot.wim to C:\bootcd\mount, where you can browse and modify the contents.
5. Type **dir C:\bootcd\mount** and press **Enter**. This is the content of boot.wim.
6. Type **dir C:\bootcd\mount\dism.exe /s** and press **Enter**. This command searches through the mount folder to find instances of dism.exe. You can see from the results that it is already in boot.wim and boot.wim does not need to be modified.
7. Type **dism /unmount-image /mountdir:C:\bootcd\mount /discard** and press **Enter**.
8. Type **MakeWinPEMedia.cmd /iso C:\bootcd C:\winpe.iso** and press **Enter**. This command creates a bootable .iso file that can be burned to CD or DVD based on the content in C:\bootcd.

Provisioning

Windows ICD is a new tool in the Windows 10 ADK. It is used to support new deployment workflows for **provisioning** and operating system deployment. Provisioning configures an already installed copy of Windows 10. In addition to managing desktop versions of Windows 10, Windows ICD can also be used to deploy and provision Windows 10 Mobile.

Provisioning an operating system image is a relatively new concept in Windows 10. Windows ICD creates provisioning packages that are deployed to computers with Windows 10 already installed. The purpose of a provisioning package is to customize an existing installation of Windows 10.

Using provisioning speeds up the deployment process for new computers and mobile devices. In the past, computers were reimaged with a new operating system to meet the configuration standards of the organization. With provisioning, a provisioning package is deployed to the operating system installation already in place. It is much faster to apply a provisioning package than to reimage an entire operating system.

Provisioning packages support the following scenarios:

- *New computers from a manufacturer*—When your organization purchases new computers, there is typically an operating system already installed. Most of the time, this operating system is Windows 10 Pro. However, many large organizations use Windows 10 Enterprise. In addition to applying configuration settings and joining the domains, a provisioning package can be used to update the operating system from Windows 10 Pro to Windows 10 Enterprise.

- *Bring your own devices (BYOD)*—Some organizations have moved to a model where employees select and purchase their own devices that are used on the company network. A provisioning package is a quick way to make various devices meet organizational standards and deploy universal applications. Universal applications are obtained from the Windows Store.

For a complete list of settings that can be configured by using a provisioning package, see Windows Provisioning settings reference at *https://msdn.microsoft.com/library/windows/hardware/dn965990%28v=vs.85%29.aspx.*

Provisioning packages are stored in .ppkg files that you need to apply on computers or devices. The permissions required to deploy a provisioning package vary depending on what is being configured. For a provisioning package that performs administrative functions, such as creating local user accounts, an administrator account must be used.

When you create a provisioning package, you are given the option to encrypt the package. Encrypting the package ensures that any sensitive information in the package, such as passwords, cannot be accessed without the encryption key. However, you also need the encryption key to deploy the package, which makes it more difficult to deploy. After encrypting a package, you should document the encryption key and keep it in a safe place.

Activity 2-10: Creating and Applying a Provisioning Package

Time Required: 10 minutes

Objective: Create and apply a provisioning package to an already deployed Windows 10 computer

Description: To enable imaging, you need to have a portable operating system with the ability to run DISM. In this activity, you create an .iso file that can be burned to a CD and used for imaging operations.

1. Click the **Start** button, type **windows imaging**, and click **Windows Imaging and Configuration Designer**.

2. In the User Account Control dialog box, click **Yes**.

3. In the Windows Imaging and Configuration Designer window, click **New provisioning package**.

4. In the New project window, in the Name box, type **SetLocalAdmin** and click **Next**.

5. On the Choose which settings to view and configure page, click **Common to all Windows desktop editions** and click **Next**.

6. On the Import a provisioning package (optional) page, click **Finish**.

7. In the Available customization pane, expand **Deployment assets** and read the list of categories. You can add universal applications, drivers, and Windows updates here.

8. Click **Runtime settings**, click **Accounts**, and click **Users**.

9. In the Users pane, type **LocalAdmin** and click **Add**.

10. In the Available customizations pane, click **UserName: LocalAdmin**. Notice that the Password field is marked as a validation error because no password has been defined.

11. In the Password box, type **password**. Notice that the validation error is gone.

12. In the UserGroup box, select **Administrators**, as shown in Figure 2-8.

Figure 2-8   User settings in WICD

13. Click the **Export** menu and click **Provisioning package**.

14. In the Build window, click **Next** to accept the default settings.

15. On the Select security details for the provisioning package page, notice that the package will be encrypted because it contains sensitive settings.

16. Copy the encryption key to the Clipboard, and click **Next**. This encryption key is required to use the provisioning package. It is important that you do not lose this key.

17. On the Select where to save the provisioning package page, click **Next** to accept the default location in your user profile.

18. On the Build the provisioning package page, click **Build**.

19. On the All done page, click **Finish**.

20. Close Windows Imaging and Configuration Designer and save the project.

21. On the taskbar, click **File Explorer** and browse to **Documents\Windows Imaging and Configuration Designer (Windows ICD)\SetLocalAdmin**.

22. Read the list of files and identify the RunTime Provisioning Tool.

23. Double-click the **SetLocalAdmin** file of type **RunTime Provisioning Tool**, as shown in Figure 2-9. This is the .ppkg file that you run to apply the package.

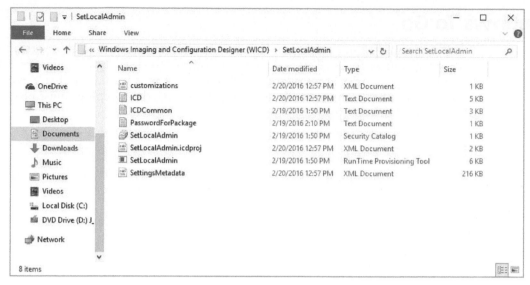

Figure 2-9   WICD project and provisioning package files

24. In the User Account Control dialog box, click **Yes**.

25. In the Enter the package password window, paste the encryption key that you copied during package creation and click **OK**.

26. In the Is this package from a source you trust window, click **Yes, add it**.

27. Right-click the **Start** button and click **Command Prompt** (**Admin**).

28. At the command prompt, type **net users** and press **Enter**.

29. Read the list of users and verify that LocalAdmin exists.

30. Close all open windows.

Windows ICD is also capable of performing Windows 10 deployment to computers and devices. The following process is used for deployment:

1. Create a new Windows image customization project.

2. Select an install.wim file from Windows 10 installation media. You also need to select the edition of Windows 10 from those that are in the .wim file.

3. Specify customizations for the installation. These customizations are used to create a provisioning package that is applied to the image during deployment.

4. Select the media type. Recovery media is used by OEM to automate the deployment process and has the option to enter audit mode. Clean install media is provided to end users and boots into OOBE for user input. Recovery media is used to boot a device and recover data after the operating system has become unusable.

5. Select the image format. The WIM format is used for desktop computers and the FFU (full flash update) format is used for mobile devices.

6. Select the deployment media. Save to a folder if you want to run the installation manually. Create a bootable USB drive if you want to boot automatically from a USB drive. A bootable USB drive is recommended.

7. Boot a computer from the bootable USB drive, enter the product key, and accept the licensing agreement.

Windows To Go

In Windows 10 Enterprise, you have the option to create a portable version of Windows 10 called Windows To Go. This is done from Control Panel, as shown in Figure 2-10. **Windows To Go** is a fully functional installation of Windows 10 on a USB drive that you can take with you and use in other computers. To use Windows To Go, the computer must be configured to boot from a USB drive.

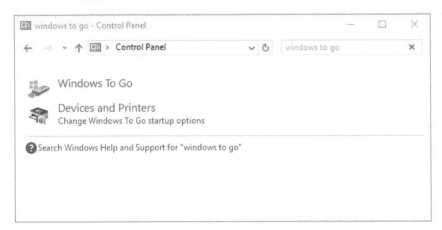

Figure 2-10   Windows To Go in Control Panel

The main benefit of using Windows To Go is that an organization can provide a standard-ized version of Windows that users can use at home. It is much easier for an organization to sup-port a standard Windows deployment than home computers with various configurations.

Some considerations for creating a Windows To Go workspace:

- You need the install.wim file from the Windows 10 installation media.

- The USB drive must be at least 25 GB.

- All data is removed from the USB drive during installation.

- Implement a BitLocker password to encrypt data on the USB drive.

- If BitLocker is implemented on the host computer, you need to suspend BitLocker before changing the boot order in the host computer.

For a click-by-click description of configuring Windows To Go, see Creating a Portable Windows 10 Environment with Windows To Go at *https://www.microsoft.com/en-us/download/details.aspx?id=48127.*

Chapter Summary

■ The three primary ways to install Windows 10 are DVD boot installation, distribution share installation, and image-based installation. DVD boot installations have low custom-ization and are only suitable for infrequent installations. Distribution share installations allow you to add extra drivers and packages. Image-based installations can include installed and configured applications along with the operating system.

■ Clean installations require user settings and data to be migrated from the old computer to the new computer. Upgrades are simpler because the process automatically migrates user settings and data.

- An attended installation requires you to answer questions during the installation.

- The Windows 10 ADK provides tools such as ACT, Windows PE, Windows SIM, and Windows ICD to help you migrate to Windows 10 and automate deployment.

- An unattended installation uses an answer file to pass configuration to Setup, with a network administrator answering questions. The two most common names for answer files are autounattend.xml and unattend.xml.

- During a basic installation, the windowsPE, offlineServicing, specialize, and oobeSystem configuration passes are performed. When Sysprep is used, the generalize, auditSystem, auditUser, and oobeSystem configuration passes can be triggered.

- Windows SIM is used to create answer files, add device drivers or packages to an answer file, create a configuration set, or apply offline updates to a Windows 10 image.

- Sysprep is used to prepare computers for imaging. After Sysprep is run, Windows 10 can be configured to enter audit mode or start the out-of-box experience.

- DISM is used to capture, modify, and apply WIM images. WIM is file-based imaging and allows you to store multiple images in a single image file. Single-instance storage reduces the size of an image file.

- DISM is also used to maintain Windows 10 images. DISM can be used to apply Windows updates and enable features.

- You can create a bootable CD, DVD, or USB drive to perform imaging operations. The necessary files are included with Windows 10 ADK.

- Windows ICD is used to create provisioning packages that are applied to Windows 10 computers that are already deployed. Provisioning avoids the need to reimage new computers and BYOD devices. Windows ICD can also create boot media for Windows 10 installation.

- Windows To Go allows users to take a portable version of Windows 10 on a USB drive to use at home or another alternate location.

Key Terms

answer file   An XML file used during an unattended setup to provide configuration to Setup.exe. Windows 10 answer files are created by using Windows (SIM).

Application Compatibility Toolkit (ACT)   A set of utilities and resources from Microsoft to help organizations run legacy software on Windows 10.

attended installation   An installation when a network administrator must be present to answer configuration questions presented during Windows 10 installation.

auditSystem configuration pass   The configuration pass that is performed *before* user sign-in when Sysprep triggers Windows 10 into audit mode.

auditUser configuration pass   The configuration pass that is performed *after* user sign-in when Sysprep triggers Windows 10 into audit mode.

autounattend.xml   An answer file that is automatically searched for during the windowsPE, offlineServicing, and specialize configuration passes.

catalog file   A file used by Windows SIM to read the configurable settings and their current status for a WIM image.

clean installation   An installation that is performed on a new computer, or does not retain the user settings or applications of an existing computer.

configuration set   The subset of files from a distribution share that are required for a particular answer file. A configuration set is more compact than a distribution share.

Deployment Image Servicing and Management (DISM)   A command-line tool that can be used to service Windows 10 images offline or online and perform imaging operations.

distribution share   A share configured through Windows SIM to hold drivers and packages that can be added to Windows 10 during installation.

distribution share installation   An installation of Windows 10 that is started by running Setup.exe over the network from a distribution share.

DVD boot installation   An installation of Windows 10 that is started by booting from DVD to run Setup.exe.

generalization   A process performed by Sysprep to prepare a computer running Windows 10 for imaging. The computer SID, computer name, and hardware information are removed during generalization.

generalize configuration pass   The configuration pass that is performed when Sysprep is run to generalize Windows 10.

Hardware Abstraction Layer (HAL)   A low-level system driver in Windows 10 that controls communication between Windows 10 and the computer hardware.

image   A collection of files captured using DISM and stored in an image file.

image-based installation   An installation that uses DISM to apply an image of an operating system to a computer. The image can include applications as well as the operating system.

image file   A file that stores one or more images (typically operating system installations). The size of an image file is minimized through the use of single-instance storage when a file exists in multiple images.

offlineServicing configuration pass   The second configuration pass that is performed after the Windows image has been copied to the local hard drive. This configuration pass applies packages such as security updates, language packs, and device drivers before Windows 10 is started.

offline update   An update that is applied to Windows 10 during installation before Windows 10 is started. The packages used for offline updates are supplied by Microsoft.

oobeSystem configuration pass   The final configuration pass before installation is complete, applied during the user out-of-box experience (OOBE). This configuration pass is typically used in conjunction with Sysprep and DISM.

product activation   A process put in place by Microsoft to reduce piracy. Unique information about your computer is sent to Microsoft to ensure that the package of Windows 10 purchased is installed on only a single computer.

provisioning   A new configuration process for Windows 10 that modifies the configuration of an already installed Windows 10 operating system to match corporate standards. Windows ICD creates provisioning packages that perform that configuration.

specialize configuration pass   The configuration pass that is performed after hardware has been detected. This is the most common configuration pass to apply settings.

Sysprep   A tool that is used to generalize Windows 10 and prepare computers for imaging.

System Audit Mode cleanup action   An option in Sysprep that triggers the computer to enter audit mode and run the auditSystem and auditUser configuration passes on reboot.

System Out-of-Box Experience cleanup action   An option in Sysprep that triggers the computer to run the oobeSystem configuration pass and start Windows Welcome on reboot.

unattend.xml   An answer file that is automatically searched for during the generalize, auditSystem, auditUser, and oobeSystem configuration passes.

unattended installation   An installation that does not require any user input because all necessary configuration information is provided by an answer file.

Universal Naming Convention (UNC)   A naming system used by Windows computers to locate network file shares and network printers. The format is \\servername\sharename.

upgrade installation   An installation that migrates all of the settings from a preexisting Windows operating system to Windows 10.

User State Migration Tool (USMT)   A set of scriptable command-line utilities that are used to migrate user settings and files from a source computer to a destination computer. USMT is typically used by large organizations during deployments of desktop operating systems.

Volume Activation Management Tool (VAMT)　A tool that can be installed to provide volume activation with KMS activation keys used with volume licensing. It is equivalent to the Volume Activation Service in Windows Server 2012 R2 and Windows Server 2016.

Windows 10 Assessment and Deployment Kit (ADK)　A collection of utilities and documentation for automating the deployment of Windows 10.

Windows Imaging and Configuration Designer (ICD)　A utility that is used to create provisioning packages for Windows 10. Windows ICD can also create bootable media that includes a Windows 10 installation image and a provisioning package.

Windows Imaging Format (WIM)　A file-based image format developed by Microsoft to store multiple images in a single file.

Windows PE　A limited version of Windows that can be used to perform recovery tasks and install Windows 10.

Windows System Image Manager (SIM)　A utility that is used to create answer files for Windows 10 unattended installations. Windows SIM can also create distribution shares and configuration sets.

Windows To Go　A portable version of Windows 10 that can be created on a USB drive.

windowsPE configuration pass　The first configuration pass performed during Setup, which can be used to perform tasks such as disk partitioning and entering the product key.

Review Questions

1. Which task cannot be performed by using DISM?

   a. Create an image.

   b. Add files to an image.

   c. Add service packs to an image.

   d. Delete an image.

   e. Apply an image.

2. Which utility is used to create answer files for unattended installations?

   a. DISM

   b. Windows PE

   c. Windows System Image Manager

   d. Windows ICD

   e. Sysprep

3. Which utility is used to prepare computers for imaging by removing specific information, such as the computer name and computer SID?

   a. DISM

   b. Windows PE

   c. Windows System Image Manager

   d. Windows Deployment Services

   e. Sysprep

4. Which installation methods require booting into Windows PE before Windows 10 starts? (Choose all that apply.)

   a. DVD boot installation

   b. distribution share installation

   c. upgrade installation

   d. image-based installation

5. Which installation method can be used to distribute Windows 10 with applications already installed?

   a. DVD boot installation

   b. distribution share installation

   c. unattended installation

   d. image-based installation

   e. attended installation

6. The _____ installation method is best suited to small organizations that install Windows 10 only occasionally.

7. Which methods can you use to migrate user settings from a previous operating system to Windows 10? (Choose all that apply.)

   a. Copy the user profile from the old computer to the new computer.

   b. Perform an upgrade over the top of the old operating system.

   c. Use Windows Easy Transfer.

   d. Use the User State Migration Tool.

   e. Use Remote Desktop to copy to files.

8. Which folder is used to store user profiles in Windows 10?

   a. C:\Documents and Settings

   b. C:\Profiles

   c. C:\Windows\Profiles

   d. C:\Users

   e. C:\Documents and Settings\Profiles

9. Which methods can you use to place applications from a previous operating system on Windows 10? (Choose all that apply.)

   a. Copy the applications from the previous computer to the new computer.

   b. Perform an upgrade over the top of the previous operating system.

   c. Use Windows Easy Transfer.

   d. Use the User State Migration Tool.

   e. Reinstall the applications on the new computer.

10. Which utility can be used to update drivers in an existing Windows 10 image?

    a. WISM

    b. Windows ICD

    c. DISM

    d. Package Manager

    e. Windows Update

11. Which configuration passes automatically search for an autounattend.xml file, if an answer file is not specified? (Choose all that apply.)

    a. windowsPE

    b. offlineServicing

    c. specialize

    d. generalize

    e. oobeSystem

12. Which configuration pass can be used to perform disk partitioning operations?

    a. windowsPE

    b. offlineServicing

    c. specialize

    d. generalize

    e. oobeSystem

13. Which configuration pass is performed by Sysprep?

    a. windowsPE

    b. offlineServicing

    c. specialize

    d. generalize

    e. oobeSystem

14. A WIM image file containing two Windows 10 images will be approximately twice as big as a WIM image file containing one Windows 10 image. True or False?

15. Which options must be used with DISM to save changes to an image? (Choose two.)

    a. /mount-image

    b. /mountrw

    c. /unmount-image

    d. /commit

    e. /save

16. Which of the following are benefits of DISM? (Choose all that apply.)

    a. WIM image file size is minimized by single instance storage.

    b. Images can be taken of an entire partition or just a single folder.

    c. Partitions can be created automatically.

    d. Images are always compressed to save disk space.

    e. There is no charge to use DISM for Windows 10 imaging.

17. Windows To Go is available in Windows 10 Pro and Windows 10 Enterprise. True or False?

18. Which of the following are scenarios where you could use provisioning? (Choose all that apply.)

    a. deploying Microsoft Office

    b. updating Windows 10 Pro to Window 10 Enterprise

    c. upgrading Windows 8.1 to Windows 10

    d. deploying new Windows Store applications

    e. performing a clean installation of Windows 10

19. Which tool is used to create provisioning packages?

    a. Windows PE

    b. Windows ICD

    c. Windows SIM

    d. ACT

    e. PCmover Express

20. Windows ICD cannot be used to completely automate the deployment of Windows 10. True or False?

Case Projects

Case Project 2-1: Installation for a Small Organization

Buddy's Machine Shop has 30 computers. Computers are replaced only as required by hardware failure or new software requirements. Jeff performs network administration tasks for Buddy's 25 percent of the time and spends 75 percent of his time doing computer automated design work. What is the best way for Jeff to start implementing Windows 10 for Buddy's Machine Shop?

Case Project 2-2: Using Image-Based Installation

Superduper Lightspeed Computers builds over 100 computers per week for customers. The computers use a wide range of hardware depending on whether they are built for gaming, home use, or office use. Create a plan for Superduper Lightspeed Computers to start using imaging, including audit mode, to install Windows 10 on their new computers.

Case Project 2-3: Migrating User Settings and Files

Hyperactive Media Sales has 10 Windows 7 laptop computers used by salespeople in the organization. Each laptop computer has several customized applications that are used during the sales process as well as customer relationship management software. All of the applications on the laptops are difficult to configure and have large data files. If all of the laptops have current hardware, what is the easiest way to install Windows 10 on them?

Case Project 2-4: Installation for a Large Organization

Gigantic Life Insurance has 4000 users spread over five locations in North America. They have hired you as a consultant to provide a solution for standardizing Windows 10 configuration. There is a mix of desktop computers and tablets running Windows 10. The computers and tablets come from a variety of vendors because Gigantic Life Insurance allows agents to purchase their own computers. How do you recommend they standardize their Windows 10 installations?

chapter 3

Using the System Utilities

After reading this chapter and completing the exercises, you will be able to:

- Understand and use Settings to configure Windows 10
- Understand the Administrative Tools
- Manage hardware components
- Understand and configure power management
- Configure displays
- Use Task Scheduler
- Use Windows PowerShell

Windows 10 includes a wide range of system utilities in Settings and in Administrative Tools. A thorough knowledge of these utilities can help you manage, tune, and improve your system. Some of the more advanced tools are Microsoft Management Console (MMC) snap-ins. A snap-in is the standardized format for creating system management utilities in Windows 2000 and later versions of Windows.

This chapter provides an overview of Settings and Administrative Tools. There is also a description of the MMC. As well, there is in-depth coverage of how to manage hardware components, configure power management, configure the display, and use Task Scheduler.

Settings Overview

Most of the configuration options for Windows 10 can be accessed through **Settings,** shown in Figure 3-1. The settings are organized into categories to make it easier to find the specific settings you are looking for. To access Settings, click the Start button and then click Settings.

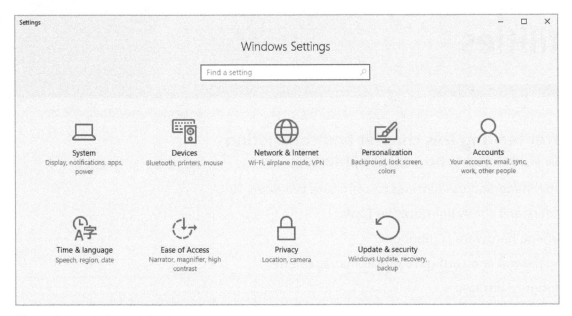

Figure 3-1   Windows 10 Settings

In Windows 7 and earlier versions of Windows, **Control Panel** was used to access configuration settings. Control Panel, shown in Figure 3-2, is still available in Windows 10. Most configuration options can be accessed through Settings, but some are still accessible only through Control Panel. In some cases, a configuration option can be accessed through both Settings and Control Panel. Newer configuration options are available only in Settings.

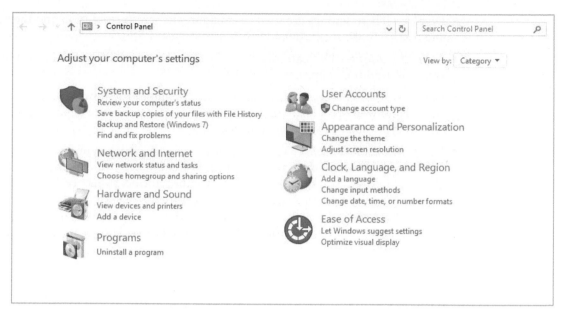

Figure 3-2   Control Panel

Options in Settings can vary depending on the hardware present in a computer running Windows 10. Some settings listed might not be visible in the screenshots or on your computer due to differences in hardware.

System

In Settings, the System category, shown in Figure 3-3, contains general-purpose settings for Windows 10. In the System category are the following settings:

Figure 3-3   System settings

- *Display*—These settings are used to configure the screen resolution and the scaling for apps and text.

- *Apps & features*—This category is used to remove or modify apps. Both Windows Store apps and traditional apps are listed here.

- *Default apps*—These settings define the default app to use for email, maps, music, photos, videos, and web browsing. You can also access settings for the default apps to use for various file types such as Word documents.

- *Notifications & actions*—These settings configure which types of notifications are displayed and where they are displayed. For example, you can enable or disable tips about Windows. You can also control whether notifications are displayed on the lock screen. You can also configure which system icons are displayed in the notification area of the taskbar. Finally, you can configure quick actions that are displayed as buttons in the taskbar **Action Center** for easy access. The Action Center is shown in Figure 3-4.

- *Power & sleep*—These settings define how long the computer must be inactive before it turns off the screen or goes to sleep. If the device has a battery, you can configure settings separately for when the device is plugged in and when it is running on battery.

- *Battery*—These settings help conserve battery power on mobile devices by limiting apps that run in the background. You can also enable and disable screen dimming when the device is running on battery power. Only devices with a battery display this category of settings.

- *Storage*—This category allows you to see how much storage is being used by various applications. You can also choose the default save locations for apps, documents, music, pictures, and videos.

- *Offline maps*—These settings allow you to define how maps are downloaded to the device. Offline maps can be used when the device does not have data connectivity.

- *Tablet mode*—If you have a device with a touch screen, you can use tablet mode to make the Windows 10 user interface easier to use. You can use these settings to enable tablet mode and define when tablet mode should be used. For example, you can configure whether a convertible laptop automatically switches to tablet mode or whether you need to confirm the switch to tablet mode.

- *Multitasking*—These settings control how you work with multiple windows and apps in Windows 10. Snap settings control how windows snap to the edge of the screen. Virtual desktop settings control how apps in different virtual desktops are displayed on the taskbar and accessed with Alt+Tab.

- *Projecting to this PC*—These settings allow you to project the display from a Windows phone or another Windows 10 computer on this computer.

- *Apps for web sites*—These settings allow you to define whether a website should be opened by a specific app or a web browser. Some websites have specific apps for displaying their content.

- *About*—This category displays information about the computer and operating system, such as the version of Windows, processor type, and amount of memory. You can also modify the computer name and domain membership here.

Figure 3-4   Action Center

Activity 3-1: Configuring Settings

Time Required: 10 minutes
Objective: View and configure settings

Description: The System category in Settings includes a wide variety of tools for managing Windows 10. In this activity, you use some of those tools to view system status and configure Windows 10. You also use Control Panel.

1. If necessary, start your computer and sign in.
2. Click the **Start** button and click **Settings**.
3. Click **System** and click **About**.
4. Read the information that is displayed about your computer. Information about your computer is located here, such as processor type and speed, memory, and computer name.
5. Click **Apps & features** and read the list of installed apps. Verify that Windows Assessment and Deployment Kit – Windows 10 is listed.
6. Click **Multitasking** and read the default configuration for the settings.
7. Click **Tablet mode** and read the default configuration for the settings.
8. Turn **Off** the Hide app icons on the taskbar in tablet mode option.
9. Click **Storage,** click **This PC (C:),** and read the list of data categories stored on the C drive.
10. Close the System window.
11. Click the **Start** button, type **Control Panel,** and then click **Control Panel.**
12. Click **System and Security** and click **System.**
13. Read the system settings and close the System window.

Devices

The Devices category, shown in Figure 3-5, contains settings for configuring hardware that your computer connects to. This includes local hardware such as devices connected to a USB port. It also includes devices connected over a network such as a printer. Most categories in Devices have links for more detailed configuration settings.

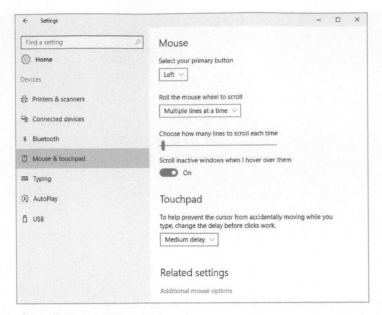

Figure 3-5   Devices settings

The settings in Devices are:

- *Printers & scanners*—This category displays printers and scanners that are connected to the computer locally or over the network. You can add or remove devices here, but there are no advanced configuration options.

- *Connected devices*—This category displays devices that are not printers and scanners that have been detected. For example, a Plug and Play monitor would be shown here. USB devices are also displayed. Again, you can add or remove devices, but not perform advanced configuration.

- *Bluetooth*—These settings are available only on a device with Bluetooth. Use this category to pair with Bluetooth devices.

- *Mouse & touchpad*—These settings control the configuration of the mouse or touch pad. For example, you can specify the primary mouse button or how quickly the scroll wheel works.

- *Typing*—This category has settings to configure how Windows 10 works with input that you type. For example, you can turn AutoCorrect for misspelled words off or on. Devices with a touch screen have additional typing options for the touch keyboard that can be displayed on screen. For example, you can turn text suggestions while typing on or off.

- *Pen*—These settings let you configure a tablet pen for your Windows 10 computer. A tablet pen is used to write on a touch screen and also includes buttons. Only some hardware and applications support using a tablet pen.

- *Wheel*—These settings let you configure a wheel with programmable buttons if your computer has one.

- *AutoPlay*—These settings control whether media connected to Windows 10 automatically plays. This is on by default, and asks for an action to perform.

- *USB*—This category has a single setting to enable notifications when there are issues connecting USB devices.

Activity 3-2: Configuring AutoPlay

Time Required: 10 minutes
Objective: Configure AutoPlay in Windows 10

Description: You do a lot of work with digital images and find it useful to automatically open removable media in File Explorer when they are inserted. You need to configure Windows 10 to automatically open File Explorer when a removable drive or memory card is inserted.

1. If necessary, start your computer and sign in.
2. Click the **Start** button and click **Settings**.
3. In the Settings window, click **Devices** and then click **AutoPlay**.
4. In the Removable drive box, select **Open folder to view files (File Explorer)**.
5. In the Memory card box, select **Open folder to view files (File Explorer)**.
6. Close the Devices window.
7. Click the **Start** button, type **Control Panel**, and then click **Control Panel**.
8. In the Control Panel window, click **Hardware and Sound** and click **AutoPlay**.
9. Scroll through the list of options. Notice that the settings for Removable drive and Memory card match what you configured in Settings, but there are many more detailed options.
10. Close the AutoPlay window.

Network & Internet

The Network & Internet category, shown in Figure 3-6, contains commonly configured settings for network connectivity. If the device has wireless data connectivity, settings for wireless connectivity are included.

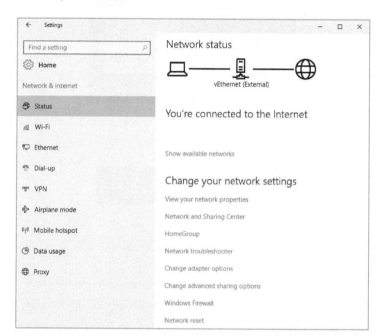

Figure 3-6   Network & Internet settings

Settings in the Network & Internet category are:

- *Status*—This section shows the status of the network connection and whether there is connectivity to the Internet.
- *Wi-Fi*—This category contains settings for Wi-Fi networks. You can select a network to connect to and there are links to advanced configuration settings.
- *Ethernet*—This category allows you to view information about connections to wired networks. You can view the IP address configuration of a network adapter.
- *Dial-up*—This category allows you to create a new dial-up connection if there is a modem in your computer.
- *VPN*—These settings allow you to create virtual private network (VPN) connections and manage when the VPN connections are active. For example, you can turn off the option to allow VPN connections over metered networks.

- *Airplane mode*—This section has settings to disable wireless network communication. If you turn on airplane mode, all wireless communication is disabled. You also have the option to disable wireless communication such as Wi-Fi and Bluetooth individually.

- *Mobile hotspot*—These settings let you configure your computer as a Wi-Fi hotspot to share an Internet connection with other devices.

- *Data usage*—This category shows the overall data usage for Windows 10 by network type. You have the option to drill down and view the network usage by application.

- *Proxy*—These settings configure when Windows 10 uses a proxy server. By default, Windows 10 automatically detects proxy settings if they are available. If no proxy settings are available, then Windows 10 connects directly to the network. You can also manually configure a proxy server.

Personalization

The Personalization category, shown in Figure 3-7, has settings for configuring the look and feel of Windows 10. These settings are primarily cosmetic and don't affect the function of Windows 10.

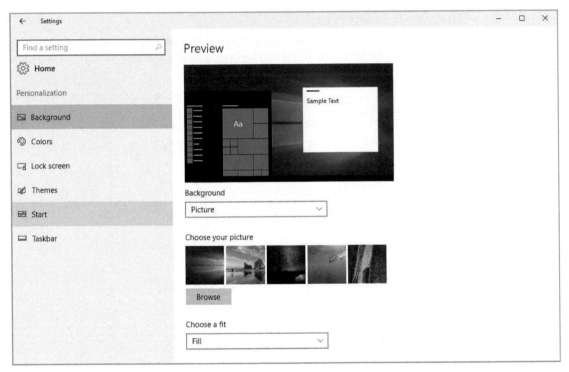

Figure 3-7   Personalization settings

Settings in the Personalization category are:

- *Background*—This category configures the look of your desktop. You can select a picture to display as the background. In earlier versions of Windows, this was referred to as wallpaper.

- *Colors*—You can use this category to select an accent color that Windows uses for the display. There is an option to allow Windows 10 to automatically select an accent color based on the background.

- *Lock screen*—These settings control the picture that is displayed on the lock screen and additional information that can be displayed. You can select one application to show detailed status on the lock screen. You can select additional applications to show quick status.

- *Themes*—This category provides a link to Personalization in Control Panel.

- *Start*—These settings allow you to customize the Start menu. You can control the size of the area showing tiles in the Start menu and control what information is automatically populated. For example, you can turn off showing the most used apps.

- *Taskbar*—This category provides taskbar configuration settings such as Lock the taskbar and Automatically hide the taskbar.

Accounts

The Accounts category, shown in Figure 3-8, has settings to create and configure user accounts. Settings in the Accounts category are:

- *Your info*—These settings allow you to configure a picture for your user account. You can also change a local account to authenticate by using a Microsoft account.

- *Email & app accounts*—These settings allow you to configure accounts for email and other apps.

- *Sign-in options*—The settings in this category vary depending on how the user account is being authenticated. A local user account only has the option to change the password. A Microsoft account has sign-in options to use a PIN or picture password.

- *Work access*—This category allows you to configure connectivity to your work or Office 365. If you connect to your work, you are participating in Mobile Device Management (MDM) where policies from your work are applied to your Windows 10 device. For example, MDM could be used to wipe your device after you lose it.

- *Family & other people*—You can use these settings to create additional local user accounts. If you are using a Microsoft account, you can configure family settings to control web browsing and other aspects of computer usage. Family settings can only be configured for Microsoft accounts.

- *Sync your settings*—These settings are available only if you are connected to a work account or using a Microsoft account. When syncing is enabled, user-specific configuration is synchronized across devices. For example, if you use the same Microsoft account to sign in on a laptop and desktop computer running Windows 10, the desktop theme can be synchronized between them.

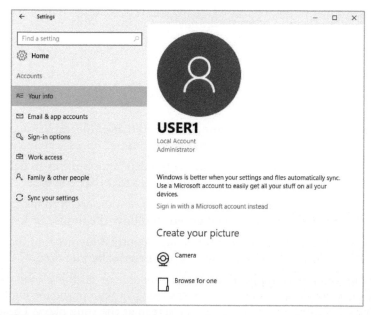

Figure 3-8   Accounts settings

Time & Language

The Time & language category, shown in Figure 3-9, has settings to manage time, display language, and speech. Settings in the Time & language category are:

- *Date & time*—These settings are used to configure time and date formatting. You can also configure the time zone. The option to set time automatically enables Windows 10 to synchronize time from *windows.time.com* on the Internet by using the Network Time Protocol (NTP). In a domain, client computers get time from domain controllers instead of the Internet.

- *Region & language*—These settings can be used to configure the country or region where you are located. The country or region that you select is used by some apps to customize content. Cortana, the personal assistant, is only available for some regions. The languages configured control which languages that Windows 10 can use to display information.

- *Speech*—This category allows you to configure voice recognition for Cortana and select the voice for Cortana. Depending on the country or region that you selected, specific languages are available.

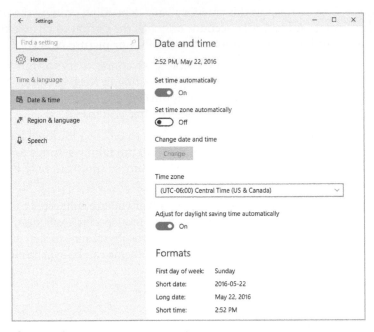

Figure 3-9   Time & language settings

Ease of Access

The **Ease of Access** category, shown in Figure 3-10, has settings to simplify access for those with visual, physical, or hearing impairment. Settings in the Ease of Access category are:

- *Narrator*—The narrator reads text in window title bars and buttons to help the visually impaired. You can also select for the narrator to read text that you type.

- *Magnifier*—The magnifier enlarges a specific point on the screen to make it easier to read for the visually impaired. It can be configured to follow the mouse or keyboard typing.

- *High contrast*—You can select from multiple high-contrast themes that make it easier to read text and differentiate between windows for the visually impaired.

- *Closed captions*—In media applications, you can enable or disable closed captions to display text on the screen that matches the words being spoken in the media. For example, closed captions can display song lyrics on the screen as the song plays. These settings control how the closed captions are displayed on the screen.

- *Keyboard*—Some people with physical disabilities have problems using the keyboard due to shakiness or other factors affecting mobility. You can turn on filter keys to ignore quickly repeated keystrokes, and turn on toggle keys to hear an audible tone when Caps Lock, Num Lock, and Scroll Lock are pressed. Sticky keys allows key combinations such as Alt+R or Ctrl+Alt+Delete to be pressed sequentially one key at a time rather than together.

- *Mouse*—These settings control how the mouse pointer is visually displayed and how the mouse pointer moves.

- *Other options*—This category contains several settings that control how notifications are displayed. You can also turn on an option to flash the title bar of the active window when a sound is played.

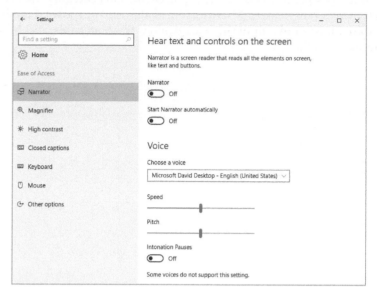

Figure 3-10　Ease of Access settings

Activity 3-3: Using Ease of Access Features

Time Required: 10 minutes
Objective: Explore the Ease of Access features in Windows 10

Description: Your organization has several people with visual and hearing impairments. You need to explore the Ease of Access features in Windows 10 to ensure that you understand how to best support them.

1. If necessary, start your computer and sign in.
2. Click the **Start** button and click **Settings**.
3. In Settings, click **Ease of Access**, click **Magnifier**, and then click the **Magnifier** switch to turn it **On**.
4. Move the mouse pointer to the edges of the screen to change the portion of the screen that is visible.
5. Click the **Invert colors** switch to turn it **On**.
6. Click the **magnifying glass** icon to display the Magnifier window and close the Magnifier window. This returns the screen to the normal view.
7. In the left pane, click **High contrast,** then in the Choose a theme box, select **High Contrast #1** and click **Apply**.
8. In the Choose a theme box, select **None** and click **Apply**.
9. In the left pane, click **Keyboard** and click the **Turns on the On-Screen Keyboard** switch to turn it **On**. This can be useful for someone with limited hand movement who cannot use a regular keyboard.
10. Close the On-Screen Keyboard window.
11. Close the Ease of Access window.

Privacy

The Privacy category, shown in Figure 3-11, has many settings to control whether apps have access to specific items in Windows 10. For example, you can prevent apps from accessing your location, camera, microphone, contacts, calendar, or email. This category also contains settings that control which data is sent back to Microsoft for diagnostic purposes. Finally, you can configure which apps are allowed to run in the background. In some cases, disabling background apps might extend battery life.

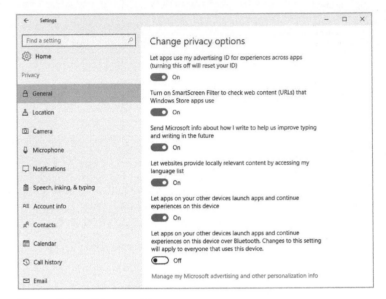

Figure 3-11   Privacy settings

Activity 3-4: Configuring Privacy Settings

Time Required: 10 minutes
Objective: Configure privacy settings in Windows 10

Description: You are concerned about your privacy and want to further restrict how your information is shared with apps. The default configuration is relatively good, but you want additional privacy.

1. If necessary, start your computer and sign in.
2. Click the **Start** button and click **Settings**.
3. In the Settings window, click **Privacy**.
4. Click the **Let apps use my advertising ID for experiences across apps** switch to turn it off.
5. In the navigation pane, click **Location** and scroll down to confirm that no apps are able to use your location.
6. In the navigation pane, click **Camera** and turn off camera access for all apps except **Messaging + Skype**.
7. In the navigation pane, click **Microphone** and turn off microphone access for all apps except **Messaging + Skype** and **Voice Recorder**.
8. In the navigation pane, click **Feedback & diagnostics** and then click **Privacy Statement**.
9. Review the Microsoft Privacy Statement and then close Microsoft Edge.
10. Close the Privacy window.

Update & Security

The Update & security category, shown in Figure 3-12, has settings to control update installation, Windows Defender, Backup, and Recovery. Settings in the Update & security category are:

- *Windows Update*—This category shows Windows updates that are available and lets you choose when to install them.

- *Windows Defender*—These settings control the anti-malware functionality of Windows Defender. From here, you can disable real-time protection temporarily for troubleshooting and control whether samples are submitted to Microsoft.

- *Backup*—These settings let you configure the File History feature that makes a backup of files to an external drive.

- *Recovery*—This category lets you reset the device to try and restore operating system functionality. Windows 10 is reinstalled.

- *Activation*—From here, you can view the activation status of the device and change the product key.

- *Find My Device*—If the device has a battery, then this option is available to try and locate the device. This option is off by default.

- *For developers*—These settings control the apps that you can install. By default, Windows Store apps can only be installed from the Windows Store. You can configure additional trusted locations from which to sideload apps. For example, your organization might have internally developed a Windows Storage app that needs to be installed.

- *Windows Insider Program*—Settings for computers that receive pre-release versions of Windows 10 updates before general availability.

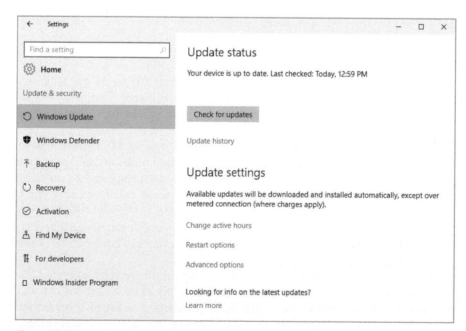

Figure 3-12　Update & Security settings

Administrative Tools

Windows 10 includes a collection of system configuration utilities that are grouped in a category called **Administrative Tools** and found in System and Security in Control Panel. Most of the tools in this category use the **Microsoft Management Console (MMC)**. The MMC is a framework that simplifies the development of administrative tools. The Administrative Tools are shown in Figure 3-13. Brief descriptions of these tools follow; later chapters offer more detailed coverage.

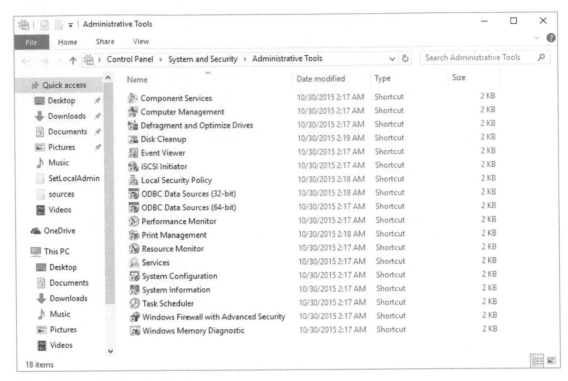

Figure 3-13   Administrative Tools

Component Services is used to configure settings for some apps. It includes settings for COM1, DCOM, and Distributed Transaction Coordinator. Typically, these settings are only modified if you receive instructions from an application developer or as part of a troubleshooting document.

Like Windows 8, the Administrative Tools in Windows 10 include disk management tools. The **Defragment and Optimize Drives** tool moves file blocks around on the disk to make individual files contiguous and faster to access. It is seldom required to perform this task manually because defragmentation is performed once per week automatically. The **Disk Cleanup** tool helps you identify unneeded files that can be removed.

Event Viewer is used to view messages from apps or Windows 10. These messages are useful for troubleshooting errors. The version of Event Viewer in Windows 10 is unchanged from the version in Windows 7.

The **iSCSI** protocol allows computers to communicate with external disks over standard Ethernet networks. External storage devices that support iSCSI are known as iSCSI targets. The computers that access iSCSI targets are iSCSI initiators. The iSCSI Initiator tool lets you configure Windows 10 to communicate with iSCSI targets and use the iSCSI targets as external disks over the network. The iSCSI protocol is used only in corporate environments and mostly on servers rather than workstations.

The Local Security Policy tool allows you to edit a wide variety of security settings on the local computer. Some of the settings include password policies, account lockout policies, auditing policies, user rights assignment, and software restriction policies. When Group Policies are used in a corporate environment, the Group Policy settings configured centrally by the administrator override the settings configured locally.

Open Database Connectivity (ODBC) is a standard mechanism for applications to access databases. Applications written to use ODBC can communicate with any supported database such as Microsoft SQL Server, Microsoft Access, or Oracle databases. A network administrator must then configure an ODBC data source to communicate with the proper database. This isolates the application from the database, makes application development easier, and provides greater flexibility when choosing a database. Windows 10 includes separate tools for configuring ODBC connections for 32-bit apps and 64-bit apps.

Performance Monitor is used to monitor and troubleshoot performance issues in Windows 10. It includes the ability to monitor many system resources, including the processor, disk, memory, and the network. Performance Monitor can log resource status over time and generate reports.

Print Management is a tool for monitoring and managing printers. In a single view, you can monitor and manage local and network printers.

Resource Monitor is a tool that provides detailed information about the processes running on your computer. You can use it to view the processor utilization, memory utilization, network utilization, and disk activity of individual processes. It is like a more advanced version of Task Manager.

Services allows you to configure Windows 10 services. You can also start and stop services if required for troubleshooting. This functionality is also available in Computer Management.

System Configuration gives you access to boot configuration, service startup, startup applications, and system tools. The General tab, shown in Figure 3-14, lets you select the type of startup you want to perform. The Boot tab lets you configure boot options such as Safe Mode. The Services tab lets you enable or disable services. The Startup tab provides a link to Task Manager where you can disable any of the applications that Windows 10 is starting automatically. The Tools tab gives you easy access to a variety of system tools such as the Registry Editor.

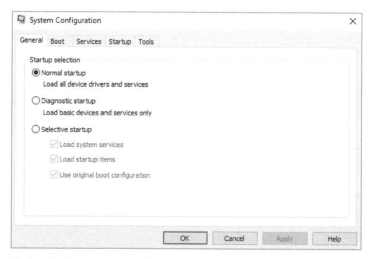

Figure 3-14   System Configuration

Task Scheduler lets you create system maintenance tasks that are performed on a regular schedule or when system events occur. Windows 10 uses Task Scheduler to perform many background maintenance tasks. You can also create your own tasks.

Windows Firewall with Advanced Security is an advanced editor for configuring Windows Firewall. It allows you to configure advanced settings for Windows Firewall that are not available through the Windows Firewall applet in Control Panel. In addition, Windows Firewall with Advanced Security can also configure IPSec settings. IPSec is a protocol used to encrypt data communication over the network.

The **Windows Memory Diagnostics Tool** is used to perform tests on the physical memory of a computer running Windows 10. The physical memory of a computer cannot be tested when Windows 10 is running because the memory diagnostics tool needs access to test all of the memory, including the memory used by Windows 10. So, when you choose to use the Memory Diagnostics Tool, your computer reboots to run the tool without Windows 10 in memory.

Microsoft Management Console

The MMC is a graphical interface shell that provides a structured environment to build management utilities. The MMC provides basic functionality, such as menus, so that management utility developers do not have to. This also provides a consistent user interface for all management utilities, which makes network administrators more productive.

Network administrators use **MMC consoles** with **MMC snap-ins** to perform management tasks. Each MMC console can host one or more snap-ins. A snap-in is a component that adds control mechanisms to the MMC console for a specific service or object. For example, the Disk Management snap-in is used to manage hard disks. Within a snap-in, there are typically multiple functions. For example, the Disk Management snap-in can partition and format hard disks.

An MMC console, shown in Figure 3-15, is composed of a console menu bar, console tree, details pane, and an Actions pane. The contents of the Action and View menus in the console menu bar change based on the snap-in that is active in the console. The console menu bar also contains a mini-icon toolbar of shortcuts to common tasks in the Action and View menus. The console tree is the left pane of the console and displays the snap-ins that are loaded into the console. The details pane is the middle pane of the console and displays the details of the item selected in the console tree. The Actions pane on the right is used to provide easy access to the options in the Action menu.

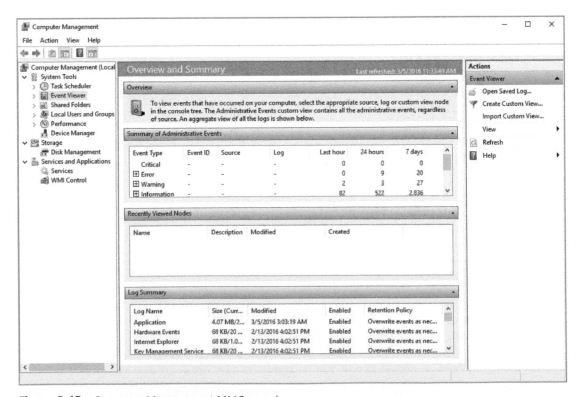

Figure 3-15   Computer Management MMC console

You can create a customized MMC console by adding the snap-ins you want to a single console and then saving the console as an .msc file. You can share .msc files between users and computers. This allows network administrators to be more productive.

The Actions pane is now favored by Microsoft over the taskpad views available in previous versions of the MMC. Snap-ins written for MMC 3.0 do not support taskpad views. Creation of taskpad views using snap-ins written for MMC 2.0 is still supported. MMC 2.0 was included in Windows Server 2003 and Windows XP.

When you share MMC consoles, you might want to restrict the ability of others to modify them. This ensures that the MMC consoles are consistent each time they are used. To prevent modification of an MMC console, you can change the console access mode. The available console access modes are listed in Table 3-1.

Table 3-1   MMC console access modes

Console access mode	Description
Author mode	Full customization of the console is allowed. This is the default console access mode.
User mode–full access	Removes the ability to add or remove snap-ins, change snap-in console options, create Favorites, or create taskpads.
User mode–limited access, multiple window	Limits access to only the portion of the console tree that was visible when the console was saved. Users are able to create new windows, but not close existing windows.
User mode–limited access, single window	Limits access to only the portion of the console tree that was visible when the console was saved. Users are not able to create new windows or close existing windows.

Limiting access to MMC consoles is not an effective security mechanism. You must limit user rights and permissions to limit a user's ability to perform administrative tasks.

Computer Management

Computer Management is an MMC console that serves as a common troubleshooting and administrative interface for several snap-ins. The Computer Management console is divided into three sections: System Tools, Storage, and Services and Applications.

The System Tools section contains:

- *Task Scheduler*—This provides a way to schedule programs to run at a particular time or when a particular event occurs.

- *Event Viewer*—This is another way to access the same information as is found in the Event Viewer administrative tool.

- *Shared Folders*—This is a way to view the shared folders on the local system. The Shares folder lets you see all shares, including hidden shares, the path of each share, and the number of clients connected to each share. The Sessions folder lets you view which users are connected to the local system over the network, how many files they have open, and the computer they are using. The Open Files folder lets you see which files are open and which user has them open.

- *Local Users and Groups*—This is a way to access similar information as Accounts in Settings. However, this option is more advanced, and provides additional options.

- *Performance*—This is another way to access the same information as is available in the Performance administrative tool.

- *Device Manager*—This provides a way to view and modify the configuration of hardware devices in your computer.

The Storage section contains:

- *Disk Management*—This is used to manage hard disks. You can partition and format hard disks.

The Services and Applications section contains:

- *Services*—This is used to enable, configure, and disable Windows 10 services.

- *WMI Control*—This provides a way to back up and restore, control security, and specify a default namespace for Windows Management Instrumentation (WMI). WMI is used to perform remote monitoring and management of Windows.

Activity 3-5: Using Computer Management

Time Required: 5 minutes
Objective: Use the Computer Management MMC console

Description: The Computer Management MMC console is one of the most commonly used administrative tools. It has several useful snap-ins, such as Event Viewer, Disk Management, and Services. In this activity, you open Computer Management using two different methods.

1. If necessary, start your computer and sign in.

2. Click the **Start** button, type **Control Panel**, and then click **Control Panel**.

3. Click **System and Security** and click **Administrative Tools**.

4. Double-click **Computer Management**. Notice that there are a number of options to manage Windows 10 using this single MMC console, as shown previously in Figure 3-15.

5. In the left pane, expand **Services and Applications** and click **Services**. This is the same information you can see in the Services MMC console that is available in Administrative Tools.

6. Close Computer Management.

7. Close the Administrative Tools window and close the System and Security window.

8. Right-click the **Start** button and click **Computer Management**. This is another way to start the Computer Management MMC console.

9. Close Computer Management.

You can also open Computer Management by pressing Win+X and selecting Computer Management from the menu.

Services

A **service** is a type of Windows application that runs in the background without user interaction. Services typically perform tasks for other software applications or perform housekeeping tasks for Windows 10. For example, the DHCP Client service is responsible for communicating on the network to get a network address that allows Windows 10 to access servers and the Internet. Windows Firewall also runs as a service.

The **Services** administrative tool, shown in Figure 3-16, is used to manage Windows 10 services. The details pane of Services has a standard view and an extended view that can be selected from tabs at the bottom of the console. The extended view shows the description of the selected service at the left side of the details pane and includes shortcuts for starting. stopping, and restarting the selected service.

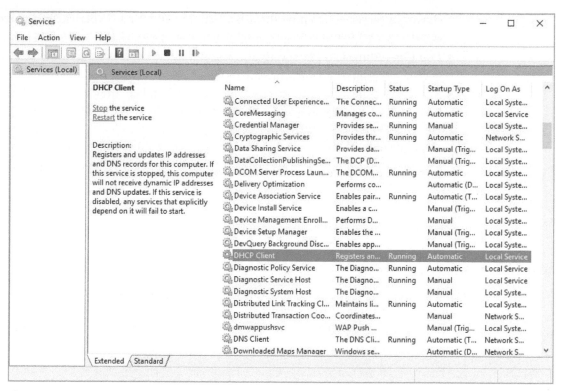

Figure 3-16 Services administrative tool

Both views show the following service information:

- *Name*—Each service is given a name to identify it. You can modify the name of a service, but it is not recommended. If you call a vendor for support, the vendor will expect services to be using standard names.

- *Description*—The description of a service provides information about what tasks the service performs. Descriptions for Windows services are provided by Microsoft, while descriptions for other services are provided by the vendor.

- *Status*—The status of a service indicates whether it is started or stopped. In rare cases, a service may have a status of starting or stopping if the service is experiencing problems during startup or shutdown.

- *Startup Type*—Services with an Automatic startup type are started when Windows 10 boots. Services with an Automatic (Delayed Start) startup type are started several minutes after Windows 10 boots. Services with a Manual startup type must be started manually by a user, or by another application. Services with a Disabled startup type cannot be started.

- *Log On As*—Each service logs on to Windows to determine its permissions to perform tasks such as file manipulation. Services can log on as the Local System account, which has full access to Windows 10 or a specific user account. Most Windows 10 services log on as Local System. However, logging on as a specific user account is more secure. Some Windows 10 services log on as Network Service or Local Service. Both of these accounts are more limited than Local System.

When you view the properties of a service, you can see additional information about it. You can also modify characteristics of the service. The Properties dialog box of a service, shown in Figure 3-17, includes the following tabs:

- *General*—Displays the service name, description, path to executable, and start parameters. In addition, there are buttons to start, stop, pause, and resume the service. Stopping and starting a service is often performed when the service has experienced an error. Pausing and restarting a service is typically done when testing service functionality.

- *Log On*—Allows you to specify the account name used by a service to log on to perform its tasks.

- *Recovery*—Allows you to specify which action is taken after first, second, and subsequent failures. The actions include taking no action, restarting the services, running a program, and restarting the computer.

- *Dependencies*—Shows you which other services require this service to be running before they can start. In addition, this tab shows you the other services that must be running for this service to start.

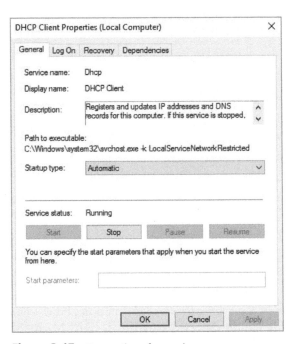

Figure 3-17   Properties of a service

Activity 3-6: Managing Services

Time Required: 10 minutes

Objective: Manage Windows 10 services by using the Services MMC snap-in

Description: Windows 10 has a number of services that run in the background performing system tasks. As part of a troubleshooting process, you often need to verify the status of services and occasionally stop or start services. In this activity, you manage services by using the Services MMC snap-in.

1. If necessary, start your computer and sign in.

2. Click the **Start** button, type **Services**, and then click **Services**.

3. Click the **Computer Browser** service. The extended view in the Services snap-in shows a description of the service at the left side of the window. This description can also be viewed when you are looking at the properties of a service.

4. Click the **Standard** tab at the bottom of the window. This view removes the service description and makes it easier to see information about the services.

5. Right-click **DHCP Client,** click **Restart,** and click **Yes.** This stops and starts the DHCP Client service and any dependent services. It is occasionally necessary to stop and start a service if it is not functioning properly.

6. Double-click **DHCP Client.** The General tab shows most of the same information that was visible in the summary of services you have already been viewing. Notice that this tab shows the executable file that runs as a service.

7. Click the **Log On** tab. If a service is configured to run as a particular user account to limit its permissions, then the credentials are entered here.

8. Click the **Recovery** tab. This tab contains settings for the actions to be taken if this service fails one or more times. Notice that this service is automatically restarted after each of the first two failures.

9. Click the **Dependencies** tab. Notice that the DHCP Client service requires several services to run properly, and several services depend on the DHCP Client service.

10. Click **Cancel.**

11. Close the Services window.

Hardware Management

Managing and maintaining computer hardware is a task performed regularly by network administrators. Windows 10 supports a wide variety of internal and external hardware components that you should be familiar with. Internal hardware components include network cards, video cards, and hard disk drives. External components are typically peripheral devices such as a mouse, printer, or USB drive.

Windows 10 requires **device drivers** to manage and communicate with hardware components. Device drivers are written specifically for a particular type and model of component. For example, a 3C905 network card driver is different from an E1000 network card driver.

Microsoft does not provide a list of hardware that is compatible with Windows 10. In most cases, hardware that functioned properly in Windows 7 or newer works with Windows 10. If you have a Windows 7 SP1 or Windows 8.1 computer, you can install the Get Windows 10 app to verify hardware and software compatibility, as described in Chapter 1, Introduction to Windows 10.

To manage hardware in Windows 10, you should understand:

- Device drivers
- Device driver compatibility
- Device Manager
- Device driver signing
- Procedures for adding new hardware components

Device Drivers

Hardware devices such as modems, network adapter cards, and video cards are manufactured by a wide variety of vendors. The capabilities and functions of these devices vary depending on the model and manufacturer. A device driver is software that allows Windows 10 to properly communicate with and use the functionality of a device.

Device drivers act as intermediaries between a hardware component and an operating system such as Windows 10. A device driver contains the instructions on how to use the full capabilities of a device properly. After they are installed, device drivers load automatically as part of the boot process each time Windows 10 is started.

In some cases, a device driver not specifically designed for a hardware component may allow that component to function. For example, the Microsoft Basic Display Adapter driver works with almost all video cards. If an incorrect device driver works, it is because the basic functionality of a class of hardware devices, such as video cards, is similar. However, installing the wrong device driver for a hardware component results in poor performance and does not let you use the advanced features of a device. Using the incorrect device driver for a hardware component may also make Windows 10 unstable.

Vendors regularly release updated device drivers. Device drivers are updated to improve performance, add additional features, or fix flaws. It is a best practice to use the latest device drivers that are available from the manufacturer's website. When a device is not working properly, installing the latest device driver should be one of the first troubleshooting steps.

 Some device drivers can be obtained through Windows Update. They are distributed as optional updates.

Device Driver Compatibility

Some device drivers designed for previous versions of Windows do not work properly with Windows 10. The driver incompatibility is due to changes that make Windows 10 more stable and secure. If a driver does not function properly in Windows 10, you must get an updated driver from the device manufacturer.

Some potential device driver compatibility issues are:

- A 32-bit version of Windows 10 requires 32-bit drivers, and a 64-bit version of Windows 10 requires 64-bit drivers.

- All driver files referenced in an .inf file must be part of the driver installation package. The .inf file for a driver describes the files that need to be installed. In some previous versions of Windows, including all files in the driver package was preferred, but not enforced. This might cause the installation of some drivers to fail.

- Installers cannot display a user interface during installation. Some older device drivers display a user interface during installation to request configuration information. You must obtain an updated device driver from the manufacturer that does not present a user interface during installation.

- All 64-bit drivers that run in kernel mode must be digitally signed by Microsoft. This means that manufacturers must submit kernel mode drivers to Microsoft for testing and approval. Previous versions of Windows allowed kernel mode drivers to be digitally signed by the manufacturer. Kernel mode drivers have unrestricted access to the computer.

- Windows 10 uses the NDIS 10.x interface for network devices. Network drivers for Windows XP are NDIS 5.x and are not compatible. To ensure the best performance, obtain an NDIS 6.0 or newer network driver. NDIS is covered in more detail in Chapter 7, Networking.

- Kernel mode printer drivers cannot be used in Windows 10. Replace Kernel mode printer drivers with newer, user mode drivers from the printer manufacturer. This affects a very small number of printer drivers. Affected printer drivers are typically specialized devices used in manufacturing environments, such as bar code printers.

Device Manager

Device Manager is the primary tool for managing device drivers. The main purpose of Device Manager is to allow you to view and modify hardware device properties. Some of the tasks that can be performed with Device Manager are:

- Determining whether installed hardware is functioning correctly

- Viewing and changing hardware resource settings

- Determining and changing the drivers used by a device
- Enabling, disabling, and uninstalling devices
- Configuring advanced settings for devices
- Viewing and printing summary information about installed devices

After installing Windows 10, you should use Device Manager to confirm that all devices are working properly. After installing a new hardware component, you should use Device Manager to confirm that the specific component is functioning properly. Any hardware component that is not functioning correctly is displayed with a yellow exclamation mark. A hardware component that has been manually disabled is displayed with a down arrow, as shown in Figure 3-18.

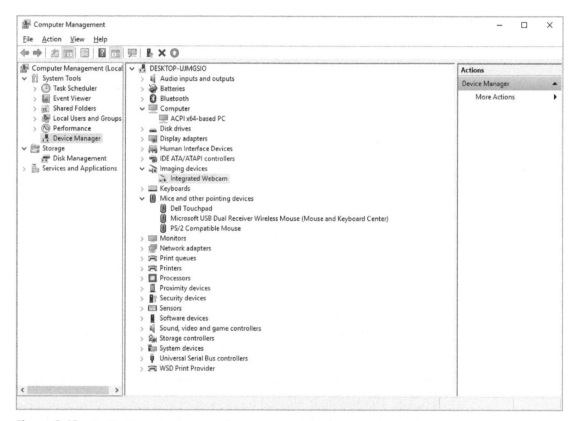

Figure 3-18   Device Manager

If a hardware component is not functioning properly, you should install an updated driver for it. You can install an updated device driver from the Driver tab in the Device Properties, shown in Figure 3-19. To access the properties for a device, right-click the device and click Properties. You can also install an updated device driver by using the Hardware Update Wizard that is accessible by right-clicking the device.

Although vendors perform extensive testing, occasionally an updated device driver causes problems. You can roll back a device driver to the previous version when an updated device driver causes problems.

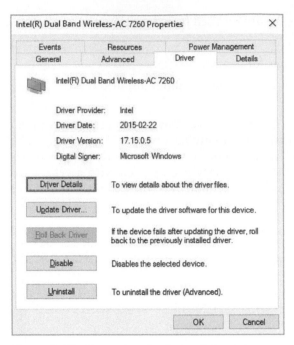

Figure 3-19 Properties of a device, Driver tab

Activity 3-7: Using Device Manager

Time Required: 10 minutes

Objective: Use Device Manager to configure hardware components and device drivers

Description: Device Manager is an MMC snap-in that can configure hardware components and device drivers. You can use it to install updated drivers and disable devices that are not functioning properly. In this activity, you view the status of the network card in your computer.

1. If necessary, start your computer and sign in.

2. Right-click the **Start** button and click **Device Manager**. If some devices are listed with a yellow question mark, it means that no device driver is loaded for those devices.

3. Expand **Network adapters** and double-click your network card to display the Properties dialog box (the name of the network card will vary depending on your hardware). The General tab gives general information about your network card, including its status.

4. Click the **Advanced** tab. The contents of the Advanced tab vary depending on the model of network card. The settings are defined by the device driver.

5. Click the **Driver** tab. This shows information about the device driver, including date, version number, and publisher. You can also update drivers here.

6. Click the **Driver Details** button. This displays the files that are used as part of the device driver.

7. Click **OK** and click the **Details** tab. The Details tab has an option box that lets you select and view all of the device driver details.

8. Click the **Property** option box and browse through the list of details you can view.

9. Click the **Events** tab. This tab displays information about actions taken by the device, such as loading or starting the device driver.

10. If present, click the **Resources** tab. You can view and modify the resources used by a device on this tab. This tab might not be available if your Windows 10 installation is virtualized.

11. If present, click the **Power Management** tab. You can use this tab to control how the network adapter interacts with power management. This tab might not be available if your Windows 10 installation is virtualized.

12. Click **Cancel**.

13. Close Device Manager.

Device Manager is also included in the Computer Management administrative tool.

Device Driver Signing

Windows 10 uses file signatures on system files to ensure system stability. Device drivers can also be signed. **Device driver signing** ensures that a driver for a specific hardware component has been verified by Microsoft to be from a known software publisher (meaning it is authentic). Device driver signing also ensures that the device driver has not been modified in any way since it was signed (meaning it has integrity). Viruses are unable to spread by using device drivers because digital signing shows an infected device driver as corrupted.

If you attempt to install an unsigned device driver in Windows 10, one of the following messages will appear:

- *Windows can't verify the publisher of this driver software*—This message appears when no digital signature is present, or the digital signature cannot be verified as valid. You should install unsigned drivers only if you are confident it is from a legitimate source.

- *This driver software has been altered*—This message appears if the device driver has been altered since the developer added the digital signature. In most cases, this message indicates that the original device driver has been infected by a malicious program and it should not be installed.

- *Windows cannot install this driver software*—This message appears only on the 64-bit versions of Windows 10. The 64-bit versions of Windows 10 do not allow unsigned device drivers to be installed by default. However, for testing purposes, you can disable the check for driver signing by using bcdedit.exe.

You can verify that existing drivers and system files are signed by running the **File Signature Verification utility** (sigverif.exe). The file name, location, modification date, and version number are returned for each unsigned file. You can then investigate whether signed versions of these files are available. It is a best practice to use only signed device drivers.

A signed device driver does not indicate that Microsoft has performed stability or quality testing.

Hardware Component Installation

When hardware components are installed in a computer, they are assigned resource settings that allow them to access the system processor and memory in different ways. Each type of hardware component has different requirements.

The four main resources a hardware component might use are:

- *Direct memory access (DMA) channels*—A legacy method for allowing devices to communicate directly with system memory instead of passing data through the processor. This method is typically used for sound cards.

- *Input/output (I/O) ranges*—Addresses at which a device can be communicated with. A single device can have several addresses, with each address allowing access to a particular device feature or component.

- *Interrupt request (IRQ) lines*—A mechanism for devices to request time from the CPU.

- *Memory address ranges*—Address ranges in system memory that are dedicated to the device.

Devices for modern computer and operating systems, such as Windows 10, support Plug and Play, which automatically assigns resources to devices. Universal Serial Bus (USB) devices are also Plug and Play. Only settings for legacy ports such as parallel ports and serial ports might require manual configuration of resources in Windows 10.

To install a Plug and Play device:

1. Install or attach the new hardware component.

2. Windows 10 automatically detects the new device.

3. A device driver is loaded automatically if Windows 10 contains an appropriate device driver.

4. If Windows 10 does not contain an appropriate device driver, you are prompted to provide one.

Some USB devices require you to install the driver before attaching the USB device the first time. This is required to ensure that Windows 10 does not attempt to load an incompatible driver before the correct driver is available. Read the instructions that come with the device to be sure.

Windows 10 might not contain the latest device driver for your hardware component. You can update the device driver after installation, if required.

To simplify the location of device drivers, you can make them available to computers by staging the drivers in the **driver store** or by providing a location to search. Windows 10 contains a driver store with a large set of device drivers included on the Windows 10 installation media. You can add new drivers to the driver store by using pnputil.exe. By adding a device driver to the driver store, you ensure that Windows 10 is able to find and install the driver when the matching hardware is attached. For example, you could stage the driver for a new USB printer on all Windows 10 computers. Then, when that printer is attached to any Windows 10 computer in the office, the appropriate driver is automatically loaded without asking the user to locate the appropriate driver.

You can also store drivers in a centralized network location. If you store drivers in a network location, you need to modify a registry key on the Windows 10 computers to configure the computers to search in that location when looking for drivers. Edit the following registry key: HKLM\Software\Microsoft\Windows\CurrentVersion\DevicePath.

Generally, you should use an automated tool to update this registry key on all of the computers to simplify deployment.

Using Regedit.exe to edit the registry is covered in Chapter 9, Windows 10 Application Support.

Power Management

Power management is becoming a major concern for corporate and personal computer owners alike. Hardware manufacturers have started to address this concern by focusing on reduced power consumption in their new products. However, a computer and monitor can still easily consume over 100 watts of power while they are running. Minimizing power usage is driven by both cost and environmental factors.

Windows 10 relies on power management capabilities built in to a computer to perform power management. Computers must meet the specifications of the **Advanced Configuration and Power Interface (ACPI)** standard to be managed by Windows 10. All current computers meet this standard, but can implement varying options.

The ACPI standard defines power states for global power management and individual devices. Power states define which devices are drawing power in the system. Power states can be implemented at different times based on the power plan you have configured. For multimedia computers, **Away Mode** provides a way to have instant power-on, similar to other consumer electronics such as a television.

 Power management can be centrally controlled by using Group Policy in a corporate environment.

ACPI States

The ACPI standard defines a number of global power management states. However, not all states are used by Windows 10. Table 3-2 lists the ACPI power states used by Windows 10.

Table 3-2   ACPI power states used by Windows 10

Power state	Description
S0 (or G0) Working	The **S0 state** is the fully functioning computer. While in this state, individual devices, such as the processor and hard disks, can be in varying power states. For example, the spinning of a hard disk can be stopped after a few minutes of inactivity to reduce power usage.
	For faster recovery from sleep mode, some hardware manufacturers support **Modern Standby** in the S0 state. Modern Standby maximizes power savings while still providing an instant-on experience. Systems capable of using Modern Standby do not use the typical S3 state for sleep.
S3 Sleep	The **S3 state** is also known as suspend to RAM. In this state, all system devices are powered down except the RAM. The RAM retains the state of all running applications. Returning from S3 to S0 requires only that the hardware be reinitialized.
	If power is lost while the computer is in the S3 state, all data from memory is lost. This is equivalent to losing power while the computer is running.
	ACPI also defines sleep states S1 and S2, but they are less commonly implemented by hardware manufacturers. They also stop processing data, but provide slightly less power savings.
S4 Sleep	The **S4 state** is also known as suspend to disk. In this state, the contents of RAM are saved to disk and all devices including RAM are powered off. During restart, the contents of RAM are loaded from disk rather than booting the operating system. When a computer system has a large amount of RAM, restarting from the S4 state can take a long period of time. For example, a computer with 2 GB of RAM needs to load 2 GB of data from disk during startup from the S4 state. This state is commonly known as **hibernate**.
	If power is lost while the computer is in the S4 state, all data is unaffected. Because the contents of memory are stored on disk, a power failure does not affect the S4 state.
S5 (or G2) Soft Off	In this state, the operating system is not running. This is the power state triggered when the operating system is shut down. Minimal hardware functionality is maintained, such as the ability to start booting the computer by using Wake on LAN. To start a computer from this state, the operating system must go through a complete boot up.
G3 Mechanical Off	In this state, the operating system is not running and no power is supplied to any devices in the computer. This is the only state in which hardware can be serviced. A computer that is in the G3 state can be unplugged and not be affected. The only power consumption for a computer in the G3 state is from a small battery that maintains BIOS settings and the clock.

Windows 10 also implements a hybrid sleep mode. **Hybrid sleep** saves the contents of memory to disk when entering the S3 state. This effectively means the computer is in the S3 state, but prepared for the S4 state. Hybrid sleep is available depending on the hardware capabilities of the computer. When available, it is enabled by default.

Hybrid sleep provides the following advantages:

- If power is lost in the S3 state, the computer can recover from the S4 state on reboot. No data is lost when there is a power outage in the S3 state.

- Hybrid sleep eliminates the requirement to leave sleep mode to enter hibernation.

Modern Standby

Windows 10 supports Modern Standby if the computer or device has support for Modern Standby. When compared with the standard S3 sleep state, a computer using Modern Standby resumes faster, providing an "instant-on" experience. In addition, because they are in the S0 state, background processes can continue to run. Therefore, the system can wake and respond to events such as receiving an instant message and sounding a notification. The system can also wake to perform scheduled maintenance.

Windows 8 had similar functionality called Disconnected Standby. In Windows 8.1, the InstantGo feature had similar functionality. Modern Standby in Windows 10 provides longer battery life than Disconnected Standby and InstantGo because it performs fewer wakeups.

Fast Startup

Windows 10 makes shutting down and restarting your computer faster with Fast Startup. When you shut down a Windows 10 computer with Fast Startup enabled, it signs out all of the user accounts, closes all applications, and hibernates Windows 10. When you turn your computer back on again, it resumes from hibernation rather than performing a complete startup. Fast Startup is enabled by default.

The benefit of Fast Startup is faster restart times after performing a shutdown. However, this means that your computer never completely shuts down the operating system and if any part of the operating system becomes unstable, a shutdown and restart won't fix it. Instead, you need to do a restart. A restart always completely unloads Windows 10 and starts it again.

When Windows 10 is in hibernation mode, the contents of memory are stored in C:\hiberfil. sys. This file can be several GB in size. This can be a concern on computers with small hard disks and little free space.

Power Plans

Windows 10 uses **power plans** to control how your computer implements power management. There are three default power plans. Some of the details of each default power plan for a laptop computer are listed in Table 3-3. In addition, you can create your own power plans. The options available to you when creating or modifying a power plan vary depending on the capabilities of your computer hardware. For example, settings for running on battery power only apply to portable computers with a battery.

Table 3-3   Default power plans

Parameter	Balanced		Power Saver		High Performance	
	AC	Battery	AC	Battery	AC	Battery
Turn off display after	10 min	5 min	5 min	2 min	15 min	10 min
Turn off hard disk after	20 min	10 min	20 min	5 min	20 min	20 min
Minimum processor state	5%	5%	5%	5%	100%	5%
Maximum processor state	100%	100%	100%	100%	100%	100%
Sleep after	30 min	15 min	15 min	10 min	Never	Never
Hibernate after	Never	Never	180 min	180 min	Never	Never

Activity 3-8: Configuring a Power Plan

Time Required: 5 minutes

Objective: Configure a power plan to reduce power consumption

Description: Windows 10 includes three default power plans to maximize performance, maximize power savings, and provide balanced power savings and performance. Most office computers do not need to maximize performance; it is more beneficial to maximize power savings. In this activity, you configure your computer to maximize power savings.

1. If necessary, start your computer and sign in.
2. Click the **Start** button and click **Settings**.
3. Click **System** and click **Power & sleep**. The options available here are very limited.
4. Click **Additional power settings**.
5. In the Power Options window, under Preferred plans, click the **Power Saver** option button.
6. Next to the Power saver plan, click **Change plan settings**. Notice that when using the Power saver plan, the display turns off after 5 minutes. The content displayed here will vary depending on whether your computer is ACPI compliant. An ACPI-compliant computer will also have a setting for when the computer goes to sleep, as shown in Figure 3-20.
7. Click **Change advanced power settings**. This allows you to see more detailed information about the power plans.
8. Expand **Processor power management** and expand **Minimum Processor State**. The minimum processor state is 5%. A virtualized version of Windows 10 might not have this setting.
9. Expand **Maximum processor state**. The maximum processor state is 100%. You could reduce the maximum processor state to reduce battery utilization, but it will also decrease system performance.
10. Click **Cancel** twice.
11. In the Power Options window, in the left pane, click **Choose what the power button does**. At the bottom of this window, you can enable or disable Fast Startup. This option might not appear in a virtualized version of Windows 10.
12. Close the System Settings window.

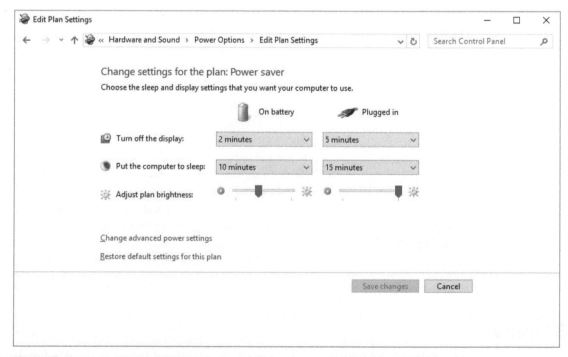

Figure 3-20 Power plan settings

Away Mode

If your computer does not support Modern Standby, you can get similar functionality by using Away Mode. Away Mode is implemented entirely in software and does not require hardware support. Computers in Away Mode are still in the S0 state. However, the computer looks and sounds like it is off. Away Mode maximizes all of the device-level power savings while continuing to work in the background if required.

In some situations, even resuming from the S3 state in 5 seconds or less is not fast enough. Computers that are used for services such as media streaming or as a personal video recorder need almost instant functionality. Away Mode is designed for these types of devices. Away Mode is not designed to be implemented on most computers. The default power management configuration is a better option in most situations.

After Away Mode is enabled, it replaces Standby requests. For example, if shutdown normally puts the computer in the S3 state, it now puts the computer in Away Mode instead. You configure Away Mode in the Multimedia settings of a power plan. Configure the *When sharing media* option to *Allow the computer to enter Away Mode*.

Away Mode has the following characteristics:

- Video is blanked
- Audio is muted
- Keyboard and mouse input is filtered out
- S0 power state

Powercfg.exe

Windows 10 includes the command-line utility **powercfg.exe** to manage power plans and query additional information. Powercfg.exe can be a bit tedious to use sometimes because you need to refer to power plans by their GUID (a long hexadecimal number) rather than by name. Some of the more commonly used options for powercfg.exe are listed in Table 3-4.

Documentation for powercfg.exe can be found at *technet.microsoft.com* (search for powercfg.exe). You can also get help for powercfg.exe by using the */?* command-line option.

Table 3-4   Options for powercfg.exe

Option	Description
/List	Lists all power plans.
/Query	Displays the settings in a power plan.
/DuplicateScheme	Copies the settings from an existing power plan to a new one.
/DeleteSetting	Deletes a setting from a power plan.
/SetActive	Sets the power plan that is active.
/AvailableSleepStates	Lists the sleep states that are and are not supported by the computer.
/Energy	Analyzes the computer for common energy and battery problems.
/BatteryReport	Creates a report of battery usage.
/SleepStudy	Generates a report about InstantGo. This is only available on systems that support InstantGo. This feature is also referred to as connected standby.

Display

As a network administrator, your main concern for displays is the display drivers that are required for Windows 10. Windows 10 requires a display driver that supports the Windows Display Driver Model (WDDM) and DirectX 9. This is approximately the same video requirements that were in place for Windows 7.

Windows 8 and newer do not use the Aero Glass interface that was available for Windows 7. This removes the window transparency that was available in Windows 7. The solid windows for applications in Windows 10 require less graphics processing and are easier to view. Some features introduced with Aero Glass such as live thumbnail previews of minimized applications are still present in Windows 10.

To manage displays for Windows 10 computers, you should understand the following display settings and functions:

- Display settings
- Visual effects
- Themes
- Desktop backgrounds
- Screen savers
- Multiple monitors
- Virtual desktops

Display Settings

The Display settings, shown in Figure 3-21, allow you to modify commonly configured display settings. You can change the size of text and applications if you have a very high-resolution screen and want to make items appear larger. You can change the orientation of monitors to be landscape or portrait to match the physical orientation of the monitor. For mobile devices that sense brightness, you can also control when the screen brightness is automatically adjusted.

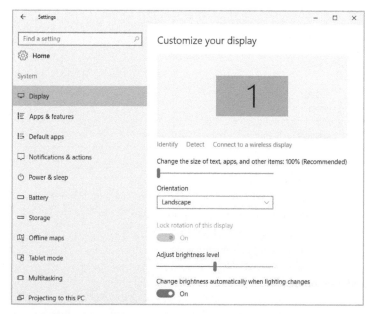

Figure 3-21 Display settings

The **screen resolution** is the number of pixels that are displayed on your monitor or LCD panel. A **pixel** is a single dot on the screen. The resolution is expressed as the number of horizontal pixels by the number of vertical pixels. For example, a resolution of 1366 × 768 means that there are 1366 pixels across the screen and 768 pixels up and down the screen.

The optimal screen resolution varies depending on the display you are using and your video card. In general, LCD panel monitors should be used at their native resolution. If you set your screen resolution at less than the native resolution, the display will appear fuzzy.

Modern monitors are Plug and Play and Windows 10 queries the optimal screen resolution for the monitor. This is why the basic display settings don't provide the option to set the screen resolution. You can set the screen resolution in the advanced display settings.

The advanced display settings include options for:

- *Color calibration*—Leads you through a wizard that adjusts the display based on you selecting the best configuration.

- *ClearType text*—Leads you through a wizard that adjusts font smoothing to make text more legible.

- *Advanced sizing of text and other items*—Allows you to change the text size for specific items such as title bars or elements without affecting other elements. Use this option sparingly as many applications do not properly adjust their display to use these settings.

- *Display adapter properties*—Shows detailed information about the display adapter, as shown in Figure 3-22. Drivers from some vendors include additional tabs to configure features specific to that display adapter.

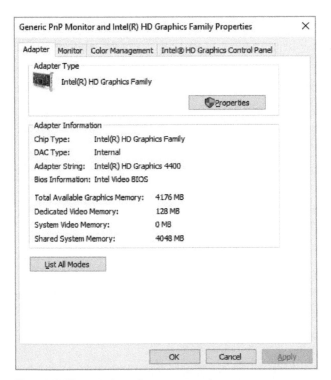

Figure 3-22   Display adapter properties

Activity 3-9: Configuring Display Settings

Time Required: 5 minutes

Objective: Configure the screen resolution and color resolution for your computer

Description: Windows 10 automatically selects display settings based on the display device that is connected to your computer during installation. However, you might want to modify the display settings to suit your own preferences. Or, you might want to modify the display settings after getting a new display such as an LCD panel. In this activity, you change the screen resolution and color resolution of your display.

1. If necessary, start your computer and sign in.
2. Right-click the desktop and click **Display settings.**
3. Under **Change the size of text, apps, and other items,** move the slider completely to the right. Notice that the text on the screen gets larger.
4. Under **Change the size of text, apps, and other items,** move the slider completely to the left.
5. Click **Advanced display settings.**
6. In the Advanced display settings window, configure the resolution to be **800 × 600 pixels** and click **Apply.** Your screen resolution changes and all of the graphics become larger on the screen. If your screen resolution is already at 800 by 600 pixels, select a different resolution. If you are using a virtual machine, the virtual machine viewing window might become smaller instead of the graphics becoming larger.
7. Click **Revert** to prevent keeping the settings.
8. Click **Display adapter properties**
9. In the adapter Properties window, click the **List All Modes** button. This displays all of the screen resolution, color depth, and refresh rate combinations that your display and video card are capable of providing.
10. Click **Cancel.**
11. Click the **Monitor** tab. This tab shows you what type of monitor is installed and allows you to configure the screen refresh rate.
12. Close all open windows.

Visual Effects

The performance options for Windows 10 includes a variety of visual effects that can be enabled or disabled, as shown in Figure 3-23. In most cases, you should use the *Let Windows choose what's best for my computer* option. When this option is selected, Windows enables and disables specific options based on the performance capabilities of your computer. These options are accessible from Performance in the advanced system settings.

Figure 3-23   Visual Effects settings

 Disabling the effects in Windows 10 might make third-party remote control programs such as VNC update the display faster. The Remote Desktop function in Windows 10 is typically not affected by these features, or they can be disabled in the Remote Desktop client.

Desktop Backgrounds

Personalizing the desktop background is one of the most common actions users want to perform when receiving a new computer. Some corporate environments dictate that a standard desktop background must be used. Standardizing the desktop background has no effect on the performance of a computer. However, a standardized background can be used to display information such as contact information for the help desk.

Windows 10 comes with a number of desktop backgrounds to choose from. However, most people want to use their own pictures for a desktop background. This is the computer equivalent of putting a picture on your desk. When you use your own image for a desktop background, it must be in bitmap (.bmp), Joint Picture Experts Group (.jpeg, .jpg), Graphics Interchange Format (.gif), or Portable Network Graphics (.png) format.

When you select a desktop background, you must also select how the graphic is laid out on the page. You can choose to stretch the picture to the size of the screen, center the picture on the screen, or tile the picture. Stretching the picture distorts the image if the original graphic is not the same proportion as the screen. Centering the picture ensures that the image is not distorted, but may leave blank spaces around the picture. Tiling the picture repeats the image if the size of the picture is less than the screen resolution.

You have the option to configure a slideshow for your background. You can define how often the pictures are changed and use the Shuffle option to randomize how they are displayed.

Screen Savers

At one point in time, screen savers were used to prevent screen burn-in. Screen burn-in occurred in monitors that displayed the exact same image for an extended period of time. After screen burn-in occurs, a ghosted image appears on the screen. Screen savers were meant to combat screen burn-in by constantly changing the information displayed on the screen.

Screen savers are no longer required to prevent screen burn-in. Modern displays are much less susceptible to screen burn-in than older devices. In addition, power-saving features in modern computers turn off displays quite quickly, often in the same time frame you would configure a screen saver to turn on.

Screen savers are now a security mechanism for locking a computer. By default, no screen saver is configured in Windows 10 and the screen does not lock. To increase security, you should enable the *On resume, display logon screen* option, shown in Figure 3-24. After you enable this option, you can define how many minutes of inactivity are required before the screen saver starts. If no screen saver is selected, the screen is blanked instead. When you resume using the computer, you are forced to sign in again. This ensures that if you leave your computer unattended, no one can access your work.

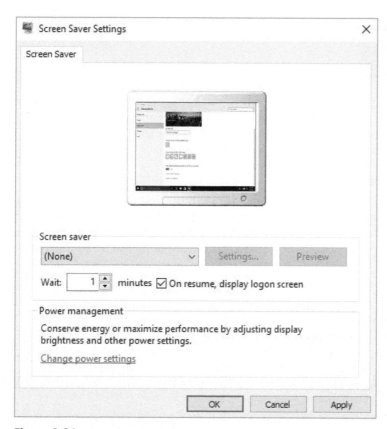

Figure 3-24   Screen Saver settings

Multiple Monitors

Windows 10 supports **multiple monitors** attached to a single computer. When you use multiple monitors, there are three configuration options; each option is useful in different scenarios:

- *Duplicate*—The default option for multiple monitors is to mirror the desktop on both displays. This is most useful when one display is a projector and you are performing a presentation or demonstration.
- *Extended*—When the desktop is extended onto the second display, you have additional screen space to perform your work. You can move windows back and forth between the

two displays and even stretch windows across both monitors. Although this does not sound important if you have not used it before, it is a very handy feature. A network administrator can perform remote desktop operations on one display, while reading documentation on the other display. Office workers can perform Internet research on one display while creating a document on the other display. Productivity is greatly increased by eliminating or reducing window switching.

- *Second screen only*—When you are running a laptop on batteries, it is useful to turn off the LCD panel display and use only an external projector during presentations and demonstrations. This can also be useful when connecting a laptop or tablet to a larger monitor.

The hardware requirements for multiple monitors vary depending on whether your computer is a laptop computer or a desktop computer. Most laptop computers allow the external video connector to be used for multiple monitors. Desktop computers require either multiple video cards to be installed, or a multihead video card. A multihead video card has connectors for multiple monitors on a single card. You can also use USB video adapters to connect multiple monitors.

You can have as many displays as your system supports. You are not limited to two displays.

When you have multiple displays, you can configure which display is primary. The primary display is the one that displays the taskbar and Start button. Both displays are shown in Display settings. You can configure whether the taskbar is displayed on additional monitors and which apps are listed on the taskbar of the secondary monitor.

Multiple Desktops

A new feature in Windows 10 is support for **multiple desktops.** When you use multiple desktops with a single monitor, you can group related apps on a desktop and switch between them easily. For example, you could have a web browser on one desktop and edit documents on a second desktop. Some operating systems refer to this functionality as virtual desktops.

Activity 3-10: Using Multiple Desktops

Time Required: 10 minutes
Objective: Use multiple desktops to organize running apps

Description: Before deploying Windows 10 for users, you want to better understand how multiple desktops can be used to organize running apps. You think this will be very useful for users without multiple monitors.

1. If necessary, start your computer and sign in.
2. On the taskbar, click **Microsoft Edge.**
3. On the taskbar, click **Task View** and click **New desktop** in the lower-right corner of the desktop.
4. Click **Desktop 2.**
5. On the taskbar, click **File Explorer.**
6. Press **Windows+right arrow** to snap File Explorer to the right side of the screen.
7. Click the **Start** button, type **notepad,** and then click **Notepad.**
8. Press **Windows+left arrow** to snap Notepad to the left side of the screen.
9. On the taskbar, click **Task View** and click **Desktop 1.**
10. Review the open apps on the taskbar. Notice that only apps from the current desktop are active.

11. On the taskbar, click **Task View** and close **Desktop 2**. Notice that all of the apps are now on Desktop 1.

12. Close all open windows.

Task Scheduler

Network administrators seldom have enough time to visit workstations and perform preventive maintenance. In most cases, the only time a network administrator sees a workstation is after it is already having problems.

Task Scheduler, shown in Figure 3-25, allows you to be proactive about computer maintenance. You can schedule a task to run at a particular time or after a particular event. For example, you could trigger disk maintenance to be performed each day at noon, when the network users are typically having lunch. If the computer is in standby, it wakes up, performs the scheduled task, and then goes back into standby. Many Windows maintenance tasks are now performed automatically by the Task Scheduler instead of relying on services to remain running.

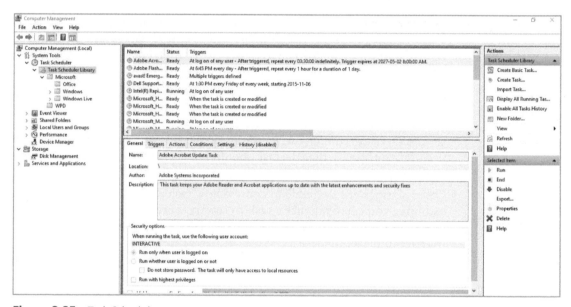

Figure 3-25   Task Scheduler

Tasks are configured with a user account, which defines the permissions used when the task runs. You can provide a local user account or a domain user account with the necessary permissions. When you provide a user account, you are prompted to provide a password for the user account and those credentials are stored locally on the computer. A domain user account is required when the scheduled task needs to access network resources.

You can also specify built-in accounts:

- *NT AUTHORITY\SYSTEM*—This account provides full access to the local computer. Any scheduled task using this account can perform any action on the local computer.

- *NT AUTHORITY\LOCAL SERVICE*—This account has user access equivalent to the Users group. This account only has access to the local computer.

- *NT AUTHORITY\NETWORK SERVICE*—In a domain environment, this account has permissions equal to the computer account in the domain. This account can access resources over the network.

Some features of Task Scheduler are:

- Scheduled tasks do not need to store credentials locally in most cases. The Service for Users (S4U) and Credential Manager can be used to manage credentials. S4U eliminates the need to store credentials locally in a corporate environment where domains are used. CredMan stores passwords locally, but ensures that each password needs to be updated only once for each set of credentials.

- The Task Scheduler in Windows 10 allows all users to create scheduled tasks. Security is not compromised because users cannot schedule a task to run using permissions higher than their own.

- The Task Scheduler Summary shows the status of previously run and currently active tasks. In addition, each task has a History tab that allows you to view detailed information about that particular task. However, by default history for tasks is disabled. To enable history for all tasks, click *Enable All Tasks History*.

- You can schedule a task to run at a particular scheduled time. However, there are many additional triggers, including at sign-in, at startup, on idle, on an event, on registration, on Terminal Server session connect, on Terminal Server session disconnect, on workstation lock, and on workstation unlock. If multiple triggers are specified, all triggers must be activated to run the task.

- You can include multiple actions in a single task. When multiple actions are specified, they are completed in order. This allows you to complete an entire process that has multiple actions that must be performed in a particular order. Each action can run a program, send an email, or send a message. The options to send an email or display a message have been deprecated and you should avoid using them. Instead, run a program or script to accomplish the same task.

- Conditions include power states and network conditions. Power states let you specify that certain tasks are run only when the computer is or is not in a sleep state. Network conditions let you specify that the task should only be run if certain network connections are available.

- Other settings are available to control how tasks behave when they start or fail. For example, you can configure a task to restart every few minutes if it fails. You can also control whether the task can be run manually regardless of the triggers and conditions that are in place.

Activity 3-11: Using Task Scheduler

Time Required: 10 minutes
Objective: Use Task Scheduler to schedule a task

Description: The Task Scheduler is used extensively by Windows 10 to run background processes. As a network administrator, you might want to add your own scheduled tasks to Windows 10 to perform maintenance. In this activity, you view a scheduled task that defragments your computer hard drive.

1. If necessary, start your computer and sign in.
2. Right-click the **Start** button and click **Computer Management**.
3. In the left pane, click **Task Scheduler**. This displays the Task Scheduler Summary in the middle pane, which shows the status of currently running tasks and previously run tasks. As well, all tasks scheduled to run in the future are listed under active tasks.
4. In the Actions pane, click **Enable All Tasks History**.

5. In the left pane, expand **Task Scheduler**, expand **Task Scheduler Library**, expand **Microsoft**, expand **Windows**, and click **Defrag**. You can see in the left pane that many categories of tasks have been created for system maintenance. ScheduledDefrag is one task.

6. In the middle pane, click the **Triggers** tab. You can see that the ScheduledDefrag task does not have a schedule. This is because the task is triggered by automatic maintenance.

7. Click the **Actions** tab. You can see that this task runs the program defrag.exe.

8. Click the **Conditions** tab. You can see that this task runs only if the computer is on AC power. If the computer switches to battery power, the task stops.

9. Click the **Settings** tab. You can see that if the computer is turned off when the task is configured to run, the task starts as soon as possible once the computer is turned on.

10. Click the **History** tab. This shows you all of the event log entries for this task, including when it started, when it completed, and if there were any errors.

11. Close Computer Management.

Windows PowerShell

Windows PowerShell is a command-line interface for performing system configuration in Windows 10. First introduced in Windows Vista, Windows PowerShell has become an essential administrative tool. You can perform many configuration tasks by using Windows PowerShell, but the real usefulness for Windows PowerShell is scripting. Windows PowerShell scripts are an effective replacement for batch scripts and Visual Basic scripts. Most people find it significantly easier to work with Windows PowerShell than batch scripts or Visual Basic scripts.

Each version of Windows PowerShell adds additional capabilities for managing Windows. Some of the things you can do with Windows PowerShell are:

- Manage services
- Manage processes
- Manage networking
- Edit the registry
- Manipulate files and folders
- Retrieve event log events

The individual commands in Windows PowerShell are cmdlets (pronounced command-lets). Each **cmdlet** is a verb-noun format. The verb describes what you want to do and the noun describes what you want to do it to. For example, Start-Service is used to start a service. Some of the common verbs are: Get, Set, Remove, Start, and Stop.

Most cmdlets have parameters that are used to provide instructions to the cmdlet. The parameters of a cmdlet are similar to using switches to modify the actions of an executable. A dash is used at the beginning of all parameter names, for example, "Start-Service -Name W32Time".

There are several ways you can learn to use cmdlets:

- *Do a search for examples*—If you are trying to accomplish a specific task, search for that task plus the word PowerShell. Many people have well-written blog postings and sample scripts.

- *Do a search for the cmdlet*—If you do a search for a specific cmdlet, the Microsoft help information for that cmdlet is at the top of the list. That help information includes a description of all the available parameters and examples.

- *Use the Get-Help cmdlet*—The Get-Help cmdlet provides a description of parameters and examples for a cmdlet. Use the -Full parameter to get all of the available information. For example, "Get-Help Get-Service -Full" shows all of the available help for the Get-Service cmdlet.

To minimize typing mistakes when entering PowerShell commands, you can use Tab completion. When you have partially typed in a cmdlet or parameter name, press Tab to autocomplete the remainder of the cmdlet or parameter. If there are multiple matches to what has already been typed, pressing Tab multiple times cycles through the matches.

Objects and Properties

When you use a Get-* cmdlet to retrieve a list of items such as services or processes, the items retrieved are objects that you can examine and manipulate. There are two important characteristics of objects. First, objects have properties that can be examined and modified. For example, when you use Get-Service to retrieve a list of services that are running, each service returned is an object that has properties. Properties for a service include things like Status, Name, and StartType.

When you query a list of objects, you can pipe those objects to another cmdlet for further processing. To pipe objects between cmdlets, you use the pipe symbol (|), which is a vertical line. The following example sorts services based on their status:

Get-Service | Sort-Object Status

To view all information about an object type, you use the Get-Member cmdlet. This cmdlet accepts an object as input and then displays all of the properties in that object type. Get-Member also displays methods that can be used to manipulate that object type. The following example shows all of the properties and methods available for services:

Get-Service | Get-Member

Formatting Output

Each cmdlet has a default output format that identifies which properties are displayed in list format or table format. Typically, a cmdlet displays only a subset of properties on the screen. If you need to see the value of other properties, you can modify the output to display specific properties. The two common display formats are:

- *List*—Displays each property as a separate line and each object is listed consecutively. This format allows you to see more detail about objects. Pipe output to Format-List to display output in a list format.

- *Table*—Displays object properties in a table format where each object is a row and each property is a column. This makes object information easily readable if there is a limited amount of information you want to display on the screen. Pipe output to Format-Table to display output in a table format.

Script Editing

Although it is possible to create PowerShell scripts by using a simple text editor such as Notepad, you should use a more advanced editor such as the Windows PowerShell Integrated Scripting Environment (ISE). **Windows PowerShell ISE**, shown in Figure 3-26, provides color coding of the script as you type it to help you identify when syntax errors are entered. It also includes debugging functionality.

Figure 3-26   Windows PowerShell ISE

Windows PowerShell scripts are saved with the .ps1 file extension.

Activity 3-12: Using Windows PowerShell

Time Required: 10 minutes
Objective: Use Windows PowerShell to display information about Windows 10

Description: Windows 10 includes many PowerShell cmdlets for viewing information and configuring Windows 10. In this activity, you query information and format it.

1. If necessary, start your computer and sign in.

2. Click the **Start** button, type **powershell,** and then click **Windows PowerShell.**

3. At the Windows PowerShell prompt, type **Get-Service** and press **Enter.** This displays the running services with the default view.

4. Type **Get-Service | Sort-Object Status** and press **Enter.** This sorts the services by Status.

5. Type **Get-Service -Name w32time** and press **Enter.** This gets information for just one service.

6. Type **Get-Service w32time | Format –List** and press **Enter.** This displays the information for the service in a list format.

7. Type **Get-Service w32time | Format –List *** and press **Enter.** This displays all properties in a list format.

8. Type **Get-Service w32time | Format-Table Name,DisplayName,Status,StartType** and press **Enter.** This displays specific properties in a table format.

9. Type **Get-Process | Out-GridView** and press **Enter.** This displays information in a sortable grid view similar to a spreadsheet. Note that the information is a snapshot and does not update.

10. Close all open windows.

Chapter Summary

- Settings provides access to change the most commonly manipulated settings in Windows 10. For more advanced settings, Control Panel is still used.

- Administrative Tools is a collection of system maintenance utilities. All of the administrative tools are MMC consoles. Two of the most commonly used administrative tools are Computer Management and Services.

- Windows 10 uses device drivers to properly communicate with various hardware components in a computer. Most device drivers designed for Windows 7 and newer versions of Windows are compatible with Windows 10.

- Device Manager is the MMC snap-in that is used to manage device drivers and hardware components. You can use Device Manager to update drivers, roll back to previous driver versions, or view the resources a hardware component is using.

- Windows 10 allows 32-bit systems to install unsigned device drivers, but will warn you that the driver publisher cannot be determined. The 64-bit versions of Windows 10 require signed device drivers.

- Power Management in Windows 10 reduces power utilization by allowing the computer to go to sleep or hibernate when not in use. Fast Startup uses hibernation to speed up the boot process. Power plans are used to define how power management is implemented for various devices.

- Windows 10 requires a video card and video driver that support the Windows Display Driver Model (WDDM) and DirectX 9. Multiple monitors can also be used to increase employee efficiency. Windows 10 also has virtual desktops to simplify app management with a single monitor.

- The display on a Windows 10 computer can be customized by controlling the display resolution, color depth, and refresh rate. The optimal configuration for display settings varies depending on the display device. Desktop backgrounds let you display a picture on your desktop. Screen savers are used to implement security.

- Task Scheduler has been enhanced with security improvements for credentials, improved logging, and expanded triggers for starting tasks. Multiple actions are allowed per task, and additional conditions can be required for a task to run.

- Windows PowerShell is a command-line interface for managing Windows 10. Many cmdlets are included and Get-Help can be used to find out more information about a cmdlet. Use the Windows PowerShell ISE for creating and editing PowerShell scripts.

Key Terms

Action Center   A place where you can review and resolve system messages.

Administrative Tools   A group of MMC consoles that are used to manage Windows 10. Computer Management, Event Viewer, and Services are the most commonly used.

Advanced Configuration and Power Interface (ACPI)   The current standard for power management that is implemented in Windows 10 and by computer manufacturers.

Away Mode   An instant-on power-saving mode that keeps the system in the S0 state.

cmdlet   A Windows PowerShell command in verb-noun format. Most cmdlets have parameters that can be used to pass options to the cmdlet.

Computer Management   One of the most commonly used administrative tools. This MMC console contains the snap-ins to manage most Windows 10 components.

Control Panel   An alternative location to configure Windows 10 settings. Used when advanced settings are not available in Settings.

3

Defragment and Optimize Drives An administrative tool that moves file blocks around in the disk to make individual files contiguous and faster to access.

device driver Software that manages the communication between Windows 10 and a particular hardware component.

device driver signing A system that ensures that a device driver is from a known publisher and that the device driver has not been modified since it was signed.

Device Manager An MMC snap-in that is used to manage hardware components and their device drivers.

Disk Cleanup An administrative tool that identifies temporary files that are no longer required and provides an option to remove them.

driver store A central location in Windows 10 where drivers are located before they are installed. A large set of drivers is included with Windows 10.

Ease of Access A collection of settings to make Windows 10 easier to use for those who have physical, visual, or hearing impairment.

Event Viewer An MMC console that is used to view messages generated and logged by Windows 10, applications, and services.

File Signature Verification utility A utility (sigverif.exe) that verifies the digital signature on operating system files and device drivers.

hibernate See S4 state.

hybrid sleep The sleep method used by Windows 10 that combines the S3 state and S4 state. When the computer moves to the S3 state, it also saves the memory file required for the S4 state.

iSCSI A protocol for transferring files between a computer and external disk storage over an Ethernet network.

Microsoft Management Console (MMC) A graphical interface shell that provides a structured environment to build management utilities.

MMC console A collection of one or more snap-ins that are saved as an .msc file for later use.

MMC snap-in A small software component that can be added to an MMC console to provide functionality. An MMC snap-in typically manages some part of Windows.

Modern Standby A new "instant-on" sleep mode in Windows 10. The computer remains in the S0 state but powers down as much hardware as possible.

multiple desktops A new feature in Windows 10 that allows you to switch between multiple desktops on a single monitor. Each desktop can have different applications.

multiple monitors Attaching two or more displays to a single computer. The information can be exactly the same on each display, or each display can be used independently by using extended mode.

Open Database Connectivity (ODBC) A standard mechanism for applications to access databases.

Performance Monitor An MMC console used to monitor and troubleshoot the performance of your computer.

pixel A single dot on a display.

power plan A set of configuration options for power management. The Balanced, Power saver, and High performance power plans are created by default.

powercfg.exe A command-line utility for configuring power management.

S0 state An ACPI power-saving mode that disables power to specific devices as requested by the operating system, but keeps the overall system running.

S3 state An ACPI power-saving mode that disables power to all devices except RAM.

S4 state An ACPI power-saving mode that saves the contents of RAM to disk and then disables power to all devices including RAM.

screen resolution The number of pixels that are displayed on your display.

service A Windows application that runs in the background without user interaction.

Services An MMC console used to manage Windows services.

Settings   A central interface for managing common Windows 10 settings. It is available from the Start menu.

System Configuration   The administrative tool that gives you access to control the boot configuration, service startup, application startup, and system tools.

Task Scheduler   A utility that allows you to schedule tasks to run at a particular time or based on specific events occurring.

Windows Memory Diagnostics Tool   A utility used to perform tests on the physical memory of a computer.

Windows PowerShell   An enhanced command-line interface that can be used to perform administrative tasks.

Windows PowerShell ISE   An integrated scripting environment for Windows PowersShell that includes color coding as you type and debugging functionality.

Review Questions

1. Which of the following accurately describe the administrative tools available in Control Panel? (Choose all that apply.)
   a. Most are MMC consoles.
   b. You can schedule tasks.
   c. You can change the screen resolution.
   d. You can change power options.
   e. You can manage device drivers.

2. Which Settings category allows you to control whether apps can access your location?
   a. System
   b. Devices
   c. Network & Internet
   d. Accounts
   e. Privacy

3. A _____ is a type of Windows application that runs in the background without user intervention.

4. Which of the following is used by apps to connect to databases?
   a. DB sources
   b. ODBC
   c. SQL
   d. RPC
   e. local ports

5. Which of the following are found in Administrative Tools? (Choose all that apply.)
   a. Event Viewer
   b. Windows Memory Diagnostic
   c. Computer Management
   d. Installed Programs
   e. Task Scheduler

6. You can build a customized MMC console by adding _____ to the console.

7. Which MMC access mode allows users to create new windows, but prevents them from viewing some of the console tree?

   a.   Author mode

   b.   User mode—full access

   c.   User mode—limited access, multiple window

   d.   User mode—limited access, single window

8. Which snap-ins are available in Computer Management? (Choose all that apply.)

   a.   Task Scheduler

   b.   Folder Options

   c.   Services

   d.   Security Configuration Management

   e.   Device Manager

9. Which tasks can you accomplish using the Services administrative tool? (Choose all that apply.)

   a.   Stop a service.

   b.   Configure a service to start automatically.

   c.   Configure the credentials for a service.

   d.   Schedule the time when a service will start.

   e.   Configure the dependencies for a service.

10. A _____ is software used to manage communication between hardware components and Windows 10.

11. To find a list of hardware components certified to run on Windows 10, you should consult the Hardware Compatibility List. True or False?

12. Which new function in Windows 10 allows you to switch a single monitor between sets of open apps?

   a.   virtual desktops

   b.   application virualization

   c.   multiple monitors

   d.   app groups

   e.   multiple desktops

13. Which tasks can you perform in Device Manager? (Choose all that apply.)

   a.   Determine which devices do not have a driver loaded.

   b.   Disable devices.

   c.   Install new hardware.

   d.   View hardware resource configuration.

   e.   Roll back a device driver.

14. You can use the Get-Member cmdlet to view the properties available for an object. True or False?

15. With a signed device driver, which of the following can Windows 10 do? (Choose all that apply.)

    a. Determine if a driver has been modified.

    b. Determine if a driver has been adequately tested.

    c. Determine if the publisher is valid.

    d. Determine if the driver is 32-bit or 64-bit.

    e. Automatically download updates.

16. Hybrid sleep is a combination of which ACPI power states? (Choose two.)

    a. S0

    b. S3

    c. S4

    d. S5

    e. G3

17. Modern Standby puts the computer in which ACPI power state?

    a. S0

    b. S3

    c. S4

    d. S5

    e. G3

18. Which requirements must be met for display adapters in Windows 10? (Choose all that apply.)

    a. minimum 256 MB of RAM on the video card

    b. support for WDDM

    c. support for DirectX 9

    d. do not use Windows 10 Starter Edition

    e. computer is certified as "Designed for Windows 10"

19. The primary purpose of a screen saver is to prevent screen burn-in. True or False?

20. Windows 10 supports attaching more than two monitors to a computer and extending the desktop across all of them. True or False?

Case Projects

Case Project 3-1: Mobile Users

All of the salespeople in Hyperactive Media Sales use laptops, so that they can take their applications and data on the road to client sites. One of the salespeople, Bob, has a docking station so that his laptop easily connects to a printer and external monitor when he is in the office. What should you do to ensure that Windows 10 uses the proper device drivers when Bob is in and out of the office?

Case Project 3-2: Saving Money by Using Power Management

Gigantic Life Insurance is always looking for ways to save money. This month, the saving theme at the managers meeting was power consumption. The operations manager has proposed changing some of the incandescent lighting to fluorescent lighting. As the IT manager, what can you propose for Windows 10 computers?

Case Project 3-3: Fuzzy Displays

Superduper Lightspeed Computers sells LCD panel displays to their customers. One of those customers phoned complaining that the text on his display is too small. He is very upset that he is unable to easily read text on the display. What might you be able to do to fix the small text?

Case Project 3-4: Accessibility Options

Over the last few months, the accountant for Buddy's machine shop has been having problems reading his computer display, but has been too embarrassed to tell anyone. Today, he finally lets you know about his problem and asks if there is anything you can do to help him. The accountant (Sanjay) is using Windows 10 on his computer. What can you suggest?

Case Project 3-5: Managing Device Drivers

One Windows 10 computer in the Engineering department of Way North University has been having network connectivity problems. This computer is a different brand and model than all of the other computers because it was purchased directly by a professor as part of a research project. As a result, you are not sure whether the problem is hardware or software. You were able to test that the network cabling is functioning properly. What can you suggest for solving this problem?

chapter 4

Managing Disks and File Systems

After reading this chapter and completing the exercises, you will be able to:

- Describe common disk technologies
- Describe disk partition styles
- Distinguish between basic and dynamic disk storage technology
- Explain Storage Spaces technology
- Use disk management tools
- Prepare and manage physical disks
- Create and manage virtual hard disks (VHDs)
- Use Storage Spaces to create and manage storage pools, storage space volumes, and resilience
- Describe Windows 10 file system features, limits, and tasks
- List file and folder attributes used in Windows 10 file systems
- Understand Windows 10 file and folder permissions

When a computer is turned off, the operating system files and local data must be available the next time the computer is started. Many types of devices are used to store this information and organize the data into individual files and folders. Common examples of such devices include USB memory keys, solid-state disks, battery-backed memory, and electromechanical hard disk drives.

As computers are evolving to support a cloud-enabled world, some data and key information, such as the user's preferred look and feel for the device, are stored in the cloud. That information is obtained over the network, but even that cloud data must be stored locally, even if it is just for temporary processing on the device. Details about how files are organized and managed are similar for most long-term file storage devices. This chapter looks at how storage is managed by Windows. Windows 10 combines old and new disk management technology such as basic MBR disks that have been around for decades and new software-controlled Storage Spaces technology with resiliency options. The chapter looks at how space on local disks is divided into units of storage called partitions or volumes. These volumes must be formatted with a file system to store and organize data, and Windows 10 has several file systems to choose from. Different file systems include different management features. The management features can be basic, such as including management attributes to mark data as read-only, or hidden. Other management features can offer advanced security settings that control what specific identities can do with the data. In this chapter, you learn the factors involved in choosing various storage solutions.

Disk Technology

Windows 10 supports many different disk interface technologies. These interface technologies apply limits for how disk hardware connects to the computer and how the disks can be used with Windows 10.

When long-term storage for files is described as disk storage, it traditionally brings to mind the idea of a spinning disk inside an electromechanical hard drive. As technology has advanced, the term *disk storage* is better applied to any device capable of storing files for a long period of time. The device might indeed have a spinning disk, or it might be made entirely from electronic circuitry without any moving parts, or it might be a virtual device operated through software but presented to Windows 10 as if it were a physical disk drive.

Disk technology can be categorized by how it is connected to the computer and how it is presented to Windows 10. When you are reviewing disk technology available on a computer for use with Windows 10, consider these disk technologies:

- Internal disk
- External disk
- Virtual hard disk (VHD)
- Multiple disks as one logical disk

Internal Disk

Devices that run Windows 10 are usually designed with consumer-grade technology and not server-grade components. Typical hardware disk interface types include SATA, USB, PCI bus, or custom electrical device integration. Internal disks are commonly realized with electromechanical drives, solid-state drives, or custom embedded chip memory. Electromechanical drives are an older technology that must rotate physical disks to read and write data so they are slower, bulkier, and consume more power but provide more storage at a lower cost. Solid-state drives (SSD) with no moving parts can be smaller and faster than electromechanical drives, but they can also be more expensive and have a limited operational lifetime. Device manufacturers can also embed chip memory into the user's computer at the factory, some of which is used to emulate an internal disk drive, which is typically not upgradable or replaceable by the user. These common nonremovable disk types are attached to the device's internal interface(s) and provide a suitable location to store operating system files required to start the computer.

External Disk

External interfaces are used to connect removable, portable disk storage. External disk interface types include USB, eSATA, wireless, and **Thunderbolt**. External storage is useful for expanding a computer's bulk file storage to contain application and user data files, but it is not typically suitable for operating system files that are essential and must always be present. Windows 10 is not normally installed on removable disk media; using removable storage for operating system files is supported only as a special feature for Windows 10 Enterprise called Windows To Go, described in Chapter 2, Installing Windows 10.

Virtual Hard Disk (VHD)

A **virtual hard disk** (VHD) is an image format that replicates the contents of a hard drive, with all the data and structural elements of the drive, but is accessed and installed in a virtual machine infrastructure. Windows 10 natively supports VHD operations, and the VHD specification is publicly available from Microsoft for use by any third-party company for free. Files can be stored in a VHD storage location just like any other disk technology once the VHD is made available in the Windows 10 operating system. All file data stored in a VHD is actually stored in a single file on the file system of a real disk drive. A VHD may contain thousands of individual files from the user's perspective, but it still only appears as one physical file on the real disk drive.

All versions of Windows 10 support VHD operations. For example, double-clicking a VHD file automatically opens the VHD file as a mounted drive on the local operating system.

Multiple Disks as One Logical Disk

A logical disk appears to the Windows 10 operating system as if it is one disk drive. Single internal, external, and VHD disks can all be examples of logical disks. Multiple physical drives can also be grouped together to appear as one logical disk to Windows 10. Two reasons for grouping multiple physical drives in this way include creating a logical disk that has more combined space than one physical disk alone could have and adding fault tolerance, which allows for a physical disk in a combined set to fail without losing access to the logical disk and its data.

Previous editions of Windows such as Windows 7 could combine multiple disks as one logical disk using RAID-based software built in to the operating system. Windows 10 includes support for an updated Microsoft technology introduced with Windows 8 called Storage Spaces. Storage Spaces can also combine multiple disks as one logical disk using technology that is similar to RAID but is enhanced beyond that legacy technology. You learn more about Storage Spaces later in this chapter.

For simplicity, the remainder of this chapter uses the term *disk* to refer to a logical disk.

Partition Styles

Windows 10 can organize data on disk drives using one of several partition styles. When a blank disk is first configured for use by Windows, one of these styles must be selected:

- Master Boot Record (MBR)
- GUID Partition Table (GPT)

Master Boot Record (MBR)

When a computer is first started, the computer must find and load the operating system after required boot hardware components are tested and initialized. That startup code must be built in to the computer hardware and is commonly referred to as boot firmware. The firmware in older computers is based on an IBM firmware standard called the basic input/output system (BIOS). The BIOS disk management design introduced the concept of a **Master Boot Record (MBR)** disk. The MBR disk partition style defines where the BIOS examines the disk drive to determine where blocks of data are stored on the disk and the types of data in those blocks, or partitions. The MBR style is proprietary to the original IBM standard and has limitations due to its age.

MBR disk technology is still common today because the startup routines for most x86 32-bit and x64 64-bit computers before Windows 8 were based on it. MBR disk technology is limited to organizing partitions on a disk up to 2 TB in size. With MBR, if the disk is larger than 2 TB, the space beyond 2 TB is visible in Windows 10 but is not able to be used for any purpose. This is a limitation of MBR, not Windows 10. As disks larger than 2 TB in size become common, the alternative to MBR is the GPT partition style.

 MBR has a limit of four partitions.

GUID Partition Table (GPT)

In the 1990s, Intel created a new standard to replace the traditional BIOS called Extensible Firmware Interface (EFI), now developed and promoted as the Unified Extensible Firmware Interface (UEFI).

Like the older BIOS standard, the UEFI firmware controls the startup process of the computer and eventually loads the operating system. Most new computers designed to run Windows 10 are sold with UEFI firmware. Computers that support UEFI typically also support the option of emulating legacy MBR-based boot firmware to run older operating systems. However, this reintroduces the legacy limitations of the MBR standard for device support. UEFI firmware that is up to date and running in full UEFI mode provides the best support for Windows 10 device operation and management.

Part of the UEFI specification defines the GUID Partition Table (GPT) as a replacement for MBR disk partitioning. One of the primary advantages to using the GPT partition style instead of MBR is that it supports disks larger than 2 TB. Only computers that start from UEFI firmware can boot from a disk that uses the GPT partition style. If a computer's firmware is using the older BIOS specification, it can boot only from an MBR disk.

Types of Disks

Empty space on disk drives can be organized using three different methods in Windows 10: basic disks, dynamic disks, and Storage Spaces.

Basic Disks

Basic disks provide a simple means to logically organize disk space within Windows. When a new hard disk is added to a computer, it is initially configured as a **basic disk**. A basic disk can be partitioned using either MBR or GPT.

All versions of Windows support MBR-style basic disk storage and can interpret basic disk data. Because basic disks have been in use for so long, many people and most computer utilities understand how to work with basic disks.

A basic disk can have its space organized into one or more defined areas of storage called partitions. Each partition is identified by its size and the type of data it is supposed to hold. Most of these partition attributes are stored in a data table on the disk that is part of the MBR or GPT specifications. This table is commonly called the **partition table**.

Dynamic Disks

Dynamic disks were first introduced as an alternative to basic disks. Disks using either MBR or GPT partition styles can be **dynamic disks**.

Dynamic disks use a different method to organize how blocks of space are reserved on a hard disk and were meant to replace basic disks. On dynamic disks, the blocks of space are called **volumes** instead of partitions. Dynamic disks add support for distributing data over multiple hard drives, with or without fault tolerance. Also, there is no four-partition limit on a dynamic disk. You can use a single dynamic disk to create many partitions.

The use of dynamic disks never really caught on and their use is not recommended. Most disk recovery utilities were never updated to work with dynamic disks, which can cause problems if there are disk errors. The advanced features enabled by using dynamic disks are now available in Storage Spaces.

Storage Spaces

Windows Server 2012 introduced the disk virtualization technology called **Storage Spaces**, an inexpensive way to combine, or pool, the storage of multiple physical disk drives. Storage Spaces can also provide fault tolerance with data redundancy across multiple disks. Implementing Storage Spaces is easier and less expensive than most consumer-level, hardware-based solutions for disk redundancy.

For disk pooling and fault tolerance, older operating systems typically relied on custom software or hardware-based RAID technology installed on the local computer, which could require expensive or proprietary mechanisms. These custom RAID solutions can be quirky and expensive, but high-end solutions such as external disk enclosures, network-attached storage (NAS), or storage area network (SAN) devices are typically even more expensive and difficult to implement.

Windows 10 supports Storage Spaces, a software-based storage technology without the need for specialized storage hardware. This mitigates the risk of failed hardware, such as storage controllers, rendering disks inaccessible. You can move disks using Storage Spaces to another Windows 10 computer to get access to the data.

 Because Storage Spaces is designed to work with common standard components, if a disk is attached to the computer using RAID-based technology, it should not be used with Storage Spaces.

Storage Spaces technology combines selected physical disks into a managed logical group called a storage pool. The storage pool acts as a container for data storage and can grow or shrink as physical disks are added or removed from the pool. The storage pool in turn presents the user a portion of that space as a virtualized representation of a disk capable of storing the user's files. That virtualized disk is also called a storage space. Note that the terms *Storage Spaces volume* and *storage space* are commonly used interchangeably to describe a volume hosted by Storage Spaces technology. Before the virtual storage space is available to the user, at least one storage pool must be created.

Storage Pool   The first step in configuring Storage Spaces is creating a **storage pool**. You do this by identifying one or more physical disks that should be assigned to the pool. Once disks are assigned to a storage pool, Storage Spaces has access to the disks. There can be more than one storage pool on the same computer; however, a disk can only be assigned to one storage pool. Disks can be added and removed from a storage pool, making the storage technology flexible to the capacity needs of the user.

 When a disk is assigned to a storage pool, all of its previous contents are erased. If the contents of the disk need to be preserved before the disk is added to the storage pool, the data on it must be backed up or moved somewhere else before it is added to the pool.

If a storage pool is running low on free drive space, additional disks can be added to the computer while it is up and running and then assigned to the storage pool to increase its capacity. To accommodate this flexible technology, Microsoft designed Storage Spaces to work with a wide variety of disks at the same time. Some disk technologies are limited by the number of physical devices that can be added or by speed limitations built in to those technologies (such as USB). Storage Spaces does not remove those limitations, but it allows multiple disks to be combined using different interface technologies simultaneously.

Disks can be removed from a storage pool if the remaining disks in the pool can store the information that was on the disk being removed. During the removal process, that disk has its data moved to the remaining disks in the pool. If there is not enough space in the pool to hold that data, the disk will fail to be removed from the pool.

The storage pool hides the details of the physical disks it combines into what appears as one large reservoir of storage. Users do not interact directly with the storage pool and have no way of knowing which disks in the pool their data is stored on. Users see only a virtual view into the pool with one or more virtualized volumes that they can work with called storage spaces.

Storage Space   After disks have been added to a storage pool, you need to allocate space from the pool for data storage. The space you allocate from the storage pool is called a **storage space**. To users, a storage space is a logical disk, but it can contain space from one or more disks in the storage pool.

Storage Spaces technology allows for the overallocation, or overbooking, of storage spaces created from storage pools. The size of the storage pool does not restrict the specified maximum size of the storage space created from it. The maximum size of a storage space volume is a logical limit and can be larger than the storage pool physical disk capacity. For example, if a storage pool has 500 GB of capacity, a 900 GB storage space volume can be created from it without generating an error. This maximum volume size is a theoretical limit, not a measured quantity in this case.

The size of the physical storage pool does set a practical limit of how much actual data can be saved to a storage space volume. If the storage pool used to create a 900 GB volume only has 500 GB of physical disk space available, Windows 10 completes write operations to the volume without an issue as long as there is free space in the pool hosting that volume. As the available free space in the physical storage pool gets low, Windows warns users that they need to add more disks to the storage pool, delete some other data in the pool, or save less data to the pool.

If a storage pool is too small to accommodate the storage requirements of the storage spaces built from it, the user can add additional physical disk drives to expand the storage pool. The point of Storage Spaces is to make it easy for the user to work with the technology. When a disk is added to a storage pool, the storage spaces built from the pool continue to operate normally. By default, data written to the storage pool via the storage space volume is organized and spread by Windows 10 among the pool member disk drives to maximize efficiency and redundancy in an automated fashion.

All the disks that belong to a storage pool are known to each other as members of the same group. If one physical disk member fails, the storage space volumes created from the pool may fail or survive depending on how the volume was configured for resiliency. Storage Spaces volume resiliency is reviewed later in this chapter.

Managing Storage Spaces technology in Windows 10 requires the use of new administrative tools such as the Storage Spaces Control Panel application or PowerShell commands, instead of the legacy Disk Management console.

Disk Management Tools

After the operating system is installed, the computer's disks are usually managed from within Windows 10 with two tools: Disk Management and DiskPart.

Disk Management

The **Disk Management console** is an MMC console snap-in that is usually found as part of the Computer Management utility. Disk Management provides a graphical interface that allows a member of the Administrators group to observe and make changes to the computer's disk configuration. Disks that are part of a storage pool are not visible in the Disk Management console but Storage Spaces virtual disks are.

The Disk Management console allows changes to be made interactively and usually takes effect immediately without requiring the computer to be restarted.

As shown in Figure 4-1, the Disk Management console is divided into two views, a top view and a bottom view. The top view defaults to a summary of the volumes and partitions on the computer. The bottom view defaults to a graphical view of the disks and the volumes/partitions they contain.

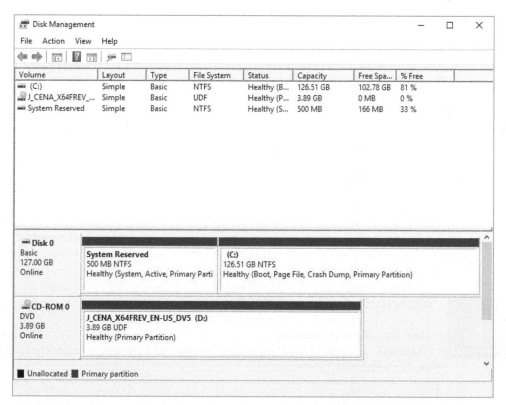

Figure 4-1   Disk Management console

DiskPart

DiskPart, shown in Figure 4-2, is a command-line tool that allows disk and volume operations to be performed from a text-based screen interactively or from within a scripted file using command-line parameters.

```
Administrator: Command Prompt - diskpart                                 —  □  ×
EXIT          - Exit DiskPart.
EXTEND        - Extend a volume.
EXPAND        - Expands the maximum size available on a virtual disk.
FILESYSTEMS   - Display current and supported file systems on the volume.
FORMAT        - Format the volume or partition.
GPT           - Assign attributes to the selected GPT partition.
HELP          - Display a list of commands.
IMPORT        - Import a disk group.
INACTIVE      - Mark the selected partition as inactive.
LIST          - Display a list of objects.
MERGE         - Merges a child disk with its parents.
ONLINE        - Online an object that is currently marked as offline.
OFFLINE       - Offline an object that is currently marked as online.
RECOVER       - Refreshes the state of all disks in the selected pack.
                Attempts recovery on disks in the invalid pack, and
                resynchronizes mirrored volumes and RAID5 volumes
                that have stale plex or parity data.
REM           - Does nothing. This is used to comment scripts.
REMOVE        - Remove a drive letter or mount point assignment.
REPAIR        - Repair a RAID-5 volume with a failed member.
RESCAN        - Rescan the computer looking for disks and volumes.
RETAIN        - Place a retained partition under a simple volume.
SAN           - Display or set the SAN policy for the currently booted OS.
SELECT        - Shift the focus to an object.
SETID         - Change the partition type.
SHRINK        - Reduce the size of the selected volume.
UNIQUEID      - Displays or sets the GUID partition table (GPT) identifier or
                master boot record (MBR) signature of a disk.

DISKPART> _
```

Figure 4-2   DiskPart running in interactive mode

Operations in the DiskPart utility are driven by a sequence of commands. Each command must have a specific object to focus its action on. For example, before a partition can be created, the DiskPart utility must be told which disk the partition will be created on. Items such as disks and partitions are usually numbered, with the first disk or partition object starting at 0.

To see a list of DiskPart commands, type *help* at the diskpart command prompt. To see more details about a specific diskpart command, type *help command_name*, where *command_name* is the command of interest.

The DiskPart utility is powerful; it can contain a series of maintenance or repair commands that can be executed as part of a scheduled task or automated response on the local computer or remotely from another computer. It is considered an advanced tool that is not normally used for day-to-day administration.

Activity 4-1: Using DiskPart

Time Required: 10 minutes
Objective: Start the DiskPart utility, browse its help menu, and use DiskPart to explore fundamental disk properties

Description: In this activity, you start the DiskPart utility, browse its help utility, and try out basic DiskPart commands.

1. If necessary, start your computer and sign in.

2. Right-click the **Start** button and click **Command Prompt (Admin)** on the shortcut menu.

3. Type **diskpart** and press **Enter** to start the DiskPart utility in its interactive mode. Note that the prompt changes to DISKPART>.

4. Type **help** and press **Enter** to see a list of DiskPart commands.

5. Type **help select** and press **Enter** to see information about the select command.

6. Type **help select disk** and press **Enter** to see information and examples for the select disk command.

7. To see what disks can be selected, type **list disk** and press **Enter**.

8. The DiskPart utility has not been focused on a particular disk yet, so some commands will not be able to run. For example, type **list partition**, press **Enter**, and note the error message.

9. To focus attention on the first disk, type **select disk = 0** and press **Enter**.

10. Type **list partition**, press **Enter**, and note that the error message is gone.

11. To see what volumes are visible to the DiskPart utility, type **list volume** and press **Enter**.

12. To leave the DiskPart utility, type **exit** and press **Enter**.

13. Close the Administrator: Command Prompt window.

 Note that a DVD-ROM might be included in the volume listing, which does not rely on the selected disk.

Managing Physical Disks

When disks are installed in a computer, several administrative tasks must be carried out to make them usable as a location to store end-user data. The major activities for proper disk administration include:

- Installing or moving disks
- Preparing hard disks

Installing or Moving Disks

When a brand-new drive is connected to a computer, the drive is typically not initialized by Windows and is not configured as either a basic or dynamic disk. This style of drive requires preparation by Windows before it can be used. Some consumer-grade external drives are already prepared and formatted at the factory and can be recognized once they are connected to the computer.

A single physical disk configured as a basic disk can be moved from one computer to another computer and it will remain a basic disk. There are no special considerations for moving basic disks.

For dynamic disks, a database identifies all volume components on all dynamic disks in that computer. The database also stores the name of the computer to which the dynamic disk belongs. When a dynamic disk is moved to a different computer, this computer identification in the database must be changed.

To change this name in the moved disk's database, the dynamic disk must be removed as a member of the source computer and imported into the destination computer's current dynamic disk database with either the Disk Management console or the DiskPart command-line utility. This updates the database on the moved disk and on every other dynamic disk that might already exist in both computers.

The Disk Management console reports the status of the disk as a Foreign Disk when it recognizes that the disk does not belong to that computer. You must right-click the disk in the graphical portion of Disk Management and select Import Foreign Disk from the shortcut menu to initiate the import process.

If a dynamic disk contains a volume that is spread across multiple dynamic disks, such as a striped or spanned volume, all member disks must be moved at the same time. Failure to do so leaves the volume broken even if the dynamic disk's computer membership is correctly updated.

Because there is some risk in moving a dynamic disk between computers, it is always best practice to ensure that a backup copy of the volume data exists before the move is performed. Before a disk is moved, its status should report as healthy in the Disk Management console.

Storage Spaces technology is similar to dynamic disk technology in that it keeps track of each disk that is a member of a storage pool. There is additional data used by Windows to manage the storage pool that goes far beyond just identifying membership. When a storage pool is moved from one computer to another, all disk members of the pool should be moved at the same time. Once the disks are connected to the target Windows 10 computer, the pool and its virtual disk storage spaces will mount automatically as read-write storage.

This behavior is not the same as moving storage pools in server-class operating systems because Storage Spaces technology in Windows 10 is designed for clients' ease of use. When you are researching Storage Spaces technology, do not assume that server features and operations are the same as those found in Windows 10.

Preparing Hard Disks

A hard disk can be connected to the computer using many different connection technologies; SATA and USB are two common examples. The hard disk might be responsible for loading the operating system or it might just provide a location for bulk data storage. Drives that provide bulk storage and that are physically portable often use Plug and Play technology to connect. These hard disk devices must be prepared to work with the computer before data can be stored on them by ensuring that three tasks are performed:

- Scan for new hardware changes
- Scan for disks
- Initialize new disks

Scanning for New Hardware Changes
A hard disk is a singular device, but the hardware used to connect it to the computer may consist of many individual components. For example, a USB-connected hard disk has a USB controller between itself and the computer that must be working correctly before the hard disk is visible to the operating system. A hardware-based RAID solution typically has a dedicated controller between the disks and the computer that hides the physical disk arrangement from the operating system.

If these intermediate devices are not functional, or if the drivers and their settings are not operational, the disks are not usable. This is not common with devices built specifically for Windows 10; however, legacy computer systems upgraded to Windows 10 might experience difficulty with legacy hardware and drivers. It is also possible that the computer running Windows 10 did not detect the new device when it was added.

When adding new hard disks, the Device Manager utility is used first to detect device driver issues and trigger a manual scan for hardware changes if the Plug and Play system did not detect the change.

Scanning for Disks
Once all connection technologies for hard disks are properly detected and their corresponding device drivers are fully functional, the hard disks should be visible. The operating system might not see the new disks immediately. Windows 10 can be forced to manually recheck all of the connected hardware for a change in disk availability by using the Disk Management console.

Initializing New Disks When a new hard disk is installed, it cannot be used to store files as a single disk until it is initialized as an MBR or GPT disk. This process is called disk initialization and is triggered by Windows 10 when it sees a blank new hard disk for the first time.

The Disk Management console can be used to trigger the initialization process manually. An administrator can right-click the unknown disk in the Disk Management console and select Initialize Disk from the shortcut menu to trigger the process.

Once a disk is initialized, any data it might have held is lost.

Until a new disk is initialized, its status is reported as Unknown and the disk cannot be used to store data. Once the disk is initialized, it becomes a basic disk without any partitions defined.

An alternative to initializing the unknown disk is to add it to a storage pool. Once it is added to the pool, the disk's status and data structures are invisible through the Disk Management console; it simply becomes a member of the pool and is managed by Windows 10 using Storage Spaces controls from Control Panel.

Virtual Disk Management Tasks

Windows 10 provides native support for working with VHDs. Note that PowerShell commands for VHD management apply only to versions of Windows 10 that support and have the Hyper-V role installed. This includes Windows 10 Enterprise, Professional, and Education versions. The Disk Management snap-in and the DiskPart command utility work for all versions of Windows 10.

This chapter provides an overview of VHDs. More detailed information about VHDs is provided in Chapter 12, Client Hyper-V.

Creating VHDs

A VHD in Windows 10 is created as a single file on a physical disk drive. All versions of Windows 10 support the ability to create a VHD. VHDs can be created using the Disk Management snap-in, the New-VHD PowerShell command, or the DiskPart command-line utility.

To create a VHD, you must specify the following information:

- *Location*—The name and physical location of the file that will hold the VHD data. The location needs to be large enough to hold the VHD file and all of its data.

- *Virtual Hard Disk Format*—VHD or VHDX. VHD is an older format that supports virtual disks up to 2 TB. VHDX is a newer format that supports virtual disks up to 64 TB and has better performance.

- *Virtual Hard Disk Size*—A maximum storage limit specified in MB, GB, or TB.

- *Virtual Hard Disk Type*—Dynamically expanding or fixed size. A fixed-size VHD immediately takes up the full size allocated to the VHD. A dynamically expanding VHD takes up only the disk space required to hold the data inside it and has a maximum size allocated. A dynamically expanding VHD behaves much like a compressed folder (.zip) that expands as you add content to it.

VHD disks created through the graphical Disk Management utility automatically attach to the operating system and appear as a new operational disk drive that is uninitialized. The drive must be initialized, just like a new hard drive, before it can be configured with partitions to store files.

VHDs are restricted to basic disk technology due to their transient existence in the operating system.

In Activities 4-2 through 4-9, you will be creating VHDs and using them to illustrate disk management and Storage Spaces features. Because VHDs are not automatically reattached after signing out, shutting down, or rebooting, you should not sign off, shut down, or reboot during or between any of these activities. There are also dependencies between some activities. Dependencies are noted before each activity with a Caution like this one.

Activity 4-3 relies on a VHD that is mounted in Activity 4-2. Do not sign out, shut down, or reboot during or between Activities 4-2 and 4-3.

Activity 4-2: Creating VHD Disks

Time Required: 10 minutes
Objective: Create a new VHD disk

Description: In this activity, you perform the typical steps required to create a new VHD disk hosted on drive C:.

1. If necessary, start your computer and sign in.
2. Right-click the **Start** button and select **File Explorer**.
3. Click to select **Local Disk (C:)** and create a new folder in the root of C: called **VHD Storage**.
4. Right-click the **Start** button and select **Disk Management**.
5. In the Disk Management window, click to open the **Action** menu and select **Create VHD**. This launches the Create and Attach Virtual Hard Disk window.
6. Click the **Browse** button and navigate to **C:\VHD Storage**. In the File name field, enter the text **VHDExample** and click the **Save** button to close the Browse Virtual Disk Files window.
7. In the Create and Attach Virtual Hard Disk window, enter the value **5** in the **Virtual hard disk size** field. Click to change the unit size from MB to **GB**.
8. Confirm that **VHD** is the virtual hard disk format selected.
9. Select **Dynamically expanding** under Virtual hard disk type to allow the VHD file to grow as required and not allocate all the disk space when it is first created.
10. Click **OK** to create the VHD and automatically attach it.
11. Note that a new disk appears in the graphical disk view with an Unknown disk type and a status of Not Initialized. The free space on the drive appears as 5 GB of unallocated space and the graphical drive icon next to the disk identifier is light blue.
12. Right-click the 5 GB of unallocated space from the VHD disk and note the available volume creation options are all grayed out and unavailable.
13. Right-click the VHD's disk name next to the blue drive icon and select **Initialize Disk** from the shortcut menu.
14. Note in the Initialize Disk window which partition styles are available for use with the VHD disk. Select **MBR** and click **OK**.
15. Right-click the unallocated space from the VHD disk and select **New Simple Volume**.
16. Click **Next**. Click **Next** again. Note the drive letter assigned to the new simple volume and then click **Next**.

17. Change the default volume label of New Volume to **VHDVOL**. Click **Next** and then click **Finish** to complete the New Volume Wizard. During the creation and formatting of the drive, Windows might mistakenly prompt you to format the new volume even though the wizard is performing that task for you. Just click **Cancel** on the prompt asking "Do you want to format it?"

18. Note the size of the newly created partition in Disk Management. It is reported as the full size of 5 GB you specified in the New Volume Creation Wizard.

19. Switch to the File Explorer window and browse to **C:\VHD Storage**. Note the size of the VHD file in that folder and the fact that it is much smaller that the reported volume size.

20. In the File Explorer window, right-click the drive letter assigned to the VHD disk and select **Properties** from the shortcut menu. Note the Used Space and Free Space values shown on the General tab. Compare this with the actual size of the VHD file noted in the previous step.

21. Click **OK** to close the drive Properties window.

22. Close all open windows, but do not sign out or restart.

Attaching and Detaching VHDs

A VHD must be attached, or mounted, to be available to the operating system and the user. When a VHD is attached, it can be managed with typical disk and partition operations. All versions of Windows 10 can attach an existing VHD file. VHDs can be attached by double-clicking the VHD file in File Explorer.

VHDs can also be attached using methods that offer more control, such as the Mount-VHD PowerShell command, the Disk Management snap-in, or the DiskPart command-line utility. When a VHD file is attached via these methods, it can optionally be opened in read-only mode where its file contents cannot be accidentally modified, only read from.

When a computer is restarted, the VHD files currently attached do not automatically re-attach. They must be manually attached again after the computer restarts. The only time a VHD automatically mounts as the computer starts is the special case in which Windows 10 is configured to boot from a VHD file.

A VHD must be detached, or dismounted, to make it unavailable to the operating system and the user. All versions of Windows 10 support the ability to detach an existing VHD file. VHDs can be detached using the Disk Management snap-in, the Dismount-VHD PowerShell command, or the DiskPart command-line utility.

Activity 4-3 relies on a VHD that is mounted in Activity 4-2. Do not sign out, shut down, or reboot during or between Activities 4-2 and 4-3.

Activity 4-3: Managing VHD Disks

Time Required: 5 minutes
Objective: View VHD attributes using DiskPart and detach a VHD

Description: In this activity, you use DiskPart to view a VHD's details, detach it, and confirm that it is no longer visible as an active disk.

1. Right-click the **Start** button and click **Command Prompt (Admin)**. If you are prompted by User Account Control for permission to run this application, click **Yes**.

2. Type **diskpart** and press **Enter**.

3. To focus attention on the VHD created in the previous activity, type **select vdisk file= "C:\VHD Storage\VHDExample.vhd"** and press **Enter**.

4. Type the command **detail vdisk** and press **Enter** to display detailed information about the VHD. Note the Virtual size and Physical size attributes listed in the output of the command.

5. Type **detach vdisk** and press **Enter** to dismount the VHD.

6. To leave the DiskPart utility, enter the command **exit**.

7. Close all open windows and sign out.

Managing Storage Spaces

Management of Storage Spaces is not integrated into any of the existing disk management utilities. A new graphical control interface called the Manage Storage Spaces view, managed by the Storage Spaces agent, is found in the System and Security Control Panel section. This tool allows administrative users to create and manage storage pools and storage spaces.

The Manage Storage Spaces view allows changes to be made interactively and take effect immediately without requiring the computer to be restarted. Physical disks that are added to storage pools can be managed with the Disk Management console before they are added to a storage pool, but once they are added to a storage pool, they must be managed within the Manage Storage Spaces view.

Creating an Initial Storage Pool and Storage Space

The initial Manage Storage Spaces view shows only a link to launch the Storage Spaces agent software, which triggers a wizard that creates a new storage pool and storage space, as shown in Figure 4-3. The Windows 10 Storage Spaces agent is designed to simplify the experience for the user and combines the process of building a storage pool and creating a virtual disk in one pass of the setup wizard.

Figure 4-3   Initial Storage Spaces settings

If there are no disks except for the system disk (i.e., drive C), the Storage Spaces agent wizard notifies the user that no drives are available for use with the technology. Before a storage pool can be created, at least one additional drive must be added to the computer and must be recognized by the system. Once a storage pool exists, the Manage Storage Spaces view changes to provide management options for existing storage pools and storage spaces, as shown in Figure 4-4.

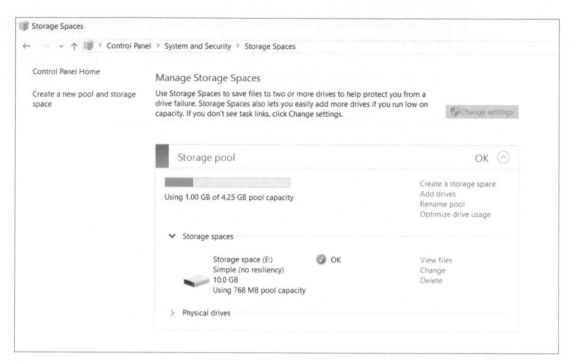

Figure 4-4   Storage Spaces settings after initial setup

Do not sign out, shut down, or reboot during or between Activities 4-4, 4-5, and 4-6. All three activities share the same VHD files that must remain attached.

Activity 4-4: Creating the Initial Storage Pool and Storage Space Volume

Time Required: 15 minutes

Objective: Create a storage pool and storage space volume using the initial Storage Spaces Wizard

Description: In this activity, you create a new virtual disk that is attached and empty. Using the initial Storage Spaces Wizard, you create a new storage space pool and volume from that virtual disk. Finally, you confirm the storage space volume's settings in the Disk Management console to note key information.

Because VHD files are not automatically reattached after a reboot, using them for Storage Spaces is not officially supported by Microsoft. Virtual disks are being used with Storage Spaces technology in this lab setting only to illustrate concepts and should never be used in a production environment. Do not sign off or restart your computer during this activity.

1. If necessary, start your computer and sign in.

2. Right-click the **Start** button and select **Disk Management**.

3. In the Disk Management window, click to open the **Action** menu and select the **Create VHD** menu item. This launches the Create and Attach Virtual Hard Disk window.

4. Click the **Browse** button and navigate to the location **C:\VHD Storage**, which was created in Activity 4-2.

5. In the File name field, enter the text **VHDPoolDisk1** and click the **Save** button to close the Browse Virtual Disk files window. This defines the name and location of the VHD file.

6. In the Create and Attach Virtual Hard Disk window, enter the value 5 in the **Virtual hard disk size** field. Change the unit size from MB to **GB**.

7. Confirm that **VHD** is the virtual hard disk format selected.

8. Select **Dynamically expanding** under Virtual hard disk type.

9. Click **OK** to create the VHD and automatically attach it.

10. Right-click the **Start** button and select **Control Panel**.

11. Click **System and Security** and click **Storage Spaces**.

12. Click the link **Create a new pool and storage space**. When you are prompted by User Account Control for permission to run the application, click **Yes**.

13. Note that the Storage Spaces agent has discovered the attached VHD as an available disk and has already selected it by default. Click the **Create pool** button.

14. Switch to the Disk Management window and note that the VHD is no longer displayed as a disk visible to Disk Management.

15. Switch back to Create a storage space.

16. Under the Resiliency settings, click the Resiliency type drop-down and select **Simple (no resiliency)**.

17. Under the Size settings, in the Size (maximum) field enter the value **10**.

18. Accept all other default settings in the initial wizard. Click the **Create storage space** button.

19. Switch to the Disk Management window and note that a new basic disk has been created that is hosting a volume sized just smaller than the value entered in Step 17. The wizard has formatted that volume and assigned it a new drive letter. Note the drive letter the volume has been assigned.

20. Right-click the **Start** button and select **File Explorer**.

21. Navigate to the folder **C:\Program Files**. Right-click the folder **Common Files** and select **Copy**.

22. Navigate to the drive letter for your storage space and paste the Common Files folder. This content is used to provide some data within the storage space volume for later activities.

23. Close all windows but do not sign out or restart your computer.

Maintaining Storage Pools and Storage Spaces

Each storage pool is identified by the physical disk members that are grouped within that pool. Metadata about the pool and its members is stored on each physical disk that is a member of the pool. The end user has the option to customize that storage pool by:

- *Renaming a storage pool*—The default name for the first storage pool is just the name "Storage pool." If the end user intends to have multiple storage pools, it might be desirable to rename this pool based on some attribute of the data or disks that are contained within the pool.

- *Adding disk drives to the pool*—The end user can add more disks to the storage pool after the disk is connected to the computer and visible to Windows 10. The physical disk must be at least 4 GB in size; if it is smaller, the Storage Spaces agent does not allow that disk to be selected. If the disk contains any previous data, it is destroyed once the disk is joined to a storage pool.

- *Creating or deleting a storage space volume assigned to the pool*—The maximum size of a volume created from the storage pool is not limited by the storage pool, and similarly, the number of volumes created from one storage pool is not limited by just having one storage pool. The biggest limitation to the number of storage space volumes is the availability of free drive letters to assign to those volumes.

- *Optimizing drive usage within the pool*—When data is written to a storage pool, Windows 10 manages the placement of the data on the physical disks. As physical disks are assigned to the pool, Windows by default tries to rebalance the data across all the disks that belong to the pool. If a storage pool was created with an earlier version of Windows and upgraded for use with Windows 10, or automatic rebalancing was not enabled when a disk was added to a storage pool, you can manually trigger the optimization and rebalancing of data across all drives in the pool as a background activity.

Do not sign out, shut down, or reboot during or between Activities 4-4, 4-5, and 4-6. All three activities share the same VHD files that must remain attached.

Activity 4-5: Managing Storage Pools and Storage Space Volumes

Time Required: 20 minutes

Objective: Manage a storage pool and storage space volumes using the Storage Spaces section in Control Panel

Description: In this activity, you rename the storage pool to aid the end user's recognition of the storage pool, plus add a second virtual disk to the existing storage pool. The activity looks at removing a disk but does not actually trigger the removal. Using the larger storage pool, you also create and remove a new simple storage volume.

1. You should already be signed in from the previous activity.

2. Right-click the **Start** button and select **Disk Management**.

3. In the Disk Management window, click to open the **Action** menu and select **Create VHD**. The Create and Attach Virtual Hard Disk window displays.

4. Click the **Browse** button and navigate to the location **C:\VHD Storage**, which was created in Activity 4-2. In the File name field enter the text **VHDPoolDisk2** and click the **Save** button.

5. In the Create and Attach Virtual Hard Disk window, enter the value 5 in the Virtual hard disk size field. Click to change the unit size from MB to **GB**.

6. Confirm that **VHD** is the virtual hard disk format selected.

7. Select **Dynamically expanding** under Virtual hard disk type and click **OK**.

8. Right-click the **Start** button and select **Control Panel**.

9. Click **System and Security** and click **Storage Spaces**.

10. Note that the links to manage the existing storage pool and its storage spaces are grayed out. Click the **Change settings** button to elevate the Storage Spaces settings window to Administrator equivalent levels.

11. When you are prompted by User Account Control for permission to run the application, click **Yes**. Note that the links to manage the existing storage pool and its storage spaces are now active.

12. Click the **Rename pool** link.

13. In the Name field, type the title **USB Archive Disks – Spring**. Click the **Rename pool** button to complete the rename operation. Note that the title of the original storage pool has now been updated.

14. Click the **Add drives** link.

15. Note that a list of available unformatted drives is presented in the Add drives wizard. Confirm that the **Optimize drive usage to spread existing data across all drives** option is checked.

16. Confirm that the virtual disk added earlier in the activity is selected and click the **Add drives** button. Note that the disk optimization feature triggers and runs in the background. The Optimize drive usage link changes to Stop optimization while the background task is in progress.

17. Click the **Optimize drive usage** link. Note that there are no configurable options. Click the **Optimize Drive Usage** link button to trigger the process manually.

18. Click the arrow to the left of the **Physical drives** title to expand and display the list of drives that belong to the pool. Note the percentage of disk space used for each disk and the fact that they are similar but not identical.

19. In the list of physical drives belonging to the storage space, note that there are two disks listed as Microsoft Virtual Disk. Because this is a lab setting, it is not clear which virtual disk is associated with a specific VHD file on disk. Select the top disk in the list of physical drives. Click the link next to it called **Prepare for removal**.

20. Because we are using virtual disks for this activity, Windows 10 will not proceed correctly with the removal. Note the warning that the removal process will take some time, and that the disk will be ready for physical removal when the drive status is changed to Ready to remove. Click the **Cancel** button.

21. Under the name of the storage pool, click the link **Create storage space**.

22. Under the Name and drive letter settings, change the Name field to **STORVOL2**.

23. Under the Resiliency settings, click the Resiliency type drop-down and select **Simple (no resiliency)**.

24. Under the Size settings, in the Size (maximum) field enter the value **20**.

25. Accept all other default settings in the initial wizard. Click the **Create storage space** button. Note that the storage space is now listed under the storage pool title within the category of Storage spaces.

26. Click the **Delete** link next to the STORVOL2 storage space. Note the warning that appears regarding the recovery of the files the volume contains. Click the **Delete storage space** button.

27. Close all windows but do not sign out or restart your computer.

Configuring Storage Spaces Fault Tolerance

Consider the fault tolerance of earlier disk technology. Individual physical disks configured as basic disks are not fault tolerant themselves. If the data is not backed up, the loss of a basic disk results in permanent data loss.

Dynamic disks support two types of fault-tolerant volumes: mirrored RAID 1 and parity-based RAID 5. Mirrored volumes consist of identical data duplicated across two dynamic disks. One disk can fail and the other remains to continue operations. RAID 5 requires three or more disks to implement but adds calculated parity data, which allows for the recovery of a failed disk using less wasted disk space than mirrored drives. Windows 10 supports dynamic disks, but dynamic disks are not the preferred method to enable fault tolerance for end-user data within Windows 10. The preferred technology for storing user data in a fault-tolerant fashion is Storage Spaces.

This chapter provides disk fault-tolerance information specific to Windows 10 and storage spaces. If you would like to review generic RAID disk fault tolerance, please see Standard RAID levels on Wikipedia at *https://en.wikipedia.org/wiki/Standard_RAID_levels*.

A storage space volume can be configured for fault tolerance when it is initially created if the proper starting conditions are met. Individual drives within the storage pool are used by Windows 10 transparently to provide the level of fault tolerance requested. Different levels of fault tolerance are available that are similar to traditional RAID levels but are customized to operate with additional functionality not normally found in traditional RAID. These fault-tolerant options are listed in Table 4-1.

Table 4-1 Storage Spaces resiliency types

Resiliency type	Description
Simple (no resiliency)	The simple storage space volume is contained within the storage pool with no regard to fault tolerance. If a disk fails in the pool and it contains a portion of the simple volume, the volume would no longer be available to the end user. A storage pool made up of one physical drive can only host simple storage space volumes. Simple storage volumes are useful for temporary data where performance is more important than the reliability of the volume.
Two-way mirror	A storage space volume configured with resiliency set to two-way mirror forces Windows 10 to keep two copies of its data on two different physical disks. This is similar to the traditional RAID 1, where one disk in the pool can fail and the volume survives. Two-way mirror volumes protect the user's data files while offering high performance for disk read and write operations. Because data is distributed to at least two physical drives in the storage pool, the practical limit of how much data you can store in a two-way mirror storage space is limited by the size of the smallest physical drive hosting each copy of the volume's data. For example, if the first physical drive added to a new storage pool is 1 TB in size, and the second disk added is 2 TB in size, a two-way mirrored volume created from that pool could not store more than 1 TB of data, even though there is remaining space on the 2 TB drive.
Three-way mirror	A storage space volume configured with resiliency set to three-way mirror forces Windows 10 to keep three copies of its data on three different hard drives. This allows up to two disks in the pool holding this volume's data to fail and the volume remains available. Counterintuitively, the data and metadata required to store data in a three-way mirror needs more than just three disks in the pool. A three-way mirror requires a minimum of five different physical disks in the storage pool. Three-way mirror volumes protect the end user's files while still offering high performance for disk read and write operations, plus the luxury of handling multiple disk failures. The extra cost required to have a minimum of five disk drives in the pool must be considered against the need for the extra protection.
Parity	When a storage space volume is configured with resiliency set to parity, Windows 10 calculates and includes error-correcting data that is stored together with the volume's data. This is similar to RAID 5. The minimum number of drives required in the storage pool to support parity fault tolerance is three. This allows a single drive to fail. To handle a double drive failure, the parity fault tolerance requires a minimum of seven drives in the pool. The calculation of parity information during writes and during a disk failure can slow the end user's interactions with the volume. Parity storage space volumes are best used with data that requires fault tolerance but not high performance, such as archive data.

Do not sign out, shut down, or reboot during or between Activities 4-4, 4-5, and 4-6. All three activities share the same VHD files that must remain attached.

Activity 4-6: Creating a Fault-Tolerant Storage Space

Time Required: 5 minutes
Objective: Create a fault-tolerant storage space volume

Description: In this activity, you create a two-way mirror storage space volume using the two virtual disks attached to the current storage pool.

1. You should already be signed in from the previous activity.
2. Right-click the **Start** button and select **Control Panel**.
3. Click **System and Security** and click **Storage Spaces**.

4. Click the **Change settings** button and click **Yes**.

5. Under the name of the storage pool, click the link **Create a storage space**.

6. Under the Name and drive letter settings, change the Name field to **STORVOL3**.

7. Under the Size settings, in the Size (maximum) field, enter the value **30**.

8. Under the Resiliency settings, click the Resiliency type drop-down and select **Parity**. Notice that the Create storage space button remains grayed out because there are not enough drives in the pool to support that resiliency type.

9. Under the Resiliency settings, click the Resiliency type drop-down and select **Two-way mirror**. Click the **Create storage space** button.

10. Once the new storage space volume is created, note that there are now two volumes listed in the Storage Spaces settings screen. One volume has its resiliency set to simple, the other is set to two-way mirror.

11. Close all windows and sign out.

File Systems

Once a volume is available to store data, its free space must be organized into files and folders using a file system. A user typically has different file storage requirements for different devices. For example, some files must be portable and interchangeable with other operating systems, while other files must be secure and efficiently stored. Some devices, such as hard disks, support multiple file systems on one device. This section discusses the common file systems used in Windows 10, the properties of files stored on them, and securing those files.

A file system allows the operating system to store and organize files. The choice of file system can limit the total amount of data stored in a partition or volume, the number of files, the size of the files, their names, attributes, and other properties. Windows 10 supports several common file systems:

- File Allocation Table (FAT)
- NT File System (NTFS)
- Resilient File System (ReFS)
- Universal Disk Format (UDF)

The choice of basic or dynamic disk technology has no impact on file system features described in this section.

File Allocation Table

The earliest file system used for hard disks by the MS-DOS operating system is the **File Allocation Table (FAT)**. All Microsoft operating systems since MS-DOS support a version of this file system. Different versions of FAT can be used with Windows 10: FAT, FAT32, and exFAT.

FAT is a simple and basic method to organize files on partitions that are no larger than 4 GB in size. FAT32 was introduced with Windows 95 OSR2 to support hard disks that were becoming much larger than 2 GB in size. Windows 10 does not use FAT32 as a file system for new partitions or volumes larger than 32 GB.

Microsoft introduced exFAT with Windows Vista Service Pack 1 and continues to license the technology to memory device manufacturers, such as USB memory sticks. ExFAT has the simplicity of the FAT file system but with capacity limits that are so large that it can be used with almost any portable bulk storage device. As memory device sizes exceed 32 GB, exFAT will likely be the file system of devices preformatted at the factory.

 A volume can't be formatted with exFAT using a graphical tool, but the command format *volume /FS:exFAT* formats a connected volume with the exFAT file system from the command line.

In Windows 10, FAT should be used for file systems only when portability to non-Microsoft operating systems is a concern. Generally, this means that FAT is used only for portable media such as USB memory sticks and memory cards for phones and digital cameras. FAT does not provide file system security. To provide enhanced features for security, usability, and larger partitions, NTFS is a better alternative.

New Technology File System

The **New Technology File System (NTFS)** was first introduced with Windows NT and a newer version of it is supported by Windows 10. NTFS stores files and folders in a way that looks very similar to the FAT file system. The difference is in how that data is secured, reliably managed, and allowed to grow. The major advantages of NTFS are in Table 4-2.

Table 4-2   Advantages of the NTFS file system over FAT

Advantage	Description
Log file and checkpoint consistency checks	Information about files and folders stored on the disk is kept in a special file called the Master File Table (MFT), which is named $MFT on the disk. To safeguard this information, the NTFS system files are protected by a transactional file system. Any changes that are made to the system files are recorded in log files. The log files keep a record of changes that were made; in the event of a failure or problem, changes made to the NTFS system files can be rolled back to a known good state.
Automatic bad cluster management	An NTFS system file called the Bad Cluster File keeps a record of all the clusters that are considered unusable by the file system within that volume. When the operating system detects that a cluster cannot be trusted to store data, the cluster's identification is automatically added to this file. If the bad cluster is currently used by a file or folder to store data, the operating system tries to move that data to a different cluster. The move is transparent to the user and does not require user intervention.
Transactional NTFS	Transactional NTFS is similar to the transactional system used to protect NTFS system files, such as $MFT, but it is used in Windows 10 to protect file data. Updates using a transactional system utilize change logs and checkpoints to validate that updates have successfully completed. If there is a problem with the updates to a file, the changes can be replayed or rolled back to a known good state.
File names stored in Unicode format	Files and folders on an NTFS file system in Windows 10 can use Unicode characters in the file name. This allows a file to use characters from many different international languages, not just the English-based ASCII character set.
Alternate data streams	A file stored on an NTFS file system can have multiple streams of data associated with it. Each stream is a sequence of data bytes. Every file has one unnamed stream that is used to store the byte data typically associated with the file and visible to users and applications. Applications can create additional named streams and link them to the file in addition to the unnamed stream. This is only visible and useful to the application itself, as the user does not have direct access to the named streams. A common example is a named stream that could be used to store a thumbnail of a large image for quick and easy previews within a graphic application.
Encrypting File System (EFS)	Files that are stored on an NTFS file system can have their contents encrypted to protect the information from unauthorized users who gain access to the file. The encryption key for the file is stored in an alternate data stream for the file. EFS is covered in more details in Chapter 6, Windows 10 Security Features.
File and folder permissions	Each file and folder on an NTFS file system has its own list of permissions that determine the actions that users or groups are allowed to perform with that item. This list of permissions is known as the access control list (ACL).
Compression	Files can be compressed to save space on NTFS volumes. The compression process is transparent to the user and their applications. When a compressed file is accessed, Windows 10 decompresses the file and presents it to the user and their applications. When the file is closed, it is compressed once again.

(continues)

Table 4-2   (*continued*)

Advantage	Description
Disk quotas	The amount of disk space used by a user can be restricted to ensure that one user does not exhaust or monopolize available space in an NTFS partition. By default, **disk quota** limits are not enabled for NTFS partitions.
Shrinkable/extendable partitions and volumes	As long as there is available free space on a disk, you can expand a partition or volume to use that free space. You can also shrink a partition or volume if there is empty space.
Volume mount points	Instead of giving a partition or volume a drive letter, you can mount the partition or volume to an empty folder in an existing drive letter.
Symbolic links	A symbolic link is stored in the directory of a folder as a file system object. The purpose of a symbolic link is to point to a file or folder located somewhere other than that folder. To applications and the user, it appears as if the file or folder pointed to is actually located in the folder containing the symbolic link.

Disk Quotas   Disk quotas are set using the Disk Management console or the general-purpose *fsutil* command-line utility. Administrative permissions are required on the computer to access quota settings. By viewing the NTFS volume's properties from within Disk Management, an extra tab called Quota displays. This tab displays quota settings for that partition or volume (see Figure 4-5). Control and reporting of disk quota details can also be managed from the command line with *fsutil* to simplify repetitive tasks such as setting up a new user or running periodic reports.

To see quota control options for the *fsutil* utility, enter the command *fsutil quota help* at the administrative command prompt.

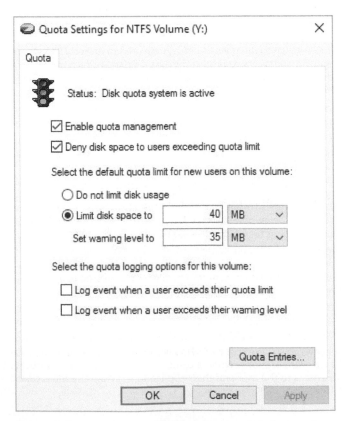

Figure 4-5   NTFS-formatted disk properties, disk Quota tab

4

Once disk quotas are enabled for a partition, the operating system calculates the amount of disk space used by each unique owner listed for all files on the volume. The first time quota management is turned on, the system takes some time to identify all the owners and count up all the file sizes attributed to each owner.

Compressed files count against the disk quota based on their uncompressed size, not their compressed size.

Even if disk quotas are enabled, the initial configuration reports only the amount of data in use by different owners; no limits or warnings are enforced. The options on the Quota tab allow for limits to be configured as a default setting for all users.

As users approach those limits, warnings can be issued; when they finally reach the maximum limit, they are denied additional disk space within the partition. Warnings to users can be ignored, misinterpreted, and not noticed, so the warnings can be optionally recorded to the application event log as a permanent reference of the event for administrators.

Some users may require special consideration and should have a different warning or deny limit in place. The Quota Entries button on the Quota tab in Figure 4-5 opens a Quota Entries window (see Figure 4-6) where user-specific limits can be defined that override the default settings.

Changes in the ownership of a file change the amount of data that is considered to belong to a user.

Status	Name	Logon Name	Amount Used	Quota Limit	Warning Level	Percent Used
OK		BUILTIN\Administrators	69 KB	No Limit	No Limit	N/A
OK		NT AUTHORITY\SYSTEM	4 MB	No Limit	No Limit	N/A
OK	Leon Plesniarski	DESKTOP-BTK24LI\UserX	346 KB	No Limit	No Limit	N/A

Quota Entries for NTFS Volume (Y:)

Quota   Edit   View   Help

3 total item(s), 1 selected.

Figure 4-6   NTFS-formatted disk properties, disk Quota tab, quota entries listed by owner

Activity 4-7: Enabling Disk Quotas for an NTFS Partition

Time Required: 10 minutes
Objective: Enable disk quotas

Description: Disk quotas can be used to limit disk utilization, but they can also be used just to identify the amount of disk space that each user is using. For example, if you enable quotas on the C: drive of a computer running Windows 10, you can see how much application data and profile space is used. In this activity, you enable disk quotas on the C: drive of your computer and log events when limits are reached.

1. If necessary, start your computer and sign in.
2. On the taskbar, click **File Explorer** and browse to **This PC**.
3. Right-click **Local Disk (C:)** and click **Properties**.
4. In the Local Disk (C:) Properties window, click the **Quota** tab and click **Show Quota Settings**. Note that the traffic light indicator on the Quota tab is red and that the status is reported as "Disk quotas are disabled."
5. Select the **Enable quota management** check box and click **Limit disk space to**.
6. In the Limit disk space to box, enter **2** in the numeric field and select **GB** from the units drop-down list.

7. In the Set warning level to box, check that **1** is entered in the numeric field and select **GB** from the units drop-down list.

8. Select the **Log event when a user exceeds their quota limit** and **Log event when a user exceeds their warning level** check boxes.

9. Click **Apply**.

10. A warning appears that enabling the disk quota system will take some time to complete. Click **OK** in the warning window to continue.

11. When the traffic light indicator on the Quota tab turns green and the status is reported as "Disk quota system is active," click the **Quota Entries** button on the Quota tab.

12. The Quota Entries for (C:) window displays and lists the current owners who have files on the volume. The Logon Name column is initially populated with the security identifiers (SIDs) of the owners found on the volume. After a period of time, the SID codes are resolved into their friendly names. Depending on the speed of your system, you might not see the SIDs.

13. Right-click the **Start** button, select **Command Prompt (Admin)**, and click **Yes** in the User Account Control dialog box.

14. At the command prompt, enter the text **fsutil quota query C:** and press **Enter**. Note the detail reported in the text output by the command in comparison to the detail visible in the Quota Entries for (C:) window opened in Step 11. Consider which report could be generated by a scheduled task for routine reporting.

15. Close all open windows.

Volume Mount Points

A partition or volume has a finite amount of space available. The partition or volume can be extended or spanned, but in some cases, this is not an option. Volume **mount points** allow an empty folder in an NTFS-formatted file system to point to another partition or volume in the local computer. Volume mount points are also known as junction points and are created with the Disk Management console. The user performing the task must have administrator privileges on the local computer.

To the users, it appears they are accessing a folder in the original NTFS partition, but in fact they are accessing the file system on the other partition. The partition connected via the volume mount point can be formatted with a different file system. The disk space reported for the NTFS volume hosting the mount point does not increase; the volume mount point is just a pointer. The free space and control of the target pointed at by the volume mount point is separately reported and managed.

A folder must be empty before it can be converted into a volume mount point. A single volume mount point can only point to one partition or volume. However, multiple mount points can point to the same target partition or volume. Volume mount points can be added or removed for a partition, but they cannot be modified.

If a partition or volume is deleted and it is pointed to by one or more mount points, those mount points revert to empty folders.

Activity 4-8: Managing Mount Points

Time Required: 30 minutes
Objective: Link additional space to an existing volume using a volume mount point and observe the changes to the view in File Explorer

Description: You can use a mount point to expand the capacity of an existing partition or volume. This can be useful when you need to add a large amount of storage space and there is no available space on the physical disk. For example, you can create a mount point for application data. In this activity, you create a mount point on the C: drive to hold data for an application.

Because VHD files are used in this activity, and VHD files are not automatically reattached after a reboot, do not sign out or restart your computer during this activity.

1. You should already be signed in from the previous activity.

2. On the taskbar, click **File Explorer** and browse to **C:**.

3. In File Explorer, on the **Home** tab, click **New folder**, type **MyAppData,** and press **Enter.**

4. Browse to C:\VHD Storage\ and double-click **VHDExample.** This mounts the VHD; take note of the drive letter for VHDVOL.

5. Browse to VHDVOL, click the **Home** tab, click **New item,** and click **Text Document.**

6. Type **DataFile** and press **Enter** to name to file.

7. Close File Explorer.

8. Right-click the **Start** button and click **Disk Management.**

9. Right-click **VHDVOL** (*driveletter:*) and click **Change Drive Letter and Paths.**

10. In the Change Drive Letter and Paths for *driveletter:* (VHDVOL) window, select the drive letter, and click **Remove.**

11. In the Disk Management window, click **Yes** to acknowledge the warning.

12. Right-click **VHDVOL** and click **Change Drive Letter and Paths.**

13. In the Change Drive Letter and Paths for VHDVOL window, click **Add.**

14. In the Add Drive Letter or Path window, click **Mount in the following empty NTFS folder,** type **C:\MyAppData** in the text box, and click **OK.**

15. On the taskbar, click **File Explorer** and browse to C:\. Notice that MyAppData is displayed with a different icon and shows a size.

16. Close File Explorer.

17. Right-click the **Start** button and click **Command Prompt.**

18. At the command prompt, type **dir C:\my*** and press **Enter.** Notice that MyAppData is a junction point.

19. Type **cd \MyAppData** and press **Enter.**

20. Type **dir** and press **Enter.** Verify that DataFile.txt is there.

21. Close the command prompt.

22. In Disk Management, scroll down in the list of disks, right-click the disk containing VHDVOL, and click **Detach VHD.**

23. In the Detach Virtual Hard Disk window, click **OK.**

24. Close Disk Management.

Symbolic Links   A symbolic link can point to a file or folder on the local computer or to a remote location identified with a UNC path. If the target is remote, the other computer hosting the target must also support symbolic links. There are two special types of symbolic links known as hard links and junction points. Only administrators can create symbolic links using the command-line utility *mklink.*

Symbolic links are different from a shortcut because a shortcut is a file that defines how Windows can locate content somewhere else. To other applications, the shortcut appears as just another file with a .lnk extension. Symbolic links appear as a file or folder with a given name that may be different or the same as the target. The majority of applications would be oblivious to the fact that the file or folder they are accessing is really located somewhere else.

A hard link can only point to a file on the same partition or volume as the hard link object. A hard link is a duplicate directory entry that points to the *contents* of a target file. When users or applications access a hard link, they believe the file content exists in the folder holding the hard link. Multiple hard links can point to the same target file. If the hard link's target file is deleted from the target's original location, the content can still be accessed through any hard link that still points to the content. The file's content is preserved until the original file and all hard links that point to it are deleted.

A junction point is a special type of symbolic link that points to folders only. The path to the target folder must be specified using an absolute path. The absolute path points to a target that can be located without needing to know the location of the original junction point object. Windows 10 makes frequent use of junction points to organize and optimize system data such as user profile folders, for example. Most end users are not aware of or recognize the use of junction points.

Resilient File System

The **Resilient File System (ReFS)** is a newer file system introduced with Windows Server 2012 that is now included in Windows 10. It is continuously being developed with new features that will potentially make it a candidate to replace NTFS as the default file system for persistent local storage. Currently, ReFS offers a subset of NTFS features and several new enhancements, but it is not a general-purpose file system that is ready to replace NTFS.

Currently, ReFS can only be selected for a Storage Spaces volume when it is configured as a resilient two-way or three-way mirror configuration. Windows 10 does not currently allow the end user to format ReFS on a basic simple volume, dynamic volume, or Storage Spaces–based simple or parity volumes. These limits may change in the future as ReFS evolves.

The ReFS file system on a Windows 10 system is complementary to the resilient nature of mirrored storage spaces. ReFS is designed to verify and autocorrect data faults on the volume without having to bring the volume down for maintenance. Data integrity and correction testing is performed routinely as a background task to ensure that the file system has the highest level of uptime possible.

ReFS cannot be used to format the system boot volume, or on removable media. Some NTFS features have been removed from the current ReFS file system in Windows 10, including some major features such as file and folder compression, disk quotas, and the Encrypting File System (EFS). These features can be served well by NTFS for now, while ReFS improves the experience with bulk storage when used together with Storage Spaces technology.

Universal Disk Format

The Universal Disk Format (UDF) is a file system developed as a standard to allow file interchange between different operating systems. This makes it ideal for storing files on portable CD-ROM and DVD media.

Windows 10 supports both reading and writing of files to the UDF file system.

File System Tasks

After a partition or volume is formatted with a file system, few changes to its base configuration are possible. The most common file system changes are changing the assigned drive letter and converting the installed file system.

Changing Drive Letters   Drive letters are used by applications and users as a quick reference to locate files. A drive letter points to a partition or volume formatted with a file system.

Once a drive letter has been used to reference a particular group of files, users and their applications expect the same drive letter to be used when the files are accessed again. In some instances, the drive letter assigned to a partition or volume must change. For example, a new application might be installed that requires a specific drive letter to access data files, perhaps to mirror old settings hard-coded into an application. In another example, a CD-ROM might be using a drive letter on one computer that is different from the CD drive letter on another computer. The user or application might be confused by the drive letter difference.

It is possible to change the drive letter, or assign a new one, to a partition or volume using the Disk Management console.

When a new partition or volume is created, one of the New Simple Volume Wizard's tasks asks if a drive letter should be assigned. Any unused drive letter can be selected. A single drive letter can only be assigned to one partition or volume.

After a drive letter has been assigned to a volume or partition, it can be changed to a different available drive letter, but some applications might become confused. If this happens, the applications will require modifications to update their drive letter expectations.

Drive letters can also be removed from a partition or volume. If a drive letter is removed, the files might become inaccessible to the user.

The number of drive letters is limited (that is, A–Z), and some drive letters are reserved for specific purposes. For example, C is reserved for the boot partition.

Converting File Systems

There are no conversion utilities to change NTFS- or FAT32-formatted volumes to ReFS. FAT can be converted to NTFS using a command-line utility.

To manually convert an ReFS or NTFS file system to FAT, perform the following steps:

1. Back up the data on the partition.
2. Reformat the partition with FAT32.
3. Restore the data originally backed up from the NTFS partition.

To convert a FAT file system to NTFS, perform these steps:

1. Back up the data on the partition.
2. Ensure free space remains on the partition.
3. Convert the partition using the *convert* command-line utility.

The file system conversion should not affect data, but any file system conversion has a risk of failure. The backup of the original data should be verified as correct and accessible before the conversion begins.

The *convert* command-line utility has the syntax of *convert drive_id /FS:NTFS*.

The *drive_id* is the drive letter, mount point, or volume name used to identify which partition to convert. The command-line option */FS:NTFS* tells the utility to convert the existing file system to NTFS.

For example, the command to convert drive N: to NTFS is

```
convert N: /FS:NTFS
```

Converting a partition requires that the convert utility runs with full administrative access to the local computer. If the file system is currently in use, the computer might have to reboot several times to complete the conversion process.

File and Folder Attributes

The FAT, ReFS, and NTFS file systems use attributes to describe general information about a file or folder. To see the general attributes of a file or folder, view the properties of the item in File Explorer. The General tab displays basic attributes such as dates and times the item was created, last accessed, and last modified. The General tab also reports the size, location, and control attribute settings.

The details reported for the properties of a file or folder change slightly depending on the type of item, file, or folder, and the file system (FAT, NTFS, or ReFS). However, for the most part, they have the same general information shown in Figure 4-7. The Security tab shown in Figure 4-7 is not available for the FAT file system.

A few items worth noting in the properties of a file:

- The Size on disk and Size are not exactly the same. This is because disk space is allocated based on the cluster size you chose when you formatted the drive.

- Created, Modified, and Accessed time can all be useful when trying to identify the current version of file that users are working on.

- If you modify the application that a file type opens with, it is changed for all files with that file extension, not just the file you are modifying.

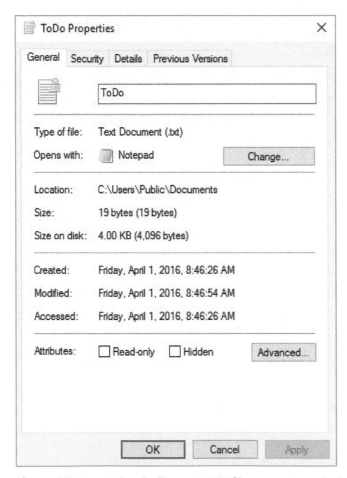

Figure 4-7   Properties of a file on an NTFS file system, General tab

Advanced attributes for a file on an NTFS file system include (see Figure 4-8):

- *File is ready for archiving*—A check box to indicate that the file has changed since the last backup

- *Allow this file to have contents indexed in addition to file properties*—A check box to enable or disable including the file in the indexing process

- *Compress contents to save disk space*—A check box to enable or disable compression of the file contents

- *Encrypt contents to secure data*—A check box to enable or disable encryption of the file

- *Details*—A button used to view which accounts are configured to access the file when encrypted

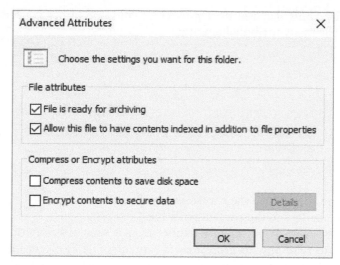

Figure 4-8   Properties of a file on an NTFS file system, General tab, Advanced attributes

Changes to advanced attributes for compression and encryption for folders are only saved after you click the Apply button or the Properties window is closed by clicking the OK button. If there are contents in the folder, you are asked if you want to apply your changes to the folder alone or to the folder and all of its current contents (see Figure 4-9).

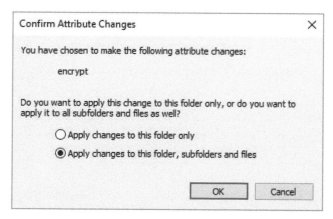

Figure 4-9   Confirm scope of advanced attribute change to a folder

Changes to the folder alone apply the setting to all new files created in the folder. This has the advantage that existing files in the folder keep their original setting.

Attribute Flags

Each file and folder has its own attribute flags to control some aspects of how the operating system interacts with the object. Most attribute flags can be viewed in File Explorer as part of the object's properties. The *attrib* command-line utility is used to manage the System and other advanced attributes, such as *no scrub* and *integrity* attribute flags, which cannot be accessed using File Explorer. (Advanced attributes such as *no scrub* and *integrity* are only relevant with the ReFS file system when it is used with Storage Spaces; therefore, there is no need to make those attributes generally available through File Explorer.) The compression and encryption attribute flags cannot be managed by using *attrib*. Instead, the *compact* command-line utility is used to manage the *compress* attribute flag and the *cipher* command-line utility is used to manage the *encrypt* attribute flag. The main attribute flags are:

- Read-only
- Archive
- Hidden
- System
- Compress
- Encrypt

Read-Only   Files and folders use the *read-only* attribute flag differently. Files that have the *read-only* flag set block changes to the contents of a file.

Folders that have the *read-only* attribute flag set trigger special behavior in File Explorer. Folders are not marked as *read-only* to protect their contents; File Explorer largely ignores this setting. Instead, the *read-only* flag is used to indicate that the folder is a system folder and should be treated differently. That is why when viewing the properties of a folder, the *read-only* setting is grayed out by default.

Archive   The *archive* attribute flag is set by the operating system when a file or folder changes. This is used as a signal to the user and backup applications that the contents have changed since the last time the file was backed up. The next time the backup runs, the backup program can clear this attribute flag to avoid repeatedly backing up the same file or folder when its contents have not changed.

Hidden   The *hidden* attribute flag is set by the user or the operating system to hide folders and files from the user. To view hidden files and folders in File Explorer, change the folder View option (see Figure 4-10).

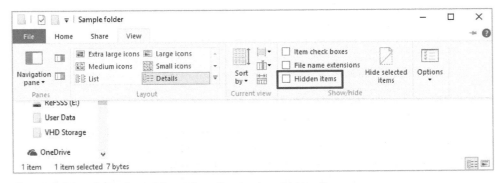

Figure 4-10   File Explorer, View tab option to show hidden items

To see all objects in a command prompt window, including hidden files and folders, use the command *dir /a*. To see only hidden objects in a command prompt window, use the command *dir /ah*.

System   The *system* attribute flag is set by the operating system for specific folders and files. The *system* attribute flag is not exposed through File Explorer. The *attrib* utility must be used to view or change this attribute. A file or folder that has this attribute flag set is typically important to the operation of the computer and hidden from the user.

Compress   The *compress* attribute is only supported on volumes and partitions formatted with the NTFS file system. A folder or file that is set to the compressed state cannot be encrypted. By default, compressed files and folders are displayed with a modified icon in File Explorer (see Figure 4-11).

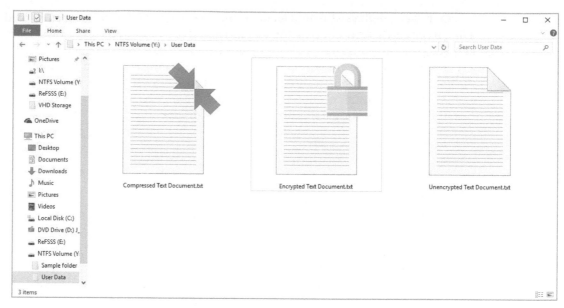

Figure 4-11   Modified icons indicate compressed and encrypted files in File Explorer

A folder that is set as compressed does not take up less space on the disk. The *compress* attribute flag for a folder indicates the default setting for new files created in that folder. A file that is set as compressed immediately becomes compressed on the disk.

Moving Compressed Files   NTFS attributes for a file are stored in NTFS system files within the partition's file system. Each NTFS-formatted partition has its own set of NTFS system files.

When a file is moved from its current location to a new location in the same NTFS partition, its attributes do not change. This means the *compress* attribute on the file remains the same regardless of the target folder default setting.

When a file is moved from its current location to a new location in a different NTFS partition, new attributes are created in the destination's NTFS system files. This means the *compress* attribute on the file becomes the same as the target folder's *compress* attribute setting.

When a file is moved to a destination folder that does not support compression (formatted with the FAT or ReFS file system for example), the file is uncompressed.

Copying Compressed Files   When a file is copied, the original file is left in its old location and a new file is created in the target folder. The newly created file always receives new attributes in the NTFS system files. This means the *compress* attribute on the file becomes the same as the target folder's *compress* attribute setting. This is true whether the destination folder is in the same NTFS partition or another NTFS partition.

When a file is copied to a destination folder that does not support compression (formatted with the FAT file system), the copy of the file is uncompressed.

Encrypt   The *encrypt* attribute is only supported on volumes and partitions formatted with NTFS in earlier versions of Windows. Windows 10 adds support for encrypted files stored on the FAT32 file system. A folder or file that is set to be encrypted cannot be compressed. By default, encrypted files and folders are displayed with an alternate icon in File Explorer.

When you encrypt files on a FAT32 file system, it looks similar to EFS, but Windows 10 uses a different mechanism to store the encryption keys called Enterprise Data Protection.

A folder that is set as encrypted is not encrypted itself. The *encrypt* attribute flag for a folder indicates the default setting for new files created in that folder. A file that is set as encrypted immediately becomes encrypted on the disk.

Only users with valid digital security keys can decrypt and access an encrypted file's contents. The Details button of a file or folder's advanced attribute settings allows users to be granted access to the encrypted file (see Figure 4-12).

If a user is not on the list of users who can access the encrypted file, that user cannot access the encrypted file's contents, even if the user is an administrator of the computer. The recovery agent is a special user account(s) set by domain policy to allow access to encrypted content in case the local users with access are accidentally deleted.

Figure 4-12   Managing user access to an encrypted file or folder

Moving and Copying Encrypted Files

Once a file is encrypted, it remains encrypted unless the *encrypt* attribute is disabled or the file is saved to a destination volume that does not support encryption.

If an encrypted file is saved to a destination device that does not support encryption (such as a FAT or ReFS volume), the user receives a warning message to indicate that the security will be lost (see Figure 4-13).

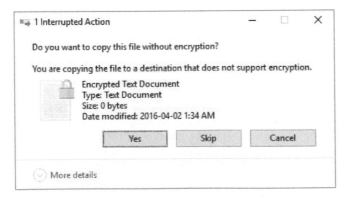

Figure 4-13   Warning that encryption will be lost when saving an encrypted file to a FAT or ReFS volume

File and Folder Permissions

Every file and folder stored on an NTFS or ReFS partition has its own **access control list** (**ACL**). The ACL is a collection of **access control entries** (**ACEs**) that identify a specific security identifier that (that is, who) can perform a given action (that is, what) to a file or folder. The ACL specifies what a user or group is allowed to do with the file or folder. Files and folders stored with other file systems such as FAT or FAT32 do not have an ACL. ReFS security is designed as a subset of NTFS technology from a client-facing perspective. In the following section, note that NTFS permission settings apply equally to ReFS security, but ReFS cannot be used to format the C: partition.

NTFS permissions apply security to files and folders that impact any user trying to access the object. This applies equally to local users and network users. If the ACL in a file system has denied access to a file, then access is denied regardless of how the file is being accessed.

Windows 10 applies specific default permissions to folders when a partition is first formatted with the NTFS file system.

Default Folder Permissions

The first level of folder in an NTFS partition is the root folder. The default permissions assigned to this folder on the C: drive are:

- Members of the computer's Administrators group have full control.
- The operating system has full control.
- Members of the computer's Users group have the ability to read and execute programs.
- Authenticated users have the ability to create folders in this folder.
- Authenticated users have the ability to create files and write data in subfolders only.

By default, users cannot create files in the root folder of an NTFS-formatted drive.

To see the permissions for the root folder of an NTFS-formatted volume, view the Security tab of the drive's Properties window (see Figure 4-14). Select a specific user or group to view the permissions assigned to that user or group.

Figure 4-14 Security tab for an NTFS drive's properties

The default permissions assigned to subfolders on the C: drive and the root folder on all other NTFS partitions are:

- Members of the computer's Administrators group have full control.
- The operating system has full control.
- Members of the computer's Users group have the ability to read and execute programs.
- Authenticated users have the ability to create, modify, and delete files and folders in this folder and its subfolders.

As additional folders and files are created, they inherit permissions from the parent object that contains them. Inheritance allows a permission setting to be configured at a higher level in the file system and have it propagate to lower subfolders and files.

NTFS permissions are assigned using two formats:

- NTFS standard permissions
- Individual NTFS permissions

NTFS Standard Permissions

Standard NTFS permissions represent a collection of predetermined individual NTFS permissions. The combination of individual permissions provides a general level of access specific to the type of standard permission assigned. For example, the standard NTFS permission of Modify is a collection of individual NTFS permissions that allows a file to be read, written to, renamed, or deleted. The names of standard NTFS permissions are meant to be intuitive and easy to understand. The standard NTFS permissions are listed in Table 4-3.

Table 4-3 Standard NTFS permissions

Permission	Description
Write	This permission used for folders allows new files and folders to be created in the current folder. The folder attributes can be changed and the folder's ownership and security can be viewed. This permission used for files allows file data to be rewritten. The file's attributes can be changed and the file's ownership and security can be viewed.
Read	This permission used for folders allows files and folder data, attributes, ownership, and security to be viewed. This permission used for files allows the file's data, attributes, ownership, and security to be viewed.
List folder contents	This permission applies only to folders. Without this permission, the files and folders contained in a folder cannot be listed. The users or applications can still access the files if they have permission and know the exact file or folder name.
Read & execute	This permission used for folders allows read access to files and folders below this point. This is the equivalent of enabling Read and List folder contents. This permission used for files allows read access to the file's information and, if it is an executable file, the user is allowed to run it. This permission automatically includes the Read permission.
Modify	This permission used for folders allows the same actions as Write and Read & execute permissions combined. The folder can also be deleted. This permission used for files allows the same actions as Write and Read & execute permissions combined. Files can also be deleted.
Full control	This permission used for folders allows the same actions as Modify plus the ability to change permissions and allow a user to take ownership of the folder. This permission used for files allows the same actions as Modify plus the ability to change permissions and allow a user to take ownership of the file.
Special permissions	Special permissions are the individual permissions that can be assigned when the predefined standard permissions are not adequate to achieve desired results.

Individual NTFS Permissions

Many individual NTFS permissions exist to fine-tune access and control for files and folders. The list of individual permissions is visible only when editing a permission entry in the Advanced security view (see Figure 4-15).

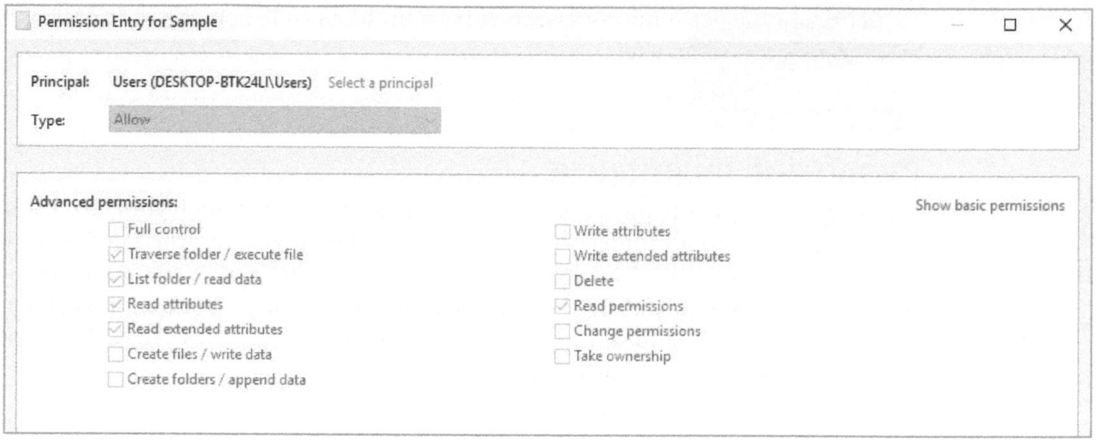

Figure 4-15   Viewing advanced individual NTFS permissions on a file

Individual NTFS permissions are not typically used to apply security to files and folders directly. The name and purpose of the individual permissions is often not intuitive. It is a best practice to use standard NTFS permissions wherever possible. This avoids complex special security settings that are unnecessarily difficult to manage.

Permission Scope

When an NTFS permission setting is applied to a file or folder, it also has a scope assigned. The scope determines what other objects are impacted by the assigned permission. For files, the scope is limited to *this object only*, which is just the file itself. In that case, the scope is not displayed in the advanced security view (see Figure 4-15).

For folders, the scope can be set to:

- This folder only
- This folder, subfolders, and files
- This folder and subfolders
- This folder and files
- Subfolders and files only
- Subfolders only
- Files only

The permission scope is visible as *Applies to* information in the advanced security view (see Figure 4-16).

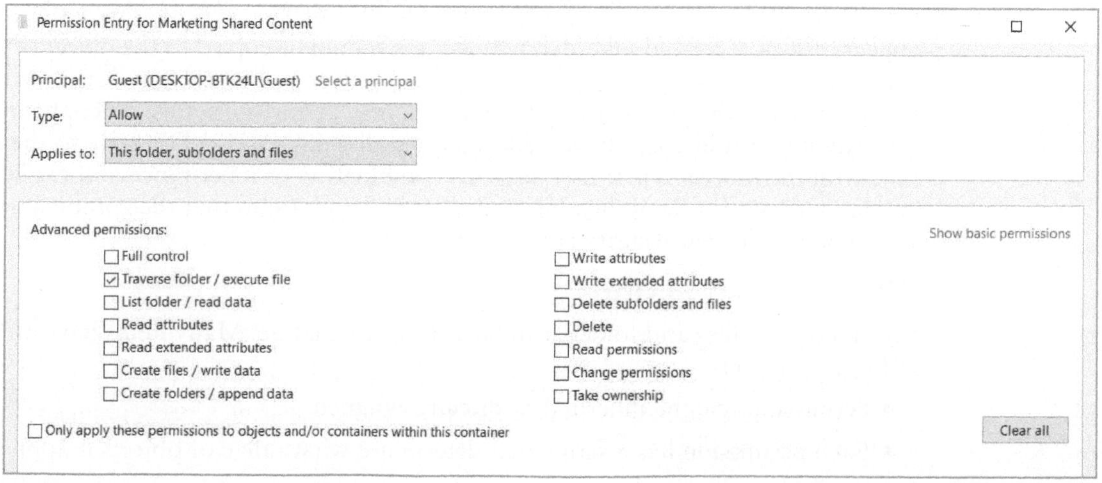

Figure 4-16   Viewing advanced individual NTFS permissions on a folder

The permission scope must be carefully considered to obtain the desired effect.

Permission Inheritance

NTFS permissions for folders apply to the first folder on which they are used. The permission then propagates to all folders below that point. When viewing the Permissions tab in advanced security settings for a folder, the *Inherited from* column shows where a permission setting was first applied (see Figure 4-17). Further changes to those permission assignments automatically propagate through folders and files below that point. Any files created in those folders inherit permissions from the folder they are located in.

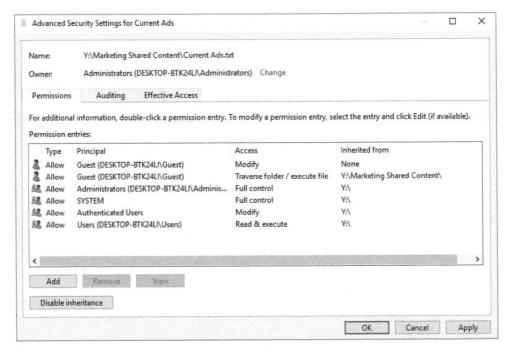

Figure 4-17   Permissions in Advanced Security Settings

Inheritance of permissions is convenient, but it might not be desired for all situations. Each file or folder has an option called *Disable inheritance* in the Advanced Security Settings window to enable or disable inheritance at that object (see Figure 4-17).

Disabling inheritance blocks inheritance of permissions from higher levels of the file system. Once inheritance is blocked, though, the object needs new permissions assigned to it. A prompt appears asking if the old inherited permissions should be copied to the object or removed entirely. If the permissions are copied, they provide a starting point and can be customized to meet any requirements. If the permissions are removed, new permissions must be configured from scratch.

Any file or folder can have additional permissions assigned directly to the object that combine with the inherited permissions. This combination of inheritance and explicit permissions at any level allows for flexibility, but you must be very careful that the combination of permissions gives you the desired security result.

Effective Permissions

Permissions on files and folders can be difficult to analyze. Many items have an impact on calculating permissions:

- Permissions can be inherited or directly assigned.
- Each permission has a scope that determines what range of objects it applies to.

- Permissions can be allowed or denied.
- Permissions can be applied to groups, and any member of that group receives those permissions.
- Users can be members in multiple groups that have different permissions to the same object.
- Owners of a file or folder have full control of the object.

To simplify the analysis, the Advanced Security Settings window for any file or folder includes an Effective Access tab (see Figure 4-18).

A group or user name can be selected for analysis. The window shows which individual NTFS permissions are effective for that group or user for that object. This tool does not show how those effective permissions were obtained; it only shows what they are. You still need to review permissions on folders above to identify how the permissions were obtained.

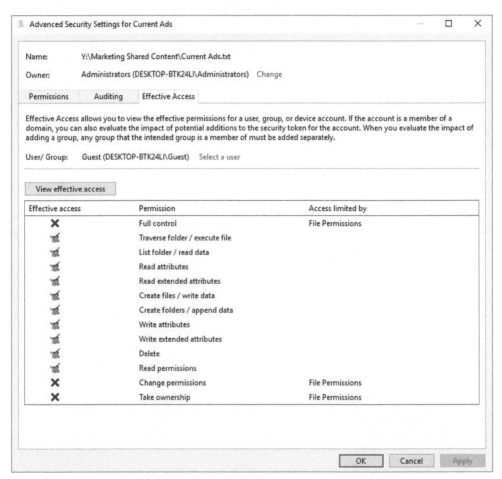

Figure 4-18   Effective Access tab in advanced file or folder security settings

Ownership

Each NTFS file or folder has an owner assigned to it. The owner of a file or folder always has the ability to assign permissions to that file or folder, regardless of what existing permissions are assigned. This ensures that the owner can always assign himself Full control permission and modify a file.

The current owner of a file or folder is visible by viewing a file or folder's Advanced security view and inspecting the Owner field (refer to Figure 4-17).

Members of the Administrators group have the right, by default, to assign or take ownership of a file or folder. Users with the Full control standard permission or the individual NTFS permission Take ownership can also assume ownership of a file.

Once a user is the owner of a folder or file, that user implicitly has full control of the object.

Permission Changes when Content Is Copied or Moved

When files and folders are first created in a volume that is formatted with NTFS, they take on the permission settings of the folder in which they are created. Copy operations always create new versions of the content that is being copied. Those new versions take on the permission settings of the target location, which might be different than the permission settings of the source content. Move operations affect permissions differently depending on the destination location relative to the source location.

Each single volume or partition formatted with the NTFS file system has its own database to track permissions and attributes for each file and folder it stores. When files and folders are moved from one location on the volume to another location on the same volume, new content is not created; only pointers to the content are moved in the database. In that case, the destination content keeps whatever permissions it originally had, regardless of the destination folder's permissions.

When files and folders are moved from one volume to a different volume formatted with NTFS, new content is created in the destination location. Just like a copy operation, the new content takes on the permission settings of the target location. Any permission settings assigned to the source content are lost.

Permission Strategy Considerations

Assigning and managing file permissions is seldom required for computers running Windows 10. Administrators have full access to the entire file system as required for any maintenance. Users have full access to their own profiles to store documents and application data. Users do not have access to the profiles of other users or the ability to modify system files. In the vast majority of scenarios, this is what you want.

In rare cases, there might be an application that requires you to modify the file system permissions to run properly. For example, some applications that use a nonstandard update process require you to give users modify permission to the application folder. Then, the user is able to run the script that copies files and updates the application.

Most of the detailed considerations about applying file and folder permissions are more relevant for configuring permissions on a shared folder on a server. On a server, you might have a shared folder with multiple folders inside it. Each of the folders in the share might have different permissions for different departments.

Shared folders and share permissions are covered in Chapter 7, Networking.

Activity 4-9: Managing File and Folder Permissions

Time Required: 30 minutes
Objective: Configure a new folder with unique NTFS security settings

Description: In this activity, you create a new folder called Marketing Documents on the C: drive. The default permissions are removed and replaced with permissions that allow only your user account to access the folder. You then create a file in the folder and investigate its resulting inherited permissions.

Because VHD files are used in this activity, and VHD files are not automatically reattached after a reboot, do not sign out or restart your computer during this activity.

1. You should already be signed in from the previous activity.

2. Right-click the **Start** button and click **File Explorer.**

3. In the left pane, click **Local Disk (C:).**

4. Create a new folder called **Marketing Documents** in **C:\.**

5. Right-click the **Marketing Documents** folder and click **Properties.**

6. In the Marketing Documents Properties window, click the **Security** tab and review the users and groups assigned permissions.

7. Click the **Advanced** button and review the specific permissions that have been applied to the users and groups.

8. In the Advanced Security Settings for Marketing Documents window, click the **Effective Access** tab.

9. Click the **Select a user link** to open the **Select User or Group** window.

10. Type your user name and click **OK** to continue.

11. Click the **View effective access** button. On the Effective Access tab, notice which individual NTFS permissions have a check mark next to them. You have all available permissions because your account is a local administrator.

12. Note the current owner of the folder. Your account is the owner of the folder because you created it. Click the **Change** link to the right of the name in the Owner field.

13. In the Select User or Group window, type the name **Administrators** and click **OK** to change the owner of the folder to the local Administrators group and any user that belongs to that group.

14. Select the **Replace owner on subcontainers and objects** check box.

15. If necessary, click the **Change Permissions** button to enable the controls for changing permissions.

16. Click the **Disable inheritance** button.

17. In the Block Inheritance warning dialog box, click the **Remove all inherited permissions from this object** to start with blank security settings for the Marketing Documents folder.

18. Click the **Add** button in the Advanced Security window to open the **Select User or Group** window.

19. Click **Select a principal** link.

20. Enter your user name and click **OK** to continue.

21. In the list of basic permissions, place a check next to the **Full control** permission.

22. Note that all other individual permissions are automatically assigned and that the permission scope is set to **This folder, subfolder and files.**

23. Click **OK** to continue.

24. Note the new permission entry on the **Permissions** tab in the Advanced Security Settings window.

25. Notice that the Inherited from column shows as None for the directly assigned permission.

26. Click **OK** to close the Advanced Security Settings window.

27. Notice the new permission setting and the simpler view on the **Security** tab of the folder's properties.

28. Click **OK** to close the Marketing Documents Properties window.

29. Create a new text document called **First Quarter Report.txt** in the **C:\Marketing Documents** folder.

30. Right-click **First Quarter Report.txt**, click **Properties,** and click the **Security** tab. Notice that the permissions from the Marketing Documents folder are inherited by this file.

31. Click **Cancel** and close all windows.

32. To release all open and attached VHDs, plus the active storage pool created with virtual disks, restart your computer. These virtual disks will not reattach automatically the next time you sign in.

Chapter Summary

- Windows 10 supports MBR and GPT partition styles that use basic and dynamic disk technology to organize data into partitions and volumes on physical disks. Basic and dynamic disks are managed using the Disk Management console or the DiskPart command-line utility.

- Initial disk management activities include preparing new disks for use and moving disks. Disks that are added to the computer might not be immediately recognized and Windows 10 can be told to check for new hardware and disks. When disks are moved from one computer to another, the drive letters they use might have to change. Dynamic disks must be imported when moved to update their membership with other dynamic disks that belong to a computer.

- Virtual hard disks (VHDs) are natively supported by Windows 10 and can be managed as a basic disk once the VHD is attached in the operating system. VHD files can either be a fixed size or allowed to grow dynamically to a maximum size. When a computer is restarted, the VHDs mounted before the reboot are not automatically attached. Windows 10 has the ability to boot from a VHD file.

- Storage Spaces technology is software-based and used to combine physical disk drives into a managed pool, which is then used to create virtual volumes from that combined space. Depending on the number of physical disks in the pool, Storage Spaces volumes can be created with a selected resiliency level. The most basic resilience level is a two-way mirror, which requires two physical drives at minimum in the storage pool. If one drive fails, the other will keep the two-way mirror volume operational.

- The primary file systems used to format bulk storage are FAT, NTFS, ReFS, and UDF. The NTFS file system is preferred in Windows 10 because it supports advanced features such as security, disk quotas, compression, and encryption that FAT does not. Small partitions can still benefit from the legacy support and simplicity of FAT. ReFS has a subset of NTFS features, but does not support disk quotas, compression, or encryption. ReFS is designed and limited initially in Windows 10 to complement the flexibility of Storage Spaces volumes configured with mirror resilience. Other disk and volume types cannot use ReFS at this writing, but it might be updated in later versions. UDF is a suitable file system for CD/DVD media.

- Users and applications can use drive letters or mount points to access partitions and volumes. Mount points are features available only with NTFS-formatted volumes. A mount point allows an empty folder in an NTFS partition to link to another volume or partition without changing the drive letter the user is using to access the data. To the user, it appears that the original partition has extra capacity.

- NTFS allows the use of file system objects called symbolic links that transparently point to files and folders in other locations. Symbolic links can point to content that is located relative to the symbolic link's location or else at a specific absolute location. A volume mount point is a special type of symbolic link called a junction point. Hard links that point at files are duplicate directory entries that point at the content of a target file. Hard links are limited to point to content on the same volume as the one holding the hard link itself.

- Files stored in FAT, ReFS, and NTFS partitions use attributes to control and limit file access. NTFS supports additional attributes for advanced features such as compression and file encryption. Encryption and compression cannot both be enabled for a file. Compression and encryption processing is automatic for file data. Encrypted files are protected even if the local disk is stolen or accessed by starting the computer with a different operating system. Windows 10 adds support for storing encrypted files to FAT32-formatted volumes.

- Given an NTFS-formatted source location, a copy operation creates content in a destination location. A move operation only creates content in a destination location when the destination is in a different NTFS volume. Newly created content takes on the permissions of the destination folder they were created in.

- NTFS and ReFS share a security model, as ReFS appears to the user as a subset of NTFS functionality. NTFS and ReFS files and folders are protected by standard permissions.

Standard permissions are made out of more complex individual permissions. NTFS/ReFS permissions have a scope applied to limit what type of data they apply to. NTFS/ReFS permissions are inherited from higher levels to lower levels. If desired, inheritance can be blocked at the file or folder level. It is difficult to manually analyze NTFS/ReFS permissions, so an Effective Access tool is available for each file and folder. Owners of a file or folder always have the ability to update permissions on the object they own.

Key Terms

access control entry (ACE)   A specific entry in a file or folder's ACL that uniquely identifies a user or group by its security identifier and the action it is allowed or denied to take on that file or folder.

access control list (ACL)   For those file systems that support ACLs for files and folders, such as NTFS, the ACL is a property of every file and folder in that file system. It holds a collection (that is, list) of ACE items that explicitly defines what actions are allowed to be taken on the file or folder to which it is attached.

basic disk   An older, IBM-originated method used to organize disk space for x86 computers into primary, extended, and logical partitions. Basic disk technology is supported by many legacy operating systems and may be required in certain multiboot configurations.

Disk Management console   An MMC console snap-in used to administer hard disks in Windows 10.

DiskPart   A command-line tool for managing disks. You can perform advanced operations with DiskPart that are not available in Disk Management.

disk quota   A system of tracking owners for file data within an NTFS-formatted partition or volume and the total disk space consumed by each owner. Limits or warning can be established to restrict disk space usage.

dynamic disk   A method for organizing disks introduced in Windows 2000 as a replacement for basic disks, but was never very popular. Dynamic disks can have a large number of volumes and also support some fault-tolerant disk configurations.

File Allocation Table (FAT)   A file system used to organize files and folders in a partition or volume. The common versions of FAT supported by Windows 10 include FAT, FAT32, and exFAT.

Master Boot Record (MBR)   The Master Boot Record exists at the very first sector of an IBM-formatted hard disk. It contains code to start the load process for an operating system from a partition or volume on the disk, a partition table to indicate what space has been reserved as partitions, and a signature sequence of bytes used to identify the disk to the operating system.

mount point   An empty folder in an NTFS-formatted file system that is used to point to another FAT, FAT32, or NTFS partition.

New Technology File System (NTFS)   A file system introduced with Windows NT. NTFS supports advanced features to add reliability, security, and flexibility that file systems such as FAT and FAT32 do not have.

partition table   A data structure contained in the MBR that is used to identify reserved areas of disk space for hard disks formatted for x86 computers. The partition table holds a maximum of four entries originally tasked to point to a maximum of four primary partitions, or three primary and one extended partitions.

Resilient File System (ReFS)   A file system introduced with Windows Server 2012 that supports basic NTFS-like features and self-healing technology for resilient bulk file storage when used together with Storage Spaces technology.

storage pool   A logical collection of disks that have been allocated to Storage Spaces. Disks must be assigned to a storage pool before Storage Spaces can use them.

storage space   A virtual disk created from the space made available by a storage pool in Storage Spaces.

Storage Spaces   A Microsoft software-based disk pooling technology that allows for different levels of resiliency to disk failure and provides virtualized volume storage within the disk pool.

Thunderbolt   A trade name for a high-speed, hardware-based interface to connect external devices to a computer, codeveloped by Apple and Intel.

virtual hard disk (VHD)   A file that is internally structured to store data like a file system. A VHD can be attached in Windows 10 and the contents accessed like a hard disk. VHDs can be fixed size or dynamically expanding. For Windows 10, they can also be VHD or VHDX format.

volume   A term used to refer to a region of disk space reserved to store file data. The term is used to generically refer to both dynamic disk volumes and basic disk partitions.

Review Questions

1. What type of startup firmware best supports Windows 10 with regard to device operation and management?

   a.   BIOS

   b.   GPT

   c.   UEFI

   d.   MBR

2. A VHD has been created using the Disk Management utility. Before the newly created VHD can be used to store files, it must be _____.

   a.   detached

   b.   configured as a dynamic disk

   c.   set to GPT partition style

   d.   initialized

   e.   set to MBR partition style

3. A storage _____ acts as a logical container grouping multiple physical disks.

4. A drive is attached to a custom hardware RAID controller. It does not show up as being available for use with Storage Spaces. To make the drive appear for use with Storage Spaces, the hardware RAID controller must be _____.

   a.   configured as mirrored RAID 1

   b.   BIOS managed

   c.   configured as parity RAID 5

   d.   UEFI managed

   e.   removed

5. You have just plugged a USB portable hard drive into an older laptop and the disk has not appeared as available. You are concerned that the hard disk controller hardware has not been recognized by the computer. What utility would you use to verify that the controller is functioning correctly?

   a.   DiskPart

   b.   Disk Management console

   c.   USB Management console

   d.   Device Manager

   e.   none of the above

6. You have recently added a new USB portable hard disk to your computer. You have received a notice that new hardware has been detected, but the disk does not appear as a storage location. Which utility would you use to verify that the hard disk's logical disk information is recognized by Windows 10? (Choose all that apply.)

    a. DiskPart

    b. Disk Management console

    c. USB Management console

    d. Device Manager

    e. none of the above

7. The number of physical disks required to implement three-way resilience for a Storage Spaces volume is _____.

    a. 1

    b. 2

    c. 3

    d. 5

    e. 7

8. The preferred technology to set up disk storage with mirrored fault tolerance for a user's backup data is _____.

    a. basic disks

    b. dynamic disks

    c. hardware-based RAID 5

    d. Storage Spaces

    e. hardware-based RAID 1

9. An NTFS partition has disk quotas enabled. You would like to run a weekly report that summarizes how much space each user is consuming. The _____ utility allows you to review quota details from the command line.

    a. convert

    b. fsutil

    c. get-diskquota

    d. diskpart

    e. dsquota

10. A 127 GB volume on a dynamic disk can be formatted with which file system?

    a. FAT

    b. FAT32

    c. NTFS

    d. ReFS

11. Windows 10 supports locally encrypted files stored on which of the following types of partitions? (Choose all that apply.)

    a. NTFS

    b. ReFS

    c. FAT

    d. FAT32

12. The _____ file system is the only one that supports file compression in Windows 10.

    a. FAT32

    b. ReFS

    c. NTFS

    d. FAT

13. A file is currently compressed in its local file system. For security reasons, the file is required to be encrypted. The file can be both compressed and encrypted. True or False?

14. A user is given Read permission to a file stored on an NTFS-formatted volume. The file is then moved to a different folder on a different NTFS-formatted volume where the user has been given Modify permission for that folder. The file is then moved to a folder on a FAT32-formatted volume. When the user signs in to the computer holding the file and accesses it via a drive letter, what is the user's effective permission to the file?

    a. Read

    b. Change

    c. Full control

    d. Modify

    e. No permissions apply

15. When assigning NTFS permissions, an ACE entry can explicitly define who is denied access to a resource. True or False?

16. A user is assigned Read permission to the NTFS folder C:\ACCOUNTING. The user requires full access to the folder C:\ACCOUNTING\FORMS and its contents. This can be accomplished by _____.

    a. not possible

    b. blocking permission inheritance at C:\ACCOUNTING\FORMS and assigning the user Full control to C:\ACCOUNTING\FORMS

    c. assigning the user Full control to C:\ACCOUNTING

    d. blocking permission inheritance at C:\ACCOUNTING and assigning the user Full control to C:\ACCOUNTING\FORMS

    e. assigning the user Full control to C:\ACCOUNTING\FORMS

17. A user checks the free space in a folder, Y:\BusReports, and notices that 3 GB of disk space is reported as available. When the user checks free space in Y:\BusReports\Archive, he notices that 5 GB of disk space is reported as available. The difference in available disk space is probably because the folder Y:\BusReports\Archive is _____.

    a. archived

    b. compressed

    c. encrypted

    d. dynamic

    e. a mount point

18. Upon opening the Disk Management console, you notice a disk whose status is reported as Foreign Disk. This is most likely because _____.

    a. the disk's Unicode property is enabled

    b. the disk has been corrupted

    c. the disk is shared on the network

    d. the disk was moved from another computer

19. A user is given Read permission to a file stored on an NTFS-formatted volume. The file is then moved to a different folder on a different NTFS-formatted volume where the user has been given Full control permission to that folder. When the user signs in to the computer holding the file and accesses its new location via a drive letter, what is the user's effective permission to the file?

    a. Read

    b. Full control

    c. No access

    d. Modify

    e. none of the above

20. A user is given Read permission to a file stored on an NTFS-formatted volume. The file is then moved to a folder on the same NTFS-formatted volume where the user has been given Modify permission to that folder. When the user signs in to the computer holding the file and accesses its new location via a drive letter, what is the user's effective permission to the file?

    a. Read

    b. Full control

    c. No access

    d. Modify

    e. none of the above

Case Projects

Case Project 4-1: Selecting a File System and Security Settings

You decide to share the annual report for your company from your computer. You decide that the data will be stored in its own partition, so you create a 20 MB logical partition for the report. If a user signs in to your computer locally, that user must have read-only access to the files. What file system would you select for the partition? What security settings would you use to achieve the desired results?

Case Project 4-2: Designing a Shared File System with Security

You are responsible for creating a shared file system to support a new branch office. The manager has requested shared locations for branch staff to access files. An area is required for all staff to access common forms and notices. Staff members are required to have read-only access to this location, but the manager requires full access to all content. A different area is required for all staff to share files without restrictions. The last area required is for the manager's private files, and only the manager has access to this location. A second manager will be hired in the next month to share the current manager's duties for job training. Both managers will require the same access throughout the file system. Only the IT administrator should have the ability to change file and folder permission settings for any area. Network permissions are not a concern because they will be configured appropriately based on the NTFS permissions you select. What groups would you create to simplify permission assignment? What folder structure and corresponding file-level permission settings would you use to achieve the desired results?

Case Project 4-3: Designing Storage Spaces

You have created a new storage space using a single 500 GB external USB 3.0 drive. The drive is becoming full, so you add another external 1 TB USB 2.0 drive to the storage pool. Now that you have two drives, you would like to create a volume with storage space resiliency set to two-way mirror. You create the new volume with two-way resiliency and a size limit of 1 TB. As you are copying files from the C: drive to this new volume, you receive a warning that you are running out of space. Only a few hundred megabytes have been copied; why might you be receiving the warning so quickly? What can you do about it?

chapter 5

User Management

After reading this chapter and completing the exercises, you will be able to:

- Describe local user accounts and groups
- Create and manage user accounts
- Manage user profiles
- Configure advanced authentication methods
- Describe Windows 10 integration with networks

User accounts are the most basic level of Windows 10 security. Authenticating as an individual user account is the basis for all other Windows 10 security mechanisms. In this chapter, you learn about local user accounts and groups, including how to create and manage user accounts. Each user has customized settings, such as desktop and program configuration data, stored in a user profile.

Windows 10 includes advanced authentication methods such as picture password, PIN, and Windows Hello. It is important to understand how these newer authentication methods can be used to increase security. In addition, the creation of user accounts for different network environments is important for efficiently controlling security.

User Accounts

User accounts are required for individuals to sign in to Windows 10 and use resources on the computer. Each **user account** has attributes that describe the user and control access. Some user account attributes are:

- Name
- Password
- Group membership
- Profile location

When a Windows 10 computer is not part of an Active Directory domain, you can sign in by using a **local user account** or a **Microsoft account.** Both types of accounts function similarly on a Windows 10 computer. The main difference between them is where the account credentials (user name and password) are stored. A local user account exists only on the one local Windows 10 computer and cannot be used to sign in to other computers. A Microsoft account is stored online by Microsoft and can be added to multiple Windows 10 computers and mobile devices.

Using a Microsoft account to sign in has several advantages:

- *Single set of credentials across devices*—If you configure multiple computers and mobile devices to use the same Microsoft account for authentication, you need to remember only one account name and one password for authentication. When you change the password for the Microsoft account, it automatically takes effect for all devices.

- *Password reset capability*—If you forget the password for a local user account, it can only be reset by another user on the same computer with administrator permissions or a password reset disk, neither of which might be readily available. If you are authenticating with a Microsoft account, you can reset the password on the Microsoft account by using an alternate email account you've provided, a mobile phone number, or by answering security questions.

- *Synchronization of some profile information*—A Microsoft account includes cloud storage that can be used to synchronize some settings among devices running Windows 10. You can synchronize settings such as the theme, web browser settings, stored passwords, language preferences, ease of access settings, and printers.

- *Integration with family settings*—For home computers, Microsoft accounts integrate with family settings to control web browsing and track computer usage.

- *Integration with other Microsoft apps*—A Microsoft account can be used for multiple Microsoft apps, such as OneDrive, Skype, or Xbox Live. When you use your Microsoft account to authenticate on Windows 10, those same credentials can automatically be used to access the Microsoft apps that use a Microsoft account. For example, when you authenticate using a Microsoft account in Windows 10, you are automatically authenticated to the OneDrive storage for that account.

Detailed information about how user accounts are used on networks and in domains is covered later in this chapter.

Whether you authenticate by using a local user account or a Microsoft account, a user account is stored in the **Security Accounts Manager (SAM) database** of Windows 10. If a user signs in locally, the SAM database is used to verify sign-in credentials. If a user signs in by using a Microsoft account, the Microsoft account credentials for the user account in the SAM database are verified with Microsoft over the Internet. If the computer is part of an Active Directory domain, and the user signs in using a domain user account, the SAM database is not used.

You can successfully sign in using a Microsoft account if you are disconnected from the Internet because cached credentials are used. Cached credentials are covered later in this chapter.

Within the SAM database, each user account is assigned a **security identifier (SID)**. Windows 10 uses the SID when assigning permissions to resources. For example, when a user is assigned permissions to access a folder, the SID is written to the folder access control list, not the user account name. Using an SID for security ensures that accounts can be renamed without losing security information. The SID for each user account is unique.

To fully comprehend user accounts, you should understand the following:

- Sign-in methods
- Naming conventions
- Default user accounts
- Default groups

Sign-In Methods

Users must sign in to Windows 10 before they can access resources and interact with the system. Windows 10 supports several sign-in methods; which method you choose depends on your requirements as network administrator, user needs, and whether the computer is a member of a domain.

The available sign-in methods are:

- Windows sign-in screen
- Secure sign-in
- Fast user switching
- Automatic sign-in
- Assigned access

Windows Sign-In Screen   For computers that are not joined to a domain, the Windows sign-in screen shown in Figure 5-1 displays a list of local user accounts that you can select from for authentication. For domain-joined computers, only the most recently used account is listed. The SAM database typically has only a few user accounts, so a graphical sign-in screen that displays each local user account is reasonable. In a domain-based environment with hundreds or thousands of accounts, it would not be possible to display an icon for each user account.

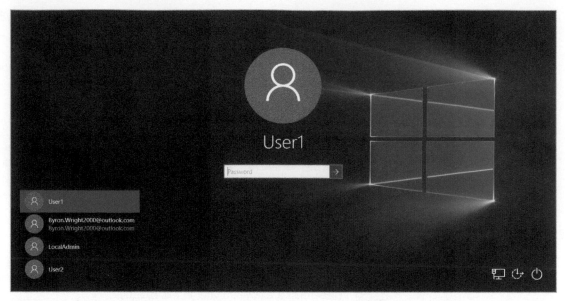

Figure 5-1   Windows 10 sign-in screen

On the Windows sign-in screen, each user is represented by an icon and name. The name is the name of the user account. The icon is selected when the user account is created, but can be changed at any time. For home users with children, the icon can be customized to be anything from their favorite cartoon character to their own picture. This makes Windows 10 more usable for small children and more fun for parents.

Secure Sign-In   Secure sign-in increases security on your computer by forcing you to press Ctrl+Alt+Delete before signing in. This protects your computer from malware that might attempt to steal your password by imitating the Windows sign-in screen.

The key sequence Ctrl+Alt+Delete is filtered by Windows operating systems, including Windows 10. The key sequence is captured by the operating system and not passed to applications. A virus or spyware never sees that Ctrl+Alt+Delete is pressed. Therefore, if you press this key combination and a sign-in window is displayed, it is the legitimate Windows sign-in screen. Secure sign-in can be enabled on the Advanced tab of the advanced User Accounts applet, shown in Figure 5-2.

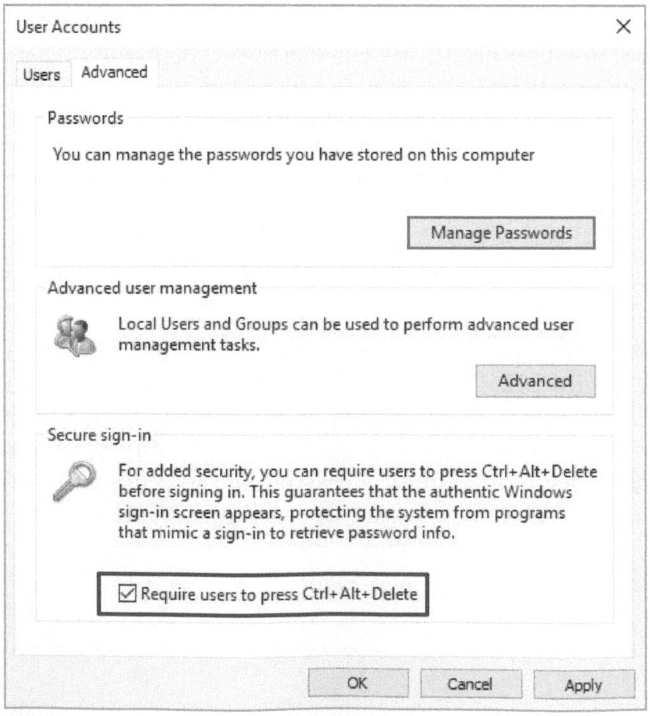

Figure 5-2   Enable secure sign-in

For domain users, this sign-in method automatically uses the most recently used domain unless otherwise specified.

Activity 5-1: Implementing Secure Sign-In

Time Required: 5 minutes
Objective: Implement secure sign-in for all users

Description: Secure sign-in makes Windows 10 more secure by ensuring that no malicious software running in Windows 10 is creating a false sign-in screen and capturing user names and passwords. In this activity, you implement secure sign-in, which forces users to press Ctrl+Alt+Delete before signing in.

1. If necessary, start your computer and sign in.
2. Click the **Start** button, type **netplwiz**, and then press **Enter**.
3. Click the **Advanced** tab.
4. Select the **Require users to press Ctrl+Alt+Delete** check box and click **OK**.
5. Sign out. Notice that the screen indicates that you must press Ctrl+Alt+Delete to sign in.

Fast User Switching   Fast user switching allows multiple users to have applications running in the background on a Windows 10 computer at the same time. However, only one user can be actively using the computer at a time. For example, User1 signs in to Windows 10 and starts creating a document in Word. User1 then locks the computer before leaving for lunch with the Word document still open. User2 comes to the computer during lunch, signs in to check email, and then signs out. After lunch, User1 returns, signs in, and continues to compose the Word document. Fast user switching allows this to happen. Without fast user switching, User1 would have been signed out automatically when User2 signed in and any unsaved work in the Word document would have been lost.

In environments where multiple users share the same computer, fast user switching is a very important feature. This is commonly desired in lab environments and for reception computers.

Automatic Sign-In   In some environments, it is desirable for the computer to automatically sign in as a specific user each time it is started. This is appropriate for libraries and other public locations where users are not assigned their own sign-in credentials. The term kiosk is sometimes used to refer to an environment where automatic sign-in is desired.

Automatic sign-in is configured on the Users tab of the User Accounts applet, shown in Figure 5-3. When you deselect the *Users must enter a user name and password to use this computer* check box and click OK, you are prompted for the credentials to be used for the automatic sign-in. From this point forward, Windows 10 automatically signs in using the credentials you specified.

When you need to do system maintenance on a computer with automatic sign-in enabled, you must stop the automatic sign-in from occurring. Holding down the Shift key during the boot process stops the automatic sign-in from occurring. Then you can sign in with your own credentials to perform the maintenance tasks. Alternatively, you can sign out after the user is automatically signed in to access the Windows sign-in screen.

Assigned Access   Assigned access is an advanced sign-in option for configuring Windows 10 as a kiosk. A kiosk is a computer in a public space that is dedicated for a single purpose. This can be used when a company has Windows 10 tablets being used for filling in surveys or when a public access computer is being used to search a catalog.

Figure 5-3   Enable automatic sign-in

When you enable assigned access, you select a local user account and a Windows Store app, as shown in Figure 5-4. At that point, the selected user account is limited to using that one app when signed in. Many normal functions such as closing the application are not possible.

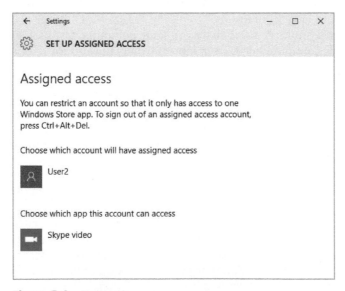

Figure 5-4   Assigned access

Although a wide range of Windows Store apps are available for many purposes, at the time of this writing, Microsoft has not made a web browser available as a Windows Store app.

Naming Conventions

A naming convention is a standard process for creating names on a network or stand-alone computer. Corporate environments establish a naming convention for user accounts, computers, folders, network shares, printers, and servers. Names should be descriptive enough that anyone can figure out what the resource is. For example, computer names are often the same as their asset tracking number (inventory tracking number) or include the name of the person who uses the computer most often.

Using a naming convention for small networks might seem unnecessary, but even small networks benefit from resources with meaningful names. For example, in a small network with two servers named "Files" and "Email," it is easy to guess what resources are on each server. In another network where the two servers are named "Sleepy" and "Dopey," there is no logical way to know what resources are on each server. If your network grows, you will be happy you implemented a naming convention early in the process.

Some common naming conventions for user names are:

- *First name*—In small environments, there is little risk that two users will have the same first name. This approach is easy for users to remember.

- *First name and last initial*—This naming convention helps ensure that user sign-in names are not duplicated. In small and mid-sized environments, if two users have the same first name, they are unlikely to have the same last initial.

- *First initial and last name*—Most large environments use this naming convention or a variation of it. Last names are more likely to be unique than first names, so this convention reduces the risk of duplicate user sign-in names.

No matter which naming convention you select, you must have a plan to deal with duplicate user sign-in names. For example, there might be Byron Wright and Blair Wright in the same organization. If your naming convention is first initial and last name, both users will have the same user sign-in name of "bwright." To fix this, you could add a numeral to the end of the second user account created, to make the user sign-in name "bwright2." You could also use two letters of the first name, in which case the user sign-in names would be "bywright" and "blwright."

When creating new local users, you must be aware of the restrictions imposed by Windows 10 on the user name, such as the following:

- *User names must be unique*—No two users can have the same sign-in name because the sign-in name is used by the computer to identify the user and verify the password associated with it during sign-in.

- *User names must be 20 characters or less*—This restriction is typically not a problem because no users want to type in a sign-in name of more than 20 characters.

- *User names are not case sensitive*—You cannot change the case of letters to create unique user sign-in names; Windows 10 reads any case changes as the original name. Also, users do not need to be concerned about case when they type in their user name. However, passwords are case sensitive.

- *User names cannot contain invalid characters*—Windows 10 uses some characters for special functions, so they cannot be used in user sign-in names. The invalid characters are: "/\[]:;|=,+*?<>.

Default User Accounts

Each Windows 10 computer has an **Administrator account** and a **Guest account** that are created during installation. The Administrator and Guest accounts are called built-in accounts because they are created on every Windows 10 computer. They also have unique characteristics. In addition, a user-specified **initial account** is created during installation. The initial account is not a built-in account.

Administrator   The Administrator account is the most powerful local user account possible. This account has unlimited access and unrestricted privileges to every aspect of Windows. The Administrator account can manage all security settings, other users, groups, the operating system, printers, shares, and storage devices. Because of these far-reaching privileges, the Administrator account must be protected from misuse.

The Administrator account has the following characteristics:

- It is not visible on the sign-in screen.
- It has a blank password by default.
- It cannot be deleted.
- It cannot be locked out due to incorrect sign-in attempts.
- It cannot be removed from the local Administrators group.
- It can be disabled.
- It can be renamed.

To protect the Administrator account from misuse, it is disabled by default in Windows 10. However, the Administrator account is automatically enabled when you enter Safe Mode so that you can use it for troubleshooting. Safe Mode is a boot option you can use when troubleshooting Windows 10.

Because the Administrator account is available only in Safe Mode, it is typically used only for troubleshooting or as an account of last resort when signing in.

The password for the Administrator account is blank by default. This password should be changed immediately after installation. This prevents users from starting in Safe Mode and signing in as Administrator. If users sign in as Administrator, they can perform any system action such as adding software, deleting files, creating a new account with administrative privileges, or increasing the privileges of an existing account.

Windows 10 restricts accounts with blank passwords to console access only. This means that no one can sign in over the network using an account with a blank password, including the Administrator account.

The Administrator account is special because it is considered an account of last resort for signing in and troubleshooting. Therefore, the Administrator account cannot be deleted or locked out after too many incorrect sign-in attempts. The Administrator account also cannot be removed from the local Administrators group because the local Administrators group is where the Administrator account derives most of its privileges.

Guest   The Guest account is one of the least privileged user accounts in Windows. This account has extremely limited access to resources and computer activities and is intended for occasional use by low-security users. For example, a company might have a computer in the lobby with Internet access for customers. The customers would sign in as a guest. The Guest account has no ability to change the computer settings.

The Guest account has the following characteristics:

- It cannot be deleted.
- It can be locked out.
- It is disabled by default.
- It has a blank password by default.
- It can be renamed.
- It is a member of the Guests group by default.
- It is a member of the Everyone group.

Most organizations have no need for a Guest account. To ensure that the Guest account is not accidentally assigned privileges that are used by anonymous users, the Guest account is disabled by default. This way, even if privileges are assigned to the Guest account by accident, no one can sign in as the Guest account and use those privileges.

The Guest account derives all of its privileges from being a member of the Guests group and the Everyone group. Both of these groups have very limited privileges. The Guests group is explicitly created for assigning permissions to Guest users. The Everyone group encompasses all users who have signed in, including the Guest account. Windows security has evolved so that the Everyone group has very limited privileges. Most privileges formerly assigned to the Everyone group are now assigned to the Authenticated Users group. Authenticated Users includes all users who have signed in except for the Guest account.

 If you enable the Guest account, the Everyone group includes anonymous users. This allows you to give users access to resources on a computer over the network without requiring a valid user name and password.

Initial Account   During installation, you are prompted for the information required to create a user. The user created from that information is given administrative privileges. Having administrative privileges means that the initial account created during installation is able to perform all of the same tasks as the Administrator account. The initial account can be used to configure Windows 10, including creating other user accounts.

Differences between the Administrator account and the initial account include the following:

- The initial account is visible on the sign-in screen.
- The initial account does not have a blank password by default.
- The initial account can be deleted.
- The initial account can be locked out due to incorrect sign-in attempts.
- The initial account can be removed from the Administrators group.

DefaultAccount   A new account in Windows 10 is DefaultAccount. This account is disabled and does not display on the sign-in screen and should not be modified in any way. DefaultAccount is undocumented and managed by Windows 10.

Default Groups

Groups are used to simplify the process of assigning security rights and permissions. When users are members of a group, they have access to all of the resources that the group has been given permissions to access. It is easier to assign permissions to a group and make five users a member of that group than to assign permissions directly to five users, particularly if the permissions change.

Windows has a number of **built-in local groups** that exist by default and cannot be deleted. These groups are assigned rights and permissions to Windows 10. Like local user accounts, local groups are stored in the SAM database and can only be assigned permissions to resources on the local computer.

The Windows 10 built-in groups are:

- *Access Control Assistance Operators*—Members of this group can access authorization attributes and permissions for resources on this computer remotely. There are not default members of this group.
- *Administrators*—Members of this group have full access to the computer. The local Administrator account is always a member of this group. The initial account created during installation is also a member of this group by default. If the computer has joined a domain, the Domain Admins group is a member of this group. Making Domain Admins a member of the local Administrators group provides centralized control of domain computers through a single sign-in.
- *Backup Operators*—Members of this group can back up and restore all files and folders on the computer. However, the ability to read and modify files is still controlled by file system security. Backup operators cannot automatically read and modify files; they must be assigned the necessary file permissions. By default, this group has no members.

- *Cryptographic Operators*—Members of this group are able to perform cryptographic operations. Only members of this group are able to modify encryption settings for IPSec in Windows Firewall when configured in Common Criteria mode. Common Criteria is a standard for security.

- *Distributed COM Users*—Members of this group are able to run and activate Distributed COM objects on the computer. This group is relevant only when using DCOM applications, which is relatively rare.

- *Event Log Readers*—Members of this group have the ability to read event logs on the local computer. You can add members to this group if you want them to be able to review the event logs for errors, but not have the ability to erase the logs.

- *Guests*—Members of this group have the same access to the system as members of the Users group. Members are able to sign in and save files, but are not able to change system settings or install programs. The exception to this is the Guest account, which has additional restrictions.

- *Hyper-V Administrators*—Members of this group can manage all aspects of Hyper-V on this computer.

- *IIS_IUSRS*—A group used to configure security for Internet Information Services (IIS). Only the system account NT AUTHORITY\IUSR is a member by default. The rights and permissions assigned to this group are applied to all IIS users who are not authenticated.

- *Network Configuration Operators*—Members can configure network components and change IP address information. This group is useful if you need to delegate the ability to change IP address configuration to other users, but do not want to give those users full administrative rights. By default, this group has no members.

- *Performance Log Users*—Members of this group are able to monitor performance counters and access performance logs on the computer. This group has no members by default. In a domain environment, domain users and groups can be added to this group to perform remote monitoring.

- *Performance Monitor Users*—Members of this group are able to monitor performance counters on the computer, but cannot access performance logs. This group has no members by default. In a domain environment, domain users and groups can be added to this group to perform remote monitoring.

- *Power Users*—Members of this group have almost all administrative permissions. It was common in previous versions of Windows to use this group for all users to ensure that they could make changes to their systems. In Windows 10, this group has been deprecated and Microsoft recommends using it only when necessary to support legacy applications that do not run when a user has lower privileges.

- *Remote Desktop Users*—Members of this group can sign in remotely by using Remote Desktop. This group has no members by default.

- *Remote Management Users*—Members of this group can query and configure Windows Management Instrumentation (WMI) objects over the network.

- *Replicator*—This group is used by special user accounts to perform file replication between computers. This group has no members by default.

- *System Managed Accounts Group*—Members of this group are managed by Windows 10 and should not be manually modified.

- *Users*—Members can operate the computer and save files, but cannot install programs, modify user accounts, share resources, or alter system settings. All user accounts created on the system are a member of this group by default. In addition, the system accounts NT AUTHORITY\Authenticated Users and NT AUTHORITY\INTERACTIVE are members of the group. In a domain environment, the Domain Users group is also a member.

Creating and Managing User Accounts

Creating a user can be done from Settings, Control Panel, or the **Local Users and Groups MMC snap-in.** The process varies depending on which tool is used, but the options are similar in each tool.

User accounts can also be created by using the *net user* command at a command prompt. However, this is rarely done. For more information, open a command prompt and type *net user /?*.

A **standard user account** derives its privileges from being a member of the local Users group. As a member of the local Users group, a user account can use software, but not install or remove software. A standard user also is not able to change computer settings that affect other users or delete operating system files. Effectively, a standard user cannot compromise the security or stability of Windows 10.

Some older software requires administrative rights to run properly. In this case, User Account Control prompts the user for the password of a user with administrative rights. To avoid being prompted for a password, you might want to make the user an administrative user.

An **administrator account** derives its privileges from being a member of the local Administrators group. Administrator accounts have complete access to the system. An administrator can make changes that compromise the stability and security of Windows 10, such as installing software, changing file system security, and updating device drivers.

In Windows 10, most actions that are triggered by an administrator do not result in a prompt from User Account Control. However, changes triggered by software do result in a prompt from User Account Control. This ensures that changes are not made by malicious software.

Accounts

From the Accounts settings, you manage your own user account and create additional user accounts. For your own account, you can switch authentication between a local account and a Microsoft account. When you switch between these options, your account settings remain the same and no data is lost. You are just changing the process used to sign in.

The wizard for adding new accounts starts by asking how the user will sign in. If you indicate that you don't have sign-in information for the user (the user's Microsoft account), you are prompted to create a Microsoft account for the user. If you don't want to use a Microsoft account for authentication, you can add a user without a Microsoft account.

Activity 5-2: Creating a Local User Account in Settings

Time Required: 10 minutes
Objective: Create a local user account

Description: Local user accounts are required to sign in to Windows 10. The Accounts window in Settings provides a simplified way to create accounts. In this activity, you create one user account that authenticates locally.

1. If necessary, start your computer and sign in.
2. Click the **Start** button and click **Settings.**
3. Click **Accounts** and click **Family & other users.**
4. Click **Add someone else to this PC.**
5. On the How will this person sign in screen, click **I don't have this person's sign-in information.**
6. On the Let's create your account screen, click **Add a user without a Microsoft account.**

7. On the Create an account for this PC screen, enter the following information and then click **Next**:

   • User name: **Bob**

   • Password: **password**

   • Password hint: **Like Activity 1-1**

8. Sign out as User*x* and sign in as Bob. Notice that it takes a few minutes to build Bob's profile during the first sign-in.

9. Click the **Start** button, click **Settings**, and click **Accounts**. Notice that the Family & other users option is not available because Bob is a standard user instead of an administrator.

10. Sign out as Bob.

Activity 5-3: Creating a Microsoft Account in Settings

Time Required: 10 minutes
Objective: Create a Microsoft account

Description: Microsoft accounts are an optional method for signing in to Windows 10. The Accounts window in Settings provides the option to create a new Microsoft account. In this activity, you create a user account that authenticates by using a Microsoft account.

1. If necessary, start your computer and sign in.

2. Click the **Start** button and click **Settings**.

3. Click **Accounts** and click **Family & other users**.

4. In the Accounts window, click **Add someone else to this PC**.

5. On the How will this person sign in screen, click **I don't have this person's sign-in information**.

6. On the Let's create your account screen, in the First name box, type your first name.

7. In the Last name box, type your last name.

8. Click **Get a new email address**.

9. In the New email box, type *yourfirstname.yourlastname*@outlook.com and press **Tab**.

10. If the email address is not available, try different combinations until the address is available.

11. In the Password box, type a password that you will remember. Use a strong password because the Microsoft account you are creating is accessible on the Internet.

12. Select the correct country, enter your birth date, and click **Next**.

13. On the Add security info screen, in the phone number box, type your phone number and click **Next**.

14. On the See what's most relevant to you screen, click **Next**. Notice that the new account has been added to the list of users.

15. Click the new account and click **Change account type**.

16. In the Change account type window, in the Account type box, select **Administrator** and click **OK**.

17. Sign out as User*x* and sign in as your Microsoft account.

18. When prompted to set up a PIN, click **Skip this step**.

19. On the Get your files here, there, and everywhere screen, click **Next**.

20. Click the **Start** button, click **Settings**, and click **Accounts**. Notice that the Family & other users option is available because the Microsoft account is an administrator instead of a standard user.

21. Sign out as your Microsoft account.

User Accounts Applet

In Windows 7, the preferred interface for creating and managing user accounts was the **User Accounts applet** in Control Panel. The User Accounts applet in Control Panel, shown in Figure 5-5, is still available in Windows 10, but has less functionality. For example, you cannot create a new user account in the User Accounts applet.

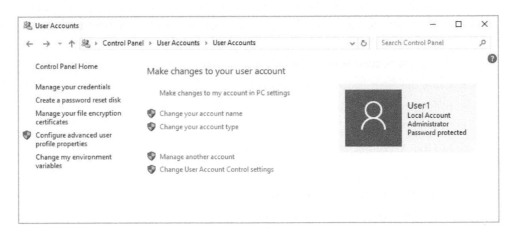

Figure 5-5   User Accounts applet in Control Panel

The administrative options with a shield beside them in the applet are restricted to administrative users. If a standard user tries to perform these tasks, the user is prompted to provide the credentials of an administrator account.

Administrative options for user accounts include the following:

- *Change your account name*—Allows administrators to change the account name of a user. This option is not available for the Administrator account.

- *Change your account type*—Allows administrators to change the user account from one type of account to another. For example, you can change a standard user to an administrative user.

- *Manage another account*—Allows administrators to select a different account to manage.

- *Change User Account Control settings*—Allows administrators to modify when prompts from User Account Control (UAC) are presented.

Additional available tasks include:

- *Manage your credentials*—This option opens the window for configuring Credential Manager. Credential Manager allows users to add, remove, and edit network locations with stored credentials. Network locations can include websites, FTP sites, and servers. Storing credentials avoids having to type in the credentials each time a resource is accessed. If your password for the resource changes, you need to edit the network location to change the password. In domain-based networks, this is not required to access domain resources.

- *Create a password reset disk*—This option creates a password reset disk. If users forget their password, the disk allows them to reset their password to a new password. Once created, a password reset disk does not need to be updated when the user password is changed. The password reset information is stored on a USB drive.

- *Manage your file encryption certificates*—This option allows users to manage the certificates used to support Encrypting File System (EFS). EFS encrypts specific files that are stored on the hard drive. Within this wizard, you can select or create a file encryption certificate, back up the certificate, configure EFS to use a smart card, and update a previously encrypted file to a new certificate.

- *Configure advanced user profile properties*—This option opens the dialog box that allows you to manage user profiles. For example, you can configure a roaming user profile. This option is seldom used.

- *Change my environment variables*—This option allows you to configure the environment variables for your computer that define characteristics such as the location of temporary files. This option is seldom used.

Activity 5-4: Using the User Accounts Applet

Time Required: 10 minutes
Objective: Manage a local user account by using the User Accounts applet in Control Panel

Description: You can use the User Accounts applet in Control Panel to manage existing user accounts. In this activity, you change a local user account to being an administrator from a standard account.

1. If necessary, start your computer and sign in.
2. Click the **Start** button, type **control**, and click **Control Panel**.
3. In Control Panel, click **User Accounts**.
4. In User Accounts, click **User Accounts**.
5. In User Accounts, click **Manage another account**.
6. In the Choose the user you would like to change box, click **Bob**.
7. Read the options you have for managing the account and click **Change the account type**.
8. In the Change Account Type window, click **Administrator** and click **Change Account Type**.
9. Close the Change an Account window.

Local Users and Groups MMC Snap-In

The Local Users and Groups MMC snap-in allows you to create and manage both user accounts and groups. The fastest way to access this snap-in is through the Computer Management Administrative Tool. The Users node contains all of the users and the Groups node contains all of the groups, as shown in Figure 5-6.

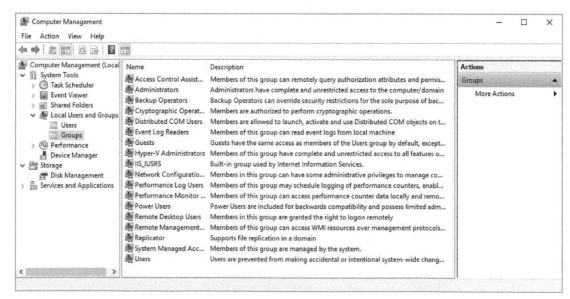

Figure 5-6   Local Users and Groups in Computer Management

The general user tasks you can perform are:

- Create a new user.
- Delete a user.
- Rename a user.
- Set a user password.

 Setting a user password is only relevant for local user accounts. Accounts that are authenticating by using a Microsoft account do not use a local password even though the option to reset the user's password appears in the interface.

Other user options can be configured in the properties of the user account. The General tab, shown in Figure 5-7, lets you view and configure the following:

- *Account name*—This information is displayed at the top of the tab but cannot be changed on this tab. To change the account name, you must right-click the user account and select Rename.

- *Full name*—This is the full name of the person using the account. This can be changed.

- *Description*—This is an optional text box that can be used to describe the purpose or use of the account.

- *User must change password at next logon*—This option forces users to change their password the next time they log on. Forcing a password change is common in corporate environments after a temporary password has been assigned.

- *User cannot change password*—This option prevents users from changing their passwords. Preventing a password change is often done for user accounts that are used as credentials for multiple services, such as scheduling system maintenance tasks. A password change would need to be updated on all services, and this ensures that it does not happen accidentally.

- *Password never expires*—This option exempts the user from the account policy that defines the maximum lifetime of a password. Preventing password expiry is useful for accounts that are used as credentials for services, such as scheduled tasks.

- *Account is disabled*—This option locks the account to prevent anyone from signing in and using the account. However, the account is retained and can be enabled again at any time. Disabling an account is often done when a user is away for an extended period of time. Disabling an account is also often done as an intermediary step before the account is deleted when a user leaves the organization.

- *Account is locked out*—This option is selected when an account is locked out because of too many incorrect sign-in attempts. When an account is locked, no one can sign in by using the account. To unlock the account and allow the user to sign in again, deselect this option.

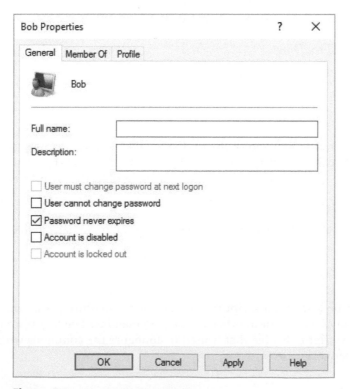

Figure 5-7   User Properties, General tab

The Member Of tab, shown in Figure 5-8, lists the groups of which the user account is a member. Any rights and permissions assigned to these groups are also given to the user account. You can add and remove the user account from groups on this tab. Be aware that changes in group membership do not take effect until the user has signed out and signed in again. This is because the security token that contains group memberships and is used to access resources is generated during sign-in.

Figure 5-8   User Properties, Member Of tab

The Profile tab is not typically used on stand-alone computers or workgroup members. Similar information is available for user accounts in a domain. It is much more common for these properties to be set in a domain.

This tab can be used to define:

• The location of a roaming user profile

• A logon script

• A home folder

The profile path specifies the location of the profile for this user. By default, profiles are stored in C:\Users\%USERNAME%, where %USERNAME% is a variable representing the name of the user account. If you specify a network location for the profile, the profile becomes a roaming user profile.

Detailed information about user profiles is provided later in this chapter.

The logon script box defines a script that is run each time during sign-in. This script can be located on the local computer or another workgroup member. The logon script is typically a batch (.bat) file or VBScript (.vbs) file that is used to configure the computer with mapped drive letters for accessing network shares.

The home folder defines a default location for saving files. If a network location is used as a home folder, a mapped drive letter is created that points to the network location. The default location for saving files is defined by the application being used. Some applications use the home folder, while others use the Documents folder. If you do not define a home folder, it resolves to the Users profile folder, for example, C:\Users\User1.

When you view the properties of a group, there is only a single tab, as shown in Figure 5-9. The General tab provides a description of the group and a list of the group members. You can add and remove users from the group here.

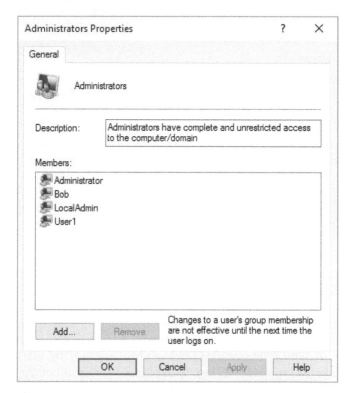

Figure 5-9 Group Properties

Activity 5-5: Using the Local Users and Groups MMC Snap-In

Time Required: 10 minutes

Objective: Manage users and groups by using the Local Users and Groups MMC snap-in

Description: The Local Users and Groups MMC snap-in is the only management tool for creating and managing groups. You can also use it for creating and managing users. The user management options in the Local Users and Groups MMC snap-in are more detailed than in the User Accounts applet. In this activity, you create a new user, create a new group, and place the new user in the new group.

1. If necessary, start your computer and sign in.

2. Right-click the **Start** button and click **Computer Management**.

3. In the left pane, expand **Local Users and Groups,** and click **Users**. Notice the users who are listed here: Administrator, Bob, DefaultAccount, Guest, LocalAdmin, User**x**, and your Microsoft account.

4. Right-click **Users** and then click **New User**.

5. In the User name box, type **Jacob**.

6. In the Full name box, type **Jacob Smith**.

7. In the Password and Confirm password boxes, type **password**. Notice that, by default, the User must change password at next logon check box is selected.

8. Click **Create** and then click **Close**.

9. In the left pane, click **Groups**. Notice all of the built-in groups that exist by default.

10. Right-click **Groups** and then click **New Group**.

11. In the Group name box, type **TestGroup**.

12. Click the **Add** button.

13. In the Enter the object names to select box, type **Jacob**, click **Check Names**, and click OK.

14. Click **Create** and then click **Close**.

15. In the left pane, click **Users**.

16. Right-click **Jacob** and then click **Properties**.

17. Click the **Member Of** tab. Notice that Jacob is a member of TestGroup and Users.

18. Click **Cancel** and close Computer Management.

19. Switch the user to **Jacob Smith**. Notice that you are given a message indicating that the password must be changed.

20. Click **OK**.

21. In the New password and Confirm password boxes, type **password2**, and then press **Enter**.

22. Click **OK**, click **Sign In**, and wait for the new profile to be created.

23. Sign out as Jacob.

Managing User Profiles

A **user profile** is a collection of desktop and environment configurations for a specific user or group of users. By default, each user has a separate profile stored in C:\Users. Many of the folders in the profile are not visible by default in File Explorer because they are marked as hidden or system files. You can change the view settings in File Explorer to make all of the folders visible.

A profile contains the following folders and information:

- *AppData*—A hidden folder containing user-specific information for applications, such as configuration settings.

- *Application Data*—A hidden shortcut to AppData for backward compatibility with Windows 2000 and Windows XP applications.

- *Contacts*—A folder to hold contacts and their properties. Contact properties include addresses, phone numbers, email addresses, and digital certificates. Contacts can be used by various applications, but the most common are email applications.

- *Cookies*—A hidden shortcut to the storage location for Internet Explorer cookies. This shortcut is for backward compatibility with previous versions of Internet Explorer. Microsoft Edge uses a location in the AppData folder for cookies.

- *Desktop*—A folder that contains all of the shortcuts and files on the user desktop.

- *Documents*—A folder that is typically the default location for saving documents.

- *Downloads*—A folder that is used to store files and programs downloaded from the Internet.

- *Favorites*—A folder that holds Internet Explorer favorites. Microsoft Edge uses a location in the AppData folder for favorites.

- *Links*—A folder in Windows 8 that contained links that were displayed as Favorites in File Explorer. This folder is not used by File Explorer in Windows 10.

- *Local Settings*—A hidden shortcut that is included for backward compatibility with Windows 2000 and Windows XP applications.

- *Music*—A folder for storing music files.
- *My Documents*—A hidden shortcut that is included for backward compatibility with Windows 2000 and Windows XP applications.
- *NetHood*—A hidden shortcut to a location storing user-specific network information such as drive mappings. This is included for backward compatibility.
- *OneDrive*—A folder that is synchronized with cloud storage in Microsoft OneDrive. All Microsoft accounts are allocated storage space online in OneDrive.
- *Pictures*—A folder for storing picture files. It appears as My Pictures in Windows Explorer.
- *PrintHood*—A hidden shortcut to a location storing user-specific printing information such as network printers. This is included for backward compatibility.
- *Recent*—A hidden shortcut to a location storing shortcuts to recently used documents. This is included for backward compatibility.
- *Saved Games*—A folder for storing saved games that are in progress.
- *Searches*—A folder that stores saved search queries so that they can easily be accessed again.
- *SendTo*—A hidden shortcut to the location storing shortcuts that appear in the Send To menu when right-clicking a data file. This is included for backward compatibility.
- *Start Menu*—A hidden shortcut to the location storing the shortcuts and folders that appear in the Start menu. This is included for backward compatibility.
- *Templates*—A hidden shortcut to the location storing application templates, such as Word document templates. This is included for backward compatibility.
- *Videos*—A folder for storing videos.
- *Ntuser.dat*—A file that stores user-specific registry information.
- *Ntuser.dat.logx*—A file that tracks changes in Ntuser.dat. This file is used to recover Ntuser.dat if the system shuts down unexpectedly.
- *Ntuser.dat{guid}.tm.blf*—A temporary file used for controlling registry changes.
- *Ntuser.ini*—A file that controls which portions of a profile are not to be copied up to a server when roaming profiles are enabled.

In addition to the details of an individual profile, you should understand the following:

- The default profile
- Mandatory profiles
- Roaming profiles
- Folder redirection
- The public profile
- Start menu configuration

The Default Profile

The **default profile** is used when new user profiles are created. When a new user signs in for the first time, Windows 10 copies the default user profile to create a profile for the new user. The folder structure in the default profile is the same as a user profile. However, the folders are empty by default.

In older versions of Windows such as Windows XP, you created a consistent environment for users by configuring the default profile on each computer to be the same. In a modern computer network, it is rare to manually configure the default profile. Instead, you should use centralized management tools such as Group Policy to enforce consistent settings on computers.

Although you can see user profiles in the file system, you cannot copy them using File Explorer. If you copy a profile using File Explorer, the security permissions are incorrect, and the user experiences many errors. If you want to configure the default profile, the only supported method is by using Sysprep.

To configure the default profile:

1. If desired, create a new local user with administrative privileges to allow for creation of a blank user profile. Domain users are not supported.

2. Sign in as the designated local user with administrative privileges.

3. Modify the user's profile as desired and delete all other user profiles. You must delete the other profiles to ensure that the correct user profile is copied.

4. Create an answer file with the CopyProfile parameter set to true.

5. Run Sysprep with the /generalize option and specify the location of the answer file.

6. Image the computer and deploy the image. When the image is started after deployment, the default user profile is created from the profile of local user account used in the preceding steps.

There are many online blog postings where users are complaining about inconsistent functionality of CopyProfile with Windows 10. Instead of configuring a default profile, use Group Policy to provide consistent user settings. This is preferable to a default profile because you can update Group Policy settings at any time. A default profile is only applicable when a user signs in to a computer the first time and a new profile is created.

Mandatory Profiles

A **mandatory profile** is a profile that cannot be modified. Users can make changes to their desktop settings while they are signed in, but the changes are not saved. This means that if there is a configuration problem, all the user needs to do is sign out and sign back in to get pristine settings again.

You can implement mandatory profiles for a single user that is causing problems or for a group of users. Most times, a single consistent desktop is implemented for a group of users. Most mandatory profiles are implemented as roaming user profiles.

To change a profile to a mandatory profile, you rename the file Ntuser.dat to Ntuser.man. After this change is made, user modifications to the profile are not saved.

If you implement mandatory profiles, you need to ensure that users are aware that any files that they save to their Desktop or Documents folders are lost when they sign out.

Roaming Profiles

A **roaming profile** is stored in a network location rather than on the local hard drive. The main benefit of roaming profiles is that settings move with a user from computer to computer on the network. Typically, roaming profiles are used in large corporations where users move among different computers each day, such as a call center.

When roaming user profiles are in place, users have a consistent work environment regardless of which computer they sign in at. This means that any customization application settings and configuration files move with the user between computers.

To configure a roaming profile, you must edit the user account to point the profile directory at a network location. Then you copy the existing user profile up to the network location.

Each time a user signs in, the roaming profile is copied to the local computer. If a user signs in and cannot contact the server with the roaming profile, the local copy of the profile is used.

Many administrators prefer not to implement roaming user profiles for the following reasons:

- *Slow sign-in and sign-out*—If users store large files in their user profile, sign-in and sign-out are slow. The slowness is caused because the user profile is copied over the network each time the user signs in and signs out.

- *Corrupted profiles*—Although not as common as with older versions of Windows, roaming user profiles can become corrupted. When a profile is corrupted, users are signed in with a temporary profile and do not have access to their normal settings. Intervention by an administrator is required to remove the corrupted profile.

Folder Redirection

Most organizations that want the ability to roam between computers implement **folder redirection**. Folder redirection lets you specify a network location for specific profile folders as an alternative to storing the data on the local client. Because the folders are redirected rather than copied, there is no impact on the speed of signing in or signing out. To users, the redirected folders appear and function the same as if the folder were stored locally.

You can combine folder redirection with roaming profiles to mitigate the shortcomings of roaming profiles. Redirecting folders avoids the slow sign-in and sign-out process that can occur with large files. Profile corruption is also minimized because the sign-out process is faster and access to the registry is more likely to be terminated properly during sign-out.

You can manually redirect some folders, such as Documents, as shown in Figure 5-10. However, in most cases, folder redirection is implemented by using Group Policy.

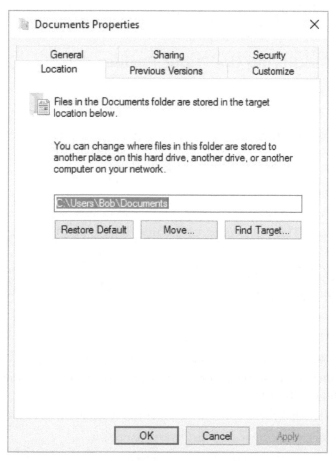

Figure 5-10   Folder redirection for Documents

The Public Profile

The **public profile** is different from other profiles because it is not a complete profile. The public profile does not include an Ntuser.dat file and consequently does not include any registry settings. The public profile is a series of folders. The content of these folders is merged into the profiles of other users when they sign in. For example, shortcuts or files placed in the Public Desktop Folder are placed on the desktop of each user. Many applications place a shortcut in the

Public Desktop Folder as part of installation to make it available to all users. Only users with administrative permission can modify the contents of the Public profile.

The public profile includes the following folders:

- *Libraries*—Libraries stored here do not appear in user profiles, but are available to all users in File Explorer.
- *Public Account Pictures*—Pictures selected by users for display with their user accounts are stored here.
- *Public Desktop*—Files and shortcuts stored here appear on the desktop of each user.
- *Public Documents*—Files stored here appear in the Documents library of each user.
- *Public Downloads*—Files stored here do not appear in profiles, but the files in it are available to all users.
- *Public Music*—Files stored here appear in the Music library of each user.
- *Public Pictures*—Files stored here appear in the Pictures library of each user.
- *Public Recorded TV*—This folder is used to store recorded television programs for personal video recorder (PVR) functionality. This folder does not appear in user profiles, but the files in it are available to all users.
- *Public Videos*—Files stored here appear in the Videos folder of each user.

Activity 5-6: Modifying the Public Profile

Time Required: 5 minutes
Objective: Modify the public profile and see how it affects users

Description: The public profile is merged into the profile of all users. Adding content to the public profile means that the content is available to all users. In this activity, you place a file in the Public Documents folder, which makes it available to all users.

1. If necessary, start your computer and sign in.
2. On the taskbar, click **File Explorer**.
3. In the left pane, expand **This PC**, expand **Local Disk (C:)**, expand **Users**, expand **Public**, and click **Public Documents**.
4. In the right pane, right-click an open area, point to **New**, and then click **Shortcut**.
5. In the Type the location of the item box, type **C:\Windows\notepad.exe** and click **Next**.
6. In the Type a name for this shortcut box, type **Notepad** and click **Finish**.
7. Right-click the **Notepad** shortcut and click **Cut**.
8. In the File Explorer address bar, type **C:\Users\Public\Desktop** and press **Enter**.
9. Right-click an empty area and click **Paste**. Notice that even an administrative user is prompted for permission to copy files here.
10. Click **Continue**. Notice that there is now a shortcut to Notepad on your desktop.
11. Double-click the **Notepad** shortcut on your desktop to test it.
12. Close Notepad.
13. Close File Explorer.

The Start Menu

In Windows 7, the Start menu was a collection of folders and shortcuts to applications. You could modify the Start menu by creating folders and shortcuts. In Windows 10, you cannot manually create folders and shortcuts in the Start menu. Instead, for your own profile, you can add and remove programs from the Start menu by right-clicking the program and pinning it to the Start menu. You can also create your own groups in the Start menu to organize items.

If your organization uses Windows 10 Enterprise or Windows 10 Education, you can use Group Policy to customize the Start screen. The layout of the Start menu is defined by an XML file that you create. The XML file is stored in a central location and the Group Policy points computers at the XML file. You can apply a full Start layout, which users cannot modify, or a partial Start layout, in which the specified groups cannot be modified but other groups can.

You can also customize the Start menu by using Windows Imaging and Configuration Designer (ICD). Windows ICD can create provisioning packages that configure a customized Start layout. The provisioning packages that customize the Start layout can also only be applied to Windows 10 Enterprise or Windows 10 Education.

For detailed information about customizing the Start layout, search for Manage Windows 10 Start layout options at *http://technet.microsoft.com*.

5

Activity 5-7: Customizing the Start Layout

Time Required: 10 minutes
Objective: Modify the Start layout and see how it affects users

Description: You can customize the Start menu for Windows 10 Enterprise and Windows 10 Education editions. In this activity, you customize the Start menu and then export it so that it can be used on other computers. You also test applying the Start layout by using a local Group Policy.

1. If necessary, start your computer and sign in.
2. Click the **Start** button, type **Notepad**, right-click **Notepad**, and click **Pin to Start.**
3. Click the **Start** button, move the mouse pointer above Notepad, and click **Name group.**
4. Type **Tools** and press **Enter.**
5. Click **Tools** and drag it above Life at a glance.
6. Click the **Start** button, type **Computer**, right-click **Computer Management**, and click **Pin to Start.**
7. Click the **Start** button and drag **Computer Management** to the **Tools** group.
8. Click the **Start** button, type **PowerShell**, right-click **Windows PowerShell**, and click **Pin to Start.**
9. Click the **Start** button and drag **Windows PowerShell** to the **Tools** group.
10. Click **Windows PowerShell.**
11. At the Windows PowerShell prompt, type **md C:\Start** and press **Enter.**
12. Type **Export-StartLayout –Path C:\Start\Start.xml** and press **Enter.**
13. Type **notepad.exe C:\Start\Start.xml** and press **Enter.**
14. Review the contents of the file and close Notepad.
15. Click **Start**, type **mmc**, and click **mmc.**
16. In the User Account Control dialog box, click **Yes.**
17. In the Console1 window, click **File** and click **Add/Remove Snap-in.**
18. In the Add or Remove Snap-ins window, click **Group Policy Object Editor**, click **Add**, click **Finish,** and click **OK.**
19. In the Console1 window, browse to **\Local Computer Policy\User Configuration\ Administrative Templates\Start Menu and Taskbar** and double-click **Start Layout.**
20. In the Start Layout window, click **Enabled.**

21. In the Start Layout File box, type **C:\Start\Start.xml** and click **OK**.
22. Leave the Console1 window open.
23. Switch users to your Microsoft account.
24. Click the **Start** button and verify that the Tools group is there.
25. Sign out of your Microsoft account and sign in as User*x*.
26. In the Console1 window, double-click **Start Layout**, click **Disabled**, and click **OK**.
27. Close all open windows.

After disabling the customized Start layout, user profiles with the customized layout will retain it but are now able to edit it.

Advanced Authentication Methods

Windows 10 includes advanced authentication methods to make using your computer more convenient and more secure. PIN or picture password authentication allows you to sign in with unique information other than your user name and password. Biometric authentication allows you to sign in based on facial recognition, fingerprints, or iris scanning.

When you use a user name and password to authenticate to Windows 10, there is a risk that the user name and password could be stolen. They can be stolen by someone watching over your shoulder when you sign in. They can also be stolen by keylogging malware installed on your computer. After your credentials are stolen, an unauthorized person can use your credentials to get access to all of your resources. Advanced authentication methods avoid this problem because you no longer type in your user name and password.

Multifactor authentication increases security by requiring you to have a thing in addition to a user name and password. The advanced authentication methods add multifactor authentication because they are unique to the device you are authenticating on. For example, if you enable PIN-based authentication, the PIN you select is different for each device. If someone steals your PIN, that person also needs your device for that information to be useful. In the case of biometric authentication, the thing is you.

Picture Password

After **picture password authentication** is configured, to sign in, you perform gestures on a picture that you have selected. To configure picture password authentication, you need to select a picture and then provide gestures on that picture. The gestures are typically going to be tracing out significant features on the picture, but they can be any gesture that you like.

When you configure picture password authentication, it is unique for each computer or device. Knowing your gestures and picture are only useful if someone also gets physical access to your device. Malware is unable to capture and use this information.

PIN

Configuring **PIN authentication** provides similar benefits to picture password authentication. When you configure PIN authentication, you provide a unique PIN for authenticating instead of your user name and password. This PIN is unique to a specific computer. Knowing the PIN is only useful if someone also gets physical access to your device.

Activity 5-8: Configuring PIN Authentication

Time Required: 10 minutes

Objective: Configure PIN authentication for a user

Description: PIN authentication enhances security in Windows 10 by avoiding reuse of a user name and password. In this activity, you enable and test PIN authentication for a user.

1. If necessary, start your computer and sign in.
2. Click the **Start** button and click **Settings**.
3. Click **Accounts** and click **Sign-in options**.
4. Under PIN, click **Add**.
5. In the First, verify your account password window, type **password** (or your password) and click **OK**.
6. In the Set up a PIN window, in the New PIN and Confirm PIN boxes, type **123456** and click **OK**.
7. Sign out and sign back in by using your PIN.
8. Click the **Start** button and click **Settings**.
9. Click **Accounts** and click **Sign-in options**.
10. Under PIN, click **Remove**.
11. Read the message about removing the PIN and click **Remove**.
12. In the First, verify your account password window, type **password** (or your password) and click **OK**.
13. Close all open windows.

Windows Hello

Biometric authentication has long been available for Microsoft operating systems. Many mobile computers include fingerprint readers that were compatible with Windows XP and even earlier versions of Windows. As new versions of Windows were released, Microsoft enhanced the operating system support for biometric authentication. This made it easier for manufacturers of biometric readers to develop drivers because the operating system provided specific support for the process. In Windows 10, **Windows Hello** is the latest level of support for biometric authentication.

Windows Hello supports the following biometric authentication methods:

- *Fingerprint*—To authenticate with a fingerprint, you place your finger on a fingerprint reader (or swipe, depending on the type of reader).

- *Facial recognition*—To authenticate with facial recognition, you place your face in front of the camera. This can happen immediately when you sit down in front of your computer.

- *Iris scanning*—To authenticate with iris scanning, you place your eye in front of the computer camera. Depending on the camera, this can be done at a distance such as several feet away. So, the experience is similar to facial recognition.

To make biometric authentication more secure, Windows Hello requires biometric readers to have advanced functionality to ensure accurate authentication. For example, cameras for facial recognition need to have infrared support (which prevents someone from using a picture of you to sign in). Consequently, most biometric readers available before the release of Windows 10 are not compatible with Windows Hello. If you want to use Windows Hello, verify that any new biometric readers are compatible.

Before you enable Windows Hello, you need to configure PIN authentication. PIN authentication is used as a backup authentication method if biometric authentication fails.

When Windows Hello is enabled, you need to provide your biometric information during configuration. However, Windows Hello does not store a picture of your fingerprint, face, or iris. Instead, Windows Hello stores information about the unique pattern that your biometric information provides. This ensures that data from Windows Hello cannot be used to re-create your biometric information.

In domain-based networks, Windows Hello is not dependent on the user password. If the password for the user is reset in the domain, Windows Hello can still be used for authentication without any user intervention. This also applies for PIN and picture password authentication.

Microsoft Passport

Many people use the same user name and password for Windows and multiple websites. In such a case, your credentials are only as secure as the weakest website. If your credentials are stolen from a website, an unauthorized person can reuse them for other websites. If you have reused the same user name and password for Windows 10, the stolen credentials can be used to sign in to the corporate network.

Microsoft Passport is a new authentication system in Windows 10 that leverages Windows Hello to avoid credential reuse in multiple locations. Each identity provider that supports Microsoft Password identifies you by using a unique certificate with a public key and private key. The identity provider, such as a website, retains the public key while Windows 10 retains the private key. Access to the private key in Windows 10 is secured by Windows Hello. When you access an identity provider, Windows Hello authenticates you and then uses the private key to verify your identity with the identity provider holding the corresponding public key.

If your computer has a **trusted platform module (TPM)**, the private keys for Microsoft Passport are stored in the TPM. If no TPM is present, the private keys are stored and secured by software. A TPM is a chip on the motherboard of a computer that is used to store encryption keys and certificates. Not all computers have a TPM.

Smart Cards

You can use smart cards as another form of multifactor authentication in Windows 10. A **smart card** contains a certificate that is used for authentication in much the same way as Microsoft Passport. However, smart card authentication is applicable only to signing in to Windows and not additional resources such as websites.

To use smart cards for authentication, each computer must have a smart card reader. You also need to install and configure a certification authority to issue the certificates that are stored on the smart cards. The cost of hardware and relatively high complexity of smart cards has prevented most organizations from implementing smart cards even though they have been supported since Windows 2000.

When users sign in by using a smart card, they first need to put the smart card in the smart card reader. Then, the user is prompted to enter a PIN number that is associated with the smart card. The PIN number is required to access the certificate on the smart card.

Windows 8 and newer versions of Windows also have the ability to use virtual smart cards. A **virtual smart card** stores the certificate in the TPM of the computer instead of on a physical smart card. However, like a physical smart card, the user needs to enter a PIN to use the virtual smart card.

When a virtual smart card is present in a computer, it functions like a smart card that is permanently attached to the computer. To authenticate by using the smart card at the sign-in screen, you need to select the correct sign-in option and then provide the PIN.

Virtual smart cards can be created by using the same certificate infrastructure that you would use for physical smart cards. However, you can also use the Tpmvscmgr.exe command-line tool. To use Tpmvscmgr.exe, you must have administrative rights on the computer.

Smart card sign-in can only be used in domain-based networks.

Network Integration

Additional considerations must be taken into account when you place Windows 10 on a network and want to interact with other network users. User sign-in and authorization is very different in a networked environment. A networked environment requires you to understand the configuration of the local computer and other networked computers. You need to understand both peer-to-peer and domain-based network types. You should also understand how cached credentials work in Windows 10.

Peer-to-Peer Networks

A **peer-to-peer network** (or workgroup) consists of multiple Windows computers that share information. No computer on the network serves as a central authoritative source of user information. Each computer maintains a separate list of users and groups in its own SAM database. Figure 5-11 shows a peer-to-peer network.

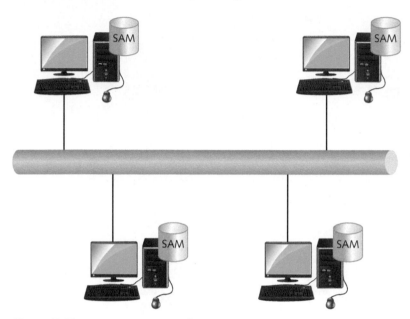

Figure 5-11   Peer-to-peer network

This type of network is most commonly implemented in homes and small offices. Windows 10 has a limit of 20 concurrent connections, which makes it impractical for sharing files and printers in larger environments.

In a peer-to-peer network, when you access shares or printers on a remote computer, you must authenticate as a user that exists on the remote computer. In most cases, it is preferred that the remote computer has a user account with the exact same name and password as the local machine. This allows **pass-through authentication** to occur. Pass-through authentication occurs when Windows attempts to authenticate to a remote resource by using the local Windows credentials to sign in to the remote computer. This requires a user account with the same user name and password to exist on the remote computer.

Pass-through authentication is the simplest authentication method for users. However, managing the user accounts and passwords on each computer is difficult. There is no automated mechanism to synchronize user accounts and passwords between computers in a peer-to-peer network. As a consequence, security management for peer-to-peer networks is progressively more difficult as the number of computers expands.

Newer authentication methods, such as Windows Hello, PIN, picture password, and Microsoft accounts, do not work with pass-through authentication because you are no longer using a local password to authenticate and you cannot synchronize the alternate credentials.

Windows 10 includes the homegroup feature to simplify the configuration of peer-to-peer networks. A homegroup removes the need to synchronize users and passwords on each computer by using a password for the homegroup instead.

More information about homegroups is available in Chapter 7, Networking.

Domain-Based Networks

User accounts for **domain-based networks** are much easier to manage than user accounts for peer-to-peer networks. A central server called a domain controller is responsible for maintaining user accounts and computer accounts. All computers in the domain share the user accounts on the domain controller. So, user accounts only need to be created once and there are no concerns about synchronizing passwords between multiple accounts. Figure 5-12 shows a domain-based network.

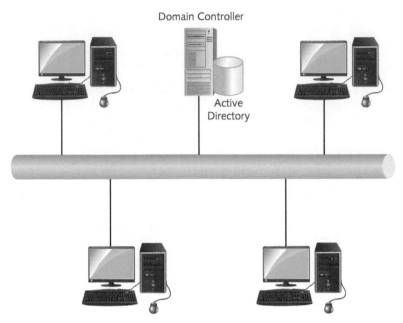

Figure 5-12   Domain-based network

To participate in a domain, Windows 10 computers are joined to the domain. The joining process creates a computer account for the Windows 10 computer and integrates Windows 10 security with the domain. The Domain Admins group becomes a member of the local Administrators group to allow centralized administration by the domain administrators. The Domain Users group becomes a member of the local Users group to allow all users in the domain to sign in to Windows 10.

Cached Credentials

When you use Windows 10 and sign in to a domain, your authentication credentials are automatically cached in Windows 10. This **cached credentials** capability is important for mobile computers that are not always connected to the domain. After credentials are cached locally, you can sign in to a computer using a domain user account, even when the domain cannot be contacted. For example, users with mobile computers can sign in with their domain account when on the road at a client site or at home.

By default, the credentials of the last 10 users to sign in are cached. However, if required, you can increase this up to 50 users, or disable cached credentials entirely. You might want to disable cached credentials because there are known methods for decrypting cached credentials if you are able to sign in as an administrator of the local computer.

 Cached credentials can be disabled by editing the local Group Policy object or by applying a domain-based Group Policy object.

Cached credentials are also used when you select to sign in with a Microsoft account in non-domain networks. Cached credentials for Microsoft accounts ensure that you can sign in when your computer does not have access to the Internet.

Chapter Summary

- User accounts are required for users to sign in to Windows 10 and use resources on that computer. Local user accounts are stored in the SAM database of each computer. You can authenticate by using local credentials or a Microsoft account.

- Windows 10 sign-in security can be enhanced by enabling secure sign-in.

- Fast user switching allows multiple users to be signed in to a computer at the same time.

- For kiosk computers, you can configure automatic sign-in and assigned access. Both features simplify using a kiosk computer.

- Three default accounts are created upon installation of Windows 10: Administrator, Guest, and the initial user account. The Administrator account does not have a password, but cannot be accessed remotely over the network. The initial user account is configured as an administrator. The DefaultAccount is also created during installation, but should not be modified in any way because it is undocumented and used by Windows 10.

- Groups help to simplify management by organizing users. Many built-in groups are created by default. The Administrators group and the Users group are the most commonly used.

- User accounts can be created from Settings, Control Panel, or the User and Groups MMC snap-in. The Accounts settings provide access to the current function, such as Microsoft accounts that older tools do not recognize. The User Accounts applet in Control Panel can still be used for managing users, but it is not preferred. The Local Users and Groups MMC snap-in allows you to manage users and groups.

- User profiles store user-specific settings. Profiles contain a number of folders and an Ntuser.dat file. New profiles are based on the default profile and are created the first time a user signs in. The default location for user profiles is C:\Users.

- You can modify profiles to make them mandatory or roaming. Mandatory profiles cannot be modified by users. Roaming profiles move with users when they sign in to different computers. Folder redirection is generally preferred to roaming user profiles. Information in the public profile is applied to all users.

- You can modify the Start menu by using an XML file defined in Group Policy. You can also use Windows ICD to create a provisioning package that modifies the Start menu.

- Windows 10 includes advanced authentication methods to increase security by tying authentication to a specific device. Picture password and PIN authentication can be implemented without any special hardware. Windows Hello requires biometric readers that meet the strict requirements of Windows Hello. You can use smart cards and virtual smart cards in a domain environment.

- In a peer-to-peer network, each computer authenticates users by using the local SAM database. User accounts and passwords are not synchronized between computers automatically.

- In a domain-based network, user authentication is controlled centrally by a domain controller. Credentials are cached at first sign-in, so users can sign in even if a domain controller cannot be contacted.

Key Terms

administrator account   The type of user account that is made a member of the Administrators local group and has full rights to the system.

Administrator account   The built-in Windows 10 account that is created during installation and has full rights to the system. This account cannot be deleted or removed by the Administrators group.

assigned access   A sign-in option that you can configure for a single local user account that restricts the user to using only an assigned Windows Store app; often used to configure Windows 10 as a kiosk.

biometric authentication   Authentication that is based on physical characteristics of the user, such as a fingerprint or facial recognition.

built-in local groups   Groups that are automatically created for each Windows 10 computer and stored in the SAM database.

cached credentials   Credentials that are stored in Windows 10 after a user has signed in to a domain or Microsoft account. Cached credentials can be used to sign in when a domain controller cannot be contacted or when there is no network connectivity.

default profile   The profile that is copied when new user profiles are created.

domain-based network   A network where security information is stored centrally in Active Directory.

fast user switching   A sign-in method that allows multiple users to have applications running at the same time. However, only one user can be using the console at a time.

folder redirection   A feature that redirects profile folders from the local computer to a network location.

Guest account   A built-in Windows 10 account with minimal privileges intended to give very limited access to Windows 10. This account is disabled by default.

initial account   The account with administrative privileges created during the installation of Windows 10.

local user account   A user account that is defined in the SAM database of a Windows 10 computer. Local user accounts are valid only for the local computer.

Local Users and Groups MMC snap-in   An MMC snap-in that is used to manage users and groups.

mandatory profile   A profile that cannot be changed by users. Ntuser.dat is renamed to Ntuser.man.

Microsoft account   An account that is stored online by Microsoft. You can use it to authenticate to multiple Microsoft cloud services and Windows 10.

Microsoft Passport   A multifactor authentication system in Windows 10 that enhances security by avoiding the use of a user name and password. Biometric authentication on the client allows access to the remote system.

Ntuser.dat   The file containing user-specific registry entries in a user profile.

pass-through authentication   Automatic authentication to a remote resource when the local computer passes the local credentials to the remote computer.

peer-to-peer network   A network where all computers store their own security information and share data.

picture password authentication   An authentication method where you trace gestures on a picture.

PIN authentication   An authentication method where you enter a device-specific PIN rather than a user name and password.

public profile   A profile that is merged with all other user profiles. The public profile does not contain an Ntuser.dat file.

roaming profile   A user profile that is stored in a network location and is accessible from multiple computers. Roaming profiles move with users from computer to computer.

secure sign-in   A sign-in method that adds the requirement to press Ctrl+Alt+Delete before signing in.

Security Accounts Manager (SAM) database   The database used by Windows 10 to store local user and group information.

security identifier (SID)   A user- or group-specific number that is added to the access control list of a resource when a user or group is assigned access.

smart card   A physical card containing a certificate that can be used as an authentication method.

standard user account   A type of user account that does not have privileges to modify settings for other users. This type of account is a member of the Users local group.

trusted platform module (TPM)   A chip on the motherboard of a computer that is designed to securely store encryption keys and certificates.

user account   Required account used for authentication to prove the identity of a person signing in to Windows 10.

User Accounts applet A legacy interface for user management in Control Panel.

user profile A collection of desktop and environment configurations for a specific user or group of users. By default, each user has a separate profile stored in C:\Users.

virtual smart card An authentication method similar to a smart card, but the certificate is stored in a TPM on the motherboard rather than on a physical card.

Windows Hello Biometric authentication functionality in Windows 10. At release, Windows Hello supported fingerprints, facial recognition, and iris scanning.

Review Questions

5

1. Local user accounts are stored in the SAM database. True or False?

2. Each user account is assigned a(n) _____ to ensure that security is kept intact if the account is renamed.

3. How do you reset the password for a Microsoft account?

   a. A local administrator can reset the password in the User Accounts applet in Control Panel.

   b. The user needs to reset the password on the Microsoft website for Microsoft accounts.

   c. Use a password reset disk.

   d. A local administrator can reset the password in Accounts settings.

   e. A local administrator can reset the password by using the Local Users and Groups MMC snap-in.

4. Which sign-in method requires users to press Ctrl+Alt+Delete before signing in?

   a. assigned access

   b. secure sign-in

   c. fast user switching

   d. automatic sign-in

5. Which sign-in method allows multiple users to have applications running on the computer at the same time?

   a. assigned access

   b. secure sign-in

   c. fast user switching

   d. automatic sign-in

6. Which characters are not allowed in user account names? (Choose all that apply.)

   a. \

   b. 1

   c. $

   d. *

   e. !

7. Because user names are case sensitive, you can use capitalization to ensure that they are unique. True or False?

8. Which characteristics apply to the Administrator account? (Choose all that apply.)

   a. It has a blank password by default.

   b. It cannot be deleted.

   c. It cannot be renamed.

   d. It is visible on the sign-in screen.

   e. It can be locked out.

9. Which characteristics apply to the Guest account? (Choose all that apply.)

    a. It has a blank password by default.

    b. It cannot be deleted.

    c. It cannot be renamed.

    d. It is disabled by default.

    e. It can be locked out.

10. Because the initial user account created during installation is a member of the Administrators group, it has all of the characteristics of the Administrator account. True or False?

11. Standard users are members of which built-in local group?

    a. Administrators

    b. Guests

    c. Remote Desktop Users

    d. Users

12. Which user management tool is required to assign a logon script to a user?

    a. User Accounts in Control Panel

    b. Local Users and Groups MMC snap-in

    c. Advanced User Accounts applet

    d. Advanced Users and Groups MMC snap-in

13. Which file in a profile contains user-specific registry settings?

    a. AppData

    b. Ntuser.dat

    c. Ntuser.man

    d. System.dat

    e. Local Settings

14. Which profile is copied to create a profile for new user accounts?

    a. Default User

    b. Public

    c. Blank

    d. Default

    e. New

15. A roaming profile is located on a network server. True or False?

16. Which profile is merged into each user profile when the user is signed in?

    a. Default User

    b. Public

    c. Blank

    d. Default

    e. New

17. After you set a PIN for a domain account on your laptop, that PIN can be used only on your laptop. True or False?

18. Which authentication method can use a fingerprint scanner to authenticate users?

    a. Microsoft account

    b. domain account

    c. Windows Hello

    d. Microsoft Passport

    e. smart card

19. In a domain-based network, each server authenticates users by using the SAM database. True or False?

20. The _____ group becomes a member of the Administrators local group when a Windows 10 computer joins a domain.

Case Projects

Case Project 5-1: Network Integration

You are an IT manager at Gigantic Life Insurance. You have a new desktop support person starting today whose experience is limited to supporting peer-to-peer networks. What do you need to tell him about how Windows 10 integrates into a domain-based network?

Case Project 5-2: Public Use Computer

Buddy's Machine Shop has a lounge for customers to wait in while their parts are being retrieved. Sometimes customers arrive a little early and have to wait up to an hour for their parts to be ready. Buddy has decided that it would be nice to give waiting customers Internet access. Describe how you would configure Windows 10 for public use.

Case Project 5-3: Secure Authentication Methods

At the most recent staff meeting of Hyperactive Media Sales, the general manager gave you instructions to make the laptops used by the salespeople as secure as possible. You have decided to implement a new advanced sign-in process for the users. How will you explain to the general manager how using new authentication methods makes the laptops more secure?

chapter 6

Windows 10 Security Features

After reading this chapter and completing the exercises, you will be able to:

- Use the local security policy to secure Windows 10
- Enable auditing to record security events
- Describe and configure User Account Control
- Describe the malware security features in Windows 10
- Use the data security features in Windows 10
- Secure Windows 10 by using Windows Update

Security is a fundamental consideration for how you configure Windows 10. Computers that are not secure are susceptible to malware that can destroy data and steal passwords. Windows 10 includes many security features. Most of the security features are enabled by default and you have options to optimize them for your environment.

In this chapter, you learn how to configure security by using the Local Security Policy, including AppLocker, and how to enable auditing. You also learn about User Account Control, which requires approval to perform administrative actions. Windows Defender, for malware protection, is also covered. Data encryption using Encrypting File System and BitLocker Driver Encryption are also covered. Finally, using Windows Update and the new Windows 10 update processes are covered.

Windows 10 Security Policies

Windows 10 includes a **Local Security Policy**, shown in Figure 6-1, which can be used to control many facets of Windows. You can access the Local Security Policy in Administrative Tools.

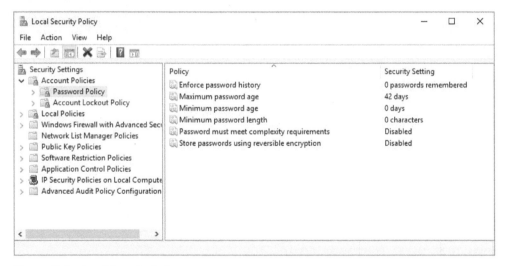

Figure 6-1   Local Security Policy

The Local Security Policy contains the following categories of settings:

- Account Policies
- Local Policies
- Windows Firewall with Advanced Security
- Network List Manager Policies
- Public Key Policies
- Software Restriction Policies
- Application Control Policies
- IP Security Policies on Local Computer
- Advanced Audit Policy Configuration

The Local Security Policy is part of a larger Windows management system called Group Policy, which can be implemented on a local computer, but is typically part of a domain-based network. A variety of tools and security templates can be used to configure and analyze security policies.

Account Policies

The Account Policies category contains the Password Policy and the Account Lockout Policy. The Account Policies in the Local Security Policy affect only local user accounts. The account policies do not affect domain accounts. To control domain accounts, the account policies must be configured at the domain level.

Password Policy   The **Password Policy** controls password characteristics for local user accounts. The available settings are:

- *Enforce password history*—This setting is the number of password changes that must occur before a password can be reused. For example, if the setting is 3, a password can only be reused every third time. The default value is 0 passwords remembered and the maximum is 24 passwords remembered.

- *Maximum password age*—This setting is the maximum amount of time that a user can keep the same password without changing it. Forcing password changes reduces the risk of a shared or hacked password being used over an extended period of time. The default value is 42 days.

- *Minimum password age*—This setting is the shortest amount of time that a user can use a password before changing it. A minimum password age is often used to ensure that users do not change their password several times in quick succession to continue using a single password. The default value is 0 days.

- *Minimum password length*—This setting is the minimum number of characters that must be in a password. In general, longer passwords are more secure. A minimum password length of 6 or 8 characters is typical for most organizations. The default value is 0 characters.

- *Password must meet complexity requirements*—This setting applies a number of tests to a new password to ensure that it is not too easy to guess or hack. This setting is enforced when a password change is made, but is not applied to existing passwords. The default value is Disabled. The complexity requirements include the following:

  - Cannot contain part of the user's account name

  - Must be at least six characters long

  - Must contain characters meeting three of the following characteristics: uppercase characters, lowercase characters, numerals (0–9), nonalphanumeric characters (e.g., !, @, #, $)

- *Store passwords using reversible encryption*—This setting controls how passwords are encrypted in the Security Accounts Manager (SAM) database that stores user credentials. By default, this setting is Disabled, and passwords are encrypted in a nonreversible format. Storing passwords by using reversible encryption is required only for compatibility with specific applications, such as remote access when using Challenge-Handshake Authentication Protocol (CHAP). Enabling this option stores passwords in a less secure way and should not be enabled unless absolutely required to support a specific need.

Account Lockout Policy   The **Account Lockout Policy** is used to prevent unauthorized access to Windows 10. Using the Account Lockout Policy, you can configure an account to be temporarily disabled after a number of incorrect sign-in attempts. This prevents automated password guessing attacks from being successful.

The settings available to control account lockouts are:

- *Account lockout duration*—This setting determines how many minutes an account remains locked. The default value is 30 minutes; however, this value is not configured until the Account lockout threshold has been configured.

- *Account lockout threshold*—This setting determines the number of incorrect sign-in attempts that must be performed before an account is locked. The default value is 0 invalid sign-in attempts, which means that account lockouts are disabled.

- *Reset account lockout counter after*—This setting determines within what time frame the incorrect sign-in attempts must occur to trigger a lockout. The default value is 30 minutes; however, this value is not configured until the Account lockout threshold has been configured.

Activity 6-1: Implementing a Password Policy

Time Required: 10 minutes
Objective: Implement a password policy that applies to local users

Description: A password policy is used to control the passwords that can be selected by users. One of the most effective password policy settings for increasing security is requiring complex passwords that are difficult to hack. In this activity, you configure a password policy to require complex passwords.

1. If necessary, start your computer and sign in.

2. Click the **Start** button, type **control**, and click **Control Panel**.

3. Click **System and Security** and click **Administrative Tools**.

4. Double-click **Local Security Policy**.

5. In the left pane, expand **Account Policies** and click **Password Policy**. This shows all of the password policy settings that are available to you.

6. Double-click **Password must meet complexity requirements**, click **Enabled**, and click **OK**. Now all passwords must meet complexity requirements when they are changed.

7. Close all open windows.

8. Press **Ctrl+Alt+Delete** and click **Change a password**. Note that this option is not available if you are signed in by using a Microsoft account.

9. In the Old password box, type **password**.

10. In the New password and Confirm password boxes, type **simple**, and press **Enter**. You receive an error indicating that the new password is not acceptable due to length, complexity, or history requirements.

11. Click **OK**.

12. In the Old password box, type **password**.

13. In the New password and Confirm password boxes, type **S1mpl3**, and press **Enter**. This time, the password is changed successfully.

14. Click **OK**.

Local Policies

Local Policies are for auditing system access, assigning user rights, and configuring specific security options. Auditing lets you track when users sign in and which resources are used. Details about auditing are covered later in this chapter. User rights control what system task a particular user or group of users can perform. The specific security options are a variety of settings that can be used to make Windows 10 more secure. Figure 6-2 shows some of the settings available in User Rights Assignment.

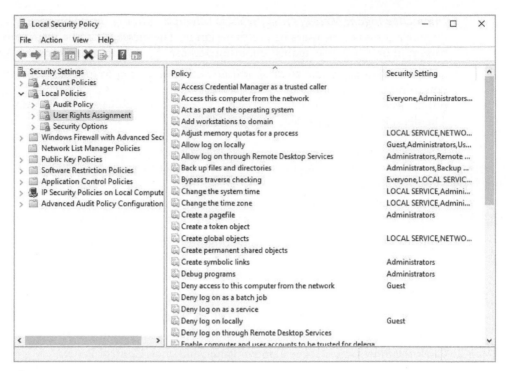

Figure 6-2   User Rights Assignment settings

Some of the settings available in User Rights Assignment are:

- *Allow log on locally*—This setting controls which users are allowed to sign in to the computer at the console, but does not affect who can access the computer over the network. Administrators, Backup Operators, Guest, and Users are assigned this right by default.

- *Back up files and directories*—This setting controls which users are allowed to back up files, regardless of whether they have the necessary file permissions to read those files. Administrators and Backup Operators are assigned this right by default.

- *Change the system time*—This setting controls which users are allowed to change the system time. Administrators and Local Service are assigned this right by default.

- *Load and unload device drivers*—This setting controls which users are able to install and remove device drivers. Only Administrators are assigned this right by default.

- *Shut down the system*—This setting controls which users are able to shut down Windows 10. For a public access computer, you might restrict this right. Administrators, Backup Operators, and Users are assigned this right by default.

Some of the settings available in Security Options are:

- *Devices: Prevent users from installing printer drivers*—This setting controls whether standard users are allowed to install network printer drivers. It does not affect the installation of local printer drivers. The default value is disabled, which allows all users to install network printer drivers.

- *Interactive logon: Do not display last username*—This setting allows you to remove the last user name from the sign-in screen. This makes sign-in more secure by not giving away user names to potential hackers. The default value is Disabled.

- *Interactive logon: Message text for users attempting to log on*—This setting allows you to display a message for users before they sign in. The message can be instructions about how to sign in or a warning against unauthorized use. By default, there is no message.

- *Shutdown: Allow system to be shut down without having to log on*—This setting allows you to require sign-in before allowing the system to be shut down. This is important for public access computers when you want to restrict which users can shut down the system. The default value is Enabled.

Activity 6-2: Configuring a Sign-In Message

Time Required: 10 minutes

Objective: Configure a warning message that appears for users before signing in

Description: The security policy of some organizations dictates that users are presented with a warning message about appropriate use before signing in. This warning is used to ensure that users are properly informed about organizational policies. In this activity, you configure Windows 10 with a warning message that appears before users sign in.

1. If necessary, start your computer and sign in. Remember that the password has been changed to S1mpl3.
2. Click the **Start** button, type **Control Panel**, and click **Control Panel**.
3. Click **System and Security** and click **Administrative Tools**.
4. Double-click **Local Security Policy**.
5. In the left pane, expand **Local Policies**, and click **Security Options**.
6. Scroll down and double-click **Interactive logon: Message title for users attempting to log on**.
7. In the text box, type **Acceptable Use**, and click **OK**.
8. Double-click **Interactive logon: Message text for users attempting to log on**.
9. In the text box, type **This computer should be used only for approved company business. Please see the acceptable use policy for more details**, and click **OK**.
10. Close Local Security Policy.
11. Sign out and press **Ctrl+Alt+Delete**. Notice that the warning message is displayed.
12. Click **OK** to display the sign-in screen.

AppLocker

AppLocker is used to define which programs are allowed or disallowed in the system. The most common use for AppLocker is malware prevention. Much malware installs itself by running from within a user profile. You can use AppLocker to restrict the locations that executables can run from and potentially avoid the problem.

A particularly nasty type of malware is known as ransomware. Ransomware encrypts files and requires payment for a key to decrypt the files. AppLocker is an effective tool to prevent ransomware.

You can audit or enforce AppLocker rules. When you audit an AppLocker rule, an event is logged when an action matching the rule is performed, but the software is allowed to run. When you enforce an AppLocker rule, software is blocked from running. If you do not define whether rules are enforced or audited, the default is enforced. When you first implement AppLocker rules, it is a good idea to use audit rather than enforce the rules. This allows you to review the logs and verify that your rules allow all of the necessary software to run. Figure 6-3 shows the configuration of AppLocker auditing and enforcement.

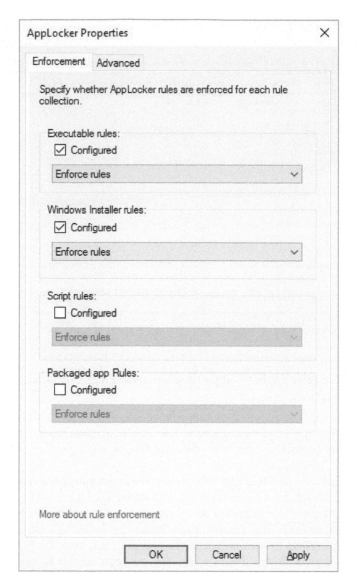

Figure 6-3 Configuring AppLocker enforcement

The enforcement or auditing of AppLocker rules relies on the configuration of appropriate rules and the Application Identity service. The Application Identity service must be running for AppLocker rules to be evaluated. This service is configured for Manual startup and is stopped by default. If you are implementing AppLocker rules, you should configure the Application Identity service for Automatic startup.

Rule Collections AppLocker rules are divided into categories called rule collections, as shown in Figure 6-4. Each rule collection applies to different types of files.

The rule collections are:

- *Executable*—These rules apply to .exe and .com files. Use these rules to control which applications users can run.

- *Windows Installer*—These rules apply to .msi and .msp files. Use these rules to control which users can install applications and from what locations.

- *Script*—These rules apply to .ps1, .bat, .cmd, .vbs, and .js files. Use these rules to control which users can run scripts.

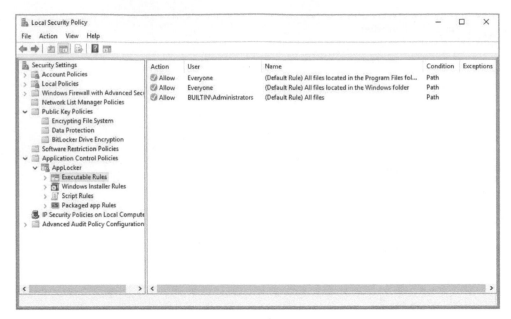

Figure 6-4   AppLocker rule collections

- *Packaged app*—These rules apply to .appx files. Use these rules to control which users can run Windows Store apps.

- *DLL*—These rules apply to .dll and .ocx files. Use these rules to verify that the DLLs used by applications are not modified or unknown. These rules are not enabled by default due to negative performance impact.

Many Windows applications use DLL files when they are executing programs. DLL files contain code that is shared across many applications, and many DLLs are included as part of the operating system. DLL files are considered a lower risk than executable files and are not evaluated by default. Evaluating DLL files creates a significant performance impact because DLLs are accessed many times during program execution, and the DLL must be evaluated each time it is accessed. However, if performance is not a concern, you can choose to evaluate DLL files in addition to executable files to enhance security.

For each rule collection, you can:

- *Create a New Rule*—This allows you to manually specify the characteristics of a rule. To create rules in this way, you must understand the exact end results that you are trying to achieve.

- *Automatically Generate Rules*—This scans your computer and creates rules that match the current configuration of your computer. In a larger corporate environment, you can create the rules on a standardized reference computer and then apply them to all computers in the organization. You should review the rules before applying them.

- *Create Default Rules*—This creates standardized rules for a rule collection that meet the needs of many users and organizations. Because these rules are very general, they provide less security than automatically generated rules but are generally easier to manage. The default rules created vary for each rule collection.

Rule Permissions   Each rule contains permissions that define whether the rule allows or denies software the ability to run, as shown in Figure 6-5. It is important to remember that until a rule is created in a rule collection, the default permission is Allow. For example, if there are no executable rules, all executables are allowed. As soon as a single executable rule is created, the default permission is Deny and only specifically allowed executables can run. For example, if you create a rule that prevents users from running cmd.exe, access to all other applications without an Allow rule is prevented.

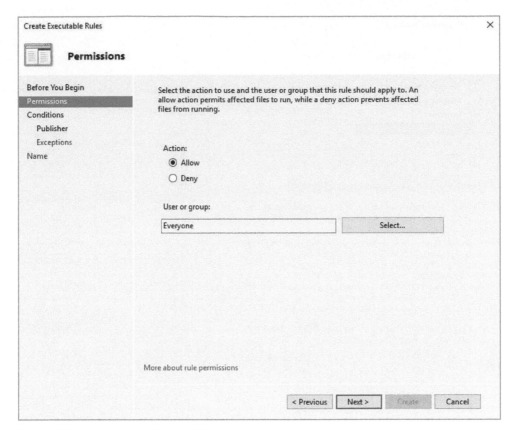

Figure 6-5   AppLocker rule permissions

Permissions also define which users the rule applies to. A rule can be applied to an individual user or group, but not multiple users or groups. This means it is very important to plan out which groups to use for allowing access.

In general, the best strategy for applying rules is to begin by creating rules that allow access for larger groups of users. Then, you can restrict smaller groups or individuals with a rule that denies access or create an exception within the original rule. The Deny permission overrides the Allow permission when multiple rules apply for a user.

Rule Conditions   A rule condition defines the software that is affected by the rule. There are three conditions that can be used:

- Publisher
- Path
- File Hash

The Publisher rule condition, shown in Figure 6-6, identifies software by using a digital signature in the software. If the software is not digitally signed, you cannot use a Publisher rule condition to identify it. Consider using a File Hash rule condition instead.

To begin configuration of a Publisher rule condition, you specify a reference file. The wizard reads the digital signature from this reference file as the basis for the condition. After a reference file has been defined, you can use the slider to select the specific information that must be matched. You can make it as specific as a particular file and file version or make it more generic and restrict it only to a specific product name or publisher. You can also define custom values that do not match the information read from the reference file.

The Path rule condition, shown in Figure 6-7, identifies software by file location. You can specify a single file or a folder path from which software can be run. This type of rule condition tends to be much less secure than a Publisher rule condition. For example, if you use a Path

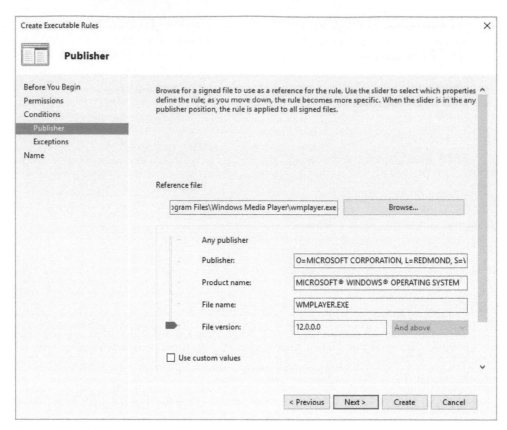

Figure 6-6   Publisher rule condition

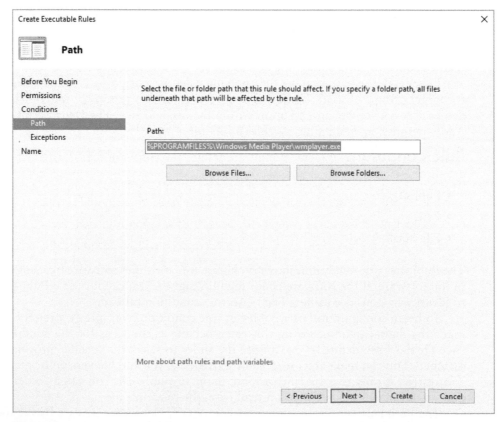

Figure 6-7   Path rule condition

rule condition that allows software to be run from C:\Program Files\, any malware accidentally installed by a user and located in C:\Program Files\ can be run. At minimum, you should avoid using Path rule conditions that allow executables to be run from file locations where standard users can copy files. Variables can be used as part of the path to simplify rule creation.

The File Hash rule condition generates a unique identifier for the specified files called a hash value. If the file is modified in any way, the hash value no longer matches and the software no longer matches the rule. If you use a File Hash rule condition, application updates will require the rule to be updated.

Rule Exceptions   An AppLocker rule exception defines software that the rule does not apply to. In general, you use rule conditions to define a large set of software and then use exceptions to define a smaller set of software that the rule does not apply to. Similar to rule conditions, when you add an exception, it can be based on publisher, path, or file hash. You can add multiple exceptions to a single rule.

Activity 6-3: Configuring AppLocker

Time Required: 10 minutes
Objective: Implement AppLocker rules

Description: AppLocker rules can be used to limit which software is allowed to run on a workstation. An administrator can use this to prevent a particular piece of software from running or allow only specific software to run. In this activity, you create and review default AppLocker rules and audit the use of cmd.exe.

1. If necessary, start your computer and sign in. Remember that the password is changed to S1mpl3.
2. Click the **Start** button, type **local**, and click **Local Security Policy**.
3. In the left pane, expand **Application Control Policies** and then click **AppLocker**.
4. Scroll down and notice that no rules are created by default, but they are enforced.
5. Click **Executable Rules.**
6. Right-click an open area in the right pane and click **Create Default Rules**.
7. Review the default rules. These rules allow administrators to run all applications and allow Everyone to run applications in C:\Program Files\ and C:\Windows\.
8. Right-click an open area in the right pane and click **Automatically Generate Rules**.
9. On the Folder and Permissions page, click **Next** to accept the default of scanning C:\Program Files\.
10. On the Rule Preferences page, read the default options that are selected and click **Next**. Notice that the rules are being created based on digital signatures and file hashes rather than file path.
11. On the Rule Preferences page, read the default settings, and click **Next.**
12. On the Review Rules page, click **View Rules that will be automatically created.**
13. Read the rules and then click **OK**. These rules are based on the software installed on your computer.
14. On the Review Rules page, click **Cancel.**
15. In the left pane, right-click **Executable Rules** and then click **Create New Rule.**
16. On the Before You Begin page, click **Next.**
17. On the Permissions page, click **Deny** and click **Next.**
18. On the Conditions page, click **Path** and click **Next.**
19. On the Path page, in the Path box, type **C:\Windows\System32\cmd.exe** and click **Next.**
20. On the Exceptions page, click **Next** to accept the default of no exceptions.
21. In the Name box, delete the existing name, type **Deny Command Prompt,** and then click **Create.**

22. In the left pane, click **Windows Installer Rules**, right-click **Windows Installer Rules**, and then click **Create Default Rules.**

23. Review the default rules that are created. These rules allow Everyone to install digitally signed software and allow administrators to install any software.

24. In the left pane, click **AppLocker** and click **Configure rule enforcement.**

25. Under Executable rules, select the **Configured** check box, select **Audit only** in the drop-down list, and then click **OK.**

26. Close Local Security Policy.

27. Right-click the **Start** button and click **Computer Management.**

28. Expand **Services and Applications** and click **Services.**

29. Click the **Application Identity** service, read the description, and then click **Start.**

30. Wait a few seconds for the service to completely initialize, and then right-click the **Start** button and click **Command Prompt.**

31. In the left pane of Computer Management, expand **Event Viewer**, expand **Applications and Services Logs**, expand **Microsoft**, expand **Windows**, expand **AppLocker**, and click **EXE and DLL.**

32. Click the **Warning** event and read the description. Notice that cmd.exe was allowed to run because it is only being audited rather than enforced.

33. In the left pane of Computer Management, scroll down and click **Services.**

34. Click the **Application Identity Service** and click **Stop.**

35. Close all open windows.

Software Restriction Policies

Software Restriction Policies are an older technology that you can use to control application usage similar to AppLocker. Software Restriction Policies are still functional in Windows 10. If both AppLocker rules and Software Restriction Policies are defined on a Windows 10 computer, only the AppLocker rules are enforced.

AppLocker is preferred over Software Restriction Policies because it provides the following enhancements:

• Rules can be applied to specific users and groups rather than all users.

• The default rule action is Deny to increase security.

• There is a wizard to help create rules.

• There is an audit-only mode for testing that only writes events to the event log.

To use AppLocker, you must implement Windows 10 Enterprise or Windows 10 Education. However, many smaller organizations use Windows 10 Pro instead because they receive it with new computers. For these smaller organizations that cannot use AppLocker, Software Restriction Policies offer an effective way to restrict malware from running.

 Because Software Restriction Policies are an older technology, they are much less likely to be tested on the Windows 10 exam than AppLocker.

Other Security Policies

Windows Firewall with Advanced Security is used to configure the firewall in Windows 10. This policy lets you configure both inbound and outbound rules for packets. In addition, you can configure specific computer-to-computer rules. In Windows 10, this area can also be used to configure IP Security (IPsec) rules.

The Network List Manager Policies are used to control how Windows 10 categorizes networks to which it is connected and how users can interact with the process. For example, unidentified networks can be automatically defined as either public or private, and the user can restrict the ability of other users to change it. These policies also control whether users can rename networks that they connect to.

Public Key Policies have settings for the **Encrypting File System (EFS)**, BitLocker Drive Encryption, and certificate services. You can add recovery agents for EFS files or BitLocker-encrypted drives. A recovery agent is allowed to decrypt files protected by EFS or BitLocker. More detailed information about EFS and BitLocker Drive Encryption is provided later in this chapter.

IP Security Policies on Local Computer are used to control encrypted network communication. By default, network communication is not encrypted. However, you can configure encrypted network communication for certain hosts or communication on certain port numbers. This policy is deprecated in Windows 10 and included only for backward compatibility with Windows 2000 and Windows XP. When configuring IPsec rules, you should use Windows Firewall with Advanced Security.

Advanced Audit Policy Configuration is a simplified way to configure advanced audit policies in Windows 10. These policies first appeared in Windows Vista, but needed to be edited at a command line. More detailed information about auditing is provided later in this chapter.

Security Templates

Security templates are .inf files that contain settings that correspond with the Account Policies and Local Policies in the Local Security Policy. In addition, security templates can contain settings for the event log, restricted groups, service configuration, registry security, and file system security. You can use security templates to apply security settings or compare existing security settings against a corporate standard.

In a corporate environment using a domain, the security settings are typically configured by using Group Policy. Security templates can be imported into a Group Policy.

Security templates are edited by using the Security Templates snap-in, shown in Figure 6-8. The Security Templates snap-in automatically opens to the C:\Users\%Username%\Documents\Security\Templates folder. You can add additional locations if desired, but typically security templates are stored here.

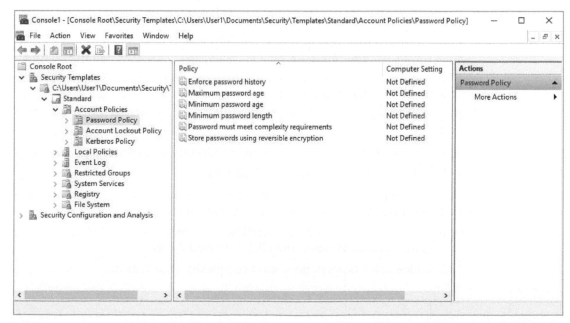

Figure 6-8   Security Templates MMC snap-in

 Windows 10 provides no default security templates.

Security templates are used by the Security Configuration and Analysis tool and Secedit. Both tools perform approximately the same tasks. The **Security Configuration and Analysis tool** is an MMC snap-in that is easy to use when working with a single computer. **Secedit** is a command-line utility that is better for scripting and working with multiple computers.

Tasks you can perform with the Security Configuration and Analysis tool are:

- *Analyze*—You can compare the settings in a security template against the settings on a computer. This is useful when you want to confirm that computers meet the minimum security requirements defined in a security template.

- *Configure*—You can apply the settings in a security template to a computer. This is useful to enforce the security requirements defined in a security template.

- *Export*—You can export the settings on a computer to a security template. This is useful if a computer has been properly configured and you want to apply these security settings to an additional computer.

Activity 6-4: Using Security Templates

Time Required: 25 minutes

Objective: Create a security template, analyze a computer, and then apply the security template

Description: One method for analyzing and enforcing security settings on a Windows 10 computer is security templates. You can create your own security templates that define the security settings you require. After the security template has been created, you can use it to analyze computers or apply security settings. In this activity, you create a security template, analyze a computer, and then apply the security template.

1. If necessary, start your computer and sign in. Remember that the password is changed to S1mpl3.
2. Click the **Start** button, type **mmc,** and click **mmc.**
3. In the User Account Control dialog box, click **Yes.**
4. In the MMC window, click the **File** menu, and click **Add/Remove Snap-in.**
5. In the Available snap-ins box, scroll down, double-click **Security Templates,** double-click **Security Configuration and Analysis,** and click **OK.**
6. In the left pane, expand **Security Templates,** and click **C:\Users\User***x***\Documents\Security\ Templates.** Notice that there are no templates stored here by default.
7. Right-click **C:\Users\User***x***\Documents\Security\Templates** and click **New Template.**
8. In the Template name box, type **Standard.**
9. In the Description box, type **Standard workstation security configuration,** and click **OK.** This creates a new blank security template that you can configure.
10. In the left pane, expand **C:\Users\Userx\Documents\Security\Templates,** expand **Standard,** expand **Account Policies,** and click **Password Policy.**
11. Double-click **Password must meet complexity requirements.**

12. Select the **Define this policy setting in the template** check box, click **Disabled**, and click **OK**. Disabling password complexity is not recommended for corporate environments. In this case, it is being used as an example of one setting that can be configured using security templates.

13. In the left pane, expand **Local Policies** and click **Security Options**.

14. Scroll down and double-click **Interactive logon: Message title for users attempting to log on**.

15. Select the **Define this policy setting in the template** check box and click **OK**. You are leaving the text blank to undo the changes made in Activity 6-2.

16. Double-click **Interactive logon: Message text for users attempting to log on**.

17. Select the **Define this policy setting in the template** check box and click **OK**. You are leaving the text blank to undo the changes made in Activity 6-2.

18. In the left pane, right-click **Standard**, and click **Save**.

19. In the left pane, click **Security Configuration and Analysis**. Notice that instructions are provided in the middle pane. In this case, no database of security settings is created, so you are creating a new database. The database holds the security settings that are analyzed or applied.

20. Right-click **Security Configuration and Analysis** and click **Open Database**.

21. In the File name box, type **analyze** and click **Open**. This creates an empty database that security settings can be imported into.

22. In the Import Template dialog box, click **Standard**, and click **Open**. This imports the security settings from the Standard security template into the database.

23. Right-click **Security Configuration and Analysis**, click **Analyze Computer Now**, and click **OK**. This compares the security settings in the database with the security settings on this computer. The comparison is then displayed in Security Configuration and Analysis.

24. Expand **Security Configuration and Analysis**, expand **Account Policies**, and click **Password Policy**. Notice that there is a red "x" beside the Password must meet complexity requirements setting because the setting in the database is different from the setting on the computer.

25. Expand **Local Policies** and click **Security Options**. Notice that there is a red "x" beside both Interactive logon: Message title for users attempting to log on and Interactive logon: Message text for users attempting to log on because the settings in the database are different from the settings on the computer.

26. Right-click **Security Configuration and Analysis**, click **Configure Computer Now**, and click **OK**. This applies the settings in the database to your computer.

27. Right-click **Security Configuration and Analysis**, click **Analyze Computer Now**, and click **OK**.

28. Expand **Account Policies** and click **Password Policy**. Notice that there is a check mark next to Password must meet minimum complexity requirements because the setting in the computer now matches the setting in the database. The setting is disabled.

29. Close the MMC and click **No** when asked to save the console settings.

30. Press **Ctrl+Alt+Delete** and click **Change a password**.

31. In the Old password box, type **S1mpl3**.

32. In the New password and Confirm password boxes, type **password**, and press **Enter**. Notice that the password was changed successfully because the requirement for complex passwords has been removed.

33. Click **OK**.

Auditing

Auditing is the security process that records the occurrence of specific operating system events in the security log. Every object in Windows 10 has audit events related to it. Log entries can be recorded for successful events or failed attempted events. For example, logging all failed sign-in attempts may warn you when an attack that might breach your security is occurring. In addition, monitoring sensitive documents for read access lets you know who is accessing the documents and when.

It is more common to use auditing to monitor access to server-based resources than resources on desktop computers. However, there are some cases where you might want to know which users are signing in to a specific workstation. For example, if security logs indicate that someone was attempting unauthorized access to resources from a particular workstation, it is useful to see which user was signed in at the time.

Windows 10 has basic auditing policy settings and advanced audit policy settings. In general, the advanced audit policy settings are more detailed than the basic audit policy settings. Using the advanced audit policy settings allows you to limit the amount of audit data that you capture. In this way, you capture only relevant data and simplify the task of reviewing the audit logs. The Advanced Audit Policy settings are shown in Figure 6-9. Table 6-1 describes the categories for Advanced Audit Policy settings.

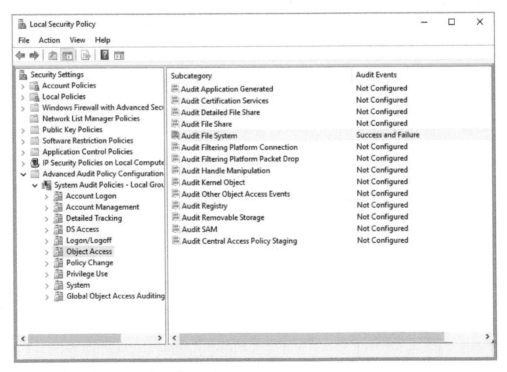

Figure 6-9   Advanced Audit Policy settings

Basic auditing is enabled through the Local Security Policy or by using Group Policy. The **audit policy** for basic auditing is located in the Local Policies node of the Local Security Policy.

Advanced auditing is enabled through the Local Security Policy, by using Group Policy, or by using auditpol.exe. The tool auditpol.exe provides the most accurate view of which Advanced Audit Policy settings are applied.

The default configuration for the Advanced Audit Policy settings can be viewed only by using auditpol.exe. If you review the configuration in the Local Security Policy, it appears that no settings are enabled. Be aware that after you enable settings in the Local Security Policy, the default configuration is lost and does not return if the Advanced Audit Policy settings are removed from the Local Security Policy. Table 6-1 describes the default configuration for the Advanced Audit Policy settings.

 Basic audit policy settings and advanced audit policy settings should not be combined as the results are unpredictable. To prevent conflicts when using the advanced audit policy settings, you can enable the security option policy setting *Audit: force audit policy subcategory settings* (Windows Vista or later) to override audit policy category settings.

Table 6-1 Event categories for Advanced Audit Policy settings

Event category	Description
Account Logon	Tracks when users are authenticated by a computer. If a local user account is used, the event is logged locally. If a domain user account is used, the event is logged at the domain controller. Account Logon events are not audited by default.
Account Management	Tracks when users and groups are created, modified, or deleted. Password changes are also tracked. Success events for user management are audited by default. Success and failure events for group management are audited by default.
Detailed Tracking	Tracks how a computer is being used by tracking application activity. This includes identifying the creation and termination of processes, encryption events, and remote procedure call (RPC) events. No events are audited by default.
DS Access	This category is not relevant for Windows 10 and is not audited by default. It is used only for domain controllers.
Logon/Logoff	Tracks user activity events, including local and domain logons, at the local computer. This category is similar to, but different from, auditing account logon events. Signing in with a local account generates both an account logon event and a logon event on the local computer. Signing in with a domain account generates an account logon event at the domain controller and a logon event at the workstation where the sign-in occurred. Success events for logon, logoff, and account lockout are audited by default. Failure events for logon are also audited.
Object Access	Tracks access to files, folders, printers, and registry keys. Each individual object being accessed must also be configured for auditing. Only files and folders on NTFS-formatted partitions can be monitored. Object access is not audited by default.
Policy Change	Tracks changes to user rights assignments, audit policies, and trust policies. Success events for audit policy changes and authentication policy changes are audited by default.
Privilege Use	Tracks when tasks are performed that require a user rights assignment, such as changing the system time. You can define which categories of privilege use are audited. None are audited by default.
System	Tracks when system events occur, such as restarting the system. By default, success and failure events are audited for system integrity and other system events. Only success events are audited for security state change.
Global Object Access Auditing	Provides an easy way to specify that all access to files or registry keys should be audited. This avoids the need to configure auditing at the file, folder, or registry key level after enabling auditing for object access to files or registry keys. However, this must still be used in combination with auditing enabled for object access. This category does not appear when using auditpol.exe.

Once the audit policy is configured, the audited events are recorded in the Security log that is viewed by using Event Viewer. Event Viewer is available as part of the Computer Management MMC console, or as a stand-alone MMC console in Administrative Tools. Security events are listed by selecting the Windows Security log, as shown in Figure 6-10.

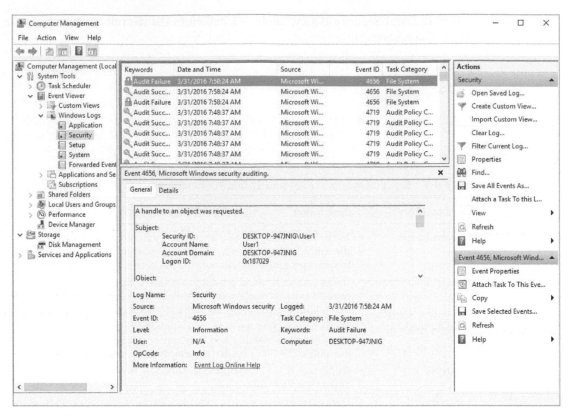

Figure 6-10   Windows Security log

Activity 6-5: Auditing File Access

Time Required: 15 minutes
Objective: Audit file modification for users

Description: In a corporate environment, it is useful to track all of the users who have modified sensitive files. You can use auditing to track file modification. In this activity, you enable auditing of file modification creation, configure a file to be audited, and view user modification of that file.

1. If necessary, start your computer and sign in. Remember that the password is changed back to **password**.

2. Right-click the **Start** button and click **Command Prompt (Admin)**.

3. In the User Account Control dialog box, click **Yes**.

4. At the command prompt, type **auditpol /get /category:*** and press **Enter**. This displays a list of all the advanced audit policy settings that are in place.

5. Read the list of policy settings that are enabled. This is the default configuration for Windows 10. Notice that under Object Access, File System auditing is not enabled. After you enable policy settings in the local security policy, these settings are removed and only the settings explicitly applied in the policy are effective.

6. Close the command prompt.

7. Click the **Start** button, type **local**, and click **Local Security Policy**.

8. In the left pane, expand **Local Policies** and click **Audit Policy**. Review the list of categories for basic auditing and notice that none are enabled in the local security policy.

9. In the left pane, expand **Advanced Audit Policy Configuration**, expand **System Audit Policies - Local Group Policy Object**, and then click **Object Access**.

10. Double-click **Audit File System**. This option enables auditing for file access.

11. In the Audit File System Properties window, select the **Configure the following audit events** check box and then select the **Success** and **Failure** check boxes.

12. Click the **Explain** tab, read the explanation, and click **OK**. The system is now able to track successful file access when users have permission to access a file and unsuccessful file access when users do not have permission to access a file. However, auditing must still be enabled for the individual files.

13. Close Local Security Policy and close all open windows.

14. On the taskbar, click **File Explorer** and click **Documents**.

15. Right-click an open area in the **Name** column, point to **New**, and click **Text Document**.

16. Type **Audit** and press **Enter**.

17. Right-click **Audit**, click **Properties**, and click the **Security** tab.

18. Click **Advanced** and click the **Auditing** tab. Notice that auditing information is protected by UAC.

19. Click **Continue** to open the auditing information. Notice that no auditing is configured by default.

20. Click **Add**, click **Select a principal**, type **Everyone**, click **Check Names**, and click **OK**. This configures auditing to track access by all users. You can limit auditing to certain users or groups.

21. In the Type box, select **All**. This configures auditing of successful and failed access.

22. Under Basic permissions, select the **Full control** check box. This configures auditing to track all changes to the file.

23. Click **OK** three times to close all open dialog boxes.

24. Double-click **Audit** to open the file and then add some content to the file.

25. Click the **File** menu, click **Exit**, and click **Save**.

26. Close File Explorer.

27. Right-click the **Start** button and click **Computer Management**.

28. In the left pane, expand **Event Viewer**, expand **Windows Logs**, and click **Security**. This displays all of the events in the security log.

29. Right-click **Security** and click **Filter Current Log**.

30. In the Event sources box, select **Microsoft Windows security auditing**.

31. In the <All Event IDs> box, type **4663** and click **OK**. Notice that multiple events are listed. These events were generated by editing the file.

32. Starting with the first event, read the Account Name identified in the event. Continue down until the Account Name referenced is User$x$. Read the description of the event. The description indicates that a file was written by User$x$, where x is the number assigned to you; the file opened was Audit.txt; and the program used to write the file was notepad.exe.

33. Close Computer Management.

User Account Control

User Account Control (UAC) is a feature that makes running applications more secure. Security is enhanced by reducing the need to sign in and run applications using administrator privileges. Reducing the use of administrative privileges makes it less likely that malicious software can adversely affect Windows 10.

In some organizations, all user accounts are configured as administrators on the local workstations. This is done to ensure that users are able to perform any local maintenance tasks that may be required, such as installing printers or software. In Windows 10, there have been major efforts to ensure that most tasks do not require administrative privileges. However, even if users are still given administrative privileges, UAC increases security.

When UAC is enabled and an administrative user signs in, the administrative user is assigned two access tokens. One access token includes standard user privileges and the other access token includes administrative privileges. The standard user access token is used to launch the Windows 10 user interface. Therefore, all applications started by using the user interface also start with standard user privileges. This approach keeps any malicious software from having access to restricted areas like system files.

Admin Approval Mode ensures that the access token with administrative privileges is used only when required. When you use an application that requires administrative privileges, you are prompted to continue or cancel running the program with administrative privileges. If you select to continue, the program is run using the access token with administrative privileges. The Application Information Service is responsible for launching programs by using the access token with administrative privileges.

When UAC is enabled and a standard user signs in, the user is assigned only one access token with standard user privileges. If the user attempts to run an application that requires administrative privileges, the user is prompted to supply credentials for a user with administrative privileges.

Application Manifest

Newer Windows applications use an **application manifest** to describe the structure of an application. The structure includes required DLL files and whether they are shared. The application manifest can include information about UAC. An entry must be included in the application manifest to trigger the privilege elevation prompt for an application that requires administrative privileges.

Applications that are not designed for Windows 10 and that require administrative privileges do not properly request elevated privileges, generating an error. You can eliminate this error by using the Application Compatibility Toolkit.

Detailed information about the Application Compatibility Toolkit is covered in Chapter 9, Windows 10 Application Support.

UAC Configuration

When UAC was introduced in Windows Vista, it prompted even administrative users for just about every administrative action that was attempted. Windows 10 reduces the number of UAC prompts presented to administrative users with a default configuration that does not prompt if the user initiated the action. If a program initiates the action, a UAC prompt is still presented.

Windows 10 also introduces a simplified interface for managing UAC settings, shown in Figure 6-11. The new interface has only four options:

- *Always notify me*—This setting is equivalent to the configuration in Windows Vista where even administrative users are prompted every time an administrative task is attempted.

- *Notify me only when apps try to make changes to my computer*—Administrative users are prompted only when a program attempts to perform an administrative task. When the administrative task is initiated by the user, a prompt is not displayed. This is the default setting.

- *Notify me only when apps try to make changes to my computer (do not dim my desktop)*— This setting is the same as the default setting except that when the UAC prompt is displayed, the screen is not dimmed.

- *Never notify me*—This setting disables UAC and is not recommended.

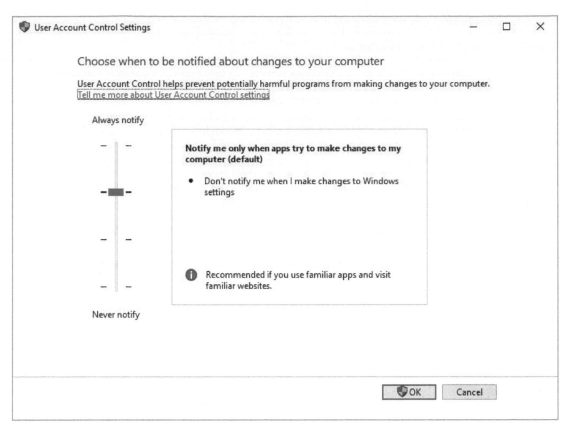

Figure 6-11   UAC settings

For advanced configuration, UAC is configured by using either the Local Security Policy or Group Policy. The policy settings for configuring UAC are listed in Table 6-2. In most cases, it is easier to manage UAC in the simplified interface.

Table 6-2   UAC configuration options

Option (User Account Control)	Description
Admin Approval Mode for the built-in Administrator account	Used to enable or disable Admin Approval Mode for the built-in administrator account. The default configuration is disabled.
Allow UIAccess application to prompt for elevation without using secure desktop	Used to allow UIAccess programs, such as Remote Assistance, to automatically disable the screen dimming that normally occurs when a UAC prompt displays. This is a less secure configuration but can speed up screen drawing over slow connections. This is disabled by default.
Behavior of the elevation prompt for administrators in Admin Approval Mode	Used to configure the elevation prompt for Administrators only. The default configuration is to prompt for consent for non-Windows binaries. However, you can also configure a prompt for administrative credentials instead of a simple approval. You can also disable the prompt. Entirely disabling the prompt effectively disables UAC for administrators because applications can then request elevation to administrative privileges and are automatically approved. However, applications do run with standard user privileges until they request elevation.
Behavior of the elevation prompt for standard users	Used to configure the elevation prompt for standard users only. The default configuration is to prompt for credentials. You can also select Automatically deny elevation requests, in which case the user must manually use Runas to elevate the privileges of the application.
Detect application installations and prompt for elevation	Used to automatically detect whether an application is being installed and generate a prompt to elevate privileges. The default configuration is enabled. If this option is disabled, many legacy application installations will fail.

(continues)

Table 6-2 (Continued)

Option (User Account Control)	Description
Only elevate executables that are signed and validated	Used to limit privilege elevation to only applications that are digitally signed. The default configuration is disabled, which allows older unsigned applications that require administrative privileges to be elevated.
Only elevate UIAccess applications that are installed in secure locations	Used to force applications using the UIAccess integrity level in their application manifest to be located from a secure location. Secure locations are C:\ProgramFiles\ and C:\Windows\System32\ and their subfolders. The default configuration is enabled.
Run all administrators in Admin Approval Mode	Used to limit all user processes to standard user privileges unless they are elevated to administrator privileges. The default configuration is enabled. When this option is disabled, UAC is disabled for administrators and standard users.
Switch to the secure desktop when prompting for elevation	Used to secure communication between the elevation prompt and other processes. When enabled, the UAC elevation prompt is limited to communication with processes that are part of Windows 10. This prevents malware from approving elevation. The default configuration is enabled.
Virtualize file and registry write failures to per-user locations	Used to enable non-UAC compliant applications to run properly. Applications that write to restricted areas are silently redirected to space in the user profile. The default configuration is enabled.

Activity 6-6: Configuring UAC

Time Required: 5 minutes

Objective: Identify the differences in simplified UAC settings

Description: In most cases, UAC with the default configuration makes using a computer more secure for administrative users because many tasks performed by administrative users do not need administrative privileges, such as reading email or researching on the Internet. The default configuration does not prompt administrative users for approval when they initiate the action. However, in some cases, you might want administrators to be prompted so that they realize they are performing an administrative task. In this activity, you review how the simplified UAC settings modify the user experience.

1. If necessary, start your computer and sign in.

2. Click the **Start** button, type **local**, and click **Local Security Policy**.

3. Expand **Local Policies** and click **Security Options**.

4. Scroll down to the bottom of the list of security options and read the options available for User Account Control.

5. Close Local Security Policy.

6. Click the **Start** button, type **control**, and click **Control Panel**.

7. In Control Panel, click **System and Security** and click **Change User Account Control settings**. Notice the shield symbol next to this item that indicates it is an administrative task that could be subject to UAC. Also notice that a UAC prompt was not displayed because you initiated the action.

8. In the User Account Control Settings window, move the slider up to **Always notify**, and click **OK**.

9. Click **Yes** to allow the changes. Notice that you are prompted by UAC because a program is changing the setting. Also notice that the screen is dimmed, indicating that the secure desktop is being used.

10. Click **Change User Account Control settings**. Notice that this time you are prompted to elevate.

11. In the User Account Control dialog box, click **Yes**.

12. In the User Account Control Settings dialog box, move the slider down to **Notify me only when apps make changes to my computer (do not dim my desktop)**, and click **OK**.

13. Click **Yes** to allow the changes.

14. Click the **Start** button, type **diskpart,** and then press **Enter.** Notice that a UAC prompt appears, but the desktop is not dimmed. Secure desktop is not being used.

15. In the User Account Control dialog box, click **No.**

16. Click **Change User Account Control settings.**

17. Move the slider back to the default setting and click **OK.**

18. Click **Yes** to approve the change.

19. Close all open windows.

Malware Protection

The Internet has become an essential tool for business and home users. For many business users, the primary application used is email. Many home users buy a computer specifically to access the Internet.

Although the Internet is a great source of information, it is also the biggest source of **malware** (malicious software). Most viruses and spyware come from the Internet. Protection from malware is an important feature in Windows 10, provided by Windows Defender, shown in Figure 6-12.

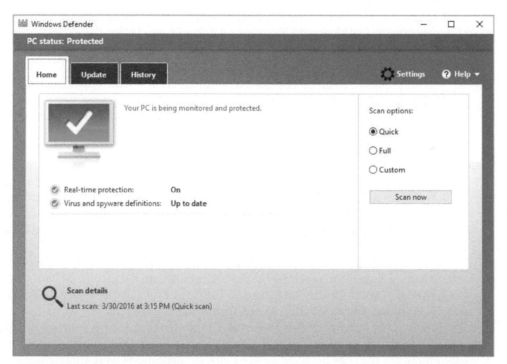

Figure 6-12   Windows Defender

Spyware

Spyware is software that is silently installed on your computer, monitors your behavior, and performs actions based on your behavior. Some spyware displays advertising based on websites you visit, others report back your web browsing activity to a central location, and others even make system changes like changing your home page.

The most important aspect of spyware is that you do not choose to install it. Spyware is sometimes installed when you visit a website. Other times, spyware is installed unwittingly along with other software. For example, many of the early file-sharing programs installed spyware.

Viruses

Viruses are a different type of malware than spyware. Like spyware, viruses are installed without your permission. Viruses are typically self-propagating and much more destructive than spyware. However, the important thing about viruses is not how we classify them. The important thing is to keep them off of your computer.

Some of the things viruses can do include:

- Sending spam from your computer to the Internet
- Capturing user names and passwords for websites, including online banking
- Stealing enough personal information for identity theft
- Allowing others to remotely control your computer and use it as a launching point for il-legal activities

In an enterprise environment, you might choose to use third-party antivirus software, not because that software detects and removes viruses better than Windows Defender, but because it offers better management capabilities. Most corporate antivirus software has a centralized console for distributing signature updates and monitoring computers. Windows Defender provides no centralized monitoring or control. Consequently, it is best suited to small environments.

Windows Defender

In Windows 7, Microsoft provided Microsoft Security Essentials for antivirus and Windows Defender for antispyware. In Windows 10, **Windows Defender** provides both antivirus and antispyware capabilities. Windows Defender has a simple interface for configuration and is enabled by default.

If you decide to install additional anti-malware software, ensure that Windows Defender is disabled. When two anti-malware programs are active, it can significantly reduce system performance.

Scanning   Real-time scanning constantly monitors activity on your computer. It monitors actions, files that are being downloaded, and disk activity. The goal of real-time scanning is to detect malware before it is installed on your computer. For example, if you download a file that contains malware, real-time scanning identifies it during the download process and prevents it from executing on your computer.

On-demand scanning is used to identify malware that is already present on your computer. A quick scan looks for malware in the most common locations. When a quick scan is running, user performance is not affected. A full scan looks at the entire disk system and running processes to find spyware. This type of scan is more complete, but will affect user performance. A full scan is typically performed when you think that spyware is on your computer.

Windows 10 automatically runs scheduled scans in the background. This is important to catch malware that has installed before malware definitions were updated.

Definitions   Windows Defender uses definitions to identify known and potential malware. The definitions should be updated regularly to ensure you can catch the most recent malware. By default, definitions are updated automatically by Windows Update. However, you also have the option to manually update the definitions on the Update tab in Windows Defender.

History   In Windows Defender, you can view the history of items that were detected. There are three options for viewing the history:

- *Quarantined items*—When Windows Defender detects potential malware that is low risk, the item is placed in quarantine. This prevents the item from running on your computer and gives you the option to release from quarantine if it was a false positive.

- *Allowed items*—These are items that Windows Defender detected as potential malware, but you selected to allow them because they were a false positive.

- *All detected items*—These are all of the items detected, including malware that was automatically deleted.

Configuration Settings   Windows Defender has a very limited set of configuration options available in the Update & security settings. In most cases, you want to leave these options at the default setting. The settings you can configure are:

- *Real-time protection*—Unless there is a specific need to disable real-time protection, you should leave this on. If you are copying a large number of files, disabling real-time protection might speed up the copying process. Also, if you are trying to a download a file that you know is safe and Windows Defender is seeing the file as a false positive, you can temporarily disable real-time scanning.

- *Cloud-based protection*—This option allows Windows Defender to communicate with the Microsoft Active Protection Service to report malware and scanning activity on your computer. This information is used by Microsoft to improve Windows Defender. Cloud-based protection is enabled by default.

- *Automatic sample submission*—When this option is enabled, samples of detected malware are sent back to Microsoft for further analysis. This is particularly important for malware identified by heuristics. After submission to Microsoft, the malware signature can be included in definitions. Automatic sample submission is enabled by default.

- *Exclusions*—Some applications such as databases might not run properly when real-time scanning is performed on them. In such a case, you can create an exclusion for specific files or folders. No exclusions are configured by default.

Some malware is able to hide itself when resident in memory and avoid detection. In some cases, the malware is capable of restarting itself after infection and remaining undetectable by anti-malware software such as Windows Defender. For this type of malware, you need to do an offline scan where Windows is not running so that the malware is not in memory. For this scenario, use Windows Defender Offline. Windows Defender Offline restarts your computer and does a scan while your installation of Windows 10 is not running.

Group Policy Configuration   The user interface for configuring Windows Defender has very few options. If you need fine-grained control over Windows Defender, you can use Group Policy. In a domain-based environment, the Group Policy settings can be easily deployed to multiple computers. The Group Policy settings for Windows Defender are located in Computer Configuration\Administrative Templates\Windows Components\Windows Defender. Each of the settings is documented in the Group Policy editor.

Activity 6-7: Using Windows Defender

Time Required: 10 minutes
Objective: Use Windows Defender to prevent spyware on a computer

Description: Windows Defender is used to prevent malware installation and remove malware. You can test the functionality of anti-malware software by using the EICAR anti-malware test file. The test file has a specific text string that all anti-malware software detects, but there is no risk of a malware infection. In this activity, you test real-time scanning and on-demand scanning.

1. If necessary, start your computer and sign in.
2. On the taskbar, click **Microsoft Edge**.
3. In the Search or enter web address box, type **www.eicar.org** and press **Enter**.
4. On the Eicar website, click **ANTI-MALWARE TESTFILE** and then click **DOWNLOAD**.

5. Scroll down and under Download area using the standard protocol http, click **eicar_com.zip**. You should be notified that Windows Defender detected malware and is removing it.

6. In the 1 Interrupted Action dialog box, click **Cancel**. This window may be hidden behind other windows.

7. Leave Microsoft Edge open for later in this activity.

8. Click the **Start** button and click **Settings**.

9. Click **Update & security** and click **Windows Defender**.

10. Click the **Real-time protection** switch to turn it **Off**.

11. In Microsoft Edge, click **eicar_com.zip**.

12. Click **Open folder** and verify that the file is downloaded.

13. Close all open windows.

14. Click the **Start** button, type **defender**, and click **Windows Defender**.

15. In Windows Defender, notice that real-time protection is off, and click **Turn on**.

16. Under Scan options, click **Custom** and click **Scan now**.

17. In the Select the drives and folder you want to scan box, expand **Local Disk (C:)**, select the **Users** check box, and click **OK**.

18. When prompted that a potential threat was found, click **Show details**.

19. In the Potential threat details box, read the recommended action and click **Apply actions**.

20. When the file is removed, click **Close** and close Windows Defender.

Data Security

The most basic level of data security in Windows 10 is NTFS permissions. NTFS permissions stop signed-in users from accessing files and folders for which they do not have read or write permission. However, NTFS permissions are only effective in protecting data when the original operating system is running.

There are many ways to work around NTFS permissions and gain access to data. The following are two examples:

- You can start a computer from a USB drive or CD-ROM and run Linux with an NTFS driver. Linux with an NTFS driver is able to read NTFS-formatted partitions and ignores the security information. This allows you to copy or modify data on the NTFS-formatted partition without even a valid user name.

- You can attach a hard drive from one Windows 10 computer to another. Local administrators always have the ability to take ownership of files and then read or modify them. When you move a hard drive, the local administrators of the new system can take ownership of files and then read or modify them.

As you can see, it is relatively easy to work around NTFS permissions when you have physical access to the computer. NTFS permissions are a very secure method of securing data when you have network access to files, but do not have physical access to the computer storing the files. This makes NTFS permissions excellent for servers, which are typically physically secured, but not as effective for desktop computers and laptops. Laptops are particularly at risk because they are more often lost or stolen.

To secure data on desktop computers and laptops, encryption is required. Windows 10 includes Encrypting File System (EFS) and BitLocker Drive Encryption to encrypt files.

Encryption Algorithms

Encryption is the process of taking data and making it unreadable. In most cases, encryption is a two-way process, where data can be encrypted to make it unreadable, then decrypted to make it readable again. The process for encrypting data is an algorithm. For computerized encryption of data, algorithms are math formulas that scramble the data into an unreadable format.

There are three main types of encryption algorithms:

- Symmetric
- Asymmetric
- Hashing

Symmetric Encryption   A **symmetric encryption algorithm** uses the same key to encrypt data and decrypt data. This is very similar to how a deadbolt lock works. When you leave your house, you lock the door with your key and when you return, you unlock the door with the same key. Figure 6-13 shows Bob and Susan accessing encrypted data by using the same key.

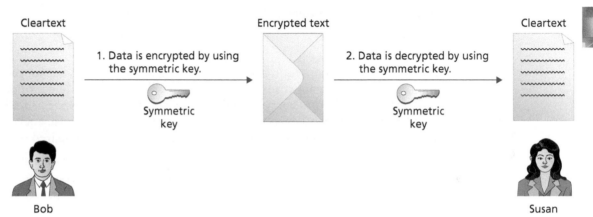

Figure 6-13   Symmetric encryption

In computerized encryption, the key is a long number that is very hard to guess. The longer the key, the harder it is to guess. One of the most common key lengths is 128 bits. Data that is symmetrically encrypted with a 128-bit key would take years to decrypt by guessing the key. Other solutions offer stronger encryption, with longer keys of 4096 bits or more.

Symmetric encryption is strong and fast. This makes it well suited to encrypting large volumes of data such as files. Most file encryption is done with a symmetric encryption algorithm. Both EFS and BitLocker Drive Encryption use symmetric encryption to secure data.

The biggest problem with symmetric encryption is securing the key. Anyone who has a copy of the encryption key can decrypt the data. In Figure 6-13, both Bob and Susan need to have a copy of the same symmetric key. EFS and BitLocker Drive Encryption both use different methods to secure the key.

Asymmetric Encryption   An **asymmetric encryption algorithm** uses two keys to encrypt and decrypt data. Data encrypted by one key is decrypted by the other key. This is similar to an electronic safe, where one person has a code that allows him to deposit money, but the other person has a code that allows her to remove money from the safe.

The keys used in asymmetric encryption are part of a digital certificate. Digital certificates are obtained from certificate authorities (sometimes also called certification authorities). Some of the better-known certificate authorities are VeriSign and Digicert. Companies can also generate their own digital certificates internally. Most server operating systems, including Windows Server 2016, have certificate authority functionality as an option.

The digital certificate from the certification authority contains a public key and a private key. The public key is meant to be known to other people. The private key is protected and known only to you. By using both of these keys, encrypted data can be sent securely without the risk of transferring a symmetrical key. For example, in Figure 6-14, Bob is encrypting data for Susan. When Bob performs the encryption, he uses Susan's public key. Then, only Susan can decrypt the data by using her private key. Only Susan can decrypt the data because only Susan has the private key.

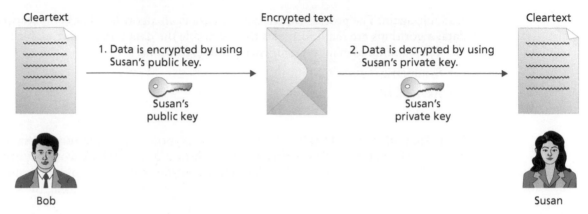

Figure 6-14 Asymmetric encryption

Asymmetric encryption requires more processing power and is less secure than symmetric encryption. This makes asymmetric encryption unsuitable for large volumes of data. Asymmetric encryption is typically used to encrypt small amounts of data. Many systems for encrypting data use symmetric encryption to encrypt the data and then use asymmetric encryption to protect just the symmetric key because a symmetric key is relatively small compared with the data it has encrypted.

Hashing   **Hashing algorithms** are used for a very different purpose than symmetric and asymmetric encryption algorithms. A hashing algorithm is one-way encryption, which means that it encrypts data, but the data cannot be decrypted.

Hashing is used to uniquely identify data rather than prevent access to data. Sometimes hash values for data are referred to as fingerprints. Some websites give you an MD5 value for downloadable software. MD5 is a hashing algorithm. The MD5 value is the unique value that is created when the MD5 hashing algorithm is run on the downloadable software. You can verify that the software has not been modified or corrupted by verifying the MD5 value after you download the software. If the software has been changed in any way, the MD5 value is also changed. Figure 6-15 shows how a hash value is used to verify that software has not been modified.

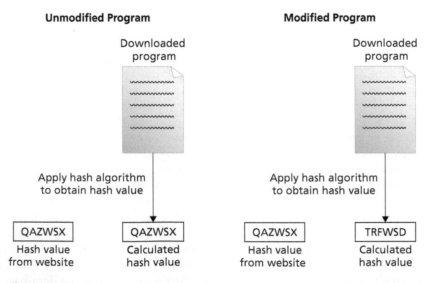

Figure 6-15 Hash encryption

Hashing algorithms are also used for storing passwords. The actual passwords entered by users are not actually checked. The operating system verifies that the hash value of the password entered by the user matches the hash value that is stored for the user's password. When passwords are stored as only a hash value, it is impossible to decrypt the password. The password can only be guessed by brute force.

Encrypting File System

EFS is a technology that was first included with Windows 2000 Professional. It encrypts individual files and folders on a partition. This makes it suitable for protecting data files and folders on workstations and laptops. However, it can also be used to encrypt files and folders on network servers. This section focuses on encrypting local files.

To encrypt a file or folder by using EFS, the file or folder must be located on an NTFS-formatted partition. FAT- and FAT32-formatted partitions cannot hold EFS-encrypted files. FAT and FAT32 file systems are not able to hold the information required to decrypt the files.

When a file is encrypted, the data in the file is encrypted using a symmetrical key that is randomly generated for that particular file. The symmetrical key is then encrypted by asymmetric encryption, based on user-specific keys. This protects the symmetrical key from unauthorized users.

To use EFS, users must have a digital certificate with a public key and a private key. Unless specifically configured otherwise, users do not have a digital certificate by default. If a user encrypts a file and does not have a digital certificate, Windows 10 generates a certificate automatically. The public key from the digital certificate is used to encrypt the symmetrical key that encrypted the file. Only the user who encrypted the file is able to decrypt the symmetrical key because only that user has access to the private key required to decrypt the symmetrical key. The EFS encryption and decryption process is shown in Figure 6-16.

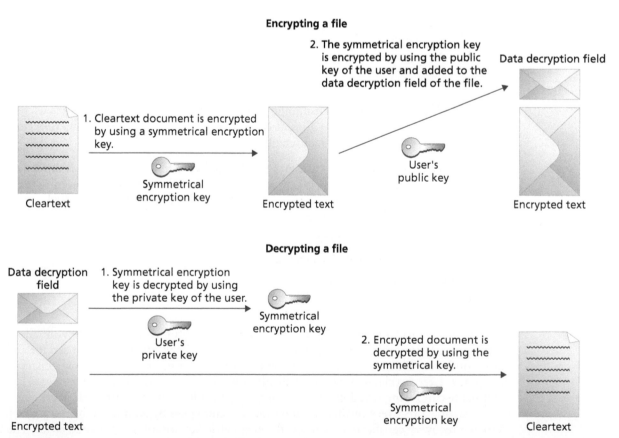

Figure 6-16   EFS encryption and decryption process

Digital certificates are stored in the user profile.

From the user perspective, encryption is a file attribute like compression, hidden, or read-only. To encrypt a file, a user needs to access the Advanced Attributes of the file, shown in Figure 6-17.

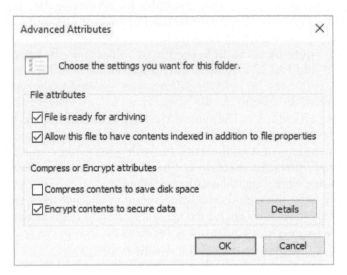

Figure 6-17   Advanced Attributes of a file

Files that are encrypted cannot also be compressed.

Files can also be encrypted using the command-line utility *cipher*. *Cipher* is useful for scripting or making changes to many files at once. For more information about *cipher* options, run *cipher* with the /? switch from a command prompt.

Lost Encryption Keys   If a user loses the EFS key, an encrypted file is unrecoverable with the default configuration. The only ways an encrypted file can be recovered is if the user has backed up the EFS key or if a recovery certificate has been created and installed.

Some ways EFS keys may be lost:

- The user profile is corrupted.
- The user profile is deleted accidentally.
- The user is deleted from the system.
- The user password is reset.

In User Accounts in Control Panel, there is an option for you to manage your file encryption certificates. This option allows you to view, create, and back up certificates used for EFS. You can also configure EFS to use a certificate on a smart card and update previously encrypted files to use a new EFS certificate. Once a certificate is backed up, it can be used whenever required. This certificate can be imported back into a new user profile or even a different user.

Creating a recovery certificate allows the files encrypted by all users to be recovered if required. When a recovery certificate is in place, the symmetric key for all files is stored twice. The first copy of the symmetric key is encrypted by using the public key of the user encrypting the file. The second copy of the symmetric key is encrypted by using the public key of the recovery certificate.

The steps for creating and using a recovery certificate are:

1. *Create the recovery certificate*—This is done by running *cipher* with the */r:filename* option, where *filename* is the name of the recovery certificate.

2. *Install the recovery certificate*—This is done by importing the recovery certificate into the local security policy as a data recovery agent. After this point, all newly encrypted files will include a symmetric key that is accessible to a user using the recovery certificate.

3. *Update existing encrypted files*—This is done by running *cipher* with the */u* option. Encrypted files can only be updated by a user who is able to decrypt the files. This means that multiple users might need to update files. Updating encrypted files adds an additional encrypted copy of the symmetric key that is accessible to a user using the recovery certificate.

To recover files, you import the recovery certificate into a user profile using the Certificates MMC snap-in. After the recovery certificate is imported, that user can decrypt any files necessary.

In a domain-based environment, the recovery certificate is deployed by using Group Policy rather than individually on each computer. To do this, browse to Computer Configuration\Windows Settings\Security Settings\Public Key Policies\Encrypting File System, right-click Encrypting File System, and click Add Data Recovery Agent. A wizard then guides you through the process of importing the certificate that will be used as a data recovery agent.

Sharing Encrypted Files   In a domain-based environment, it is easy to store encrypted files on a server and access them from multiple workstations or share them with other users. The necessary certificates are automatically created and stored on the remote server, and the files are encrypted and shared. On workstations that are part of a workgroup, the process takes more work.

For a single user to work with encrypted files on multiple computers, follow these steps:

1. Encrypt the file on the first computer.

2. Export the EFS certificate, including the private key from the first computer.

3. Import the EFS certificate, including the private key on the second computer.

4. Open the encrypted file on the second computer.

To share encrypted files with other users, follow these steps:

1. Export the EFS certificate of the first user, but do not include the private key.

2. Import the EFS certificate of the first user into the profile of the second user as a trusted person.

3. The second user encrypts the file and shares it with the first user. A copy of the symmetric key is encrypted with the public key of each user.

 **NOTE**   Encrypted files are typically not shared within a workgroup because of the complexity involved in exporting and importing certificates between computers. Sharing encrypted files is typically only done between users on the same computer or within a domain where no additional configuration is required.

Moving and Copying Encrypted Files   The encryption of files and folders behaves differently than NTFS permissions and compression when files and folders are moved and copied. When files and folders are copied, they always take on the NTFS permissions or compression attribute of the folder they are copied into. However, this is not the case for encrypted files.

The following rules apply for moving and copying encrypted files:

- An unencrypted file copied or moved to an encrypted folder becomes encrypted.

- An encrypted file copied or moved to an unencrypted folder remains encrypted.

- An encrypted file copied or moved to a FAT partition, FAT32 partition, or floppy disk becomes unencrypted if you have access to decrypt the file.

- If you do not have access to decrypt a file, you get an access-denied error if you attempt to copy or move the file to a FAT partition, FAT32 partition, or floppy disk.

Activity 6-8: Using EFS

Time Required: 10 minutes
Objective: Use EFS to encrypt and protect files

Description: EFS is used to encrypt individual files and folders. Once a file is encrypted, only authorized users are able to read the data in the file. In this activity, you encrypt a file and test it to ensure that only authorized users can decrypt the file.

1. If necessary, start your computer and sign in.
2. On the taskbar, click **File Explorer**.
3. In File Explorer, browse to **C:\Users\Public\Public Documents**.
4. Right-click an open area in the **Name** column, point to **New**, and click **Text Document**.
5. Type **encrypt** as the file name and press **Enter**.
6. Double-click **encrypt** to open it and type a line of text.
7. Click the **File** menu, click **Exit**, and click **Save**.
8. Right-click an open area in the **Name** column, point to **New**, and click **Text Document**.
9. Type **other** as the file name and press **Enter**.
10. Double-click **other** to open it and type a line of text.
11. Click the **File** menu, click **Exit**, and click **Save**.
12. Right-click **encrypt** and click **Properties**.
13. Click the **Advanced** button, select the **Encrypt contents to secure data** check box, and click **OK**.
14. Click **OK**, click **Encrypt the file only**, and click **OK**. Notice that the file encrypt now has a lock icon to indicate that it is encrypted.
15. Close File Explorer.
16. Switch user to **Bob**.
17. On the taskbar, click **File Explorer**.
18. In File Explorer, browse to **C:\Users\Public\Public Documents**.
19. Double-click **other**. Notice that you are able to open and read this file.
20. Close Notepad.
21. Double-click **encrypt**. You receive an error indicating that access is denied because the file is encrypted.
22. Click **OK** to close the error dialog box and close Notepad.
23. Sign out as **Bob**.

Activity 6-9: Recovering Lost Encryption Keys

Time Required: 10 minutes
Objective: Back up and restore an EFS encryption key

Description: A lost EFS encryption key means that an encrypted file cannot be accessed. To avoid this problem, you can back up the encryption key of a user. If a user's encryption key is backed up, you can restore it and then the user regains access to his files. In this activity, you back up and restore the encryption key for a user.

1. If necessary, start your computer and sign in.
2. Click the **Start** button, type **control**, and click **Control Panel**.

3. Click **User Accounts** and click **User Accounts**.

4. In the left pane, click **Manage your file encryption certificates**.

5. Click **Next** to start the Manage your file encryption certificates wizard.

6. Click **Next** to accept the default certificate.

7. If necessary, click **Back up the certificate and key now**.

8. To set the Backup location, click the **Browse** button, type **CertBak**, and click **Save**. The default location is your Documents directory. Typically, you would save the backed-up certificate on removable storage and keep it in a secure location.

9. In the Password and Confirm password boxes, type **password**, and click **Next**. It is important to secure the backup with a password because it contains your private key.

10. Click **Next** to skip updating encrypted files with a new key.

11. Click **Close**.

12. Click the **Start** button, type **mmc**, and press **Enter**.

13. Click **Yes** to start the Microsoft Management Console.

14. Click the **File** menu and click **Add/Remove Snap-in**.

15. In the Available snap-ins area, click **Certificates** and click **Add**.

16. Click **Finish** to accept managing certificates for your user account, and click **OK**.

17. In the left pane, expand **Certificates—Current User**, expand **Personal**, and click **Certificates**.

18. In the middle pane, right-click the **User*x*** certificate, and click **Delete**. If there are multiple certificates, delete all of them.

19. Read the warning message about losing the ability to decrypt files and click **Yes**.

20. Sign out and sign in again. This clears the certificate from memory.

21. On the taskbar, click **File Explorer**.

22. In File Explorer, under Recent files, double-click **encrypt**. You receive an error indicating that access is denied because the file is encrypted.

23. Click **OK** to close the error dialog box and close Notepad.

24. Click the **Start** button, type **mmc**, and press **Enter**.

25. Click **Yes** to start the Microsoft Management Console.

26. Click the **File** menu and click **Add/Remove Snap-in**.

27. In the Available snap-ins area, click **Certificates** and click **Add**.

28. Click **Finish** to accept managing certificates for your user account, and click **OK**.

29. In the left pane, expand **Certificates—Current User**, and click **Personal**.

30. Right-click **Personal**, point to **All Tasks**, and click **Import**.

31. Click **Next** to start the Certificate Import Wizard.

32. Click the **Browse** button, change the file type to **Personal Information Exchange (*.pfx,*. p12)**, click **CertBak**, and click **Open**.

33. Click **Next**.

34. In the Password box, type **password**.

35. Select the **Mark this key as exportable. This will allow you to back up or transport your keys at a later time** check box, and click **Next**.

36. Click **Next** to accept the default certificate location, click **Finish**, and click **OK**. Now you have a personal certificate again.

37. Close the MMC and click **No** to saving the console settings.

38. In File Explorer, double-click **encrypt**. Now you are able to open the file because you have restored the certificate that contains your private key. Your public key was used to encrypt the symmetrical key that was used to encrypt the file.

39. Close all open windows.

BitLocker Drive Encryption

BitLocker Drive Encryption is a data encryption feature included with Windows 10 that addresses some of the shortcomings of EFS. EFS is designed to encrypt only specified files. There are some files, such as the operating system files, that cannot be encrypted by using EFS. In addition, in some cases it might be possible to introduce low-level software that is able to steal EFS certificates.

When you use BitLocker Drive Encryption, an entire volume is encrypted. This protects not only your data, but also the operating system. Protecting the operating system ensures that additional software is not placed on the drive when the operating system is shut down. Figure 6-18 shows the screen used to enable BitLocker Drive Encryption.

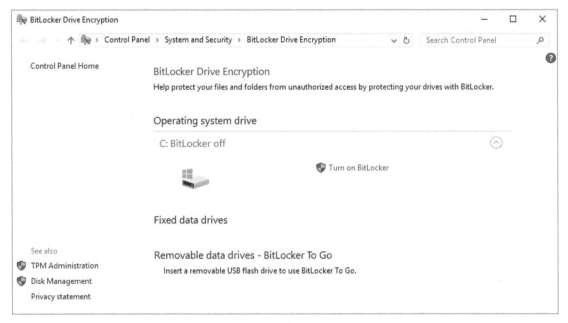

Figure 6-18 BitLocker Drive Encryption

BitLocker Drive Encryption is designed to be used with a trusted platform module (TPM). A TPM is part of the motherboard in your computer and is used to store encryption keys and certificates. Not all computers have a TPM module and you should verify whether a TPM is present when buying a newer computer. BitLocker Drive Encryption can be used on computers without a TPM, in which case the encryption keys are stored on a USB drive or you need to enter a PIN at startup.

When a TPM is used, BitLocker Drive Encryption has two modes:

- *TPM only*—In this mode, the user is not aware that BitLocker is activated because the keys stored in the TPM are automatically used to start Windows 10. This option protects data from offline modification, but does not add any extra protection to the boot process to prevent password guessing.

- *Startup key*—In this mode, the user must supply a startup key to boot Windows 10. The startup key can be configured on a USB drive or as a PIN entered by the user. This adds additional protection because password guessing to sign in to the operating system cannot be performed without first obtaining the startup key.

BitLocker Hard Drive Configuration   To use BitLocker Drive Encryption, your hard drive must be divided into two partitions. One partition is used as the operating system volume. The operating system volume is the volume that is encrypted. This volume contains both the operating system and user data.

The second required volume is the system volume. The system volume is not encrypted and contains the necessary files to boot the operating system. This volume must be at least 300 MB and formatted as an NTFS volume. Windows 10 automatically creates this volume as part of the installation process unless you specifically prevent it.

BitLocker Encryption Keys   BitLocker actually uses two keys to protect data. The **Volume Master Key (VMK)** is used to encrypt the data on the operating system volume. The VMK is then encrypted using a **Full Volume Encryption Key (FVEK)**. This multiple-key method for data encryption makes it faster to change the encryption key. Changing the VMK would require re-encrypting all of the data, which is time consuming. Changing the FVEK requires only re-encrypting the VMK, which is very fast. Figure 6-19 illustrates how the encryption keys are used to protect data.

6

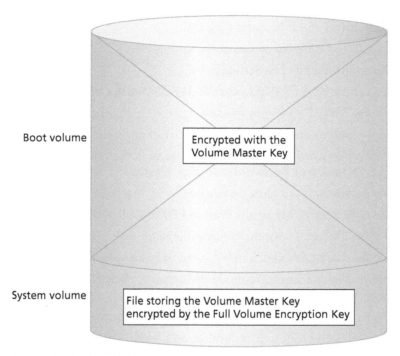

Boot volume

Encrypted with the
Volume Master Key

System volume

File storing the Volume Master Key
encrypted by the Full Volume Encryption Key

Figure 6-19   BitLocker encryption keys

Accessing BitLocker-encrypted data is seamless for the user. A filter driver is used by Windows 10 to encrypt and decrypt data transparently as it is accessed from the hard drive. All data saved on the operating system volume is encrypted, including the paging files and hibernation file. Although there is a slight decrease in disk performance, it should not be noticeable to users under most circumstances.

Activity 6-10: Enabling BitLocker Drive Encryption

Time Required: 15 minutes
Objective: Enable BitLocker Drive Encryption

Description: BitLocker Drive Encryption encrypts the contents of a hard drive so that unauthorized users cannot gain access to it. This is typically implemented in mobile computers.

For the best experience, you should use a computer with a TPM. However, you can enable BitLocker on computers without a TPM. In this activity, you encrypt the C: drive of a computer without a TPM.

1. If necessary, start your computer and sign in.
2. Click **Start**, type **mmc**, and press **Enter**.
3. Click **Yes** to start the Microsoft Management Console.
4. Click the **File** menu and click **Add/Remove Snap-in**.
5. In the Available snap-ins area, click **Group Policy Object Editor** and click **Add**.
6. Click **Finish** to edit the Local Computer Group Policy object and click **OK**.
7. Expand **Local Computer Policy**, expand **Computer Configuration**, expand **Administrative Templates**, expand **Windows Components**, expand **BitLocker Drive Encryption**, and click **Operating System Drives**.
8. Double-click **Require additional authentication at startup**.
9. In the Require additional authentication at startup window, click **Enabled**.
10. Select the **Allow BitLocker without a compatible TPM (requires a password or startup key on a USB flash drive)** check box and click **OK**.
11. Close the MMC and click **No** to saving the settings.
12. Click the **Start** button and click **Settings**.
13. In the Find a setting box, type **BitLocker** and click **Manage BitLocker**.
14. In the BitLocker Drive Encryption window, for the C: drive, click **Turn on BitLocker**.
15. On the Choose how to unlock your drive at startup page, click **Enter a password**.
16. On the Create a password to unlock this drive page, in the Enter your password and Reenter your password boxes, type **password**, and click **Next**.
17. On the How do you want to back up your recovery key page, click **Print the recovery key**.
18. In the Print window, click **Microsoft Print to PDF** and click **Print**.
19. In the Save Print Output As window, in the File name box, type **BitLocker** and click **Save**.
20. On the How do you want to back up your recovery key page, click **Next**.
21. On the Choose which encryption mode to use page, click **New encryption mode (best for fixed drives on this device)** and click **Next**.
22. On the Are you ready to encrypt this drive page, click **Continue**.
23. In the BitLocker Drive Encryption dialog box, click **Restart now**. This dialog box may be hidden behind other windows. If there is a DVD mounted, you are prompted to remove the DVD.
24. On the BitLocker screen, in the Enter the password to unlock this drive box, type **password** and press **Enter**.
25. Sign in to your computer.
26. Right-click the **Start** button and click **Command Prompt (Admin)**.
27. In the User Account Control dialog box, click **Yes**.
28. At the command prompt, type **manage-bde -status**. This shows the percentage of encryption completed.
29. Close the command prompt.

BitLocker Network Unlock   One potential issue with BitLocker-encrypted systems is maintenance. If TPM and a PIN are required for startup, it prevents remote maintenance.

For example, if a wake-on-LAN is used to start a computer remotely, it remains at the BitLocker screen waiting for the PIN to be entered and an administrator cannot remotely control it and updates cannot be installed. To resolve this issue, BitLocker Network Unlock allows computers to start automatically when connected to the corporate network.

When Network Unlock is enabled, the computer requests a certificate from the network during startup. A Windows Deployment Services (WDS) server provides a certificate capable of unlocking BitLocker. This functionality is only possible if the computer has UEFI firmware. BIOS firmware is not supported for Network Unlock.

For more information about Network Unlock, go to *technet.microsoft.com* and search for BitLocker Network Unlock.

Recovering BitLocker-Encrypted Data   When BitLocker Drive Encryption is enabled, a recovery password is generated automatically. The recovery password is a random number that you can save to a USB drive or folder, display on the screen, or print. It is important to keep the key in a secure location because it can be used to access data on the BitLocker-encrypted volume.

In Windows 10, there is also an option to configure a data recovery agent for BitLocker. Like a data recovery agent for EFS, a data recovery agent for BitLocker is able to access BitLocker-encrypted data even if a user forgets the PIN or password. In domain-based environments, this is configured by importing a certificate for a data recovery agent into Group Policy at Computer Configuration\Windows Settings\Security Settings\Public Key Policies.

In domain-based environments, you have the option to store the recovery password for BitLocker-encrypted drives in Active Directory. When this option is enabled, the recovery password is stored as an attribute of the computer object in Active Directory. You can also configure BitLocker to not allow encryption unless the recovery password is successfully stored in Active Directory. In a Group Policy Object, enable Store BitLocker recovery information in Active Directory Domain Services (Windows Server 2008 and Windows Vista) in Computer Configuration\Administrative Templates\Windows Components\BitLocker Drive Encryption.

The recovery password is required when the normal decryption process for BitLocker Drive Encryption is unable to function. The most common reasons that the recovery password is required are:

- *Modified boot files*—If one of the boot files on the system volume is modified, BitLocker Drive Encryption stops the system from starting because the operating system has been tampered with.

- *Lost encryption keys*—If there is a problem with the TPM and the encryption keys stored in it are lost or corrupted, the encrypted volume cannot be decrypted normally. The recovery password is also required if the encryption keys are stored on a USB drive that is lost or erased.

- *Lost or forgotten startup PIN*—If the requirement for a startup PIN is selected and the user forgets the startup PIN, the recovery password is required to access the encrypted data.

The recovery process is as follows:

1. Turn on your computer.
2. Enter the BitLocker Drive Encryption Recovery Console.
3. Provide the recovery password by inserting a USB key or typing it in.
4. Your computer restarts and boots normally.

Previous versions of Windows required you to use the function keys when typing in the recovery password. In Windows 10, you can use the function keys or normal number keys.

Disabling BitLocker Drive Encryption
If you no longer need BitLocker Drive Encryption, you can turn it off or disable it. Turning off BitLocker Drive Encryption decrypts all of the data on the hard drive and makes it readable again. Once BitLocker Drive Encryption is turned off, the disk can be moved to another computer and read by other operating systems.

Disabling BitLocker Drive Encryption does not decrypt the files on the volume. BitLocker Drive Encryption stores the FVEK as a clear key, which effectively removes the data protection associated with using BitLocker Drive Encryption. A clear key is one that is not encrypted or protected in any way. Disabling BitLocker Drive Encryption is not sufficient for other operating systems to read the BitLocker-encrypted data.

Activity 6-11: Recovering a BitLocker-Encrypted Drive

Time Required: 20 minutes
Objective: Recover a BitLocker-encrypted drive

Description: BitLocker Drive Encryption protects your data from anyone who might steal your computer. However, it can also render your data unavailable if the keys in the TPM are corrupted or you forget a startup password. In this activity, you recover the C: drive of a computer after forgetting the password.

1. If necessary, start your computer and sign in.
2. On the taskbar, click **File Explorer**, and under Recent files, double-click **BitLocker**.
3. Read the contents of BitLocker.pdf. This content should be stored in a safe location that is not on the encrypted drive.
4. Print a copy of BitLocker.pdf so that you can use it later in this activity to recover the drive. If you do not have access to a printer, copy the recovery key on a piece of paper. If you are working with a virtual machine, you can take a screenshot.
5. Restart your computer.
6. On the BitLocker screen, press **Esc** to enter BitLocker Recovery.
7. On the BitLocker recovery screen, in the Enter the recovery key for this drive box, type the recovery key from BitLocker.pdf and press **Enter**.
8. Sign in to your computer.
9. Click the **Start** button and click **Settings**.
10. In the Find a setting box, type **BitLocker** and click **Manage BitLocker**.
11. For the C: drive, click **Suspend protection**.
12. In the BitLocker Drive Encryption window, click **Yes**.
13. Restart your computer and sign in. Notice that you did not need to enter the password even though the drive is still encrypted.
14. Click the **Start** button and click **Settings**.
15. In the Find a setting box, type **BitLocker** and click **Manage BitLocker**.
16. For the C: drive, click **Turn off BitLocker**.
17. In the BitLocker Drive Encryption window, click **Turn off BitLocker**.
18. Close all open windows.

BitLocker To Go   Windows 10 includes **BitLocker To Go** as a method for protecting data on removable storage such as USB drives. When you choose to enable removable storage for BitLocker To Go, you are prompted for how the storage will be unlocked. This process for unlocking the encryption keys is different for BitLocker To Go because you must be able to unlock the removable drive on multiple computers.

The options for unlocking removable storage are:

- *Use a password to unlock the drive*—When this option is selected, you enter a password that protects the encryption key for the data. When you take the removable storage to another computer, you are prompted for the password before getting access to the data on the removable drive.

- *Use my smart card to unlock the drive*—When this option is selected, you identify a smart card that will protect the encryption key for the data. When you take the removable storage to another computer, you must provide the smart card and the PIN for the smart card before getting access to the data on the removable drive. This method is the most secure, but the second computer must have a smart card reader, which is not common.

When you enable BitLocker To Go for a removable drive, you are prompted to save or print the recovery key, just as you are when you enable BitLocker for a fixed hard drive.

BitLocker To Go can only be enabled for a device when using Windows 10 Pro, Enterprise, or Education editions. However, any edition of Windows 10 can view or modify data encrypted by BitLocker To Go. There is also a BitLocker To Go Reader that can be used on Windows Vista and Windows XP computers. The BitLocker To Go Reader is automatically included on removable storage encrypted by BitLocker To Go, and is accessible while the drive is still encrypted.

BitLocker To Go can be configured to automatically unlock a protected drive when it connects to a particular computer when a particular user is signed in. This simplifies access to the drive when used in a trusted environment, but still prompts for a password when the protected drive is used in another location.

There are many BitLocker and BitLocker To Go settings that can be managed through Group Policy. For example, you can force all removable storage to be encrypted with BitLocker To Go.

Windows Update

Scheduling automatic updates with Windows Update is the most important security precaution you can take with Windows 10. The vast majority of exploits used by viruses, worms, and other malware are addressed by updates available from Microsoft. Often, computers are vulnerable to many of these threats only because the necessary updates have not been applied.

When a Windows security flaw is found by a security company or ethical hacker, the flaw is reported to Microsoft. The person or company that found the flaw does not release their findings until Microsoft has created and released an update to fix the problem. Typically, this takes a few weeks or months.

After the update has been released, the person or company that found the flaw releases detailed information about the flaw. Microsoft releases the information on their website as well. Malware creators then begin to create software that takes advantage of the flaw. Computers that do not apply patches in a timely way are still vulnerable to malware using the flaw. Computers that are updated regularly are not vulnerable.

Servicing Branches

Microsoft has fundamentally changed the update process in Windows 10. In previous versions of Windows, Microsoft released security updates for varying service pack levels, which made it difficult for Microsoft to test and verify compatibility. Microsoft now releases updates for specific builds of Windows 10 only for a specified period of time. Before the end of the support period, a new build is released and computers upgrade to the new build, which then gets new updates until the next build is released.

 New builds of Windows 10 are installed similarly to an upgrade. The install of a new build typically takes 30–45 minutes.

There are now four distinct servicing branches:

- *Windows Insider Preview Branch*—This branch is updated irregularly, but can be updated as often as once per week. Consider this branch beta software. Windows Insider Preview should be used only on test computers if you want an early look at new features.

- *Current Branch*—This branch is maintained with updates for four months. Any computer configured to use Current Branch installs new builds immediately when released by Microsoft.

- *Current Branch for Business*—This branch installs new builds four months after they are released to Current Branch and provides updates an additional four months after that. This branch is available only on Windows 10 Pro, Enterprise, and Education editions.

- *Long Term Servicing Branch*—This branch is a specific edition of Windows 10 that does not receive feature updates. Windows Updates are provided for Long Term Servicing Branch for 10 years. This is meant for controlled environments, such as equipment controllers, where changes cannot be tolerated.

Controlling Windows Updates

The default configuration of Windows 10 uses the Current Branch and installs updates automatically when they are available. You have the option to check for updates immediately, but typically this is not required. You also have the option to view your update history here. Viewing the update history can be useful when trying to identify if a recent update introduced instability.

In the settings for Windows Update, you can configure active hours and restart options to control how your computer behaves after updates are installed. When you define active hours, your computer will not be automatically restarted during those active hours. The restart options allow you to define a specific time that you prefer to restart your computer after updates. There are also a few Advanced options, shown in Figure 6-20. These options are:

- *Give me updates for other Microsoft products when I update Windows*—In most cases, you will want to leave this option enabled to get updates for a wide variety of Microsoft products. Malware is capable of taking advantage of flaws in multiple products, not just the operating system.

- *Defer feature updates*—Selecting this option configures the computer to use Current Branch for Business and delay installation of new builds by four months.

- *Use my sign in info to automatically finish setting up my device after an update*—When a sign-in is required to complete installing an update, this option allows it to happen automatically, which avoids having to wait for the installation to complete the next time you sign in to your computer.

- *Choose how updates are delivered*—This option lets you select whether the download updates via peer-to-peer delivery from other computers. This option is on by default, but limited to only computers on the local network. You can also allow downloading and sending updates with computers on the Internet.

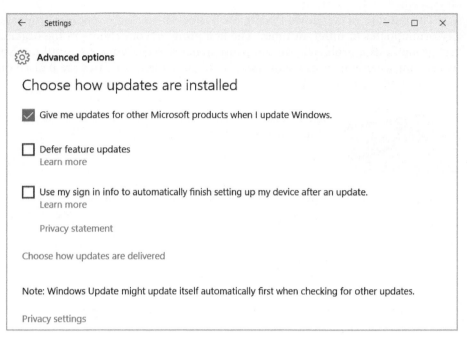

Figure 6-20   Windows Update Advanced options

Windows Update for Business

To allow more detailed control of update delivery to computers in a business environment, you can use Windows Update for Business. Windows Update for Business is a Group Policy setting that controls when updates are delivered after the updates are released. The Defer Upgrades and Updates setting (Figure 6-21) is found in Computer Configuration\Administrative Templates\Windows Components\Windows Update.

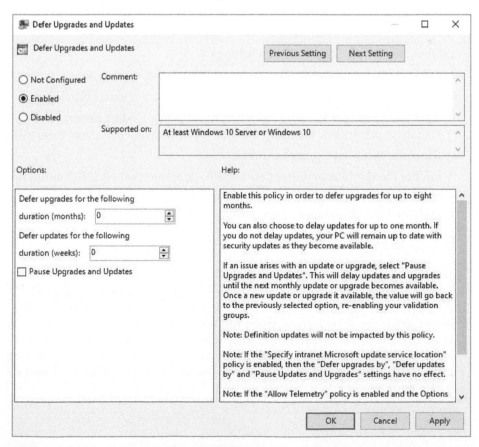

Figure 6-21   Defer Upgrades and Updates Group Policy setting

The purpose of Windows Update for Business is to create separate groups of computers that perform updates at different times. The first group is your testers in the organization. If the testers group finds a problem, you can pause updates to everyone else until the issue is resolved. Be aware that when you pause updates, it is not permanent. Updates are paused only until the next round of updates is released.

 Upgrades can be delayed up to eight months and updates can be delayed up to four weeks.

The standard Windows Update process can also be modified to use Windows Server Update Services (WSUS). WSUS provides greater control over the update process by allowing individual updates and upgrades to be approved for delivery to groups of computers. When WSUS is used, the Defer Upgrades and Updates setting is not used. Detailed information about WSUS is covered in Chapter 13, Enterprise Computing.

Activity 6-12: Protecting Your Computer by Using Windows Update

Time Required: 5 minutes
Objective: Protect your computer by configuring Windows Update to use Current Branch for Business

Description: One of the simplest methods for protecting your computer from malware that uses known exploits is regular installation of patches and security updates. For better stability in a business environment, you can configure Windows Update to use Current Branch for Business instead of Current Branch. In this activity, you configure Windows Update to use Current Branch for Business.

1. If necessary, start your computer and sign in.
2. Click the **Start** button and click **Settings**.
3. Click **Update & security**. This screen indicates whether Windows 10 is up to date or not.
4. Click **Advanced options** and select the **Defer feature updates** check box.
5. Click the **back** button at the top of the screen, click **Update history,** and then in the Windows Update window click **Uninstall updates.** You can remove updates from this window.
6. Close the Installed Updates window.
7. On the Update history screen, click the **back** arrow, and click **Advanced options.**
8. Click **Choose how updates are delivered** and verify that your computer is now downloading updates from computers on the Internet.
9. Close all open windows.

Updating Windows Store Apps

Windows Store apps are not updated by using Windows Update. Windows Store apps are updated through the Windows Store. To access settings related to Windows Store app updates, click the Start button, open the Windows Store app, and then click the person icon just to the left of the Search box. This icon is your profile picture if you have configured one. If you select Download and updates, you are presented with the options shown in Figure 6-22. From here, you can check for updates, download all updates, or download specific updates.

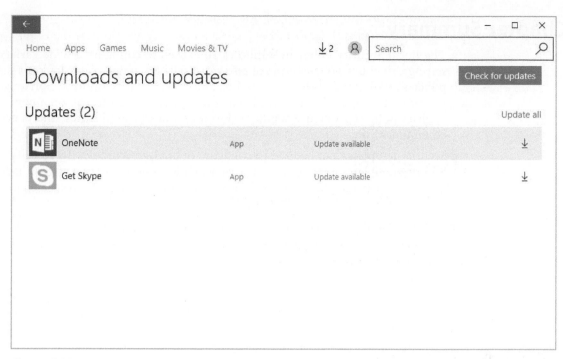

Figure 6-22   Windows Store Downloads and updates

If you select Settings, you are presented with the options shown in Figure 6-23. From here, you can enable or disable automatic updates for Windows Store apps. Update apps automatically is on by default. This is the preferred option in most scenarios.

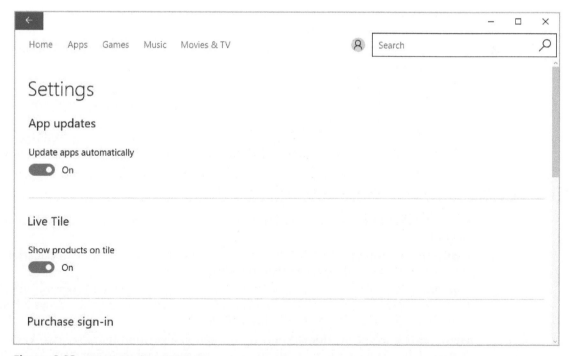

Figure 6-23   Windows Store Settings

Chapter Summary

- The Local Security Policy in Windows 10 is used to configure a wide variety of security settings. Account policies control password settings and account lockout settings. Local policies configure auditing, user rights, and other security options. Software restriction policies and AppLocker control what software is allowed to run on a computer. Other security policies configure Windows Firewall and EFS certificates, and encrypt network communication.

- Security templates can be used to configure or analyze Windows 10 security options. Security templates include account policy and local policy settings from the local security policy. Security templates also include settings for the event log, restricted groups, service configuration, registry security, and file security.

- Analyzing and applying security templates is done with Secedit or the Security Configuration and Analysis MMC snap-in. Secedit is a command-line tool that is useful for scripting mass operations.

- Auditing is used to record specific operating system events to the security log. Event categories that can be configured are Account Logon, Account Management, Detailed Tracking, DS Access, Logon/Logoff, Object Access, Policy Change, Privilege Use, System, and Global Object Access.

- User Account Control (UAC) increases security by allowing users to sign in and perform their jobs with standard user accounts. UAC also limits administrators to standard user privileges until administrative privileges are required by using Admin Approval Mode.

- Windows Defender is anti-malware software. It scans for viruses and spyware. It provides real-time scanning and can perform on-demand scanning.

- Encrypting File System (EFS) is used to protect individual files by encrypting them. Only the person who encrypted a file can decrypt it, unless that file has been properly shared. A recovery certificate can be used to decrypt files, if the certificate is configured.

- BitLocker Drive Encryption is used to encrypt an entire volume. To use BitLocker Drive Encryption, there must be at least two partitions on the hard drive. BitLocker Drive Encryption also protects the operating system from being modified. BitLocker To Go allows removable storage to be encrypted.

- Windows Update is used to ensure that updates are applied to Windows 10 as they are made available. Windows 10 uses the Current Branch update of Windows 10 by default, but can be configured to use the Current Branch for Business.

- Windows Store apps are updated by the Windows Store instead of Windows Update. Windows Store apps are automatically updated by default.

Key Terms

account lockout policy A collection of settings, such as lockout duration, that control account lockouts.

application manifest An XML file that describes the structure of an application, including required DLL files and privilege requirements.

AppLocker A feature in Windows 10 that is used to define which programs are allowed to run. This is a replacement for the software restriction policies found in Windows XP and Windows Vista, but it is not available in Windows 10 Pro.

asymmetric encryption algorithm An encryption algorithm that uses two keys to encrypt and decrypt data. Data encrypted with one key is decrypted by the other key.

audit policy   The settings that define which operating system events are audited.

auditing   The security process that records the occurrence of specific operating system events in the Security log.

BitLocker Drive Encryption   A feature in Windows 10 that can encrypt the operating system partition of a hard drive and protect system files from modification. Other partitions can also be encrypted.

BitLocker To Go   A new feature in Windows 10 that allows you to encrypt removable storage.

Encrypting File System (EFS)   An encryption technology for individual files and folders that can be enabled by users.

Full Volume Encryption Key (FVEK)   The key used to encrypt the Volume Master Key (VMK) when BitLocker Drive Encryption is enabled.

hashing algorithm   A one-way encryption algorithm that creates a unique identifier that can be used to determine whether data has been changed.

local security policy   A set of security configuration options in Windows 10. These options are used to control user rights, auditing, password settings, and more.

malware   Malicious software designed to perform unauthorized acts on your computer. Malware includes viruses, worms, and spyware.

password policy   A collection of settings to control password characteristics such as length and complexity.

Secedit   A command-line tool that is used to apply, export, or analyze security templates.

Security Configuration and Analysis tool   An MMC snap-in that is used to apply, export, or analyze security templates.

security template   An .inf file that contains security settings that can be applied to a computer or analyzed against a computer's existing configuration.

symmetric encryption algorithm   An encryption algorithm that uses the same key to encrypt and decrypt data.

User Account Control (UAC)   A feature in Windows 10 that elevates user privileges only when required.

Volume Master Key (VMK)   The key used to encrypt hard drive data when BitLocker Drive Encryption is enabled.

Windows Defender   Anti-malware software included with Windows 10.

Review Questions

1. Which security feature in Windows 10 prevents malware by limiting user privilege levels?
   a.   Windows Defender
   b.   User Account Control (UAC)
   c.   Microsoft Security Essentials
   d.   Service SIDs

2. Which of the following passwords meet complexity requirements? (Choose all that apply.)
   a.   passw0rd$
   b.   ##$$@@
   c.   ake1vyue
   d.   a1batr0$$
   e.   A%5j

3. Which password policy setting should you use to prevent users from reusing their passwords too quickly?

    a. maximum password age

    b. minimum password age

    c. minimum password length

    d. password must meet complexity requirements

    e. store passwords using reversible encryption

4. Which account lockout policy setting is used to configure the time frame in which incorrect sign-in attempts must be conducted before an account is locked out?

    a. account lockout duration

    b. account lockout threshold

    c. reset account lockout counter after

    d. account lockout release period

5. The _____ local policy controls the tasks users are allowed to perform.

6. Which type of AppLocker rule condition can uniquely identify any file regardless of its location?

    a. publisher

    b. hash

    c. network zone

    d. path

7. How would you create AppLocker rules if you wanted to avoid updating the rules when most software is already installed?

    a. Manually create rules for each application.

    b. Automatically generate rules.

    c. Create default rules.

    d. Download rule templates.

8. Evaluating DLL files for software restrictions has a minimal impact on performance because of caching. True or False?

9. Which utilities can be used to compare the settings in a security template against a computer configuration? (Choose all that apply.)

    a. Secedit

    b. Windows Defender

    c. Security Templates snap-in

    d. Group Policy Object Editor

    e. Security Configuration and Analysis tool

10. To which event log are audit events written?

    a. Application

    b. Security

    c. System

    d. Audit

    e. Advanced Audit

11. An _____ is used to describe the structure of an application and trigger UAC when required.

12. What are you disabling when you configure UAC to not dim the desktop?

    a. Admin Approval Mode

    b. file and registry virtualization

    c. user-initiated prompts

    d. secure desktop

13. To prevent malware installation, you should configure Windows Defender to perform _____.

14. Which type of encryption is the fastest, strongest, and best suited to encrypting large amounts of information?

    a. symmetric

    b. 128 bit

    c. asymmetric

    d. hash

    e. public key

15. To encrypt a file by using EFS, the file must be stored on an NTFS-formatted partition. True or False?

16. How can you recover EFS-encrypted files if the user profile holding the digital certificate is accidentally deleted? (Choose all that apply.)

    a. Restore the file from backup.

    b. Restore the user certificate from a backup copy.

    c. Another user who has access to open the file can decrypt it.

    d. Decrypt the file by using the recovery certificate.

    e. Decrypt the file by using the EFS recovery snap-in.

17. Which of the following is *not* true about BitLocker Drive Encryption?

    a. BitLocker Drive Encryption requires at least two disk partitions.

    b. BitLocker Drive Encryption is designed to be used with a TPM.

    c. Two encryption keys are used to protect data.

    d. Data is still encrypted when BitLocker Drive Encryption is disabled.

    e. You must use a USB drive to store the startup PIN.

18. BitLocker Drive Encryption is user aware and can be used to protect individual files on a shared computer. True or False?

19. Which servicing branch for Windows Update should be used for computers where changes cannot be tolerated?

    a. Windows Insider Preview Branch

    b. Current Branch

    c. Current Branch for Business

    d. Long Term Servicing Branch

    e. Stable Service Branch

20. What is the name of the Group Policy setting that configures Windows Update for Business?

   a. Defer Upgrades and Updates

   b. Windows Update for Business

   c. Windows Update Delay

   d. Enterprise Windows Update

   e. Windows Update Deployment

Case Projects

Case Project 6-1: Virus Prevention

Buddy's Machine shop has been infected with a virus for the second time in six months. Several machines cannot run antivirus software because it interferes with specialized software used to carve machine parts from blocks of metal. What can you do to mitigate the risk of viruses infecting the computers?

Case Project 6-2: Applying Security Settings

Gigantic Life Insurance has thousands of insurance brokers selling their services. The security officer has recently identified a list of security settings that she wants configured on all Windows 10 computers used by the insurance brokers. What is the best way to apply these security settings?

Case Project 6-3: Data Encryption

The salespeople at Hyperactive Media Sales all use laptop computers so they can have easy access to important data on the road. The salespeople regularly take customer lists and other sensitive company information with them. Occasionally a laptop is lost or stolen. Which data encryption features in Windows 10 can prevent hard drive data from being used after a laptop is stolen? Which features would you implement and why?

chapter 7

Networking

After reading this chapter and completing the exercises, you will be able to:

- Understand Windows 10 network components
- Describe and configure Internet Protocol version 4
- Describe and configure Internet Protocol version 6
- Perform and monitor file sharing
- Connect Windows 10 to the Internet
- Describe and configure wireless networking
- Configure Windows Firewall
- Describe homegroup networks

The vast majority of computers in corporations and small offices are networked. Many homes have multiple computers that are used to share files and access the Internet. As a computer professional, it is essential that you understand how to configure Windows 10 for networking in these situations.

In this chapter, you learn how to configure networking in Windows 10, including both IPv4 and IPv6, and how to implement network file sharing and monitor file shares. Internet connectivity is discussed. You learn about configuring connectivity to wireless networks, including the new Wi-Fi Sense feature in Windows 10. You also learn to secure network connectivity by using Windows Firewall. Finally, you learn how a homegroup can be used for file sharing in small networks.

Networking Overview

Windows 10 includes the basic components of networking such as clients, services, protocols, and network drivers; however, additional features have been added. The basic components of Windows 10 that support networking are:

- Network and Sharing Center
- Networks
- Connections

Network and Sharing Center

Network and Sharing Center is a central point in Windows 10 for managing the configuration of the network you are currently connected to. The areas of Network and Sharing Center, as shown in Figure 7-1, are:

- *View your active networks*—This area shows summary information for the network you are connected to. It displays the network you are connected to, the type of network it is, the type of access you have, and the connection being used to access the network.

- *Change your networking settings*—This area displays links to common configuration and troubleshooting wizards.

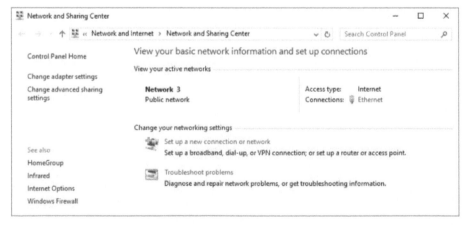

Figure 7-1 Network and Sharing Center

Networks

In early versions of Windows, the operating system was simply aware of a network card being physically connected (or not connected) to a network. Windows 10 has been enhanced to be network location aware. When you move a computer from one network to another, Windows 10 is aware that it is connected to a different network. Windows 10 keeps track of enough network properties to profile the network it is connected to. If the network is disconnected and reconnected later,

Windows 10 may recognize the network from a list of stored network profiles. Windows 10 can associate certain properties with that network profile, such as its assigned network **location type.**

Network location awareness allows you to configure the security settings for each location differently. For example, for the network in your office, you might allow your computer to be discoverable by other computers on the network, but not when you are traveling on the road in hotels and airports. The configuration settings for each network are saved so that you do not need to reconfigure your computer as you move from one frequently used network location to another.

Network Name   When you first connect to a network, the network is given a name to identify it by Windows 10. Wireless networks are named after the broadcast ID of the wireless access point. For example, connecting to the wireless network at work could create a network profile called Corp-Private. For Ethernet networks, the new network is assigned the prefix "Network" followed by a sequence number of the next available network number in the network profile history. For example, plugging into a new wired network at a hotel could create a network profile called Network 5.

Location Types   Each network location is assigned a location type. When you first connect to a network, Windows 10 prompts you if your computer should be visible, or discoverable, to other computers on the network, as shown in Figure 7-2. Depending on how you respond, different security settings are applied. Components that are configured include **Windows Firewall** and **network discovery**. Previous editions of Windows differentiated between home and work locations, but Windows 10 simplifies the location list to locations that are trusted for computer discovery and those that are not.

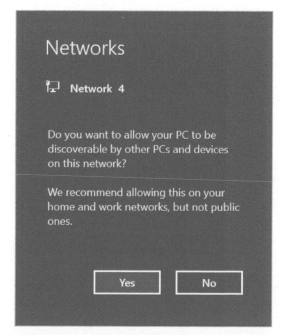

Figure 7-2   Confirming if you want your computer discoverable on a new network

The location types are:

- *Private network*—The **private network** category is used when the computer is connected as part of a peer-to-peer network in a trusted location. Typically, this is used at home or at work for peer-to-peer networking. The computer is able to access other network computers and you are able to share files and printers on your computer. Computers on a private network can belong to a homegroup.

- *Public network*—**Public network** is the default location type for a new network, and is used when the computer is connected in an untrusted public location such as an airport.

In a public location, you cannot be sure of who else is using the network. Other network computers have limited or no visibility to your computer on the network. Your computer can connect to publicly available network resources, but you are not able to share files and printers on your computer. Connections initiated from other computers on the public network are blocked by default.

- *Domain network*—The **domain network** category is used in corporate environments when your computer is part of a domain network. When Windows 10 can communicate with a domain controller, the network connection is automatically placed in this location category. You cannot manually place a computer in this category. The computer settings for computers on a domain network are determined by Group Policy settings configured by the network administrator.

Network Discovery   One of the network characteristics you can configure is network discovery. Network discovery provides you with an easy way to control how your computer views other computers on the network and advertises its presence on the network. Network discovery settings can be reviewed or modified by selecting the *Change advanced sharing settings* task from the Network and Sharing Center, as seen previously in Figure 7-1. This opens the Advanced sharing settings screen where for each type of network location, you can adjust the network discovery behavior of that type of location, as shown in Figure 7-3.

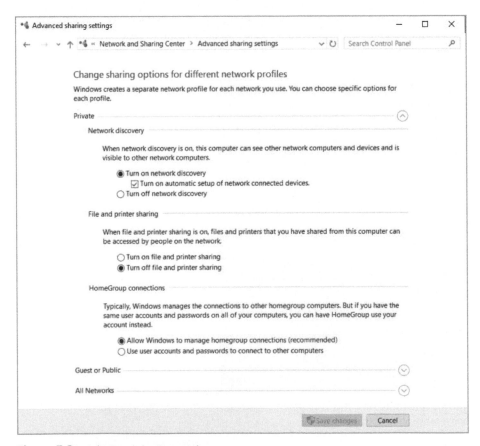

Figure 7-3   Advanced sharing settings

The options for network discovery are:

- *Turn on network discovery*—You can see and access other computers and devices on the network. Other computers can also see your computer on the network and access shared resources. This is the default configuration when the network is in the Private location type.

- *Turn off network discovery*—You cannot see or access other computers and devices on the network. Other computers also cannot see your computer on the network or access shared resources. This is the default configuration for networks in the Public location type.

Activity 7-1: Exploring Network and Sharing Center

Time Required: 5 minutes

Objective: Become familiar with the options that are available in Network and Sharing Center

Description: Network and Sharing Center provides you with an overview of the network configuration on your computer. In this activity, you explore a few of the options available to you in Network and Sharing Center.

1. If necessary, start your computer and sign in.

2. Right-click the **Start** button and click **Control Panel**.

3. Click **Network and Internet** and then click **Network and Sharing Center**.

4. In the section titled View your active networks, review the name of the network listed there and note if it is a public or private network.

5. To the right of that network name, note the network Connections section and the link to its settings. Click that link to bring up the connection's status window.

6. Click the **Details** button and note the type of information visible. Much of the same information is visible by running the command *ipconfig /all* from a command prompt window, but note that the user does not have to perform those extra steps. Note that key information such as DHCP enabled, Physical Address, IPv4 Address, IPv4DHCP Server, and IPv4 DNS Server are displayed.

7. Close the Network Connection Details window.

8. In the connection's Status window, click **Diagnose**.

9. If no problems were found (none are expected in the lab environment), note the message that troubleshooting couldn't identify the problem. Click **Close**.

10. Close all open windows.

Connections

Connections in Windows 10 are fundamentally the same as in previous versions of Windows. For each network device installed in your computer, a connection is created to manage that network device. For example, if your computer has an Ethernet network card and a wireless network card, there will be two connections in Windows 10, one to manage each device. The properties of a connection are shown in Figure 7-4. If your computer has multiple network cards, you will see an additional Sharing tab when viewing connection properties. Connections are composed of:

- Clients and services
- Protocols
- Network drivers

Clients and Services   Clients and services are the applications that use the network to communicate. A **client** allows you to connect to a particular service running on a remote computer. A **service** allows your computer to accept connections from and provide resources to a remote computer.

The clients and services included with Windows 10 are:

- *Client for Microsoft Networks*—**Client for Microsoft Networks** allows Windows 10 to access shared files and printers on other Windows computers.

- *File and Printer Sharing for Microsoft Networks*—**File and Printer Sharing for Microsoft Networks** allows Windows 10 to share files and printers with other Windows computers.

- *QoS Packet Scheduler*—This service controls the flow of network traffic in Windows 10. It is responsible for optimizing network communication by controlling the Quality of Service (QoS). Corporate environments can use QoS policies to give certain network

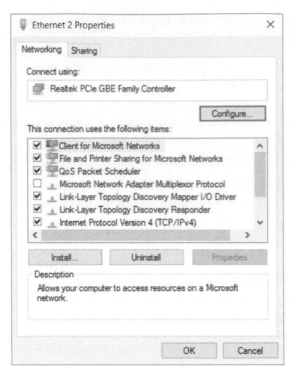

Figure 7-4 Network connection Properties

content types higher priority within Windows 10. For private networks, QoS incorporates Quality Windows Audio/Video Experience (qWAVE) to ensure that A/V streams get higher network priority than data streams, which are more tolerant of network delays.

 All three client and service components in Windows 10 are installed by default.

Both the Client for Microsoft Networks and File and Printer Sharing for Microsoft Networks use the **Server Message Block** (**SMB**) protocol. Early versions of Windows included a client for accessing Novell NetWare networks. This legacy client has been removed from Windows 10.

Protocols Protocols are the rules for communicating across the network. They define how much data can be sent and the format of the data as it crosses the network. Windows 10 includes several protocols for network communication.

- *Internet Protocol Version 4 (TCP/IPv4)*—**Internet Protocol Version 4** (**TCP/IPv4**) is the standard protocol used on corporate networks and the Internet. This protocol is installed by default and cannot be removed. However, it can be disabled.

- *Internet Protocol Version 6 (TCP/IPv6)*—**Internet Protocol Version 6** (**TCP/IPv6**) is an updated version of TCP/IPv4 with a larger address space and additional features. It has not yet gained widespread popularity, but will in the future. Windows 10 uses this protocol for some peer-to-peer networking applications. This protocol is installed by default and cannot be removed. However, it can be disabled.

- *Link-Layer Topology Discovery Mapper I/O Driver*—The Link-Layer Topology Discovery Mapper I/O Driver protocol is responsible for discovering network devices on the network, such as computers and routers. It is also responsible for determining the network speed.

- *Link-Layer Topology Discovery Responder*—The Link-Layer Topology Discovery Responder protocol is responsible for responding to discovery requests from other computers.
- *Microsoft LLDP Protocol Driver*—This protocol is used by network devices to advertise their identity, capabilities, and neighbors on a local network.

Detailed information about TCP/IPv4 and TCP/IPv6 is found later in this chapter.

Network Drivers A **network driver** is responsible for enabling communication between Windows 10 and the network device(s) in your computer. Each make and model of network device requires a driver specifically developed for that device, just as each printer requires a printer driver specific to that make and model of printer.

Windows 10 includes network drivers for network devices from a wide variety of manufacturers. However, if the network driver for your network device is not included with Windows 10, you can obtain the driver from the manufacturer's website.

Activity 7-2: Viewing a Network Connection

Time Required: 5 minutes
Objective: View the properties and status of a network connection

Description: To configure Windows 10 for network connectivity, you need to understand the components of a network connection and how to view their status. In this activity, you view the status and properties of a network connection.

1. If necessary, start your computer and sign in.
2. Right-click the **Start** button and click **Control Panel**.
3. Click **Network and Internet** and click **Network and Sharing Center**.
4. Under the View your active networks heading, and to the right of Connections, click the named network connection. The name of the network connection will be different on different computers, but will likely be called Ethernet. This shows the current connection status.
5. Click the **Properties** button. This displays all of the clients, services, and protocols that are installed.
6. Click the **Configure** button. This allows you to modify the configuration of the network card or network card driver.
7. Click the **Advanced** tab. This tab allows you to configure many settings for your network card. The options available here vary depending on the card. However, all cards allow you to in some way configure the connection speed and duplex. These are important settings to ensure proper connectivity when connecting to some network switches in the event that autonegotiation fails.
8. Click the **Driver** tab. This tab lets you view driver details, update the driver, roll back the driver to a previous version, disable the device, and uninstall the driver.
9. Click the **Details** button. This shows you the files used as part of the device driver as well as additional information about the driver, such as version and the company that provided the driver.
10. Click the **Events** button. This shows you a history of driver events that may assist with troubleshooting in the event of a problem.
11. Close all open windows.

Windows 10 includes several interfaces that make it easier for developers to create clients, services, protocols, and network drivers. These interfaces provide a standard way for clients and services to communicate with protocols and a standard way for protocols to communicate with network drivers. TCP/IP is by far the most common protocol used.

IP Version 4

TCP/IP is the most popular networking protocol in the world today. Although Windows 10 has the ability to use multiple protocols, only TCP/IP is included with Windows 10 for network communication such as file sharing or accessing the Internet. Part of the IPv4 standard defines how to specify and decipher the address of a computer that sent a piece of TCP/IP data, and the address of the computer that will receive it. The IPv4 addressing scheme works whether the computers are right next to each other or if they are located on opposite sides of the globe.

IP Addresses

Each computer must have a unique **IP address** to communicate on the network. If any two computers on the same network have the same IP address, it is impossible for information to be correctly delivered to them.

IPv4 addresses are actually a binary number, 32 bits (binary digits) wide. Each bit can have the value 1 or 0. IPv4 addresses are most commonly displayed in dotted decimal notation. In this format, an IP address is displayed as four decimal numbers, called octets, which are separated by periods. An example of an IP address written in dotted decimal notation is 192.168.5.66. In this example, 192 is the first octet, 168 is the second, 5 is the third, and 66 is the fourth and last octet. Each octet represents the decimal number equivalent of the 8 binary bits in that portion of the 32-bit address. An octet value can range between 0 and 255.

The value of the first octet determines the general class of an IPv4 address, as shown in Table 7-1.

Table 7-1 IPv4 address classes

First octet value range	Corresponding class
0 to 127	A
128 to 191	B
192 to 223	C
224 to 239	D
240 to 255	E

There are special cases and considerations in the IPv4 class–based system:

- If the first octet is zero, the remaining octets identify local machines on the same network as the computer sending data. The special IPv4 address 0.0.0.0 is used in routing logic to represent "all other computers."

- A first octet value of 127 identifies a destination that is local to the computer sending data. The address in this range that is commonly seen is 127.0.0.1, or the loopback address. Data sent to the **loopback address** returns to the computer that sent it and does not appear on the actual network.

- A first octet identifying a Class D address represents a multicast address. Computers that belong to the same multicast group have the same multicast address assigned to them. Data sent to that multicast address attempts to deliver copies of the data to all multicast members with the same address. Class D addresses are not used to identify a single host computer with a unique IPv4 address.

- A first octet identifying a Class E address is reserved for future use and special purposes. Class E addresses are not used to identify a single host computer with a unique IPv4 address. The special IPv4 address 255.255.255.255 is used as a **broadcast address** that represents the destination "all computers in this network." Data sent to this broadcast address cannot leave the local network through a router.

Several ranges of IP addresses are reserved for internal private network use and cannot be routed on the Internet. However, they can be routed internally on corporate networks. A proxy server or Network Address Translation (NAT) must be used to provide Internet access to computers using these addresses. Table 7-2 shows the network addresses that are reserved for internal networks.

Table 7-2   Addresses for internal networks

IP address range	Network (in CIDR notation)
192.168.0.0.–192.168.255.255	192.168.0.0/16
172.16.0.0–172.31.255.255	172.16.0.0/12
10.0.0.0–10.255.255.255	10.0.0.0/8

Subnet Masks

An IP address is composed of a network ID and a host ID. Using the concept of a postal address for comparison, the network ID is similar to a street name and the host ID is similar to a house number. When a packet of information is being delivered on a corporate network, the network ID is used to get the packet to the proper area of the network and the host ID is used to deliver the packet to the correct computer. The total number of binary bits used to define a network ID plus the host ID must equal 32 bits exactly in order to fit in an IPv4 address.

A **subnet mask** is used to define which part of an IP address is the network ID and which part of the IP address is the host ID. If the subnet mask is configured incorrectly, Windows 10 might not be able to communicate with computers on other parts of the network. Two computers cannot be active on the same local network with the same network ID and same host ID. This would cause an IP address conflict and other computers would not know which computer to communicate with.

The subnet mask is another 32-bit binary number, specified separately from the IP address itself. For discussion sake, consider this example of a subnet mask value in binary form (blank spaces inserted for readability):

Subnet mask = 1111 1111 1111 1111 1111 1111 0000 0000

The subnet mask's bits set to 1 identify what part of an assigned IPv4 address belongs to the network ID. The bits set to 0 identify what part of an address belongs to the host ID. In this example, this would be interpreted by a computer as the first 24 bits of the IPv4 address identify the computer's network ID; the last 8 bits of the IPv4 address identify the computer's host ID. For convenience, the dotted decimal notation is used to enter the subnet mask value into the IP settings of a network interface. Using dotted decimal notation, the preceding subnet mask binary value would be entered as 255.255.255.0.

The subnet mask octet value of 255 indicates that the corresponding IPv4 address octet belongs to the network ID. The subnet mask octet value of 0 indicates that the corresponding IPv4 address octet belongs to the host ID. For example, consider the following breakdown of an IPv4 address into its network and host ID components given a subnet mask:

IPv4 address = 192.168.4.1

Subnet mask = 255.255.255.0

Network ID = 192.168.4.0

Host ID = 0.0.0.1

If two computers have the same network ID in their respective assigned IPv4 address, they should be able to directly communicate on the same local network through a common device such as a network switch. If the network ID is not the same, routers must receive the data from one computer and pass it to the destination network for delivery to the target computer. For example, consider the following three IPv4 addresses and a given subnet mask:

IPv4 address A = 172.16.4.254

IPv4 address B = 192.168.4.254

IPv4 address C = 172.16.4.1

Subnet mask = 255.255.0.0

If these three IP addresses are assigned to three different computers on the same local network, it is assumed that all three computers have the same subnet mask assigned. Each computer would analyze the network ID of each address as:

Network ID of address A = 172.16.0.0

Network ID of address B = 192.168.0.0

Network ID of address C = 172.16.0.0

From the perspective of a computer assigned address A, address C is reachable by sending data directly over the local network, as expected. However, the computer assigned address A considers address B to only be reachable through a router. This is because the network ID of address B does not match its own. The computers assigned address A and B do not realize that they are on the same local network. They might fail to transfer data between each other if a router is not present or configured to relay data between the two computers.

Analyzing how subnet masks can be used to group hosts, and how to analyze subnet mask octet values other than 255 or 0, is an advanced TCP/IP design topic beyond the scope of this book.

Documenting subnet mask values with dotted decimal values is not the only way to write a subnet mask value using a shorthand notation. Another way to specify a subnet mask is to write the IPv4 address followed by a slash and a number that identifies the number of contiguous binary ones on the left-hand side of the subnet mask. For example, consider this subnet mask expressed in binary and dotted decimal notation:

Subnet mask (binary) = 1111 1111 1111 1111 0000 0000 0000 0000

Subnet mask (dotted decimal) = 255.255.0.0

In the case of the preceding example, there are 16 ones in the subnet mask value; therefore, the IP address and subnet mask value can be written as *IPaddress*/16. If this subnet mask was applied to the IP address 172.16.34.1, it would be written as 172.16.34.1/16. This notation is commonly referred to as **classless interdomain routing (CIDR)** notation.

Default subnet mask values were originally defined by the class of the IPv4 address, as shown in Table 7-3.

Table 7-3   Class-based default subnet mask values

Class	Default subnet mask value	Default subnet mask value (in CIDR notation)
A	255.0.0.0	/8
B	255.255.0.0	/16
C	255.255.255.0	/24

For more detailed information about advanced IP addressing and deeper binary-level information, see TCP/IP Fundamentals for Windows at *http:// technet.microsoft.com/en-us/library/bb726995.aspx*.

Default Gateways

The Internet and corporate networks are large networks that are composed of many smaller networks. Routers control the movement of packets through the networks. An individual computer is capable of delivering packets on the local network, but not to remote networks. To deliver packets to a remote network, the packet must be delivered to a router. The router sends the packet on toward its final destination.

A computer's **default gateway** is a router on the local network that is used to deliver packets to remote networks. The default gateway is identified in the computer's IP settings by entering the IP address assigned to the router's local network connection. If a computer has multiple network interfaces configured for IPv4, only one should be configured with a default gateway setting. If the default gateway is configured incorrectly, the computer cannot communicate outside the local network. This means Internet connectivity is not possible and corporate computers will likely not have access to all resources.

Windows 10 stores the default gateway setting internally as part of a larger table, called the **routing table,** as shown in Figure 7-5. The routing table is revisited later in this chapter.

7

```
Command Prompt

C:\Windows\System>route print
===========================================================================
Interface List
 23...dc 4a 3e a7 dd 12 ......Realtek PCIe GBE Family Controller
  2...18 5e 0f 99 3d c0 ......Microsoft Wi-Fi Direct Virtual Adapter
 42...1a 5e 0f 99 3d bf ......Microsoft Wi-Fi Direct Virtual Adapter #2
 11...18 5e 0f 99 3d bf ......Hyper-V Virtual Ethernet Adapter
  6...18 5e 0f 99 3d c3 ......Bluetooth Device (Personal Area Network)
  1...........................Software Loopback Interface 1
 13...00 00 00 00 00 00 00 e0 Teredo Tunneling Pseudo-Interface
  7...00 00 00 00 00 00 00 e0 Microsoft ISATAP Adapter #2
===========================================================================

IPv4 Route Table
===========================================================================
Active Routes:
Network Destination        Netmask          Gateway       Interface  Metric
          0.0.0.0          0.0.0.0  192.168.100.254  192.168.100.105     25
        127.0.0.0        255.0.0.0         On-link        127.0.0.1    306
        127.0.0.1  255.255.255.255         On-link        127.0.0.1    306
  127.255.255.255  255.255.255.255         On-link        127.0.0.1    306
    192.168.100.0    255.255.255.0         On-link  192.168.100.105    281
  192.168.100.105  255.255.255.255         On-link  192.168.100.105    281
  192.168.100.255  255.255.255.255         On-link  192.168.100.105    281
        224.0.0.0        240.0.0.0         On-link        127.0.0.1    306
        224.0.0.0        240.0.0.0         On-link  192.168.100.105    281
  255.255.255.255  255.255.255.255         On-link        127.0.0.1    306
  255.255.255.255  255.255.255.255         On-link  192.168.100.105    281
===========================================================================
Persistent Routes:
  None

IPv6 Route Table
===========================================================================
Active Routes:
 If Metric Network Destination      Gateway
 13    306 ::/0                     On-link
  1    306 ::1/128                  On-link
 13    306 2001::/32                On-link
 13    306 2001:0:5ef5:79fd:18f2:1e4:305e:dc30/128
                                    On-link
 11    281 fe80::/64                On-link
 13    306 fe80::/64                On-link
 13    306 fe80::18f2:1e4:305e:dc30/128
                                    On-link
 11    281 fe80::bdf4:30b0:19ea:8e1e/128
                                    On-link
  1    306 ff00::/8                 On-link
 11    281 ff00::/8                 On-link
 13    306 ff00::/8                 On-link
===========================================================================
Persistent Routes:
  None
```

Figure 7-5   Windows networking routing table displayed with *route print* command

DNS

Domain Name System (DNS) is essential to communicate on a TCP/IP network. The most common use for DNS is resolving host names to IP addresses. When you access a website, you access a location such as *www.microsoft.com*. This is a **fully qualified domain name (FQDN)**, which is a combination of host name and domain name. Computers cannot connect to a service on the Internet directly by using a host name. Instead, they convert the host name to an IP address and then access the service by using the IP address.

DNS is essential for Internet connectivity because most people use domain names, not IP addresses, to access Internet servers such as websites. DNS is required to convert the name of a website to an IP address. As well, DNS is required for Windows 10 computers in a domain-based network to find domain controllers and sign in.

A primary and secondary DNS server address can be defined for any network connection. To avoid operational problems, it must be clear how Windows 10 will use multiple DNS server entries if they are defined. When a program asks Windows 10 to translate a host name to an IP address, it picks the IP of one of the DNS servers and sends it a DNS query. There is no guarantee that the primary DNS server will always be the server queried first but typically it is checked first.

When the computer receives a response from a DNS server telling it an answer has been found, or a response that no matching information is available, Windows 10 considers the DNS server active and functional. It is only when the DNS server fails to respond at all that Windows 10 sends the request to one of the other defined DNS servers. A response that a name couldn't be translated into an IP address is still a valid response and the other DNS servers will not be queried for an answer to the same question.

Windows 10 also provides a text file called hosts in the folder C:\Windows\System32\ drivers\etc\ that maps IP addresses to host names. Entries in the hosts file take precedence over data retrieved from DNS servers. Custom data can be entered into the hosts file to override DNS server data; however, this is a local file and can be difficult to remotely administer.

WINS

Windows Internet Naming Service (WINS) is a legacy technology used to resolve NetBIOS names to IP addresses. In addition, it stores information about services such as domain controllers. WINS is primarily used for backward compatibility with older NetBIOS-based networks. NetBIOS names can be used to access network services, such as file shares. Windows 10 is capable of using WINS, but uses DNS as its primary name-resolution mechanism. IPv6 does not support using WINS.

Methods for Configuring IPv4

All IP configuration information can be manually entered on each Windows 10 computer, but this approach is not very efficient. With each manual entry, there is risk of a typographical error. In addition, if the IP configuration changes, visiting each computer to modify the configuration can be an enormous task. Manually entering IP configuration information is called static configuration. Figure 7-6 shows TCP/IP version 4 configured with a static IP address.

Dynamic Host Configuration Protocol (DHCP) is an automated mechanism used to assign IP addresses, subnet masks, default gateways, DNS servers, WINS servers, and other IP configuration information to network devices. Automating this process avoids the problem of information being entered incorrectly. If a change needs to be made to the IP address information, you modify the configuration of the DHCP server. The DHCP server can be configured with a range of IP addresses to hand out, specific exclusions to never hand out, or specific reservations that are given out to DHCP client computers with specified MAC addresses. Obtaining IP configuration information automatically is called dynamic configuration.

If Windows 10 is configured to use dynamic IP configuration and is unable to contact a DHCP server, the default action is to use an **Automatic Private IP Addressing (APIPA)** address. These addresses are on the 169.254.0.0/16 network.

APIPA is designed as a solution for very small networks with no Internet connectivity requirements. When two computers generate APIPA addresses, they are able to communicate with each other because they are considered to be on the same local network, with a randomly generated unique host address. Unfortunately, APIPA addresses have little benefit in most scenarios because no default gateway is configured and no DNS server is assigned. This means that

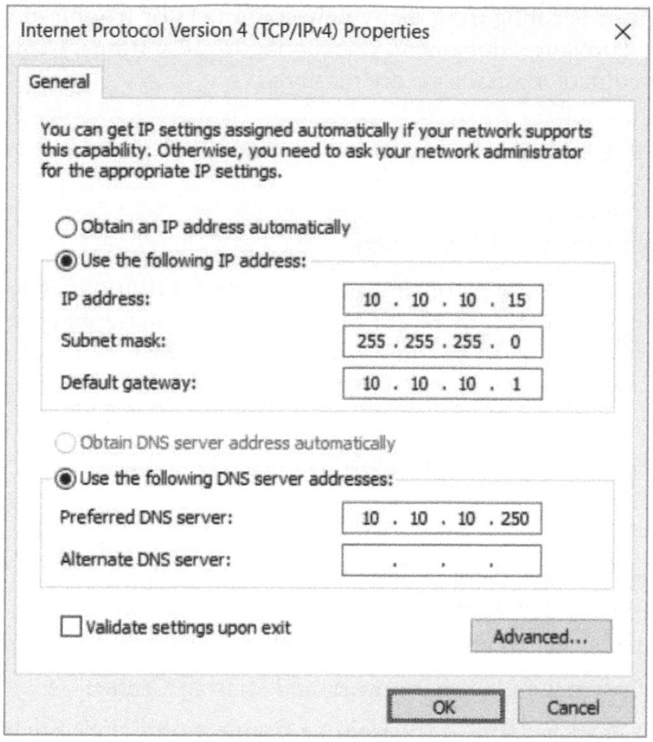

Figure 7-6   Static IPv4 configuration

the computers cannot access the Internet. Consequently, a computer using an APIPA address is usually just a sign that the computer could not contact a DHCP server.

When a network connection is set to obtain its IP address automatically, Windows 10 also allows you to configure a static set of alternate IP configuration options. If a DHCP server cannot be contacted, the **alternate IP configuration** is used instead. When an alternate IP configuration is enabled, APIPA is not used. Figure 7-7 shows the Alternate Configuration tab for Internet Protocol Version 4.

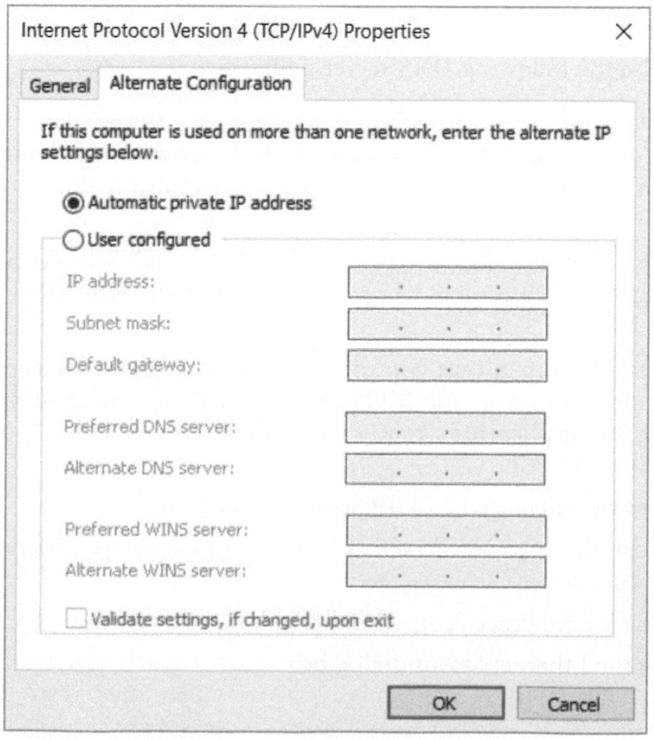

Figure 7-7   Alternate IP configuration for IPv4

When an administrator is configuring many new computers or troubleshooting, scripts can be run to automatically configure, document, or reconfigure IP settings. Utilities such as *netsh* are powerful once their control mechanisms are mastered.

Activity 7-3: Viewing and Configuring IPv4

Time Required: 5 minutes

Objective: View and configure IPv4 settings

Description: When you are troubleshooting network connectivity, it is essential that you understand how to view the existing IPv4 configuration to evaluate whether it is a problem. The graphical interface can be used to view and configure IPv4. In this activity, you view and configure IPv4 by using the graphical interface.

To avoid disrupting communications, the changes you are making in this activity are not saved.

1. If necessary, start your computer and sign in.
2. Right-click the **Start** button and click **Control Panel**.
3. Click **Network and Internet** and click **Network and Sharing Center**.
4. Under the Network heading, and to the right of Connections, click **Ethernet** (or whatever the network connection for your machine in the lab is called).
5. Click the **Properties** button.
6. Click **Internet Protocol Version 4 (TCP/IPv4)** and click **Properties**. This shows you the basic configuration of IPv4. By default, an IP address and DNS server address are obtained automatically through DHCP.
7. Click **Use the following IP address**. This allows you to enter in a static IPv4 configuration.
8. In the IP address box, type **192.168.1.100**.
9. If necessary, in the Subnet mask box, type **255.255.255.0**.
10. In the Default gateway box, type **192.168.1.1**.
11. If necessary, click **Use the following DNS server addresses**.
12. In the Preferred DNS server box, type **192.168.1.5**.
13. Click the **Advanced** button. In the Advanced TCP/IP Settings, you can configure additional options. On the IP Settings tab, you can configure multiple IP addresses and default gateways.
14. Click the **DNS** tab. This tab allows you to control how DNS lookups are performed and whether this computer attempts to register its name with the DNS servers by using dynamic DNS.
15. Click the **WINS** tab. This tab allows you to configure how WINS lookups are performed. Some networks prefer to disable NetBIOS over TCP/IP to reduce network broadcasts. However, some legacy applications require NetBIOS, so test your applications before disabling NetBIOS over TCP/IP.
16. Click **Cancel** to close the Advanced TCP/IP Settings dialog box.
17. Click **Cancel** to close the Internet Protocol Version 4 (TCP/IPv4) Properties dialog box without saving any changes.
18. Click **Cancel** to close the Ethernet Properties dialog box.
19. Click **Close** to close the Ethernet Status dialog box.

20. Close Network and Sharing Center.

21. Close all open windows.

Activity 7-4: Using Ipconfig and Netsh

Time Required: 10 minutes

Objective: Use *ipconfig* and *netsh* to view and configure IPv4

Description: Windows 10 includes *ipconfig* and *netsh* to view and configure IPv4 at the command line. These utilities can also be used for scripting. *Ipconfig* is used to view IPv4 configuration or release and renew IP configuration from a DHCP server. *Netsh* can be used to configure IPv4. In this activity, you use *ipconfig* and *netsh* to view and configure IPv4.

1. If necessary, start your computer and sign in.

2. Right-click the **Start** button, click **Command Prompt (Admin)**, and click **Yes** when prompted by UAC to allow this application to make changes to your computer.

3. At the command prompt, type **ipconfig** and press **Enter**. This command displays a summary of your IPv4 and IPv6 information.

4. Type **ipconfig /all** and press **Enter**. This command displays more detailed IP configuration information.

5. Type **ipconfig /release** and press **Enter**. This command releases the DHCP address on your computer. Notice that no IPv4 address is listed in the results.

6. Type **ipconfig /renew** and press **Enter**. This command renews a DHCP address on your computer or obtains a new one. Notice that the newly acquired IPv4 address is displayed.

7. Type **netsh** and press **Enter**. *Netsh* can be used in an interactive mode where you navigate through menu levels to view information.

8. Type **interface** and press **Enter**. This command changes to the interface context, where you can get more information about network interface configuration.

9. Type **ipv4** and press **Enter**. This command changes to the IPv4 context, where you can get more information about IPv4 configuration.

10. Type **show** and press **Enter**. This command displays a list of the information that can be displayed.

11. Type **show addresses** and press **Enter**. This command shows the IPv4 addresses that are used by this computer.

12. Type **set address** and press **Enter**. This command shows help information on how to configure an IP address for DHCP or as static. If a command is missing required information, the help screen for that command is automatically output.

13. Type **exit** and press **Enter**.

14. Close the command prompt and all other open windows.

Activity 7-5: Testing Alternate IP Configuration

Time Required: 10 minutes

Objective: Learn how APIPA and an alternate IP configuration can be used

Description: By default, Windows 10 uses an APIPA address (169.254.x.x) when it is configured for dynamic IP addresses, but it cannot contact a DHCP server. However, you can configure Windows 10 to use a specific set of IP configuration information instead of using APIPA. In this activity, you see how to configure an alternate IP configuration.

All DHCP servers in the classroom must be disabled for this activity. If you are using virtual machines, this can be accomplished by configuring the virtual machines to use a local network that does not have access to the actual classroom network.

1. If necessary, start your computer and sign in.

2. Right-click the **Start** button, click **Command Prompt (Admin)**, and click **Yes** when prompted by UAC to allow this application to make changes to your computer.

3. At the command prompt, type **ipconfig /release**. This removes the current IP address from your computer.

4. Type **ipconfig /renew** and press **Enter**. The renewal was unsuccessful and your computer is now using an APIPA address on the 169.254.x.x network.

5. Type **ipconfig** and press **Enter**. This command displays a summary of your IPv4 and IPv6 information. If the IPv4 address is not an APIPA address, the DHCP server was likely not properly disabled for this activity.

6. Close the command prompt.

7. Right-click the **Start** button and click **Control Panel**.

8. Click **Network and Internet** and click **Network and Sharing Center**.

9. Under the View your active networks heading, and to the right of Connections, click **Ethernet** (or the name of your wired or wireless connection). You also can use that connection name in the remaining steps instead of Ethernet.

10. Click the **Properties** button.

11. Click **Internet Protocol Version 4 (TCP/IPv4)** and click **Properties**.

12. Click the **Alternate Configuration** tab and click **User configured**.

13. In the IP address box, type **192.168.*x*.100**, where *x* is the number assigned to you by your instructor at the start of class. For example, if your user name is User1, your number is 1.

14. If necessary, in the Subnet mask box, type **255.255.255.0**.

15. Click **OK** to save the alternate configuration.

16. Click **Close** to close the Ethernet Properties dialog box.

17. In the Ethernet Status dialog box, click **Details**. Notice that the computer is using the alternate IP address you configured in Step 13 instead of an APIPA address.

18. Click **Close** to close the Network Connection Details box.

19. Click **Close** to close the Ethernet Status box.

20. Close Network and Sharing Center.

21. Close all open windows.

Your instructor can enable DHCP for the classroom again once the activity has been completed by all students. You can confirm that your network connectivity is working by visiting an Internet website. It might be necessary to renew your IP address to obtain a valid address from the DHCP server.

Essential IPv4 Utilities

Several key utilities can be used at the command line or within a script to configure and diagnose IP settings. Some of these utilities make low-level changes to the TCP/IP functionality. Some of these changes will be denied unless the commands are run from a command window that has administrator privileges on the computer. Table 7-4 shows some of the common IP troubleshooting utilities.

Table 7-4   IP troubleshooting utilities

Utility	Description
hostname	Displays the host name of the computer that it is run on. This is useful when you are at a computer and do not know the computer name.
ipconfig	Shows the current IPv4 and IPv6 configuration. You can also display some DNS information.
ping	Verifies connectivity to a destination by sending an ICMP request packet.
tracert	Provides similar information as the ping command, but shows response times for every router on the path to the destination. Note that the routers consider ICMP requests low priority, which can provide unreliable latency information.
pathping	Provides similar information as tracert, but sends 100 ICMP requests per router in an attempt to identify packet loss.
route	Displays and modifies information in the local routing table.
netstat	Displays statistics and information about network connections.
nbtstat	Displays information about legacy NetBIOS over TCP/IP. It can display the NetBIOS names known to the computer and purge the cache.
getmac	Displays MAC addresses associated with network adapters. Use *getmac /v* to obtain verbose output that includes the adapter name in addition to the adapter identifier. Use *getmac /s HostIP /u userid /p password* to obtain MAC addresses from a remote system.
arp	Displays and modifies the contents of the address resolution protocol (ARP) table, which maps IP addresses to MAC addresses. Use *arp -a* or *arp -g* to display the contents of the ARP table. Uses *arp -d HostIP* to delete an entry from the ARP table.
netsh	Modifies network configuration. Most of this functionality is now replicated in Windows PowerShell cmdlets.
nslookup	Queries DNS records directly from a DNS server. This is used to verify whether DNS records on various servers are configured correctly.

Ipconfig   The *ipconfig* command displays the basic TCP/IP settings of all active network connections. There are several command-line options that make the command versatile in troubleshooting TCP/IP settings. Table 7-5 shows some of the most useful.

Table 7-5   Common ipconfig options for troubleshooting TCP/IP

Command	Description
ipconfig /all	Displays all TCP/IP configuration settings in verbose detail. This includes DNS servers, the default gateway, and DHCP server (if applicable).
ipconfig /release	Removes dynamically assigned IP addresses from network connections. This disables TCP/IP operations on those interfaces.
ipconfig /renew	Attempts to renew IP addresses for all network connections that are configured to obtain an IP address automatically. If the renewal of a network connection's current IP address is refused by the DHCP server, the IP address is lost and a new IP address must be assigned by the DHCP server.
ipconfig /registerdns	Forces Windows 10 to register its name and IP address with the DNS server defined on a network interface's properties. This process is performed on startup. So, it is typically done manually only if the IP address has recently changed.
ipconfig /displaydns	Displays all cached DNS lookup data.
ipconfig /flushdns	Deletes the cached DNS lookup data.

DNS lookup results are cached by a service on the Windows 10 computer called the DNS client (dnscache) service. The cache itself is called the DNS resolver cache. Displaying the DNS resolver cache reveals if cached DNS data from DNS server lookups is responsible for improper or unexpected operations. This can be caused by bad data stored in the DNS server hierarchy, performing the lookup against the wrong custom DNS server, or holding stale data in the cache that has since changed to different values on the DNS server.

The cached data will display positive results, where data has been returned, and negative results, where a response came back from the DNS server stating that a value matching the lookup request does not exist. Both types of responses are considered valid responses.

From these results, the technician may determine that the DNS server pointed to might be incorrect, or that data held by a DNS server might be wrong. These changes by themselves will not change the result returned by a DNS lookup for names that already exist in the DNS resolver cache. The results will persist in the cache until the TTL (Time to Live) for a cache result has expired, the DNS client service is restarted, or the command *ipconfig /flushdns* is issued on the computer.

Ping   The *ping* command confirms basic IP connectivity between the computer that it is run on and a specified target host. The *ping* command tests the ability of network data to reach a target and return; it does not confirm that applications on the target computer are operating properly. The target host may be identified with an IP address or DNS name. The *ping* utility sends out a special type of packet called an ICMP request packet. The computer that receives this packet may reply with a response ICMP packet. The *ping* utility measures the total time it takes for the request to get to the destination and response packet to get back to the computer running the *ping* command. This latency time is measured in milliseconds (ms). Some network devices and firewall software, such as Windows Firewall, may actively block *ping* ICMP traffic even though the network connection is perfectly healthy.

The *ping* ICMP process is repeated four times by default to check if the results are consistent. The number of times the test actually runs is configurable through command-line options. It can be increased to get a better profile of latency and losses over a period of time. Lost replies are tracked to reveal percent loss. Any loss could be an indication of a failing component between the computer and the target host. Table 7-6 shows some useful command-line switches for the *ping* command.

Table 7-6   Common ping options for troubleshooting

Command	Description
ping -t	Continues pinging indefinitely
ping -a	Forces a reverse DNS lookup to identify the FQDN associated with an IP address
ping -n	Specifies the number of requests to send
ping -4	Forces use of IPv4
ping -6	Forces use of IPv6

Route   The *route* command can alter or display the IP routing table. The routing table is displayed by issuing the *route print* command, as seen previously in Figure 7-5.

The Network Destination 0.0.0.0 with Netmask 0.0.0.0 in the routing table is the default route, also known as the default gateway. In rare cases, multiple default routes can be created, which cause unreliable network connectivity even though the default gateway appears correctly configured with using *ipconfig*.

Routes can be manually added or removed in the routing table using the *route add* or *route delete* commands, respectively. Any custom changes that are made will be lost between reboots unless the additions are flagged as persistent with the –*p* command-line option. Changes to the routing table are not typical for workstations. It is common to review the routing table to confirm what routing entries are present but not manage its settings directly.

Netstat   The *netstat* command can display different types of TCP/IP statistics for active software and connections. Many options are available that can be reviewed by typing *netstat /?* at the command line. Several common *netstat* command-line options used in troubleshooting network connections are shown in Table 7-7.

Table 7-7 Common netstat options for network troubleshooting

Command	Description
netstat -a	Displays all connections and active ports waiting for a connection
netstat -e	Displays statistics about total data sent and received
netstat -r	Displays the routing table
netstat -b	Displays the name of a program responsible for a connection or listening for one
netstat -o	For each connection, displays the process ID of the process that owns the connection

The *netstat* command is useful for documenting the network activity and connections at a moment in time. You can view the information on screen, but it is often easier to view if you direct the output to file.

You can obtain information similar to *netstat* by using the graphical tool Resource Monitor.

Nslookup   The *nslookup* command can be used at the command prompt to look up a DNS entry from a specific DNS server or it can provide an interactive text-based console for advanced DNS queries.

Nslookup is a powerful tool because it can query a DNS server directly, even if it is a different one than the network settings are using right now. The *debug* feature allows the administrator to deeply diagnose what data can be returned to the Windows 10 client and why.

To fully appreciate the utility, the administrator must have knowledge of the type of records a DNS server includes, such as:

- *A*—Maps a host name to an IPv4 address
- *AAAA*—Maps a host name to an IPv6 address
- *PTR*—Maps an IPv4 or IPv6 address to a host name
- *MX*—Identifies the mail server(s) responsible for managing email for a domain
- *NS*—Identifies the DNS servers that authoritatively hold custom DNS data for a domain

To review *nslookup* commands, start *nslookup* in its interactive mode by entering *nslookup* on the command line and pressing Enter. At the *nslookup* interactive prompt, >, type *help*.

Troubleshooting IPv4

To successfully troubleshoot IPv4-based communications, the technician should follow an incremental process that has proven successful in most situations. IPv4 has been in use for a very long time. Many problems actually have simple causes, such as a connection being in the wrong state or a feature turned off unexpectedly.

A common approach is to perform the following in order:

1. Confirm current settings.
2. Validate IPv4 connectivity.
3. Verify DNS name resolution.
4. Verify data connections.

Confirm Current Settings   The existing IPv4 settings should be confirmed. Assumptions about what settings are active lead to incorrect troubleshooting progress. The *ipconfig* and *netsh* utilities can display the current settings. If the IPv4 address settings look valid, it is possible that the default route or routing table is incorrect. The default route can be displayed with the *ipconfig* or *route* command. If all settings appear correct, the computer's connectivity with those settings must be validated.

Validate IPv4 Connectivity   If all settings appear correct, the *ping* utility can be used to confirm that the computer can ping its own loopback address. If the command is successful, the TCP/IP IPv4 protocol is functional on the computer.

The computer keeps track of which computers it recently communicated with, and some of that information can be out of date. The IPv4 system uses an ARP table to keep track of network devices it last connected to. If the ARP table data is in doubt, it can be cleared with the *arp* utility.

The *ping* command can be used to ping a local host such as the default gateway. If the local default gateway can be pinged, connectivity to the local network and the default gateway are validated in one attempt.

If the router can be pinged, attempt to ping a remote host using its IPv4 address. If this fails, confirm the path the traffic is taking with either the *pathping* or *tracert* commands. If IPv4 communications to remote hosts work when the raw address is specified in a command, but not by name, there is likely a DNS issue.

Verify DNS Name Resolution   Confirm the correct DNS servers are specified on network settings manually or automatically through DHCP with the *ipconfig* utility. If the wrong servers were entered, that should be corrected first. While troubleshooting, if there are multiple DNS servers specified, consider simplifying the list to just one server that you expect has the correct data.

The DNS resolver caches data and that data may contain obsolete data or invalid responses. Once the DNS servers are corrected, the cache data can be purged with *ipconfig /flushdns* to provide a clean start to name resolution. The DNS data being cached can also be displayed with *ipconfig /displaydns* to confirm that expected answers are being correctly obtained by the Windows computer.

The DNS cached data tells you what answer the workstation received, but not from which DNS server, and not if the data the DNS server is holding is correct. The data stored on the DNS server itself should be verified. This can be verified from the workstation with the *nslookup* utility or you can ask the administrator of the DNS server.

A common mistake is configuring a domain-joined workstation with an ISP's DNS server in addition to a corporate domain DNS server. When the workstation tries to look up DNS data to find corporate domain servers, it may ask the ISP's DNS server where they are located instead of the domain DNS server. You can specify a preferred order for Windows 10 to query DNS servers, but you cannot restrict Windows 10 from using both interchangeably. The ISP DNS server sends back a valid response—the domain server's DNS data doesn't exist in its database—and the client caches the response as a valid lookup result. As a result, domain operations are disrupted and fail to operate correctly on the workstation. When the workstation is restarted by the user, it might go back to working with the correct domain DNS server. The workstation user might report intermittent overall failures and annoyance as a result.

Verify Data Connections   If basic IP communications and name resolution appear healthy, the problem might be a result of data filtering by a firewall restriction or corruption. Any computer or device between the local client and the destination might be filtering data connections, disallowing them entirely. Windows 10 has a firewall component built in to filter inbound and outbound data connections, which is covered later in this chapter.

Many server-based data services listen on a specific data port. The Transmission Control Protocol (TCP) portion of TCP/IP allows an application to identify itself with a specific port value. The IP address identifies the computer itself; the TCP port identifies the listening application on that computer. Many third-party tools report the status of TCP ports for a given remote IP address. Windows 10 can report active port connections on the computer using the *netstat* command.

A crude test to check for connectivity to remote servers is to use the *telnet* application on the local computer to attempt a connection to a remote active TCP port. The *telnet* utility is available for installation as part of Windows, but it is not installed by default. It can be installed by opening Control Panel, Programs, Programs and Features, and selecting the task Turn Windows features on or off. The *telnet* client can then be selected and installed.

The *telnet* program provides an interactive interface that normally connects to a telnet server on its default TCP port number. A different port number can be specified on the command line, one that is used by a service other than telnet. For example, the mail server protocol for the Simple Mail Transfer Protocol (SMTP) is port 25. The *telnet* command *telnet mail.example .com 25* opens an interactive session with the mail server, identified by the name *mail.example .com*, which is listening for connections on TCP port 25. If the data connection is allowed, the mail server greeting should be displayed. If it is, this confirms that there is some level of data connectivity allowed.

Additional filtering or data corruption may happen after the initial TCP connection to give the impression of a data communication problem. To see the full network conversation between two computers, a utility such as the Microsoft Message Analyzer would have to be employed. Message Analyzer is a utility that is not included by default with Windows 10 but can be downloaded for free. The implementation and usage of Message Analyzer is an advanced topic beyond the scope of this book. Before Message Analyzer, Microsoft produced and used a tool called Network Monitor. Network Monitor has been deprecated and should not be used with Windows 10.

A popular open source alternative to Message Analyzer is Wireshark. For more information, see *https://www.wireshark.org.*

IP Version 6

IPv6 is the replacement for IPv4. The creators of IPv4 could not have anticipated the expansion of the Internet and, as a result, IPv4 has some serious shortcomings when used for global networking. IPv6 addresses these shortcomings.

Improvements found in IPv6 include:

- Increased address space
- Hierarchical routing to reduce the load on Internet backbone routers
- Simpler configuration through automatic address management
- Inclusion of encryption services for data security
- Quality of service
- Extensibility to support new features

IPv6 Address Notation

The address space for IPv4 on the Internet has essentially been depleted; IPv6 has a significantly larger address space. IPv6 addresses are 128 bits long, while IPv4 addresses are only 32 bits long. IPv6 provides many more addresses than are available in IPv4.

IPv6 has many more addresses than would normally be required for computing devices, but it is designed for ease of use rather than efficiency of allocation. Many of these addresses will probably never be assigned to a host. In fact, only one-eighth of the total address space is allocated for Internet-accessible addresses.

IPv6 addresses are represented in hexadecimal, with each four-digit segment separated by colons. Each hexadecimal digit can be converted to an equivalent four-bit binary value. The total address length is a maximum of 32 hexadecimal digits. An example of an IPv6 address is 222D: 10B5:3355:00F3:8234:0000:32AC:099C.

To simplify the expression of IPv6 addresses, any group of four hexadecimal digits can drop leading zeros, leaving at least one digit visible. The IPv6 address in the previous example can be simplified to: 222D:10B5:3355:F3:8234:0:32AC:99C.

When an IPv6 address contains a long set of zeros, the zeros can be compressed to a double colon. "::". For example, the multicast address FF02:0:0:0:0:0:112A:CC87 could be shortened to FF02::112A:CC87. This type of zero compression can only be used once per address. In general, it doesn't matter if the compression is done on the right or left side of the address; what really matters is that it can only be done once.

IPv6 Address Types

The format of an IPv6 address is more complex than an IPv4 address. Depending on the purpose of the IPv6 address, understanding how to decompose the different parts of the address changes. The full decomposition of different address types is an advanced topic beyond the scope of this book. The numbers on the left side of a written IPv6 address provide a clue as to what type of address it is, which is covered in this chapter.

IPv4 addresses had only two parts, the network address and the host address. The subnet mask value identified where the split between network and host bits was placed in the 32-bit IPv4 address. The IPv6 address has a similar concept, but it is not written in dotted decimal notation. Instead, it uses the CIDR notation of adding a slash and a number after the slash to the end of the IPv6 address. That number indicates the number of bits on the left side of the written address that makes up the network portion of the address. This network portion of the address is referred to in general as the **address prefix**. For example, 10F0:0:0:6501::/64 is a possible IPv6 prefix.

The address prefix contains information that helps devices such as routers decide how to move data between networks and the links between those networks. When an address prefix is specified, be careful to avoid using zero compression incorrectly. The previous example of 10F0:0:0:6501::/64 is a valid address prefix that uses zero compression to shorten the full address 10F0:0:0:6501:0:0:0:0/64. A common mistake is to write the address as 10F0::6501/64, which will be interpreted incorrectly as 10F0:0:0:0:0:0:0:6501/64.

Depending on the address type, the address prefix can be composed of multiple components that are more complicated than the IPv4 network ID. It is important to recognize that IPv6 is a young standard and it is still evolving. Some of the format information current today may change over time.

Knowing the type of address helps to set expectations of how data can be delivered to an interface. The designers of IPv6 knew that the end point for delivery could be a physical device such as a network card, a wireless device, or some program that is receiving data and acting as an end point for IPv6 data. The end point for IPv6 data delivery is called an interface. A single computer is typically called a node, which is capable of running multiple interfaces. Each interface can have one or more IPv6 addresses assigned to it. Recognizing the address type by its address prefix (see Table 7-8) is a required skill to analyze IPv6 addresses assigned to an interface.

Table 7-8   Common IPv6 address prefixes

IPv6 address type	Address prefix
Link-local unicast	FE80::/64
Global unicast	2000::/3
Unique local unicast	FC00::/7
Multicast	FF00::/8
Anycast	Any valid unicast address
Teredo	2001::/32

Link-Local Unicast   A unicast address defines a delivery destination that identifies a specific single interface. Data sent to or from link-local unicast addresses is not allowed to pass through IPv6-aware routers. A link-local unicast address is automatically assigned to any active interface on the computer by Windows 10. A link-local address allows computers in a local network to communicate with each other without requiring the use of a router. In IPv4, this same link-local behavior is provided by Automatic Private IP Addressing (APIPA), which generates IP addresses in the range 169.254.0.0 to 169.254.255.255.

The address prefix of a link-local address in IPv6 is FE80::/64. The last 64 bits of the address are randomly generated by Windows 10 as the host ID. An example of a link-local unicast address is FE80::F9:1435:305E:DFF2.

A computer can have more than one link-local address if it has multiple network interfaces. The address prefix for each link-local address on that computer is exactly the same. When the computer is sending to a link-local address, the routing table cannot tell which interface to use to send data to a destination link-local address. If this causes a problem, the link-local address can be extended with a zone ID.

Each network interface in Windows 10 is assigned a network interface ID, otherwise known as a zone ID. The zone ID can be used to identify what network interface is used to send the data. The syntax to specify a zone ID is *IPAddress%ZoneID*, where *IPAddress* is the destination link-local address and *ZoneID* is the interface ID of the network interface.

To see the current identifier for each network interface, open a command window and issue the command *ipconfig* or *netsh interface ipv6 show interface*. The output of the *netsh* command lists a column titled Idx, as shown in Figure 7-8, which identifies the interface ID for each interface listed. The *ipconfig* output lists it at the end of each link-local address displayed beneath each connection, but there is a lot more information displayed than necessary with the *ipconfig* command.

```
C:\WINDOWS\system32>netsh interface ipv6 show interface

Idx     Met         MTU          State                Name
---  ----------  ----------  ------------  ---------------------------
  1         50  4294967295   connected     Loopback Pseudo-Interface 1
  6         40        1500   disconnected  Bluetooth Network Connection
  2          5        1500   disconnected  Local Area Connection* 2
 13         50        1280   connected     Teredo Tunneling Pseudo-Interface
 23          5        1500   disconnected  Ethernet 2
 42          5        1500   disconnected  Local Area Connection* 3
  7         50        1280   disconnected  isatap.gateway.mts.net
 11         20        1500   connected     vEthernet (Public Virtual Switch)

C:\WINDOWS\system32>
```

Figure 7-8   *Netsh* output displaying network interface ID

If a command such as *ping fe80::613a:325f:5e1b:d9b4* returns the error result "Destination host unreachable" or "PING: transmit failed. General failure," it may be due to the command using the wrong interface to send the *ping* request. As an example, consider that the *netsh* command was issued to display the interface IDs and the correct one was determined to be 15. The *ping* command could be modified to include it as *ping fe80::613a:325f:5e1b:d9b4%15*.

Global Unicast   A global address can be routed as a public address on the Internet through routers and networks. Global unicast IPv6 addresses are usually assigned by an ISP or public registration authority.

Note that a global unicast address can be generally identified with the address prefix 2000::/3. Even though that is the current block of IPv6 addresses being handed out to public end points, this may change in the future. There are still large portions of the IPv6 address space that are unused. An example of a global unicast address is: 2001:0:4137:9E76:F9:1435:304E:DFF2.

Unique Local Unicast   The unique local address type is a replacement address type for the deprecated site-local address type. These addresses are intended for local communications within a private site. These addresses are similar in function to IPv4 internal private addresses (see Table 7-2) in that they are not intended to be directly routable over the Internet.

The unique local address type allows an administrator to identify a site and route internally within that private site. Routers that connect to the global Internet will drop data with this address type if it is sent directly out to the Internet. Note that a unique local unicast address can be generally identified with the address prefix FC00::/7.

Multicast An IPv6 **multicast** address serves the same purpose as an IPv4 multicast address. One or more computers can be assigned a multicast address that identifies them as members of the same group of computers. When data is sent to a multicast address, all computers with an interface that belongs to that multicast group will receive a copy of the data.

The address prefix of a multicast address is FF00::/8. Multicast addresses include a scope setting that determines the distribution level of the data, such as local or global distribution. Managing multicast addresses is not a typical administration task for Windows 10, so these settings are not reviewed in detail here.

Some multicast addresses are reserved and have a special meaning. Two examples include the "all nodes" and "all routers" multicast address. The all nodes multicast address FF02::1 is used to send data to all computers on the same local network. This is the same functionality as the broadcast address for IPv4. The all routers multicast address FF02::2 is used to send data to all routers on the same local network.

Anycast The assignment of **anycast** addresses to a network interface is currently restricted to routers only. The anycast address is not assigned to client computers. The anycast address has the same format as any unicast address. What makes an address an anycast address is the fact that a single unicast address is assigned to more than one network interface, and those interfaces can be on different computing devices. Multiple devices can share the same anycast address and respond to other computers without an IP address conflict. This technique allows client computers to find the closest instance of a service. The closest computer or device with a specific anycast address responds to the client.

The device configured with an anycast address must know that it is an anycast address. The format of the address does not tell a computer that an address is an anycast address. The anycast address is typically managed as part of a large enterprise or ISP managing backbone routers.

Special Addresses Two special addresses exist in IPv6, the loopback address and the unspecified address. The loopback address in IPv6 is specified as 0:0:0:0:0:0:0:1, otherwise written as ::1 or ::1/128. The loopback address is only assigned to a virtual interface, never to a physical one. Any data sent to the loopback address for a computer will deliver in software back to the computer that sent it. The data will not be sent out on the physical network; the entire process will happen in software using the virtual interface only.

The unspecified address is 0:0:0:0:0:0:0:0, otherwise written as :: or ::/128. The unspecified address is never assigned to a computer. It indicates the absence of an address. This can be observed when an IPv6 address is unspecified in a configuration window or when a computer is sending an IPv6 packet, but it doesn't have a source address yet.

Teredo The Teredo client is built in as part of Windows 10, but it is inactive unless its services are required. **Teredo** is a technology that allows IPv6 data to be tunneled over an IPv4 network that is using **Network Address Translation (NAT)**. In an IPv4 network using NAT, the identity and availability of a computer is hidden by the NAT device. This makes it difficult for a computer using IPv6 addressing to tunnel directly through an IPv4 network.

The Teredo client typically connects to two types of special servers: the Teredo server and Teredo relay server. The Teredo client connects to a Teredo server to register itself as a client. Windows 10 creates a virtual network interface called the Teredo Tunneling Pseudo-Interface. This interface is assigned a specially formatted Teredo IPv6 address. Teredo addresses have a fixed address prefix of 2001::/32.

The Teredo server acts as a broker while a connection is being created to another computer. Control and status messages are read from the Teredo server. The bandwidth required to run a

Teredo server is low, so public Teredo servers such as *teredo.ipv6.microsoft.com* exist that can be used by any Teredo client.

The Teredo relay server connects a Teredo client indirectly to another computer on an IPv6-only network to transfer data. The Teredo relay server can send status and control messages to the Teredo server, where the Teredo client picks them up. A Teredo relay server will have a lot of data flowing through it, so there are typically no public Teredo relay servers.

Methods for Configuring IPv6

A computer running Windows 10 automatically configures its network interfaces with a link-local address. These can be displayed by entering the *ipconfig* command at the command line, as shown in Figure 7-9. The link-local addresses allow the computer to interact with other computers on the local network but not through a router to other networks.

```
C:\WINDOWS\system32>ipconfig

Windows IP Configuration


Ethernet adapter Ethernet 2:

   Media State . . . . . . . . . . . : Media disconnected
   Connection-specific DNS Suffix  . :

Wireless LAN adapter Local Area Connection* 2:

   Media State . . . . . . . . . . . : Media disconnected
   Connection-specific DNS Suffix  . :

Wireless LAN adapter Local Area Connection* 3:

   Media State . . . . . . . . . . . : Media disconnected
   Connection-specific DNS Suffix  . :

Ethernet adapter vEthernet (Public Virtual Switch):

   Connection-specific DNS Suffix  . : gateway.mts.net
   Link-local IPv6 Address . . . . . : fe80::bdf4:30b0:19ea:8e1e%11
   IPv4 Address. . . . . . . . . . . : 192.168.100.105
   Subnet Mask . . . . . . . . . . . : 255.255.255.0
   Default Gateway . . . . . . . . . : 192.168.100.254

Ethernet adapter Bluetooth Network Connection:

   Media State . . . . . . . . . . . : Media disconnected
   Connection-specific DNS Suffix  . :

Tunnel adapter Teredo Tunneling Pseudo-Interface:

   Connection-specific DNS Suffix  . :
   IPv6 Address. . . . . . . . . . . : 2001:0:5ef5:79fd:18f2:1e4:305e:dc30
   Link-local IPv6 Address . . . . . : fe80::18f2:1e4:305e:dc30%13
   Default Gateway . . . . . . . . . : ::

Tunnel adapter isatap.gateway.mts.net:

   Media State . . . . . . . . . . . : Media disconnected
   Connection-specific DNS Suffix  . : gateway.mts.net

C:\WINDOWS\system32>
```

Figure 7-9 *Ipconfig* command output

To configure IPv6, you can use:

- Static configuration
- Automatic configuration
- Scripts

A network connection's properties include settings for IPv6. By default, the properties are configured to obtain an IPv6 address automatically. It is not common to configure an IPv6 address statically. To configure a static address, a network interface's IPv6 properties must be reconfigured to use a specific IPv6 address with a specified subnet prefix length, as shown in Figure 7-10.

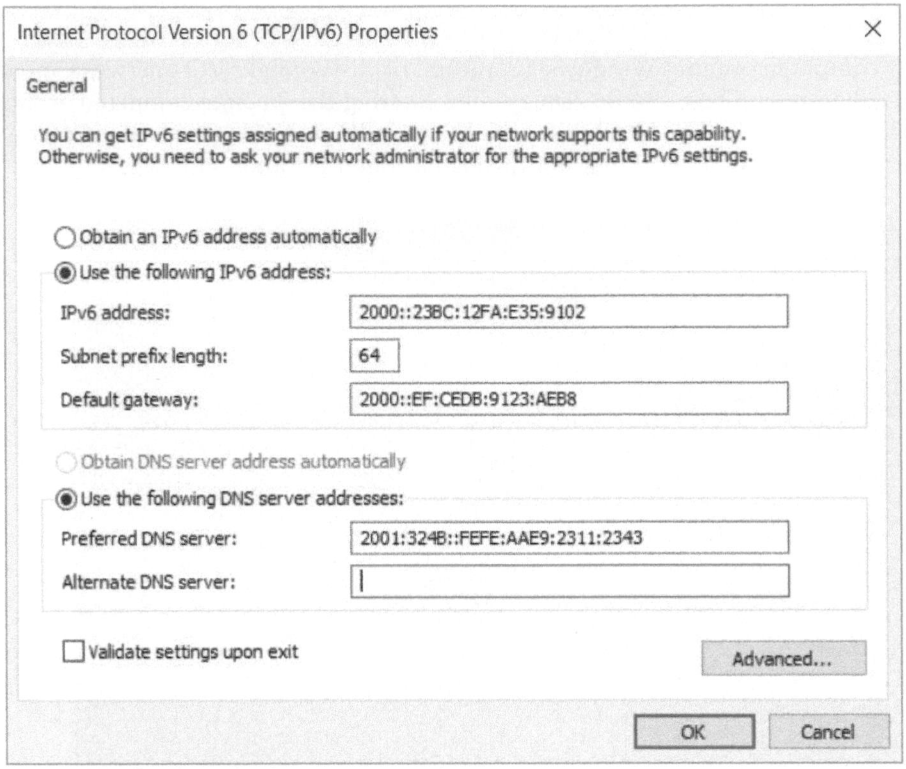

```
Internet Protocol Version 6 (TCP/IPv6) Properties                              ✕

┌ General ┐

  You can get IPv6 settings assigned automatically if your network supports this capability.
  Otherwise, you need to ask your network administrator for the appropriate IPv6 settings.

  ○ Obtain an IPv6 address automatically
  ◉ Use the following IPv6 address:

     IPv6 address:                    2000::23BC:12FA:E35:9102

     Subnet prefix length:            64

     Default gateway:                 2000::EF:CEDB:9123:AEB8

  ○ Obtain DNS server address automatically
  ◉ Use the following DNS server addresses:

     Preferred DNS server:            2001:324B::FEFE:AAE9:2311:2343

     Alternate DNS server:            |

  ☐ Validate settings upon exit                              [ Advanced... ]

                                                    [   OK   ]  [ Cancel ]
```

Figure 7-10   Static IPv6 configuration

The Advanced button in the IPv6 Properties window allows the interface to be assigned one or more default gateways, multiple IPs, and custom DNS settings. IPv6 does not implement NetBIOS over TCP/IP, so there are no WINS configuration options.

Automatic configuration can be done in two ways: stateful and stateless. To enable automatic configuration of the IPv6 address, a network interface's IPv6 properties must be configured, as shown in Figure 7-11.

Stateful automatic address configuration involves one or more devices that track the state of the client in internal data tables. Traditional IPv4 address allocation through DHCP is an example of stateful address allocation. IPv6 can also obtain an address from an IPv6 DHCP server (DHCPv6) if one is configured on the local network. Windows Server 2008 or later can support IPv6 configuration as a DHCP server, but earlier versions of Windows Server cannot. A compatible IPv6 DHCP relay can also be used with IPv6 addressing to enable a client to interact with a DHCPv6 server on a different network.

In stateful address allocation, the DHCPv6 server tracks details about the client while it is operational with a leased address assigned by that DHCP server. This can restrict the mobility of a client as it has to coordinate its address assignment with servers and other devices while it moves from one network to another. The client and DHCP server present a DHCP Unique Identifier (DUID) to identify themselves when exchanging DHCPv6 messages. The clients DHCPv6 DUID can be seen by issuing the command *ipconfig /all* at a command prompt.

Stateless automatic address configuration empowers the client to collect as many settings as possible from the network around it and have it create its own IPv6 address. The subnet address in use on a local network is advertised by an IPv6-aware router as the subnet ID.

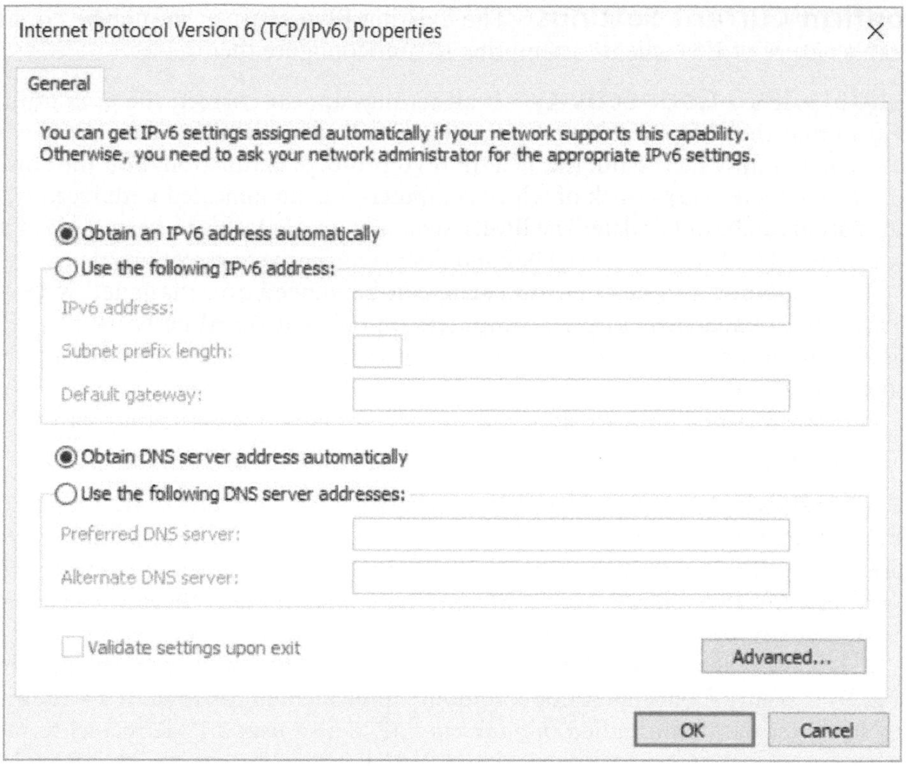

Figure 7-11   Automatic IPv6 configuration

The client generates a random interface ID and combines it with the subnet ID to create its own IPv6 address. Configuration options such as DNS server settings are collected from DHCP servers or the router connected to the local network. If there is no router connected, the interface can only automatically configure a link-local address. The advantage to stateless configuration is that less equipment and configuration effort is required to set up the IPv6 address for a network.

In small networks, even settings such as the DNS server settings may not be required. Windows 10 can resolve local client names using the **Link-Local Multicast Name Resolution (LLMNR)** protocol and related supporting services. This allows a computer to query the names of other computers on the local network using IPv4 and IPv6 without relying on NetBIOS, WINS, or DNS name resolution. This can minimize the requirement to have name configuration servers defined ahead of time and configured for clients.

The Teredo tunneling interface is a special case of address autoconfiguration because the computer attempts to connect to a Teredo server and obtain reply information used to create a Teredo-class IPv6 address.

Script commands using *netsh* can be used to configure IPv6 settings on the computer. Changes to a network interface's settings may take multiple commands to completely configure the interface.

Troubleshooting IPv6 Settings

Because IPv6 addressing is new and there are new details of how to configure it, many people assume that troubleshooting is different. The overall troubleshooting methodology is similar to IPv4 troubleshooting with the following notable considerations in each troubleshooting stage:

1. Confirm current settings.

2. Validate IPv6 connectivity.

3. Verify DNS name resolution.

4. Verify data connections.

Confirm Current Settings   The existing IPv6 settings should be confirmed due to the default nature of IPv6 clients attempting to autoconfigure themselves.

Validate IPv6 Connectivity   If all settings appear correct, the *ping* utility can be used to confirm that the computer can ping its own loopback address by issuing the command *ping ::1*. If the command is successful, the TCP/IP IPv6 protocol is functional on the computer.

The computer keeps track of which computers it communicated with recently, and some of that information can be out of date. The IPv4 system uses an ARP table to keep track of network devices it last connected to. IPv6 uses a neighbor and destination cache to essentially do that as well.

The neighbor and destination cache can be viewed and managed with the *netsh* utility. The neighbor cache lists known computers on the same local network as the client computer. The destination cache lists the next IPv6 address the computer should send data to, to reach a particular destination.

If either the neighbor or destination cache data is in doubt, they can be cleared with the *netsh* utility.

Verify DNS Name Resolution   Different types of records are registered with the DNS server depending on the IP data the client is registering. An IPv4 address and host name are stored in the DNS server using an A record. The A record maps the name of the computer to its IP address. An IPv6 address and host name are stored in the DNS server using an AAAA record. The AAAA record maps the name of the computer to its IPv6 address.

A DNS server may be configured to map the IP address back to the name of the computer using PTR records, but this is not commonly implemented for IPv6. IPv4 addresses are stored in a DNS server data table called *in-addr.arpa*. IPv6 also uses a PTR record to match an IPv6 address to a name, but it uses a data table called *ip6.arpa*.

DNS servers may resolve a name to either an IPv4 address or an IPv6 address. There is no guarantee the DNS server will respond with IPv4 or IPv6 data in all cases. A computer may have a valid IPv4 A record stored in DNS but no IPv6 AAAA record. To restrict troubleshooting to IPv6 addresses, the *ping* command can be forced to only use IPv6 addresses by issuing the command *ping -6 TargetName*, where *TargetName* is the target name of the remote computer. If the DNS server cannot provide an answer that is a valid IPv6 address, the command reports that the host name could not be found.

Verify Data Connections   Using the *telnet* application is a common tool for administrators to test application connectivity. The *telnet* utility does not guarantee it will use IPv6 to connect to a remote service unless the target address is specified as an IPv6 address. Carefully consider that specifying a target DNS host name to connect to does not guarantee that an IPv6 address will be used instead of an IPv4 address.

File Sharing

There are many different ways you can share files between two computers. For example, you can copy files on a USB drive, send files by using instant messenger software, upload files to a website or cloud storage for sharing, or send files using email. However, all of these options are flawed because they do not maintain a single central copy of the file. When there are multiple copies of a file in multiple locations, it is difficult to track which version has the latest changes, and sometimes changes are made to multiple versions of the file, which are difficult to reconcile at a later time. Due to security restrictions and firewalls, you might need to use some of these options over the Internet. However, on a LAN you can use file and printer sharing instead.

File sharing in Windows 10 allows you to share files from any folder on your computer or the Public folder with other computer users on your LAN. In a home environment, the homegroup feature allows each homegroup member computer to share personal libraries. (Homegroups are covered later in this chapter.) In a small business environment, each user may store their business files in the Public folder only, so that all users have access to the files on all of the Windows 10 computers. In a larger corporate environment, files are typically stored on centralized servers rather than shared from individual Windows 10 computers.

Windows 10 includes controls to allow the user and administrator to customize how much they want to share over the network, with whom, and with what access rights. When security is a concern, Windows 10 provides options to configure settings based on the convenience and knowledge level of the person making changes. In trusted environments, such as at home, shared folder security can be configured with simple wizards that can apply some or no security checks at all. In corporate environments, specific shared folder permissions can be applied that combine with NTFS file-level permissions to fine-tune and customize access.

If users commute between home and corporate networks with portable computers, they might need to authenticate with several user and password combinations. Windows 10 includes the Credential Manager utility to assist with remembering those details and automating authentication.

Sharing data is an essential feature, and the most generic form of that built in to Windows 10 is the idea of a shared public folder.

Sharing the Public Folder

The Public folder is typically located at C:\Users\Public. Sharing the Public folder is a simplified way to perform file sharing on home and small office networks. Public folder sharing is disabled by default when a computer is joined to a domain. By default, all files in the Public folder are shared between users who sign in to the local computer. If a user signs in to the local computer, she may be restricted from seeing local data files belonging to other users of that computer. The Public folder gives those users a way to share data locally. However, the Public folder can also be shared with network users. Sharing for the Public folder is configured by using the Public folder sharing option in Advanced Sharing settings in the Network and Sharing Center, shown in Figure 7-12.

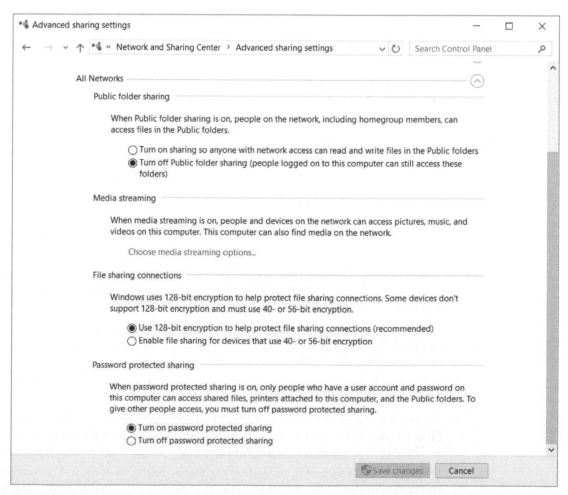

Figure 7-12 Public folder sharing controls

The options for sharing the Public folder are:

- *Turn on sharing so anyone with network access can read and write files in the Public folder*—When this option is selected, all network users are able to read, change, delete, and create files in the Public folder. A Public folder configured this way could be used as a central storage location for business documents in a small business to ensure that files can be easily found and are able to be backed up each night.

- *Turn off Public folder sharing*—When this option is selected, only local users can access files in the Public folder.

You also have options for Password protected sharing that also apply to the Public folder, shown in Figure 7-12. Password protection offers two options. These options also apply to other shared folders and printers.

- *Turn on password protected sharing*—When this option is selected, network users must sign in to the sharing computer by using a user account that has been granted access to the sharing computer. The account can be either a local user account or a domain user account. This allows you to restrict access to the shared public folder to valid user accounts, but you cannot select which user accounts have access. All valid user accounts are able to access the shared Public folder.

- *Turn off password protected sharing*—When this option is selected, anyone can access the information in the public folder, even if they do not have a valid user account on the sharing computer. Effectively, this allows anonymous users access to the Public folder.

Activity 7-6: Sharing the Public Folder

Time Required: 10 minutes
Objective: Share data in the public folder with network users

Description: Windows 10 includes a Public folder feature to make sharing files with other network users easier. Public folder sharing is performed from Network and Sharing Center. In this activity, you use Network and Sharing Center to share the Public folder.

1. If necessary, start your computer and sign in.
2. Right-click the **Start** button and click **Control Panel.**
3. Click **Network and Internet** and click **Network and Sharing Center.**
4. Click **Change advanced sharing settings** on the left-hand side of the Network and Sharing window.
5. Scroll down to the All Networks section and click the down arrow on the right of the section title to open it if it is not already expanded.
6. Scroll down to Password protected sharing and click **Turn off password protected sharing** if it is not already selected. This allows any user on the network to access your shared folders and printers without specifying a password.
7. Scroll up to Public folder sharing, and click **Turn on sharing so anyone with network access can read and write in the Public folders** if it is not already selected. Now all users have access to the shared public folder.
8. If it is highlighted because you made a change to a setting, click **Save Changes.** Notice that file sharing must be enabled to share the Public folder.
9. Right-click the **Start** button and select **File Explorer.** On the left-hand side, select **Network.** Find the computer icon with your computer name in the right-hand pane and double-click it. This opens a window that displays the shares on your computer. Users is listed as a share.
10. Double-click **Users** and double-click the **Public** folder to open it. You can see that all of the subfolders in the Public folder are available for storing and retrieving files. With the settings you have selected, these folders and the files inside them are available to all users on the network, regardless of whether they have a valid user account on your computer.

11. Double-click **Public Documents**, right-click in the empty area, point to **New**, and click **Text Document**.

12. Type **NetworkDoc** and press **Enter**.

13. Double-click **NetworkDoc** and type in some text.

14. Click the **File** menu, click **Save**, and close Notepad.

15. (Optional) Test the Public folder of another computer.

    a. In File Explorer, click **Network**.

    b. Double-click your partner's computer.

    c. Double-click **Users**, then **Public**, and double-click **Public Documents**.

    d. Right-click in the empty area, point to **New**, and click **Text Document**.

    e. Type **RemoteDocUser**X, where X is your student number, and press **Enter**.

    f. Double-click **RemoteDocUser**X.txt and type in some text.

    g. Click the **File** menu, click **Save**, and close Notepad.

16. Close all open windows.

Sharing Any Folder

Sharing files from any folder on your computer gives you more options to control which users have access to your files and what those users can do to your files. You are able to set the permissions for users when you share individual folders. For example, in a small business, the users in your project team may be given permission to view and change your shared files, but your other coworkers are only able to view the files.

The ability to configure permissions may be confusing for inexperienced users, but for experienced users the level of control allows you to configure file sharing just the way you want it. In a domain-based network, you can select users from the domain to share files with. In a workgroup-based network, you must create local accounts for the users you want to share files with. For example, if you want to share files with Bob, who signs in to another computer, you must create a user account for Bob on your Windows 10 computer, and then give the local user Bob permission to access files.

In a workgroup-based network, when a user account is created for Bob on your computer, it becomes difficult for Bob to ensure that the passwords used for his account on his own computer and your computer remain synchronized. However, Bob can use Credential Manager to save the password for the remote account so that he does not have to remember it.

Activity 7-7: Using Credential Manager

Time Required: 15 minutes

Objective: Use Credential Manager to save the password for a network account

Description: Credential Manager allows users to save the user names and passwords for remote systems. This avoids the requirement for users to remember many passwords on a peer-to-peer network. In a domain-based network, this is not required to access domain resources because the domain account can be used to access resources on all computers in the domain. A domain user may still need to use Credential Manager to store credentials to a resource outside the domain, such as a sign-in to Office 365 services. In this activity, you enter a user account into Credential Manager.

1. If necessary, start your computer and sign in.

2. Right-click the **Start** button and click **Computer Management**.

3. In the left pane, expand **Local Users and Groups** and click **Users**.

4. Right-click **Users** and click **New User**.

5. In the User name and Full name boxes, type **WorkgroupUser**.

6. In the Password and Confirm password boxes, type **password**.

7. Deselect the **User must change password at next logon option**. This user account will be shared by multiple users to access this computer. Therefore, you do not want the password to change automatically.

8. Select the **User cannot change password option**. If the account is shared by multiple users, you also do not want any users to change the password.

9. Select the **Password never expires option** and click **Create**. After this user is created, it can also be used to sign in to the local computer, not just access network resources.

10. Click **Close** to close the New User dialog box.

11. Close the Computer Management window.

12. Right-click the **Start** button and click **Control Panel**.

13. Click **User Accounts** and then click **Credential Manager**.

14. Under the Manage your credentials title, click **Windows Credentials**. This option allows you to configure passwords that are required for remote computers. The other option to manage Web Credentials stores application credentials that are used to connect to Internet applications and are not what people would consider user credentials. The Windows Credentials section includes generic credentials that can sign in a user to a web-based service.

15. Next to the row titled Windows Credentials, click the **Add a Windows credential** link to begin adding a new cached Windows user account.

16. In the Internet or network address box, type the name of your partner's computer.

17. In the User name box, type **WorkgroupUser**.

18. In the Password box, type **password**.

19. Click **OK**. Now whenever you access your partner's computer, Windows 10 uses the credentials you just entered. This allows you to specify different user names and passwords than the local account where you are currently signed in. Note that the credential is now listed based on the target computer it holds a credential for.

20. At the top of the credentials listing, click the **Back up Credentials** link.

21. Click the **Browse** button and accept the default folder location of the Documents folder. Note that the file extension for the Credential Manager backup file ends in .crd. In the File name field, enter the text **LabCredentialBackup** and then click the **Save** button.

22. Click **Next** to proceed with the credential backup operation.

23. When prompted, press **Ctrl+Alt+Delete**. To ensure that the backup operation is happening using a trusted code level, you must press Ctrl+Alt+Delete to switch to the secure desktop. If you cannot press Ctrl+Alt+Delete because you are running Windows 10 in a virtual environment, you will not be able to complete the save operation.

24. After you press Ctrl+Alt+Delete, you will be prompted for a password to secure the backup file. Enter the word **Backup1** in both the Password and Confirm password fields, and then click **Next**. Note the warning that the credential backup file should be removed from the computer and stored on some other media, and then click **Finish**.

25. Close the Credential Manager window.

26. Close all open windows.

Creating and Managing Shared Folders

There are two user interfaces for sharing folders in Windows 10:

- Share tab or "Share with" menu item
- Advanced sharing

Share Tab or "Share with" Menu Item   The Share tab is shown on the ribbon when the File Explorer window is open to show folders and files on the local computer. It is designed for users with basic needs, users who are not trying to fine-tune or tweak shared item security.

It simply enables the users to get what they want—the selected item shared with basic read or read/write permissions. The options can change depending on the type of network the computer is connected to. The Share tab options for a private connected computer are shown in Figure 7-13. You can also access sharing options by right-clicking a file or folder in File Explorer and choosing "Share with" from the shortcut menu. When the computer is domain joined, the homegroup menu options are not displayed.

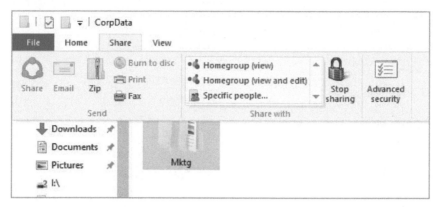

Figure 7-13   Share tab in File Explorer

This method simplifies folder and file sharing by controlling both NTFS and share permissions at the same time. The knowledge and complexity of what those permissions are is hidden from the users when they decide to change the sharing status of an item. The choices in the "Share with" group on the Share tab include:

- *Stop sharing*—Permission to access the selected item as a general shared resource is denied. NTFS permission inheritance on that folder or file is disabled and new permissions are applied so that only the owner of the item, members of the local Administrators group, and the operating system itself have full control permission to access it.

- *Homegroup (view)*—This option appears only if the computer considers itself connected to a private network location. The local HomeUsers group on the computer is granted access to only read the selected file or folder contents. This effectively gives all homegroup members this permission.

- *Homegroup (view and edit)*—This option appears only if the computer considers itself connected to a private network location. The local HomeUsers group on the computer is granted read and write permission to the selected file or folder contents. This effectively gives all homegroup members this permission.

- *Specific people*—This option opens the File Sharing Wizard to select people to share the selected item with. Individual user accounts can have their permission to the selected item set to: read, read/write, or removed to discontinue access. The Owner permission is given to the person who first shares a folder. Owner status cannot be assigned to a user or groups. Owners can perform any action on the selected folders and files plus edit the permission levels for the shared resource.

Some system folders are considered protected and cannot have custom shared settings applied. The Public folder is one such example. Any attempt to modify its shared status with the Sharing tab or "Share with" menu opens the Advanced Sharing settings options from Control Panel.

Advanced Sharing   If you click Advanced Sharing on an item's Properties screen (shown in Figure 7-14), you can configure options that are not available in the simpler "Share with" interface. When you view a folder's properties, the Sharing tab identifies if the folder is shared and provides a button to activate Advanced Sharing controls. However, advanced folder sharing configures only share permissions; it does not configure NTFS permissions. To complete the security configuration for a shared folder created through advanced folder sharing, you must configure NTFS permissions as a separate task.

Configuring NTFS permissions is covered in Chapter 4, Managing Disks and File Systems.

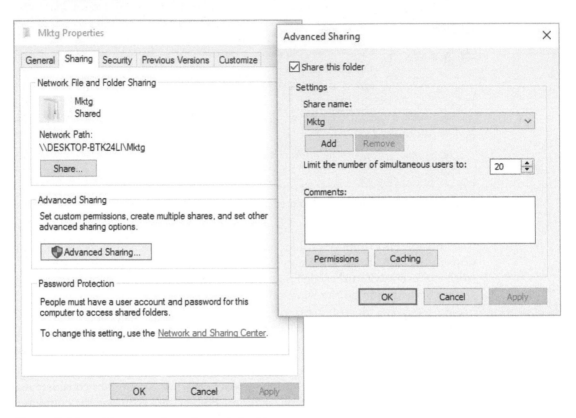

Figure 7-14   Folder properties, Advanced Sharing

When shared folder permissions are combined with NTFS permissions, the most restrictive permissions are effective. For example, if a user is assigned Read share permissions and Full control NTFS permissions, the user will have only read access when accessing the folder over the network. If a user is assigned Full Control share permissions and Read NTFS permissions, the user will also only have read access.

To simplify the management of permissions, you can assign the Full Control share permission to the Everyone group and then use NTFS permissions to apply more restrictive access to the folders and files in the shared folder. This has the added benefit of ensuring that user permissions are the same for accessing folders and files whether a user accesses the content over the network or by signing in to the local computer.

The settings you can configure in Advanced Sharing are:

- *Share this folder*—This option enables the folder as shared.

- *Share name*—This option allows you to specify one or more names that the folder is shared as. Users access the shared folder by using the UNC path *computername**sharename*.

- *Limit the number of simultaneous users to*—Windows 10 supports up to 20 concurrent connections from network users. With this setting, you can reduce this to a lower number to ensure that the computer is not overwhelmed by network users. However, this is typically not done because sharing files has very little effect on performance.

- *Comments*—This box contains text that is displayed for users when they view the share on the network. Typically, the text describes the content in the shared folder.
- *Permissions*—This button lets you configure the share permissions for the shared folder.
- *Caching*—This button lets you control how network clients cache files from this share as offline files. You can prevent file caching, allow users to select files for caching, or force file caching. Caching files for offline use is typically done only for mobile computers.

 Share names ending in a dollar sign ($) are hidden shares that cannot be seen by browsing the network, but can still be accessed by using the appropriate UNC path.

Advanced Sharing lets you allow or deny permissions, as shown in Figure 7-15. When a permission is denied, it overrides any permissions that are allowed. For example, if the Everyone group is given Read permission and the user Bob is denied Read permission, Bob will not have access to the share.

Figure 7-15   Folder properties, Advanced Sharing, Permissions

The share permissions available in Windows 10 are:

- *Full Control*—Allows users complete control over files and folders in the share and sets permissions on files and folders in the share. In addition, Full Control allows users to configure the share permissions on the shared folder.
- *Change*—Allows users complete control to create, modify, and delete files in the shared folder, but not to set permissions.
- *Read*—Allows users to read the contents of files in the shared folder, but not to modify the files in any way.

You can access advanced sharing only by clicking the Advanced Sharing button on the Sharing tab in the Properties of a folder. This is not the same option as the Advanced security button available through the Share tab in File Explorer.

Activity 7-8: Creating Shared Folders

Time Required: 15 minutes
Objective: Create shared folders for network users

Description: There are multiple methods to create shared folders. To ensure that shared folders meet your needs, you need to understand the differences between the methods for creating shared folders. In this activity, you create shared folders using multiple methods.

1. If necessary, start your computer and sign in.
2. Click the **Start** button and click **File Explorer**. In the left pane, click to select the **Documents** location.
3. Right-click the empty area in the right pane, point to **New**, and click **Folder**.
4. Type **SimpleShare1** and press **Enter**.
5. Click **SimpleShare1** and click the **Share** menu on the toolbar.
6. Select **Specific people** from the sharing toolbar. Click the drop-down list, click **WorkgroupUser**, and click the **Add** button. Notice that the default permission given to WorkgroupUser is Read.
7. To the right of WorkgroupUser, click **Read**, and click **Read/Write**. This allows WorkgroupUser to modify files.
8. Click the **Share** button.
9. Read the results in the File Sharing window. Notice that the UNC path for this share is long and goes through the C:\Users folder. All folders shared by using simple file sharing in your Documents folder use this long UNC path.
10. Click **Done**.
11. In the file browser window currently displaying the Documents library, double-click **Local Disk (C:)** under Computer in the left-hand pane.
12. Right-click an open area in the right-hand pane, point to **New**, and click **Folder**.
13. Type **SimpleShare2** and press **Enter**.
14. Right-click an open area, point to **New**, and click **Folder**.
15. Type **AdvancedShare** and press **Enter**.
16. Right-click **SimpleShare2** and click **Share with**. Select **Specific people**.
17. Click the drop-down list, click **WorkgroupUser**, and click the **Add** button.
18. To the right of Workgroup User, click **Read**, and then click **Read/Write**.
19. Click the **Share** button.
20. Read the results on the File Sharing window. Notice that the UNC path is directly to the shared folder when the folder is not inside your Documents folder.
21. Click **Done**.
22. Right-click **AdvancedShare** and click **Properties**.
23. Click the **Sharing** tab and click **Advanced Sharing**.
24. Select the **Share this folder** option. Notice that the Share name setting is the same name as the folder by default, but it can be changed.

25. Click the **Permissions** button. This displays the share permissions for this share. Advanced sharing configures only share permissions, not NTFS permissions. NTFS permissions for this folder must be configured manually by using the Security tab. Using "Share with" sharing configures both share permissions and NTFS permissions.

26. Select the **Allow** option next to the **Change** permission and click **OK**. This allows all users to modify files through the share, but not to change the share permissions.

27. Click **OK** to close the Advanced Sharing dialog box.

28. Click the **Security** tab and click the **Edit** button.

29. Click **Add**, type **WorkgroupUser**, click **Check Names**, and click **OK**.

30. In the Group or user names box, click **WorkgroupUser**.

31. In the Permissions for WorkgroupUser box, select the **Allow** option next to the **Modify** permission and click **OK**. NTFS permissions work with the share permissions to control what tasks a user is able to perform on a network share.

32. Click **Close** to close the AdvancedShare Properties dialog box.

33. Close all open windows.

Monitoring Shared Folders

Over time, you might lose track of all the folders that are shared on your computer. The most comprehensive way to monitor shares is by using Computer Management, shown in Figure 7-16. The Shared Folders System Tool has three nodes for monitoring and managing shared folders:

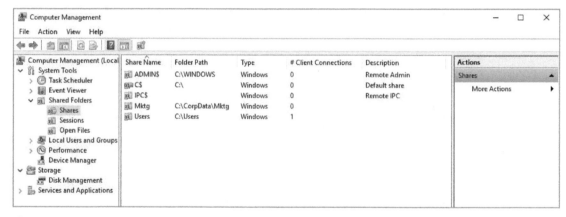

Figure 7-16   Shares view in Computer Management

- *Shares*—This node allows you to create new shares, configure existing shared folders, and optionally stop sharing them. It shows all of the shared folders on this computer, including hidden shares. The summary view here even allows you to see how many clients are connected to each share.

- *Sessions*—This node allows you to see which users are connected to this computer. The summary view shows which computer each user is connecting from, how many files each user has open, and how long each user has been connected. If your system has the maximum of 20 sessions already connected and you need to allow another user access, you can disconnect an existing session from here.

- *Open Files*—This node allows you to see which files and folders are opened through file shares on this computer. You can see which users have the files open and whether the file is open for writing. Occasionally, due to system problems, users will be disconnected from files, but Windows 10 keeps the file locked. You can force a file to close here so that it can be reopened and modified.

Activity 7-9: Monitoring Shared Folders

Time Required: 5 minutes
Objective: Monitor shared folders by using Computer Management

Description: When you share folders on your computer, it is useful to see who is using those files. For example, if you want to reboot your computer, you must be sure that no files are open. Rebooting a computer with shared files open can corrupt the files. In this activity, you monitor shared folders on your computer.

1. If necessary, start your computer and sign in.

2. Right-click the **Start** button and click **Computer Management.**

3. In the left pane, expand **Shared Folders** and click **Shares.** This displays all of the shares on your computer, including the hidden shares. You can see the Users, SimpleShare2, and AdvancedShare shares from previous activities. You can also see the number of clients connected to each share and the folder each is sharing.

4. Right-click **SimpleShare2** and click **Properties.** The General tab allows you to configure the name of the share, description, user limit, and offline settings.

5. Click the **Share Permissions** tab and click **Everyone.** This tab allows you to configure the share permissions for the share. Notice that the Everyone group has Full Control.

6. Click the **Security** tab, and in the Group or user names box, click **WorkgroupUser.** This tab displays the NTFS permissions for the folder. Notice that WorkgroupUser has Full Control NTFS permissions. These NTFS permissions were automatically configured by the Share with... sharing in the previous activity.

7. Click **Cancel** to close the SimpleShare2 Properties dialog box.

8. Click the **Start** button and select **File Explorer.** Click **Network**, double-click your computer, double-click **Users**, double-click **Public**, double-click **Public Documents**, and double-click **NetworkDoc.txt** to open it. This opens NetworkDoc.txt through the UNC path and creates a network connection to your computer.

9. In Computer Management, select the **Refresh** button in the toolbar to update the shared folder details. Read the # Client Connections for the Users share. There is now one connection for the file you have opened. You can also press **F5** to refresh the screen contents to update the # Client Connections value.

10. In the left pane, click **Sessions.** The Sessions folder shows you which users are connected to your computer and from which computer they are connected.

11. In the left pane, click **Open Files.** The Open Files folder shows you which files and folders are open on your computer and by which user.

12. Close all open windows.

Internet Connectivity

Today, almost every computer is configured to communicate on the Internet. However, depending on your needs, how your computer connects to the Internet will vary. The way you connect to the Internet will also vary depending on whether a single computer or multiple computers are using an Internet connection.

Single-Computer Internet Connectivity

Many homes have one or more computers sharing the Internet. How a computer is configured to connect to the Internet depends on the type of Internet connection you have.

For some Internet connection types, the IP address provided to you is usually a fully routable IP address on the Internet. This means that anyone on the Internet can connect to and communicate with your computer. In those cases, it is important to enable Windows Firewall to protect your computer.

Detailed information about Windows Firewall is provided later in this chapter.

7

Cable
Almost all cable companies offer high-speed Internet connectivity as an option to their subscribers. In most cases, this is the simplest way to connect to the Internet.

When you subscribe to an Internet connection with your cable provider, you will be supplied with a cable modem that connects to the same cable that you hook up to your TV. The cable modem is responsible for converting signals from a format that travels properly over the cable provider network to standard Ethernet in your home. You connect an Ethernet cable from your computer to the cable modem.

By default, Windows 10 networking is configured to use DHCP to obtain IP configuration information. When you connect your computer to the cable modem, the cable provider's DHCP server provides IP configuration information to Windows 10. Moments after you plug in the Ethernet cable, you should be able to access the Internet.

For more detailed information about Internet connectivity over cable systems, see the Internet Service description at *http://technet.microsoft.com/ en-us/library/cc750549.aspx*.

DSL
Digital subscriber line (DSL) is a high-speed Internet connection over telephone lines. This type of Internet connectivity is often as fast as cable, but slightly more difficult to configure.

When you subscribe to DSL, you are supplied with a DSL modem that connects to a phone line. The DSL modem is responsible for converting signals from a format that travels properly over the phone system to standard Ethernet in your home. The DSL modem is commonly combined with a router/firewall appliance in one physical box. You connect an Ethernet cable from your computer to the DSL modem to connect to the Internet.

DSL connections usually use **Point-to-Point Protocol over Ethernet (PPPoE)** to secure connections. Your DSL provider supplies you with a PPPoE user name and password to connect to the network. In a home situation, the installer can program this information into the DSL modem for you. Only after you are authenticated by using PPPoE will you be able to obtain IP configuration information from the DSL provider and connect to the Internet.

If the DSL provider has only supplied a DSL modem, and it does not have a router/firewall supplied with it, Windows 10 has built-in support to connect directly via PPPoE. You can connect to a network requiring PPPoE by creating a broadband connection from the Network and Sharing Center. The options in a broadband connection are similar to a dial-up connection.

For more detailed information about Internet connectivity over DSL systems, see the Internet Service description at *http://technet.microsoft.com/ en-us/library/cc750549.aspx*.

Dial-Up
Although progressively becoming much less common, some people still access the Internet using a dial-up connection over a phone line by using a modem. This is a much slower way to access the Internet. However, it is suitable when there are no other options available. Windows 10 includes support for dial-up connections.

Wireless WAN
Wireless wide area networks (WWANs) are fully supported by Windows 10 using cellular data network devices that connect through broadband cell towers and Wi-Fi hotspots for Internet data transfer. Those cellular data network devices can be built in to the Windows 10 device, plugged in as an add-on device via USB, or a wired/wireless attached device such as a smartphone. These devices have a SIM card to identify the user to the cellular data network, enabling connectivity to the Internet.

There are several requirements in order for this option to work. The provider of the broadband service must enable this option for the portable device, typically for an extra fee. Most broadband vendors refer to this feature as "tethering" the computer to the mobile device. The mobile device must also be configured to recognize that this feature is active. The advantage to this technology is that broadband support for mobile devices is now widespread. The disadvantage is that the data plan contract to pay for the bandwidth used by the mobile device while it operates in this mode can be expensive. Windows 10 works with this type of connection fully aware that it is a WWAN service.

Shared Internet Connectivity

It is possible for multiple computers to share a single Internet connection. This is not commonly done for dial-up connections, but is quite common for cable modem and DSL Internet connections. For multiple computers on your network to share a single Internet connection, there must be a mechanism in place to share the single IP address given to you by your ISP. The two most common mechanisms for sharing an IP address are a router or Internet Connection Sharing (ICS).

Router Connection Sharing
Multiple computers can share an Internet connection with a dedicated router appliance. The router is assigned an IP address from the ISP to connect to the public Internet. Computers on the router's internal network are assigned private IP addresses that are not routable on the Internet. The computers on the internal network use the router as their default gateway, sending Internet-bound traffic to the router for delivery.

The hardware routers sold in retail stores are also simple firewalls that perform Network Address Translation (NAT). NAT is the process that allows multiple computers to effectively share the single IP address assigned by the ISP.

Internet Connection Sharing
Internet Connection Sharing (ICS) is an older technology that allows a Windows 10 computer with multiple network interfaces to act as an Internet router for other local computers. The ICS computer is called the host computer. To use ICS, the host computer must have an Internet connection (public interface) plus one additional network connection (private interface). The public interface obtains an Internet-routable IP address from your ISP. The private interface uses a private IP address to communicate with other computers that you are sharing the Internet connection with.

You use the Sharing tab in the Properties of the public interface to enable ICS. The Sharing tab, shown in Figure 7-17, is only available when there are at least two connections on the computer.

Figure 7-17   ICS Sharing settings on network interface properties

 It is strongly recommended to use a router instead of ICS.

Wireless Networking

Network connections allow data to flow from the local computer to other computers that share that network. Many networking technologies rely on a wire-based physical data connection to the local computer. Different types of cables, connectors, and expansion equipment make up the wired network. Instead of relying on wires to connect computers, a wireless network transfers data without a physical connection. The most common type of wireless technology uses radios to transmit and receive data. Many different types of radios have been developed for wireless technology.

Standards are written by organizations such as the **Institute of Electrical and Electronics Engineers (IEEE)** to guide the manufacturers of wireless network products and help make them functional and compatible with each other. The IEEE standard most commonly used for popular wireless networking products is IEEE **802.11**.

The Wireless Fidelity (Wi-Fi) Alliance was created in 1999 as a nonprofit body to help manufacturers test and certify wireless products that would work together. These wireless standards are summarized in Table 7-9. IEEE 802.11n performance is fast and currently preferred because it is more tolerant of interference and supports a wide range of devices. Many portable devices such as smartphones and newer laptops include support for IEEE 802.11ac, which is becoming a popular alternative to 802.11n.

Table 7-9   IEEE 802.11 wireless standard comparison

Wireless standard	Primary radio frequency	Maximum data throughput (Mbps)
IEEE 802.11a	5 GHz	54
IEEE 802.11b	2.4 GHz	11
IEEE 802.11g	2.4 GHz	54
IEEE 802.11n	2.4 and 5 GHz	600
IEEE 802.11ac	5 GHz	867
IEEE 802.11ad	2.4, 5, and 60 GHz	7168

Windows 10 provides a strong foundation for wireless technology, leaving the manufacturer with less responsibility for code development and a smaller chance of creating unstable software. Wireless adapters now appear as their own media type, not as an Ethernet 802.3 connection.

Even though Windows 10 supports a range of IEEE 802.11 standards, several are becoming obsolete. For example, it is rare to find 802.11a and 802.11b hardware in use. Each standard defines limits on how many devices can interact at once, resistance to radio interference, how fast they transfer data, and over what range they can operate. Exceeding any of those limits can cause performance issues that Windows 10 cannot compensate for with software alone. For example, the 802.11ad standard can operate at a very high data rate but only for a short distance, typically within the same room.

A computer running Windows 10 may have a wireless adapter installed in the computer. It may be installed as an add-on card, plugged into a USB port, or built in to the system itself. If the wireless adapter is built in, such as in a laptop, there is often a power switch that toggles the adapter on or off to save power or ensure privacy.

The wireless adapter can communicate with a base station or other wireless adapters. A base station is commonly called a wireless access point (WAP). The WAP itself connects to the wired network and allows wireless clients to ultimately use that wired connection. The WAP may be part of a firewall device sharing access to the Internet or it may be a stand-alone unit. The WAP and wireless adapter must use the same 802.11 standard to communicate with each other. If they are not compatible, one or the other hardware component may need to be replaced. When a WAP is purchased, consider that many support a combination of IEEE 802.11 standards, which can give them a price or feature set competitive advantage over other WAPs.

Most WAP devices have a web server built in to them that allows the device to be configured initially using a wired network connection. The manufacturer's instructions provide connection details and initial sign-in credentials. The manufacturer identifies a default management IP address, an initial connection URL (for example, *http://192.168.0.1/admin*), and a default administrator ID and password.

The most common configuration details for a WAP include:

- *Security Set Identifier (SSID)*—The **Security Set Identifier (SSID)** is the name assigned to the WAP to identify itself to clients. The SSID may or may not be configured to broadcast its identity to all wireless clients. If the SSID is not broadcast, the wireless client can still connect if it knows the name ahead of time and has the right connection settings preconfigured.

- *802.11 mode*—This includes the versions of 802.11 in which the radio operates, such as 802.11n. Choices will be limited to the modes supported by the WAP hardware.

- *Security method*—This includes the methods used to encrypt and restrict wireless client connections to the WAP.

Wireless encryption methods and client connection restrictions are required because the range of a wireless signal does not have a specific boundary. A private system may be detected by clients in unauthorized and unexpected areas. Newer technology has a greater range than ever before. Simply upgrading existing wireless hardware may expose companies to risks they did not think about before. A wireless client must be configured with correct security settings to enable it to communicate with a secured WAP. If the WAP is unsecured, it is referred to as an open or unsecured system.

Connecting to an open system may be dangerous because your computer may be connecting to an untrusted WAP that has been configured purposely to help unauthorized users gain access to your system or monitor the traffic you move through the WAP. If there is no choice, ensure that the connection is identified as a Public network connection to maximize the protection of Windows Firewall and to disable your computer's advertising of its identity.

Creating a Wireless Connection

Wireless network connections can be created using several methods:

- *Manually connect to a wireless network*—This wizard is available by clicking *Set up a new connection or network* in Network and Sharing Center and selecting the Manually Connect to a Wireless Network option. All settings are manually configured.

- *Connect to a network*—By clicking the network icon in the notification area of the taskbar, a list of wireless networks is displayed, as shown in Figure 7-18. The list of visible networks shows the signal strength of each connection, if it is secure or open (no security), and if Windows 10 is connected to one of them. Selecting a network from the list and clicking the Connect button triggers the client to attempt a connection. If a security passphrase is requested, the user must enter a correct value before the connection is fully established.

- *Copy a profile from USB flash drive*—A wireless configuration profile can be saved to a USB flash drive. That USB drive stores configuration information for the wireless network, optionally including the security passphrase as well. The XML files on the USB drive can be used to program multiple computers and devices labeled as Windows Connect now compatible.

- *Use a command-line utility*—The *netsh* command-line utility supports a command section for wireless LAN configuration, *wlan*. This advanced utility is not typically used in day-to-day network administration, but it is available for advanced management. More options can be seen by issuing the command *netsh wlan /?*.

Figure 7-18 Wireless networks displayed from taskbar notification area

- *Configure in Group Policy*—Wireless network settings can be applied to domain computers using Group Policy settings defined in Active Directory. A list of allowed or denied wireless networks can be specified.

- *Use Wi-Fi Sense*—Wireless network settings could be shared among contacts using Outlook.com, Skype, and Facebook contacts who decide to share certain Wi-Fi connections with their contacts; however, this feature has been disabled by Microsoft due to its complexity and low demand for this feature.

Windows 10 keeps a list of SSIDs sorted by preference based on what you connected to in the past. The last used SSID is the preferred connection to connect to by default. If you are connected to one SSID in the list but you want to select a different one, simply select the other one from the list and connect to it. Windows 10 will remember that choice for next time.

Wireless Network Properties   When a new wireless connection is created, the key settings stored to describe it in Windows 10 are:

- *Network name*—The name of the wireless connection and its profile in the operating system

- *Security type*—The type of security methods the WAP expects the wireless client to use

- *Encryption type*—The method used to encrypt data, if a choice exists, as a customization of the selected security type

- *Security key*—A passphrase that acts as a password, allowing the wireless client to authenticate and connect

- *Connect automatically when this connection is in range*—The setting that identifies this SSID as preferred; tries to connect automatically once the client detects the WAP is operating in range

- *Look for other wireless networks while connected to this network*—A setting that allows the client to attempt to connect to a preferred wireless connection if it becomes available while connected to this SSID

- *Connect even if the network is not broadcasting its name (SSID)*—A setting that allows the client to attempt to connect even if it does not notice the WAP broadcasting its SSID wirelessly

Note that the last three connection settings enable a preference to be set for connecting to WAPs. A preferred connection can be set to automatically connect. A secondary connection can be used, but the client can change to a preferred WAP if it becomes available. If none of those are available, Windows can search for a specifically named WAP that is not broadcasting its name to clients. A WAP that is not configured to broadcast its name is sometimes seen as a security measure; however, there are applications available that can spot the SSID from other types of packets the WAP generates, making the name known to others if they really want to look for it.

Wireless Network Security   A wireless network connection has settings for both security type and encryption type. The security type defines how authentication is performed. The encryption type defines the algorithm that is used to encrypt data while in transit over the wireless network. In general, these settings are automatically detected when you connect to a wireless network for the first time.

The following security types are available:

- *No authentication (open)*—This service type is used by public Wi-Fi networks where you are not required to provide credentials.

- *WPA2-Personal*—**WPA2-Personal** uses a pre-shared key (password) for authentication and is suitable only for small environments.

- *WPA2-Enterprise*—**WPA2-Enterprise** uses 802.1x for authentication and is suitable for larger environments.

- *802.1x*—This option is an older method for supporting 802.1x authentication that is less secure that WPA2-Enterprise. This method should be avoided.

The **802.1x** protocol is a standard for network devices, such as a Windows 10 computer, to be authenticated by switches or WAPs. Windows 10 provides authentication credentials to the WAP and then the WAP queries a RADIUS server to verify the credentials. In a Windows-based environment, the RADIUS server can verify authentication for Active Directory user accounts or computer accounts.

There are three encryption types available:

- *None*—Data is transmitted as cleartext. This option is available only for open networks.

- *Wired Equivalent Privacy (WEP)*—This older encryption protocol has known flaws and should be avoided whenever possible. This option is available only for open networks and 802.1x.

- *Advanced Encryption Standard (AES)*—This is the preferred encryption type and is used by WPA2-Personal and WPA2-Enterprise.

Managing Wireless Connections

Managing a wireless network connection is similar to managing a wired network connection. There are typically very few tasks required to manage a wireless network after it is configured, except for troubleshooting when there are connectivity issues.

If there are connectivity issues, you can view the status of the wireless network, as shown in Figure 7-19. This shows which wireless network you are connected to and the signal strength. In the unlikely event you need to change the settings for the wireless network, you can do it manually in the wireless properties, but it is typically faster and easier to forget the existing network and reconnect to autodetect the settings again.

Figure 7-19   Wireless connection status

Windows 10 keeps a record of all wireless networks that it has connected to, including the settings that were used. To delete older wireless networks that are no longer in use, you can choose to forget them. However, there is no technical benefit to doing so.

From a user perspective, temporarily disabling Wi-Fi can be useful for air travel. If you activate Airplane mode, it disables Wi-Fi and Bluetooth connectivity. You can enable Airplane mode in Settings or from the network icon on the taskbar, as shown in Figure 7-18.

Troubleshooting Wireless Connections

Wireless technology is flexible, but there are several issues that commonly arise. The first thing to check is whether the wireless radio on the device running Window 10 is turned on. This can be controlled by a switch, key, or just plugging in an antenna.

Wireless technologies are typically radios restricted to specific radio frequencies. Other devices, such as microwaves and cordless telephones, can interfere with the signal. If the interference cannot be eliminated, the signal between the computer and WAP might need to be improved with better antennas or better antenna placement. If that does not help enough, the WAP and wireless network adapter might have to be reconfigured to use a different frequency. Each of the 802.11 standards is designed to operate on one or perhaps more frequencies. Purchasing new hardware might be a requirement in some situations where the existing hardware and its supported 802.11 settings fail to operate effectively. Options are limited by the manufacturer's support for both the WAP and wireless network adapter.

Some 802.11 standards are limited to what channels, in addition to specific frequencies, they can use to communicate with the wireless client. Channel selection may be limited by the number of active clients and sources of interference nearby. Making changes to those wireless adapter settings might require updates to the WAP configuration as well.

The SSID assigned to a WAP identifies that device. There is no automatic method to force two WAP devices in the same area to have different SSID values assigned. If they have the same

SSID, the wireless client may become confused about which one to connect to and unreliable connectivity will result. This is common when WAP devices are installed with factory settings in areas where multiple offices or homes are clustered together. A WAP's SSID and administrator credentials (i.e., user ID and password) should always be changed when it is installed for the first time.

A Windows 10 client can be configured to connect to a WAP automatically when it is in range. If the same client is configured for multiple WAPs and they are all active and in range, it may disconnect from one WAP and reconnect to another as the signal strength varies. This can cause the client to appear slow and unresponsive. The wireless client can be moved closer to one of the WAPs to change the signal strength—the closer it is, the stronger the signal will appear. Another strategy is to set one wireless SSID as preferred and all others enabled with the option to connect to a more preferred network if it is available.

WAP devices in public places may be untrusted, even if they have a passphrase configured. If a computer is being connected to an untrusted network, always consider setting the network location type as Public and confirming that Windows Firewall is up to date and configured without unsafe exceptions. Not all open WAPs are considered dangerous; some are designed to be open to allow devices to connect and access a paid secure wireless connection. By default, Windows 10 allows access to an open wireless connection to determine if paid Wi-Fi is available through that SSID. Turn off the Paid Wi-Fi Services option in Wi-Fi Settings to disable this functionality.

If the problem doesn't seem to be the external wireless environment, the user can trigger the network troubleshooter by right-clicking the network icon in the taskbar and selecting Troubleshoot problems from the shortcut menu. This wizard is designed to work with users who are not as technically inclined; however, it should not be dismissed as a superficial troubleshooting tool. Microsoft has compiled a lot of intelligence into the network troubleshooter and it can correct many conditions with little effort from the user.

Windows 10 includes advanced troubleshooting tools for wireless connections that are used by network administrators and normally not by the average user. A history of wireless activity is collected by Windows 10 and can be used to generate a report called the Wireless LAN Report, or WlanReport for short. This is an .html and .xml file created by opening an elevated administrative command prompt and issuing the command *netsh wlan show wlanreport*. The report will be generated and include the date that the report was run in the file name. The location of the report will be reported by the command, but it is typically stored in the hidden folder C:\ProgramData\Microsoft\Windows\WlanReport.

The WlanReport.html file can be viewed in a browser and contains an interactive summary graph, as shown in Figure 7-20. This graph is useful for a quick review of the wireless connection history, but the report also contains general system information, user information, network adapter inventory details, output of an *ipconfig /all* command, details of the wireless devices, drivers, wireless profiles, and a detailed wireless network session analysis.

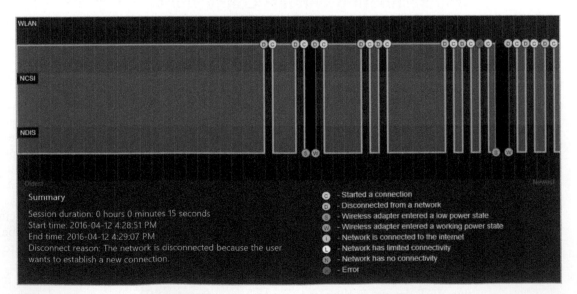

Figure 7-20   Wireless LAN report summary

Activity 7-10: Viewing the Wireless LAN Report

Time Required: 10 minutes

Objective: Generate and view a wireless LAN report

Description: The *netsh* utility can be used to generate a wireless LAN report that can be used for advanced troubleshooting. In this activity, you generate a wireless LAN report and then view the contents.

 It is only possible to complete this activity if you have a wireless network card in your computer.

1. If necessary, start your computer and sign in.
2. Right-click the **Start** button, click **Command Prompt (Admin)**, and click **Yes** in the User Account Control dialog box.
3. At the command prompt, type **netsh wlan show wlanreport** and press **Enter**.
4. On the taskbar, click **File Explorer**, browse to **C:\ProgramData\Microsoft\Windows\ WlanReport**, and double-click **wlan-report-latest.html**.
5. Scroll down and read the information in the report.
6. Close all open windows.

Some Windows 10 computers that have been updated from an earlier operating system might have an old device driver installed for the wireless network adapter that is not fully compatible with Windows 10. In that case, consider updating the device drivers for the wireless network driver using Device Manager. If the problems showed up only after the driver was recently updated, Device Manager also presents the option to roll back the device driver. If neither of those options install a stable version of the device driver, look for a new device driver and advice from the wireless card manufacturer's website. Ensure you are downloading the correct driver based on the manufacturer, make, and model number of the wireless adapter.

Even if a wireless network card driver is correct, the problem with connectivity can be caused by malicious software (malware), poorly written software, or people making low-level changes to network settings in the registry and making a mistake. This is not that common, but the attempted fix is fairly straightforward. Several command-line commands can reset the basic TCP/IP configuration of the computer. These commands should be run in the sequence listed below in an elevated command prompt window (right-click the Start button, select Command Prompt (Admin)):

- *Netsh winsock reset*—Reset the Winsock catalog tracking what applications are associated with ports linked to TCP/IP interfaces.
- *Netsh int ip reset*—Reset the TCP/IP protocol (i.e., re-install it).
- *Ipconfig /release*—Discard any previously obtained DHCP IP address information.
- *Ipconfig /renew*—Attempt to obtain new DHCP IP address information.
- *Ipconfig /flushdns*—Purge any previous DNS cached responses, which map names to IP addresses or "name not found" responses.
- *Shutdown /r /f /t 60*—Restart the computer (i.e., /r), forcing open applications to close (i.e., /f), waiting for 60 seconds to elapse before triggering the actual restart (i.e., /t 60).

If the network settings on the network adapter and the TCP/IP protocol are not the problem, it is possible that antivirus, Windows Firewall settings, or anti-malware settings may have contributed to the problem. Antivirus and anti-malware performance and configuration issues should be escalated to their vendor for support. Windows Firewall settings are reviewed in the next section.

As a last resort, consider the option of running the command *netcfg –d* from an elevated command prompt. This cleans up and removes all network devices from the Windows 10 computer, and then triggers a restart. The Windows 10 computer detects the installed network devices it can see and attempts to reinstall drivers to default settings. This can help if the computer has been upgraded from an older operating system and old VPN software components or devices no longer used litter the system settings, causing a general network failure. This command might have to run more than once to completely remove the old network devices.

Windows Firewall

A standard firewall protects your computer by restricting which network packets are allowed to reach your computer from another network, such as the Internet. A host-based firewall, like Windows Firewall in Windows 10, evaluates each packet as it arrives or leaves and determines whether that packet is allowed or denied. By default, all packets are denied when they arrive from external sources and only a few are allowed for specific purposes. For example, when you join a domain, Windows 10 automatically configures Windows Firewall to allow the correct packets through for domain-based communication. Other packets are denied.

One way to improve security on computers is by reducing the attack surface, the elements of a computer system, device, applications, and operating system that can be attacked by hackers and malware. Disabling and removing unnecessary services is a common way to reduce the attack surface. Using a host-based firewall restricts communication with your computer and further reduces the attack surface. By reducing the attack surface, it is less likely that worms, viruses, and other malware are able to install on your computer.

Basic Firewall Configuration

The Windows Firewall Control Panel window provides basic firewall configuration options. Windows 10 allows custom firewall settings for each type of network location, private or public, as shown in Figure 7-21. When the computer is domain joined, there are additional options available in the advanced firewall settings window, which is reviewed later in the chapter. When a network interface becomes active, it has a specified network location. The matching firewall settings for that type of network location applies to traffic through that interface. If a Windows 10 computer has multiple network interfaces active, each can be assigned a different network location, each with different firewall settings based on their assigned network location.

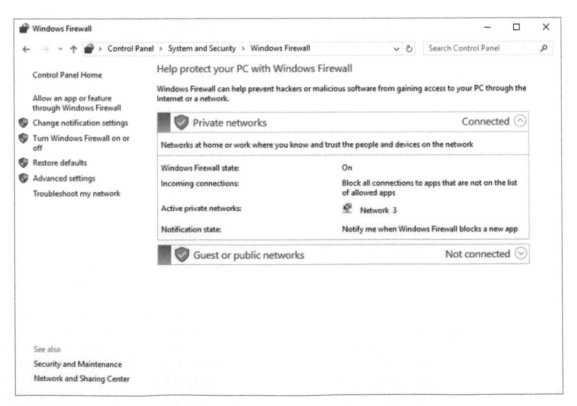

Figure 7-21   Windows Firewall, main window

When Windows Firewall is enabled, the default configuration blocks all incoming packets except for specifically configured exceptions. This allows Windows Firewall to be configured to support applications such as instant messenger programs. Instant messenger programs, for example, typically require some exceptions on Windows Firewall to receive messages. This is typically the behavior you want.

When *Turn Windows Firewall on or off* is selected from the Windows Firewall Control Panel window, the Customize Settings window is displayed, as shown in Figure 7-22. For each network type, you can disable Windows Firewall, but this should only be done for troubleshooting.

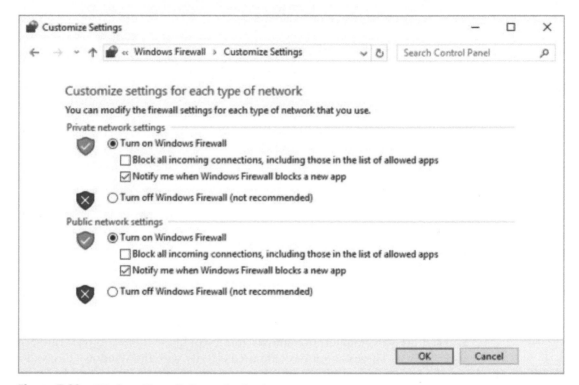

Figure 7-22   Windows Firewall, Customize Settings

There is an option to block all incoming connections. When this option is selected, no exceptions are allowed. You are still able to initiate communication with other computers, but other computers cannot initiate communication with your computer. This is recommended only when you are connected directly to public networks, such as the wireless network in a café.

When *Allow a program or feature through Windows Firewall* is selected from the Windows Firewall Control Panel window, the Allowed apps window is displayed, as shown in Figure 7-23. This allows you to configure which programs are able to accept network communication requests. A program can be allowed access through the firewall depending on the network location type, private or public. The firewall exception can be enabled for one, both, or none of the network location categories.

This allows some applications, such as Remote Assistance, to be available when the user is connected in supported situations. Many corporate offices do not want Remote Assistance enabled when the user is connected in unsupported locations, or in locations where other support methods are available. The choice of what application to make an exception for and the type of network location to enable it for are defined by situational requirements.

When you create an exception for a program, the exception applies to that program no matter what port number it uses. The exception is also only valid when the program is running. If the program is stopped, the exception poses no risk.

When Restore defaults is selected from the Windows Firewall Control Panel window (refer to Figure 7-21), the option to restore default settings for Windows Firewall is presented. If you have performed many customized configurations and did not document them, you might want to reset Windows Firewall back to the default configuration as part of the troubleshooting process.

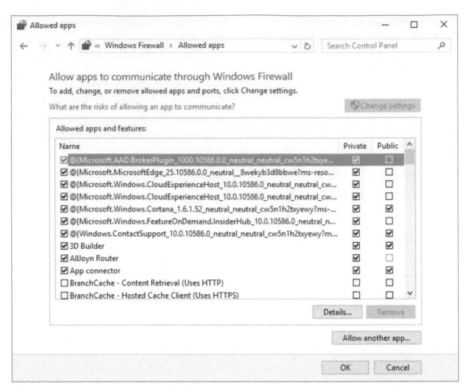

Figure 7-23   Windows Firewall, Allowed apps

Advanced Firewall Configuration

Advanced firewall configuration allows you to configure more complex rules, outgoing filtering, and **IPsec** rules. These cannot be configured directly with the Windows Firewall utility in Control Panel. Advanced firewall configuration is useful in corporate and enterprise computing situations. The basic Windows Firewall utility is usually sufficient in home and small business situations. The tools available to perform advanced firewall configuration are:

- *Windows Firewall with Advanced Security utility*—This utility is a graphical tool to configure all of the Windows Firewall features on a single computer.

- *Netsh*—This is a command-line utility for managing network configuration. It is also capable of configuring all of the Windows Firewall features on the local computer. This tool can be used in a script that is run on multiple computers.

- *Group Policy*—To quickly and easily manage the Windows Firewall settings in a corporate environment, you should use Group Policy. It allows firewall settings to be applied to hundreds or thousands of computers very quickly. Some Windows 10 Group Policy configuration options were not available for previous versions of Windows and these settings are ignored by previous versions of Windows.

- *Windows PowerShell*—There are Windows PowerShell cmdlets that can be used to configure advanced firewall settings. To view the list of cmdlets, use Get-Command *firewall* and Get-Command *ipsec*.

The **Windows Firewall with Advanced Security utility** is shown in Figure 7-24.

You will practice using the Windows Firewall with Advanced Security utility in Activity 7-11.

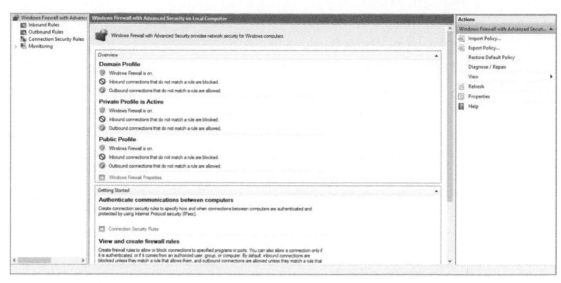

Figure 7-24   Windows Firewall, Advanced Settings window

Configuring Firewall Properties   Windows 10 stores the firewall properties based on location types. The configuration of each location type is referred to as a profile. When the Windows Firewall with Advanced Security on Local Computer node is selected, a summary is displayed showing the configuration of each profile. You can edit the configuration for each profile, as shown in Figure 7-25. The tabs for editing each profile have exactly the same options.

Figure 7-25   Windows Firewall, profile settings for network locations

In each profile, you can:

- Enable or disable Windows Firewall.
- Configure inbound connections.
  - ○ *Block (default)*—All inbound connections are blocked unless specifically allowed by a rule.
  - ○ *Block all connections*—All inbound connections are blocked regardless of the rules.
  - ○ *Allow*—All inbound connections are allowed unless specifically blocked by a rule.
- Configure outbound connections.
  - ○ *Allow (default)*—All outbound connections are allowed unless specifically blocked by a rule.
  - ○ *Block*—All outbound connections are blocked unless specifically allowed by a rule.
- Customize protected network connections.
  - ○ *Select which network interfaces this firewall state applies to*—All are selected by default.
- Customize settings.
  - ○ *Display notifications to the user when a program is blocked from receiving inbound connections*—This is useful for users to be notified when something unusual is happening on the network.
  - ○ *Allow unicast response to multicast or broadcast network traffic*—Some network attackers use multicast and broadcast requests to map out the network and determine client IP addresses. Disabling this reduces that possibility.
  - ○ *Apply local firewall rules*—This option allows firewall rules from Group Policy and the local computer to both be applied. If there is a conflict between Group Policy-based rules and local rules, the Group Policy-based rules are effective. You can only configure this option in Group Policy.
  - ○ *Apply local connection security rules*—This option allows connection security rules from Group Policy and the local computer to both be applied. If there is a conflict between Group Policy-based rules and the local rules, the Group Policy-based rules are effective. You can only configure this option in Group Policy.
- Customize logging.
  - ○ *Name*—This identifies the name and location of the Windows Firewall log. By default, this is C:\Windows\system32\LogFiles\Firewall\pfirewall.log.
  - ○ *Size limit*—This limits the size of the Windows Firewall log to ensure you do not run out of disk space.
  - ○ *Log dropped packets*—This specifies whether blocked packets are logged. By default, this option is turned off and blocked packets are not logged.
  - ○ *Log successful connections*—This specifies whether successful connections are logged. By default, this option is turned off and successful connections are not logged.

Configuring IPsec   By using the Windows Firewall with Advanced Security utility, you can configure IPsec settings, as shown in Figure 7-26. If the settings are configured as Default, they can be overridden by Group Policy-based settings.

The IPsec default settings you can configure are:

- *Key exchange*—This setting controls which method is used to securely transmit the keys used for data encryption between both computers.
- *Data protection*—This setting controls which methods are used to encrypt and protect the integrity of data.
- *Authentication method*—This setting controls which method is used to authenticate the two computers creating an IPsec connection. The simplest method is a pre-shared key (password), but it is also the least secure. By default, Kerberos authentication is used.

Figure 7-26   Windows Firewall, IPSec settings

The IPsec exemption settings you can configure are:

- *Exempt ICMP from IPsec*—This is a Yes or No setting. ICMP packets are commonly used by troubleshooting tools (such as *ping*), and if they are exempted from IPsec by the network administrator it could assist in diagnosing issues during troubleshooting. Note that exempting ICMP packets from IPsec doesn't automatically allow them through the Windows Firewall. The Windows Firewall rules must be enabled separately to allow ICMP traffic as well.

The IPsec tunnel authorization settings you can configure are:

- *None*—No user or computer authorization is required to use a tunnel mode connection from a remote computer to the local computer.

- *Advanced, Custom*—List specific users or computers that are either allowed (i.e., authorized) or denied (i.e., exceptions) the use of the tunnel mode connection from a remote computer to the local computer.

Viewing and Editing Firewall Rules   A large number of inbound and outbound rules are created by default in Windows 10. Figure 7-27 shows a sample list of inbound rules. In the

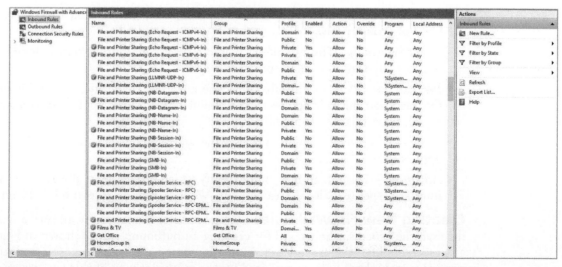

Figure 7-27   Windows Firewall, inbound rule listing

list of rules, you can see the name of the rule, a group of rules it belongs to, profiles the rule can belong to, when the rule is enabled, and whether the rule allows or denies packets.

The icons for each rule also give you information about that rule. Rules that allow packets have a green arrow icon. Rules that deny packets have a red circle with a slash. If the icon has a down arrow on it, the rule is disabled.

You modify an existing rule by opening its properties. Figure 7-28 shows the properties of the Echo Request ICMPv4-In rule.

Figure 7-28   Windows Firewall, inbound rule properties

The tabs in the properties of an inbound rule are:

- *General*—This tab allows you to configure the rule name, configure the rule description, enable or disable the rule, and choose the rule action (e.g., allow, block, or allow if secured by user or computer identity).

- *Programs and Services*—This tab allows you to select programs, application packages, and services that this rule applies to.

- *Remote Computers*—This tab allows you to restrict connections to include or exclude specific computers or groups of computers. IPsec authentication is required.

- *Remote Users*—This tab allows you to restrict connections to include or exclude specific users or groups of users. IPsec authentication is required.

- *Local Principals*—This tab allows you to restrict connections to include or exclude specific users or application package properties.

- *Protocols and Ports*—This tab allows you to specify the protocol type this rule applies to, the local port this rule applies to, the remote port this rule applies to, and which ICMP packet types this rule applies to.

- *Scope*—This tab allows you to specify the source and destination IP addresses this rule applies to.

- *Advanced*—This tab allows you to specify which profiles (e.g., domain, private, public) and interface types (e.g., local area network, wireless, remote access) this rule applies to.

Creating New Firewall Rules   When you create a new firewall rule, a wizard guides you through the process. The wizard for creating an outbound rule is shown in Figure 7-29. Using a wizard simplifies the process of rule creation because it limits the options during the creation process to only those options you need for the particular type of rule you are creating.

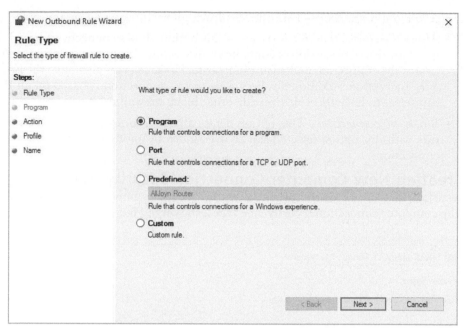

Figure 7-29   Windows Firewall, New Outbound Rule Wizard

The rule types you can create with the Outbound Rule Wizard are:

- *Program*—A program rule allows or denies traffic for a specific program that is specified by selecting an executable file. You can specify which profiles this rule applies to.

- *Port*—A port rule allows or denies traffic for a specific TCP or UDP port. You can specify which profiles this rule applies to.

- *Predefined*—A predefined rule creates a group of rules to allow or deny Windows functions, such as file and printer sharing or Remote Assistance. In most cases, these rules are already created and do not need to be re-created. These rules allow you to define source and destination computers (endpoints) that the rule applies to. You can also specify to which profiles this rule applies.

- *Custom*—A custom rule lets you configure programs, ports, protocols, endpoints, and profiles. You can use this type of rule when the other rule types do not meet your needs.

When you define the actions for a rule, as shown in Figure 7-30, you can specify:

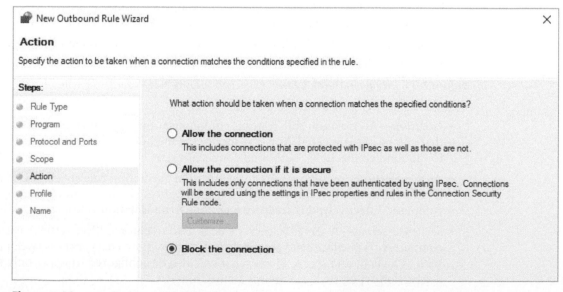

Figure 7-30   Windows Firewall, New Outbound Rule Wizard, rule actions

- *Allow the connection*—This option allows connections based on this rule.

- *Allow the connection if it is secure*—This option allows connections based on this rule only when an IPsec connection is configured. By default, this option requires that IPsec authenticates the connection and ensures integrity. However, you also have the option to require data encryption. Additionally, because a secure connection is based on an IPsec rule, you can select to have this rule override other block firewall rules.

- *Block the connection*—This option denies all connections based on this rule. However, a rule with this option selected can be overridden by another rule that allows only secure connections.

Creating New Computer-Connection Security Rules   Computer-connection security rules use IPsec to authenticate and secure communication between two computers. The computer-connection security rule types, shown in Figure 7-31, are:

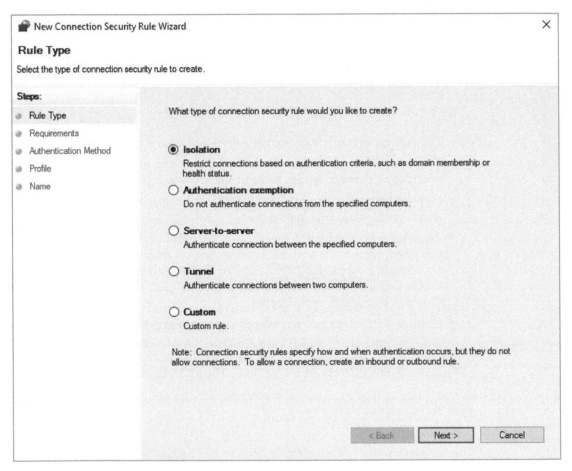

Figure 7-31   Windows Firewall, New Connection Security Rule Wizard, rule type

- *Isolation*—An isolation rule restricts communication with other computers to only those that can be authenticated. You can specify the method of authentication. The rule can apply to inbound connections, outbound connections, or both.

- *Authentication exemption*—An authentication exemption rule specifies IP addresses or IP address ranges that do not need to be authenticated when communicating with this computer. Effectively, this creates exceptions to an isolation rule.

- *Server-to-server*—A server-to-server rule is used to enforce IPsec settings between two computers. Typically, this type of rule is used to require encryption between two computers, such as a client and server. However, it can also be configured to apply only for certain connection types, such as wireless connections.

- *Tunnel*—A tunnel rule is used to configure Windows 10 as the endpoint of a secure communication tunnel. Other computers use the Windows 10 computer as their default gateway to secure communication through the IPsec tunnel. This type of rule is seldom used.

- *Custom*—A custom rule allows you to configure a customized rule if the standard rule types do not meet your needs.

Monitoring Windows Firewall Rules and Connections   When you view the inbound or outbound rules for Windows Firewall, there is a large list of rules that includes enabled or disabled rules. The Firewall node under Monitoring in Windows Firewall with Advanced Security, shown in Figure 7-32, allows you to see all of the rules that are enabled in one screen. This quickly shows you how your system is configured. This is also useful to see the rules that are being applied by Group Policy.

Figure 7-32   Windows Firewall, monitoring

The Connection Security Rules node under Monitoring allows you to see the computer connection security rules that are enabled and any security associations that are active. A security association is the set of rules for communication negotiated between two computers. If two computers have a security association, they are using IPsec to communicate.

Security associations are listed in two categories:

- *Main Mode*—Used for the initial configuration of an IPsec connection, including authentication

- *Quick Mode*—Signifies a secure IPsec communication channel has been negotiated

Activity 7-11: Configuring Windows Firewall

Time Required: 15 minutes

Objective: Configure Windows Firewall by using the Windows Firewall with Advanced Security utility

Description: Windows Firewall in Windows 10 is capable of performing outbound filtering as well as inbound filtering. In this activity, you create a rule to block access to Internet websites and then disable the rule.

1. If necessary, start your computer and sign in.

2. On the taskbar, click **Microsoft Edge**.

3. In the Search or enter web address box, type **http://www.microsoft.com** and press **Enter**. When the Microsoft website loads, it confirms that your computer is able to connect to the Internet properly right now.

4. Close Microsoft Edge.

5. Click the **Start** button, type **firewall**, press **Enter**, and click **Continue**. This opens the simple Windows Firewall Control Panel window.

6. Click the **Advanced settings** link. This opens the Windows Firewall with Advanced Security utility.

7. Read the overview of Windows Firewall configuration. Windows Firewall is on for all network location profiles, inbound connections that do not match a rule are blocked by default, and outbound connections are allowed by default. In the Overview pane, click the **Windows Firewall Properties** link.

8. Click the **Private Profile** tab. These settings apply for all Private networks.

9. In the Settings area, click the **Customize** button. Here, you can configure whether notifications are displayed when inbound connections are blocked and how local firewall rules are combined with firewall rules defined in Group Policy.

10. Click **Cancel** to close the Customize Settings for the Private Profile dialog box.

11. In the Logging area, click the **Customize** button. Here, you can configure logging for Windows Firewall.

12. In the Log dropped packets box, select **Yes**, and click **OK**. Now all blocked connections will be logged to C:\Windows\system32\LogFiles\Firewall\pfirewall.log.

13. Click **OK** to close the Windows Firewall with Advanced Security on Local Computer Properties dialog box.

14. In the left pane, click **Outbound Rules**. These are the rules that control outbound communication. However, none of the default rules block outbound communication.

15. In the left pane, right-click **Outbound Rules** and click **New Rule**.

16. In the Rule Type window, click **Custom** and click **Next**.

17. In the Program window, click **All programs** and click **Next**.

18. In the Protocol type box, click **TCP**.

19. In the Remote port box, click to select **Specific Ports** and type **80,443**. This rule will apply to outbound packets addressed to port 80 and port 443. Ports 80 and 443 are used by web servers.

20. Click **Next**.

21. Click **Next** to select the default option of applying to all computers.

22. If necessary, click **Block the connection**, and click **Next**. This rule will block connections to port 80 and port 443.

23. Click **Next** to accept the default configuration of this rule applying to all profiles. You can also limit it to specific profiles.

24. In the Name box, type **Block Web** and click **Finish**. The Block Web rule is now at the top of the list of outbound rules. Notice that it is enabled and the action is block.

25. On the taskbar, click **Microsoft Edge**.

26. In the Search or enter web address box, type **http://www.microsoft.com** and press **Enter**. You are unable to load the Microsoft website because the Block Web rule is blocking access to all websites.

27. Close Microsoft Edge.

28. In Windows Firewall with Advanced Security, right-click **Block Web** and click **Disable Rule**.

29. Close Windows Firewall with Advanced Security.

30. On the taskbar, click **Microsoft Edge**.

31. In the Search or enter web address box, type **http://www.microsoft.com** and press **Enter**. This verifies that web connectivity is working again.

32. Close Microsoft Edge.

Homegroup Networks

Networking for a small group of computers outside the corporate office is more about convenience than security. Security is still required but might not be as strict or feature rich. The goal is to share information without a lot of administrative knowledge or configuration steps. Homegroups were introduced originally to service the home user's need to share files with family members.

A **homegroup network** uses IPv6 and link-local addresses to enable communications between homegroup members. Discovery of computers and their names on the local network is automatic by default. This technology is designed to be used in a private network. A computer can create a homegroup only when it has a network interface connected as a private network location and it is not domain joined. All editions of Windows 10 are allowed to join a homegroup, including older Windows operating systems such as Windows 7, Windows 8, and Windows 8.1. A domain-joined computer is not allowed to share its files with the homegroup, but it can access the files shared by other homegroup members.

Security in a homegroup is simple. When a homegroup is created on the first member computer, a password is generated that other computers must use to join the homegroup. Homegroup settings can be managed from Control Panel with the options shown in Figure 7-33.

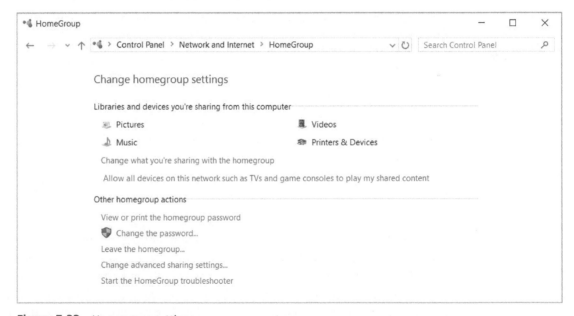

Figure 7-33   Homegroup settings

Each member of the homegroup can decide what to share with other members of the homegroup. Deciding what to share is a personal decision. Libraries can be selected or deselected for sharing with only a few mouse clicks. Each library is a collection of folders on the local drive that stores an expected type of content, such as pictures. Each user can manage the folders that make up a library, even if they are in different folder locations on the local machine. This is much easier than configuring individual shared folders with older style workgroups; however, it requires the use of IPv6 and several services for naming and peer management.

Homegroup members show up in the computer browser window as a different category of browsable locations. There is no complicated procedure to browse a homegroup resource; the intent is to just point, pick, and use.

Windows automatically manages homegroup connections. Homegroups were restricted in older Windows operating systems to the home network location. In Windows 10, there is no home network location, only the private network location. This allows the network administrator to use the homegroup feature in a small branch office where there are no domain services available. Two services are started when a homegroup is active, the HomeGroup Provider and HomeGroup Listener, and both must be running for the homegroup to function. When a computer or device moves from a private network to a public one, the homegroup function deactivates for that computer or device.

Chapter Summary

- Network and Sharing Center is a central location to view and access networking information, such as viewing active networks, network status, and connection status, and to access configuration and troubleshooting wizards.

- Windows 10 is network-aware and can sense which type of network location it is connected to and change settings accordingly. Network location types are Private, Public, or Domain.

- Network connections are composed of clients, services, protocols, and network drivers. Windows 10 includes both IPv4 and IPv6 protocols, neither of which can be removed.

- The important configuration concepts in IPv4 are IP addresses, subnet masks, default gateways, DNS, and WINS. If any of these components are configured incorrectly, network communication may be affected.

- Windows 10 can obtain IP configuration information from static configuration data, DHCP, APIPA, or an alternate IP configuration. DHCP is the most common.

- Windows 10 uses IPv6 to support peer-to-peer and general networking applications. IPv6 is becoming more common and the address types must be recognized. Teredo allows IPv6 traffic to be tunneled through an IPv4 network even when NAT is used on the IPv4 network.

- Sharing the Public folder is an easy way to share files on the network. However, access cannot be controlled per user. All files are shared with all valid users. Valid users can be defined as user accounts with access to Windows 10 or any other users.

- When you share any folder, you can use the Share tab in File Explorer or the "Share with" menu item when you right-click a file or folder, or you can use advanced sharing. The Share tab or "Share with" configure sharing and NTFS permissions at the same time. Advanced sharing configures only share permissions. NTFS permissions must be configured separately.

- The primary technologies for connecting a single computer or device to the Internet are cable, DSL, WWAN, and dial-up. Cable and DSL are high-speed connection methods, while dial-up is slow. DSL commonly requires the configuration of PPPoE. WWAN requires a broadband device to supply Internet connectivity, a cable to tether (connect) the computer to the mobile device, and a paid contract from the broadband supplier to use the feature.

- When an Internet connection is shared by multiple computers, there must be a mechanism to share the single IP address assigned by your ISP. You can use a router or Internet Connection Sharing (ICS). ICS configures Windows 10 as a router to share an Internet connection.

- Wireless networking in Windows 10 supports different versions of the IEEE 802.11 standard that defines how a wireless adapter in a computer connects to a wireless access point (WAP). The WAP's SSID and security settings must be correctly configured to enable the wireless client to connect. Wireless clients can automatically reconnect when they are in range of a WAP. Network location settings and Windows Firewall can help secure the data connection.

- Windows Firewall is a host-based firewall included with Windows 10. Windows Firewall can perform inbound and outbound filtering. Also, IPsec rules are combined with firewall rules in Windows 10. Windows Firewall can be configured by using the basic Control Panel interface, Windows Firewall with Advanced Security utility, or Group Policy.

- Homegroup networking allows home users to share categories of data through libraries with each other. Homegroup networks use IPv6 addressing and specialized services to automatically track peer names and connections. Homegroup security uses a simple password to control computer membership. This technology is not intended to be used inside the corporate or typical workplace environment, so there are some functional limits applied by default.

Key Terms

802.1x   An IEEE standard designed to enhance security of wireless networks by authenticating a user to a central authority.

802.11   A group of IEEE standards that define how to transfer data over wireless networks.

address prefix   The network portion of an IPv6 address.

alternate IP configuration   A set of static IP configuration information that is used instead of APIPA when a computer is unable to contact a DHCP server.

anycast   An IPv6 unicast address that has been assigned to multiple devices. Only one closest device responds to requests on this address.

arp   A command-line utility that can be used to display and manage the ARP table.

Automatic Private IP Addressing (APIPA)   A system used to automatically assign an IP address on the 169.254.x.x network to a computer that is unable to communicate with a DHCP server.

broadcast address   An address that indicates the destination for that packet is all available computers.

classless interdomain routing (CIDR)   A notation technique that summarizes the number of binary bits in an IP address that identify the network an IP address belongs to, counted starting from the left-hand side of the IP address as written in binary form. The number of bits is written at the end of the IP address with a slash "/" symbol separating the two values (e.g., 192.168.1.0/24 or FE80::/64).

client   A client allows you to communicate with a particular service running on a remote computer.

Client for Microsoft Networks   The client that allows Windows 10 to access files and printers shared on other Windows computers by using the SMB protocol.

default gateway   A router on the local network that is used to deliver packets to remote networks.

Domain Name System (DNS)   A system for converting computer host names to IP addresses.

domain network   The location type that is used when a computer joined to a domain is on the domain network, for example, a corporate office.

Dynamic Host Configuration Protocol (DHCP)   An automated mechanism to assign IP addresses and IP configuration information over the network.

File and Printer Sharing for Microsoft Networks   The service that allows Windows 10 to share files and printers by using the SMB protocol.

fully qualified domain name (FQDN)   The full name of a host on the network, including its host and domain name. For example, the FQDN *www.microsoft.com* includes the host name *www* and the domain name *microsoft.com*.

getmac   A command-line utility that can be used to display the MAC address for network adapters on a system.

homegroup network   A feature that allows file sharing between computers on a private network without a complicated setup process.

hostname   A command-line utility that can be used to identify the name of the computer.

Institute of Electrical and Electronics Engineers (IEEE)   A professional society that promotes and nurtures the development of standards used in the application of electronic technology.

Internet Connection Sharing (ICS)   A Windows 10 feature that allows multiple computers to share an Internet connection by performing NAT.

Internet Protocol Version 4 (TCP/IPv4)   The standard protocol used on corporate networks and the Internet.

Internet Protocol Version 6 (TCP/IPv6)   An updated version of TCP/IPv4 with a much larger address space.

IP address   The unique address used by computers on an IPv4 or IPv6 network. An IPv4 address is commonly displayed in dotted decimal notation. For example, 10.10.0.50.

ipconfig   A command-line utility that can be used to display and manage IP address settings for network interfaces on a computer.

IPsec   A protocol that is used to secure and authenticate an IPv4 connection.

Link-Local Multicast Name Resolution (LLMNR)   A protocol that defines methods for name resolution of local neighboring computers without using DNS, WINS, or NetBIOS name resolution services. LLMNR can operate on IPv4 and IPv6 networks with the use of specially crafted multicast addresses to query client names on other computers.

location type   The type of network: public, private, or domain. Different configuration settings are applied based on the location type.

loopback address   The IP address 127.0.0.1 that is used to represent the local computer itself on the network. Traffic sent to the loopback address does not get passed over an actual network; it is processed within the operating system without using an actual network connection.

multicast   A type of address that is shared by multiple computers or devices. All hosts in the multicast group listen for communication on the shared address and all can respond.

nbtstat   A command-line utility that can be used to display protocol statistics and current TCP/IP connections using NetBIOS over TCP/IP.

netsh   A command-line utility that can be used to display, change, add, and delete network configuration settings on a computer, including basic and advanced settings.

netstat   A command-line utility that can be used to display protocol statistics and current TCP/IP network connections.

Network Address Translation (NAT)   A system that allows multiple computers to share a single IP address when connecting to the Internet.

Network and Sharing Center   A central location to view network status and configure network settings.

network discovery   A setting that controls how your computer views other computers on the network and advertises its presence on the network.

network driver   The software responsible for enabling communication between Windows 10 and the network device in your computer.

network location awareness   The ability for Windows 10 to detect when it is connected to a different network and perform actions based on the change.

nslookup   A command-line utility that can be used to view or debug the data returned from a DNS server in response to a DNS name resolution query.

pathping   A command-line utility that can be used to test IP communications between the computer running the utility and a remote target. In addition to the basic IP communication test, the *pathping* utility traces the routers involved in establishing the IP communication path.

ping   A command-line utility that can be used to test IP communications between the computer running the utility and a remote target.

Point-to-Point Protocol over Ethernet (PPPoE)   A protocol used to secure connections over most DSL lines.

private network   The location type that is used for trusted networks where limited security is required, for example, a small office.

protocol   A standard set of rules that defines how different components of a system operate together.

public network   The location type that is used for untrusted networks where high security is required, for example, a public wireless hotspot.

route   A command-line utility that can be used to display and manage the routing table.

routing table   A data table that is used by Windows 10 to select the next IP address data must be delivered to, to ultimately deliver data to a given target address.

Security Set Identifier (SSID)   A unique ID that identifies a wireless access point to the wireless networking clients that send data to it.

Server Message Block (SMB)   The protocol used for Windows-based file and printer sharing.

service   An application that provides functionality to remote clients over the network.

stateless automatic address configuration   In IPv6, this is automatic address configuration obtained from the network routers.

stateful automatic address configuration   In IPv6, this is automatic address configuration by using DHCPv6.

subnet mask   A number that defines which part of an IP address is the network ID and which part is the host ID.

Teredo   A system to tunnel IPv6 addressed packets over an IPv4 network, even if NAT is used on the IPv4 network.

tracert   A command-line utility that can be used to trace the routers involved in establishing an IP communication path between the computer running the command and a target address.

unicast   A type of network address that is assigned to a single computer or device.

Windows Firewall   A host-based firewall included with Windows 10 that can perform inbound and outbound packet filtering.

Windows Firewall and Advanced Security utility   A utility that is used to configure Windows Firewall and IPsec rules.

Windows Internet Naming Service (WINS)   A system used to resolve computer NetBIOS names to IP addresses.

wireless access point (WAP)   A device that allows wireless devices to connect through it to a wired network.

WPA2-Enterprise   A modern security type for wireless networks that uses 802.1x authentication.

WPA2-Personal   A modern security type for wireless networks that uses a pre-shared key for authentication.

Review Questions

1. Your computer is configured to obtain an IPv4 address and DNS server address automatically. What utility will help you to find the IPv4 address of your computer? (Choose all that apply.)

   a. tracert

   b. ipconfig

   c. nslookup

   d. netsh

2. Which location type would be most appropriate to select when using your laptop computer to access the Internet by using a wireless hotspot at a tradeshow?

   a. trusted network

   b. untrusted network

   c. domain network

   d. private network

   e. public network

3. _____ provides you with a way to control how your computer views other computers on the network and advertises its presence on the network.

   a. Windows Firewall

   b. SMB

   c. Network discovery

   d. IPv6

   e. Network location

4. Your computer is configured to obtain an IPv4 address and DNS server address automatically. You are concerned that the IPv4 routing table is incorrect. What utility will display the IPv4 routing table? (Choose all that apply.)

   a. route

   b. netstat

   c. nslookup

   d. netsh

   e. route4

5. Which components are part of a Windows 10 network connection? (Choose all that apply.)

   a. clients

   b. services

   c. protocols

   d. network drivers

   e. cabling

6. Which protocol is used by the Client for Microsoft Networks and File and Printer Sharing for Microsoft Networks to communicate with each other and share files?

   a. FTP

   b. IPv4

   c. IPv6

   d. HTTP

   e. SMB

7. For a Class C IPv4 address, what is the correct default subnet mask value, specified as either a dotted decimal address or a CIDR value? (Choose all that apply.)

   a. 255.0,0,0

   b. /24

   c. 255.255.255.0

   d. C::/24

   e. 255.255.256.0

8. Which of these addresses represents a valid IPv6 link-local address?

   a. 169.254.12.1

   b. ::1

   c. FE80::2cab:2a76:3f57:8499

   d. 2001:0:4137:9e74:2cab:2a76:3f57:8499

   e. FF::1:2

9. A user has been given Full Control permission to a shared folder. The user has been given Modify permission at the NTFS level to that folder and its contents. What is that user's effective permissions to that folder when accessed through the shared folder from another computer?

   a. Full Control

   b. Modify

   c. Read

   d. No access

10. Which IPv4 configuration options must be configured properly to communicate with websites on the Internet? (Choose all that apply.)

    a. IP address

    b. subnet mask

    c. default gateway

    d. DNS

    e. WINS

11. Which of the following IP addresses can be used by a host on the global Internet? (Choose all that apply.)

    a. 192.168.0.55

    b. 172.32.0.1

    c. 169.254.99.208

    d. 38.15.222.299

    e. 99.99.99.99

12. Which method can be used to assign IPv4 configuration settings when a DHCP server is not available? (Choose all that apply.)

    a. static configuration

    b. DNS

    c. WINS

    d. APIPA

    e. alternate IP configuration

13. To convert host names to IP addresses on the Internet, _____ is used.

14. Which of the following IPv4 addresses has the same network ID as 192.168.112.45 given the subnet mask 255.255.255.0?

    a. 10.0.0.45

    b. 192.168.113.46

    c. 192.168.112.257

    d. 172.16.112.45

    e. 192.168.112.5

15. Which sharing method should you use if you want to configure share and NTFS permissions for a user in a single process?

    a. Public folder sharing

    b. Share with

    c. advanced sharing

    d. Create A Shared Folder Wizard

16. Which sharing method does *not* allow you to pick the folder that is being shared?

    a. Public folder sharing

    b. simple sharing

    c. advanced sharing

    d. Create A Shared Folder Wizard

17. Which of the following IPv4 addresses have the same network ID as 10.16.112.45 given the subnet mask 255.255.0.0? (Choose all that apply.)

    a. 10.16.160.45

    b. 192.168.172.46

    c. 10.16.122.2

    d. 10.16.185.45

    e. 10.18.114.3

18. What is the most accurate way to view all of the shares on your system?

    a. Browse your computer on the network.

    b. View the shares in Computer Management.

    c. Use the Show me all the shared network folders on this computer link.

    d. Use the Show me all the files and folders I am sharing link.

    e. View the shares in Network and Sharing Center.

19. The Internet connection technology that requires a mobile broadband device and a data plan that activates this feature is known as a _____ connection.

    a. cable modem

    b. 802.11n

    c. DSL

    d. WWAN

    e. dial-up

20. Which Internet connection type is most likely to require the use of PPPoE?

    a. cable

    b. DSL

    c. dial-up

    d. wireless hotspot

21. A user has been complaining that his wireless connection has been connecting and disconnecting too frequently. What command could you use to generate a detailed HTML-based report for analysis of the wireless connection on this computer in the past?

    a. *netcfg wlan show report*

    b. *netsh int ip report*

    c. *netsh wlan show wlanreport*

    d. *netcfg -d*

22. Which of these addresses represents a valid IPv6 global unicast address?

    a. 169.254.12.1/64

    b. 2001::1::FEA

    c. FE80::2cab:2a76:3f57:8499

    d. 2001:0:4137:9e74:2cab:2a76:3f57:8499

    e. FF::1:2

23. Which of these addresses represents a valid loopback address? (Choose all that apply.)

    a. ::1

    b. ::/0

    c. FF::1

    d. 127.0.0.1

    e. 127::1/32

24. Which utilities can be used to perform advanced firewall configuration? (Choose all that apply.)

    a. Windows Firewall Control Panel applet

    b. Netsh

    c. Group Policy

    d. Windows Firewall and Advanced Security

    e. Windows PowerShell

25. A computer has the IPv4 address 192.168.0.23 and a subnet mask of 255.255.255.0. Which of these addresses represents a possible default gateway address? (Choose all that apply.)

    a. 192.168.0.254

    b. 193.168.0.1

    c. 0.0.0.1

    d. 127.0.0.1

    e. 192.168.0.1

7

Case Projects

Case Project 7-1: Networking Concepts

Superduper Lightspeed Computers helps many customers configure small home networks. A new staff person has started with very limited networking experience. How would you explain the basics of Windows 10 networking to the new person?

Case Project 7-2: Configuring Windows Firewall

Gigantic Life Insurance has thousands of desktop computers and has just completed a major security audit. One of the recommendations in the security audit was to implement a host-based firewall on all workstations. Explain how Windows Firewall could be used by Gigantic Life Insurance and the method you would use to configure Windows Firewall on all the workstations.

Case Project 7-3: Network Awareness

The salespeople at Hyperactive Media Sales all use laptop computers so they can take data with them on the road. You are a salesperson for Superduper Lightspeed Computers talking to Hyperactive Media Sales about upgrading the laptops to Windows 10. Explain how network location awareness in Windows 10 would make the laptops more secure.

chapter 8

User Productivity Tools

After reading this chapter and completing the exercises, you will be able to:

- Describe features for file management in File Explorer
- Use OneDrive to store documents
- Understand and configure Windows 10 printing
- Describe the features in Microsoft Edge and Internet Explorer

Windows 10 includes a variety of tools that are required in a modern operating system to be productive. You certainly need specialized apps like Microsoft Office to create and consume content, but the operating system also needs to provide some core tools for tasks such as managing files and accessing the Internet.

In this chapter, you learn how to use File Explorer for file management, including how to configure libraries. You also learn about how cloud-based storage provided by OneDrive can be used to make your files portable. OneDrive also serves as a backup solution if your computer hard drive fails. Despite the promise of a paperless office, printing is still important functionality in Windows 10 and you learn how to configure printing. Finally, you identify the features available in the new Microsoft Edge web browser as well as Internet Explorer, including Enterprise Mode to ease the migration to Microsoft Edge.

File Explorer

File Explorer, shown in Figure 8-1, is the interface used to view the file system in Windows 10. The left navigation pane provides a way to move quickly to various locations where files might be stored. The right pane displays the files and folders in the location that is selected in the navigation pane.

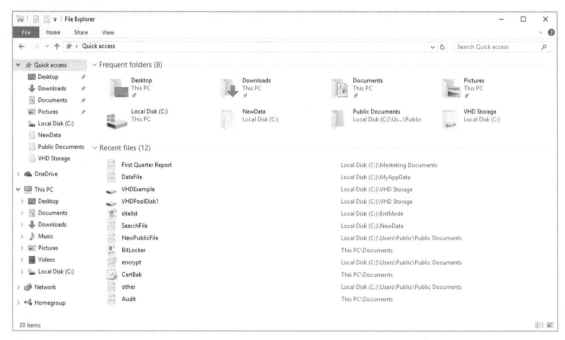

Figure 8-1   File Explorer

In the navigation pane, there are several file storage locations available by default:

- *Quick access*—When you select this node, a list of recently accessed files and folders are displayed. You also have the option to pin folders in Quick access. For example, if you are working on several projects, you can pin the folder that stores files for each project in Quick access.

- *OneDrive*—This node provides access to **OneDrive** cloud storage that is associated with a Microsoft account.

- *This PC*—This node displays the files and folder for locally attached storage. This includes hard disks, USB drives, and DVDs.

- *Network*—Use this node to display computers on the local area network (LAN). If the computers have shared resources, you can browse file shares and shared printers.

- *Homegroup*—Use this node to browse and connect to existing homegroups. You can also create a new homegroup from this node.

If you are double-clicking folders in the right pane to drill down into the folder structure, the navigation pane is not updated. You can configure the navigation pane to keep in sync with the folders you browse to. Some people prefer this because it simplifies moving between folders in the navigation pane.

Ribbon Tabs

Above the navigation pane and the right pane are ribbon tabs for various functions. The tabs available on the ribbon vary depending on the content that you have selected.

When you are viewing the file system, the following tabs are available:

- *File*—This tab provides options to open a new File Explorer window, command prompt, or Windows PowerShell prompt that is focused on the current folder. For the command prompt and Windows PowerShell prompt, this can be significantly faster than opening a prompt and then changing to the directory that you want. This tab also allows access to folder and search options.

- *Home*—This tab has buttons for manipulating files and folders. For example, there are buttons to copy, paste, and delete. There are also options to view file and folder properties and select items. Many of the options here are similar to the context menu displayed when you right-click a file or folder.

- *Share*—This tab provides options to configure folder sharing and file permissions. It also has options to share files with an app that you specify or via email. There are also options to send files to a zipped folder, burn to disc, print, or fax.

- *View*—This tab has options that control how files and folders are displayed. For example, you can select whether file details are displayed, just file names, or with various sizes of icons. You can enable display of a Details pane or a Preview pane with additional information when files are selected.

One common user complaint is the inability to distinguish between files of different types that have the same name. For example, you may have a Word document and an Excel spreadsheet that are both named Project1. Both documents have different icons, but it can be difficult to interpret the icons when files are displayed in List view. To make it easier for users to distinguish between files of different types, you can configure Windows 10 to display the file name extensions. This is done on the View tab by selecting the File name extensions check box. This is not selected by default.

Activity 8-1: Configuring File Explorer

Time Required: 5 minutes
Objective: Customize the display in File Explorer

Description: For many users, the default display in File Explorer is acceptable. However, you have the option to customize it in many ways depending on your preferences. In this activity, you perform some of the commonly implemented modifications to the default view in File Explorer.

1. If necessary, start your computer and sign in.

2. On the taskbar, click **File Explorer**.

3. In File Explorer, click the **View** tab, click the **Navigation pane** button, and, if necessary, click **Expand to open folder** to enable it.

4. In the navigation pane, click **This PC**.

5. In the right pane, double-click **Local Disk (C:)** and double-click **Windows**. Notice that the navigation pane is matching where you are browsing.

6. Scroll down in the right pane, and notice that most of the file extensions are hidden.

7. Click the **View** tab and, if necessary, select the **File name extensions** check box.

8. Scroll down in the right pane, and notice that most of the file extensions are now visible, which makes it easier to identify the type of file.

9. Click the **View** tab and click **List** in the Layout group. Notice that you can now see more files and folders at one time.

10. Click the **View** tab and click the **Options** button.

11. In the Folder Options window, click the **View** tab, click **Restore Defaults**, and click **OK**. This disables viewing of file extensions.

12. Close File Explorer.

Libraries

Libraries were introduced in Windows 7 to simplify access to files in multiple locations. Each library contains multiple file system locations and the content from all locations is placed together into a single view. A library can contain local folders or file shares.

You can modify the locations included in a library, but the location must be indexed by Windows Search. This means that if you add a file share, it must be indexed by Windows Search on the computer that is hosting the file share. This requirement ensures that content can be categorized and displayed quickly.

Some file management issues to consider for libraries are:

- When you browse down into a folder from the root of a library, you are viewing a specific location and any files created are in that specific location.

- When you are viewing the root of a library and create a new file or folder, the new item is created in the location specified as the default save location in the properties of the library.

- If you share a library via a homegroup, then other users can create files in the folder set as the public save location.

Activity 8-2: Using Libraries

Time Required: 5 minutes
Objective: Use libraries to organize files in File Explorer

Description: In Windows 10, libraries are not visible by default. Some users who upgrade from Windows 7 or Windows 8.1 may prefer to continue using this feature. In this activity, you enable libraries in File Explorer and verify their functionality.

1. If necessary, start your computer and sign in.

2. On the taskbar, click **File Explorer**.

3. In File Explorer, click the **View** tab, click the **Navigation pane** button, and click **Show libraries** to place a check mark before that item.

4. In the navigation pane, expand **Libraries** and click **Documents**.

5. Right-click **Documents** and click **Properties**.

6. In the Documents Properties window, click **Add**.

7. In the Include Folder in Documents window, in the address bar, type **C:\Users\Public** and press **Enter**.

8. Click **Public Documents** and click **Include folder**.

9. In the Document Properties window, the single green check mark identifies the Document folder as your default save location. The green check mark with the users identifies the Public Documents folder as the public save location.

10. Right-click **Public Documents**, click **Set as default save location**, and click **OK**. Notice that the view now includes both locations.

11. Click the **Home** tab, click **New item**, click **Text Document**, type **NewPublicFile** as the file name, and press **Enter**. Notice that the file was created in the Public Documents folder because that is the default save location for the Documents library.

12. Click the **View** tab, click **Navigation pane**, and click **Show libraries** to remove the check mark from that item.

13. Close File Explorer.

Search

Windows 10 includes search functionality that can be used to find files and folders. Search is made faster by an indexing function included in Windows 10. You do not need to choose whether search occurs inside or outside the index. It is context sensitive. If you are searching content that is indexed, the index is used. If you are searching content that is not indexed, the index is not used.

Indexing is automatically enabled so that all users can immediately get the benefit of index-based searches. Each time a file is updated, the index is also updated. When a user performs a search, the search results include only files that the user has access to.

By default, only the most common file system locations are indexed. This prevents the index from incorporating less relevant files, such as operating system files, which users are unlikely to search for. Search speed is improved and indexing time is decreased by indexing only specified files. You can add additional search locations depending on your needs. Figure 8-2 shows the Indexing Options where you can configure indexed locations.

The file locations indexed by default are Offline Files, the Start Menu, and C:\Users (except the AppData subfolder in each profile). Other locations are indexed for specific applications

8

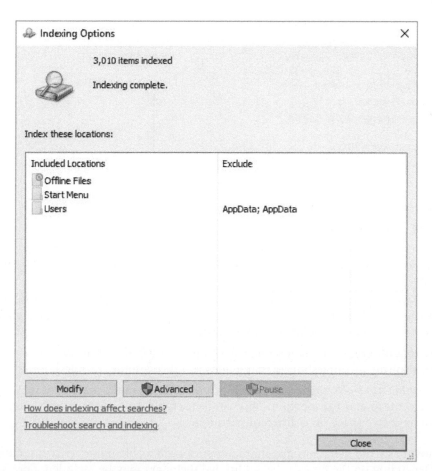

Figure 8-2 Indexing Options

if the application is in use. If you are using Internet Explorer, Internet Explorer History is indexed. If you are using Microsoft Outlook in cached mode, the cached mailbox is indexed.

In addition to defining which locations are indexed, you can also define which file types are indexed and how those files are indexed. For each file type (defined by file extension), you specify whether the contents of the files or only **metadata** about the file is indexed. For some file types, such as pictures, the content of the files is meaningless from a search perspective and should not be indexed. Other file types such as Word documents can have their content indexed so that you can search for documents based on the content. The filter for each file type is responsible for understanding how to properly index that content type. Figure 8-3 shows the configuration of file types in Advanced Options.

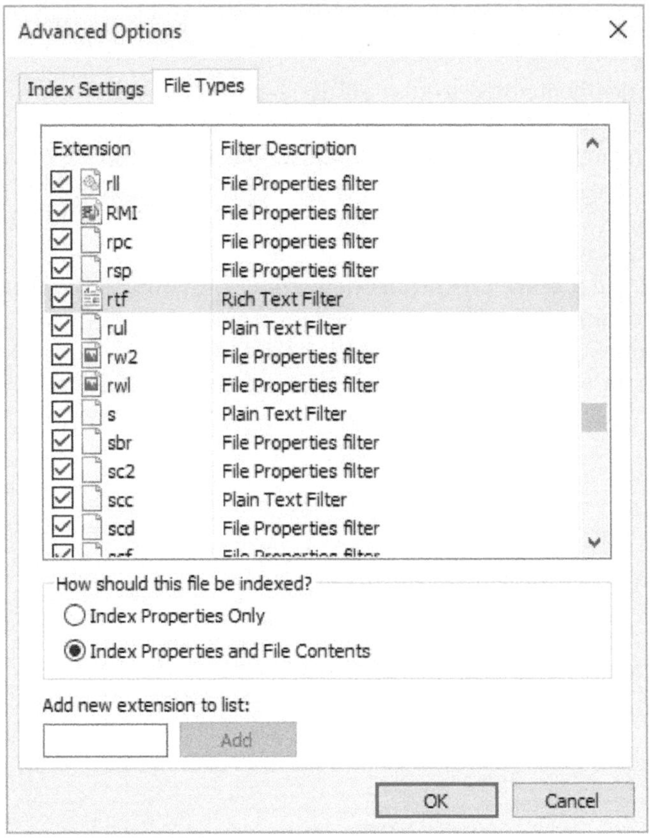

Figure 8-3   Indexing Advanced Options

On the Index Settings tab in Advanced Options, there are additional settings that you can configure:

- *File Settings*—You can select whether encrypted files are indexed. You can also select whether words with different accents are treated the same, for example, whether *resume* and *resumé* are indexed as the same word.

- *Troubleshooting*—You can rebuild the index if you believe it has become corrupted. You can also run a troubleshooter that guides you through the troubleshooting process.

- *Index location*—You can move the index from the default location of C:\ProgramData\ Microsoft to another location. This can be useful if the C drive is becoming full and you have free space on a different partition.

The most basic file metadata are characteristics such as file name, creation date, and modified date. Depending on the type of file, additional metadata may be included. For example, pictures taken with a digital camera have additional metadata that is only appropriate for pictures such as the shutter speed and lighting conditions.

Activity 8-3: Configuring Windows Search

Time Required: 10 minutes
Objective: Configure Windows Search to index a new location

Description: Indexing files makes it much faster to find specific files you are looking for. If you store files outside of your User file, they are not indexed by default. In this activity, you add an additional indexing location for Windows Search and verify that it is searchable.

1. If necessary, start your computer and sign in.

2. On the taskbar, click **File Explorer**.

3. If necessary, expand **This PC** and click **Local Disk (C:)**.

4. Click the **Home** tab, click **New folder**, type **NewData** as the folder name, and press **Enter**.

5. Double-click the **NewData** folder, click the **Home** tab, click **New item**, click **Text Document**, type **SearchFile** as the file name, and press **Enter**.

6. Double-click **SearchFile** to open the file in Notepad.

7. In Notepad, type the word **Kangaroo**, click the **File** menu, and click **Save**.

8. Close Notepad.

9. On the taskbar, in the Ask me anything search box, type **Kangaroo**. This displays web searches for Kangaroo.

10. At the top of the search box, click the **Documents** icon and click **Kangaroo**. The search didn't find anything.

11. Click the **Start** button and click **Settings**.

12. In the Settings window, in the Find a setting box, type **index**, and click **Indexing Options**.

13. In the Indexing Options window, click **Modify**.

14. In the Indexed Locations window, expand **Local Disk (C:)**, select the **NewData** check box, and click **OK**.

15. In the Indexing Options window, click **Close**.

16. On the taskbar, in the search box, type **Kangaroo** and then click **My stuff**. This time, the search found the file because it has been indexed.

17. Close all open windows.

OneDrive

OneDrive is cloud-based storage that is automatically included for free when you create a Microsoft account. Each Microsoft account is allocated 5 GB of storage space that can be used for file storage in OneDrive. Additional storage can be purchased if required.

 The OneDrive included as part of a Microsoft account is different from the OneDrive included with Office 365. The OneDrive included with Office 365 typically provides 1 TB of storage and is integrated with Share-Point Online.

Files stored in OneDrive can be accessed directly from the OneDrive website or by using the OneDrive client. The OneDrive client is included with Windows 10 and integrates into File Explorer as a separate node for accessing files.

There are several benefits to using OneDrive:

- Access files from anywhere
- Back up automatically to the cloud
- Recover deleted or modified files

- Edit files from a web browser
- Edit files on mobile devices
- Share files with others

OneDrive Client

If you sign in to Windows 10 by using a Microsoft account, the OneDrive client automatically uses that account to sign in to OneDrive also. Then, any files you save in the OneDrive node in File Explorer are automatically synchronized to OneDrive where they can be accessed from another computer, a mobile phone, or tablet. Because OneDrive files are accessible by web browser, they can be accessed from almost any device.

If you do not sign in to Windows 10 by using a Microsoft account, you need to configure the OneDrive client with the credentials for your Microsoft account.

The OneDrive node in File Explorer, shown in Figure 8-4, has Documents and Pictures folders by default, but you can create additional folders to organize your files. Files and folders that are up to date with OneDrive have a green check mark to indicate that they are successfully synchronized. When you make changes to a file, the icon changes to two arrows in a circle to indicate that the file is synchronizing. While you have a file open for editing, it is typical for the synchronizing icon to appear for the file.

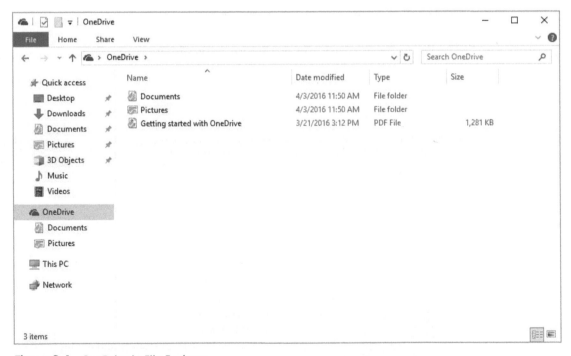

Figure 8-4 OneDrive in File Explorer

The default location for files synchronized by the OneDrive client is C:\Users\%username%\OneDrive in the user's profile. If you have a folder with preexisting data, you can change synchronization to use that folder instead. When you select a folder with preexisting data, that data is merged with the data already stored in OneDrive.

In the properties for the OneDrive client, you can also configure the following settings:

- *Start OneDrive automatically when I sign in to Windows*—This option is on by default and should be left on. If you turn off this option, files stop synchronizing with OneDrive because the client is not enabled the next time you sign in.

- *Let me use OneDrive to fetch any of my files on this PC*—This option is disabled by default. Enable this option if you want to be able to browse the file system on the computer and access files through the OneDrive website.

- *Use Office to work on files with other people at the same time*—This option is on by default and should be left on. When this option is on, you can collaborate with other users on a shared Microsoft Office document at the same time. Two or more users can perform simultaneous editing.

The OneDrive client also has autosave options. You can change the default save location for documents and pictures to OneDrive instead of the local PC. You also have the option to automatically store pictures and videos from cameras and phones in OneDrive when you retrieve them using your computer.

OneDrive Web Interface

The web interface for OneDrive, shown in Figure 8-5, provides access to all of the features of OneDrive. In the web interface, you have access to all of the files that have been synchronized to OneDrive, but in addition you can:

- Recover deleted files from the Recycle bin.
- Access previous versions of files.
- View a list of all files that you have shared.
- View the amount of storage space you have remaining in OneDrive.
- Access files on computers with the OneDrive client installed and configured.

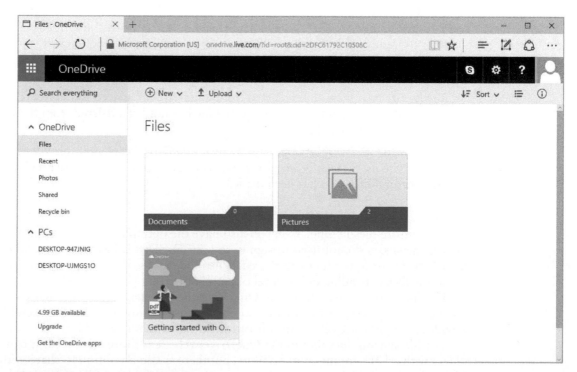

Figure 8-5   OneDrive web interface

You can access OneDrive at *http://onedrive.live.com*.

The web interface for OneDrive is not just a way to download your files on different computers. You can also use the web versions of Microsoft Office applications, such as Word and Excel, to view and edit the files online. When you open a file in the OneDrive website, it automatically opens in the appropriate online Office application in read-only mode. If you choose to edit the file, you are prompted as to whether to edit in the online Office application or use a locally installed Office application.

If you choose to use the online Office application to edit a file, you get a very functional but not full-featured version of the application. The online Office applications work with a variety of web browsers across platforms, such as Microsoft Edge, Internet Explorer, Firefox, Chrome, and Safari.

Files in online Office applications are automatically saved as you edit them. It is initially disconcerting that you do not have the option to save the file manually, but you can verify that the file has been saved in the status bar.

If you choose to use a locally installed Office application to edit a file, the file is opened directly from OneDrive. Office applications are capable of opening files over the Internet by using the HTTP protocol. When you save the file, it is saved directly back into OneDrive.

Mobile versions of Office applications are also available for tablets and phones running Windows 10, Android, and iOS. These apps are free from each operating system's app store. This means that you can install a mobile version of Word on your iPad or Android device and edit a document stored in OneDrive.

Managing Files

You can perform basic file management tasks by using both the OneDrive website and the OneDrive client in File Explorer. Both of these tools can delete, copy, move, and rename files. However, there are two functions that can only be performed in the OneDrive website:

- *Recover deleted files*—Files deleted from OneDrive are placed in the Recycle bin and then deleted after approximately 90 days. If a file has not been deleted from the Recycle bin, you can restore it and regain access to it.

- *Previous file versions*—As you modify files, OneDrive keeps multiple versions of the file, not just the most recently saved version. You can access and recover previous versions if an incorrect modification has been made.

Sharing Files and Folders

When you store files in OneDrive, you also have the option to share files and folders with other users. Other users do not need to sign in to your OneDrive; instead, you send them a URL for the specific file or folder that you shared. When they follow the URL, they are able to either view or edit the files depending on the level of permissions that you specified.

The file sharing function in the OneDrive client generates a URL that can be accessed by anyone who you send it to. It can also be accessed by anyone who they send it to. The URL provides anonymous access to the file or folder that you have shared.

The file sharing function in the OneDrive website is more advanced. It can share files and folders with a URL for anonymous users, but there is also an option to share with specific users. When you share with specific users, you specify an email address. The email address you specify must be associated with a Microsoft account. Then, that user is required to authenticate before accessing the file.

Activity 8-4: Using OneDrive

Time Required: 10 minutes
Objective: Use OneDrive to manage files

Description: OneDrive is a cloud-based service that you can use to back up and share files. In this activity, you save files in OneDrive and explore the recovery options.

1. If necessary, start your computer and sign in by using your Microsoft account.

2. On the taskbar, click **File Explorer**.

3. In File Explorer, in the navigation pane, click **OneDrive**, and then double-click **Getting started with OneDrive**. This .pdf file should be in the root of OneDrive unless you previously deleted it.

4. Quickly scan through the document and close Microsoft Edge.

5. In File Explorer, in the navigation pane, expand **OneDrive** and click **Documents**.

6. In the right pane, right-click an open area, point to **New**, click **Text Document**, type **OnlineFile**, and then press **Enter**.

7. Double-click **OnlineFile**.

8. In Notepad, type **First edit**, close Notepad, and save the changes. When the file icon has a green check mark, it has finished synchronizing to OneDrive.

9. In File Explorer, right-click **OnlineFile** and click **Delete**.

10. On the taskbar, click **Microsoft Edge**.

11. In Microsoft Edge, in the address bar, type **http://onedrive.live.com** and press **Enter**. Notice that you do not need to provide authentication credentials if you signed in to Windows 10 by using a Microsoft account.

12. In OneDrive, click **Recycle bin**. Notice that OnlineFile.txt is listed here.

13. Click **OnlineFile.txt** and click **Restore**.

14. Click **Files** and click **Documents**. Notice that the file is restored to the Documents folder.

15. Click **OnlineFile.txt** and wait for the file to open in the editor. A simple online text editor is used because this is a text file.

16. Add text **Second edit** and a new line in the file and then click **Save**.

17. In File Explorer, verify that there is a green check mark for OnlineFile, and then double-click **OnlineFile**.

18. In Notepad, verify that Second edit appears and then close Notepad.

19. In OneDrive, click **New** and click **Word document**. The creates a new Word document named Document1.

20. In Word Online, type **Version 1** and wait for the document to finish saving.

21. In the top ribbon, click **Documents**.

22. In OneDrive, click **Document1.docx**.

23. In Word Online, click **Edit Document** and click **Edit in Word Online**.

24. Add a new line with the text **Version 2** and wait for the document to finish saving.

25. In the top ribbon, click **Documents**.

26. In OneDrive, right-click **Document1.docx** and click **Version history**. The current version is automatically selected and you see a preview.

27. Select the most recent older version. Notice that this document has only the Version 1 text. You have the option to restore this version or download it.

28. Close all open windows.

8

Printing

Despite the promise of the paperless office, most organizations still do quite a bit of printing. Maintaining printers and troubleshooting their functionality can be a significant portion of your job when doing desktop support. To support printers and troubleshoot them, you need to understand:

- Printing scenarios
- Printer drivers
- Printer management tools

Printing Scenarios

As a network administrator, you need to be able to troubleshoot the printing process. One of the keys to troubleshooting is understanding how printers can be connected to Windows 10. Figure 8-6 shows the physical layout of local printing, network printing directly to a printer, and network printing to a shared printer.

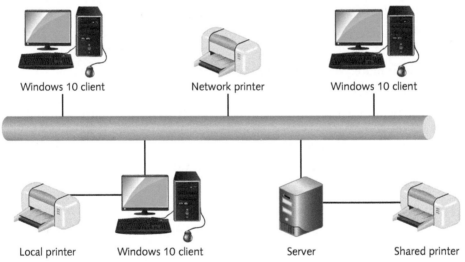

Figure 8-6   Printing scenarios

Local Printing   Local printing requires that a printer be connected directly to a Windows 10 computer by using a cable. The type of cable you select depends on which connection type is physically available on the printer. Most modern printers connect to a computer by using a USB cable. Some older printers and specialty printers are connected with parallel or serial cables.

USB printers are automatically installed in Windows 10 when they are connected because they are Plug and Play. However, before you connect a USB printer for the first time, read the documentation included with the printer. Some USB printers (particularly multifunction printers) require you to install the driver before attaching the printer for the first time. If you connect the printer before the proper driver is installed, Windows 10 attempts to load a compatible driver, which might not have full functionality for the printer. The installation process for serial and parallel printers must be triggered manually.

The most common reasons to use local printing are simplicity and security. The entire printing process occurs within the local computer, so troubleshooting is easier. Having a local printer makes printing secure because users are able to print sensitive documents in their office from the local printer rather than in an open area on a shared network printer where other users might see the document contents.

To install a local printer, you need administrator permissions if the driver is not already installed. After a local printer is installed, it is available to all users on that computer.

Printing Directly to a Network Printer   A high percentage of printers can be configured to communicate directly on a wired or wireless network. This functionality is available even in many lower-end printers for home users. When a printer is connected directly to the network, computers can send it print jobs over the network. Many computers can be connected to the network printer at the same time, but only one computer can be printing at a time.

Sharing a printer on the network saves money in the long run. Typically, it costs less to purchase a single high-capacity printer rather than many low-capacity printers for many computers. The per page consumables cost for the high-capacity printer is typically much less than for low-capacity printers.

In this scenario, print jobs are queued at the local computer and sent to the printer when the printer is not busy. This is a contention-based system, and there is no specific order in which print jobs are serviced. There is no central queue to control the order or priority of print jobs. However, a key benefit is the lack of any single computer as a single point of failure.

When you print directly to a network printer, it behaves similarly to a local printer except that connectivity is through a network port or wireless network adapter instead of USB port. To install this type of printer in Windows 10, you need administrator permissions if the driver is not already installed on the computer. After this type of printer is installed, it is available to all users on the computer.

Printing to a Shared Printer   Both Windows servers and Windows clients are capable of sharing printers on the network. When a printer is shared, multiple computers on the network can use it. Windows 10 attempts to find printers shared on the local network and install them automatically. However, if the shared printers are not on the local subnet, you need to install the printer manually.

In this scenario, all print jobs are queued on the computer that is sharing the printer. This allows all jobs to be controlled in a central location, which can make troubleshooting relatively simple. If jobs are not printing, you start by looking at the computer that is sharing the printer. However, the computer sharing the printer also becomes a central point of failure. If the computer sharing the printer is disabled or turned off, it is not possible to print documents on the shared printer.

Shared printers can be connected directly to the sharing computer or be network printers.

Standard users can install a shared printer, even if the printer driver is not already installed. For older version 3 printer drivers (Windows 7), the printer driver is copied from the computer sharing the printer. For newer version 4 printer drivers (Windows 8/8.1/10), the print job can be rendered totally on the server side and no driver installation is required. However, if the client can identify the correct version 4 printer driver through Plug and Play, the driver can be installed from local files or Windows Update to allow client-side rendering with full functionality.

For a detailed discussion of printer driver versions, search for Printer Sharing Technical Details on the TechNet website at *https://technet.microsoft.com/*.

After installation, a shared printer is installed only for the user who installed it. Other users on the same computer also need to install the printer to be able to use it.

Printer Drivers

A basic **printer driver** is software that Windows 10 uses to understand and use the features of a printer. A key part of driver functionality is formatting print jobs so that they print properly. When an incorrect printer driver is used, print jobs might have small formatting errors like misalignment or you might get what appear to be random characters printing.

Windows 10 supports **printer driver packages** that include the basic printer driver but can also include additional software. For example, a printer driver package could include additional software that shows printer status such as remaining toner in the notification area. Generally, printer packages are still referred to as printer drivers.

Page Description Languages   Many printers have support for multiple page description languages and different printer drivers are available for each of the languages. A **page description language** defines the layout of content for a print job. It is not uncommon to find that some applications work properly with a printer driver using one page description language but have small formatting errors when using the printer driver for another page description language. You might need to experiment with different versions of printer drivers to find one that works best with your applications.

Some commonly available page description languages are:

- *PostScript*—**PostScript** is the oldest and best supported page description language. If you are having issues with printer driver versions, try using the PostScript driver because printer manufacturers often put the most effort in ensuring that the PostScript drivers work properly.

- *Printer Command Language*—**Printer Command Language (PCL)** is the most common page description language after PostScript. In general, PCL offers faster printing than PostScript but is also more prone to odd formatting errors because many printer manufacturers put less time into developing PCL drivers. PCL 5 and PCL 6 drivers can provide varying results and you should try both when troubleshooting if your printer supports both.

- *Portable Document Format*—**Portable Document Format (PDF)** is most often thought of as a document format, but it is also supported by some printers as a page description language. This allows .pdf documents to be sent directly to a printer without any processing.

- *XML Paper Specification*—Microsoft designed **XML Paper Specification (XPS)** as both a document format and page description language. Microsoft uses XPS internally as part of the printing process, but most printers do not include native support for XPS.

To support using XPS as a document format, Windows 10 includes a virtual printer named Microsoft XPS Document Writer. New in Windows 10 is a virtual printer for PDF documents named Microsoft Print to PDF. Both of these printers let you print from any application and save the output as a file in either XPS or PDF format. XPS and PDF documents can both be viewed by using Microsoft Edge.

Printer Driver Store   Windows 10 has a **printer driver store** where installed printer drivers are added. Printer drivers can be added to the store before the printer is attached. This can be useful in corporate environments by preconfiguring computers with all printer drivers that may be required.

Adding a driver to the store is known as staging a driver. If a printer driver is added during the printer installation process, the driver is automatically staged as part of the process. Drivers can also be staged manually by a user with administrative rights using the pnputil.exe utility. Drivers can also be added to the store by users who have been granted device installation rights by a group policy. Table 8-1 has examples of using the pnputil.exe utility.

Table 8-1   Pnputil.exe examples

Example	Description
pnputil.exe /add-driver *driverINFfile*	Add a printer driver to the store
pnputil.exe /enum-drivers	Enumerate (list) all third-party drivers in the store
pnputil.exe /delete-driver *driverINFfile*	Delete a printer driver from the store
pnputil.exe /?	Display the help information for pnputil.exe

When drivers are added to the store, they are stored side by side. This means that multiple versions of the same driver can be contained in the store, which is useful when testing new printer drivers. Occasionally, new printer drivers result in print quality problems for specific reports or documents. When this occurs, you can change the printer driver back to a previous version.

After a printer driver is in the printer driver store, standard users can install local and network printers that use that driver. By default, standard users cannot install new printer drivers unless it is a shared printer and the driver is downloaded from the computer sharing the printer.

Because multiple driver versions are stored side by side in the driver store, you should remove old versions from the driver store after you have determined that they are not required. This ensures that an obsolete version of a printer driver is not installed accidentally by a user.

Activity 8-5: Staging a Driver

Time Required: 10 minutes
Objective: Stage a printer driver in the driver store

Description: Standard users are not able to download and install their own printer drivers from a manufacturer's website. However, if a driver is staged in the driver store before the printer is installed, Windows 10 uses the driver automatically when the printer is installed. In this activity, you download and stage a printer driver.

1. If necessary, start your computer and sign in.
2. On the taskbar, click **Microsoft Edge**.
3. In the Search or enter web address box, type **support.hp.com** and press **Enter**.
4. In the search area, click **Search all support** and select **Software, Drivers, and Updates**.
5. In the Enter your product number and keywords box, type **universal print driver** and press **Enter**.
6. On the HP Universal Print Driver Series for Windows page, click **HP Universal Print Driver for Windows**.
7. In the Select your product's operating system box, select **Windows 10 (64-bit)**.
8. Expand **Driver – Universal Print Driver (4)** and for HP Universal Print Driver for Windows PCL6 (64-bit), click **Download**, and click **Save**.
9. When the download is complete, close Microsoft Edge.
10. On the taskbar, click **File Explorer** and click **Downloads**.
11. Double-click the file you just downloaded.
12. In the WinZip Self-Extractor window, in the Unzip to file box, type **C:\HPDriver**, deselect the **When down unzipping open: .\install.exe** check box, and click **Unzip**.
13. Click **OK** and close all open windows.
14. Right-click the **Start** button, click **Command Prompt (Admin)**, and click **Yes**.
15. Type **pnputil /?** and press **Enter**. This command displays the list of available options for pnputil.exe.
16. Type **pnputil /enum-drivers** and press **Enter**. This command displays the list of third-party driver packages that have been installed. The HP Universal Print Driver package is not listed.
17. Type **dir C:\HPDriver*.inf** and press **Enter**. This command displays all INF files in the HPDriver directory.
18. Type **pnputil /add-driver C:\HPDriver\hpcu185u.inf** and press **Enter**. This command installs the printer driver package into the printer driver store. If the command prompt is not running as an administrator, this command fails. This file might not be available in your downloaded version of the driver. If this file is not available, select an alternative .inf file.

19. After the package is added, type **pnputil /enum-drivers** and press **Enter**. Notice that the driver is now listed and named oem*x*.inf, where *x* is a number. The .inf file for each driver is renamed when it is added to the driver store. This guarantees that all .inf files have a unique name.

20. Close all open windows.

Printer Management Tools

Windows 10 has several tools for managing printers. You can choose the method based on your scenario and which tool you prefer to work with. The **Print Management snap-in** and Devices and Printers were introduced in Windows 7. The option to manage printers in Settings is new for Windows 10.

Printers & Scanners   Printers & scanners, accessed from Devices on the Settings screen and shown in Figure 8-7, is a new interface for managing printers in Windows 10. You can add or remove printers here. You can also set the default printer. When the option *Let Windows manage my default printer* is turned on, the default printer is always the last printer you used rather than a printer specifically defined as the default printer.

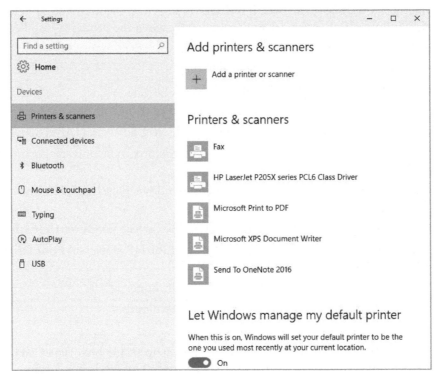

Figure 8-7   Printers & scanners

When you click *Add a printer or scanner*, Windows 10 scans the network looking for printers. If a printer is found, you click the printer to install it. If Windows 10 does not find the printer on the network, you can click *The printer that I want wasn't listed*, which opens the Add Printer Wizard that provides more advanced option for installing a printer.

After adding a printer, if you click the printer, there is an Open queue option where you can manage print jobs. There is also a Manage option where you can perform the following tasks:

- Print a test page.
- Run the troubleshooter.
- View printer properties.
- View printing preferences.
- View hardware properties.

ACTIVITY

Activity 8-6: Adding a Printer

Time Required: 10 minutes
Objective: Add a new printer from Settings

Description: In Windows 10, a USB printer will be detected automatically, but you need to manually install network printers. In this activity, you install a new network printer from Settings.

1. If necessary, start your computer and sign in.
2. Click the **Start** button and click **Settings**.
3. In the Settings window, click **Devices**.
4. Click **Add a printer or scanner**. Windows takes a few minutes to scan the network to attempt to find printers and display any printers that are found.
5. Click **The printer that I want isn't listed**.
6. In the Add Printer window, click **Add a printer using a TCP/IP address or hostname** and click **Next**.
7. In the Device type list, select **TCP/IP Device**.
8. In the Hostname or IP address box, type **172.16.99.99**. There is no printer at this IP address; it is chosen for the purposes of the lab only to see the interface.
9. Deselect the **Query the printer and automatically select the driver to use** check box and click **Next**. In most cases, you want to leave this option on. You are deselecting it because we are simulating the process.
10. On the Additional port information required page, click **Standard** and click **Next**.
11. In the Manufacturer box, click **HP**.
12. In the Printers box, scroll to the bottom and select **HP Universal Printing PCL 6** and click **Next**.
13. In the Printer name box, type **HP Printer PCL6** and click **Next**.
14. On the Printer Sharing page, click **Do not share this printer** and click **Next**.
15. Click **Finish**.

Devices and Printers   Devices and Printers in Control Panel, shown in Figure 8-8, allows you to manage printers installed on the local computer. The functionality of Devices and Printers is the same as Printers & scanners in Settings. The major tasks that you can perform in Devices and Printers are:

- *Add a printer*—This option adds a new printer to the local computer. This printer can be physically attached or a network printer. This option scans the network just as when you add a printer in Printers & scanners.
- *See what's printing*—This option allows you to see jobs in the print queue for the selected printer. Within the queue, you can pause or delete individual print jobs.
- *Set as default printer*—This option allows you to configure a printer as the default printer for apps. In an app, such as Microsoft Word, when you click the Print button in the toolbar, the default printer is used.
- *Select printing preferences*—This option allows you to configure basic printer settings and paper configuration.
- *Configure printer properties*—This option allows you to edit all printer properties, including those for printing preferences, sharing, and security.
- *Configure print server properties*—This option allows you to edit print server properties for the local computer. This includes setting available forms (page sizes), configuring ports, and managing drivers.
- *Remove device*—This option removes the printer from your computer.

When you right-click a printer, most of the configuration options are in Properties. The Properties option allows you to view some summary configuration information.

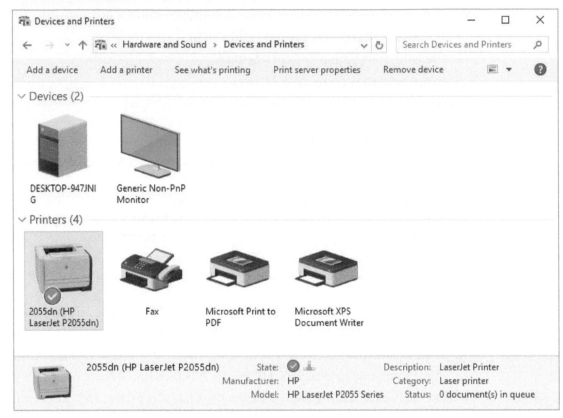

Figure 8-8   Devices and Printers in Control Panel

Print Management Snap-In   The Print Management snap-in, shown in Figure 8-9, allows you to manage printers for your entire network from a single computer. This is a big benefit for any organization with multiple print servers. Typically, you use the Print Management snap-in to manage print servers rather than individual computers.

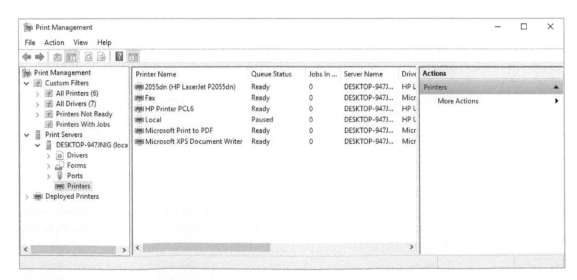

Figure 8-9   Print Management snap-in

Some features of the Print Management snap-in are:

* *Manage multiple print servers*—You can manage and configure not only printers, but also print server configuration, such as adding standard TCP/IP ports or printer drivers.

* *Filter views*—You can filter views to display only the printers that you are interested in. This can include showing only printers in an error state or in one physical location. Four filters exist by default: All Printers, All Drivers, Printers Not Ready, and Printers With Jobs.

* *Automatic installation of printers on a print server*—You can trigger an automatic printer installation process that scans the local subnet for network printers. If the appropriate drivers are located on the print server, all printers will be installed automatically. This can make configuring a new print server much faster.

* *Bulk printer management*—You can perform management operations on multiple printers at one time. For example, you can pause all of the printers on a print server before you take it down for maintenance.

* *Use Group Policy to deploy printers*—You can add printer deployment information to Group Policy Objects to automatically install printers on workstations.

* *Notification*—You can configure notifications to send an email when the conditions of a filter are met. For example, you can create a filter that shows only printers in an error condition and set a notification on that filter. Then, when any printer experiences an error condition, you will be notified by email.

The Use Group Policy to deploy printers option in the Print Management snap-in is outdated and should not be used. The updated method for deploying printers by using Group Policy is by using Group Policy Preferences. Group Policy Preferences are covered in Chapter 13, Enterprise Computing.

Activity 8-7: Using the Print Management Snap-In

Time Required: 10 minutes

Objective: Use the Print Management snap-in to install a new printer on the local computer

Description: The Print Management snap-in is capable of managing local and remote printers and print servers. In this activity, you use the Print Management snap-in to install a local printer.

1. If necessary, start your computer and sign in.

2. Click the **Start** button and click **Settings**.

3. Click the **Start** button, type **print**, and click **Print Management**.

4. If necessary, in the left pane, expand **Custom Filters** and click **All Printers**. This filter displays all of the printers installed on every print server that is being monitored. In this case, only the local printers are displayed because only the local computer is being monitored.

5. In the left pane, click **All Drivers**. This filter displays all of the printer drivers that are installed on every print server that is being monitored. This allows you to see if different printer driver versions are installed on various print servers.

6. In the left pane, if necessary, expand **Print Servers**, expand your computer, and click **Drivers**. This node displays only the printer drivers that are installed on your computer.

7. In the left pane, click **Forms**. This node displays the forms that are configured on your computer. Forms are the paper sizes the printer is configured to use. You can add, edit, or delete forms by right-clicking the Forms node and clicking Manage Forms.

8. In the left pane, click **Ports**. This node displays all the ports configured on your computer that can be used for printing. You can add additional ports or manage existing ports from here.

9. In the left pane, click **Printers**. This node displays all of the printers that are installed on your computer. You can manage the printers from here and install new printers.

10. In the left pane, right-click **Printers** and click **Add Printer**.

11. Click **Add a new printer using an existing port**, if necessary, click **LPT1: (Printer Port)**, and click **Next**. After printer installation, this printer will generate an error when you attempt to print because there is no printer physically attached to your computer on LPT1.

12. Click **Use an existing printer driver on the computer**, if necessary, click **HP Universal Printing PCL6**, and click **Next**.

13. In the Printer Name box, type **Local**.

14. Leave the option **Share this printer** checked, type **Local** in the Share Name box, and click **Next**.

15. On the Printer Found screen, click **Next**.

16. When the printer installation is finished, click **Finish**.

17. In the left pane, click **Printers**. The new printer named Local is installed here now.

18. Right-click **Local** and click **Pause Printing**.

19. Right-click **Local** and click **Print Test Page**.

20. In the Local dialog box, click **Close**.

21. In the left pane, click **Printers With Jobs**. Notice that this screen now displays the printer Local because there is a job in the queue.

22. Close all open windows.

Printer Configuration

In many cases, after installing a printer, no further configuration is required. If you install a local USB printer, all of the available options might already be configured for you. However, when you install more complex printers with multiple paper trays and finishing options like duplexing, you need to configure the printer. You might also need to manage print jobs, configure location-aware printing, or configure branch office printing.

Configuration Options   Each printer you install in Windows 10 can be configured independently. Most of the options available for configuration are standardized by Windows 10. However, the Device Settings tab, shown in Figure 8-10, has device-specific settings. These settings typically indicate whether specific hardware options such as duplexers and paper trays have been installed. The Device Settings tab might not be included for all printers.

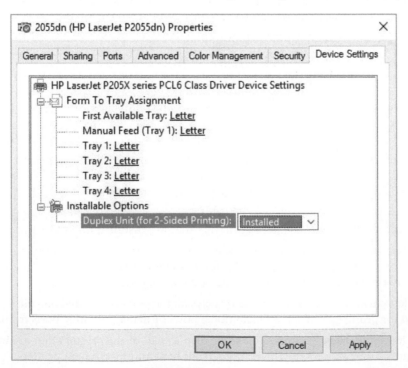

Figure 8-10   Device Settings tab of a printer

The Advanced tab, shown in Figure 8-11, has a number of options that are typically only implemented for server-based printing. However, these settings are also available for Windows 10. The options on this tab are the same regardless of the printer driver that is installed.

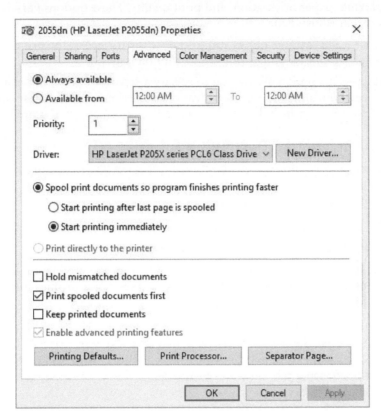

Figure 8-11   Advanced tab of a printer

Options on the Advanced tab are:

- *Availability*—You can schedule the time of day that the printer is available. This is typically used for large print jobs that are deferred until after regular work hours to prevent the printer from being busy for an extended period of time during the workday.

- *Priority*—This option is used when multiple printers are configured to use the same port. The printer with the highest priority will print first. Printers with lower priority are able to print through the port only when printers with higher priority have completed all of their jobs. This is used on busy print servers to give a few users faster access to the printer.

- *Driver*—You can update or change the printer driver here.

- *Spooling configuration*—Spooling allows you to begin using an application faster after printing by storing the print job as a file and sending the print job to the printer as a background process. If you print directly to the printer, you cannot begin using your application again until the print job is complete. When spooling is enabled, you can prevent printing from starting until the last page is spooled as a troubleshooting mechanism when print jobs are being corrupted.

- *Hold mismatched documents*—This option holds print jobs in the queue if the paper type of the print job is not correctly matched to the paper in the printer.

- *Print spooled documents first*—This option gives priority to print jobs that have completed spooling over those that are still spooling.

- *Keep printed documents*—This option keeps a copy of each print job in the queue even after the job is complete. This allows print jobs to be resubmitted later if additional copies are required.

- *Enable advanced printing features*—This option enables various advanced printing options depending on the application that you are using and the printer driver that is installed.
- *Printing Defaults*—This option includes the default configuration options for print jobs, such as duplexing, paper orientation, and print quality. These options vary based on the printer driver that is installed.
- *Print Processor*—This option allows you to choose the format of the print jobs. This is typically used when troubleshooting print job corruption issues.
- *Separator Page*—This option allows you to specify a separator page that is included at the beginning of each document. Large organizations sometimes include these on busy printers where the separator page includes the user name of the person who printed the job.

Other standard tabs on a printer's Properties window are:

- *General*—Used to view information about the printer, configure printing preferences, and print a test page.
- *Sharing*—Used to configure printer sharing.
- *Security*—Used to configure user and group permissions for printing.
- *Ports*—Used to select and configure ports that are used by this printer.
- *Color Management*—Used to configure color profiles that are used to control how screen colors are translated to colors for printers. In some cases, color profiles for specific printers are available for download.

Printer Sharing and Security Just as you can create file shares to share files with other users and computers over the network, you can also create shared printers. This is useful in a small office when you want to share the printer attached to a workstation. Sharing is enabled and controlled on the Sharing tab, shown in Figure 8-12.

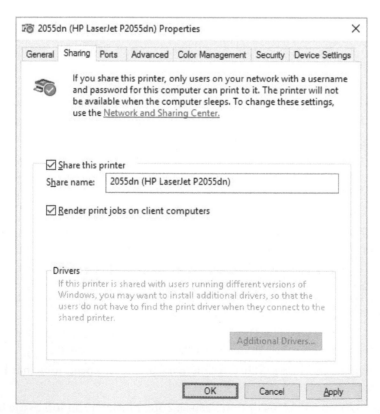

Figure 8-12   Sharing tab of a printer

The Sharing tab allows you to:

- Enable sharing for the printer.
- Define the share name for the printer.
- Specify whether print jobs are rendered on the client computer or print server.
- Add drivers for other operating systems to download by using point and print.

Whether a printer is shared or local, you can also configure security on that printer to control who is allowed to use and manage the printer. The Security tab is shown in Figure 8-13. You can allow or deny user and group permissions to print, manage printers, and manage documents.

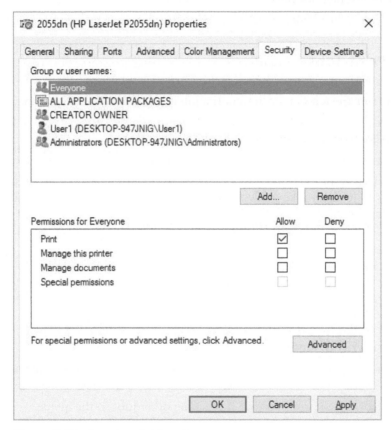

Figure 8-13   Security tab of a printer

The default permissions for printing are:

- *Everyone*—Allowed to print.
- *All Application Packages*—Allowed to print and manage documents. This allows Windows Store apps to print and manage print jobs.
- *Creator Owner*—Allowed to manage documents. This allows all users to manage their own print jobs.
- *User who installed printer (Userx)*—Allowed to print, manage printers, and manage documents.
- *Administrators*—Allowed to print, manage printers, and manage documents.

Branch Office Direct Printing   In Windows Server 2012 and Windows 8, Microsoft introduced **Branch Office Direct Printing** as a way to improve print performance for users in remote offices. Branch Office Direct Printing is designed for use when the client doing the printing and the printer are in the same physical location, but the print server that shares the printer is in a different location. Print configuration information from the print server is cached on the client computer and the client prints directly to the printer instead of sending print jobs to the print server.

Consider the following for Branch Office Direct Printing:

- You can centralize the administration of printers for remote offices but still keep WAN link utilization low because the print jobs stay local within the branch office.

- Intermittent WAN outages are not a problem because the printer configuration is cached on the client.

- The client computer is responsible for rendering the print job and must have the correct printer driver installed locally.

- Branch Office Direct Printing is enabled on a shared printer by using the Print Management snap-in.

Managing Print Jobs

In addition to controlling printers, you can also manage the individual jobs in a print queue. For each print job, you can perform the following tasks:

- *Pause*—Prevents the job from printing. If a job is partially finished printing, it stops at the end of a page.

- *Resume*—Allows a paused print job to continue printing.

- *Restart*—Restarts printing a job from the first page.

- *Cancel*—Stops a print job and removes it from the queue. The print job might not stop immediately, as it might take a few moments for the printer to remove the job from memory and complete printing the final page.

- *Edit job properties*—Allows you to change the priority of a print job or schedule the job.

Some of the situations where you might want to manage print jobs include:

- Restarting a print job when there has been a paper jam and some pages have been destroyed

- Pausing a large print job to let several other smaller print jobs be completed

- Raising the priority of a print job to ensure that it prints next

- Changing the schedule of a large print job to prevent it from printing during main office hours

- Canceling a corrupted print job that is blocking other jobs in the queue

Print jobs are managed in Windows 10 by the spooler service. When printing has inexplicably stopped for a printer on a Windows computer, a reboot usually fixes the problem, unless a corrupted print job is blocking the queue. Instead of rebooting the computer, stop and start the print spooler service to accomplish the same result faster. This can be done by using the Services snap-in or opening a command prompt as Administrator and using the *net stop spooler* and *net start spooler* commands.

If there is a corrupted print job, it is possible that you will not be able to cancel the job. In such a case, stop the spooler service and delete the job manually in the file system. Print jobs are stored in C:\Windows\System32\spool\PRINTERS. Each print job is composed of two numbered files (.spl and .shd). Delete both files for the corrupted print job and then start the spooler service.

Sometimes corrupted print jobs cause the spooler service to hang. If you can't stop the spooler service, you can kill the spoolsv.exe process by using Task Manager.

Activity 8-8: Managing Print Jobs

Time Required: 5 minutes
Objective: Manage print jobs

Description: Managing individual print jobs is seldom required. However, it can be useful for troubleshooting. In this activity, you manage a print job in the queue.

1. If necessary, start your computer and sign in.
2. Click the **Start** button and click **Settings**.
3. Click **Devices** and click **Local**. Note that the Printer local is paused.
4. Click **Open queue**. Notice that a Test Page job exists from Activity 8-7.
5. Right-click **Test Page** and click **Pause**. Notice that the status of the job changes to Paused.
6. Right-click **Test Page** and click **Resume**.
7. Right-click **Test Page** and click **Properties**. On the General tab, you can modify the priority and schedule of the job.
8. Click **OK** to close the Test Page Document Properties dialog box.
9. Right-click **Test Page** and click **Cancel**.
10. When prompted, click **Yes** to confirm canceling the job.
11. Close all open windows.

Web Browsers

Microsoft includes the new Edge browser in Windows 10. This is the default browser and is designed to be used for everyday web browsing. However, many organizations have intranet applications or access websites with ActiveX controls that are not supported in Microsoft Edge. To support those older applications, Internet Explorer 11 is also included in Windows 10.

Microsoft Edge

Over the years, Internet Explorer obtained a reputation as an unsecure browser. Despite huge security improvements in Internet Explorer, the reputation was hard to lose and Microsoft determined that it would be best to create a completely new web browser that is not limited by the requirement to support legacy technologies. **Microsoft Edge** in Windows 10 is that web browser.

Microsoft Edge works quite well for basic web browsing, and is focused on supporting Internet standards such as HTML5. This browser is not designed to support older web applications designed for specific versions of Internet Explorer. Any web-based application that requires an older version of Internet Explorer to render properly on the screen will not work properly in Microsoft Edge.

The other major feature not in Microsoft Edge is ActiveX controls. ActiveX controls were a method to allow code to be downloaded from a website and executed in the web browser. However, due to their design, ActiveX controls were a large security risk. Many older web-based applications used ActiveX controls.

Finally, Java applets are not supported in Microsoft Edge. There is no compatible plug-in or extension that allows you to run Java applets. Because Java applets were an ongoing security concern, this is a good thing. Other major browsers such as Chrome and Firefox are also ending support for Java applets.

New Features   Without the requirement to support older nonstandard features, Microsoft Edge is better performing and more secure. However, there are also new features that are improvements over Internet Explorer:

- *Web Notes*—With Web Notes, you can mark up a webpage with your own content. You can draw on the screen and make diagrams, create text notes, and highlight.

- *Reading view*—When you enable Reading view, the page layout simplifies and you can focus on reading the content. The exact results vary between webpages, but generally, sidebars, menus, and many advertisements are removed.

- *Reading list*—The Hub is a central location for favorites, web browsing history, downloads, and the reading list. The reading list is an alternate list of favorites. Now you can add webpages to your favorites or your reading list.

- *Share*—There is an option to share webpages built in to the browser interface. When you select the option, you are prompted for a Windows Store app to use to share the content. For example, you can select the Mail app that is included in Windows 10.

- *Extensions*—In web browsers such as Chrome or Firefox, browser extensions that modify the behavior of the web browser are very popular. Microsoft Edge did not support browser extensions at the initial release of Windows 10, but extension support has been added.

Configuration Settings   The Microsoft Edge browser has a much more limited set of settings for configuration than Internet Explorer did. Internet Explorer had varying security zones and many other settings. Most of this is not required for Microsoft Edge because of the redesign for improved security.

Some of the configuration settings for Microsoft Edge are:

- Configure whether Microsoft Edge opens with a home page.
- Configure the content for newly opened tabs.
- Clear browsing data.
- Ask or do not ask what to do with downloads.
- Synchronize favorites and the reading list across Windows devices.
- Configure reading view style and font size.
- Enable or disable pop-up blocking.
- Enable or disable Adobe Flash Player.
- Manage saved passwords and form data.
- Change the default search engine.
- Enable or disable SmartScreen Filter.

Activity 8-9: Using New Features in Microsoft Edge

Time Required: 5 minutes
Objective: Use new features in Microsoft Edge

Description: Microsoft Edge is a completely rebuilt web browser for Windows 10. It includes some new features that can be useful for users. In this activity, you try out some new features in Microsoft Edge.

1. If necessary, start your computer and sign in.
2. On the taskbar, click **Microsoft Edge**.
3. In the Search or enter web address box, type **www.microsoft.com** and press **Enter**.
4. In Microsoft Edge, in the upper right, click **Make a Web Note**.
5. Using the Pen tool (selected by default), write **WOW**.
6. Select the **Add a typed note** tool.
7. Click on the webpage and type **Find out pricing**.
8. Click **Exit**, click **Yes** to save the changes, and click **Save**.
9. Click **Exit**.
10. In the address bar, type **www.huffingtonpost.com** and press **Enter**.

11. Click an article on the screen to read it.

12. After the page loads, click **Add to favorites or reading list**, click **Reading list**, and click **Add**.

13. Click **Hub** and click **Reading list**. You can see the article that you added to the reading list.

14. Close Microsoft Edge.

Internet Explorer

Many organizations will be supporting Internet Explorer 11 in Windows 10 for an extended period of time to continue using legacy web-based applications. So, it is essential that network administrators are aware of how to configure Internet Explorer 11 in addition to Microsoft Edge.

Security Zones   The Security tab in the Internet Options for Internet Explorer, as shown in Figure 8-14, allows you to set Internet security options. The websites you connect to are grouped into zones and each zone can have different security options selected.

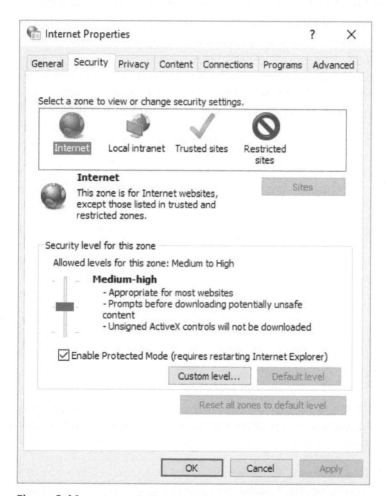

Figure 8-14   Internet Options Security tab in Internet Explorer 11

The zones for Internet Explorer security options are:

- *Internet*—The Internet zone includes all Internet websites that are not specifically assigned to another zone. The default security level is Medium-high.

- *Local intranet*—The Local intranet zone is meant to be all computers on the internal corporate network. The internal corporate network is defined by default as all sites in the local domain. However, this is only relevant if the workstation is joined to a domain. For workstations that are not part of a domain, the Intranet zone is treated the same as the Internet zone. The default security level is Medium-low.

- *Trusted sites*—The Trusted sites zone contains no sites by default; you must add sites that you consider trusted. This is useful when the Internet zone settings block functionality such as pop-up windows that are required for a site you know and trust. Adding the site to the Trusted sites zone allows that site to function properly. The default security level is Medium.

- *Restricted sites*—The Restricted sites zone is a specific list of sites that you do not trust. No sites are in this list by default. The default security level is High and cannot be changed except through custom settings.

The security options available for each zone control things like whether you are prompted when scripts or ActiveX controls are run. However, many security settings can be confusing to users. To make the process of selecting security options simpler, Microsoft has included predefined categories with groups of security settings. The five options are High, Medium-high, Medium, Medium-low, and Low. You also have the option to use custom settings for precise control over the security options.

Local Intranet Zone   The Local intranet zone is used primarily to support older web-based applications that require lowered security to function properly. By default, any website accessed by using a server name without dots (periods) is part of the Local intranet zone. For example, *http://webserver/app* is part of the Local intranet zone, but *http://webserver.mydomain.com/app* is not part of the Local intranet zone. You can also manually add websites to the Local intranet zone.

When a website is part of the Local intranet zone, Internet Explorer can pass sign-in credentials from the local workstation to the web server for authentication. Some companies use this as a method for automatically authenticating users to web-based applications. Users are prompted for sign-in credentials if the website is not part of the Local intranet zone.

Protected Mode   All Internet Explorer zones can be configured to run in **Protected Mode**. Protected Mode works in conjunction with UAC to prevent malware from installing through Internet Explorer. UAC isolates websites loaded in Protected Mode in a low (untrusted) integrity level. This limits any malware loaded from a website to low-risk areas of Windows such as Temporary Internet Files and a very small portion of the registry.

Protected Mode is disabled for the Local intranet and Trusted sites zones by default.

SmartScreen Filter   The **SmartScreen Filter** in Internet Explorer 11 warns you when you are about to access a website that is known to install malicious software or is used as part of a phishing attack. The list of unsafe websites is maintained by Microsoft and you can report new unsafe sites.

By default, the SmartScreen Filter is turned on and scans each website you access. This is the best configuration in most scenarios. However, if a computer does not have access to the Internet, you might want to disable the SmartScreen Filter to prevent users from seeing error messages about being unable to perform SmartScreen filtering for internal websites.

SmartScreen Filter is also used in Microsoft Edge.

Privacy   Internet Explorer 11 includes a number of features that enhance privacy. **InPrivate Browsing** allows you to access the Internet without any information being stored in cache or history. This can be useful when using a public computer and you do not want anyone to easily identify the websites you have been visiting. However, there are numerous other ways web activity can be monitored, such as logging on a proxy server or firewall.

Cookies are used by websites to save information related to the website on your local computer. However, they can also be used by websites to monitor your activity. The Privacy tab in Internet Options allows you to control how cookies are accepted in Internet Explorer. Be aware that completely disabling cookies prevents some websites from working properly. For example, a shopping website might rely on cookies to keep track of items in a shopping cart.

Tools   Several tools are available in Internet Explorer 11 to enhance the browsing experience and increase manageability. The **Popup Blocker** prevents most pop-up advertisements from being displayed. Pop-up advertisements are not a security risk, just annoying.

Compatibility View provides backward compatibility for websites and applications that were targeted for previous versions of Internet Explorer. Microsoft maintains a list of known websites that need Compatibility View and Internet Explorer 11 automatically downloads this list. If you choose to use the Microsoft compatibility lists, when you visit a website on the list of sites requiring Compatibility View, it is automatically enabled. If you visit a website, such as an internal application, that requires Compatibility View, you can enable Compatibility View manually.

Websites in the Local intranet zone display using Compatibility View by default.

Internet Explorer is extensible with add-ons. Add-ons increase the functionality of Internet Explorer and can include toolbars or other features. Poorly written add-ons for Internet Explorer can introduce instability to your computer. In addition, some add-ons function as spyware or adware. Users are lured into installing add-ons with promises of easy searching and cool icons for email messages. Internet Explorer 11 includes a **Manage add-ons** tool that makes it easier to identify, disable, and remove unwanted add-ons.

On the Advanced tab in Internet Options, there is a Reset button. This button resets Internet Explorer to default settings and removes all add-ons. In some cases, this can be useful to remove add-ons that you are unable to remove through Manage Add-ons. After using this option, you will need to reinstall any helper applications because they will no longer be configured in Internet Explorer.

Enterprise Mode

To ease the transition from using Internet Explorer to Microsoft Edge, you can use **Enterprise Mode**. Enterprise Mode allows you to create a list of websites that require Internet Explorer and have those websites automatically open in Internet Explorer for your users. This avoids the user frustration of needing to remember which browser to use for which websites.

To use Enterprise Mode, first you create an XML file that defines the websites that require Internet Explorer. When you specify the websites, you can also select the mode of Internet Explorer. For example, to support an older web-based application, you can specify that the site be opened in IE 7 Enterprise Mode, which emulates Internet Explorer 7.

Although you can manually create the XML file for Enterprise Mode, it is faster and easier to use Enterprise Mode Site List Manager, shown in Figure 8-15, to create the XML file. Enterprise Mode Site List Manager for Windows 10 can be downloaded from *http://go.microsoft.com/fwlink/p/?LinkId=716853*.

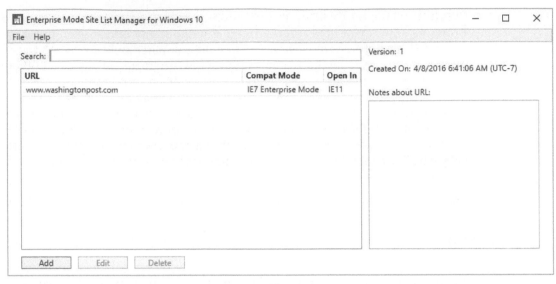

Figure 8-15   Enterprise Mode Site List Manager for Windows 10

The final step in configuring Enterprise Mode is configuring the clients to use the XML file. This is done by enabling the Configure the Enterprise Mode Site list Group Policy setting in \Administrative Templates\Windows Components\Microsoft Edge, shown in Figure 8-16. This setting is available for users and computers. When you enable this setting,

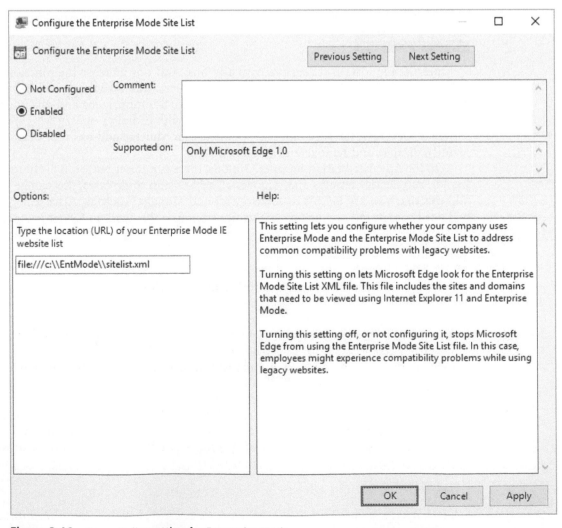

Figure 8-16   Group Policy setting for Enterprise Mode

you provide the location of the XML files. The location can be a website, network share, or local file.

Another Group Policy setting that you can use for website compatibility is *Send all intranet sites to Internet Explorer 11*. When you enable this setting, all sites that are part of the Local intranet zone are opened by using Internet Explorer 11 instead of Microsoft Edge.

Enterprise Mode can also be used with Internet Explorer to set compatibility modes for various websites. There are Internet Explorer–specific registry keys to enable Enterprise Mode for Internet Explorer, but the same XML file can be used for the site list.

Activity 8-10: Using Enterprise Mode for Compatibility

Time Required: 15 minutes
Objective: Implement Enterprise Mode to provide backward compatibility for web-based applications

Description: Many organizations have web-based applications that are not compatible with Microsoft Edge. You can use Enterprise Mode to configure a list of websites that will open by using Internet Explorer. In this activity, you implement Enterprise Mode to support legacy web-based applications.

1. If necessary, start your computer and sign in.
2. On the taskbar, click **Microsoft Edge**.
3. In the Search or enter web address box, type **http://go.microsoft.com/fwlink/p/?LinkId=716853** and press **Enter**.
4. Click **Download**.
5. Click **Save**.
6. When the download is complete, click **Run**.
7. In Enterprise Mode Site List Manager Setup dialog box, click **Next**.
8. Select the **I accept the terms in the License Agreement** check box and click **Next**.
9. On the Destination Folder screen, click **Next**.
10. Click **Install** and click **Yes** in the User Account Control dialog box.
11. Click **Finish**.
12. Click the **Start** button, type **enterprise**, and click **Enterprise Mode Site List Manager**.
13. In Enterprise Mode Site List Manager for Windows 10, click **Add**.
14. In the Add new website window, in the URL box, type **www.washingtonpost.com**.
15. In the Compat Mode box, select **IE7 Enterprise Mode**.
16. In the Open In box, select **IE11** and click **Save**.
17. In Enterprise Mode Site List Manager for Windows 10, click the **File** menu and click **Save to XML**.
18. In the Save as dialog box, click **Local Disk (C:)**, click **New Folder**, type **EntMode**, and press **Enter**.
19. Double-click **EntMode**.
20. In the File name box, type **sitelist.xml** and click **Save**.
21. Close all open windows.
22. Click the **Start** button, type **mmc**, and press **Enter**.
23. Click **Yes** in the User Account Control dialog box.
24. In the MMC window, click **File** and click **Add/Remove Snap-in**.
25. In the Add or Remove Snap-ins window, double-click **Group Policy Object Editor**, click **Finish**, and click **OK**.

8

26. Browse to \Local Computer Policy\Computer Configuration\Administrative Templates\Windows Components\Microsoft Edge and double-click **Configure the Enterprise Mode Site List**.

27. In the Configure the Enterprise Mode Site List window, click **Enabled**.

28. In the Type the location (URL) of your Enterprise Mode IE website list box, type **file:///c:\\ EntMode\\sitelist.xml** and click **OK**.

29. On the taskbar, click **Microsoft Edge**.

30. In the Search or enter web address box, type **www.washingtonpost.com** and press **Enter**. Notice that Internet Explorer starts and opens the Washington Post website.

31. Close all open windows.

Chapter Summary

- File Explorer is used to manage and access files in Windows 10. You can enable libraries to provide additional functionality. You can also index additional file system locations to make searching more effective.

- OneDrive is cloud-based storage for files that provides you with a backup location for your files and portability. You can access files in OneDrive through File Explorer or by using a web browser. You can also share files stored in OneDrive with other people.

- In the web interface for OneDrive, you can view file versions and recover deleted files from the Recycle bin. You can also edit files by using online Microsoft Office applications.

- Printing can be implemented with local or network printers. You can also share printers from a computer running Windows 10 or Windows Server.

- Printer drivers allow Windows 10 to use the full capabilities of a printer. The drivers are often available for PostScript and PCL. After installation, printer drivers are stored in the printer driver store.

- Printers can be installed and managed by using Printers & scanners in Settings, Devices and Printers in Control Panel, and the Print Management snap-in. Some of the configuration settings for printers are standardized while others are specific to the capabilities of each printer.

- The Microsoft Edge web browser is a completely new web browser in Windows 10. To maintain backward compatibility for older web-based applications, Windows 10 includes Internet Explorer 11. Enterprise Mode can be used to identify websites that should automatically be opened in Internet Explorer.

Key Terms

Branch Office Direct Printing   A feature that allows Windows 10 computers to print directly to a printer shared from a print server rather than sending the print job through the print server.

Compatibility View   A feature in Internet Explorer 11 that provides backward compatibility for websites and applications that were targeted for previous versions of Internet Explorer.

Enterprise Mode   A feature in Internet Explorer and Microsoft Edge that automatically configures various compatibility modes for websites.

InPrivate Browsing   An Internet Explorer 11 and Microsoft Edge feature that prevents caching of web content and logging of web activity in Internet Explorer.

libraries   Virtual folders in File Explorer that combine content from multiple locations to simplify file access.

Manage Add-ons   A tool in Internet Explorer 11 that makes it easier to identify, disable, and remove unwanted add-ons.

metadata   Information or properties for a file or other object. Windows 10 allows you to include tags as additional metadata for files.

Microsoft Edge   The new web browser in Windows 10 that has better support for web standards, such as HTML5, than Internet Explorer.

OneDrive   Cloud-based storage that is provided when you create a Microsoft account. You can access files in OneDrive through File Explorer or a web browser.

page description language   A language that defines the layout of content for a print job.

Popup Blocker   An Internet Explorer and Microsoft Edge feature that prevents most pop-up advertising from being displayed while you browse websites.

Portable Document Format (PDF)   A popular document format that is also supported as a page description language by some printers.

PostScript   A common page description language used by printers to describe how a page is printed.

Print Management snap-in   A printer management tool in Windows 10 that allows you to manage local and remote printers.

Printer Command Language (PCL)   A common language used by printers to describe how a page is printed.

printer driver   Software used by Windows 10 to properly communicate with a specific make and model of printer.

printer driver package   An enhanced printer driver that can contain additional software.

printer driver store   A location in Windows 10 that caches printer drivers and is capable of storing multiple versions of a printer driver.

Protected Mode   A feature in Internet Explorer 11 that isolates any code that runs within Internet Explorer to prevent malware infection.

SmartScreen Filter   An Internet Explorer and Microsoft Edge feature that warns you about websites known to install malicious software or used in phishing attacks.

XML Paper Specification (XPS)   A document format that describes how a page should be displayed. XPS is similar to Adobe Portable Document Format (PDF).

Review Questions

1. Which document format is similar to XPS?

    a. PDF

    b. TXT

    c. DOC

    d. RTF

2. Which of the following are languages used by printers? (Choose all that apply.)

    a. WPF

    b. XPS

    c. PCL

    d. PostScript

3. Which utility is used to add printer drivers to the printer driver store?

    a. pdriver.exe

    b. pnputil.exe

    c. PushPrinterConnections.exe

    d. Print Management snap-in

4. Which utilities can be used to manage printers? (Choose all that apply.)

    a. Devices and Printers in Control Panel

    b. Computer Management

    c. Device Manager

    d. Print Management snap-in

    e. Printers & scanners in Settings

5. Which of the following are features available only in the Print Management snap-in? (Choose all that apply.)

   a.   Manage remote printers

   b.   Manage local printers

   c.   Configure notifications

   d.   Bulk printer management

   e.   Update printer drivers

6. When a printer is configured with a lower priority value, the print jobs for that printer are printed first. True or False?

7. By default, all users are able to manage their own print jobs because the _____ group has the manage documents permission.

8. When you create a new document in the root of a library, where is the document created?

   a.   in the highest priority location with free space

   b.   in the first location listed in the library properties

   c.   in a location you specify when prompted

   d.   in the default save location of the library

9. Which file locations are indexed by default? (Choose all that apply.)

   a.   Offline files

   b.   the Windows folder

   c.   the Start menu

   d.   the Users folder

10. For each type of file, you can specify whether the contents of the file are indexed. True or False?

11. Which Internet Explorer 11 security zone is only relevant if the computer is joined to a domain?

   a.   Internet

   b.   Local intranet

   c.   Trusted sites

   d.   Restricted sites

12. When Internet Explorer 11 runs in Protected Mode, it runs with lower privileges than the user. True or False?

13. What is the default folder synchronized with OneDrive?

   a.   C:\OneDrive

   b.   C:\Users\%username%\SkyDrive

   c.   C:\Users\%username%\OneDrive

   d.   C:\Users\%username%\Cloud

14. Which actions for OneDrive can only be performed when accessing files through the web interface? (Choose all that apply.)

   a.   Recover deleted files from the Recycle bin.

   b.   Share files with other people.

   c.   Edit files by using web-based applications.

   d.   Simultaneously edit files at the same time as other people.

   e.   Access previous versions of files.

15. Access to shared files in OneDrive can be restricted to specific people. True or False?

16. Which of the following are characteristics of Branch Office Direct Printing? (Choose all that apply.)

    a. WAN utilization is reduced.

    b. The print server is responsible for rendering the print job.

    c. WAN outages prevent jobs from starting because the print server cannot be contacted.

    d. You can centrally manage printers for multiple locations from a single print server.

    e. The Print Management snap-in is used to enable Branch Office Direct Printing on a printer.

17. Microsoft Edge supports ActiveX controls. True or False?

18. Which steps are required to configure Enterprise Mode with Microsoft Edge? (Choose all that apply.)

    a. Create a text file with a list of websites requiring Internet Explorer 11.

    b. Create an XML file with a list of websites requiring Internet Explorer 11.

    c. Enable Enterprise Mode in Group Policy.

    d. Enable Enterprise Mode in Microsoft Edge settings.

19. The SmartScreen filter is used to prevent malware in Microsoft Edge and Internet Explorer 11. True or False?

20. The _____ service is responsible for processing print jobs.

Case Projects

CASE PROJECTS

Case Project 8-1: Virus Prevention

The accountant for Buddy's Machine shop has just received a new Windows 10 computer. His accounting software has been installed and is working well. However, he asks you to install a PDF printer that he uses to generate invoice PDFs to send out via email. This PDF printer is quite expensive. Explain why this PDF printer is not necessary for Windows 10.

Case Project 8-2: Website Compatibility

Gigantic Life Insurance is planning the implementation of Windows 10 for their internal staff. As part of the migration process, you want to standardize on using the new Microsoft Edge browser for the enhanced security over Internet Explorer. However, there are several important web-based applications that only run properly in Internet Explorer. How can you implement Enterprise Mode to make this process easy for users?

Case Project 8-3: Data Backup with OneDrive

The salespeople at Hyperactive Media Sales all use laptop computers so they can have easy access to important data on the road. However, there is a concern that the salespeople keep data on those laptop computers and the data is never backed up. If the hard drive in the laptop fails, important information would be lost. Explain how OneDrive can help in this scenario.

chapter 9

Windows 10 Application Support

After reading this chapter and completing the exercises, you will be able to:

- Describe the application environments supported by Windows 10
- Modify and back up the registry
- Install various types of apps
- Describe and implement options for app compatibility
- Configure clients for virtual desktops and RemoteApp

As a technology support worker, it is easy to lose track of the real purpose of computers. The purpose of computers is to run applications that allow workers to be more productive. Installing and troubleshooting those applications is core to the role of desktop support.

In this chapter, you review the different application environments available in Windows 10, which in turn identify the types of apps supported by Windows 10. You also learn about the structure of the registry and how to edit it. Then, you learn about different installation processes for apps, including automated deployment for larger organizations. You also identify the different options for mitigating app compatibility problems when migrating to Windows 10. And finally, you learn about how to access virtual desktops and RemoteApp programs when Remote Desktop Services has been configured.

Application Environments

Apps are written by developers to interact with a specific **application environment subsystem**. Apps use **application programming interfaces (APIs)** to request services from the application environment subsystem. The application environment subsystem is then responsible for communicating with the operating system to accomplish privileged tasks, such as accessing hardware to communicate on the network or save files to disk.

To install and use an app, the application environment it is written for must be present. If the application environment is not present, the APIs necessary for the app to request operating system functions are not available. In addition, some application environments have multiple versions and the correct version must be present for apps. In some cases, before you install an app, you might need to install Windows Updates to ensure you have the most recent version of the desired application environment.

All of the application environments in Windows 10 restrict apps to running in user mode where they are isolated from the core functionality of the operating system. Running apps in user mode ensures that a poorly written app does not affect system stability. This compares with hardware drivers that operate in kernel mode where a poorly written driver can impact system stability.

Win32 and Win64

Applications designed to interact with the **Win32** subsystem were the most common type of application in use with earlier operating systems, such as Windows XP. As new subsystems, such as **.NET Framework**, become more popular with developers, the percentage of applications that use Win32 will drop.

Each Win32 application runs in its own virtual memory space and is executed by the processor in user mode. If the Win32 application crashes, it does not affect other Win32 applications or the operating system. The number 32 refers to the binary size of the processor instructions in the applications code—32 bits. Win32 apps are also known as 32-bit apps.

Most organizations use the 64-bit version of Windows 10 rather than the 32-bit version of Windows 10. Both versions support Win32, but the 64-bit version of Windows 10 supports 32-bit applications by using a **Windows on Windows 64 (WOW64)** virtualized environment to host Win32 apps. The calls to Win32 APIs are translated to an equivalent **Win64** API call in the 64-bit version of Windows 10 to provide compatibility.

Most desktop applications are still 32-bit rather than 64-bit. For example, most organizations use the 32-bit version of Microsoft Office. On a 64-bit version of Windows 10, 32-bit applications are typically installed in C:\Program Files (x86).

Activity 9-1: Identifying Win32 and Win64 Apps

Time Required: 10 minutes

Objective: Run Win32 and Win64 apps and review how they appear in Task Manager

Description: The core apps included in the 64-bit version of Windows 10 are all 64-bit applications. However, there are 32-bit versions of some system apps included for backward compatibility for some programs. In this activity, you launch a Win32 app and a Win64 app to confirm how they are individually presented on the Processes tab in Task Manager.

1. If necessary, start your computer and sign in.
2. Click the **Start** button, type **notepad**, and click **Notepad**.
3. On the taskbar, click **File Explorer**.
4. In File Explorer, browse to **C:\Windows\SysWOW64** and double-click **notepad**.
5. Compare the two Notepad windows. Notice that there is no visual difference between the two Notepad windows.
6. Right-click the taskbar and click **Task Manager**.
7. If Task Manager is in the simplified view, click **More details**.
8. On the Processes tab, notice that there are two Notepad apps. One of the Notepad apps has (32 bit) appended to the name. The text (32 bit) identifies Win32 processes.
9. Right-click **Notepad (32 bit)** and click **Properties**.
10. In the Notepad Properties window, notice that the location for this app is C:\Windows\SysWOW64 and click **Cancel**.
11. Close all open windows.

.NET Framework

The .NET Framework is a commonly used application environment for apps on Windows 10. If the .NET Framework is required for an app, it is identified in the app documentation. Most applications that require the .NET Framework verify that the correct version of .NET Framework is available during installation. Some apps even distribute the .NET Framework during installation if required.

There are multiple versions of the .NET Framework. At the time of writing, the current version is .NET Framework 4.6.2. In theory, the latest version of .NET Framework is compatible with previous versions, but the reality is that some apps require specific versions. In general, .NET Framework 3.5 supports apps written for .NET versions 2.0, 3.0, and 3.5. Apps requiring .NET 4.0 or later are generally compatible with the latest version of the .NET Framework. Windows 10 provides .NET Framework 3.5 and .NET Framework 4.6 as features.

Updates for the .NET Framework are delivered through Windows Update. If your organization has .NET applications, you should test any new .NET Framework updates before deploying them to user computers. Updates for the .NET Framework are issued regularly.

Activity 9-2: Installing .NET Framework 3.5

Time Required: 10 minutes
Objective: Install .NET Framework 3.5 on Windows 10

Description: Some applications require an older version of .NET Framework to be installed. In Windows 10, .NET Framework 3.5 is available for backward compatibility. In this activity, you install the .NET Framework 3.5 feature on Windows 10.

1. If necessary, start your computer and sign in.
2. Click the **Start** button, type **feature**, and click **Turn Windows features on or off**.
3. In the Windows Features window, notice that .NET Framework 4.6 Advanced Services is already installed by default.
4. Select the **.NET Framework 3.5 (includes .NET 2.0 and 3.0)** check box and click **OK**.

5. In the Windows Features window, click **Download files from Windows Update**. The installation files are not included with Windows 10. In most cases, the file download takes only a few minutes.

6. When Windows has completed the requested changes, click **Close**.

Windows Store Applications

Starting with Windows 8, there is a new type of app called **Windows Store apps**. This new type of application is designed with a more modern interface that is flexible enough to accommodate multiple form factors like tablets and phones. These apps have been known as Metro apps, Modern apps, Windows Store apps, and Universal Windows Platform apps.

The most recent iteration of Windows Store apps is Universal Windows Platform apps, also known as Universal apps. Universal apps make it easier for developers to target multiple platforms. Developers can make a single application for Windows desktop computers, tablets, and Windows phones. Newer apps in the Windows Store are Universal apps.

Legacy Applications

If you are running a 64-bit version of Windows 10, you cannot run DOS or Win16 applications. DOS was the command-line precursor to Windows, and Win16 was used for apps in Windows 3.1. Both of these platforms were popular in the 1980s and early 1990s. So, there are very few apps in production use that were designed for DOS or Win16.

If you do have a legacy DOS or Win16 application that you need to run, you can use a 32-bit version of Windows 10. To support Win16 applications, a 32-bit version of Windows 10 translates Win16 API calls to Win32 API calls in the same way that 64-bit versions of Windows 10 support 32-bit applications. DOS applications are supported by a virtual instance of DOS (Ntvdm.exe).

The Registry

Windows 10 has the **registry** as a central store for application and operating system configuration information. When applications or Windows 10 starts, they read their configuration information from the registry. When you make configuration changes to applications or Windows 10, those changes are stored in the registry so that they can be retrieved later.

In most cases, you do not need to manually edit or view the registry. Applications and Windows 10 properly understand the structure of the registry and how their own information is stored in it. However, sometimes, you will find support documents that identify registry keys that need to be verified or modified. In those cases, you need to understand the structure of the registry and how to modify it.

Registry Structure

The registry is divided into sections and levels of data. Multiple sections exist to organize data by purpose. The individual sections are called hives. Each **hive** has a specific role to play and is stored in memory while it is in use. When the computer is shut down, the memory versions of the hives are written to files and folders typically found in the folder C:\Windows\System32\config. Each hive is composed of one or more files.

Within a single hive, the data is stored in keys and values identified by their name and position relative to each other. Figure 9-1 shows an example of the registry structure when viewed with a registry editing tool.

The left-hand navigation pane displays a hierarchical folder structure. Each hive appears as a top-level folder in the left pane. In the hives, each folder in the left pane is referred to as a **registry key**. Each registry key is identified by the hive it belongs to, its position relative to other keys in the hive, and its name.

The right-hand pane shows the data values that are stored at a specific level in the registry hierarchy (i.e., within a registry key). Each registry key can store multiple data values. The data values are defined by a name that is case sensitive, a type indicating how the data is formatted (e.g., binary, string, word), and the actual data stored by the value.

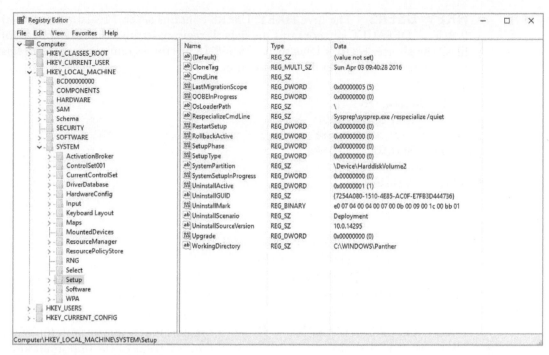

Figure 9-1   View of the registry structure

 In documentation, it is common for the registry hive names to be abbreviated. For example, HKEY_LOCAL_MACHINE is often referred to as HKLM. Also, HKEY_CURRENT_USER is often referred to as HKCU.

To aid in troubleshooting and understand why changes might be requested by a support document, it is useful to understand the contents of each registry hive. Table 9-1 describes the contents of each registry hive.

Table 9-1   Registry hives

Hive name	Description
HKEY_CLASSES_ROOT	This hive defines file types (classes) and properties associated with those types. For example, file type associations are stored here. This hive is a combination of HKCU\Software\Classes and HKLM\Software\Classes. If settings for a file type are defined in both locations, the user-specific settings take precedence.
HKEY_CURRENT_USER	This hive contains the user-specific registry information from ntuser.dat stored in the user profile. Any application or operating system settings that are user specific are stored in this hive. If you are attempting to fix a user-specific application issue, the support document will have you review and modify keys here.
HKEY_LOCAL_MACHINE	This hive contains global settings for the entire computer and the applications installed on it. If you are attempting to fix any operating system or application issue that is not user specific, the support document will have you review and modify keys here. More details about HKLM are provided later in this chapter.
HKEY_USERS	This hive contains the user-specific settings for the current user and several system services. The name of the registry key for the currently signed-in user is the security identifier (SID) of the user. The content of the key for the currently signed-in user is also available in HKCU.
HKEY_CURRENT_CONFIG	This hive contains details about the current hardware profile in use. The details report the differences between the standard configuration defined in HKLM\System and HKLM\Software and those in the active hardware profile. This hive is also a mapped view to information stored in HKLM\System\CurrentControlSet\Hardware Profiles\Current.

HKEY_USERS   The hive HKEY_USERS contains several registry keys, as shown in Figure 9-2. The .DEFAULT key contains the default registry settings that are copied for new user profiles. The shorter registry keys such as S-1-5-18 are for system services. The registry keys with a full SID are for the currently signed-in user.

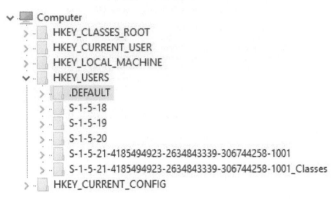

```
∨ 🖥 Computer
    >   📁 HKEY_CLASSES_ROOT
    >   📁 HKEY_CURRENT_USER
    >   📁 HKEY_LOCAL_MACHINE
    ∨   📁 HKEY_USERS
        >   📁 .DEFAULT
        >   📁 S-1-5-18
        >   📁 S-1-5-19
        >   📁 S-1-5-20
        >   📁 S-1-5-21-4185494923-2634843339-306744258-1001
        >   📁 S-1-5-21-4185494923-2634843339-306744258-1001_Classes
    >   📁 HKEY_CURRENT_CONFIG
```

Figure 9-2   HKEY_USERS hive

HKEY_LOCAL_MACHINE   This hive contains important settings for Windows 10 and applications. This hive stores all of the general settings. Some of the important keys in this hive are:

- *BCD00000000*—This key contains information from the boot configuration database that defined the Windows 10 boot process. Instead of editing these keys, you should use bcdedit.exe.

- *HARDWARE*—This key contains hardware information that is detected at startup. You should not edit this information.

- *SOFTWARE*—This key contains information for applications. Application data is typically located in a key with the following naming structure: HKLM\SOFTWARE*vendor**application*\.

- SYSTEM—This key contains information about Windows 10 and hardware drivers. Device driver and service information is in HKLM\SYSTEM\CurrentControlSet. A backup copy of this key named ControlSet001 is updated each time a user signs in. This backup can be used by Windows 10 during a recovery.

Windows 7 had a recovery option named Last Known Good that restored ControlSet001. This recovery option is not available in Windows 8 or newer.

Registry Editing Tools

The preferred method for configuring applications and Windows 10 is to use the interfaces provided for that purpose. Applications typically have Settings or Options that you can use to configure the application. Windows 10 has Settings, Control Panel, and various Microsoft Management Console (MMC) snap-ins.

If you do need to view and modify the registry entries, take the following precautions:

- Back up the portion of the registry you will be changing before you make any changes.

- Restrict the number of changes made at one time to limit the impact and identify which change actually fixed the problem.

- When possible, use a test system rather than a user's computer to verify that changes resolve the issue.

- If you are adjusting registry entries for services or drivers, ensure that the computer can boot properly after the changes have been made.

Registry Editor   The most commonly used tool for viewing and modifying the registry is the graphical **Registry Editor** (regedit). In addition to basic editing functionality, you can use this tool to search the registry and modify permissions. You can also export and import sections of the registry. Regedit is shown in Figure 9-1.

When you export registry keys for a backup, it is done to a .reg file. If you want to restore the contents of the .reg file, you can import it by using regedit. However, you can also double-click the file in File Explorer to restore the registry keys.

Activity 9-3: Using Regedit to Back Up and Modify the Registry

Time Required: 10 minutes
Objective: Use regedit to view and change registry information

Description: Startup information for services is stored in the registry. Although you should normally edit service startup information by using the Services administrative tool, you can also edit directly in the registry. In this activity, you modify the startup setting for a server by using regedit.

1. If necessary, start your computer and sign in.
2. Click the **Start** button, type **services**, and click **Services**.
3. Scroll down and double-click the **Print Spooler** service.
4. In the Print Spooler Properties (Local Computer) window, read the information for the service, and click **Cancel**. Notice that the Startup type is Automatic.
5. Click the **Start** button, type **regedit**, and click **regedit**.
6. In the User Account Control dialog box, click **OK**.
7. In the Registry Editor, browse to **HKEY_LOCAL_MACHINE\SYSTEM\CurrentControl-Set\Services\Spooler**.
8. Right-click **Spooler** and click **Export**.
9. In the Export Registry File window, click **This PC** and double-click **Local Disk (C:)**.
10. In the File name box, type **SpoolerBak** and click **Save**.
11. In the Registry Editor, double-click **Start**.
12. In the Edit DWORD (32-bit) Value window, in the Value data box, type **4**, and then click **OK**.
13. In Services, press **F5** to refresh the view, verify that the Startup type is now Disabled, and close Services.
14. In the Registry Editor, collapse all of the hives so that no keys are visible, and close the Registry Editor.

Activity 9-4: Restoring a Registry Backup

Time Required: 10 minutes
Objective: Restore registry settings from a .reg file

Description: Before modifying the registry, you should export any keys that you will be changing to a .reg file. If the registry change does not go as planned, you can import the .reg file to restore the previous level of functionality. In this activity, you restore a .reg file and verify that the contents imported properly.

1. If necessary, start your computer and sign in.
2. On the taskbar, click **File Explorer**, browse to **C:**, and double-click **SpoolerBak**.

3. In the User Account Control dialog box, click **Yes**. Notice that the Registry Editor is being started.

4. In the Registry Editor window, click **Yes** to continue.

5. Click **OK** to acknowledge the successful import and then close File Explorer.

6. Click the **Start** button, type **regedit**, and click **regedit**.

7. In the User Account Control dialog box, click **Yes**.

8. In the Registry Editor, expand **HKEY_LOCAL_MACHINE** and click **SYSTEM**.

9. Click the **Edit** menu and click **Find**.

10. In the Find window, in the Find what box, type **spooler**.

11. In the Look at area, deselect all check boxes except **Keys** and click **Find Next**.

12. Keep pressing **F3** to Find Next until the Print Spooler service identified in Activity 9-3 is located. This will take about 5–10 presses, but review the information that is found along the way.

13. Read the Start value and verify that it has been set back to 2.

14. Click the **Start** button, type **services**, and click **Services**.

15. Scroll down to the Print Spooler service and verify that the Startup Type is Automatic.

16. Close all open windows.

Reg.exe   If you need to read or write registry entries from batch files, you can use reg.exe, as shown in Figure 9-3. Reg.exe is a command-line utility with similar functionality to regedit. You may see some support documents that advise you to use reg.exe when modifying the registry. This is because it is easier to type out a single command in support documentation than to provide multiple steps to perform the task using a graphical interface. Regardless of the registry editing tool used, the end result is the same.

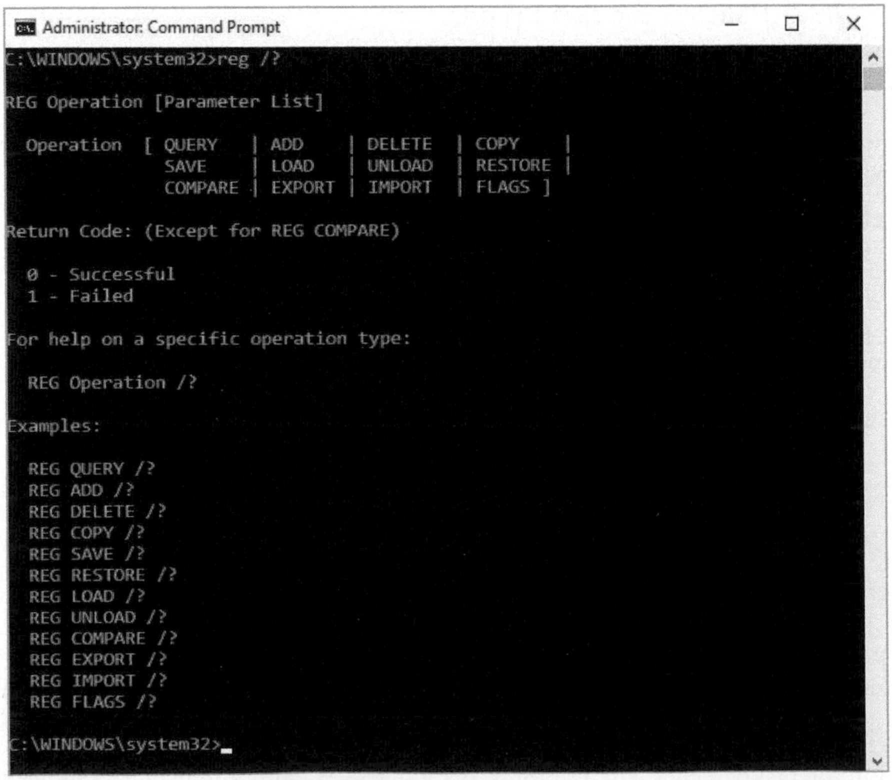

```
Administrator: Command Prompt                                    —    □    ×

C:\WINDOWS\system32>reg /?

REG Operation [Parameter List]

  Operation  [ QUERY    | ADD     | DELETE  | COPY     |
               SAVE     | LOAD    | UNLOAD  | RESTORE  |
               COMPARE  | EXPORT  | IMPORT  | FLAGS ]

Return Code: (Except for REG COMPARE)

  0 - Successful
  1 - Failed

For help on a specific operation type:

  REG Operation /?

Examples:

  REG QUERY /?
  REG ADD /?
  REG DELETE /?
  REG COPY /?
  REG SAVE /?
  REG RESTORE /?
  REG LOAD /?
  REG UNLOAD /?
  REG COMPARE /?
  REG EXPORT /?
  REG IMPORT /?
  REG FLAGS /?

C:\WINDOWS\system32>
```

Figure 9-3   Reg.exe command-line utility

Activity 9-5: Using Reg.exe

Time Required: 10 minutes
Objective: Use reg.exe to view and modify registry entries

Description: If you need to query or modify the registry from a command line or batch file, you can use reg.exe. In this activity, you view and modify registry entries by using reg.exe.

1. If necessary, start your computer and sign in.

2. Right-click the **Start** button, click **Command Prompt (Admin)**, and click **Yes** in the User Account Control dialog box.

3. At the command prompt, type **reg /?** and press **Enter** to view the general help information.

4. Type **reg query /?** and press **Enter** to view the query help information.

5. Type **reg query HKLM\SYSTEM\CurrentControlSet\Services\Spooler** and press **Enter**. Verify that the Start value is 0x2.

6. Type **reg add /?** and press **Enter** to view the add help information.

7. Type **reg add HKLM\SYSTEM\CurrentControlSet\Services\Spooler /v Start /d 0x4** and press **Enter**. This sets the Start value to 0x4.

8. Press **Y** and press **Enter** to confirm overwriting the value.

9. Type **reg query HKLM\SYSTEM\CurrentControlSet\Services\Spooler** and press **Enter**. Verify that the Start value is 0x4.

10. Type **reg import /?** and press **Enter** to view the import help information.

11. Type **reg import C:\SpoolerBak.reg** and press **Enter**.

12. Type **reg query HKLM\SYSTEM\CurrentControlSet\Services\Spooler** and press **Enter**. Verify that the Start value is 0x2 as it was restored from the backup.

13. Close the command prompt.

Windows PowerShell   In Windows 10, you can also use Windows PowerShell to view and modify registry values. This is important as administrators are more likely to create new scripts in Windows PowerShell than to create batch files and use reg.exe.

In Windows PowerShell, the registry is accessible similar to the file system. Both HKCU and HKLM are configured as drives. You can navigate through these drives by using *cd* and *dir*. However, these are actually aliases to the PowerShell cmdlets Set-Location and Get-ChildItem.

There is no built-in Windows PowerShell functionality to export or import a subtree of the registry to a .reg file. It can be done by a script, but it is significantly more complex than using regedit or reg.exe.

Activity 9-6: Viewing the Registry by Using Windows PowerShell

Time Required: 10 minutes
Objective: Use Windows PowerShell to view and modify registry entries

Description: If you need to query or modify the registry from a command line or batch file, you can use Windows PowerShell. In this activity, you view and modify registry entries by using Windows PowerShell.

1. If necessary, start your computer and sign in.

2. Click the **Start** button, type **powershell**, right-click **Windows PowerShell,** and click **Run as administrator.**

3. In the User Account Control dialog box, click **Yes**.

4. At the Windows PowerShell prompt, type **Get-PSDrive** and press **Enter**. You can see that HKCU and HKLM are available.

5. Type **Set-Location HKLM:** and press **Enter**. Notice that the prompt has changed to indicate you are in HKLM.

6. Type **Get-ChildItem** and press **Enter**. You can see the same registry keys as in regedit.

7. Type **Set-Location SYSTEM\CurrentControlSet\Services\Spooler** and press **Enter**.

8. Type **Get-ItemProperty .** and press **Enter**. The period in this command represents the current folder of Spooler. Notice that Start has a value of 2.

9. Type **Set-ItemProperty . -Name Start -Value 4** and press **Enter**.

10. Type **Get-ItemProperty .** and press **Enter**. Verify that Start has a value of 4.

11. Type **reg import C:\SpoolerBak.reg** and press **Enter**.

12. Close the Windows PowerShell prompt.

Installing Apps

There are multiple ways that apps can be packaged for deployment. The most common way traditional Win32 or .NET Framework apps are packaged is in an **.msi file**. This type of file is read by the Windows Installer service to perform the installation. The .msi file has all of the files for the app and instructions for file locations and registry keys.

For app developers, the Windows Installer service takes care of the details of app installation, repair, and removal. All the developers need to do is package the application properly.

Even though many apps have a setup.exe file, typically that setup.exe just starts the installation using an .msi file.

Some app developers do not use .msi files for their apps. Typically, you see this for small developers that want to do very simple deployment of their apps. These apps often lack repair functionality once they are installed. The installation and uninstallation are handled completely by the setup.exe file.

Automating .msi Installation

In a small organization, you can go to each computer and install apps manually on each computer. This process is typically faster than figuring out how to automate the process. However, in a larger organization, it is worth the time to identify how apps can be automatically deployed to computers. Even if it only takes 5 minutes to install an app, 5 minutes for 1000 computers is a long time.

The simplest automated deployment method is to create a batch file that does a silent install of the application. Many applications have a */q* or */quiet* option for the setup.exe file. You can configure the command to run *setup.exe /quiet* in a sign-in script. This is not very sophisticated, but can work for some simple scenarios.

There is also an msiexec.exe command-line utility, shown in Figure 9-4, which can be used with .msi files in a script. When you run msiexec.exe, you can specify a */quiet* option to suppress prompting users for input. If the app requires some input during installation, you can provide a transform file (.mst) that provides the additional information necessary for the app to install.

A more manageable way to deploy .msi-based applications in smaller environments is by using Group Policy. In Group Policy, you can deploy .msi-based apps to users or computers. If you deploy apps to users, the apps get installed on each computer that they use. If you deploy

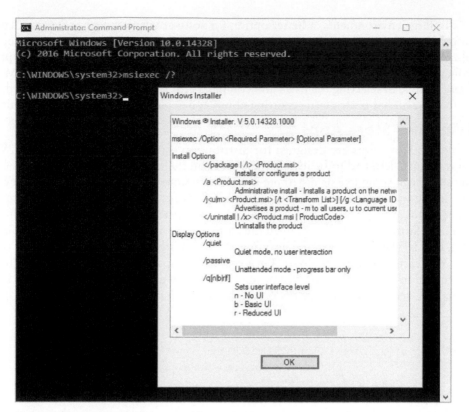

Figure 9-4   Msiexec.exe command-line utility

apps to computers, they are available to all users on that computer. Figure 9-5 shows the Group Policy setting for application deployment to a computer.

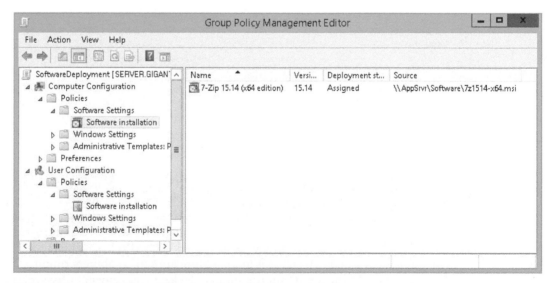

Figure 9-5   Group Policy settings for software deployment

Apps installed by Group Policy do not prompt the user for input. So, if the app typically requires user input, you need to create a transform file to provide the necessary information or repackage the app with the information already provided.

Apps are able to install even if the signed-in user does not have administrative permissions. This is because the Windows Installer service does the work and it has Local System privileges.

When you deploy software by using Group Policy, you can also update it afterwards by applying an .msp file to the application. Or, you can create a new version of the app and replace the existing version for upgrades.

In large environments, a better option for software deployment is System Center Configuration Manager. Configuration Manager has many other functions, but it also does software deployment. It is able to deploy both .msi-based apps and newer Windows Store apps. Like Group Policy, it can include transform files and do versioning. However, Configuration Manager is much more flexible in selecting the users and computers for which the apps are deployed. Configuration Manager also has centralized reporting about app deployment and can even monitor licensing.

Windows Store Apps

Windows Store apps are designed for distribution through the Windows Store. Windows Store apps are not designed to be installed manually in the same way traditional apps are. There is no option to run setup.exe or distribute a Windows Store app by using Group Policy.

If the app you want is in the Windows Store, users can install it from the Windows Store. However, it is not very manageable to instruct users to obtain apps directly from the Window Store. If you have obtained the **.appx** file for a Windows Store app, you can sideload the app, that is, install an app from a source other than the Windows Store, such as your workplace.

You can manually sideload Windows Store apps much more easily in Windows 10 than you could in Windows 8 and Windows 8.1. You can allow sideloading of apps in the Settings > Update & security > For developers screen, as shown in Figure 9-6.

Figure 9-6   Setting to enable sideloading

After sideloading is enabled, the certificate used to sign the Windows Store app must be trusted by the Windows 10 computer. If the app was signed by using a certificate from a public certification authority, no configuration is required. If the app was signed by using a self-signed certificate, that certificate needs to be imported on the computer running Windows 10 as a trusted root certification authority. Finally, you install the app by using the Add-AppxPackage cmdlet.

To automate the deployment of Windows Store apps to computers running Windows, you can use Configuration Manager. If you use mobile device management software, such as Microsoft Intune, you can deploy Windows Store apps to desktop computers, tablets, and phones.

Microsoft has also created a **Microsoft Store for Business**. Each business has its own private portal with approved Windows Store apps. This makes it much easier for users to find the correct apps than if users had to find the same apps in the Windows Store. The other benefit is that custom apps can be placed in the Microsoft Store for Business and installed without sideloading. The custom apps you place in the Microsoft Store for Business do not have to go through an approval process the way that apps for the Windows Store do.

Office 365 ProPlus

For some Office 365 licensing plans, Office 365 ProPlus is included for users. At the time of writing, Office 365 ProPlus has equivalent functionality to Microsoft Office Professional Plus 2016.

This is the full Microsoft Office suite that includes Word, PowerPoint, Excel, Outlook, OneNote, Publisher, Access, and Skype for Business.

For more information about Office 365 ProPlus, see *https://products.office.com/en-us/business/office-365-proplus-business-software.*

The volume licensed and retail versions of Microsoft Office are distributed as .msi files and can be installed by using the standard methods for .msi-based applications. Office 365 ProPlus is distributed in an entirely different way. Office 365 uses Click-to-Run for distribution.

Click-to-Run streams the installation of Office 365 ProPlus. This means that it delivers the critical components first and allows the users to begin using Office apps before installation is complete. This is important because Office 365 ProPlus is designed to be deployed by users from the Office 365 website.

The Click-to-Run deployment method is also responsible for deploying updates. When Office 365 ProPlus is updated in Office 365, those updates are streamed to clients when they start the apps.

When users install Office 365 ProPlus from the Office 365 website, there is no customization. All of the components are installed by default. If you need to limit components that are installed, you can use the Office Deployment Tool for Click-to-Run. This tool creates an XML file that can be used to limit the components that are installed. You can modify an existing installation of Office 365 ProPlus or download a local installation source so that users can access the initial installation files locally.

Licensing for Office 365 ProPlus is per user. Users have an account in Office 365 and they need to authenticate using their Office 365 every 30 days to keep the installation of Office 365 ProPlus active. This is an alternative to the traditional license key and activation process. At the time of writing, one user can install Office 365 ProPlus on up to 5 devices. This allows users to install Office 365 ProPlus on their work desktop, a mobile computer, and their home computer with a single license.

Package Management

Windows 10 is the first version of Windows to include a package management framework, named PackageManagement. Package management is a common feature in Linux distributions, but has not been found in Windows before. Package management, as a concept, differs from Windows Installer because it provides the ability to obtain software from a central repository.

There are several package managers, such as Chocolatey. The promise of package management is that you can identify a package to be installed from a repository and that package will be installed along with any required dependencies.

PackageManagement in Windows 10 integrates with package managers that already run on Windows by using providers. The end result is that you can use consistent Windows PowerShell cmdlets to access various package management systems and install apps.

At the time of writing, the package management functionality in Windows 10 is somewhat limited. It is suitable for testing and developers, but probably is not quite ready to be widely used as a deployment method in an organization.

You can get more information about PackageManagement at *http://blogs.technet.com/b/packagemanagement/archive/2015/04/29/introducing-packagemanagement-in-windows-10.aspx.*

App Compatibility

One of the primary concerns when planning a deployment of Windows 10 is application compatibility. The good news is that the vast majority of apps designed for Windows 7 and newer run properly on Windows 10. Most compatibility issues are for legacy apps created for Windows XP.

If you have older apps that do not run properly on Windows 10, the preferred option is to upgrade the app to a newer version that works properly. Unfortunately, some apps may not have an upgraded version. For example, a line-of-business application may have been custom developed many years ago and there is no easy alternative. If there is no path for upgrading, you need to explore alternate options for compatibility.

Compatibility Settings for Executables

Windows 10 includes some basic features for application compatibility that you can set when viewing the properties of an executable file, shown in Figure 9-7. Some of the common issues that can be addressed are:

- *Reliance on older Windows versions*—Some Windows apps specifically verify which version of Windows they are running on and do not run if the reported version is not recognized. For example, an app might look for Windows XP, Windows Vista, or Windows 7 as acceptable versions and not recognize Windows 10. To resolve this issue, you can set the compatibility mode as Windows Vista (RTM, Service Pack 1, or Service Pack 2), Windows 7, or Windows 8. When you set the compatibility mode, and an app queries the operating system version, the configured compatibility level is reported back to the app.

- *Display issues*—Many older apps were designed for smaller and lower-resolution displays. These apps don't display properly on newer displays with higher resolution and operating systems that expect higher color depth. Windows 10 can force the app to run in a 640×480 resolution window, eliminate scaling on high-resolution displays, and reduce color depth.

- *Reliance on administrator permissions*—Some apps require administrative permissions to run properly. This is due to poor programming practices by developers that require the user to write to privileged areas of the file system or the registry. In Windows 10, with User Access Control (UAC), even if you are an administrator of the local computer, apps are launched with standard user permissions unless a manifest file for the application indicates that the app requires elevated privileges. Older apps do not have this manifest file. However, you can specify that the apps need to run with elevated privileges by selecting the *Run this program as an administrator* option. The user still needs to be a local administrator on the computer.

Figure 9-7   Compatibility settings for an executable

If you are unsure of how to resolve compatibility issues for an application, you can run the compatibility troubleshooter. This wizard attempts to automatically detect the compatibility problem. If automatic detection fails, you can go through a wizard that asks you a series of questions to identify a likely resolution. After the wizard is complete, the settings selected are visible on the Compatibility tab and can be disabled there.

Activity 9-7: Configuring App Compatibility

Time Required: 10 minutes
Objective: Configure compatibility settings for an app

Description: Some older apps do not run properly in newer versions of Windows, including Windows 10. In this activity, you configure compatibility settings for an app.

1. If necessary, start your computer and sign in.
2. On the taskbar, click **File Explorer** and browse to **C:\Windows.**
3. In File Explorer, right-click **write,** click **Copy,** and close File Explorer.
4. Right-click the desktop and click **Paste.**
5. On the desktop, right-click **write** and click **Troubleshoot compatibility.**
6. In the Program Compatibility Troubleshooter, on the Select Troubleshooting screen, click **Troubleshoot program.**
7. On the What problems do you notice screen, select the **The program requires additional permissions** check box and click **Next.**
8. On the Test compatibility settings for the program screen, click **Test the program.**
9. In the User Account Control dialog box, click **Yes.** The UAC dialog box may be minimized on the taskbar. If so, click it to make it active.
10. Close WordPad.
11. In the Program Compatibility Troubleshooter, click **Next.**
12. On the Troubleshooting has completed screen, click **Yes, save these setting for this program.**
13. On the Troubleshooting has completed screen, click **Close.**
14. On the desktop, right-click **write** and click **Properties.**
15. In the write Properties window, click the **Compatibility** tab, verify that **Run this program as an administrator** is selected, and then click **Cancel.**

Application Compatibility Toolkit

To help identify and resolve app compatibility issues, the Windows 10 Assessment and Deployment Kit (ADK) includes the **Application Compatibility Toolkit (ACT).** This toolkit includes multiple components:

- *Application Compatibility Manager*—This is the administrative console, shown in Figure 9-8, that you use to control the overall discovery, collection, and analysis process for apps. This is the interface that you use to access information in the ACT database.

- *Inventory-collector package*—This package is deployed to the desktop computer to identify the apps that are installed. The results of the inventory are written to centralized file shares.

- *ACT Log Processing Service*—This service processes the logs collected from desktop computers and stores the information in the ACT database.

- *ACT database*—This is a Microsoft SQL Server database that stores information collected from desktop computers. It also stores compatibility information about apps. The Windows 10 ADK includes SQL Server 2012 Express for this purpose.

- *Microsoft Compatibility Exchange*—This is a web service that provides compatibility information that can be used by ACT and incorporated into the ACT database. This is how information shared by other companies is provided to you.

- *Runtime-analysis package*—This package is deployed to computers in your test environment to monitor compatibility when running apps. The Compatibility Monitor tool is included in the package for this purpose. You can also use Compatibility Monitor to send a compatibility database to Microsoft.

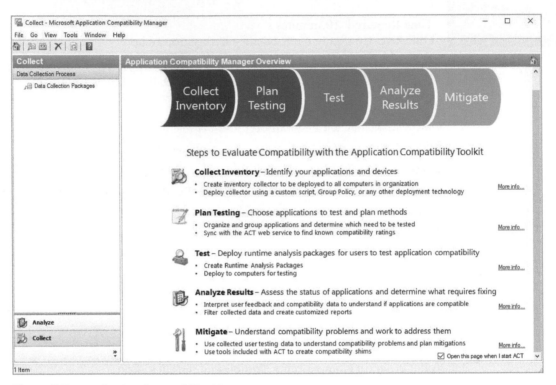

Figure 9-8   Application Compatibility Manager

Identifying App Compatibility Issues

The overall process for using ACT is to first take an inventory of your applications. This list of apps can then be compared with the information in ACT to identify if there are any known compatibility issues. If there are compatibility issues, you can identify whether there are known methods to mitigate the problems.

If you have custom applications, you can use Compatibility Monitor to help identify whether they have problems running on Windows 10. Compatibility Monitor replaces a number of specialized tools available in older versions of ACT. To use Compatibility Monitor, just start it and let it collect information while you use the apps. Data collected by Compatibility Monitor is uploaded to a share where it is incorporated into the ACT database.

Mitigating App Compatibility Issues

If you find problems with application compatibility, the preferred option is to either fix a custom application or upgrade prepackaged applications. However, for some popular applications there may be known ways to mitigate issues included in ACT. Compatibility Administrator can be used to generate a compatibility-fix database of apps fixes that can be applied to computers.

In some cases, compatibility issues with custom apps can be resolved by using the Standard User Analyzer (SUA). This tool included with Compatibility Monitor is used to closely monitor the activity of a single app and provide a resolution for problems if possible. SUA also generates a compatibility-fix database.

To apply a compatibility database (.sdb) to multiple computers, you can use sdbinst.exe. This tool can be scripted and run at sign-in or by a software management tool such as Configuration Manager.

Client Hyper-V

If an app is not compatible with Windows 10 and there is no way to mitigate the issue, you need to run an older operating system to keep using that application. For example, if all users are being upgraded to a 64-bit version of Windows 10, another operating system is required to support a legacy 16-bit Windows app. Although it is possible to maintain an older physical computer for the purpose of running the older app, that older computer will be prone to failure over time.

Client Hyper-V is virtualization software for Windows 10. It allows you to create virtual machines with a completely independent operating system that shares the hardware on the computer running Windows 10. In the virtual machine, you can install the required operating system and application.

More details about Client Hyper-V are provided in Chapter 12, Client Hyper-V.

The potential downsides to using Client Hyper-V are:

- There is no easy way to move data from the virtual machine to the host computer.
- The operating system in the virtual machine still needs to be managed with software updates and any other management considerations.
- Some users find it confusing to use a separate virtual machine for some tasks.

Virtual Desktop Infrastructure and RemoteApp

Windows Server can host and provide access to virtual desktops. This functionality is provided by **Remote Desktop Services**. There are several variations, but for all of them, the application runs on a computer and the Remote Desktop Protocol (RDP) is used to access the visual information for the app. By running the app on a remote computer, any application issues on the local computer are avoided.

More details about Remote Desktop Services are provided later in this chapter.

App-V

Application Virtualization (App-V) is a technology that both deploys and manages apps. Instead of a standard installation, apps are streamed to computers and can begin executing before all of the app files are on the destination computer. Updates are never installed directly on the client computers. Instead, the source app is updated and the updates stream to the clients. This is similar to how Office 365 ProPlus is distributed because the Click-to-Run functionality for Office 365 ProPlus is based on App-V.

Apps distributed by using App-V run in a virtualized environment within the operating system. From a user perspective, the app appears to be installed like a normal application, but conflicts with other applications running on the computer are avoided. You can use App-V to resolve compatibility conflicts when two apps cannot both be installed on the same computer. However, the apps must still be compatible with the operating system.

Remote Desktop Services

The Remote Desktop Services role in Windows Server provides a way to run apps on a remote server or virtual machine and have the display appear on the local computer. This way, users can run apps without ever installing them on their local computer. This system can be used when there are app compatibility concerns, but more often, it is used to provide remote access to apps.

The RDP protocol used by Remote Desktop Services is very efficient. This makes it feasible to provide access to remote desktops and apps over the Internet, even over public Wi-Fi. This provides flexibility to use apps from anywhere and on any device that has an RDP client. Microsoft provides Remote Desktop clients for not only Windows, but also iOS and Android devices.

Remote Desktop Services can provide two types of virtual desktops:

- *Session-based virtual desktops*—This type of virtual desktop is hosted on a Remote Desktop Session Host (RD Session Host). A single RD Session Host is shared by multiple users at one time. When the users connect, they each get their own independent desktop and run their own applications. However, the core operating system services are shared, which allows many users to share the same server.

- *Virtual machine-based virtual desktops*—This type of virtual desktop is hosted on a Windows server running Hyper-V. Each user has an independent virtual machine with a completely independent operating system. The hardware of the server is shared among the virtual machines, but each virtual machine is independent. This type of virtual desktop has lower density than session-based virtual desktops.

RemoteApp

In addition to virtual desktops, there is also **RemoteApp**. RemoteApp still uses either session-based virtual desktops or virtual machine-based virtual desktops to execute apps, but the user interface is different. Users open a RemoteApp running on a virtual desktop and it behaves like a regular application. The window is only for that application. For most users, this is a simpler interface and easier to understand.

Microsoft also has a cloud-based version of RemoteApp named **Windows Azure RemoteApp**. For Windows Azure RemoteApp, you configure your application on a server managed by Microsoft in a Microsoft data center. Then, you and your users can access the app over the Internet. It avoids the need for you to set up your own infrastructure for RemoteApp.

Accessing Virtual Desktops and RemoteApp

Unlike older virtual desktop solutions like Terminal Services, you do not directly access an RD Session Host. In a properly configured and highly available solution, the clients connect by using a Remote Desktop Web Access (RD Web Access) server or the RemoteApp and Desktop Connections client.

The RD Web Access server provides a website where users authenticate. After the users authenticate, they see the RemoteApp programs and virtual desktops to which they have been given access. Users click the RemoteApp program or virtual desktop that they want to access, and Remote Desktop Connection is launched to access it.

RemoteApp and Desktop Connections is included in Windows 7 or newer to access RemoteApp programs and virtual desktops hosted by Remote Desktop Services. This client reads the list of RemoteApp programs and virtual desktops by accessing a web feed URL on the RD Web Access server. The web feed URL is *https://<servername>/RDWeb/Feed/webfeed.aspx,* where *<servername>* is the host name of the RD Web Access server.

There are three ways to configure RemoteApp and Desktop Connections with the URL for the web feed:

- *Manually enter the URL*—You can provide users with instruction on how to configure the URL the first time they start it. This solution is not very scalable and runs the risk of users making typing errors, but it is simple to implement.

- *Use Group Policy*—You can configure the URL in a Group Policy Object at \User Configuration\Policies\Administrative Templates\Windows Components\Remote Desktop Services\RemoteApp and Desktop Connections. If all of your computers are domain joined, this is a fast way to configure all of them in a single step.

- *Based on email address*—The initial configuration for RemoteApp and Desktop Connections can use a DNS record based on an email address provided by the user. For the domain of the email address, RemoteApp and Desktop Connections looks for an _rdac TXT record. The value of that record is the URL for the web feed. This solution requires users to initiate it, but works for internal and external users.

RemoteApp and Desktop Connections refreshes data from the web feed only once per day. It can be refreshed manually if required.

The wizard for configuring RemoteApp and Desktop Connections prompts for either a URL or email address, as shown in Figure 9-9. Based on this information, the wizard connects with the web feed and downloads the list of RemoteApp programs and virtual desktops that the user has access to.

At the time of writing, Microsoft provided a quick tour option to quickly try out Azure RemoteApp by using a Microsoft account. The following activity is based on that option. If the website has changed, identify the steps necessary to try out Azure RemoteApp in the new configuration.

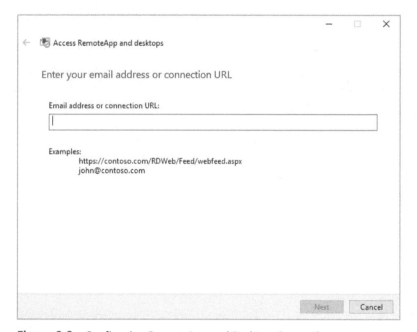

Figure 9-9   Configuring RemoteApp and Desktop Connections

Activity 9-8: Using Azure RemoteApp

Time Required: 10 minutes

Objective: Implement a password policy that applies to local users

Description: Azure RemoteApp is a cloud-based solution from Microsoft for accessing apps. These apps in Azure RemoteApp can be accessed from anywhere in the world and you do not need to worry about how to properly secure it. In this activity, you access a demo of Azure RemoteApp by using a Microsoft account.

This activity relies on a public webpage provided by Microsoft that may change over time. If the expected webpage is not available, a web search should provide a similar trial or tour webpage.

1. If necessary, start your computer and sign in.

2. On the taskbar, click **Microsoft Edge**.

3. In the Search or enter web address box, type **https://www.remoteapp.windowsazure.com/ en/tour.aspx** and press **Enter**.

4. On the Try Azure RemoteApp Now page, under 2 minute demo, click **Download the client**.

5. On the Download now page, click **Download for Windows**.

6. In the Application Install – Security Warning window, click **Install** and wait for the client to download.

7. In the Azure RemoteApp window, click **Get Started**.

8. On the Microsoft Azure screen, sign in using your Microsoft account.

9. On the Azure RemoteApp screen, click **Start free trial**.

10. In the Azure RemoteApp window, shown in Figure 9-10, double-click **Word 2013**. Word 2013 has opened on your computer, but it actually is running in the Microsoft data center.

11. Take a few minutes to explore other applications.

12. Close all open windows.

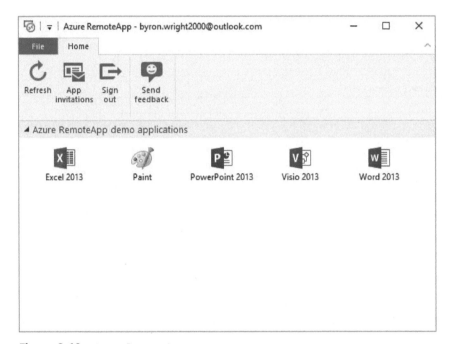

Figure 9-10 Azure RemoteApp

 To enhance the security of RemoteApp, you can digitally sign the .rdp configuration files. For more information see *https://technet.microsoft.com/en-us/library/cc754499(v=ws.11).aspx*.

Chapter Summary

- Windows 10 supports running apps by providing various application environments. You can run Win32, Win64, .NET Framework, and Windows Store apps.

- The registry is a central store of configuration information for apps and the operating system. It is composed of hives that contain registry keys and values. Two commonly accessed hives are HKCU and HKLM.

- To edit the registry, you can use the graphical Registry Editor, reg.exe, or Windows PowerShell cmdlets. Before editing the registry, you should export the keys so that you can restore them if required.

- An .msi-based app is installed by the Windows Installer service. You can automate installation of .msi-based apps by using Group Policy or Configuration Manager.

- Installation of Windows Store apps on desktop computers can be automated by using Configuration Manager. For phones, tablets, and non-domain-joined computers, you can automate deployment by using mobile device management software, such as Microsoft Intune. The Microsoft Store for Business is a customizable website that you can use to provide your users with access only to specific apps.

- Office 365 ProPlus installs by using a new technology called Click-to-Run. PackageManagement is a new package management framework that is similar to package management implemented on Linux.

- Windows 10 provides some basic functionality for resolving app compatibility issues. However, you can also use ACT, Client Hyper-V, Remote Desktop Services, and App-V.

- Remote Desktop Services provides access to virtual desktops and RemoteApp programs. A virtual desktop is a complete desktop with applications. RemoteApp provides access to only an app in a single window. Azure RemoteApp is cloud-based infrastructure to provide access to RemoteApp programs.

Key Terms

.appx file A file for installing a Windows Store app.

.msi file An app packaged for installation by the Windows Installer service.

.NET Framework A commonly required application environment for Windows apps. It is available in multiple versions.

Application Compatibility Toolkit (ACT) A collection of tools to identify and resolve app compatibility issues. It is included in the Windows 10 ADK.

application environment subsystem A software layer that exists between apps and the operating system to simplify app development.

application programming interface (API) The interface used by a program to request services from the application environment, which in turn interfaces with the operating system to provide those services.

Application Virtualization (App-V) A technology that deploys applications by streaming and isolates them in a virtual environment.

Click-to-Run A new streaming installation technology that is used to deploy Office 365 ProPlus.

Client Hyper-V A feature in Windows 10 that allows you to run virtual machines.

hive A discrete body of registry keys and values stored in files as part of the operating system.

Microsoft Store for Business A customizable online store for businesses to organize Windows Store apps for their users.

registry A central store for application and operating system configuration information in Windows 10.

Registry Editor The graphical tool included in Windows 10 to edit the registry. Commonly known as regedit.

registry key A section within a hive that can contain other registry keys and values.

RemoteApp A feature in Remote Desktop Services that presents clients with a single app in a window.

Remote Desktop Services A server role for Windows Server that is used to provide virtual desktops and RemoteApp programs to users.

Win32 Applications designed to run in a Windows 32-bit instruction environment.

Win64 Applications designed to run in a Windows 64-bit instruction environment.

Windows Azure RemoteApp A cloud-based environment hosted by Microsoft that allows you to provide your own applications through RemoteApp.

Windows on Windows 64 (WOW64) A system in Windows that allows 32-bit Windows apps to run on a 64-bit operating system.

Windows Store apps The newest application environment that is designed to be cross platform with phones, tablets, and desktop computers.

Review Questions

1. Which types of apps are not supported by a 64-bit edition of Windows 10? (Choose all that apply.)

   a. DOS

   b. Win16

   c. Win32

   d. Win64

   e. .NET Framework

2. Which registry hive is used to store global information about apps regardless of the user who is signed in?

   a. HKEY_CLASSES_ROOT

   b. HKEY_CURRENT_USER

   c. HKEY_LOCAL_MACHINE

   d. HKEY_DYN_DATA

   e. HKEY_GLOBAL_CONFIG

3. On a 64-bit version of Windows 10, where are 32-bit apps typically installed?

   a. C:\Program Files

   b. C:\Windows\SysWOW64

   c. C:\Program Files (WOW64)

   d. C:\Program Files (x86)

   e. C:\Windows\WOW64

4. Which versions of .NET Framework are included with Windows 10? (Choose all that apply.)

   a. .NET Framework 1.1

   b. .NET Framework 2.0

   c. .NET Framework 3.5

   d. .NET Framework 4.0

   e. .NET Framework 4.6

5. All Windows Store apps are universal apps. True or False?

6. You can use a 32-bit version of Windows 10 to run legacy Win16 apps. True or False?

7. Which registry hive contains settings that are imported from ntuser.dat?

   a. HKEY_CLASSES_ROOT

   b. HKEY_CURRENT_USER

   c. HKEY_LOCAL_MACHINE

   d. HKEY_DYN_DATA

   e. HKEY_GLOBAL_CONFIG

8. Which tools or methods can you use to import a .reg file? (Choose all that apply.)

   a. Registry Editor (regedit)

   b. regimp.exe

   c. reg.exe

   d. double-clicking the .reg file in File Explorer

   e. Import-Registry

9. You can automate installation of Window Store apps by using Group Policy. True or False?

10. Which types of apps can be deployed by using Configuration Manager? (Choose all that apply.)

    a. .msi

    b. .appv

    c. Click-to-Run

    d. .NET Framework

    e. .appx

11. Which cmdlet do you use to sideload Windows Store apps?

    a. Add-AppxPackage

    b. Install-WinApp

    c. Install-WinStoreApp

    d. Add-WinApp

    e. New-Sideload

12. Office 365 ProPlus never receives updates through Windows Update. True or False?

13. Which compatibility issues can be fixed for an app by using the capabilities included in Windows 10? (Choose all that apply.)

    a. wrong version of .NET Framework

    b. a version check to verify that the app is running on Windows XP

    c. poor display quality on full screen when the screen resolution is 1920×1024

    d. required to right-click and run as administrator

    e. odd colors when the color depth is greater than 16-bit

14. Which ACT tool is used to deploy compatibility fixes to computers?

    a. ACT database

    b. Microsoft Compatibility Exchange

    c. Runtime-analysis package

    d. fixinst.exe

    e. sdbinst.exe

15. If you have a computer running a 64-bit version of Windows 10 with Client Hyper-V, it is possible to run a 16-bit Windows app in a virtual machine. True or False?

16. Which of the following are true about App-V? (Choose all that apply.)

    a. Apps are streamed for installation.

    b. RDP is used to access the app.

    c. Virtual environments prevent conflicts between apps.

    d. Virtual environments allow a 16-bit app to be run on a 64-bit operating system.

    e. Apps are updated when the source on the server is updated.

17. Microsoft Store for Business contains Azure RemoteApp programs. True or False?

18. Which three methods can you use to configure RemoteApp and Desktop Connections with the URL of the web feed? (Choose all that apply.)

    a. Manually enter the URL during configuration.

    b. Create a CNAME record in DNS that includes the URL and have users enter their email address during configuration.

    c. Configure a Group Policy Object with the correct URL.

    d. Create a TXT record in DNS that includes the URL and have users enter their email address during configuration.

    e. Package an .msi file with the correct configuration information.

9

19. Which Remote Desktop Services role can users sign in to for access to RemoteApps and virtual desktops?

   a. RD Session Host

   b. Terminal Server

   c. RD Session Broker

   d. RD Virtualization Host

   e. RD Web Access

20. Which PowerShell cmdlet is used to modify a registry key value?

   a. Set-ItemProperty

   b. Set-RegKeyValue

   c. Set-ChildItem

   d. Set-LocationValue

   e. Set-ChildItemValue

Case Projects

Case Project 9-1: Application Compatibility

Gigantic Life Insurance has thousands of desktop computers running a wide variety of apps. You are planning to deploy Windows 10, but first you need to ensure that all of your applications are compatible with Windows 10. Which tool should you use to identify compatibility issues and potentially remediate issues?

Case Project 9-2: Remote Access to Apps

Hyperactive Media now has over 40 salespeople on the road meeting with customers. The salespeople currently have laptops with locally installed apps. However, this means that salespeople need to come back to the office and transfer sales orders from their laptops to the central order system. Describe how salespeople could be given remote access to this system by using RemoteApp. Are there any concerns about using RemoteApp?

chapter 10

Performance Tuning and System Recovery

After reading this chapter and completing the exercises, you will be able to:

- Describe performance tuning concepts
- Use Performance Monitor
- Use Task Manager
- Configure Performance Options
- Describe tools that you can use for troubleshooting errors in Windows 10
- Describe backup and recovery of user data using File History, Backup and Restore (Windows 7), and OneDrive
- Describe recovery options for an unstable Windows 10 computer using recovery disks, Windows Recovery, device driver rollback, system restore points, and System Reset

On most Windows 10 computers, the default configuration provides acceptable performance. When users run applications, the applications respond quickly. When users access files, the files open quickly. However, on some systems, over time performance can start to deteriorate. Performance tuning lets you optimize the performance of Windows 10 to function at acceptable standards. However, poor performance and improper operations might not simply be a matter of tweaking the system; problems might have appeared that require corrective actions to remedy.

In this chapter, you begin by learning about the performance tuning process and how Performance Monitor allows you to find system bottlenecks. Additionally, you learn how to use Task Manager and optimize system performance. If you recognize that the problems are significant enough to require a repair of the Windows system, this chapter investigates your options—including recovering old versions of data and application components, or ultimately repairing or replacing the total Windows operating system.

Performance Tuning Overview

Performance tuning is a process rather than an event. In an ideal world, an effective performance tuning process is initiated well before problems occur. However, in most cases, performance tuning is not even considered until a performance problem exists.

The performance tuning process consists of:

- Establishing a baseline
- Recognizing bottlenecks
- Tuning performance

Establishing a Baseline

To recognize system **bottlenecks**, you must first establish a baseline that defines normal performance. A **baseline** is a set of performance indicators captured when system performance is acceptable. The values of baseline performance indicators are compared with future values of performance indicators to isolate performance problems.

Windows 10, like previous versions of Windows, is capable of reporting on a wide variety of performance indicators. Performance indicators are often called **counters** because they display values for system characteristics. Some examples of counters are:

- % Processor Time
- Disk Read Byte/sec
- Memory: Available Mbytes
- IPv4: Datagrams/sec

When you establish a baseline, it is important to ensure that you are measuring the normal state of the performance indicators. If unusual activity is occurring, the baseline performance measurement is not valid, and it will be difficult to use the baseline to identify abnormal activity in the future.

To ensure that you are measuring the normal state when establishing a baseline, you should:

- Verify that no unusual activity is happening on the workstation. For example, ensure that no applications are performing large queries to databases or processing batch jobs, unless that is the normal state of the computer.

- Measure performance indicators over time. By measuring performance indicators over time, you can see an average value for the indicators. Average values are less volatile and more accurate than measuring with snapshots of short duration.

Recognizing Bottlenecks

A bottleneck occurs when a limitation in a single computer system component slows down the entire system. For any application, there is always one component in the computer system that is the limiting factor for performance. This component is the bottleneck. Performance tuning attempts to eliminate bottlenecks.

The bottleneck for each activity you perform and each application that you run may be different. For example, a database application may require fast access to the hard drive, and disk drives are a common bottleneck. A 3-D rendering program may experience limited processing power as the most common bottleneck. The most common bottlenecks to system performance are in the areas of disk, memory, processor, or the network.

Disk Bottlenecks   Disk bottlenecks occur when Windows 10 and running applications want to read and write information to the physical disk in the system faster than the disk can manage. For desktop computers running Windows 10, disk bottlenecks are not that common.

If required, disk performance can be increased in a few different ways:

- *Upgrade the disks*—Disks are rated for certain speeds of data transfer. Electromechanical hard drives that spin the disk faster typically perform faster. The rotations per minute (RPM) is a good indicator of expected performance. A 5400 RPM drive (typically used in laptop computers) performs slower than a 7200 RPM drive, but the reduced performance reduces noise, cost, heat generation, and power usage. To avoid the mechanical latency concerns, solid-state drives (SSDs) are now readily available and have no moving parts. SSDs are more expensive but are also much faster than mechanical drives.

- *Implement mirrored Storage Spaces*—Mirrored Storage Spaces volumes (see Chapter 4, Managing Disks and File Systems) increase read and write performance by spreading data manipulation tasks across multiple drives.

- *Move the paging file to a nonsystem disk*—By default, the paging file, which is accessed often by the system, resides on the same disk as the operating system files, which are also accessed often by the system. Putting the paging file on a different disk (not just a different partition) can increase performance by reducing the data manipulation that any one disk needs to perform.

Memory Bottlenecks   Most memory bottlenecks occur when the applications you are running require more memory than is physically available in the computer. This forces Windows 10 to use virtual memory to accommodate the memory requirements of all the running applications. Virtual memory is a system whereby memory is simulated on disk with a paging file. The least used memory areas are stored in the paging file. When information in the paging file is required, it is taken out of the paging file and placed in physical memory.

Accessing information from disk is much slower than accessing information from physical memory. Reducing the need for virtual memory can significantly improve system performance. You can recognize when virtual memory is being heavily used by a high volume of disk activity.

To reduce the use of virtual memory:

- *Increase the amount of physical memory*—Adding physical memory to a computer allows more information to be kept in physical memory, which reduces the need for virtual memory.

- *Run fewer applications at once*—If you are running multiple applications, more information is kept in memory. Reducing the number of applications running at the same time reduces the amount of memory used and, consequently, the need for virtual memory.

If there is heavy utilization of the paging file, moving the paging file to a faster disk such as an SSD can improve performance. Windows 10 also allows some USB drives to be used for ReadyBoost. ReadyBoost uses a USB drive as a memory cache similar to a paging file. The USB drive is faster than a mechanical disk, but offers no performance improvement when an SSD is being used.

Processor Bottlenecks   A processor bottleneck occurs when there is too much work for a processor to do. In a computer with one single-core processor, the computer can only work on one task at a time. To run multiple applications and perform system tasks, the processor switches between the required tasks very quickly to give the illusion of all activities happening at the same time. When too many tasks must be performed, or an individual task requires too much processor time, the processor becomes a bottleneck.

To resolve a processor bottleneck:

- *Change to a faster processor*—Processor performance is traditionally measured by clock speed. When comparing processors with the same architecture, a processor with a higher clock speed can perform more work in a given time frame.

- *Add additional processors*—Some computers are capable of containing multiple physical processors. Windows 10 Professional and Windows 10 Enterprise can support more than one physical processor. Windows 10 Home can support only one. Having multiple processors means that tasks can be completed more quickly because the computer can work on multiple tasks at the same time. Be aware that two processors are not twice as fast as a single processor because some inefficiency is introduced when the system coordinates the activity of two processors.

- *Change to a multicore processor*—Many processors are now multicore, which effectively means there are multiple processing centers on a single chip. A common two-, four-, or six-core processor increases processing capacity with more effectiveness than simply adding a single, faster processor.

The motherboard in a computer supports a limited range of processors. In most cases, it is not practical to upgrade only the processor. A new motherboard is also required.

Network Bottlenecks   Network bottlenecks are more common for servers than computers running Windows 10. In the rare circumstance where the network is simply too slow, you can replace the existing network with a faster system. For example, if an old 100 Mbps network is slowing down file sharing between computers, you could replace it with a 1 Gbps network system. This might involve replacing network cards, cabling, and switches. Note that the slowest networking component between two systems determines the fastest speed that the two computers can communicate with each other. It is common that the maximum speed of a network connection (for example, 1 Gbps) is not fully realized because there are overhead and random delays that use up some of the network's capacity to carry data. A 1 Gbps network connection might end up limited to around 800 Mbps of effective data transfer, which is not a bottleneck; it is expected because of administrative and operational overhead on the data stream. As wireless networks become more common at home, problems with wireless performance may have less to do with the local computer and more to do with the networking equipment's age, component position, and local interference.

Tuning Performance

The process for performance tuning is consistent regardless of the problems being experienced. In each case, you perform the following steps:

1. Create a baseline for the computer.

2. Compare the baseline with current performance indicators.

3. Identify possible causes for variations from the baseline.

4. Identify possible fixes for variations from the baseline.

5. Select a fix to implement.

6. Implement the fix and monitor for changes.

7. If the problem is not resolved, undo the fix and repeat Step 5.

8. If the problem is resolved, document the solution for future reference.

When selecting a fix to implement, you should take into account the time involved and the likelihood that the fix will resolve the problem. Sometimes, it is better to attempt several simple fixes, even if they are less likely to fix the problem, before attempting a complex fix that is likely to solve the problem.

Documentation during the performance tuning process is essential. As you attempt each fix, you should document the changes you are making. This allows you to undo each fix before you try the next one.

Monitoring Performance

Performance Monitor is an MMC snap-in that is used to monitor system performance indicators. The utility should be run by a user signed in as an administrator or the equivalent. The utility is commonly called *perfmon* by experienced administrators because it can be started from the command line by running perfmon.exe or starting the snap-in itself, perfmon.msc, from Administrative Tools in Control Panel or by manually adding it to a custom MMC console. Performance Monitor is an advanced system tool that is used by system administrators looking at low-level performance of a computer and is not commonly used for day-to-day operations. You can use Performance Monitor, as shown in Figure 10-1, to generate a baseline and find system bottlenecks. The first screen of Performance Monitor displays a system summary using text to summarize simple counters. Resource Monitor runs as a process spawned by Performance Monitor when you click the Open Resource Monitor link shown in Figure 10-1.

10

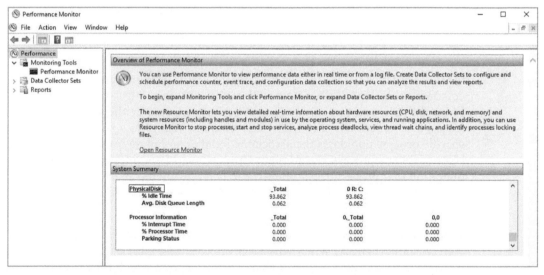

Figure 10-1   Performance Monitor

Resource Monitor

Resource Monitor, shown in Figure 10-2, provides real-time monitoring of the most common system performance indicators. Key performance indicators are also summarized in graphs at the side of the screen. The performance indicators are listed as tabs under the main menu for each system area that is monitored: CPU, Disk, Network, Memory. The displayed charts and summaries are updated in real time while monitoring is active. The screen data continuously updates itself, making it hard to read the data at times. Monitoring can be stopped and restarted to freeze the displayed values. Individual processes can be selected or sorted by column to help organize the view. Each tab's summary bars can be opened to display additional information about a specific system area. Note that the performance counters referenced in Resource Monitor are only a few key counters. Many more counters are available for advanced review and analysis in the Performance Monitor tool.

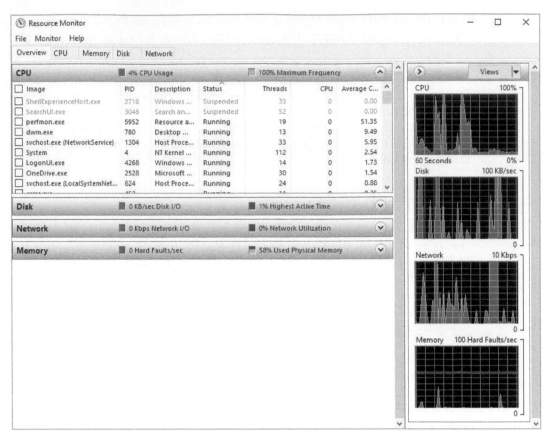

Figure 10-2 Resource Monitor

CPU The CPU area is used to monitor processor performance and determine whether the processor is a bottleneck. When you select the CPU tab, a list of running processes is displayed. From this tab, you can sort the list of active processes by their CPU activity, threads spawned, status, and process ID (PID). The PID uniquely identifies a single running process. Selecting a specific process populates the associated handles and modules summary sections accordingly. By right-clicking a process, the administrator can pause, resume, or stop the process. By toggling the operation of a process, the administrator can quickly test its net effect on the computer's performance. Note that toggling a single process can cause instability, so this advanced feature should be used carefully.

Disk The Disk area is used to monitor disk performance and determine whether the disk subsystem is a bottleneck. When you select the Disk tab, a list of processes performing disk activity is displayed. The Processes with Disk Activity reports which processes have had disk activity in the last 60 seconds. The Storage section reports overall activity of each storage location, organized by logical disk. Each logical disk reports the physical disk it is on, the percentage of time that disk is active, space usage, and the number of disk operations waiting to be completed in the disk queue. A high disk queue length is usually indicative of a disk subsystem that is overwhelmed or experiencing technical issues.

Network The Network area is used to monitor network performance and determine whether the network subsystem is a bottleneck. The Network tab displays additional information about network activity and the endpoints that are generating traffic or are capable of receiving network data. TCP connection details are provided and include statistics about packet loss and latency in milliseconds between a listed local and remote address. Heavy packet losses or high latency is a sign that the network connection is oversaturated or experiencing faults somewhere between the two addresses.

Memory   The Memory area is used to monitor memory performance and determine whether the memory subsystem is a bottleneck. The Memory tab displays additional information in a graphical form detailing how portions of memory have been allocated. The quick view can help an administrator get a general awareness of the current memory demands.

Activity 10-1: Using Resource Monitor

Time Required: 5 minutes
Objective: Use the Resource Monitor tool launched from the Performance Monitor utility

Description: The Resource Monitor utility launched from Performance Monitor gives you a quick snapshot of what is happening on your system with regard to the CPU, disk, network, and memory. In this activity, you use Resource Monitor.

1. If necessary, start your computer and sign in.

2. Right-click the **Start** button and click **Control Panel**.

3. Click **System and Security** and click **Administrative Tools**.

4. Double-click **Performance Monitor**.

5. If necessary, click **Performance** at the top of the left-hand navigation pane to display the Overview of Performance Monitor and System Summary sections in the right-hand pane.

6. Click the **Open Resource Monitor** link in the Overview of Performance Monitor section.

7. Click the **Overview** tab if it is not already selected. Review the graphs at the right side of the screen for CPU, Disk, Network, and Memory.

8. Expand the **CPU** summary bar if it is not already expanded and review the listed processes in the Image column. Review the column information available for each process.

9. Click the **CPU** column header, so that there is a down arrow in the header just to the left of the column title. This sorts the processes from highest to lowest based on their current CPU utilization. If you click again, the sort order is reversed.

10. Collapse the **CPU** summary bar and expand the **Disk** summary bar. Read the information about each process. This area provides disk usage information for each process running on the system.

11. Collapse the **Disk** summary bar and expand the **Network** summary bar. Read the information about each process. This area provides network usage information for each process running on the system.

12. Collapse the **Network** summary bar and expand the **Memory** summary bar. Read the information about each process. This area provides memory usage information for each process running on the system.

13. Close all open windows.

Performance Monitor

Performance Monitor, shown in Figure 10-3, is a tool within the Performance Monitor utility that allows you to visually display the data generated by counters. For each counter that is monitored, you can view the last, average, minimum, and maximum values. These values are based on the total time that the counter has been monitored.

Counters   Unlike Resource Monitor, Performance Monitor allows you to select the individual counters you want to view. This helps you to focus monitoring on a specific operating system element. In some cases, after finding a general problem by using Resource Monitor, you might want to find more detailed information by using the Performance Monitor counters.

10

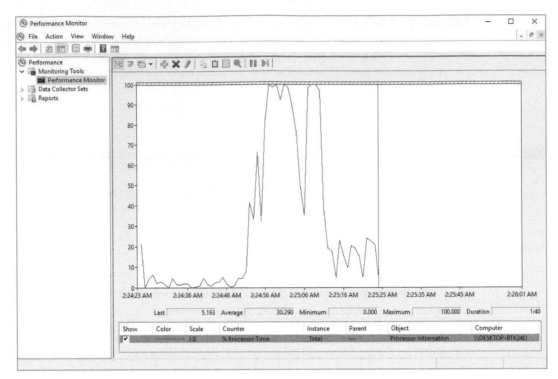

Figure 10-3 Performance Monitor tool

When you add a counter, it can be from the local computer or another computer available over the network. In most cases, you will monitor the local computer. However, some counters should be monitored over the network to prevent monitoring from affecting the validity of the data. For example, if you are logging disk activity, you should monitor it over the network to ensure that the logging process itself is not creating disk activity that affects your results.

Counters are divided into categories. Common counter categories include processor, memory, physical disk, TCPv4, system, and logical disk. Many other categories are also available that offer specialized counters of interest.

For each counter, there may be multiple instances of that counter to choose from. For example, in a computer with multiple processors, each processor is an instance. This allows you to monitor the information about each processor separately or you can choose to view a combined total for all processor instances. Selecting a counter to display will display information about that counter's collected data as a chart type.

Chart Types   Three different chart types are available for viewing performance data:

- *Line*—Displays a line for each selected counter. Each line is displayed in a different color to help distinguish them. This chart type allows you to visualize performance over time. This is the default chart type.

- *Histogram bar*—Displays a vertical bar for the current value of each performance counter. This chart type is useful for comparing similar types of counters with each other at the same time.

- *Report*—Displays the current value of each performance counter in decimal format. This is useful when you want to see the exact value of a performance counter rather than compare it with other performance counters.

Activity 10-2: Using Performance Monitor

Time Required: 10 minutes
Objective: Use Performance Monitor to view counter values

Description: Performance Monitor allows you to view the value of performance counters. You can choose to display the values in several different formats. The counters allow you to monitor system performance. In this activity, you use Performance Monitor to view system activity.

1. If necessary, start your computer and sign in.
2. Right-click the **Start** button and click **Control Panel**.
3. Click **System and Security** and click **Administrative Tools**.
4. Double-click **Performance Monitor**.
5. If necessary, in the left pane, expand **Monitoring Tools** and click **Performance Monitor**. You can see that by default % Processor Time is displayed. The default report type shown is a line chart.
6. In the toolbar, click the **plus** symbol.
7. In the list of Available counters, expand **PhysicalDisk** and click **% Disk Time**. This counter monitors how often the disk is busy.
8. In the Instances of selected object box, click **<All instances>**. This selects disk 0 for monitoring. If multiple disks were present in this computer, multiple instances would be listed.
9. Select the **Show description** check box to enable it. This displays a description of each counter as you select it.
10. Click **Add**.
11. In the list of Available counters, expand **Memory** and click **Available MBytes**. This counter monitors how much physical memory is free for use by processes.
12. Click **Add** and click **OK**. Notice that new lines are added to the graph. The graph is scaled from 0 to 100, but the new counters might provide values outside that range.
13. At the bottom of the screen, click **% Disk Time** for the Instance _Total. The Last, Average, Minimum, and Maximum values now reflect what has been measured for % Disk Time. Note the average value. A small value here might not register on the scrolling line graph. A scale value adjusts the counter values to better fit in the graph range from 0 to 100. The default scale value is 1.
14. Right-click **% Disk Time** and click **Properties**. Select a new color for the counter's displayed line that will be easy to see and differentiate from the other counters.
15. Click the **Scale** drop-down list, select **10.0** to multiply all counter values for this counter by 10 before displaying them on the line graph, and then click **OK**.
16. At the bottom of the screen, right-click **Available MBytes** and click **Scale Selected Counters**. This automatically changes the scale used to measure the counter. The line for this counter was previously at the very top of the chart and did not provide useful information.
17. In the toolbar, click the **Change graph type** button. This changes the graph to a bar chart.
18. Click the **Change graph type** button again. This changes the graph to a report.
19. In the left pane, right-click **Performance Monitor** and click **Properties**. Notice that on the General tab, you can modify the graph sample rate and the time span that is displayed.
20. Click **Cancel** and leave Performance Monitor open for the next activity.

Data Collector Sets

Data Collector Sets organize multiple counters into a single unit. This makes monitoring performance easier to manage in much the same way that assigning users to groups makes system security easier to manage for individual users.

A Data Collector Set can monitor and log the following types of data:

- *Performance counters*—This records data on a timed basis. The value of selected performance counters is recorded at defined intervals, such as 1 second.

- *Event trace*—This tracks when system events occur. In this way, real-time information is collected about the system rather than samples. The information collected is based on the selection of an event trace provider. For each provider, you can select which specific events are tracked.

- *Configuration*—This tracks changes to the registry and when they occurred. You can use this to monitor changes made by application installations.

When you configure a Data Collector Set, it is often to log performance information to disk. In fact, for event trace data and configuration data, the changes must be logged to disk.

Data Collector Sets are not always running. If they were, very large log files would be generated and system performance would suffer. You can manually start Data Collector Sets when you are performing troubleshooting or start them with an alert. If you are collecting a baseline, you should schedule the Data Collector Set to run at a regular time.

Data Collector Set scheduling is very flexible, allowing you to create multiple schedules based on a start date, end date, day of week, and time of day. Stopping a Data Collector Set is configured most often based on overall collection duration or a maximum collected data limit. When a Data Collector Set stops, you can run a task. This can be used to process the log files after data collection is complete. For example, you might have a script that looks for specific event values within the logs. Or you might simply copy logs to a network location for further analysis.

Activity 10-3: Logging Performance Data

Time Required: 15 minutes
Objective: Log performance data by using a Data Collector Set

Description: Data Collector Sets allow you to group counters for easier manageability. If you want to log performance data, it must be done with a Data Collector Set. In this activity, you create a Data Collector Set and log performance data to disk.

1. In the left pane of Performance Monitor, expand **Data Collector Sets** and click **System**. You can see that two predefined Data Collector Sets are created by the system to perform common maintenance tasks.

2. In the left pane, click **Event Trace Sessions**. These are trace providers used by the system to collect system performance data.

3. In the left pane, click **User Defined**. When you create new Data Collector Sets, they are placed in this folder.

4. Right-click **User Defined**, point to **New**, and click **Data Collector Set**.

5. In the Name box, type **CPU and Disk logging** and click **Next**. This Data Collector Set will be created from a template.

6. In the Template Data Collector Set box, select each option and read the description.

7. Click **Basic** and click **Next**.

8. Accept the default Root directory and click **Next**.

9. Click **Open properties for this data collector set** and click **Finish**.

10. On the General tab, read which user the Data Collector Set will run as.

11. Click the **Directory** tab. This tab shows you where the log files will be stored.

12. Click the **Stop Condition** tab. Notice that, by default, the Data Collector Set will stop after 1 minute.

13. Click **OK**.

14. In the left pane, expand **User Defined** and click **CPU and Disk logging**.

15. Right-click **Performance Counter** in the right pane and click **Properties**. Notice that all processor-related counters are selected by default.

16. Click **Add**, expand **PhysicalDisk**, click the section title **PhysicalDisk**, click **Add**, and click **OK**. This adds all of the counters for the physical disk.

17. Notice that the log format is binary in the Performance Counter Properties window, and click **OK**.

18. In the left pane, click **User Defined**. Notice that CPU and Disk logging has a status of stopped in the right pane.

19. Right-click **CPU and Disk logging** and click **Start**.

20. Wait 1 minute for the data collection to complete.

21. In the left pane, click **Performance Monitor** and, in the toolbar, click the **View Log Data** button. Note that if you hover the cursor over each toolbar button, the name of the button is displayed as a tooltip.

22. Under Data source, click **Log files**, click **Add**, double-click the **Admin** folder, double-click **CPU and Disk logging**, double-click the folder with today's date, click the file **Performance Counter.blg**, and then click **Open**.

23. Click **Time Range**. This displays the time range in the log file. You can select just a subset of the time range to view if you desire. The default setting is to display the entire time range.

24. Click the **Data** tab to select the counters to display from the log file, click **Remove** as required to remove any existing counters, and click **Add**.

25. Expand **PhysicalDisk**, click **% Idle Time**, and click **Add**. This adds the total % Idle Time for all physical disks that were logged.

26. Expand **Processor**, click **% Idle Time**, and click **Add**. This adds the total % Idle Time for all processors that were logged.

27. Click **OK**. Notice that the counters are now listed under Counters.

28. Click **OK** to save the settings and display the data on the Performance Monitor graph. If necessary, change the chart view's graph type to **Line**.

29. Click the **plus** symbol in the toolbar. Notice that only the PhysicalDisk and Processor counters are available because only those counters were logged.

30. Expand **PhysicalDisk**. Notice that you can select any counter in the category because they were all logged.

31. Click **Cancel** to close the Add Counters window.

32. Leave Performance Monitor open for the next activity.

Alerts   For performance counters, you can configure **alerts** instead of logging to disk. After selecting the performance counter you desire for an alert, you also state a threshold value and configure whether the alert is triggered by going above or below the threshold value. For example, you can trigger an alert when the \Memory\AvailableBytes counter drops below 50 MB.

When an alert triggers, the following can be performed:

- *Log an entry in the application event log*—Placing an event in the application log allows you to search for the event later and incorporate it into your normal system monitoring process.

- *Start a Data Collector Set*—If you have an ongoing problem that you are trying to monitor, you can start a Data Collector Set when the alert is triggered. For example, if disk utilization is high, you can start a collector set with various counters that help you find the source of the problem.

- *Run a scheduled task*—Running a task can start any program. In most cases, you will want to run a script. For example, you could run a script that sends the administrator an email notification.

Data Manager   Data Manager allows you to automatically control the log files and reports that can be generated by Data Collector Sets. You can apply a policy and specify actions. Using Data Manager, you can specify parameters such as minimum free disk space, maximum number of folders, report generation, and deletion preferences to make room for new data.

Reports

Reports are used to process log file data and display it in a meaningful way. You add rules for report processing in the properties of the Data Collector Set. In theory, you could create your own rules for processing log files, but most administrators will never need to do so. Windows 10 includes the rules you are likely to need.

Activity 10-4: Viewing Reports

Time Required: 10 minutes
Objective: View a report generated by Performance Monitor

Description: Performance Monitor can generate reports from log files. To do this, XML-based rules files are applied to the log data. Several system reports are available. In this activity, you view an existing system report.

1. In the left pane of Performance Monitor, under Data Collector Sets, click **User Defined**.

2. Right-click **CPU and Disk logging** in the right pane and click **Start**.

3. Wait approximately 1 minute for data collection to complete.

4. Right-click **CPU and Disk logging** and click **Latest Report** in the shortcut menu. The left-hand navigation pane changes focus to highlight the most recent report and the report's details are opened in the right-hand pane.

5. Review the information available in the report. Locate the Summary section and confirm the general report details available there.

6. Close Performance Monitor and close all other open windows.

Task Manager

Task Manager, shown in Figure 10-4, provides an overview of the current state of a computer. The information provided by Task Manager is less detailed than the information found in Performance Monitor and Resource Monitor.

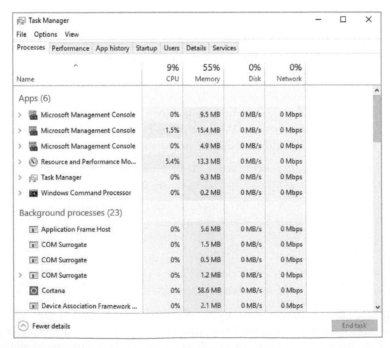

Figure 10-4 Task Manager

You can access Task Manager in several ways:

- Press Ctrl+Alt+Delete.
- Press Ctrl+Shift+Esc.
- Right-click an empty area of the taskbar and select Task Manager.
- Run taskmgr.exe from a command prompt.

Processes

The Processes tab in Task Manager shows all user applications running on the computer. For example, the process Resource and Performance Monitor appears in the list of active tasks in Figure 10-4 because it is actively running on that computer.

You can also view the process that corresponds with an application to find out more detailed information. To do so, right-click the process and click Go to details. This opens the Details tab and highlights the precise process matching the application selected on the Processes tab.

For each process, you can see:

- *Name*—The process executable file
- *User Name*—The user who started the process
- *CPU*—The percentage CPU utilization of the process
- *Memory*—The memory used exclusively by the process
- *Description*—A brief description of the process, if available

You can optimize the view of processes by adding additional columns and sorting based on column information. For example, if you want to find the process that is writing the data to disk, you can add the I/O Write Bytes column and then sort based on that column. Columns are added by right-clicking on any column header and selecting Select columns.

For each process, you have the option to set the priority of the process. In some cases, you may be able to boost the performance of a particular application by raising the priority of the application. However, this is not recommended because raising the priority of one application can be detrimental to other applications.

You can also end a specific process or process tree. Ending a process tree stops the process and all other processes that were started by the process. Ending just the process allows other processes started by the process to continue running.

On a system with multiple CPUs or a multiple-core CPU, it is possible to set processor affinity for a process. Setting processor affinity assigns a process to a particular processor. In the vast majority of situations, system performance will be better if you do not set processor affinity for a process. When processor affinity is not set, Windows 10 optimizes system performance automatically by moving processes among processors as required.

Services

The Services tab provides a list of the services running on Windows 10. The information here is approximately the same as the information found in the service portion of Computer Management. From this tab, you can also locate the process associated with a particular service and can start and stop services.

Performance

The Performance tab, shown in Figure 10-5, provides a quick overview of system performance for memory and processor utilization. The current CPU, memory, disk, and network usage is shown as line graphs together with basic statistics. A link is also available to launch Resource Monitor from this tab as a convenience.

Other Task Manager Tabs

The App history tab shows a summary of what applications have been using resources since the last startup and the total usage of those resources in comparison with each other.

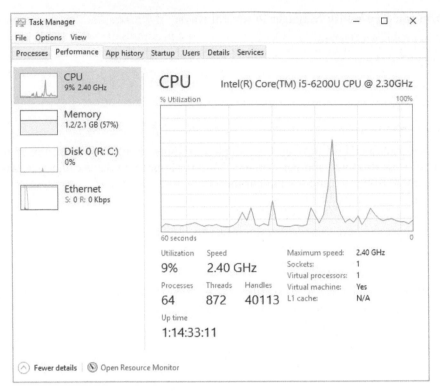

Figure 10-5   Task Manager, Performance tab

The Users tab has a list of users who are currently signed in to the system. If multiple users share a computer and use fast user switching to stay signed in, the users appear in this list. If required, you can disconnect users.

The Startup tab shows a list of applications that start automatically when Windows starts, and lets the user mark them as enabled or disabled for startup.

Activity 10-5: Using Task Manager

Time Required: 10 minutes
Objective: Use Task Manager to view system information

Description: The primary purpose of Task Manager is to provide a quick overview of system and process performance information. In this activity, you view system information and manage processes by using Task Manager.

1. If necessary, start your computer and sign in.
2. Click the **Start** button, in the search box type **cmd**, and press **Enter**.
3. In the command window, type **mspaint** and press **Enter**.
4. Right-click the taskbar and click **Task Manager**.
5. Note that the initial view for Task Manager is to just list the running applications. Click the down arrow next to **More details** to expose all of Task Manager's details if they are not already visible.
6. If necessary, click the **Processes** tab. You can see that both the command prompt and Paint are listed in the Apps section.
7. Right-click **Windows Command Processor** and click **Go to details**. This switches to the Details tab, with the command prompt process selected.
8. Right-click **cmd.exe** and click **End process tree**.
9. Read the warning and click **End process tree**. This closes both the command prompt and Paint because Paint was started by the command prompt.

10. Click the **CPU** column header once. This sorts the processes by CPU utilization. A down arrow above the column title indicates that the processes are sorted in descending order with the highest CPU utilization at the top of the list.

11. Click the **Services** tab. This tab displays the status of services running on the computer.

12. Click the **Performance** tab. This tab provides some basic CPU and memory utilization information.

13. Click the **Ethernet** mini-graph on the left side of the window. This displays an overview of network utilization and status.

14. Click the **Users** tab. This tab displays a list of all users who are signed in. Multiple users can be signed in at the same time when fast user switching is used.

15. Close Task Manager.

Performance Options

Windows 10 includes the Performance Options dialog box, shown in Figure 10-6, to optimize visual effects, processor scheduling, and virtual memory. You can access the Performance Options dialog box by right-clicking Start, selecting System, selecting the Advanced tab, and then clicking Settings in the Performance section.

Figure 10-6　Windows 10 Performance Options

The Visual Effects tab allows you to configure a wide variety of settings that improve how the Windows 10 interface performs. By default, the option *Let Windows choose what's best for my computer* is selected.

The Advanced tab lets you select whether processor time is allocated to optimize performance for programs or background services. If Programs is selected, the program running in the active window is given a slightly higher priority than other applications. This ensures that the program you are using is the most responsive on the system. If you select Background services, all programs are given the same priority.

The Advanced tab also gives you access to the setting for **virtual memory**. By default, the paging file is managed automatically by Windows. As more of the paging file is required, it is expanded from the minimum size to the maximum size.

You can manually configure the paging file if you prefer. This allows you to optimize the placement of the paging file. Moving the paging file to its own hard disk optimizes system performance because there will be less contention for disk resources when accessing the paging file. Alternatively, you can spread the paging file over multiple disks to speed access to the file.

Most Windows 10 computers have only a single hard disk, and increasing performance is not possible by adjusting the virtual memory settings. However, you might want to move the paging file to a different partition to free space on the C: drive if it is almost full.

It is also possible to specify that no paging file is to be used. However, this is not recommended as performance will suffer. Even when systems have sufficient physical memory to hold all active processes and their data, system performance suffers when the paging file is disabled.

 Moving the paging file to its own partition on the same physical disk or multiple partitions on the same physical disk has no performance benefit.

Data Execution Prevention (DEP) is a processor feature that Windows 10 is capable of using. DEP monitors processes to ensure that they do not access unauthorized memory spaces, which is done by various types of malware, such as viruses, to take control of systems. Despite the value of DEP in preventing malware, there is a performance cost. By default, DEP is enabled for only essential Windows programs and services. This protects the core components of the operating system that are likely to be targeted by malware, yet preserves system performance. You can enable DEP for all programs and services (and specify exceptions), but this has a significant performance impact and is not recommended.

Overall, Windows 10 is very sensitive and adaptive to performance levels on the computer. Tools like Task Manager and Performance Monitor help the administrator or user understand what a computer is busy doing. When the performance of a computer is suspect, these tools can help identify why. If the problem seems to be a fault within the system, the administrator may have to consider recovery.

Troubleshooting Windows 10 Errors

Sometimes Windows 10 or apps installed on Windows 10 become unstable and start to generate errors. Sometimes an error message is displayed on the screen that provides an obvious solution, but more often you need to use additional tools to do further troubleshooting. The more information that you have about a problem, the more likely it is that you can find a solution. Using precise search terms in a search engine generates results that are more likely to be applicable to your specific problem.

Steps Recorder

When a user reports an error, the information provided by the user is not always accurate. Rather than accepting a description of the error at face value, you are better off to have the user demonstrate the steps to reproduce the error. If you cannot visit or view the user desktop, you can ask the user to record the steps with **Steps Recorder**.

Steps Recorder does not capture a video of the user performing actions. Instead, a screenshot is captured each time the user clicks on a screen item. The screenshots and user actions are saved in a report that can be emailed or saved to a shared storage location. The report is an .mht file that contains both text and the screenshots. To keep the report size small, it is compressed in a .zip file.

Text typed by the user is not captured by Steps Recorder. If information being typed is important, the user needs to add a comment that includes the information being typed.

Reliability Monitor

Sometimes a computer has become unstable over time and you would like to identify when the stability problem began. **Reliability Monitor,** shown in Figure 10-7, rates the system stability of Windows 10 and lets you monitor the events that contribute to system stability.

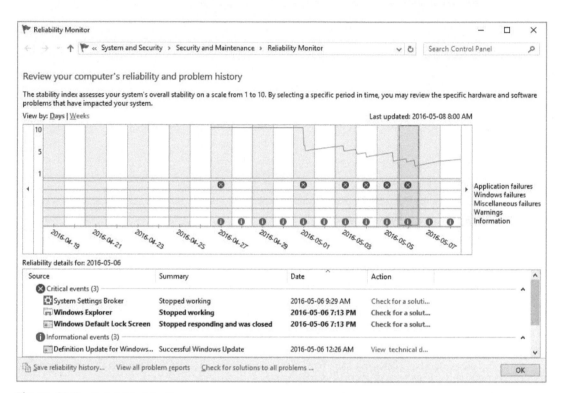

Figure 10-7   Reliability Monitor

Reliability Monitor collects the following data:

- *Software installs and uninstalls*—Software tracked here includes driver and operating system updates.
- *Application failures*—Any application that stops responding is logged here.
- *Windows failures*—Any system failure that results in blue screen errors and boot failures is logged here.
- *Miscellaneous failures*—Any event not included in other categories is logged here. One type of failure recorded here is improper shutdowns.

The Reliability Monitor graph lets you see the point in time at which significant reliability events occurred. You can use the graph to drill down and find out what event occurred in that time frame and correct the problem. For example, if frequent failures occur after adding a new driver, the driver is the likely cause of the stability problem and it should be removed.

Event Viewer

Event Viewer (introduced in Chapter 3, Using the System Utilities) is used to browse and manage events stored in system event logs, as shown in Figure 10-8. You can start Event Viewer as a stand-alone administrative tool or use it in Computer Management. The most common event types in the logs are Error, Warning, and Information.

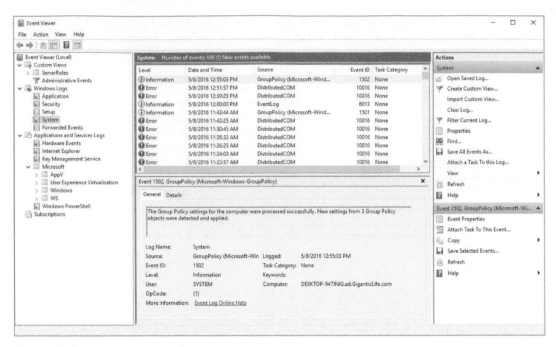

Figure 10-8   Event Viewer

The logs in the Windows Logs node of Event Viewer are the most commonly used for troubleshooting. Most non-Microsoft apps and many Microsoft apps write their events to the Application log. The Security log contains Audit Success and Audit Failure events. The System log contains general operating-system-level events such as services starting and stopping or IP address conflicts.

The Applications and Services Logs node contains event logs for many operating system services. It also contains logs for some management software such as User Experience Virtualization and App-V. In general, each service or app has its own log.

The Custom Views node is used to create filtered views that can contain specific event types from specific sources. You can create a view that gathers events you require for working with a specific application that writes information to various logs. The Administrative Events view shows Critical, Error, and Warning events from all logs.

You can use the Subscriptions node to copy events from a remote computer to yours. This can be useful when you are monitoring several computers. By default, the events from a subscription are copied into the Forwarded Events log.

You can use the events in Event Viewer to verify that a process is completing properly or to identify an error. If there is an error event, you can search for solutions to that error based on the Event ID and the Source.

You can also attach a scheduled task to a specific event. When the event appears in the event log, the scheduled task is triggered. This can be useful if you want to be notified when a specific event occurs. This can also be used to resolve problems that can be resolved simply with a script. For example, the script could restart a service when the service generates an error.

File Recovery and Backup

If user data is stored on a Windows 10 computer, it should be backed up to ensure that it can be recovered in case of a hardware failure. Getting users to back up their data before there is a problem requires the administrator to know how to advise the users of their options. Windows 10 includes two major features to aid in file recovery, File History and Backup and Restore (Windows 7).

Both of these features must be turned on and configured to be of use to the user.

Configuring File History

File History allows data that is typically important to a user to be backed up to an external hard drive or a network location. File History is a user-specific data protection mechanism that protects local resources. To access File History, the user must open Settings, click Update and Security, and then click Backup. This opens the Backup window shown in Figure 10-9. You can also configure File History from Control Panel.

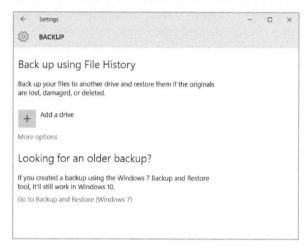

Figure 10-9   Backup settings

File History is disabled to start with because it needs someone to pick a location to store backup data that will be available if the primary drive fails. When you attach an external hard drive, Windows 10 asks you what to do with the attached drive, including the option to use the drive with File History. The user can select that option or wait to configure the drive with File History from Settings or Control Panel. For example, the user can open Settings, Update and Security, Backup, and then click the Add a drive button under the Back up using File History section, as shown in Figure 10-9.

 File History can also save to a network location, but the option to pick a network location is found only in the Control Panel File History settings.

When you attach an external hard drive and configure it for use by File History, the drive does not get erased. Backup data is added to the drive using the drive's free space. Note that if the source files include any EFS-protected files, the external drive should be formatted with NTFS to back up the source data properly.

File History creates a series of folders at the root of the drive selected to hold File History data. The path looks like this:

F:\FileHistory*username**workstationName*

where *F:* will be replaced with the drive letter assigned to the external drive selected for use by File History on that system. By default, the user's libraries are included in the backup: Music, Pictures, Videos, and Camera Roll. Local folders from the user's profile are also included: Documents, Desktop, Contacts, Favorites, Downloads, Links, Roaming, and OneDrive, to name the majority. The OneDrive folders that are included contain local data for that user that has been synchronized from OneDrive in the cloud. Some hidden folders in the user's profile that contain application data (e.g., AppData) are not included by default.

The first backup will happen in the background while the user is working on other tasks. The performance impact to the computer is slight, but there will be some activity. Successive backups will copy only files that have changed since the most recent backup, so they will be faster. New instances of a file are saved in the same backup folder, but with a different date and time stamp added to the title within parentheses.

File History content is not compressed or encrypted on the external drive. Anyone who steals the drive will have ready access to the drive's contents unless it is encrypted with a technology like BitLocker. Be careful with the security of the File History backup drive. Optionally, you can select a network location and use permissions on the network location to restrict access.

Files are backed up every hour by default. The backup frequency can be changed to as little as every 10 minutes or as much as every 24 hours. The retention period for backup data can be changed so the oldest backup data will be deleted when space is needed for newer backup files, or kept for a range from 1 month to 2 years, or to be kept forever (the default).

File History controls in Settings and those in Control Panel do not have exactly the same features. There are some options such as adding folder locations (available only in Settings) or choosing a network location to store backups (available only in Control Panel) that are not available in both. These limitations may change as Windows 10 continues to develop.

The user can see and optionally add folders to the backup using the File History controls in Settings but not those in Control Panel. The user can add folders anywhere on the local computer, and if they choose to show hidden files and folders, they can include hidden folders as well. These backup options are available by clicking the *More options* link in the Backup settings, which opens the Backup options window shown in Figure 10-10. The list of folders being backed up is listed under that window's section called Back up these folders.

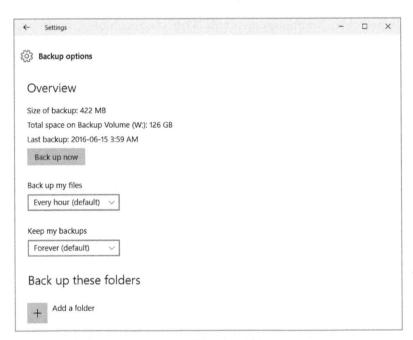

Figure 10-10   File History additional options in Settings

Note that the backup frequency, the retention period, and the folders selected for backup determine how much data is written to the external drive, potentially filling it up. A user can also limit how much disk space is used by excluding specific folders from the File History backup using the Settings or Control Panel. The *Exclude these folders* section in the Settings Backup options has an *Add a folder* link to identify folders to exclude from the backup, as shown in Figure 10-11.

Only one backup drive can be configured for use by File History at a time. If you want to switch from using one drive to another, you must first stop using the current drive and add the new one. You can click the Stop using drive button in the Backup options window, as shown in Figure 10-11. When you stop using a drive with File History, the backed-up data on that drive is not deleted.

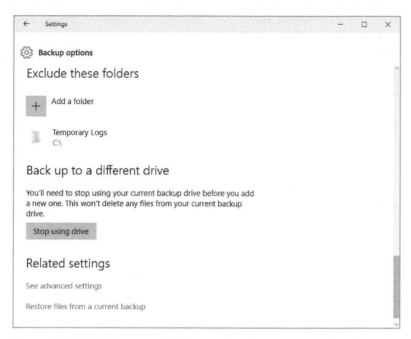

Figure 10-11   File History, additional options in Settings, continued

You select how File History retains backups. By default, files are kept forever, but if your backup drive runs out of space, the backups begin to fail. To avoid this issue, you can select to keep backups *Until space is needed*. You also have the option to select retention periods from 1 month to 2 years.

Administrator controls and utilities are limited with File History. There is a single Group Policy Object (GPO) control found in Computer Configuration > Administrative Templates > Windows Components > File History > Turn off File History. This allows the administrator to set a policy that blocks users' ability to use File History as a security measure. From the command line, there is one utility available, *FhManagew.exe*, which is used to trigger a cleanup of backup files that are older than a specified age and have a newer version of that file included in the backup data, or the file is no longer in the scope of what is being protected.

Recovering files from the File History backup is covered later in this chapter in the Restore Previous Versions of Files and Folders section.

Configuring Backup and Restore (Windows 7)

Windows Backup has been in use with many older versions of Windows. It was deprecated in Windows 8 and not included in Windows 8.1. With the upgrade potential of Windows 10, there is a good chance people would still have backups created and available that are compatible with the legacy Windows Backup utility going as far back as Windows 7. Windows 10 introduces a newer version of that utility and calls it **Backup and Restore (Windows 7)** to denote its legacy status. This utility can do more than access old backup content; it also has the ability to help protect the operating system itself. This capability is covered later in this chapter in the System Recovery section.

The Backup and Restore (Windows 7) utility can be started from the Backup Settings screen, as shown in Figure 10-9, or from the System and Security section of Control Panel. The startup screen launched from Control Panel is shown in Figure 10-12. There is also a command-line tool called *wbadmin.exe* that must be run from an elevated command prompt that allows the administrator to manage the backup process from script files and scheduled tasks.

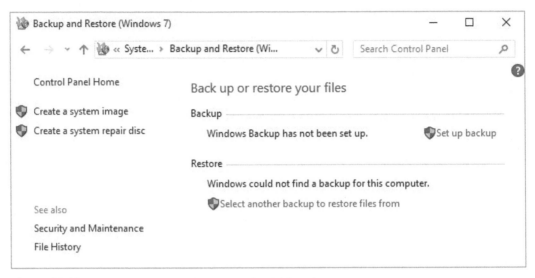

Figure 10-12   Backup and Restore (Windows 7), initial settings

The target destination to save backups to should be a different physical disk than the local drive that holds C:, in case the drive holding C: fails. The drive selected can be another drive internal to the system, an external drive, a virtual drive, or a shared network location. Consider the safety of the backup target location in the event of a disaster or a need to recover data. An external drive has the best chances of local recovery and portability in the case of local equipment failure.

When Backup and Restore (Windows 7) is started for the first time, you must select a target location (disk or network) for backup data. Backup and Restore (Windows 7) checks if there is enough space to back up critical user data and create a system image. A system image is a copy of the drives required for Windows to run. System images and restoring them are discussed later in this chapter. Users can select the data to back up or let Windows choose for them. By default, Windows selects the user's libraries, the desktop, and default Windows folders. If users choose to manually select items to back up, they can optionally include any local path on the system, all users, or just that user's libraries, and whether to create a system image or not.

Backup and Restore (Windows 7) schedules a backup task to repeat on a regular interval, plus it runs the backup task immediately, as shown in Figure 10-13.

The backup task schedule can be modified by clicking Change Settings, as shown in Figure 10-13, or it can be viewed and modified using Task Scheduler. The backup jobs for Windows Backup are stored in Task Scheduler, in the Task Scheduler Library > Microsoft > Windows > WindowsBackup folder. Modifying the schedule on the backup task with Task Scheduler allows the use of other triggers than just a schedule, such as when a workstation is locked.

 Recovering files from Backup and Restore (Windows 7) is covered in the next section.

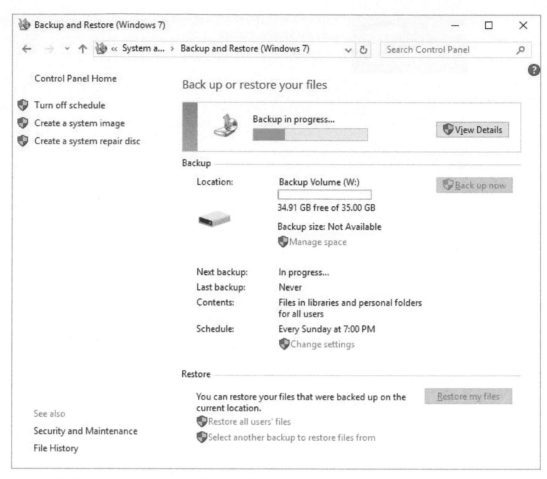

Figure 10-13   Backup and Restore (Windows 7), backup in progress

Restoring Previous Versions of Files and Folders

If File History or Backup and Restore (Windows 7), or both, have been configured to protect user data, that data can be recovered using a feature called **Previous Versions**.

The user can browse to a location in File Explorer and open the properties of a file or folder to reveal a tab called Previous Versions, as shown in Figure 10-14. A list of known previous versions is displayed. The user has the option to recover an old version of the content and restore it in the same place, or to an alternate location for inspection.

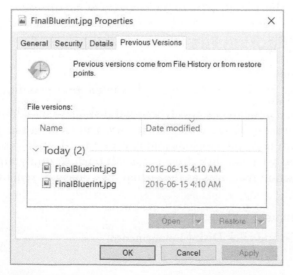

Figure 10-14   Previous Versions tab of folder Properties

Previous Versions restore points are not the same as restore points created by System Restore.

The data protected by File History can be browsed by selecting Settings > Update & security > Backup > More options > Restore files from a current backup. This opens a window that allows you to browse current and past File History backups, as shown in Figure 10-15.

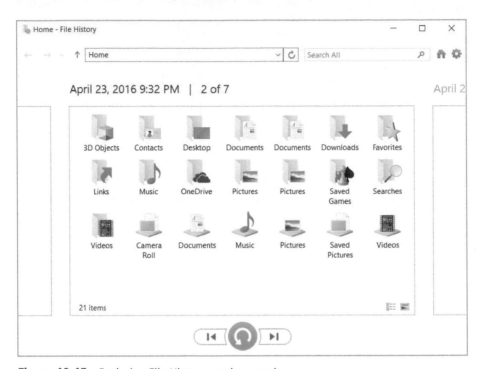

Figure 10-15   Exploring File History previous versions

When content is selected in the window, clicking the green circle arrow restores that data to its former location. Right-clicking the green circle arrow opens a menu that allows you to restore the content to an alternate location.

File History is preferred to using Backup and Restore (Windows 7) for user data. The legacy Windows Backup utility is available to browse old backups and create system images that can include system files and user data. It can be used to protect user data; however, its use is limited to Control Panel settings and command-line utilities by its legacy nature. If you create a system image of Windows 10, it can be a valuable tool to assist in the recovery of a damaged operating system.

Activity 10-6: Configuring File History

Time Required: 30 minutes

Objective: Configure basic File History settings and examine restore options

Description: In this activity, you simulate a separate internal disk drive by adding a virtual disk to the system and then configuring it for use with File History. You create a sample Grocery List file that will be backed up with multiple versions and restored to identify supporting backup data elements. Note that using a virtual disk drive is for lab purposes only and is not recommended for backing up production machines as the virtual disk does not remain attached after the system is restarted.

1. If necessary, start your computer and sign in.

2. Right-click the **Start** button and click **Disk Management**.

3. Click to open the **Action** menu and click **Create VHD.**

4. Click **Browse** and navigate to the folder **C:\VHD Storage,** which was created in the chapter activities for Chapter 4, Managing Disks and File Systems. In the File name field, type **VHDFileHistory** and click **Save.**

5. Change the Virtual hard disk size unit from MB to **GB.**

6. In the Virtual hard disk size field, type **4.**

7. Under Virtual hard disk format, click to select **VHDX.**

8. Confirm that under Virtual hard disk type, **Dynamically expanding (recommended)** is selected, and then click **OK.**

9. In the bottom pane, scroll to the new 4 GB disk, right-click the disk name, and select **Initialize disk** from the shortcut menu. Accept the default settings in the Initialize Disk window and click **OK.**

10. Right-click the 4 GB of unallocated space on that disk and select **New Simple Volume.**

11. Click **Next,** click **Next** to accept the default volume size, and note the assigned drive letter here: _____.

12. Click **Next** to accept the assigned drive letter.

13. Change the Volume label to **File History Data** and click **Next.**

14. Click **Finish** to create the new virtual disk. If there is a prompt to format the disk before using it, you can safely cancel the prompt.

15. Close the Disk Management window.

16. Click the **Start** button and click the **Settings** (gear-shaped) icon.

17. Click **Update & security** and click **Backup.**

18. Under the heading Back up using File History, click the **plus** symbol next to Add a drive.

19. When the drive search completes, click the drive labeled **File History Data.** Note that the Add a drive section is replaced with an on/off control to enable or disable the automatic backup of the user's files.

20. Click the **More options** link.

21. Under Back up my files, select **Every 12 hours.**

22. Under Keep my backups, select **Until space is needed.**

23. Under Overview, click **Back up now.** Note that the status changes in the Overview section, but no progress window opens.

24. Right-click anywhere on the desktop, select **New** from the shortcut menu, and then click **Text Document.**

25. Edit the name of the new document to be **Grocery List** and press **Enter** to save the change.

26. Double-click the **Grocery List** text document on the desktop to open it. In the Notepad editor window, enter the text **Version one – eggs.** Close Notepad and when prompted to save your changes, click **Save.**

27. Note that you could wait for the 10-minute time limit to back up the modified file; however, for the purposes of this activity, you will manually trigger the backup. In the Settings, Backup window, click **Back up now.** Note that the next backup is faster because only changed files and folders are backed up.

28. Double-click the **Grocery List** text document on the desktop to open it. In the Notepad editor window, edit the text to read **Version two – eggs, apples.** Close Notepad and when prompted to save your changes, click **Save.**

29. In the Settings, Backup window, click **Back up now.**

30. Right-click the **Grocery List** document on the desktop and select **Restore previous versions** from the shortcut menu. Note that the Properties window of the file opens and the Previous Versions tab is selected by default.

31. Click to select the oldest version of the file from the list, and then click **Restore**.

32. When you are prompted to replace or skip files, select **Replace the file in the destination**. Note that a progress indicator will be temporarily displayed and then File Explorer opens to show the restored content.

33. In the File Explorer window that opened, double-click the **Grocery List** file and note that the original version of the document has replaced version two.

34. In File Explorer, click the **Home** tab on the ribbon and select **History** from the Open section of the ribbon.

35. Note that there are multiple backups of the desktop folder available to choose from. Click the **left arrow** at the bottom of the File History window until you reach the first File History backup. Note that the Grocery List file is not listed because the first File History backup was made before the file existed.

36. Click the **right arrow** at the bottom of the File History window until you reach the latest File History backup.

37. Double-click the **Grocery List** file within the last File History backup, which previews the contents of the file in the File History window. In this preview mode, the arrows at the bottom of the screen allow you to examine different versions of the content.

38. Confirm that version two of the Grocery List content is displayed and then click the Green circular arrow button at the bottom of the File History window. Select **Replace the file in the destination**. Note that a progress indicator is temporarily displayed and then File Explorer opens to show the restored content.

39. In the Settings, Backup options window, scroll to the bottom and click **Stop using drive**.

40. In an open File Explorer window, open the drive letter you noted in Step 11.

41. Navigate to the folder *H:*\FileHistory*UserX**PcX*\Data\C\Users*UserX*\Desktop, where *H:* is the drive letter noted in Step 11, *UserX* is the user you are signed in as, and *PcX* is the name of your computer.

42. Review the versions of the Grocery List file in that folder and note the difference in the file names.

43. Close all windows.

44. Do not restart your computer or sign out before proceeding to the next activity to ensure that the File History Data virtual hard drive remains attached and available.

Recovering Files from OneDrive

Files stored in OneDrive are synchronized to the local Windows 10 computer and are cached locally. If a file is deleted within OneDrive, it is moved to a Recycle Bin in the cloud and to the local File Explorer Recycle Bin.

The OneDrive Recycle Bin is limited in capacity, typically to 10% of the storage limit purchased for OneDrive storage. If desired, more space can be purchased with OneDrive to increase the OneDrive Recycle Bin capacity.

If deleted items are emptied from the OneDrive Recycle Bin, they are deleted permanently and will not be able to be restored.

OneDrive is built based on SharePoint technology in the cloud; therefore, it includes a document version history when viewed through *OneDrive.live.com*. Right-clicking a data file such as a Word document gives the Version history option to browse the available versions based on the dates and times it was last saved. Previous versions can be restored or downloaded for further inspection.

When the user's data is securely backed up to an external drive or to the cloud, an ailing Windows 10 computer can be diagnosed and repaired using system recovery steps that might be disruptive to user data stored on the local system.

System Recovery

If there are minor problems with a computer running Windows 10, you might be able to resolve those errors by researching the issue and finding help online. However, sometimes it is not an effective use of time to spend hours troubleshooting and tinkering when you can perform a system recovery instead. If a computer running Windows 10 does not boot, you must perform a system recovery.

System Restore and Restore Points

Windows 10 is a resilient operating system, but it is a complex and dynamic product. When changes are made to the system's files and control settings, there is a chance that something could go wrong. Occasionally, damage could be caused by a recently installed program that has a fault in its design, by a transient error that occurred during installation, or perhaps by malware that introduced a defect by design. System Restore allows you to restore the computer's system files (operating system and applications) to an earlier point in time. It does not change your personal data files.

Older operating systems could use a feature called Last Known Good Configuration to start with the last known good configuration operating system settings that worked for the last full successful startup. This feature has been removed in Windows 10 in favor of more advanced options such as System Restore. **System Restore** uses a component called system protection that stores a snapshot of system files and settings about to be updated before the changes are made. That record is stored in something called a system **restore point**.

To access the System Protection settings, open Control Panel, System and Security, System, and click the System Protection link. This opens the System Properties window with the System Protection tab selected, as shown in Figure 10-16.

10

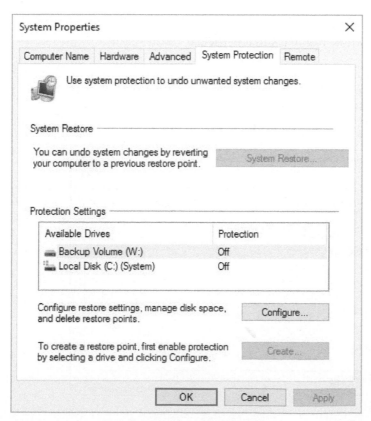

Figure 10-16   System Properties, System Protection tab

More than one restore point can be saved, creating a series of point-in-time snapshots of the system. The creation of restore points happens automatically when a major change or installation takes place in the operating system. Restore points can be manually triggered by clicking the Create button shown in Figure 10-16. Automatic triggers include Windows updates, scheduled tasks (in Task Scheduler > Task Scheduler Library > Microsoft > Windows > SystemRestore), and application installs that are System Restore aware. Even restoring a restore point triggers the creation of a new restore point for the current system before the old restore point is recovered.

System Restore can also restore a system by using data in a system image backup created by Backup and Restore (Windows 7). Note that even though the system image contains both system data and user data, only the system data is restored.

System protection can be activated from the System Properties window by selecting a drive from the Available Drives column and then clicking the Configure button. You can turn protection for that drive on or off, as well as select how much space the restore points can use on that drive. Once the history of restore points reaches that maximum, the oldest restore points will be deleted to make space for the new one. Note that a drive selected for protection must be formatted with the NTFS file system. In the background, system protection uses Volume Shadow Copy Service (VSS) to take backup snapshots of the data it includes within a restore point. The most important drive to be protected by System Restore is C:.

An administrator can also use PowerShell commands in an elevated PowerShell session to update and automate the configuration of System Restore. The five cmdlets available include:

- *Enable-ComputerRestore*— Turn SystemRestore on for specified drives, for example: Enable-ComputerRestore "C:\","W:\" enables System Restore on drives C: and W:. Note that C: must be actively protected by the same command or prior configuration. If C: is not protected by System Restore, no other drive can be protected.

- *Disable-ComputerRestore*—Turn System Restore off for a specified drive.

- *Checkpoint-Computer*—Create a new restore point, for example: Checkpoint-computer "PS Triggered restore point" creates a restore point called the same as the title provided in the command.

- *Get-ComputerRestorePoint*—Show all available restore points.

- *Restore-Computer*—Roll back to a particular restore point.

Rolling back to a restore point is relatively easy. Click the System Restore button shown in Figure 10-16 to open the Restore system files and settings utility, as shown in Figure 10-17. This screen displays a list of restore points that are available to roll back to.

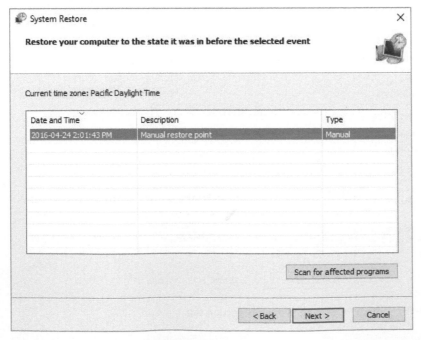

Figure 10-17   Selecting a system restore point

You can also start the Restore system files and settings utility from an elevated command prompt using the command *rstrui.exe*. This can be useful when you can only start the computer into Safe Mode with Command Prompt. You can also boot into the Windows Recovery Environment (WinRE) and run the System Restore utility from the advanced options. WinRE is reviewed later in this chapter.

If you aren't sure what changes a restore point will make, you can click to highlight a restore point of interest and then click the Scan for affected programs button. This shows programs and drivers that will be deleted or restored for you to review. Once you select a restore point, the system updates the computer and restarts. Rolling back to an earlier restore point doesn't always capture the changes that need to be made perfectly. Some drivers and programs might fail to operate after the rollback and might need to be reinstalled or repaired manually.

Activity 10-7: Configuring System Restore Points

Time Required: 15 minutes
Objective: Configure system restore points

Description: In this activity, you configure system restore points and create an initial restore point manually. After the restore point is created, you use it to roll back the computer configuration to that earlier configuration.

1. Right-click the **Start** button and click **Control Panel**.

2. Click **System and Security**, click **System**, and then click the **System protection** link.

3. In the Protection Settings section of the System Properties window, click to highlight the **File History Data** drive that was created in the previous activity, and then click **Configure**.

4. Note that you cannot turn on system protection for the drive because system protection is not enabled for drive C: first. Click **Cancel**.

5. In the Protection Settings section of the System Properties window, click to highlight **C:** and click the **Configure** button.

6. Move the slider in the Disk Space Usage section to change the maximum usage to approximately **10%**.

7. Click to select **Turn on system protection** and click **OK**.

8. In the Protection Settings section of the System Properties window, click to highlight the **File History Data** drive that was created in the previous activity, and then click **Configure**.

9. Note that you can now turn on system protection for the drive. Click **Cancel**.

10. Click **Create** to manually create a restore point. When prompted for the restore point name, enter the text **First manual restore point** and click **Create**.

11. Wait for the status message that the restore point was created successfully. Click **Close** on the message.

12. Click **System Restore**.

13. Click **Next** to pass the System Restore Wizard introduction screen.

14. Note the list of available restore points. Click to select and highlight the restore point created earlier.

15. Click **Scan for affected programs**. This checks to see if there are any programs or drivers that will change as a result of rolling back the computer configuration to this restore point.

16. Note that no changes to programs or drivers should be detected and click **Close**.

17. Click **Next** to proceed to the review screen.

18. Note that this step will restart your computer, which will detach the File History Data disk attached in an earlier activity. Click **Finish**, and when prompted to confirm the action, click **Yes**.

19. Wait for the restore to complete and then sign in.

20. Note the message that the restore has completed successfully and click **Close**.

10

Driver Rollback

Device drivers are typically vendor-supplied software that manages the communication and operation between a device and the Windows operating system. Manufacturers create device drivers to Microsoft specifications. Over time, manufacturers release updated device drivers that fix bugs and perhaps add functionality or support for updated features within Windows. Because device drivers are essential to the operation of Windows, Windows 10 automatically downloads and installs updated drivers via Windows Update.

Device drivers have low-level access directly into the kernel portion of the operating system. It is best practice to source device drivers from trusted locations such as the manufacturer's website or Windows Update. Device drivers are typically digitally signed with a trusted signature. The 64-bit version of Windows 10 enforces this; however, the 32-bit version can allow unsigned drivers to be installed.

Windows 10 comes with many driver packages that are distributed with the operating system. Many devices install using the Microsoft drivers by default. To see what device drivers are active on the current system, the administrator can use the elevated command-line tool *driver-query.exe* to obtain a list of installed device drivers. If the Microsoft default driver for that hardware device is the driver controlling a piece of hardware, it can't be rolled back. If a new driver is later installed for a device, that can be rolled back.

The most common reason for rolling back a device driver is instability in operations after the driver is upgraded. It might take time for the instability to appear, and a fix might be to locate an even newer driver rather than roll back the current driver. If there is no newer driver, rolling an unstable driver back might be the only option. If the computer is extremely unstable, the administrator can restart the Windows 10 computer into Safe Mode and roll back the driver as well.

The option to roll back a device driver is visible in Device Manager, in the properties of a device, on the Driver tab, as shown in Figure 10-18. Once a driver is rolled back, a newer version of the driver must be discovered by the administrator to effectively update that driver. That might have to wait until the vendor of the hardware releases a new driver.

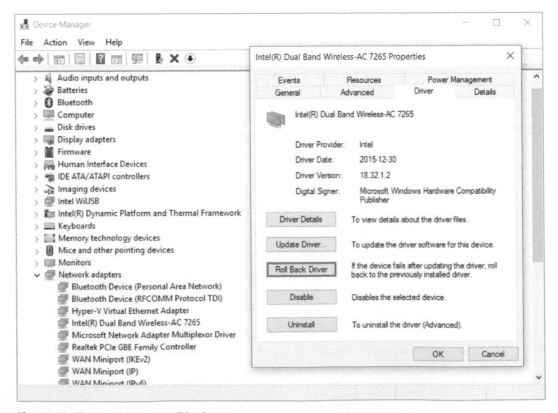

Figure 10-18   Device driver roll back

There is also the option to uninstall the driver for a hardware component, as shown in Figure 10-18. This removes the driver assigned to that device, but the driver package remains in the driver store. The next time the computer restarts, hardware detection will likely see the device and install the device driver using the driver package in the driver store. This is useful if the old driver properties were badly misconfigured during testing and the administrator wants to start over from scratch with fresh settings.

Device Manager does not have the capability to roll back printer device drivers.

If a driver update does not resolve stability with Windows 10, more intense diagnostic efforts might be required, such as rolling back to a previous system restore point, rolling back to a previous saved system image, resetting the system to a previous recovery point, or triggering a full reinstallation of Windows.

Activity 10-8: Managing Device Driver Update Settings

Time Required: 5 minutes
Objective: Configure device driver update settings

Description: In this activity, you confirm that Windows Update will obtain and install updated device drivers for your computer's hardware.

1. If necessary, start your computer and sign in.
2. Right-click **Start** and select **System**.
3. Click **Advanced system settings**.
4. Click the **Hardware** tab and click **Device Installation Settings**.
5. Confirm that **Yes (recommended)** is selected. Click **Cancel**.
6. Close all windows.

Recovery Drive

When the Windows operating system is unhealthy and won't start, an important tool to help recover it is the optional **recovery drive**. The recovery drive is created from an earlier healthy OS installation on the computer, and contains a backup of the Windows system files and recovery tools to assist in the repair process. The recovery drive is usually an external drive connected to a USB port on the computer, but some devices support the use of high-capacity memory cards as recovery drives.

The legacy command-line tool *recimg.exe* is no longer supported with Windows 10. The legacy *recimg.exe* tool let you configure a custom recovery image for Windows to use when you refresh your PC.

To create a recovery drive, use the search field on the taskbar to search for the phrase *Create a recovery drive*. The Control Panel utility *Create a recovery drive* should be highlighted at the top of the search results. Note that this utility requires administrative access to run. The option *Back up system files to the recovery drive* must be selected to copy over the current Windows installation's system files; otherwise, about 500 MB of recovery utilities are written to the external USB drive. If the Windows system files are selected, you need about 16 GB of space on the recovery drive, but you will be able to attempt the reinstallation of Windows from that data.

The utility scans your system for a compatible device to use as a recovery drive. When you select a drive, it will be formatted so all of the data that is on that drive will be lost if you

10

have not backed it up. A new volume will be created on the formatted drive with the label RECOVERY, and selected recovery information will be copied to the drive. The recovery information on that drive can't be used to recover an incompatible architecture (32-bit vs. 64-bit) or an older version of Windows (in case you rolled back to a previously installed version of Windows).

If there was already a local drive in the computer identified as a recovery drive, you might be asked if you want it deleted now that you have an external recovery drive. If you need to save space, you can answer yes.

Windows Recovery Environment (WinRE)

If Windows 10 is not working properly, there is an option to run the Windows Recovery Environment (Windows RE or WinRE) as a recovery platform based on Windows Preinstallation Environment (Windows PE). WinRE provides an automated diagnosis and repair of boot problems plus a centralized platform for advanced recovery tools, as shown in Figure 10-19. WinRE is preloaded into most Windows 10 desktop editions and is located in its own partition or in the path C:\Recovery\WindowsRE. The image to run WinRE is *winre.wim,* but it is typically flagged as a hidden system file that is not readily visible in File Explorer.

The WinRE environment can be started in several ways:

- Boot from recovery media.
- Use the computer's hardware recovery button (if available) or button combination to trigger a secondary boot to the WinRE environment.
- Restart the computer with the command-line command *shutdown.exe /r /o.*
- Press and hold the Shift key and then select the power option Restart from the sign-in screen.

After the PC starts in WinRE mode, select Troubleshoot, Advanced Options.

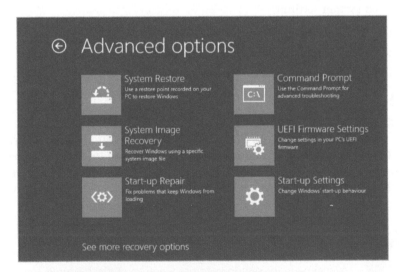

Figure 10-19   Windows Recovery, Advanced options

From the WinRE environment, advanced startup options can be selected by selecting Troubleshoot, Advanced Options, Startup Settings. This allows the administrator to reboot the system and activate the advanced startup menu.

The option to press F8 to enable a startup troubleshooting menu is no longer available with Window 10. The Advanced Options menu replaces this legacy option.

The system restarts and allows the administrator to select one of these options:

- *Enable low-resolution video mode*—Lowers the video resolution temporarily if the currently configured resolution is too high for the attached display device to display an image.

- *Enable debugging mode*—Configures additional device driver monitoring and troubleshooting for a developer.

- *Enable boot logging*—Logs a history of device drivers being loaded on startup to a file called Ntbtlog.txt.

- *Enable Safe Mode, Safe Mode with Networking, or Safe Mode with Command Prompt*—Starts Windows 10 with a minimum set of known safe drivers, services, and applications to service and troubleshoot the local operating system. Safe Mode does not include networking support unless it is optionally selected. If the GUI environment is not required or is still problematic, Safe Mode can be started with just a command-line window available to issue commands.

- *Disable device driver signature enforcement*—Allows the loading of unsigned device drivers. This option is used by developers.

- *Disable early-launch and anti-malware protection*—Disables this protection feature to see if that is what could be causing a startup issue.

- *Disable automatic restart on system failure*—Disables the automatic restart after a system failure to help collect diagnostic information.

- *Launch recovery environment*—Starts the recovery environment and selects other options from the WinRE options.

System Reset

If you were unable to repair a computer running Windows 7, you needed to reinstall the operating system. The reinstall could be done from an installation DVD or by imaging. In Windows 10, you have the option to reset the computer. When you reset the computer, it removes all apps and puts settings back at their default values. However, you have the option to keep your data files, as shown in Figure 10-20.

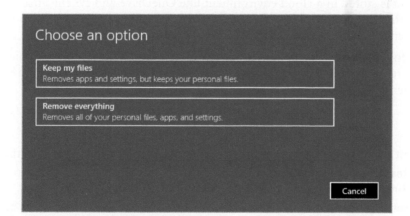

Figure 10-20   System reset options

The option to reset the PC to an initial out-of-the-box state can be triggered by going to Settings, Update & security, Reset this PC, and selecting Get started. If the computer can't be started normally but the WinRE environment can, select Troubleshoot, Reset this PC.

If your computer came from the factory with applications installed, those vendor applications will likely still be installed after the reset, but any applications that you added will be removed. When the process is complete, you can sign in and see a list of applications that were removed on the desktop.

Most of the time, you will choose to keep user data. However, if you are resetting the PC so that you can sell it or give it away, you can select the option to erase everything. This option removes all personalization and returns the computer to its initial configuration after a Windows installation.

Some vendors include customized restore information, and the option to restore factory settings might be displayed. This performs the system reset and takes you back to an experience similar to when you first unpacked the computer.

Chapter Summary

- Establishing a baseline for performance tuning allows you to recognize variations from normal system behavior and identify system bottlenecks. The four main areas that cause bottlenecks are disk, memory, processor, and network.

- Performance Monitor can be used to monitor system performance, monitor system reliability, create alerts, log performance activity, and generate reports.

- Data Collector Sets are used to control the logging of performance data and create alerts. You can schedule when Data Collector Sets are active. Data Manager is used to automatically manage the logs after creation.

- Task Manager allows you to quickly view system process information. Process information includes memory utilization and processor utilization. In addition, you can monitor network utilization.

- Performance Options allow you to configure visual effects, processor performance, virtual memory, and Data Execution Prevention. In most cases, the default configuration for these settings is acceptable.

- To gather information to help troubleshoot errors in Windows 10 or apps, you can use Steps Recorder, Reliability Monitor, and Event Viewer.

- Windows 10 recovery options include mechanisms to protect user data such as File History and Backup and Restore (Windows 7), which are optional to configure, but beneficial to enable sooner rather than later to protect user data before the system itself needs repair.

- If user data is stored in a cloud environment like OneDrive and synchronized with local copies of the data, OneDrive can be used to restore files if there is a problem with the operating system.

- The Windows 10 operating system has many tools available for improved operating system recovery: recovery disk, system image backup, system restore points, and the WinRE environment.

Key Terms

alert   An event that is triggered when a count value is above or below the specified threshold value.

Backup and Restore (Windows 7)   The legacy backup utility that is included to provide access to backups from Windows 7.

baseline   A set of performance indicators gathered when system performance is acceptable.

bottleneck   The component in a process that prevents the overall process from completing faster.

counters   The performance indicators that can be recorded in Performance Monitor.

Data Collector Set   A grouping of counters that you can use to log system data and generate reports.

Data Execution Prevention (DEP)   A feature designed to prevent the installation of malware by monitoring processes to ensure that they do not access unauthorized memory spaces.

Data Manager   The Performance Monitor component that is used to automatically manage performance logs.

File History   A feature that is used to back up user files to an external hard drive or file share.

Performance Monitor   A tool within the Microsoft Management Console (MMC) that allows you to visually display the data generated by counters.

performance tuning   The process for collecting system performance data, analyzing system performance data, and implementing system performance improvements.

Previous Versions   The tab available to restore files and folders that have been backed up by File History or Backup and Restore (Windows 7).

recovery drive   An optional drive that you can create with a system image from your currently installed operating system and apps.

Reliability Monitor   A utility that rates the system stability of Windows 10 over time and correlates system events with changes in system stability.

reports   Reports created in Performance Monitor that use XML-based rules to analyze logged data and display meaningful results.

Resource Monitor   A utility launched from Performance Monitor that provides real-time monitoring of the most common system performance indicators.

restore point   A snapshot of operating system and program files at a specific point in time that can be restored to roll back to a point in time when the operating system or apps were stable.

Steps Recorder   A tool that can be used to record the steps required to generate a problem and store the steps and screenshots in a file.

System Restore   The feature that uses system protection to create and restore system restore points.

Task Manager   A utility that allows you to view overall system information and manipulate processes.

virtual memory   The combination of physical memory and the paging file.

10

Review Questions

1. Performance monitoring is the act of changing a system's configuration systematically and carefully observing performance before and after such changes. True or False?

2. Which of the following can Task Manager monitor? (Choose all that apply.)

    a. system CPU utilization

    b. network CPU utilization

    c. user CPU utilization

    d. process CPU utilization

3. Which of the following can be used to start Task Manager? (Choose all that apply.)

    a. Ctrl+Alt+Delete

    b. running taskman.exe

    c. Ctrl+Shift+Esc

    d. Right-clicking the taskbar

4. In Performance Monitor, all performance objects have the same counters. True or False?

5. Which Performance Monitor component records log files?

    a. Performance Monitor

    b. Reliability Monitor

    c. Data Collection Sets

    d. alerts

    e. reports

6. Which Performance Monitor component analyzes logs by using XML-based rule files?

   a.   Performance Monitor

   b.   Reliability Monitor

   c.   Data Collection Sets

   d.   alerts

   e.   reports

7. Each Data Collector Set can contain only a single counter. True or False?

8. What is the most common physical symptom of insufficient memory?

   a.   excessive heat coming from the computer

   b.   graphics displayed incorrectly on the monitor

   c.   a memory error code displayed on the screen

   d.   high levels of disk activity

   e.   three short beeps from the computer

9. File History is designed to roll back device drivers. True or False?

10. When a component is the slowest part of a process, it is referred to as a (n) _____.

11. Which Performance Monitor component is used to view performance logs?

   a.   Performance Monitor

   b.   Reliability Monitor

   c.   Data Collection Sets

   d.   alerts

   e.   reports

12. You know that you will be making some major changes to your computer and you want to back up all of your user data and the local operating system. This can be accomplished by selecting all drive data to create a:

   a.   Recovery Drive

   b.   WinRE environment

   c.   system image disk

   d.   File History backup

13. The most commonly accessed event logs are located in the Applications and Services Logs node. True or False?

14. A device driver can't be rolled back in Device Manager, but you suspect that the driver is the reason you are having problems. You should:

   a.   Uninstall the driver.

   b.   Update the driver.

   c.   Restore a previous system image.

   d.   Restore a previous restore point.

15. Your computer sign-in screen is visible, but after you enter your sign-in credentials, the computer fails to sign in and present your desktop, then finally it restarts and takes you back to the sign-in screen. You want to get in to the Windows Recovery environment. What key do you hold down when you restart the computer to start the Windows Recovery environment?

   a.   F8

   b.   Ctrl

   c.   F10

   d.   Shift

16. Which backup and restore function can you use to set a computer back to its factory default settings without any additional media?

   a. System Restore

   b. File History

   c. Windows Recovery Environment (WinRE)

   d. Recovery Drive

   e. System Reset

17. Which backup and restore function can you use to create a system image that includes the apps you have installed?

   a. System Restore

   b. File History

   c. Windows Recovery Environment (WinRE)

   d. Recovery Drive

   e. System Reset

18. Which tool can you use to gather screenshots of a user demonstrating a problem?

   a. Remote Desktop

   b. Steps Recorder

   c. Reliability Monitor

   d. Event Viewer

   e. Remote Assistance

19. Which tool can you use to identify the point in time at which a computer running Windows 10 started to become unstable?

   a. Remote Desktop

   b. Steps Recorder

   c. Reliability Monitor

   d. Event Viewer

   e. Remote Assistance

20. Resource Monitor can be used to monitor the amount of data sent over various network connections. True or False?

Case Projects

CASE PROJECTS

Case 10-1: Collecting Performance Data

Gigantic Life Insurance has several batch jobs that run on Windows 10 computers overnight. The batch jobs are scheduled overnight because they require all the performance capability of the computers and must be completed by morning for staff to perform their regular work. The batch jobs always use approximately the same amount of data, but occasionally they are not finished in the morning, resulting in lost productivity. Describe how you would determine the cause of the slow processing.

Case 10-2: Upgrading System Performance

A potential employer has asked you to describe your approach to the recovery of a Windows 10 computer that is failing. Given that it contains important local user data, you are asked to describe your opinion of Windows 10 features to protect that data in advance of recovery efforts.

chapter 11

Microsoft Intune Device Management

After reading this chapter and completing the exercises, you will be able to:

- Describe Microsoft Intune as a device management solution
- Support mobile devices
- Support client computers
- Manage devices with Microsoft Intune
- Deploy software updates using Microsoft Intune
- Manage apps with Microsoft Intune

Microsoft Intune is a service based in the cloud that is used to manage computers and mobile devices. Microsoft considers the Intune service to be an essential management tool for Windows 10 devices, and is, therefore, an essential component of the exam. Domain-joined and non-domain-joined devices can be enrolled into the management service. The Intune service itself is managed using a web-based console to deploy software apps and updates, inventory hardware and software, manage endpoint protection, manage mobile devices, manage software licensing, and provide remote assistance. Supported client devices include Windows, Apple **iOS**, and **Android**. Intune can work independently or it can be integrated with an on-premises deployment of **System Center 2012 Configuration Manager (SCCM)**.

Microsoft Intune Overview

Microsoft Intune is a replacement for a former service called Windows Intune. Microsoft Intune has evolved to provide the network administrator with a full-featured management service without the overhead of building up a large, on-premises network infrastructure. In fact, Microsoft Intune can be deployed for an organization that has no on-premises server infrastructure. The most common scenario today is a managed enterprise with boundaries that reach far beyond a private network, with cloud apps and portable devices extending the business ecosystem around the globe.

Mobile devices can be managed directly or through on-premises connectors. The operating systems supported by Microsoft Intune for devices treated as mobile devices include:

- Windows 10, Windows 8.1, Windows 8/8.1 RT, Windows Phone
- Mac OS X (version 10.9 and later)
- Apple iOS (version 7.1 and later)
- Android (version 4.0 and later)

Mobile devices can extend the workplace beyond private corporate boundaries, and can come from many sources. Users might want to use the mobile devices they prefer, and have selected and purchased for themselves. These are generically referred to as **Bring Your Own Device (BYOD)**. The corporate administrator can also allow users to select a personal device from the business's inventory of devices, generically referred to as **Choose Your Own Device (CYOD)**. The business can also provide devices that service a pool of users, either with a dedicated device administrator or just kept as general-use inventory.

Capabilities for managing mobile devices include:

- *Mobile application management*—Restrict some app operations as well as provide a managed browser that restricts the sites users are allowed to visit.
- *Password management*—Manage password requirements, complexity, and operational settings.
- *Manage corporate-owned Apple iOS devices*—Support CYOD or shared devices.
- *Deploy profiles for VPN, certificates, email, Wi-Fi*—Enable access to company resources through profiles.
- *Manage device capabilities*—Control access to features such as the camera, voice recognition, and roaming settings.
- *Reset, wipe or retire devices*—Reset passcodes and lock or even wipe the data from lost or stolen devices.

Desktop computers can also be managed by Microsoft Intune if the Intune client is installed on them. Supported operating systems include:

- *Windows Vista*—Business, Ultimate, and Enterprise editions
- *Windows 7*—Professional, Ultimate, and Enterprise editions
- *Windows 8/8.1*—Professional and Enterprise editions
- *Windows 10*—Pro and Enterprise editions

The Intune desktop client is capable of:

- *Managing software updates*—Keeping the computer up to date
- *Antivirus/malware protection*—Using Intune's Endpoint Protection for antivirus and malware protection
- *Remote assistance*—Connecting to a help desk for assistance using Remote Desktop
- *Software license management*—Tracking usage against license limits for compliance monitoring and reporting

As a cloud-based service, Microsoft Intune requires the use of two administrative websites: the Office 365 Administrator Portal and the Microsoft Intune Admin console. The Office 365 Portal (*https://portal.office.com* or *https://portal.office365.com*) is used to manage user accounts and licenses to use Intune, monitor the service health, and manage billing and purchases for the Intune subscription. The stand-alone Microsoft Intune Admin console (*http://manage.microsoft.com*) is used to manage the majority of the Intune service features, such as distributing policies, performing updates, managing protection, and running reports. Over time, Microsoft is gradually moving this Intune Admin console into the Office 365 Portal so it can be launched from there instead.

End users can also connect to the Microsoft Intune Company Portal (if the Intune administrator configures and enables it) to access company data and apps. This can be accomplished through the Company Portal website (*https://portal.manage.microsoft.com*) or the Company Portal app published for that device. The goal of the Company Portal is to allow users to help themselves, including the ability to enroll their devices for Intune management, download software deployed by the organization, view the status of their devices, or contact the IT department if they need to escalate any issue for support.

If System Center 2012 Configuration Manager (SCCM) is implemented in the organization, Intune integration can maintain a consistent management experience for computers that are joined to Active Directory and those that are not. The integration is assisted by the installation of an Intune Connector site system role on-premises. This allows for the use of the on-premises SCCM console for Intune-managed devices that are also domain joined. Devices that are not domain joined can only be managed in the Intune admin console.

Office 365 supports Mobile Device Management using features that are a subset of the Intune features. Note that Office 365 subscriptions can be combined with Microsoft Intune to add full Mobile Device Management features to the Office 365 service, using a full Intune subscription per user license or the **Enterprise Mobility Suite** (**EMS**) license suite. In that case, the choice of using cloud-based Intune only is configurable in either the Intune Admin console or the Office 365 Admin center.

The EMS product contains licenses for **Azure AD Premium** (for enhanced identity options), Windows Intune (mobile device/app management), and Azure Rights Management Services (for email and document protection). The idea is that these features will help manage and protect the mobile user with a single license assignment.

The full Intune product adds the Company Portal, policies to restrict mobile app management, app profiles, secure player apps, inventory, patching, anti-malware, and the ability to integrate to on-premises SCCM.

Signing Up for Microsoft Intune

The full Intune product is available as a stand-alone cloud service or as part of the Enterprise Mobility Suite. Microsoft has also made a 30-day trial available for people to evaluate the service (see *http://aka.ms/ymo1j0*) with 100 Intune licenses.

As with most cloud-based services from Microsoft, the user accounts linked to a trial are stored in Azure AD. One common mistake made during the trial is to sign up with a new account and then find it difficult to transition to the existing corporate environment if it already uses **Azure AD** or Office 365. If the business already has Azure AD or Office 365, the Intune trial can be added to the existing subscription by an authorized administrator.

If you are evaluating Intune as part of an exercise, it is best to use a disposable identity that will expire with the Intune trial.

Activity 11-1: Signing Up for a Microsoft Intune Trial

Time Required: 10 minutes

Objective: Sign up for a Microsoft Intune trial subscription

Description: In this activity, you sign up for a 30-day trial of Microsoft Intune. As part of the sign-up process, you will be prompted to fill in a form asking for enough information to create an Office 365 trial account. 100 Intune licenses will be added to that Office 365 account. The first user created in the Office 365 account will be the administrator of that Office 365 account. The name of the Office 365 account will be based on a fictitious company nickname you select, which must be unique from all other Office 365 accounts. The Office 365 account name will be the company nickname followed by *.onmicrosoft.com*.

1. If necessary, start your computer and sign in.
2. Note the Microsoft account you signed up for in Chapter 5, Activity 5-3 (Microsoft account user ID and password).
3. Click **Start**, type **Internet Explorer**, and then press **Enter** to start Internet Explorer.
4. In Internet Explorer, enter the address **http://aka.ms/ymo1j0** and click **Try now**.
5. Complete the trial sign-up using the credentials from Step 2 as the email address. As part of the sign-up process, you must specify a fictitious company name. That name must be unique in the Azure AD directory service. If the first name you select is not available, select a different one. Note that you might need to prove that you are not an automated software bot by using a working phone to receive a security code as a text message or phone call. Entering the security code online creates a new Azure AD sign-in credential that ends with *.onmicrosoft.com*. Record the Azure AD sign-in and password:

   Azure AD user account _____

   Azure AD user password _____
6. Once the sign-up process is complete, you must create user accounts for the trial. When you are prompted to create users, click the **Start** button. This opens the Office 365 Portal.
7. The Office 365 Portal home page opens. Click the **Admin** tile in the middle of the page to open the Office 365 Admin center.
8. If you are prompted by a message welcoming you to the new Admin center, click **Next**.
9. If you are prompted by a message describing how to use the In search of... feature, read the message and click **Next**.
10. If you are prompted by a message describing how to navigate the Admin center, read the message and click **Finish**.
11. At the top left of the Admin center, click the > icon to expand the navigation menu.
12. In the Admin center, locate and click **Admin centers** in the navigation menu. This expands a list of administrative sites below that section.
13. Under Admin centers in the navigation menu, click **Intune**.
14. If you are prompted to sign in again, sign in as the Office 365 administrative user recorded in Step 5. The first time the Microsoft Intune Admin console loads, it might take a minute or two; please wait for it to load.
15. In the Microsoft Intune Admin console, click **Admin** in the left pane.
16. In the middle pane, click **Mobile Device Management**.
17. In the right pane, click **Set Mobile Device Management Authority**.
18. If Intune prompts you to confirm that Intune will be the MDM authority, check the box and then click **Yes**. For the purposes of the trial, Intune might default to itself as the authority. In that case, confirm that under the heading Mobile Device Management Authority a check mark is displayed next to **Set to Microsoft Intune**.
19. Close all open windows.

Adding Users to Intune

Microsoft Intune users are typically created as identities associated with an Office 365 tenant account. User accounts were originally configured using the discontinued Microsoft Intune

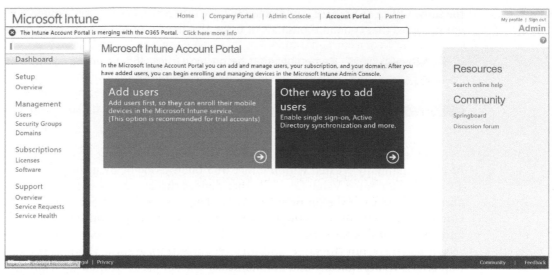

Figure 11-1 Legacy Microsoft Intune Account Portal

Account Portal website (*https://account.manage.microsoft.com*), as shown in Figure 11-1; however, Microsoft decided to unify and requires that you use the user account management part of the Office 365 Portal (*http://portal.office.com*) to configure user accounts. The Office 365 tenant account is a subscription container for Office 365 services. A company commonly sets up only one production Office 365 tenant account, and adds users to that account. Purchased Office 365 licenses within the tenant account can be assigned to the user accounts that belong to that tenant. The user accounts inside the Office 365 tenant are actually stored in the directory service, Azure AD, which provides identity management for a variety of Microsoft services, including Office 365.

The Office 365 tenant account itself has to be identified with a name in Azure AD. The default format of this name is a company nickname, followed by the suffix *.onmicrosoft.com*. For example, if a company is called Able Brothers Furniture, a suitable nickname might be ABFurniture. The nickname has to be unique within Azure AD and no other Office 365 tenant can use that nickname. During the sign-up process, the system checks a nickname to see if it is available for a new Office 365 tenant account. If it is not unique, you will have to try a different nickname. The choice of a nickname for the tenant is important because it can only be created once, and after it is defined, it can't be changed without destroying the tenant account. If the Office 365 tenant account is being used for testing purposes, it would be a mistake to assign a nickname you want to use in production.

Once the Office 365 tenant account exists, users can be created as part of that account. User account names are different for Office 365 user accounts than for on-premises legacy pre-Windows 2000 account names. The legacy pre-Windows 2000 names use the format ADDomainName\NetBIOSAccountName. For example, the user LPeters from the Active Directory domain ABFURNITURE would have a legacy logon name of ABFURNITURE\LPeters. Office 365 apps do not use this format for user names; instead they use a format called **User Principal Names (UPNs)**. Active Directory can also support identifying a user with a unique UPN. The format of a UPN is *userid@DomainName*, where *userid* is a unique name assigned to that user, and *DomainName* is a name associated with the Office 365 tenant directory, or on-premises Active Directory, to uniquely identify that directory. The domain name looks like a DNS name. In the example, the fictitious company could be assigned a suitable domain name such as *abfurniture.com*. The sample user, LPeters, could then have a UPN assigned that looks like *LPeters@abfurniture.com*. It is preferred that the UPN match the user's email address to help the user remember the UPN, but this is not a technical requirement. The domain name for UPN purposes is more commonly called a UPN suffix.

In Office 365, the number of domain names you can add to a single tenant is nearly unlimited, but you must be able to prove to Microsoft that you have administrative control of a domain name before you can add it to the tenant. The domain name must be unique and can only be assigned to one Office 365 tenant. If another individual or company is using that domain name with its tenant, you can't use it with yours.

A user account can only have one UPN assigned to it, with a unique user ID and one UPN suffix chosen from the list of available UPN suffixes for that Office 365 tenant. Different users within the same Office 365 tenant could possibly have different UPN suffixes assigned. For Office 365 tenant accounts that contain thousands of users, this flexibility is essential to supporting the enterprise.

Remember that before an Office 365 tenant account is assigned a custom domain name, a default domain name is assigned to the tenant account using the format *CompanyNickname.onmicrosoft.com*. *CompanyNickname* is selected by the corporate administrator when the Office 365 tenant account is first created.

User accounts can be added to an Office 365 tenant using a variety of methods. They can be either manually created within Office 365 one-by-one or by using a bulk import process with a Comma Separated Value (.csv) file that defines the user accounts to create. User accounts can also be copied from the on-premises Active Directory using **DirSync**, Azure AD Sync, Azure AD Connect, or some other third-party custom user synchronization tool. DirSync, Azure AD Sync, and Azure AD Connect are provided by Microsoft and represent successive generations (most recent listed last) of the same directory synchronization tool. The purpose of the synchronization tool is to periodically and automatically extract user information from on-premises identity databases (i.e., Active Directory, LDAP directories, or SQL users) and insert or update them into Office 365. For larger companies with many users, this can be a real time-saver, allowing the on-premises directory to be the source of authority for user account details in the cloud. These tools can also be configured to synchronize passwords from on-premises accounts to their Office 365 equivalent user accounts, and with later versions of the sync tool, the passwords can be synced back from Office 365 to on-premises accounts.

Once a user account exists in Office 365, and more specifically in Azure AD, it can be assigned a license to enable that identity to access a service, such as Intune. When the user no longer needs to use that service, or the user account is deleted, the license is freed up and becomes immediately available for assignment to a different user. License assignments are made by subscription administrators, commonly called Global Administrators in Office 365. This is typically accomplished through the web-based Office 365 Admin center (*http://portal.office.com*).

PowerShell commands can also be used to manage licenses for Office 365 user accounts by downloading and installing the Windows Azure Active Directory module for Windows PowerShell. These PowerShell commands are considered outside the scope of this chapter.

Activity 11-2: Adding Users to Microsoft Intune

Time Required: 10 minutes
Objective: Add a new user to Microsoft Intune and license the account

Description: In this activity, you add a new user called Sam Spade to the Azure AD directory that identifies users belonging to the Intune tenant account, and license Sam as an Intune user.

Managing Intune as the administrator is typically done through a web browser, where Internet Explorer is the preferred web browser and it is Silverlight enabled. Because you might be signed in as a user (rather than an administrator) on your computer, opening a browser window to the Intune Administration webpage might link the wrong identity. It is a common practice to activate Internet Explorer in its private mode, known as InPrivate Browsing, and then connect to the Intune administrative webpages as an administrator account. The Microsoft Edge browser is currently not supported for use with the Intune administrative webpages.

1. Click **Start,** type **Internet Explorer,** right-click **Internet Explorer** from the search results, and then select **Pin to taskbar.**

2. Right-click the **Internet Explorer** icon in the taskbar and select **Start InPrivate Browsing.**

3. In the Internet Explorer address bar, type **https://manage.microsoft.com** and press **Enter**.

4. When you are prompted for credentials to sign in to Microsoft Intune, use the user ID and password recorded in Activity 11-1, Step 5. This opens the Microsoft Intune Admin console.

5. Click the **GROUPS** workspace and select **Overview** if it is not already selected.

6. Click the **Add Users** task. This opens a new tab in Internet Explorer that displays the Office 365 Admin center, Active users view.

7. Click **+ Add a user**.

8. Required fields have a red asterisk next to the field name. Note which two fields are marked as required fields for a new user.

9. In the First name field, type the text **Sam**.

10. In the Last name field, type the text **Spade**.

11. Press the **Tab** key. If the Display Name field does not automatically update, in the Display Name field, type the text **Sam Spade**.

12. In the User name field, type the text **sspade**.

13. Confirm that the Location is set to the correct country setting. If not, select the correct country. This sets the license limits based on the country you are in.

14. Confirm that the Password setting is set to **Auto-generated**.

15. Confirm that the Roles setting is set to **User (no administrator access)**.

16. Confirm that the Microsoft Intune license is selected for this new user. Click **Save**.

17. By default, an email with the new user's temporary password will be sent to your tenant's administrator account. This account does not have its own mailbox in this activity. Clear the check mark next to **Send password in email**.

18. Note the new user's name and password:

    Azure AD user name _____

    Azure AD user password _____

19. Click **Close**.

20. Close the Active users tab but leave the Microsoft Intune Admin console tab open for the next activity.

Supporting Mobile Devices

Microsoft Intune can support a variety of devices that are mobile: BYOD, CYOD, or shared corporate resources. The current version of Microsoft Intune requires that when it is first configured, the IT administrator must select if Microsoft Intune will be the only service managing mobile devices, or if it will share the responsibility with an on-premises System Center 2012 Configuration Manager installation, as shown in Figure 11-2. This choice must be made before any mobile devices can be added because this setting is hard to change after it is made (typically requiring a call to Microsoft support to change).

Device owners must be added to Microsoft Intune so the service can recognize their identities as belonging to the managed service, which was described earlier in this chapter.

The management of mobile devices is referred to as **Mobile Device Management (MDM)**. A mobile device must be enrolled in Intune for it to be managed by Microsoft Intune. Users can enroll up to five devices themselves that will be associated, or linked, with their user account in Azure AD. The Intune administrator can also define a device enrollment manager account that has permissions to enroll more than five devices. The device enrollment manager account is limited to enrolling devices that will not operate with a user identity and that access company resources. This is useful for adding devices such as point-of-sale terminals that need to be managed by Intune but will not run any apps operating in the context of a particular Intune user account.

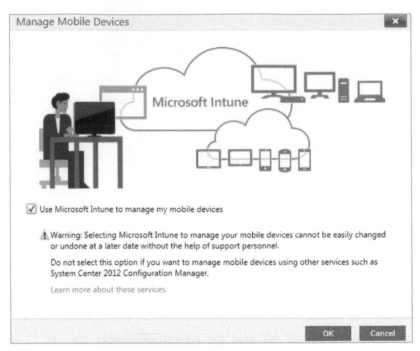

Figure 11-2   Selecting to use Microsoft Intune to manage mobile devices

Apps on a mobile device can be managed separately from the device itself, based on the identity of the user using the app. The management of mobile apps is referred to as **Mobile Application Management (MAM)**. A device can experience Intune management using either MDM, MAM, or both. The device or app must be able to accept mobile management controls. Being enrolled in Intune establishes knowledge of the managed component within Intune and the establishment of a trust between the remote component and the Intune service itself.

Note that Apple iOS devices require a special certificate to establish a trust between the device and the Intune service. Apple requires the administrator to request an **Apple Push Notification service (APNs)** certificate using a certificate-signing request issued by Intune. The Apple certificate registration process requires the company administrator to register and obtain an Apple ID user account. Note that the credentials of this Apple ID account should be well recorded because the account will need to be used every year to refresh the Apple-issued certificate. If the administrator does not monitor that account's email, the administrator may miss the warning that the previously issued certificate is going to expire. If the APNs certificate expires, iOS device management will fail as soon as the currently issued certificate expires.

The MDM enrollment process is unique to the device type:

- *Windows 8 or higher*—Installing the Intune client is sufficient for enrollment.

- *Apple iOS 7 and later*—Obtain the Microsoft Intune Company Portal app from the Apple App store, and follow the directions when the app is started.

- *Windows Phone*—Open Settings, select Company apps, and then select Install Company app or Hub.

- *Android 4.0 and later*—Obtain the Microsoft Intune Company Portal app from Google Play or an other Android app store, and follow the directions when the app is started.

- *Windows RT*—Open PC Settings, click Network, and then click Workplace. Enter the user's account name and click Turn On, completing the prompts to allow the app and services.

Note that just as the Intune service continuously evolves, so do mobile operating systems. The minimum supported mobile device operating system version number will change over time. When the supported version number is increased, older versions are usually supported for a period of time if the device using it is already enrolled. New enrollments are held to the current minimum operating system version number.

Supporting Client Computers

Microsoft Intune can manage computers that are typically not thought of as mobile devices, including domain-joined workstations and stand-alone computers. These computers can be managed via Intune by installing an Intune client on the local computer. The Intune client provides the mechanism for providing status information, installing software updates, managing apps, enabling and managing Endpoint Protection, updating Windows Firewall settings, and enabling remote assistance.

The Intune client can be downloaded from the Microsoft Intune Admin Portal (https:// *manage.microsoft.com*, click Admin workspace, and then click Client Software Download) and saved by the Intune administrator to a central location. The download includes a setup executable and a certificate that identifies the Intune client to the Intune service during enrollment. These setup files can be deployed to a computer manually, through a script, or distributed through a tool such as Group Policy.

The Intune client supports both 32-bit and 64-bit operating systems from Vista up to Windows 10 as long as it is not a Home edition and it does not already have a management client installed from an on-premises systems management solution such as SCCM or **Systems Management Server (SMS,** an earlier version of SCCM). The user installing the client must have full administrator rights to the local computer and the local Windows Installer must be at version 3.1 or higher.

It is becoming more popular to allow users to consume computer services themselves without involving the help desk. This self-service model for deploying the Intune client can be achieved by enabling and directing users to use the Intune Company Portal (*https://portal.manage.microsoft .com*). Note that the Intune client package you can download as an administrator is not normally given directly to an end user to install; instead, the Intune Company Portal website or the Company Portal app are preferred for end-user-initiated enrollment.

11

Activity 11-3: Downloading and Installing the Intune Client

Time Required: 15 minutes

Objective: Download and install the Intune client to the local computer

Description: Windows computers can be managed by Intune once the Intune client is downloaded and installed on the local computer. The client can be copied to a central server and installed with a script or Group Policy Object; however, in this lab setting, you install the local download directly.

1. Continue from Activity 11-2 by selecting the Microsoft Intune Admin console webpage. If the browser or tab was accidentally closed, open it again with these steps:

   a. Right-click the Internet Explorer icon in the taskbar and select **Start InPrivate Browsing**.

   b. In the Internet Explorer address bar, type **https://manage.microsoft.com** and press **Enter**.

   c. When you are prompted for credentials to sign in to Microsoft Intune, use the user ID and password recorded in Activity 11-1, Step 5. This opens the Microsoft Intune Admin console.

2. Click the **ADMIN** workspace. If you are prompted to reauthenticate, confirm your credentials and reselect the correct browser tab.

3. In the Administration menu, click **Client Software Download** and click the **Download Client Software** button in the right pane.

4. Select **Save As** when you are prompted to save the Microsoft_Intune_Setup.zip file. Save the file to the desktop.

5. After the zip package has completed its download, right-click the zip file on the desktop and extract its contents to the default path suggested. This creates and opens a folder on the desktop that has the Intune client setup executable and the certificate information identifying your tenant.

6. Double-click **Microsoft_Intune_Setup.exe** to run the client software on your computer.

7. When you are prompted to allow this app to install software on your PC, click **OK**.

8. When the installation wizard is complete, click **Finish**.

9. Close the File Explorer window, but leave the Internet Explorer window open for the next activity.

Managing Devices with Microsoft Intune

Once user accounts are created and Intune licenses are assigned to those users, Intune features must be configured to interact with your device ecosystem. Devices to be managed must be enrolled, and apps to be managed must be compatible with Intune features. Intune has many features, but you might not decide to use all of them at the same time. For some enterprises, it might make sense to use a only specific subset of features. Knowing what those features do is essential to selecting and configuring them.

The Microsoft Intune Admin console is accessible by browsing to *https://manage.microsoft.com* and signing in as an administrator of the Intune service. The starting view is called Dashboard view, as shown in Figure 11-3. As the Intune service is customized, tiles will update on the Dashboard to provide quick summary information and status details that would be important to the administrator, such as monitoring what devices have successfully enrolled.

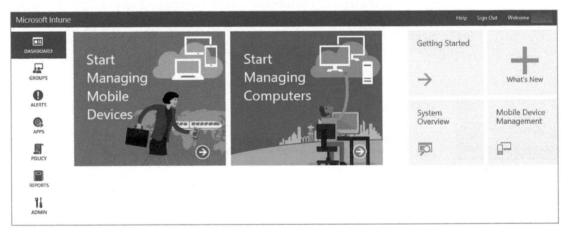

Figure 11-3   Microsoft Intune Admin console, Dashboard view

The left pane of the page has icons that represent subsections of the Intune controls, such as Groups, Alerts, and Reports. These are commonly called workspaces in Intune documentation. Clicking the icon for a workspace opens an administrative task menu in the middle of the page, with common task nodes for that workspace. The task nodes are arranged in an indexed fashion, where different levels can be expanded or collapsed by clicking the arrow next to them, as shown in Figure 11-4.

Managing devices with Intune typically involves grouping devices and users to view and manage members, create inventory reports, configure monitoring and alerts, manage policies, manage remote computers, and configure Windows or third-party updates.

Grouping Devices and Users

Intune has the ability to group users and devices for management and security purposes. Intune groups are managed from the Groups workspace in the Microsoft Intune Admin console (*https://manage.microsoft.com*). The Intune user accounts are defined in Azure AD, usually as part of an Office 365 tenant account. The user accounts may be automatically synchronized

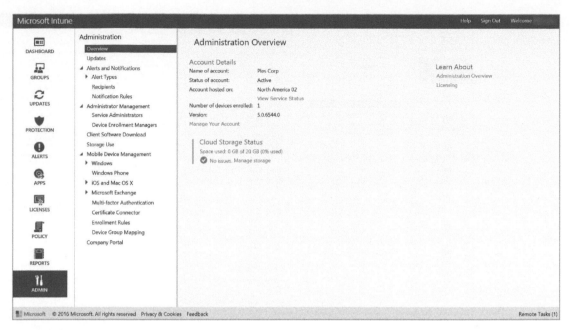

Figure 11-4   Microsoft Intune Admin console, Admin view

from an on-premises Active Directory system, or manually created using the Office 365 Admin center. Device accounts are created when devices are enrolled or discovered.

Intune groups are used within Intune and are not the same as the security groups within Azure AD. Security groups created in Azure AD, or synchronized from on-premises Active Directory to Azure AD, can be involved in determining membership of an Intune group, but they are not Intune groups themselves.

An Intune group can be a user group or a device group. A user or device can belong to more than one group. Intune group membership can be defined using membership rules that include or exclude members. Membership rules can be direct or criteria based. Direct membership specifies a list of members to include or exclude. Criteria-based membership uses security groups in Azure AD and attributes to dynamically determine what members are included or excluded.

Intune has its own starting hierarchy of groups, organized by users and devices. This default hierarchy cannot be deleted or renamed. The user-based group hierarchy starts with the default groups:

1. All Users

    1.1. Ungrouped Users

The device-based group hierarchy starts with the default groups:

1. All Devices

    1.1. All Computers

    1.2. All Mobile Devices

        1.2.1. All Direct Managed Devices

        1.2.2. All Exchange ActiveSync Managed Devices

    1.3. All Corporate Pre-Enrolled Devices

        1.3.1. By iOS Serial Number

        1.3.2. By IMEI (All platforms)

    1.4. Ungrouped Devices

Some of the default groups contain members by virtue of an attribute of the device itself, for example, whether it is a mobile device or computer device. Custom groups can be created to organize members, enabling an administrator to quickly analyze their status, as shown in Figure 11-5.

11

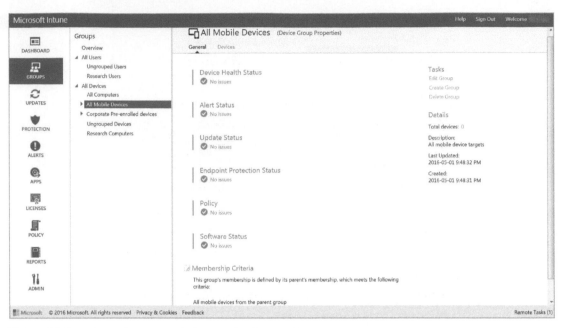

Figure 11-5 Microsoft Intune Admin console, Groups view

To maintain a hierarchy, each new group links to a parent group. Ultimately, each group will have the All Devices or All Users group as the top-level group in a group hierarchy. The logic of the design for each custom level is entirely up to the administrator who is designing it, based on how the administrator wants to use Intune. Common advice is to think about how many people you would impact if you changed a setting that applied to members within the group. Consider factors such as:

- Help desk support availability to support impacted members

- Communication complexity (i.e., small groups can require more custom communications)

- Administrator visibility

A secondary administrator called a service administrator can be specified for Intune, and the groups that the service administrator can see can be restricted to specific groups. This could be useful in the case where the group structure assists with administrative delegation.

Activity 11-4: Creating Custom Groups and Assigning a Service Administrator

Time Required: 15 minutes
Objective: Create a custom user and device group and assign a service administrator account to those groups

Description: Custom user and device groups can be created as part of the Intune group hierarchy. In this activity, you create a user group and review individual wizard pages. You also create a device group without reviewing the optional wizard pages. You configure a user created in a previous activity as a service administrator with a filtered view that assigns the newly created user and device groups.

1. Continue from Activity 11-3 by selecting the Intune Admin console webpage (*https://manage.microsoft.com*).

2. Click the **GROUPS** workspace. If you are prompted to reauthenticate, confirm your credentials and reselect the correct browser tab.

3. Click the **Create Group** task.

4. In the Group Name box, type **Research Users.**

5. Under Select a parent group, select **All Users.**

6. Click **Next.**

7. Accept the default membership criteria and click **Next.**

8. Accept the default direct membership settings and click **Next.**

9. Review the summary page and click **Finish.**

10. Click **Overview** in the middle pane.

11. Click the task **Create Group** in the right pane.

12. In the Group Name box, type **Research Computers.**

13. Under Select a parent group, select **All Devices.**

14. Click **Finish** to accept the default settings for the group attributes and create the group.

15. Click the **ADMIN** workspace.

16. Click **Administrator Management** in the middle pane.

17. Click the **Add Service Administrator** task.

18. In the user ID field, type the user account noted in Activity 11-2, Step 16.

19. Under Access permissions, click **Full access.**

20. Click **OK.**

21. Note that the right pane now lists the known service administrator accounts, with the newly created account already highlighted. Click the **Manage Groups** link.

22. In the Manage group access window that opens, click **Remove** twice to remove the default groups.

23. On the left side, click the **Research Users** group to highlight it and click **Add.**

24. On the left side, click the **Research Computers** group to highlight it and click **Add.**

25. Click **OK** to save your changes.

26. Leave the Internet Explorer window open for the next activity.

Inventory Reporting

Microsoft Intune includes several predefined reports that are available to the Intune administrator. Reports are available from the Reports workspace and individually in the other workspaces if they are applicable.

The reports are continuously evolving as part of the online service; therefore, the list you see might differ from this one. The reports that are included at this writing are:

- *Detected Software Reports*—View all software installed on the computers managed by Intune. Reports can be filtered by device group, software publisher, or software category.

- *Mobile Device Inventory Reports*—View the mobile devices in the organization. Reports can be filtered by device group, operating system, or illegally unlocked status.

- *Terms and Conditions Reports*—View the users who have accepted the terms and conditions policies you have created for them to accept, filtered by users or specific terms and condition policies.

- *Noncompliant Apps Reports*—View users and devices that are noncompliant with the company app policies, filtered by device group, operating system, or compliant/noncompliant app list.

- *Certificate Compliance Reports*—View the certificates that have been issued to users and devices via the Network Device Enrollment Service, filtered by user or device groups, certificate expiry date, or certificate state (i.e., expired, revoked, issued).

- *Device History Reports*—View a history of device retire, wipe, and delete actions, filtered by date range up to 90 days in the past.

- *Mac OS X Hardware Reports*—View Mac OS X devices in the organization, filtered by device group.

- *Mac OS X Software Reports*—View Mac OS X software in the organization, filtered by device group.

- *Health Attestation Reports*—View the data reported by the Windows Health Attestation service for mobile devices, filtered by device groups, operating systems, all devices or just devices that support health attestation, and status (i.e., BitLocker not enabled, Secure Boot not enabled, Code Integrity not enabled, Early launch anti-malware not enabled).

Because many of the reports support filters, once the filter selections are defined for a particular report, the report can be saved as a custom version of that report. The next time the administrator wants to run that report, it can be loaded from a history of saved reports.

Configuring and Monitoring Alerts

Viewing detailed reports alone can make it difficult to spot important events or problems; therefore, Intune supports the creation of alerts and notifications.

In the Microsoft Intune Admin console, Alerts workspace, the Intune administrator can view alerts that need attention plus notices from the Intune service itself. Types of alerts are predefined in Intune and can be individually enabled or disabled. Part of configuring an alert is to determine the severity of the problem: Critical, Warning, or Informational. For example, the alert type *DHCP Service Stopped* might require only a Warning status, and does not need to be flagged as Critical. Alert types can have additional configuration options defined, such as a threshold or secondary condition that must be met to trigger the alert.

 Alerts are not managed from the Alerts workspace; they are instead configured from the Admin workspace > Alerts and Notifications > Alert Types task.

Alerts are displayed as tiles in several workspaces in the Microsoft Intune Admin console; however, this might not be useful if nobody is looking at them when the problem happens. Alerts support the ability to configure notifications. The Intune service can send alerts via email to recipients defined in the Admin workspace > Alerts and Notifications > Recipients node. All that is required is the recipient's email address and the language to use to send the alert.

Once the recipient is defined, rules are updated that define what types of alerts should trigger email notices to those recipients. Alert notification rules are managed from the Admin workspace > Alerts and Notifications > Notification Rules node. By default, five notification rules are defined and enabled that cannot be deleted or edited and do not have any recipients assigned to them to start with: All Alerts, Critical Alerts, Informational Alerts, Remote Assistance Requests, and Warning Alerts. These notification rules can be individually disabled and have recipients assigned to them. If these are too generic, the administrator can create new rules based on alert type categories and the severity level that triggers a notification. Alert categories include:

- *System*—Alerts when deployments to clients have failed, or when mobile device issues are encountered

- *Monitoring*—Alerts about resource availability or levels (e.g., free disk space, automatic services that are not running)

- *Remote Assistance*—Alerts when a user has requested remote assistance

- *Updates*—Alerts when updates are waiting for approval

- *Endpoint Protection*—Alerts when Endpoint Protection on managed computers has recorded a major event (e.g., detecting malware, reporting disabled protection)

- *Policy*—Alerts when a device has a problem implementing Intune policy settings
- *Notices*—Alerts when service announcements are released

Managing Policies

One of the main goals of a device management service such as Microsoft Intune is to enable the administrator to control features and apply settings to managed devices. In an on-premises situation, the administrator may elect to use Active Directory and Group Policies to apply settings to domain-joined computers. Intune uses a similar concept to Group Policy that is generically called Microsoft Intune policies, but they apply to computers and mobile devices, domain joined or not.

Most Intune policies can be accessed from the Microsoft Intune Admin console, Policy Workspaces, as shown in Figure 11-6.

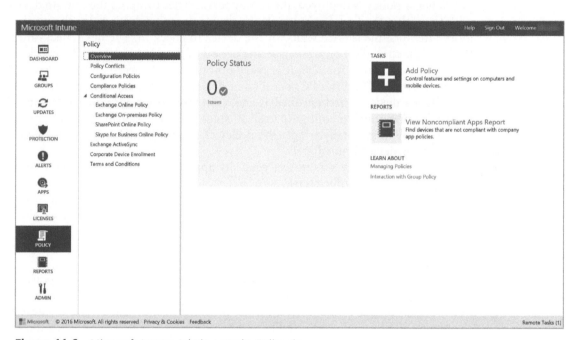

Figure 11-6   Microsoft Intune Admin console, Policy view

The main categories of Intune policies include:

- *Configuration Policies*—Manage security settings and features for different types of devices using predefined templates. If multiple configuration policies update the same setting on a device, the most restrictive setting is applied.

If an Intune configuration policy modifies the same setting as an active Group Policy for a domain-joined device, the Group Policy setting has a higher priority. If the domain-joined computer can't sign in to the domain, the Intune policy will be applied. Otherwise, the Group Policy setting will be applied instead. This mixed approach is not desirable and should be avoided by carefully planning Group Policy application within the domain. This can be accomplished using proper OU structure within the domain, security group filters, WMI filters, and perhaps even blocking Group Policy inheritance.

- *Compliance Policies*—Rules and settings devices must meet to be considered compliant, including monitoring and remediation. Compliance policies have a higher priority over configuration policies. If multiple compliance policies update the same setting on a device, the most restrictive setting is applied.

- *Conditional Access Policies*—Restrict access to app services such as Exchange on-premises, Exchange Online, SharePoint Online, or Skype for Business Online. Conditional access policies can be used in combination with compliance policies.

- *Corporate Device Enrollment Policies*—Enable enrollment policies for iOS devices.

- *Term and Conditions Policies*—Terms and conditions that users can review and potentially must accept before their devices are managed by Intune. These policies include version controls so that as terms and conditions change, users must agree to the updated agreement.

Creating an Intune policy can be done from the Overview task in the Policy workspace or from each specific policy task. Simply creating a policy does nothing until it is deployed against a group of devices.

When a policy is deployed, the Intune service tries to signal the remote device to check in for updates within the first 5 minutes. If the device doesn't acknowledge the notification after three more attempts, the service waits for the device to check in. The next check-in time will be when the device is turned on or after a specific period of time has elapsed. The check-in period depends on the device family: for iOS, it is every 6 hours; for Android and Windows Phone, it is every 8 hours; and for Windows PCs enrolled as devices, it is once every 24 hours.

When a device is first enrolled, it checks in more often for policies to apply to ensure that it has the opportunity to configure itself in stages and work through full compliance and access. If users want to manually trigger the policy check, they can sign in to the Company Portal app and sync the device immediately.

If an Intune policy was not successfully applied, it is listed as a policy conflict in the Policy workspace, Policy Conflicts task.

Configuration policies typically make up the majority of specialized Intune policies. In addition to general configuration settings, features and resources can be configured, which include VPN profiles, Wi-Fi profiles, and certificate profiles that are organized by device type. Configuration policies also include software policies and computer management settings such as Windows Firewall settings.

Software policies apply controls for managed browsers and Mobile Application Management (MAM) policies. Once a device is managed and compliant, Intune administrators can shift attention to how company data is accessed on the devices they manage. If users access corporate data, they might need to have their ability to cut and paste data restricted. They might need the ability to share data between some apps and not others. They might also need to have their ability to save information to personal storage limited to make sure that corporate data is not stored in a vulnerable location or potentially copied in violation of company policy. MAM policies can accomplish this task by working together with apps that are MAM aware, such as Microsoft Office. Custom apps can be made MAM aware by corporate developers using the Intune App Software Development Kit or the App wrapping tool. The mobile device's MAM apps keep track of the identity using it—personal or corporate—perhaps both at the same time. MAM treats data elements as protected resources and guards data isolation according to MAM policies. Note that MAM policies can apply to apps on devices that are not enrolled, as long as the app is MAM aware.

When a policy is removed or no longer applies to a user and the user's devices, the settings that have been customized will revert to earlier settings or back to their default settings.

Managing Remote Computers

Viewing the devices that are members of a group in the Microsoft Intune Admin console allows the administrator to trigger remote operations for an individual device.

The remote device management operations include:

- *Restart Computer*—Request a restart of the remote device.

- *Update Malware Definitions*—Trigger an update of malware definitions for Endpoint Protection on the device.

- *Run a Malware Scan*—Trigger a malware scan (full or quick scan) on the device using Endpoint Protection.

- *Refresh Policies*—Trigger a refresh of Intune policies from the device.

- *Refresh Inventory*—Request updated inventory information from the device.

- *Remote Lock*—Trigger a lock of the device if the user has misplaced the device and it is not set to lock automatically after a period of time.

- *Passcode Reset*—Trigger a new passcode for a device if the user has forgotten the passcode or the passcode must be reset because the user has been terminated.

- *Retire/Wipe*—Trigger a selective or full wipe of the device and remove it from Intune. A selective wipe removes company data but leaves personal data intact for the user, unlocks controls previously locked down by Intune policies, revokes management policies, and removes resource access policies (e.g., Wi-Fi or VPN). A full wipe returns the device to factory default configuration and removes all data.

Computers that are added to a trial Intune account should be retired before the end of the Intune trial or they cannot be assigned to another Intune account after the Intune trial expires.

- *Delete*—Remove the device from Intune.

Activity 11-5: Creating an Intune Policy

Time Required: 20 minutes
Objective: Create a custom policy and apply it to a Windows client

Description: In this activity, you create a custom Intune policy to configure contact information for a fictitious company called ACME. You push the new policy out to the Windows client that was added to Intune in a previous activity. You start the local app Microsoft Intune Center on the local client to review the change made by the new policy.

1. Continue from Activity 11-4 by selecting the Microsoft Intune Admin console webpage (*https://manage.microsoft.com*).
2. Click the **POLICY** workspace. If you are prompted to reauthenticate, confirm your credentials and reselect the correct browser tab.
3. Click the **Add Policy** task.
4. Click to expand the **Computer Management** category and select the **Microsoft Intune Center Settings** template.
5. Click the **Create Policy** button.
6. In the name field under General, type **Lab 11-5 Custom Policy 1**.
7. Scroll down and under Microsoft Intune Center, fill in the fields as follows:
   - Name: **ACME Administrators**
   - Phone Number: **1-800-555-1212**
   - Email Address: **Support@acme.bogus**
   - Website name: **ACME Help Desk**
   - Website name: **http://www.acme.bogus/helpdesk/contact**
   - Notes: **Monday to Friday, 7AM – 9PM EST**
8. Click the **Save Policy** button.
9. Click **Yes** when you are prompted to deploy this policy now.
10. Click **All Computers** to highlight it, click **Add** to select the group, and then click **OK**. This creates the policy and returns the view to a list of configuration policies.
11. Click the **GROUPS** workspace.
12. In the middle pane, click the **All Devices** selection.

11

13. Click the **Remote Tasks** link, and select **Refresh Policies**.

14. Click **Close** when you are notified that a request to refresh policies has been sent.

15. Click **Start** and click **Microsoft Intune Center** from the recently added section of the Start menu.

16. Review the support information that has been updated from the policy at the bottom of the Microsoft Intune Center window.

17. Close the Microsoft Intune Center window, but leave the Internet Explorer browser window open for the next activity.

Deploying Software Updates Using Microsoft Intune

Microsoft Intune can deploy software updates to devices that are managed with the Intune client. Updates to apps can be managed for approval, deployment, and installation while monitoring the deployment. The Updates workspace in the Intune Admin console is used to manage updates; however, it only appears (as shown in Figure 11-7) after at least one successful Intune client is deployed.

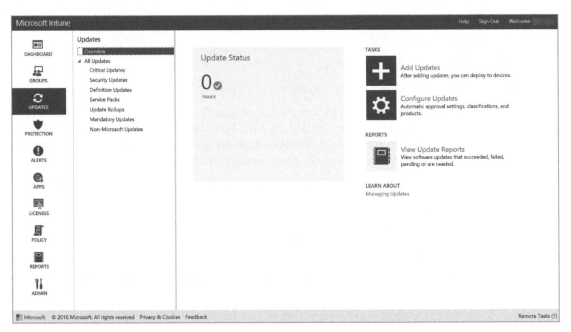

Figure 11-7 Microsoft Intune Admin console, Updates view

The Updates workspace Overview node displays status information using live tiles and a link to display update reports. The categories of updates in the middle pane are used to view updates of that type in the right-hand pane. A large number of results can be returned; therefore, a display filter is available to reduce the list, as shown in Figure 11-8.

Instead of browsing through a list, the Update Report lists computers using report criteria such as update classification (e.g., service packs) and update status (e.g., pending, failed, installed) for selected device groups. The Update Report settings can be saved and loaded in the future to toggle the report settings quickly. The generated report opens in a new window and includes the option to print or export the results to a CSV or HTML file.

An update has to be approved by the Intune administrator for it to be available for installation. The update is assigned to select groups and a deployment action is selected: required install, available install, do not install, or uninstall.

Manually approving each update might not be desirable, so Intune supports the option of automatic update approval. Automatic update approvals are configured from the Admin

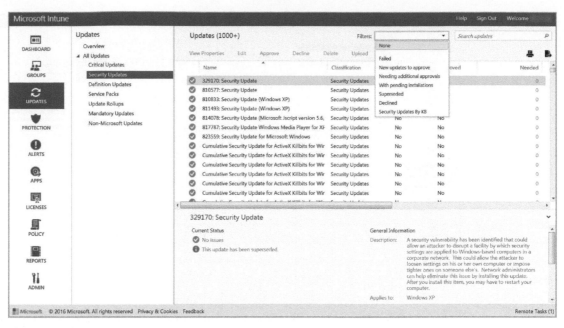

Figure 11-8   Microsoft Intune Admin console, Updates view, filter list

workspace, Updates node. This node defines what updates the Intune service monitors for the tenant as well as any automatic update rules that apply to those selected product categories. Automatic update rules are applied against a product category (e.g., Windows, Office) and update classes (e.g., critical, security, feature packs, service packs). Note that the product category selected in the automatic update rule should be selected in the general update settings as well or Intune will not apply the automatic update.

Automatic update rules can be applied to specific groups of devices that will receive the updates, and optionally an installation deadline can force those devices to install the updates—even if that requires them to reboot. The installation deadline is configurable from several options that extend from 1 day after approval up to 28 days after approval.

In addition to Microsoft updates, Intune has the ability to distribute third-party updates that are in EXE, MSI, or MSP format. In the Updates workspace, the Add Updates task can upload the update file and define the parameters for applying the update using the Microsoft Intune Software Publisher.

Managing Apps Using Microsoft Intune

Software updates help to keep a device up to date, but Intune can also publish apps to specific devices or users as specified through the Apps workspace of the Intune Admin console, as shown in Figure 11-9.

The Apps workspace Overview node displays status information using live tiles, a task to add apps, and a link to view the Detected Software Report. From the Apps workspace, in general you can add apps or links to external apps, and then deploy those apps to devices or workstations. Intune also has the ability to use MDM and MAM policies to configure and protect apps and their related data, as described earlier in this chapter.

Adding Apps Using Microsoft Intune

Apps distributed through Microsoft Intune are defined by the administrator using a utility called the Microsoft Intune Software Publisher. When the administrator clicks the Add Apps task from the Overview node, the Microsoft Intune Software Publisher is downloaded to the administrator's workstation and runs as an Add Software Wizard. This tool has its own installation requirements to operate correctly on the administrator's computer. Currently, it requires Microsoft

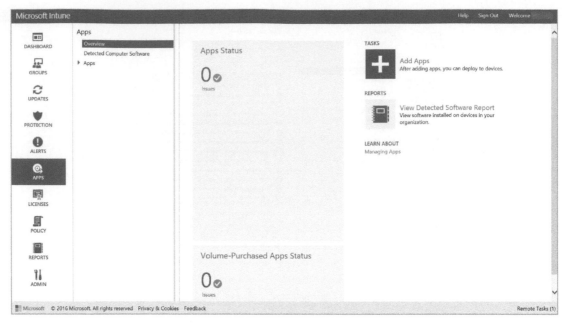

Figure 11-9   Microsoft Intune Admin console, Apps overview

.NET Framework 4.0. As the tool evolves, confirm that the Intune administrator's computer is kept up to date to meet the tool's minimum requirements.

The Add Software Wizard walks the Intune administrator through the process of adding an app to the list of Intune-managed apps. If the installation files for an app are required to enable the app's installation, Microsoft Intune offers a cloud storage space for storing those files. This cloud-based storage enables the installation of software regardless of where the device is located—on or off the corporate network. An Intune trial subscription starts with 20 GB of cloud storage, increased from the original trial amount of 2 GB. If desired, additional space can be purchased for a paid Intune subscription. Not all app types can be installed from the cloud storage space due to device limitations and restrictions.

Some devices require that an app must be loaded from a trusted location such as their respective store (e.g., Windows Store, Apple App Store). Intune can add the managed app as a pointer to an external website or store installation URL, generically referred to as *deep-linking* an app in Intune terminology.

Some apps are meant to be installed from a device's related store (e.g., Windows Store), but you might want to bypass that step and load them directly to the device. This is typically done in the enterprise environment when line-of-business apps are developed and distributed directly to end-user devices. Bypassing the Windows Store to install the app is known as *sideloading* the app. Windows 8–based devices require the device to be domain joined or licensed using a sideloading product activation key. Microsoft Intune can store sideloading keys, which allows for the installation of line-of-business devices on these older Windows devices. Windows 10–based devices do not require a sideloading product activation key. The app code must be signed by the developer using a certificate that the device trusts, and Windows 10 support for sideloading must be enabled, either via Group Policy, MDM policy, or locally on the Windows 10 device.

Custom line-of-business apps are usually developed through custom app development. To prove that the app can be trusted by the device, the developer signs the code using an SSL code-signing certificate. If the device trusts the certificate that was used to sign the code, it trusts the code. Microsoft Intune allows the administrator to upload additional code-signing certificates and sideloading keys from the Admin workspace, not the Apps workspace, as shown in Figure 11-10.

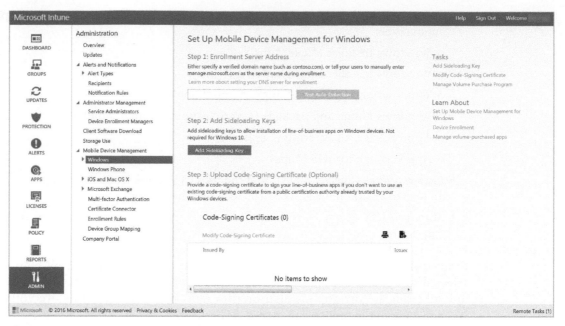

Figure 11-10   Microsoft Intune Admin console, Mobile Device Management for Windows settings

 Code-signing certificates uploaded to Intune have a .cer file extension.

11

The Microsoft Intune Software Publisher Wizard steps the administrator through more than just defining the elements of the app installation. The Add Software Wizard reauthenticates the Intune administrator as the program runs locally on the administrator's workstation. The wizard needs to confirm what type of app the administrator is adding to Intune (as shown in Figure 11-11):

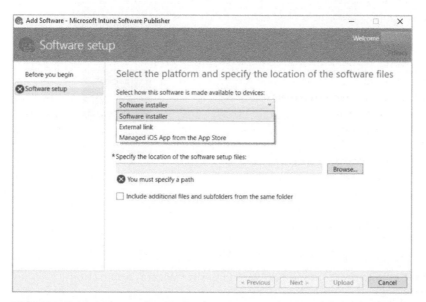

Figure 11-11   Microsoft Intune Software Publisher Wizard, application platform and installer selection

- *Software installer*—Identify the app installer type based on the device and app installation engine type:
  - o Windows Installer (*.exe, *.msi)
  - o Windows Installer through MDM (*.msi)
  - o Windows app package (*.appx, *.appxbundle)
  - o Windows Phone app package (*.xap, *.appx, *.appxbundle)
  - o App Package for Android (*.apk)
  - o App Package for iOS (*.ipa)
- *External link*—Specify a URL that the user can access from the Company Portal to install an app from an online store or run as a web-based app.
- *Managed iOS App from the App Store*—Specify a URL to deploy a free iOS app from the App Store.

If any content is uploaded to Intune's cloud storage, the files must all be in the same folder selected to upload, optionally including its subfolders. Only one local path can be selected to upload from, so any app installation files must be consolidated before you run the wizard. No single file in the upload can exceed 2 GB in size.

For a typical desktop app install using the Windows Installer, the wizard prompts for a description of the app, as shown in Figure 11-12. This includes required information, such as the publisher, app name, and app description. Optional information can be provided to help the user identify an app as the user browses for it, including a URL for software information, a privacy URL, an app category, and a custom icon. The wizard also prompts for the target computer requirements before the installation can start, including architecture (32-bit, 64-bit, or either) and operating system minimum version (Windows XP, Windows Vista, Windows 7, Windows 8, Windows 8.1, any version). Optional command-line arguments can be defined within the wizard, if they are required. Once the summary of the wizard settings is accepted, any installation files are compressed and copied to Intune cloud storage, as shown in Figure 11-13.

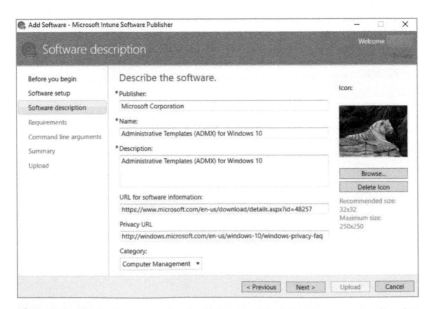

Figure 11-12   Microsoft Intune Software Publisher Wizard, application description settings

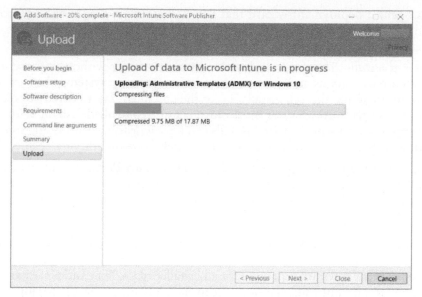

Figure 11-13   Microsoft Intune Software Publisher Wizard, application file upload to cloud storage

Once the wizard is completed and the browser is refreshed, the newly added app is visible in the Apps workspace, as shown in Figure 11-14.

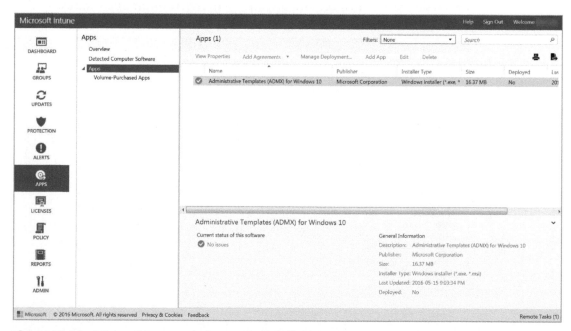

Figure 11-14   Microsoft Intune Admin console, Apps listing

Deploying Apps Using Microsoft Intune

Once an app is added to the app list, the next step is to consider deployment of the app. To deploy an app, the admin highlights the app in the App list and then clicks Manage Deployment on the top toolbar, as shown in Figure 11-14.

This opens a deployment wizard that determines which device or user groups this app is deployed to, and the deployment action for that target. The deployment action can include the following:

- *Required install*—The app is deployed to the user's device without end-user intervention. Due to licensing limits and newer mobile device operating systems, the user might still see a prompt to accept the app installation or the app might fail to deploy to older mobile operating systems. Always test the deployment in a controlled fashion before deploying a new app to your users. Required installs can have a deadline for installation defined that includes as soon as possible, one week, two weeks, one month, or a custom date and time.

- *Available install*—The app is deployed to the Company Portal and the user can choose to install it on demand. Many Intune systems are designed with the preference that the users will self-service themselves as much as possible and avoid placing a load on the help desk.

- *Uninstall*—The app is removed from the device.

- *Not applicable*—The app is not installed or displayed in the Company Portal.

Not all deployment types are supported for all installer types. For example, external links are only applicable to user groups using the Available install and Not applicable deployment actions.

If there are conflicting deployment settings applied to users and devices, settings against the device take precedence over settings for the user. Installation settings take precedence over uninstall settings.

Once an app is deployed, the effective deployment status of an app can be viewed by highlighting an app in the App list and clicking View Properties from the top toolbar to open the app's properties, as shown in Figure 11-15. The properties include a Computers and Users tab that shows which devices and users have successfully installed the app. As a general overview, the Dashboard workspace also displays an overview of the app's status.

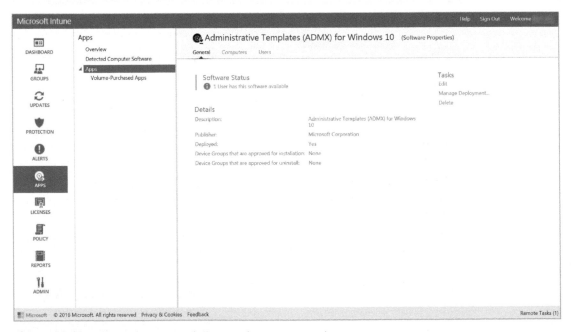

Figure 11-15   Microsoft Intune Admin console, App properties

Intune apps can also be updated by updating the app within Intune. The original app package can be edited by highlighting an app in the App list and clicking Edit from the top toolbar. New software details can be supplied and saved as an update to the original app package. When devices check for available apps, the installed app on the device is automatically updated to the latest version. If this is not suitable, another option is to set the app deployment to uninstall and deploy a different app package at a later time or as an on-demand install.

Chapter Summary

- Microsoft Intune is a device-management solution for a variety of devices: Windows PC, Mac OS X, Apple iOS, and Android devices. Devices can be domain joined or not and still be managed with Intune. Intune supports scenarios where the company issues the device or users bring their own personal devices.

- Microsoft Intune can be combined with on-premises System Center Configuration Manager (SCCM) or it can be configured to run from the cloud only. This choice is made at the beginning of the Intune deployment and cannot be changed after the choice is made.

- An administrator who wants to evaluate Microsoft Intune can sign up for a free 30-day trial with 100 Intune licenses. The Intune tenant is associated with an Office 365 tenant that stores user account details in Azure AD. If the trial is meant to be disposable, the Office 365 tenant details should not conflict with any setting desired in production.

- Once Intune is deployed into production, on-premises Active Directory identities can be synchronized to Office 365 using a tool such as DirSync or one of its newer variations.

- Mobile devices can be enrolled into Intune using several options and control settings via policies within Intune. Windows PCs can be added to Intune and managed by installing the Intune client on those computers.

- Users and computers can be grouped within Intune. Intune groups can use information from security groups, but they are not the same thing as groups defined in Azure AD. Intune groups have their own hierarchy and are linked to a parent group to build a management structure based on the administrator's style and environment management needs.

- A service administrator can be created to manage a portion of the Intune environment and restricted to visibility defined by specific device and user groups.

- To review the performance of the Intune system, the Intune administrator has a rich collection of reports that can be filtered to focus attention on desired information.

- Instead of waiting to find information on dashboard tiles and reports, Intune supports the generation of alerts and notifications that are customizable to those areas that are important to the Intune administrator.

- Devices and computers managed by Intune can have policies applied to them to configure features and settings, including resource access, compliance, and security settings.

- Remote computers can be managed from the Intune Administrator console for operations such as remote lock, passcode reset, full or partial wipe, and others.

- Updates are an important part of managing an Intune environment, and updates can be customized to be manually managed or configured for automatic application with follow-up reporting for administrative review.

- Deploying software based on managed users and devices is a major strength of Microsoft Intune, supporting a blend of devices and deployment options.

Key Terms

Android   An open source operating system currently developed by Google used for smartphones and tablet computers.

Apple Push Notification service (APNs)   A service created by Apple that allows external apps to send notification data to apps installed on Apple devices.

Azure AD   Otherwise known as Azure Active Directory; an identity and access management cloud solution that provides the ability to manage users and groups. It provides identity information for secure access to on-premises and cloud apps, including Office 365, Azure, and Intune.

Azure AD Premium   A paid-for and enhanced version of Azure AD that includes enterprise features such as self-service identity and access management and self-service password reset for on-premises users.

Bring Your Own Device (BYOD)   A policy that allows employees to bring their own computers, smartphones, and tablets to work and use them to access corporate resources.

Choose Your Own Device (CYOD)   A policy that allows employees to choose a computer, smartphone, or tablet from a corporate-owned pool of devices and use them to access corporate resources.

DirSync   A Microsoft tool for synchronizing copies of local identity information into Azure AD. Many administrators still use this name for newer versions of the synchronization software such as Azure AD Connect.

Enterprise Mobility Suite (EMS)   A license suite available for purchase from Microsoft that includes Azure AD Premium, Microsoft Intune, and Azure Rights Management Services.

iOS   An operating system used for mobile devices that are manufactured by Apple.

Mobile Application Management (MAM)   Software and services responsible for provisioning and controlling access to mobile apps that are used in a business environment, on both BYOD and corporate-assigned devices.

Mobile Device Management (MDM)   Security software used to monitor, manage, and secure employee mobile devices across mobile service providers and mobile operating systems.

System Center 2012 Configuration Manager (SCCM)   Management software developed by Microsoft to manage large groups of computers, primarily deployed on-premises.

Systems Management Server   An earlier version of SCCM.

User Principal Name (UPN)   The name that uniquely identifies a user within an identity directory, such as Active Directory or Azure Active Directory. It looks similar to an email address, with a user name followed by the @ symbol, and then a domain associated with that user. The domain name is formatted to appear like a DNS name. A sample UPN would be *Bob.Smith@example.com*. No other user in the directory could share this UPN.

Review Questions

1. Windows Intune is the latest edition of the Intune service. True or False?

2. A user can enroll _____ device(s) into Intune.
   a. 1
   b. 2
   c. 3
   d. 5

3. Group Policy settings generally take precedence over Intune configuration policy settings. True or False?

4. Intune policies that control how an app can store data are generically referred to as Mobile _____ Management policies.

5. Intune Update Reports can be exported to what type of log files? (Select two.)
   a. .txt
   b. .exe
   c. .csv
   d. .xml
   e. .html

6. A Windows PC running the Intune Client will check in how often?

    a. every hour

    b. every 6 hours

    c. every 8 hours

    d. every 24 hours

    e. never

7. Android-based phones and tablets require a Google Push Notification Service certificate to be managed with Intune. True or False?

8. Alert types are managed from the _____ workspace.

    a. Admin

    b. Reports

    c. Alerts

    d. Apps

    e. Protection

9. Automatic update rules can specify a maximum installation date deadline of _____ day(s) after approval?

    a. 1

    b. 5

    c. 15

    d. 28

    e. 30

10. All user and device groups are linked to a parent group. True or False?

11. The top parent group for computers is called All _____.

12. Which web console is used to manage Intune licenses?

    a. Office 365 Admin center

    b. Administrator console

    c. Company Portal

    d. Company app

    e. none of the above

13. If an APN certificate for Intune expires, Intune will only be able to manage _____ for iOS devices:

    a. configuration settings

    b. nothing

    c. compliance settings

    d. remote lock requests

14. The oldest Windows client operating system compatible with the Intune client is _____.

    a. Windows XP SP3

    b. Windows 2000 Professional

    c. Windows Vista

    d. Windows 7 Service Pack 1

15. Intune user accounts can be synchronized from on-premises Active Directory using the
_____ utility:

a. EMS

b. Azure RMS

c. Intune sync

d. DirSync

16. The Microsoft Edge browser is suitable for accessing and operating the Intune Admin console. True or False?

17. Intune can operate in a hybrid mode with on-premises System Center Configuration Manager. True or False?

18. Third-party updates can be uploaded to Intune and distributed via Intune if the update file is in which of the following formats? (Choose all that apply.)

a. XML

b. MSI

c. MSP

d. MDM

19. When the Intune client is being installed on local PCs, any previous System Center Configuration Manager client on the PC must be _____.

a. version 3.1 or higher

b. 64-bit

c. updated to the 2012 R2 edition

d. removed

20. The web address to open the Intune Admin console in Internet Explorer using an InPrivate Browsing session is _____.

a. *manage.microsoft.com*

b. *account.manage.microsoft.com*

c. *portal.manage.microsoft.com*

d. *portal.office.com*

Case Projects

Case 11-1: Protecting Corporate Resources

Gigantic Life Insurance has terminated a sales account manager who is traveling on the road with a company-issued mobile device. What operations can you take as the Intune administrator to ensure the mobile device is not used to access corporate resources by the sales account manager? If the user does not return the device, what can you do to help ensure that the device does not contain any corporate data?

Case 11-2: Upgrading System Performance

You are responsible for managing Windows updates on 80 Windows 10 Enterprise computers at the office. You currently receive alert notifications when a new critical or security update is available for approval. Once you approve the updates, they are eventually installed. You would like these updates to apply automatically for the Windows 10 computers, and ensure that they are applied within 1 day of approval. How can this be accomplished with Intune? How can you confirm that your workstations are applying the updates as expected and present a detailed, biweekly report to your CEO?

chapter 12

Client Hyper-V

After reading this chapter and completing the exercises, you will be able to:

- Understand how Hyper-V works and how to install it
- Create virtual machines
- Configure virtual memory
- Configure virtual processors
- Create and manage virtual hard disks
- Configure virtual network adapters
- Manage virtual machines

Virtualization is a core technology in server data centers. However, it can also be used on Windows 10 computers by implementing Client Hyper-V. Client Hyper-V allows you to create complex test environments with multiple virtual machines on a single computer as long as that computer has sufficient resources.

In this chapter, you learn the architecture of Hyper-V, use case scenarios, and learn how to install Hyper-V. You also learn how to create, configure, and manage virtual machines. This includes managing virtual machine hardware, such as virtual memory, virtual processors, virtual hard disks, and virtual network adapters. This also includes exporting virtual machines, importing virtual machines, and managing checkpoints.

Overview of Hyper-V

Hyper-V is a technology first introduced in Windows Server 2008 to allow a Windows-based server to host virtual machines. Virtualization and the use of virtual machines has become commonplace in company data centers. A variation of Hyper-V is also available in Windows 10 to allow desktop computers to run virtual machines.

Virtualization allows the hardware of a single computer to be shared by multiple operating systems running at the same time. The hardware capacity is subdivided into virtual machines. Each **virtual machine** is allocated a specific amount of resources, such as processing capacity and memory. After creating a virtual machine, you install an operating system in the virtual machine and it behaves like a physical computer.

Hyper-V Architecture

To implement virtualization, Hyper-V uses a piece of software called a **hypervisor**. The hypervisor resides between the operating system and hardware, as shown in Figure 12-1. After Hyper-V is installed, the hypervisor controls all communication with the physical hardware on the computer, even for the host operating system.

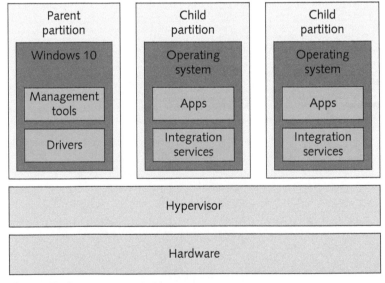

Figure 12-1   Hyper-V architecture

Microsoft documentation refers to the host operating system as the parent partition. The host operating system is important for Hyper-V because the hardware drivers for the physical computer are loaded there. If the host operating system crashes, the virtual machines cannot function.

Each of the virtual machines is a child partition. The child partition does not have access to any physical hardware and does not load drivers for the physical hardware. The operating systems in the child partition have access to virtualized hardware provided by Hyper-V. Some of the hardware components are emulated components that most operating systems have drivers for. Other hardware components are optimized virtual components that require specific drivers. Recent Windows operating systems include the drivers for the virtual components, which are called integration services.

Scenarios for Using Virtualization

In data centers, virtualization is an efficient use of hardware in servers that are generally so powerful that a single server would sit idle if only a single operating system and application were hosted on it. For computers running Windows 10, Client Hyper-V is more likely to be used for testing or application compatibility.

The checkpoint functionality for virtual machines is very useful for testing because you can almost instantly reset a computer back to a previous state. This is much more efficient than reimaging a physical computer to try alternate scenarios during testing.

Some scenarios for using Client Hyper-V are:

- *Update testing*—Testing updates on a production desktop can render it unusable. So, you need to use a separate operating system for initial testing. You could maintain a separate physical computer for testing updates, but that requires physical space and does not have the ability to do checkpoints. A support technician can easily maintain several virtual machines with various operating systems and application combinations for ensuring updates do not have unexpected results.

- *Software testing*—Support technicians often have specialized software configurations on their own computers that might not be suitable for testing the same software used by users. When a trouble ticket comes in and you need to identify the issue in the software, you need to either work with the user on his or her computer or maintain a separate computer. Again, a virtual machine is a simpler solution to maintaining a separate computer.

- *Software deployment*—Getting new software to deploy properly can be a time-consuming, finicky process. Before virtual machines became common, deployment testing involved a separate physical machine that would be reimaged between each test. This might cause each test to take 30 minutes or more. With virtualization and checkpoints, the majority of that time is avoided because the reimaging process is avoided. In addition, you can have virtual machines in various configurations to ensure the software works properly for multiple user configurations.

- *Demonstrations*—As part of software product sales, it is typically a requirement to do a demonstration of the software. Salespeople can have a laptop with virtual machines that create the required environment to demonstrate the software. The demonstration can include complex environments with multiple servers and supporting components, such as Microsoft SQL Server and domain controllers.

- *Training*—Rather than configuring physical computers in a training environment, it can be much faster to use virtual machines. The physical computers in a classroom function as hosts for the virtual machines and then students use the virtual machines. You can switch between completely different classes just by shutting down one set of virtual machines and starting another. It also allows students to have complex environments that are completely private to avoid one student impacting another. Checkpoint functionality also makes it easy to recover from mistakes.

- *App compatibility*—If an app is not compatible with Windows 10, users can have a virtual machine with an older Windows operating system to run that application. This is not an ideal situation, and it is better to upgrade the app to a compatible version if possible. However, if you cannot obtain a compatible version of an app that is no longer in development, this can be an acceptable solution.

- *Running alternate operating systems*—Some support technicians need to run specialized environments with alternate operating systems such as Linux. You can use Client Hyper-V for virtual machines with a Linux operating system. Again, this avoids the need to have a separate physical computer.

12

Because virtual machines do not have access to the physical hardware, there is no way to test hardware drivers.

Client Hyper-V in Windows 10 also includes support for **nested virtualization**. Nested virtualization allows for a single physical computer enabled as a Hyper-V host to have a virtual machine that is also enabled as a Hyper-V host. This might have some applicability for flexible deployments in data centers, but it is unlikely to be useful for Client Hyper-V.

Comparing Server and Client Hyper-V

Both Hyper-V on Windows Server and Client Hyper-V on Windows 10 offer the same core functionality that allows you to run virtual machines. So, both are suitable for use when doing simple testing using virtual machines. In fact, a virtual machine created on a Windows server can be moved to Client Hyper-V and vice versa. When you have a test virtual machine, it does not matter whether it runs on a server or your local computer.

The server version of Hyper-V has more advanced capabilities that are required in a data center to provide high availability. Some of the features in Hyper-V for Windows Server that are not available in Client Hyper-V are:

- *Live virtual machine migration*—Allows virtual machines to be moved from one Hyper-V host to another while the virtual machine is running. There is no interruption to users.

- *Hyper-V replica*—Replicates virtual machines between two Hyper-V hosts for redundancy. Data changes are replicated at a set interval. The interval is between 30 seconds, 5 minutes, or 15 minutes.

At the time of writing, the most recent builds of Windows 10 include RemoteFX 3D Video Adapter for increased graphics performance, and Fibre Channel Adapter for connectivity to a fibre channel storage area network. These were not included in the initial release of Windows 10, but have been added since then.

Client Hyper-V for Windows 10 has one feature that is not available in Hyper-V for Windows Server. Client Hyper-V supports sleep and hibernate functionality in the host operating system. This means that if you have virtual machines on your laptop, you can close the lid and not worry that Client Hyper-V is going to prevent your laptop from going to sleep and shortening the battery life. This is not available in the server version of Hyper-V because servers are expected to provide continuous service.

The other benefit of Client Hyper-V is how the virtual machines are managed. This benefit is not technical; it is administrative. In a data center, it can be a time-consuming process to go through the procedures necessary to get a new virtual machine allocated. There might also be a limit on the resources that can be allocated in the data center. When you use Client Hyper-V on your own computer, you can create virtual machines at will and allocate the necessary resources. However, this might require that your computer is upgraded with either a faster disk or more memory.

Client Hyper-V Prerequisites

You can install Client Hyper-V for Windows 10 Pro, Windows 10 Enterprise, and Windows 10 Education editions. Client Hyper-V is not included in Windows 10 Home or Windows 10 Mobile editions. The 32-bit editions of Windows 10 also do not support Hyper-V.

If you have a supported edition of Windows 10, you also need to meet the following requirements:

- *64-bit processor with Second Level Address Translation (SLAT)*—This technology is supported by most recent processors, such as Intel Core i3, i5, and i7.

- *Processor support for VM Monitor Mode Extension*—For Intel processors, this feature is known as Intel Virtualization Technology (Intel VT).

- *Virtualization enabled in firmware*—The hardware virtualization functionality in the process is often disabled by default. This functionality needs to be enabled in the firmware of the computer. The name of the feature varies depending on the computer manufacturer.

- *Hardware enforced data execution prevention (DEP)*—This option needs to be enabled in the firmware of the computer.

The simplest way to confirm that your computer meets the requirements for Client Hyper-V is to run systeminfo.exe. This utility reports back the status of the Hyper-V requirements, as shown in Figure 12-2. In Figure 12-2, all of the hardware requirements have been met, but hardware virtualization has not been enabled in the firmware.

```
Hyper-V Requirements:      VM Monitor Mode Extensions: Yes
                           Virtualization Enabled In Firmware: No
                           Second Level Address Translation: Yes
                           Data Execution Prevention Available: Yes
```

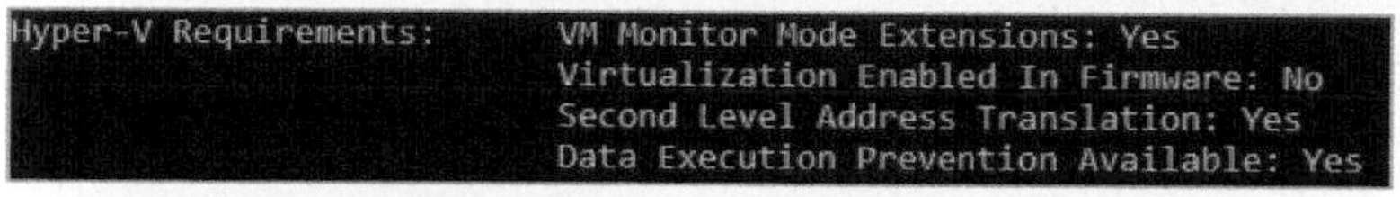

Figure 12-2   Hyper-V output from systeminfo.exe

Installing Client Hyper-V

Client Hyper-V is a feature in Windows 10. Consequently, you can install it by using any method that is available for installing Windows features. You can install Windows features by using the graphic interface in Programs and Features, Windows PowerShell, or dism.exe. Figure 12-3 shows the interface for installing Hyper-V in the graphical interface.

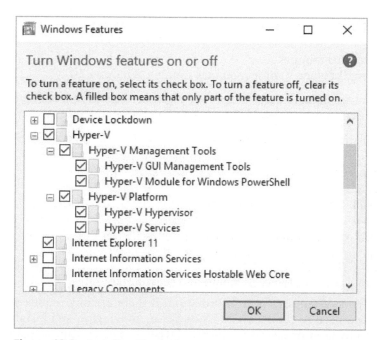

Figure 12-3   Installing Hyper-V

To install Hyper-V by using Windows PowerShell, run the following command:

Enable-WindowsOptionalFeature -Online -FeatureName Microsoft-Hyper-V-All

To install Hyper-V by using dism.exe, run the following command:

Dism /Online /Enable-Feature /Featurename:Microsoft-Hyper-V-All

To enable Hyper-V, you need administrative permissions. If you are using dism.exe or Windows PowerShell, the prompt needs to run as administrator.

After the Hyper-V feature is installed, you need to reboot for it to take effect. This allows the hypervisor to be inserted into the boot process. You can configure that the hypervisor is loaded by using bcdedit.exe. The {current} configuration shows the hypervisorlaunchtype is set to Auto, as shown in Figure 12-4.

```
Administrator: Command Prompt                                    —   □   ×
Windows Boot Loader
-------------------
identifier                 {current}
device                     partition=C:
path                       \WINDOWS\system32\winload.efi
description                Windows 10
locale                     en-US
inherit                    {bootloadersettings}
recoverysequence           {0893aaf7-8941-11e3-934d-9cebe80ccbb1}
recoveryenabled            Yes
badmemoryaccess            Yes
isolatedcontext            Yes
flightsigning              Yes
allowedinmemorysettings    0x15000075
osdevice                   partition=C:
systemroot                 \WINDOWS
resumeobject               {0893aaf5-8941-11e3-934d-9cebe80ccbb1}
nx                         OptIn
bootmenupolicy             Standard
hypervisorlaunchtype       Auto

C:\WINDOWS\system32>_
```

Figure 12-4   Bcdedit showing hypervisorlaunchtype

Activity 12-1: Installing Hyper-V

Time Required: 10 minutes
Objective: Install Hyper-V for a computer running Windows 10

Description: Computer manufacturers ship their computers in varying configurations. You need to ensure that your computer is capable of running Hyper-V and configured properly before you enable the Hyper-V feature. In this activity, you prepare your computer and enable Hyper-V.

 This activity requires a physical computer capable of running Hyper-V. Some of the instructions in this activity are general because the detailed steps will vary by manufacturer and model.

1. If necessary, start your computer and sign in.

2. Right-click the **Start** button and click **Command Prompt**.

3. At the command prompt, type **systeminfo** and press **Enter**.

4. Review the Hyper-V requirements information. If there are any requirements that are not already met, you need to resolve those issues before moving on and installing Hyper-V. If it indicates that a hypervisor has been detected, Hyper-V is or was at one point installed on the computer.

5. Close the command prompt.

6. Click the **Start** button, type **features**, and then click **Turn Windows features on or off**.

7. In the Windows Features dialog box, click the **Hyper-V** check box and click **OK**.

8. After Hyper-V completes installing, click **Close**.

9. Restart your computer to complete installing Hyper-V. In most cases, you are prompted to restart.

Creating Virtual Machines

After you install Hyper-V, you can start creating virtual machines. A virtual machine provides virtual hardware to an operating system and you can configure what hardware is provided in the virtual machines. Table 12-1 shows the basic considerations for virtual machine hardware.

Table 12-1　Virtual machine hardware

Component	Description
CPU	Each virtual machine is allocated a specific number of virtual processors. Only one virtual processor is assigned by default. In most cases, you should assign at least two virtual processors to allow the operating system to perform better multitasking.
Memory	Each virtual machine needs to be allocated enough memory for the operating system and apps. Memory allocated to a VM is no longer available to the host operating system or other virtual machines. The amount of memory in a Hyper-V host is a critical consideration in regard to the number of virtual machines that can run at one time.
Disk	Each virtual machine needs at least one virtual hard disk to store the operating system and data. Virtual hard disks can be in the .vhd or .vhdx format. They can also be a fixed size or dynamically expanding. Considerations for selecting these options are covered later in this chapter.
Network	Virtual machines do not need to be network connected, but in most cases, you want them to either connect to the same network as your Hyper-V host or to a private network that is reserved for testing.

Management Tools

To manage Hyper-V, you can use either the **Hyper-V Manager** or Windows PowerShell cmdlets. Hyper-V Manager, shown in Figure 12-5, is the graphical console that can be used to manage networking and virtual machines. This is the most commonly used method for managing virtual machines. You also have the option to connect to a remote Hyper-V host and manage the virtual machines on the remote host.

12

Figure 12-5　Hyper-V Manager

There are Windows PowerShell cmdlets for managing every aspect of Hyper-V, some of which are not accessible in Hyper-V Manager. However, it is rare that Windows PowerShell cmdlets are required to access advanced functionality. It is more common that you use Windows

PowerShell cmdlets to automate tasks and save time. For example, if you have a set of virtual machines that you need to deploy to a set of computers in a lab, you could write a PowerShell script that copies the virtual machine files from a server, imports them on the local Hyper-V host, and creates a starting checkpoint for recovery.

Virtual Switches

To provide network connectivity for virtual machines, you need to create virtual switches. Each **virtual switch** represents a network that virtual machines can connect to. In Hyper-V Manager, you can use Virtual Switch Manager to create and manage virtual switches, as shown in Figure 12-6.

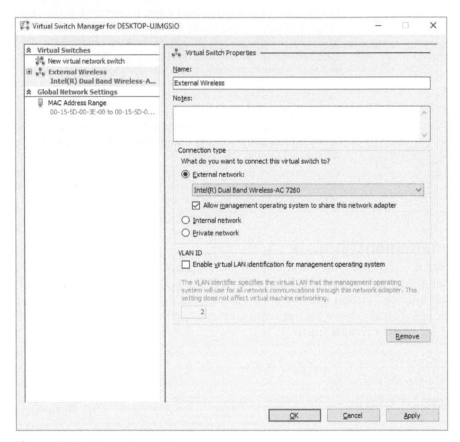

Figure 12-6   Virtual Switch Manager

The most commonly used network type is an **external network**. This type of network uses a physical network adapter in the Hyper-V host to provide virtual machines with connectivity to a physical network. When you create an external network, you need to select the network adapter that should be used for connectivity. You can select any network adapter that is present in the system, including Wi-Fi, Ethernet, or USB network adapters.

If there is only one network adapter in the computer, the Hyper-V host can have only one external network. If there are multiple network adapters, you can have up to one external network per network adapter. If you are using a laptop, it is a good idea to create an external network for both wired and wireless connectivity. Then, you can connect your virtual machines to an external network regardless of whether your physical network connectivity is wired or wireless.

You need to manually change the virtual switch that virtual machines are connected to. Virtual machines do not automatically switch between wired and wireless networks.

On an external network, the option *Allow management operating system to share this network adapter* is enabled by default. You should leave this option enabled. On a computer with only one network adapter, this allows virtual machines and the host operating system to use the network adapter. If you disable this option on a system with a single network adapter, the host operating system loses network connectivity.

A **private network** does not have connectivity to an external network or the host operating system. You can use a private network to create a completely isolated environment for testing. You can create multiple private networks on a Hyper-V host to allow for multiple isolated sets for virtual machines. Keeping your test virtual machines on a private network means you do not need to worry about conflicts like accidentally using the same name as a production server. You could also use a private network for testing antivirus and security issues without affecting the host operating system or other computers on the production network.

Like a private network, an **internal network** does not have access to a physical network. The difference is that the host operating system is connected to an internal network. This can make it easier to move files to virtual machines by copying them from the host to the virtual machines over the internal network.

Activity 12-2: Creating an External Virtual Switch

Time Required: 10 minutes
Objective: Create an external virtual switch by using Hyper-V Manager

Description: Hyper-V uses virtual switches to provide connectivity for virtual machines. An external virtual switch links to a physical network card in the Hyper-V host to provide network connectivity on the physical network. In this activity, you create an external virtual switch for virtual machines.

12

This activity requires a physical computer capable of running Hyper-V. Some of the instructions in this activity are general because the detailed steps will vary by manufacturer and model.

1. If necessary, start your computer and sign in.
2. Click the **Start** button, type **hyper**, and then click **Hyper-V Manager**.
3. In Hyper-V Manager, in the left pane, click your computer name, and in the Actions pane, click **Virtual Switch Manager**.
4. In the Virtual Switch Manager window, click **New virtual network switch**, click **External**, and then click **Create Virtual Switch**.
5. In the Name box, type **External**.
6. In the Connection type area, verify that **External network** is selected and that an appropriate network adapter is selected.
7. Also verify that **Allow management operating system to share this network adapter** is selected and click **OK**.
8. In the Apply Networking Changes window, click **Yes** to acknowledge the warning.
9. You might see a device installation window as the virtual network adapter driver is installed. If so, wait for this to complete.
10. Close all open windows.

Virtual Machine Generations

When you create a virtual machine, you are given the choice between a Generation 1 or a Generation 2 virtual machine, shown in Figure 12-7. Both types of virtual machines provide the same basic functionality, but they do have differences in the virtual hardware that they provide. Table 12-2 compares Generation 1 and Generation 2 virtual machines.

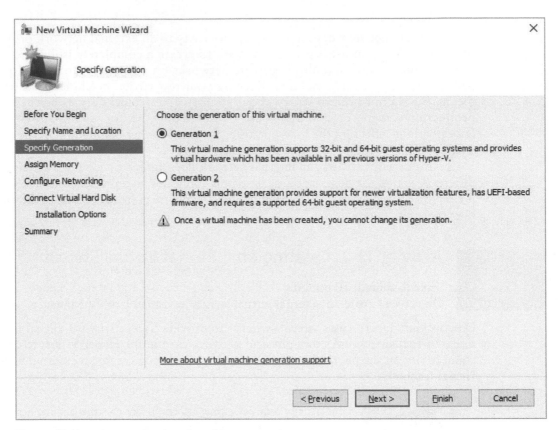

Figure 12-7   Selecting the virtual machine generation

Table 12-2   Generation 1 and Generation 2 virtual machines

Component	Generation 1	Generation 2
Firmware	BIOS-based	UEFI-based
Secure Boot	Not available	Enabled by default
Disk controller	IDE and SCSI	SCSI only
Network adapter	Legacy and synthetic	Synthetic only
Floppy disk controller	Available	Not available
DVD drive	Included by default	Available but without pass-through option

The first big difference between Generation 1 and Generation 2 virtual machines is the firmware emulation. **Generation 1 virtual machines** use BIOS-based firmware, which supports a wider range of operating systems. **Generation 2 virtual machines** use UEFI-based firmware, which is supported only by 64-bit editions of Windows Server 2012 or newer, Windows 8 or newer, and some Linux distributions. If you are installing an operating system that does not support UEFI-based firmware, you need to select a Generation 1 virtual machine.

Secure Boot is a function in UEFI-enabled firmware that is enabled by default. When Secure Boot is enabled, untrusted code cannot be executed outside the operating system. Windows operating system components are digitally signed by Microsoft and trusted when Secure Boot is enabled. Non-Microsoft operating systems are not typically trusted and you either need to configure UEFI firmware to trust the digitally signed files or disable Secure Boot.

Generation 1 virtual machines can only boot from virtual hard disks attached to a virtual IDE controller. The paging file for Windows must also be on a virtual hard disk attached to an IDE controller. IDE is limiting because you can have a maximum of two controllers and only two devices on each controller. However, you can add a SCSI controller for additional virtual hard drives. Generation 2 virtual machines have only SCSI disk controllers.

Legacy network adapters are available only in Generation 1 virtual machines. They are emulated network adapters for which most operating systems include drivers. They can be used to support older operating systems for which there are no Hyper-V Integration Services. A legacy network adapter was also required to support Preboot Execution Environment (PXE), which allows computers to boot from a network source.

The overall performance of legacy network adapters is quite low. Synthetic network adapters are completely virtual. So, they are not limited by trying to emulate real hardware. They are optimized to work with Hyper-V. In Generation 2 virtual machines, the synthetic network adapter has been improved to support PXE. Therefore, legacy network adapters are not available in Generation 2 virtual machines.

Floppy disk controllers are not present in modern computers and they are not included in Generation 2 virtual machines. If you need to connect extra data storage to a virtual machine, you can use a virtual hard drive instead. A virtual hard disk can be moved between virtual machines.

DVD drives are supported for both Generation 1 and Generation 2 virtual machines. A DVD drive is automatically added to new Generation 1 virtual machines. The DVD drive in Generation 1 virtual machines can be attached to an .iso image or use pass-through to access a physical DVD drive in the host. In Generation 2 virtual machines, the DVD drive must be added and it does not support the pass-through functionality.

Activity 12-3: Creating a Virtual Machine

12

Time Required: 45 minutes
Objective: Create a virtual machine and install an operating system

Description: After you have created a virtual switch for network connectivity, you can create a virtual machine and connect it to that network. After creating the virtual machine, you need to install an operating system. In this activity, you create a virtual machine and then install Windows 10 in that virtual machine.

This activity requires you to have an .iso image of the Windows 10 installation DVD. For the purpose of the activity, it is assumed that the file is C:\ISO\Win10.iso on your Hyper-V host. If your .iso for Windows 10 is named differently or in an alternate location, adjust the activity accordingly.

1. If necessary, start your computer and sign in.
2. Click the **Start** button, type **hyper**, and then click **Hyper-V Manager**.
3. In Hyper-V Manager, in the left pane, select your computer name, and in the Actions pane, click **New** and click **Virtual Machine**.
4. In the New Virtual Machine Wizard, on the Before You Begin screen, click **Next**.
5. On the Specify Name and Location screen, in the Name box, type **Win10-Ch12** and click **Next**.
6. On the Specify Generation screen, click **Generation 2** and click **Next**.
7. On the Assign Memory screen, in the Startup memory box, type **2048** and click **Next**.

8. On the Configure Networking screen, in the Connection box, select **External** and click **Next**.

9. On the Connect Virtual Hard Disk screen, review the default settings and click **Next**. This creates a 127 GB dynamically expanding virtual hard drive.

10. On the Installation Options screen, verify that **Install an operating system later** is selected and click **Next**.

11. On the Completing the New Virtual Machine Wizard screen, click **Finish**.

12. Right-click **Win10-Ch12** and click **Settings**.

13. In the Settings for Win10-Ch12 window, in the left pane, click **Processor**.

14. In the Number of virtual processors box, type **2**.

15. In the left pane, click **Memory** and in the Minimum RAM box, type **1024**.

16. In the left pane, click **SCSI Controller**, click **DVD Drive**, and then click **Add**.

17. In the DVD Drive area, click **Image file** and type **C:\ISO\Win10.iso**. Modify this path if your Windows 10 installation .iso is in a different location.

18. Click **Apply** and click **Firmware** in the left pane.

19. In the Boot order area, click **Network Adapter** and click **Move Down** twice to move it to the bottom of the list.

20. Click **OK**.

21. In Hyper-V Manager, right-click **Win10-Ch12** and click **Connect**.

22. In the Win10-Ch12 window, click the **Start** button.

23. Press a key to boot from the DVD and install Windows 10 by using all of the default options and the express settings. If necessary, refer back to Activity 1-1 in Chapter 1.

24. Use the same user name and password as you did for Activity 1-1.

25. Click **Yes** to allow your PC to be discoverable.

26. Close all open windows, including the Windows for Win10-Ch12.

Controlling Virtual Machines

Virtual machines have several possible states and it is important to understand what they are and when to use them. The possible states for virtual machines are:

- *Off*—A virtual machine that is off is not using any processing or memory resources. This is the equivalent of turning off a physical computer.

- *Starting*—A virtual machine is in this state briefly when you start it. It remains in this state while allocating resources. After resources are allocated, the state changes to running.

- *Running*—A virtual machine that is running is actively attempting to boot the operating system or running the operating system. Processing resources are being used and memory has been allocated. You can interact with a running virtual machine just like a physical computer that has been turned on.

- *Paused*—A paused virtual machine is not using processing resources, but it is still using the memory allocated to it. The state of the virtual machine has not been saved to disk and if the host loses power, it is like the virtual machine has also lost power. Paused is similar to a physical computer being in a sleep state.

- *Saved*—A saved virtual machine is not using process resources or memory. The contents of memory have been written to disk. This is similar to hibernation for a physical computer. For virtual machines that take a long time to start, it is sometimes faster to start from a saved state than from an off state.

Hyper-V Manager includes a **Virtual Machine Connection** utility to view and interact with virtual machines, as shown in Figure 12-8. If you keep it as a window instead of full screen, there is a toolbar that simplifies interacting with the virtual machine. The toolbar has a button to send Ctrl+Alt+Delete to the virtual machine instead of having to remember a special keystroke combination.

The keystroke combinations for Virtual Machine Connection are listed at *https://blogs.msdn.microsoft.com/virtual_pc_guy/2008/01/14/virtual-machine-connection-key-combinations-with-hyper-v/.*

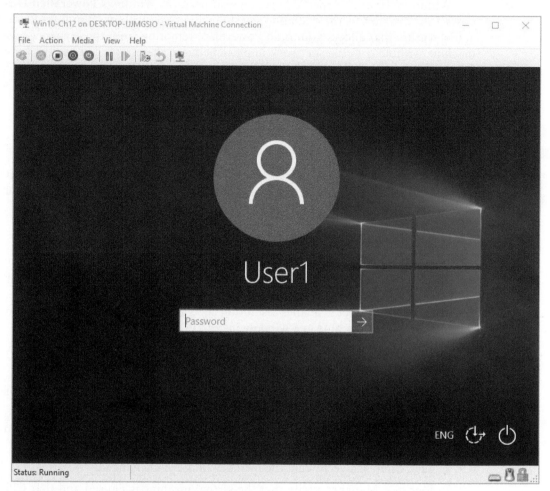

Figure 12-8   Virtual Machine Connection

Virtual Machine Connection can be used to:

- Interact with the graphical interface of the virtual machine.
- Start, pause, save, and shut down the virtual machine.
- Change the .iso mounted in the DVD drive.
- Create checkpoints and revert to the previous checkpoint.

The basic connectivity mode in Virtual Machine Connection does not allow you to cut and paste content between the virtual machine and the host operating system. There is no method for pulling data out of a virtual machine other than over a network. The only method for putting data into a virtual machine is typing the contents of the Clipboard on the host inside the virtual machine. This allows you to put a small amount of text in the virtual machine, but not full files.

There is an **enhanced session mode** that you can enable that uses RDP functionality. The enhanced session mode provides the same copy-and-paste functionality between the host and virtual machine as if you were using a Remote Desktop connection. To use enhanced session mode, Remote Desktop must be enabled in the virtual machine, and the user signing in must have permission to connect by using Remote Desktop. This mode is available if the guest operating system is Windows Server 2012 R2 and newer or Windows 8.1 or newer.

As an alternative to Virtual Machine Connection, you can use the Remote Desktop Client to connect over the network. However, to do this, you need to know either the computer name or the network address. To use Virtual Machine Connection, you do not need that information.

Windows 10 as a Hyper-V host can also perform **Windows PowerShell Direct** when Windows 10 is installed as the operating system in a virtual machine. Windows PowerShell Direct is a new feature that allows you to do PowerShell remoting from the Hyper-V host to the virtual machine without a virtual network in place between them. You can use the Enter-PSSession or Invoke-Command cmdlets with the -VMName parameter. This feature is new in Windows 10.

Activity 12-4: Controlling a Virtual Machine

Time Required: 15 minutes
Objective: Control a virtual machine and see the effects

Description: Once a virtual machine is created, you can start, stop, pause, and save it. In this activity, you control a virtual machine and monitor the effect it has on system resources.

1. If necessary, start your computer and sign in.
2. Click the **Start** button, type **hyper**, and then click **Hyper-V Manager**.
3. In Hyper-V Manager, double-click **Win10-Ch12** to connect to it.
4. In the Connect to Win10-Ch12 window, select a screen resolution less than the resolution of your physical screen and click **Connect**. For example, if your computer screen resolution is 1920 × 1200, select a smaller resolution such as 1366 × 768. This allows you to more easily use the virtual machine in a window instead of requiring full screen.
5. Verify that Win10-Ch12 is running.
6. Right-click the taskbar and click **Task Manager**.
7. In Task Manager, click the **Performance** tab and read the amount of memory in use. If the Performance tab is not available, click **More details**.
8. In the Win10-Ch12 window, on the toolbar, click **Pause** and verify that you can no longer interact with the virtual machine.
9. In Task Manager, verify that the memory in use is unchanged.
10. In Hyper-V Manager, verify that the virtual machine is Paused and that CPU Usage is 0%. Note that the Assigned Memory is about 1 GB.
11. In the Win10-Ch12 window, on the toolbar, click **Resume** and verify that you can interact with the virtual machine again.
12. On the toolbar, click **Save**. Your connection to the virtual machine will be lost.
13. In the Virtual Machine Connection dialog box, click **Close**.
14. In Task Manager, verify that memory utilization is down by about 1 GB.
15. On the taskbar, click **File Explorer** and browse to **C:\ProgramData\Microsoft\Windows\ Hyper-V\Virtual Machines**. Notice that there is a large .vmrs file that is the saved state for the virtual machine. It is somewhat smaller than the memory that was allocated, but it is still over 500 MB.
16. Close File Explorer.

17. In the Win10-Ch12 window, click **Start** and verify that you can interact with the virtual machine again.

18. Close all open windows.

Integration Services

Microsoft makes **integration services** software available for all supported virtual machine operating systems. Installing integration services in the guest operating system provides drivers for the synthetic hardware and also installs several services. For recent versions of Windows, integration services is automatically installed and updated through Windows Update.

Supported operating systems for Hyper-V in Windows 10 are:

- Windows Vista Service Pack 2 or newer
- Windows Server 2008 R2 or newer
- Major distributions of Linux and FreeBSD

The Windows services included with integration services facilitate communication with the Hyper-V host. Each service provides communication for a different purpose. To enable communication, the service needs to be running in the operating system of the virtual machine and it needs to be enabled in virtual machine settings. The services installed in a Windows 10 virtual machine for integration services are listed in Table 12-3.

Table 12-3   Integration services

Service	Description
Hyper-V Data Exchange Service	Shares registry keys and values from the virtual machine in HKLM\Software\Microsoft\Virtual Machine with the Hyper-V host to provide status information.
Hyper-V Guest Service Interface	Allows data copying between the Hyper-V host and the virtual machine when enhanced session mode is being used.
Hyper-V Guest Shutdown Service	Shuts down the operating system in the virtual machine when the option is selected in Hyper-V Manager. This avoids the need to sign in to perform a shutdown.
Hyper-V Heartbeat Service	Communicates with the Hyper-V host to verify that the operating system in the virtual machine is responding to requests.
Hyper-V Remote Desktop Virtualization Service	Accepts management requests from the Remove Desktop Virtualization Host, which is used for deployments of virtual machine-based virtual desktops.
Hyper-V Time Synchronization Service	Synchronizes time from the Hyper-V host with the virtual machine.
Hyper-V VM Session Service	Enables Windows PowerShell Direct, which allows PowerShell Remoting from the Hyper-V host to the virtual machine without a virtual network.
Hyper-V Volume Shadow Copy Requestor	Receives request by backup software running on the Hyper-V host to create a volume shadow copy before a backup of the virtual machine is performed.

Activity 12-5: Identifying Integration Services

Time Required: 15 minutes
Objective: Identify integration services and their effect on a virtual machine

Description: Integration services provide drivers for virtual hardware and facilitate communication between virtual machines and the Hyper-V host. In this activity, you review and enable all of the integration services.

1. If necessary, start your computer and sign in.

2. Click the **Start** button, type **hyper**, and then click **Hyper-V Manager**.

3. In Hyper-V Manager, right-click **Win10-Ch12** and click **Settings**.

4. In the Settings for Win10-Ch12 window, in the left pane, click **Integration Services**.

5. In the Integration Services area, notice that Guest services is not enabled by default.

6. Select the **Guest services** check box and click **OK**.

7. In Hyper-V Manager, right-click **Win10-Ch12** and click **Connect**.

8. In the Connect to Win10-Ch12 dialog box, select an appropriate screen resolution and click **Connect**.

9. Sign in to Win10-Ch12.

10. In Win10-Ch12, click the **Start** button, type **service**, and then click **Services**.

11. Scroll down, select **Hyper-V Data Exchange Service**, and then read the description.

12. Select each of the remaining Hyper-V services and read the descriptions. Notice that the Hyper-V VM Session Service is not started. It starts automatically when PowerShell Direct is used.

13. On your computer, right-click the **Start** button, type **PowerShell**, right-click **Windows Power-Shell**, and then click **Run as administrator**.

14. In the Windows PowerShell window, type **Enter-PSSession -VMName Win10-Ch12** and press **Enter**.

15. When prompted, enter your credentials for Win10-Ch12 to sign in.

16. Notice that the Windows PowerShell prompt now starts with [Win10-Ch12] to indicate that you are connected to Win10-Ch12.

17. In Win10-Ch12, in Services, press **F5** to refresh and notice that the Hyper-V VM Session Service is now started.

18. Close all open windows.

Virtual Machine Startup and Shutdown

Just like a physical computer, you have the ability to control the boot order for the virtual machine. You can set the priority for the boot devices, including the CD/DVD drive, hard drive, network adapter, or floppy drive. For Generation 1 virtual machines, the boot order is set in the BIOS node, as shown in Figure 12-9. For Generation 2 virtual machines, the boot order is set in the Firmware node.

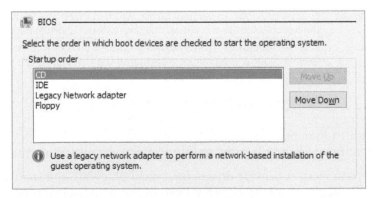

Figure 12-9   Virtual machine startup order (Generation 1 machine)

You can also set automatic start and stop actions for virtual machines. These control what the virtual machines do when the Hyper-V host is started or shut down.

The default automatic start action for virtual machines, shown in Figure 12-10, is to start a virtual machine if it was running when the Hyper-V host was shut down. Effectively, this restores your virtual machines to the state they were in when you shut down your Windows 10 computer and provides you with consistency. You can also choose to never start the virtual machine automatically or always start the virtual machine automatically.

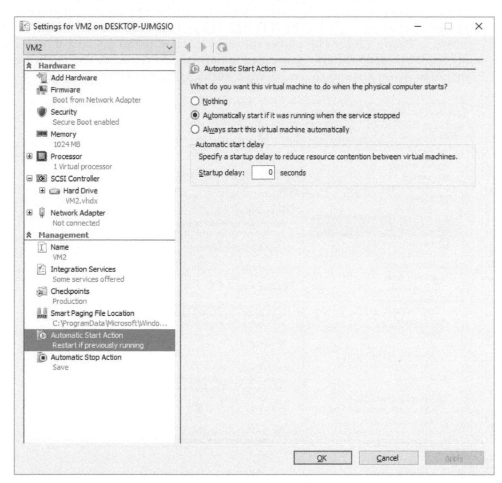

Figure 12-10   Virtual machine automatic start action

When virtual machines are automatically started, you have the option to specify a delay before they are automatically started. The delay is useful to avoid overloading the disk subsystem on startup. You can set the default for individual virtual machines to stagger their startup and even out the disk activity.

The default automatic stop action is to save the virtual machine state. This is generally faster than selecting to shut down the virtual machine and provides faster startup later. You also have the option to turn off virtual machines, but this can leave them in an inconsistent state because it is the equivalent of turning off the power on a running computer.

Virtual Memory

The Hyper-V host has a fixed amount of memory that can be allocated to virtual machines. The efficient use of that memory allows you to run more virtual machines at the same time. However, it is very difficult to exactly predict how much memory a virtual machine needs. Instead, you should use **Dynamic Memory**.

When you enable Dynamic Memory, the amount of memory from the Hyper-V host that is allocated to the virtual machine varies depending on demand from the virtual machine. As the virtual machine requires more memory, such as when starting additional applications, Hyper-V allocates that memory while the virtual machine is up and running. The end result is that the virtual machine gets the memory it needs and no more.

When you create a new virtual machine, you specify the startup memory and whether Dynamic Memory is enabled (Dynamic Memory is enabled by default). If you use this default configuration, the minimum RAM will be 512 MB and the maximum RAM will be 1048576 MB, as shown in Figure 12-11. This allows the memory allocated to the virtual machine to grow up to any level necessary and also drop down to only what is required. You might want to set a higher minimum if you know that it will impact virtual machine performance.

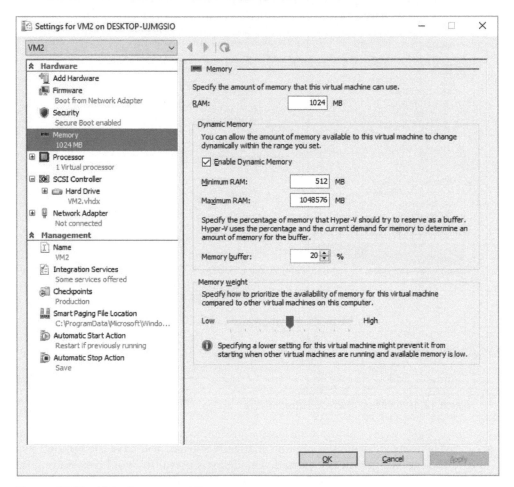

Figure 12-11   Virtual memory settings

The Memory buffer setting specifies the level of free memory required before additional memory is allocated. For example, with the default setting of 20%, a virtual machine with 2048 MB allocated and only 100 MB free would be allocated more memory because there is less than 20% free.

The Memory weight setting determines which virtual machine has the highest priority for allocating memory if multiple virtual machines need additional memory. By default, all virtual machines have the same weight. If you increase the memory weight for a virtual machine, it has higher priority when memory is required.

Some applications are not well suited to using virtual memory. For example, Microsoft SQL Server, which is used by many applications, attempts to use all available memory for caching to increase performance. This could result in a virtual machine running SQL Server being allocated more virtual memory than is required for performance.

If you do not allocate enough memory, a virtual machine might have low performance. One common problem in virtual machines with limited memory is that they have high disk activity due to high use of the paging file.

Virtual Processors

When you create a virtual machine, the default configuration has only one virtual processor. This means that the virtual machine can only run a single process at a time. To have reasonable performance, you should consider giving each virtual machine at least two virtual processors, as shown in Figure 12-12.

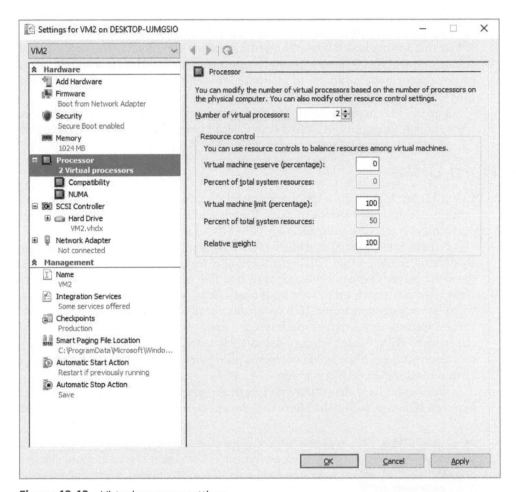

Figure 12-12 Virtual processor settings

The maximum number of virtual processors that you can assign to a virtual machine is the number of processor cores that are in the Hyper-V host. For example, if the physical processor in the Hyper-V host has four cores, you can assign up to four virtual processors to a virtual machine. This means that the virtual machine can take up to 100% of the resources on the physical processor.

Hyper-Threading presents logical processor cores to Windows instead of physical processor cores. In some cases, Hyper-Threading can increase system performance by allowing more threads to run simultaneously. When you enable Hyper-Threading in the firmware, Windows 10 identifies that the processor core count has doubled. All of the logical processors cores are available as virtual processors for a VM. So, with eight logical processor cores, a single virtual machine can be assigned up to eight virtual processors.

There are resource control settings for each virtual machine that can be used to limit the amount of processor capacity that is used. The resource control settings are:

- *Virtual machine reserve (percentage)*—This is the percentage of the virtual machine's total processing power that is exclusively reserved for this virtual machine.

- *Virtual machine limit (percentage)*—This is the percentage of the virtual processors allocated that the virtual machine is allowed to use.

- *Relative weight*—When multiple virtual machines are competing for processing capacity, the relative weight determines how much is allocated to each virtual machine. A virtual machine with a relative weight of 200 is allocated twice as much processing power as a virtual machine with a relative weight of 100.

The Compatibility node has the setting *Migrate to a physical computer with a different processor version*. This setting is disabled by default because it can lower virtual machine performance. When this setting is disabled, the virtual machine can identify the specific type of physical processor in the Hyper-V host and can be optimized for it. When this setting is enabled, the type of physical processor is hidden to facilitate moving the virtual machine between computers with different processor architectures.

The NUMA node has settings to optimize memory utilization on multiprocessor computers. Even though this option is available in Client Hyper-V, it is unlikely to be used.

Virtual Hard Disks

Client Hyper-V provides a lot of options for disk configuration. You need to understand what the options are and the benefits of each. Clearly understanding the options allows you to optimize performance and disk utilization for your virtual machines.

Generation 1 virtual machines must boot and store their paging files on an IDE controller. By default, there are two IDE controllers, allowing you to attach up to four disks, if you remove the DVD drive. There is a maximum of two IDE controllers. If you need additional virtual hard disks, you can attach up to four SCSI controllers, which can each have 64 virtual hard disks.

The requirement to use IDE controllers was for compatibility in Generation 1 virtual machines. Generation 2 virtual machines are designed for newer operating systems and only SCSI controllers are used for storage devices. Using SCSI controller might provide a small performance advantage. Also, SCSI controllers allow virtual hard disks to be added or removed from a virtual machine while it is running.

The virtual hard disks that you create are not specifically IDE or SCSI. You can move disks between IDE and SCSI controllers with no effect, other than potential issues related to booting.

 With multiple virtual machines running, one of the most common bottlenecks is disk performance. The easiest way to increase disk performance is by using a solid-state drive (SSD) instead of a traditional spinning disk.

VHD Format

Older Microsoft virtualization technologies were able to use only VHD virtual hard disks. Client Hyper-V can use either VHD or VHDX virtual hard disks. Most virtual machines using VHDs are doing so only because they have been migrated from older technologies. If you are creating new virtual hard disks, you should use the VHDX format.

A VHD has a maximum size of 2 TB. For most tasks in Client Hyper-V, this is not a limitation that you should be concerned about. However, a VHDX has a maximum size of 64 TB.

The main benefits of the VHDX format are:

- Better resilience to corruption from unexpected disk events such as power outages

- Improved performance, particularly for dynamically expanding drives

- Automatic trimming of dynamically expanding drives with unused space

When you create a new virtual hard disk, Windows 10 provides a new format of virtual hard disk called a **VHD Set,** as shown in Figure 12-13. Despite the name, a VHD Set is a single virtual hard disk, but it is composed of multiple files. There is a .vhds file and an .avhdx file. The .vhds file has metadata and the .avhdx stores the data. This is a special type of disk designed for scenarios where multiple virtual machines need to share access to the same virtual disk. This is done for high-availability scenarios using failover clustering.

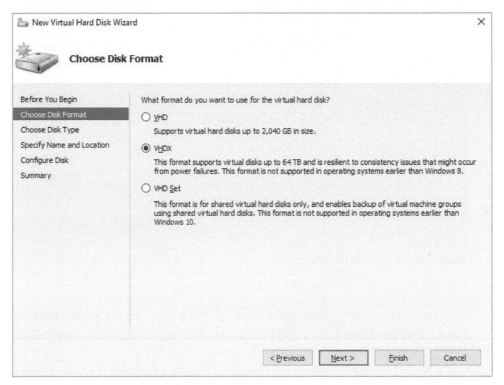

Figure 12-13   Virtual hard disk formats

VHD Type

When you create a new virtual machine and create a virtual hard disk as part of that process, the default configuration is a 127 GB dynamically expanding disk in the VHDX format. You can change the size of the disk, but unless you want it to be larger, there is no need.

A **dynamically expanding disk** takes up only the physical space required to store its contents. So, if you put 1 GB of data inside a 127 GB dynamically expanding disk, the .vhdx file for the virtual hard disk will be approximately 1 GB. This is an efficient use of space on your physical disk because space is only allocated to the virtual hard disk as required. The operating system in the virtual machine identifies the disk as being 127 GB and is unaware that it is dynamically expanding.

For VHD format disks, there were significant performance issues as the disks expanded. However, for VHDX format disks, the performance for dynamically expanding disks is significantly improved and in most cases, there is no significant benefit to using fixed-size disks instead.

If you create a **fixed-size disk,** as shown in Figure 12-14, the .vhdx file takes up all of the allocated space on the physical disk immediately. If you create a 50 GB fixed-size disk, the .vhdx file is 50 GB and never grows or shrinks.

When you need to create many virtual machines, differencing disks can be used to minimize the amount of disk space used. **Differencing disks** have a single parent disk that does not change. All changes are stored in the differencing disk and there can be multiple differencing disks that attach to a single parent.

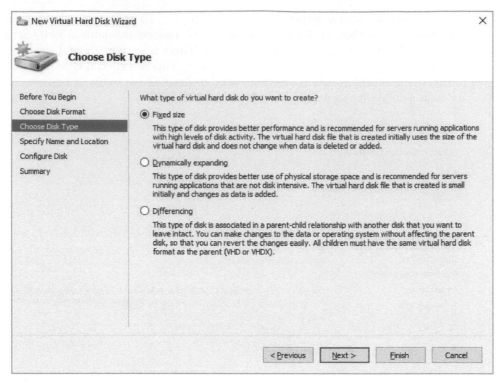

Figure 12-14   Virtual hard disk types

If you are creating multiple virtual machines that run the same operating system, you can use a single parent and one differencing disk for each of the virtual machines. You would use the following process:

1. Create a virtual machine and install the operating system you want for all of the virtual machines.

2. Run sysprep on the virtual machine and shut it down.

3. Copy the virtual hard disk from the virtual machine to a location where all of the virtual machines will use it. This is the parent virtual hard disk.

4. Create a new differencing disk that is linked to the parent.

5. Create a new virtual machine and use the differencing disk instead of creating a new virtual hard disk.

6. Start the virtual machine and configure Windows.

7. Repeat Steps 4–6 for each virtual machine based on the parent.

If the parent of a differencing disk is moved, the differencing disk ceases to work properly. You won't be able to access data on the differencing disk at all. To repair a differencing disk and relink it with the parent disk, you can inspect the differencing disk. When you inspect the differencing disk, the wizard identifies that the parent is no longer in the correct location and requests the location of the parent. After you browse and provide the new location of the parent, the differencing disk is relinked and functions properly again.

Editing Virtual Hard Disks

In most cases, you do not need to do any manual editing of a virtual disk. However, if you did not plan your disks very well initially, you might need to do some editing. The editing options available vary depending on the type of disk.

The editing options are:

- *Compact*—This option is used to remove the free space from dynamically expanding VHD disks.

- *Convert*—This option allows you to convert from one virtual hard disk format to another. The conversion process creates a new virtual hard disk in the new format and copies the data from the existing virtual hard disk. So, you need to ensure that there is sufficient disk space available.

- *Expand*—You can expand the capacity of both fixed-size and dynamically expanding virtual hard disks.

- *Shrink*—Use this option to shrink dynamically expanding VHDX disks. You will not typically need to do this as VHDX disks shrink periodically while the virtual machine is running.

- *Merge*—Use this option to merge a differencing disk with its parent. Be aware that after you do this, any other differencing disks that use the same parent will not be functional.

- *Reconnect*—You can reconnect a differencing disk to its parent by using this option. This accomplishes the same result as inspecting a differencing disk after the parent has moved.

Activity 12-6: Expanding a Virtual Hard Disk

Time Required: 15 minutes
Objective: Expand a virtual hard disk

Description: The default size of a dynamically expanding virtual hard disk that you create for a virtual machine is 127 GB. Most of the time, that is large enough, but sometimes you might need to expand a virtual hard disk. In this activity, you expand the virtual hard disk for your virtual machine.

1. If necessary, start your computer and sign in.
2. Click the **Start** button, type **hyper**, and then click **Hyper-V Manager**.
3. In Hyper-V Manager, right-click **Win10-Ch12** and click **Shut Down**.
4. In the Shut Down Machine dialog box, click **Shut Down**.
5. In the Actions pane, click **Edit Disk**.
6. In the Edit Virtual Hard Disk Wizard, click **Next**.
7. On the Locate Virtual Hard Disk screen, click **Browse**, browse to **C:\Users\Public\Documents\ Hyper-V\Virtual hard disks**, click **Win10-Ch12.vhdx**, and then click **Open**.
8. Click **Next**.
9. On the Choose Action screen, click **Expand** and click **Next**.
10. On the Expand Virtual Hard Disk screen, in the New size box, type **256** and click **Next**.
11. On the Completing the Edit Virtual Hard Disk Wizard screen, click **Finish**.
12. In Hyper-V Manager, right-click **Win10-Ch12** and click **Start**.
13. Right-click **Win10-Ch12** and click **Connect**.
14. In the Connect to Win10-Ch12 dialog box, select an appropriate screen resolution and click **Connect**.
15. In Win10-Ch12, sign in.
16. Right-click the **Start** button and click **Disk Management**.

12

17. Read the information for Disk 0. Notice that there is 129 GB of unallocated space because you expanded the disk.

18. Close Disk Management and close all open windows.

Virtual Networking

For the most part, configuring networking for a virtual machine consists of having a virtual network adapter in the virtual machine and connecting it to the appropriate virtual network. However, there are some advanced considerations for virtual local area network (VLAN) configuration that might be relevant in some scenarios.

If your organization uses VLANs as part of the networking infrastructure, you might also need to configure a VLAN ID for the network card in a virtual machine. This is required when a switch port allows hosts from multiple VLANs and the virtual machine needs to identify the VLAN where it is located.

You can also enable bandwidth management for a network adapter. When enabled, you can specify minimum and maximum bandwidth allocated to the VM in Mbps. You can use this to ensure that a virtual machine has sufficient bandwidth available. You can also ensure that a virtual machine does not monopolize the available network bandwidth. This feature is not available for legacy network adapters.

The hardware acceleration options are virtual machine queue and IPsec task off-loading. Both of these options off-load network processing tasks to the physical network adapter of the host if it is enabled and supported by the physical network adapter. Neither of these options are likely to make much difference to the performance of a virtual machine implemented using Client Hyper-V.

By default, MAC addresses for virtual machines are dynamically assigned from a pool automatically configured in the virtual network. You can also assign a static MAC address of your choice. In most cases, you would only need to manually assign a MAC address if your physical switches are restricting connectivity based on MAC address.

Some other options available in advanced features for a network adapter are:

- *Enable MAC address spoofing*—You need to enable this option if any network communication from the virtual machine will use a MAC address other than the MAC address configured in the virtual machine. The most common reason to enable this is to support Windows Network Load Balancing in virtual machines. It is also required if the virtual machine is going to be a Hyper-V host performing nested virtualization.

- *Enable DHCP guard*—This option prevents the virtual machine from acting as a DHCP server by blocking DHCP Offer packets.

- *Enable router advertisement guard*—This option prevents the virtual machine from sending router advertisements and redirection messages that could negatively impact dynamic routing configured on production routers.

- *Protected network*—This option is not valid for Client Hyper-V because it is relevant only for highly available virtual machines running in a clustered environment.

- *Mirroring mode*—Port mirroring allows you to copy packets sent and received by one virtual machine to another virtual machine for analysis. The network adapter in the virtual machine being monitored is set with a mirroring mode of Source. The virtual machine with the packet sniffing software, such as WireShark, has a network adapter set as Destination.

- *Enable this network adapter to be part of a team in the guest operating system*—You need to enable this option if you are using the Windows network teaming functionality in a virtual machine for two network adapters connected to separate virtual switches. If you do not, the team will be disconnected if one physical network adapter loses connectivity. This is rarely implemented for Client Hyper-V.

Managing Virtual Machines

In addition to the basic management tasks of starting and stopping virtual machines, you can also move virtual machine files, import and export virtual machines, and create checkpoints. Moving virtual machine files is useful when you need to change the directory structure you are using for virtual machine storage or if you have a new physical disk to which you want to move the files. Importing and exporting virtual machines is typically used to move them between computers, but you could have a standard virtual machine that you import multiple times to have a consistent starting point. Finally, checkpoints are used to allow you to revert to a known good state. You can create a checkpoint before applying an update.

Moving Virtual Machine Files

If you need to move virtual machine files to a new location, Hyper-V Manager provides a wizard for that purpose. The wizard, shown in Figure 12-15, allows you to move only specific types of virtual machine data or all of it. If you choose to move the virtual machine's data to different locations, you can move the following separately:

- *Virtual hard disks*—For most virtual machines, this is the greatest amount of storage and most likely to be moved to a new location where there is more free space or better performance.

- *Current configuration*—The configuration is a small XML file that does not affect performance.

- *Checkpoints*—Checkpoints include differencing disks that can grow quite large and might impact performance on a slow disk. These are typically kept in the same location as the virtual hard disks because they require similar performance.

- *Smart paging*—This area is used only when overuse of dynamic memory is preventing virtual machines from starting. It is rarely used and requires only a few GB of space to allow virtual machines to start.

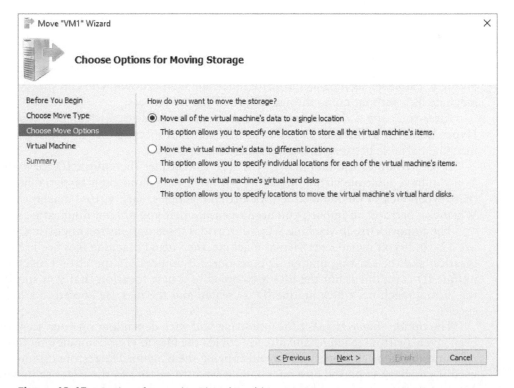

Figure 12-15   Options for moving virtual machine storage

Activity 12-7: Moving Virtual Machine Storage

Time Required: 15 minutes
Objective: Move virtual machine files to a single folder

Description: The default locations for virtual machine files are located in several places. The virtual hard disks are stored in C:\Users\Public and the checkpoints are stored in C:\ProgramData. Sometimes it is simpler to manage and track if all of the files for a virtual machine are in a single location. In this activity, you move all virtual machine files to a single folder.

1. If necessary, start your computer and sign in.
2. On the taskbar, click **File Explorer** and select the **C:** drive in the navigation pane.
3. In File Explorer, on the ribbon, on the **Home** tab, click **New Folder**, type **Win10-Ch12**, and then press **Enter**.
4. Click the **Start** button, type **hyper**, and then click **Hyper-V Manager**.
5. In Hyper-V Manager, right-click **Win10-Ch12** and click **Move**.
6. In the Move "Win10-Ch12" Wizard, click **Next**.
7. On the Choose Move Type screen, click **Next**.
8. On the Choose Options for Moving Storage screen, click **Move all of the virtual machine's data to a single location** and click **Next**.
9. In the Folder box, type **C:\Win10-Ch12** and click **Next**.
10. On the Completing Move Wizard screen, click **Finish**. Notice that the move proceeds even though the virtual machine is running.
11. After the move is complete, in File Explorer, browse to **C:\Win10-Ch12** and review the files and folder structure that are there.
12. Close all open windows.

Exporting and Importing Virtual Machines

When you want to make a copy of a virtual machine, you can use the Export option in Hyper-V Manager. If the virtual machine files are in multiple locations, this makes the process simple to perform. However, as long as the virtual machine is shut down, you can simply copy the virtual machine files without going through a formal export process.

After you copy a virtual machine, you can import it. The copy can be imported on the same Hyper-V host or a different Hyper-V host. There is no special process required to make a virtual machine portable between Hyper-V hosts.

Before you perform an import, you need to consider the unique ID for a virtual machine. You can have multiple virtual machines with the same name on a Hyper-V host. So, to ensure that Hyper-V can individually identify virtual machines, each virtual machine has a unique ID. When you perform an import, you need to ensure that you are not duplicating a unique ID.

The Import Virtual Machine Wizard provides three options for importing, as shown in Figure 12-16. If you register the virtual machine, the virtual machine files are left in their existing location and the existing unique ID is retained. If you restore the virtual machine, the existing unique ID is retained, but the files are copied to a new location that you specify. If you copy the virtual machine, a new unique ID is created and the files are copied to a location that you specify.

The option that you select for importing will vary depending on your scenario. If you have been given a virtual machine and already copied the files to your computer, registering the virtual machine would be appropriate to avoid copying them again. The restore option is typically only used if you have exported as a backup and want to restore to the exact same virtual machine. Most of the time, you are likely to copy the virtual machine and create a new unique ID to ensure that there are not any conflicts.

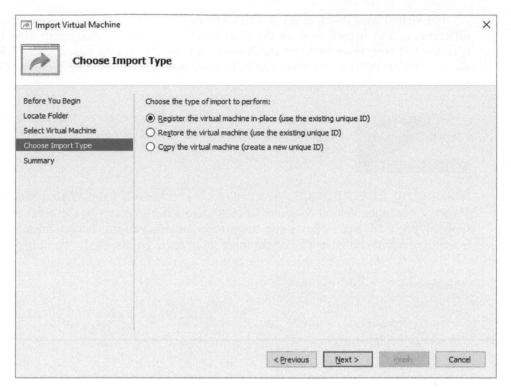

Figure 12-16   Options for importing a virtual machine

Using Checkpoints

Virtual machine **checkpoints** allow you to copy the state of a virtual machine and prevent changes to that state. If needed, at a later point in time, you can revert to a checkpoint and undo recent changes.

　　If you have a virtual machine that you use for testing, you can create a checkpoint before you do any changes. Then after you are done testing, you can revert to the checkpoint and have a clean system again. This is also useful for doing iterative testing to reset the test environment to a clean state.

   It is important to remember that a checkpoint is not a replacement for a backup. If it would take a significant amount of work to re-create a test environment, or if virtual machines contain data that is important, you need to back up the virtual machines to a separate disk drive to ensure that disk failure does not cause data loss.

　　You also need to understand how apps in your test environment affect different virtual machines. If your app has components on different virtual machines, you might need to create checkpoints on all of the virtual machines at the same time for the app to be consistent. For example, if you apply a service pack to an app server that also updates data in Active Directory, you should have a checkpoint of both the app server and the domain controller virtual machines before you apply the service pack.

Checkpoint Contents   A checkpoint includes all aspects of the virtual machine, including configuration, virtual hard disk contents, and the contents of memory. You can take a checkpoint of a running virtual machine, and if you restore to that checkpoint, the virtual machine will still be running in that state. However, the downside of checkpoints for running virtual machines is that the contents of memory are saved to disk as a .bin file. If you have many checkpoints of virtual machines, the .bin files can consume a large amount of disk space.

For virtual hard disks, creating a checkpoint triggers the creation of a differencing disk. The differencing disk is used to store the virtual hard disk changes that occur after the checkpoint is created. If you create multiple checkpoints, a new differencing disk is created for each checkpoint. Multiple differencing disks can be chained together with one differencing disk serving as a parent to another differencing disk.

 Having multiple checkpoints and a large chain of differencing disks can cause high disk activity because Hyper-V needs to read from multiple files.

Managing Checkpoints   You can create checkpoints from Virtual Machine Connect or Hyper-V Manager. Virtual Machine Connect also lets you revert to the most recent checkpoint. Only Hyper-V Manager allows you to perform more advanced checkpoint management, which is required when you have a more complex set of checkpoints, as shown in Figure 12-17.

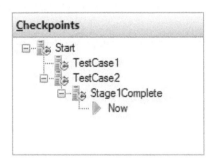

Figure 12-17   Checkpoints

Within Hyper-V Manager, you have the following options for a checkpoint:

- *Settings*—This is a read-only option to see the virtual machine settings in the checkpoint.

- *Apply*—This option applies the selected checkpoint to the virtual machine. When selected, you are provided with an option to create a checkpoint of the current state so that the current state is not lost.

- *Export*—This option allows you to export a virtual machine from a specific checkpoint. The exported virtual machine does not contain checkpoints. So, if you export a checkpoint from the middle of a checkpoint tree, no other checkpoints in that tree are included. All of the necessary content is merged in the exported virtual machine.

- *Rename*—By default, checkpoints are named based on the time they are taken. It is often useful to provide a more descriptive checkpoint name that describes the state of the virtual machine.

- *Delete Checkpoint*—This option removes the checkpoint and merges any differencing disks as necessary. Unlike older versions of Hyper-V, the differencing disks can merge in the background while the virtual machine is running.

- *Delete Checkpoint Subtree*—If there is a tree of multiple checkpoints, this is a quick way to delete the selected checkpoint and any checkpoints created after it.

Activity 12-8: Managing Checkpoints

Time Required: 15 minutes
Objective: Create and delete checkpoints

Description: Checkpoints are useful to save the state of a virtual machine in case you want to restore that state. They are commonly used for testing. In this activity, you create and then revert to a checkpoint.

1. If necessary, start your computer and sign in.

2. Click the **Start** button, type **hyper**, and then click **Hyper-V Manager.**

3. In Hyper-V Manager, right-click **Win10-Ch12** and click **Shut Down.**

4. In the Shut Down Machine dialog box, click **Shut Down.**

5. After the virtual machine is shut down, right-click **Win10-Ch12** and click **Checkpoint.**

6. In the Checkpoints area, right-click the checkpoint, click **Rename**, type **Start**, and then press **Enter.**

7. Right-click **Win10-Ch12** and click **Start.**

8. In the Connect to Win10-Ch12 dialog box, select an appropriate screen resolution and click **Connect.**

9. In Win10-Ch12, sign in.

10. Right-click the desktop and click **Personalize.**

11. In the Personalization window, on the **Background** tab, in the Background box, select **Solid color.**

12. Under Background colors, click a vibrant color, like orange, and close the Personalization window.

13. In the Win10-Ch12 window, on the toolbar, click **Revert.**

14. In the Revert Virtual Machine dialog box, click **Revert.** Notice that the virtual machine is now turned off because it was off when the checkpoint was taken.

15. In Hyper-V Manager, in the Checkpoints area, right-click **Start** and click **Delete Checkpoint.**

16. In the Delete Checkpoint dialog box, click **Delete.**

17. Right-click **Win10-Ch12** and click **Start.**

18. In the Connect to Win10-Ch12 dialog box, select an appropriate screen resolution and click **Connect.**

19. In Win10-Ch12, sign in. Notice that the background color change made before you reverted has been lost.

20. Close all open windows.

12

Chapter Summary

- Client Hyper-V allows you to run virtual machines using a computer with Windows 10. This is very similar to the version of Hyper-V available for Windows Server.

- You create virtual switches to allow virtual machines to perform network communication. You can create external, private, and internal networks.

- Virtual machines can be Generation 1 or Generation 2. If the operating system supports Generation 2, you should use Generation 2. Generation 2 virtual machines do not support legacy emulated hardware devices.

- A virtual machine behaves like a physical computer. You can start or shut down a virtual machine. You can also pause a virtual machine, which is similar to sleep, and save a virtual machine, which is similar to hibernate.

- Integration services provide drivers for the operating system in the virtual machine. They also facilitate communication with the Hyper-V host.

- In most cases, it is beneficial to use Dynamic Memory to optimize the amount of memory used by virtual machines. You should also consider giving all of your virtual machines at least two virtual processors.

- Virtual hard disks can be in either the VHD or VHDX format. There is also a .vhds file for shared set virtual hard disks. Virtual hard disks can be fixed size, dynamically expanding, or differential. You can perform editing tasks on virtual disks such as expanding them or shrinking them.

- If your network uses VLANs, you can configure a virtual network card to use a specific VLAN. You can also configure a virtual network card to allow MAC spoofing if you are using advanced network technologies such as Windows Network Load Balancing in your virtual machines.

- You can move virtual machine storage, even while the virtual machine is running. You can also export and import virtual machines to copy them. Checkpoints allow you to save the state of a virtual machine and later revert back to it.

Key Terms

checkpoint   A saved state of a virtual machine that you can revert to.

differencing disk   A type of virtual hard disk that tracks changes that would have been made to a parent disk.

Dynamic Memory   A feature of Hyper-V that allows the memory allocated to a virtual machine to be increased and decreased based on demand in the virtual machine while it is running.

dynamically expanding disk   A virtual hard disk that only uses the physical disk space required to store its contents. The disk file expands and shrinks as data is moved in and out of it.

enhanced session mode   A type of connectivity between Virtual Machine Connection and the virtual machine based on the RDP protocol that allows movement of data between the virtual machine and the Hyper-V host.

external network   A virtual network that is bound to a physical network adapter and provides access to the physical network.

fixed-size disk   A type of virtual hard disk that takes the same physical space on disk as the volume of data that it can store.

Generation 1 virtual machines   Virtual machines that are compatible with older Microsoft virtualization technologies and support older hardware standards like BIOS and IDE.

Generation 2 virtual machines   Virtual machines that are compatible only with newer versions of Hyper-V and support only newer hardware types such as UEFI. Only more recent operating systems such as Windows 8 or newer can be used.

Hyper-V Manager   The graphical administrative tool for managing virtual machines.

hypervisor   The software layer that controls access to hardware after virtualization is enabled.

integration services   A set of drivers that allows operating systems to use virtualized hardware in a virtual machine. There are also services that facilitate communication between the Hyper-V host and the operating system in the virtual machine.

internal network   A virtual network that can be accessed by virtual machines and the Hyper-V host.

nested virtualization   A new Hyper-V feature in Windows 10 that allows you to enable Hyper-V in a virtual machine, which can then host its own virtual machines.

private network   A virtual network that can be accessed only by virtual machines.

shared set   A type of virtual hard disk that is designed to be shared between multiple virtual machines.

virtual machine   A set of hardware resources that has been allocated for virtualization to run an operating system.

Virtual Machine Connection   The graphical tool that is used to connect to virtual machines and interact with them.

virtual switch   A virtual component that allows you to create virtual networks that virtual machines can use.

virtualization   A technology that allows the hardware of a single computer to be shared by multiple operating systems running at the same time.

Windows PowerShell Direct   A new feature in Windows 10 that allows you to perform PowerShell remoting from the Hyper-V host directly to the virtual machine without using a virtual network.

Review Questions

1. What is the name of the software layer that is installed when you enable the Hyper-V feature?

    a.   hardware virtualizer

    b.   hardware abstraction layer

    c.   Hyper-V hardware manager

    d.   virtual hardware layer

    e.   hypervisor

2. Which of the following scenarios would Hyper-V *not* be useful for?

    a.   testing hardware driver updates

    b.   creating a test environment for an application

    c.   testing updates

    d.   developing software deployment

    e.   demonstrations

3. Nested virtualization allows you to enable Hyper-V in a virtual machine. True or False?

4. Which editions of Windows 10 support enabling Hyper-V? (Choose all that apply.)

    a.   Windows 10 Home

    b.   Windows 10 Pro

    c.   Windows 10 Enterprise

    d.   Windows 10 Education

    e.   Windows 10 Mobile

5. Which methods can you use to install Hyper-V in Windows 10? (Choose all that apply.)

    a.   Settings

    b.   Enable-WindowsOptionalFeature

    c.   Enable-WindowsFeature

    d.   Dism.exe

    e.   Programs and Features

6. Which utility can you use to verify that your computer supports installing Hyper-V?

    a.   Dism.exe

    b.   Systeminfo.exe

    c.   Hypercheck.exe

    d.   Hwtest.exe

    e.   Virtest.exe

12

7. Which type of virtual network would allow virtual machines to access the Internet?

    a. internal

    b. external

    c. private

    d. public

8. Generation 2 virtual machines have UEFI-based firmware. True or False?

9. Which feature is supported only by legacy network adapters in Generation 1 virtual machines?

    a. VLANs

    b. MAC address spoofing

    c. DHCP guard

    d. PXE boot

    e. router guard

10. In which states does a virtual machine consume memory resources? (Choose all that apply.)

    a. Off

    b. Running

    c. Paused

    d. Saved

11. To allow pasting of data from the Hyper-V host to the virtual machine, you should enable enhanced session mode. True or False?

12. Which cmdlets can be used with Windows PowerShell Direct to send Windows PowerShell commands to a virtual machine?

    a. Enter-PSSession

    b. Connect-VM

    c. Invoke-Command

    d. Remote-Command

    e. Send-Command

13. Which Hyper-V service is required to allow proper backup of a virtual machine from the Hyper-V host?

    a. Hyper-V Data Exchange Service

    b. Hyper-V Guest Service Interface

    c. Hyper-V VM Session Service

    d. Hyper-V Volume Shadow Copy Requestor

14. For which operating systems are integration services provided? (Choose all that apply.)

    a. Windows XP Service Pack 3

    b. Windows Vista Service Pack 2

    c. Windows 7 Service Pack 1

    d. Windows Server 2008

    e. major distributions of Linux

15. When you enable Dynamic Memory, the operating system in the virtual machine reports that it has the maximum RAM available. True or False?

16. When you create a dynamically expanding disk, the operating system in the virtual machine reports that it has the maximum size available. True or False?

17. Which virtual hard disk editing option is relevant only for dynamically expanding VHD disks?

   a. Compact

   b. Convert

   c. Expand

   d. Shrink

   e. Merge

18. Which of the following is true about the unique ID of a virtual machine?

   a. An imported virtual machine always retains the same unique ID.

   b. No two virtual machines on the same Hyper-V host can have the same unique ID.

   c. An imported virtual machine always generates a new unique ID.

   d. Two virtual machines with the same unique ID on different Hyper-V hosts cannot communicate.

19. To copy a virtual machine, you must export it. True or False?

20. To create a checkpoint, the virtual machine must be stopped. True or False?

Case Projects

Case Project 12-1: Software Testing

You provide support for Buddy's Machine Shop. They currently have a server that runs Windows Server 2012 R2 and their accounting application. All of the desktop computers use Windows 10.

The accountant at Buddy's Machine Shop is considering changing to different accounting software and he wants to test it. The application vendor provides preconfigured Hyper-V virtual machines with the software already installed for testing. Explain how the accountant can use this.

Case Project 12-2: Applying Security Settings

Gigantic Life Insurance has a help desk that provides service for several thousand users. When calls come in to the help desk, the help desk staff remote control the user's computer to review and troubleshoot the problem. However, some problems require research and testing that cannot be done while connected to the user's computer.

The help desk maintains a small pool of physical computers with various configurations used by users. Sometimes, there is contention for who can use particular computers when help desk staff require access to a particular application or configuration. How can Client Hyper-V in Windows 10 help?

12

chapter 13

Enterprise Computing

After reading this chapter and completing the exercises, you will be able to:

- Understand Active Directory
- Use Group Policy to control Windows 10
- Describe enterprise deployment tools for Windows 10
- Use enterprise management tools for Windows 10
- Configure enterprise file services for Windows 10

In the computer industry, the term *enterprise* is used to describe large companies with needs that are different from smaller companies. Enterprise products typically have much better features for manageability than those used by smaller companies. Enterprise deployments of Windows 10 have unique challenges that need to be addressed.

In this chapter, you learn how Active Directory and Group Policy can be used to manage hundreds or thousands of Windows 10 computers. Enterprise deployment and management tools for Windows 10 are also described. Finally, you learn how enterprise file services differ from simple file sharing.

Active Directory

Windows networks can be either workgroup-based or domain-based. A domain-based network can be centrally managed and is much more efficient than workgroup-based networks for larger environments. Windows 2000 Server and later versions include **Active Directory** to create domain-based networks. Active Directory expands on the domain concept by linking domains in logical structures named trees, and multiple trees into forests.

Domain controllers are servers that hold a copy of Active Directory information. Domain controllers are responsible for authenticating users when they sign in to a workstation. After users are authenticated, they can access network resources. Domain controllers also respond to requests for other domain information such as printer information or application configuration.

 Starting with Windows Server 2008, Microsoft has rebranded several services under the Active Directory name and uses the term Active Directory Domain Services (AD DS) to refer to what had been previously known as Active Directory. The term Active Directory is still commonly used by IT professionals and is used throughout this book.

Active Directory Structure

The key feature of Active Directory is a **domain**. A domain has a central security database that is used by all computers that are members of the domain. This central database means that user accounts can be created once in the domain and then used to sign in at any workstation in the domain. No matter which workstation the user signs in at, the user gains access to all of the appropriate network resources. There are no concerns about synchronizing passwords because only one central account is used.

In addition to user account information, domains also store information about computers. Each computer that is a member of the domain has an account in Active Directory. Information about applications and printers is also found in Active Directory. DNS information is often stored in Active Directory.

Active Directory uses the same naming convention for domains and objects contained in these domains as DNS. For example, an Active Directory domain can be named *GiganticLife.com*. However, Active Directory domains and DNS domains contain very different content. Many organizations use the same DNS domain name for Active Directory and the Internet email, but it is not required.

Organizational Units   Each domain can be subdivided into **organizational units (OUs)**. Using OUs allows you to organize the objects in a domain. For example, you can organize the users in a domain by department by creating an OU for each department. This makes it easier to find the user accounts that you are looking for. Figure 13-1 shows how OUs are displayed when using the Active Directory Users and Computers administrative tool on the server.

OUs can also be used for delegating management permissions. For example, you can delegate the ability to create and manage objects in the Marketing OU to an administrator assigned to the Marketing department. That administrator will not be able to create and manage objects in the OUs of other departments.

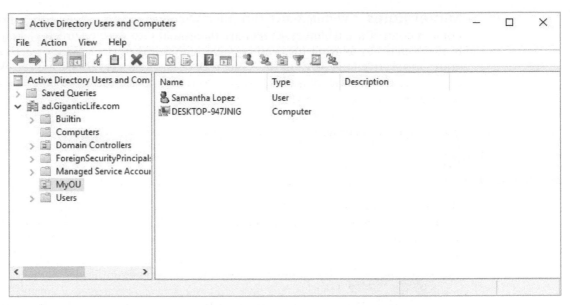

Figure 13-1 Active Directory Users and Computers

Finally, OUs are used to apply group policies. Group policies can be applied to a specific OU, which applies Group Policy settings to the user accounts or computer accounts in the OU. For example, you could create a group policy with marketing-specific settings and apply it to the Marketing OU.

Trees and Forests In most cases, a single domain subdivided into OUs is sufficient to manage a network. However, you can create more complex Active Directory structures by combining multiple domains into a **tree** and multiple trees into a **forest**. Figure 13-2 shows a single Active Directory forest with two trees. The domains using *ad.GiganticLife.com* are one tree and the domains in *EnormousLife.com* are another tree. *Europe.ad.GiganticLife* is a subdomain of *ad.GiganticLife.com*.

13

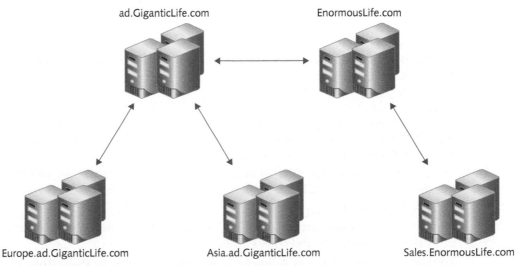

Figure 13-2 Domains, trees, and trusts

When multiple domains exist in a forest, trust relationships are automatically generated between the domains. This allows administrators to give users in one domain access to resources in another domain.

Server Roles Within Active Directory, Windows servers can be either member servers or domain controllers. Member servers are integrated into Active Directory and can participate in the domain by sharing files and printers with domain users. Windows 10 computers integrate into Active Directory in the same way as member servers. However, Windows 10 is a desktop operating system and is not able to function as either a member server or a domain controller.

Activity 13-1: Installing a Domain Controller

Time Required: 1.5 hours
Objective: Install a Windows Server 2016 domain controller

Description: To create a single centralized security database, you must have a Windows server configured as a domain controller. In this activity, you install Windows Server 2016 and configure the server as a domain controller.

The preferred method for implementing this activity is for students to have their own virtual servers in an isolated environment. The virtual machine students created in Chapter 12, Client Hyper-V, can be used with the server installed in this activity. However, you can use a single server shared by multiple students. In such a case, you need to modify the activities slightly to ensure that each student is not affecting other students, and some parts, such as this activity, must be demonstrated.

At the time of writing, Windows Server 2016 was not yet released. There may be minor variations between this lab and the release version of Windows Server 2016.

1. Place the Windows Server 2016 DVD in the computer and start it.
2. Press a key to boot from the DVD when prompted.
3. In the Windows Setup window, click **Next** to accept the default language, time, and keyboard settings.
4. Click **Install now.**
5. On the Select the operating system you want to install screen, click **Windows Server 2016 (Desktop Experience)** and click **Next.**
6. On the License terms screen, select the **I accept the license terms** check box and click **Next.**
7. On the Which type of installation do you want screen, click **Custom: Install Windows only (advanced).**
8. On the Where do you want to install Windows screen, if there are any preexisting partitions, delete them all, click **Drive 0 Unallocated Space,** and then click **Next.** The install proceeds and might reboot.
9. In the Customize settings window, in the Password and Reenter password boxes, type **Passw0rd** (0 is zero) and click **Finish.**
10. Sign in to your server as **Administrator** with a password of **Passw0rd.**
11. In the Networks area, click **Yes** to make the server discoverable.
12. In Server Manager, in the navigation pane, click **Local Server.**
13. Next to Ethernet, click **IPv4 address assigned by DHCP, IPv6 enabled.**
14. Right-click **Ethernet** and click **Properties.**

15. In the Ethernet Properties window, click **Internet Protocol Version 4 (TCP/IPv4)** and click **Properties.**

16. In the Internet Protocol Version 1 (TCP/IPv4) Properties window, enter an IP address, subnet mask, and default gateway assigned by your instructor. This server needs to be on the same IP network as the client you will be connecting to it.

17. In the Preferred DNS server box, type **127.0.0.1** and click **OK.** This server will be configured as a DNS server.

18. In the Internet Protocol Version 4 (TCP/IPv4) Properties window, click **Close.**

19. Close the Network Connections window.

20. Next to Computer name, click the computer name.

21. In the System Properties window, on the Computer Name tab, click **Change.**

22. In the Computer Name/Domain Changes window, in the Computer name box, type **DC** and click **OK.** Note: If your environment is coexisting with other students, obtain a unique name from your instructor.

23. In the Computer Name/Domain Changes dialog box, click **OK.**

24. In the System Properties window, click **Close.**

25. In the Microsoft Windows dialog box, click **Restart Now.**

26. Sign in to your server as **Administrator** with the password of **Passw0rd.**

27. In Server Manager, click **Manage** and click **Add Roles and Features.**

28. In the Add Roles and Features Wizard, click **Next.**

29. On the Select installation type screen, click **Role-based or feature-based installation** and click **Next.**

30. On the Select destination server screen, click **DC** and click **Next.**

31. On the Select server roles screen, select the **Active Directory Domain Services** check box.

32. In the Add Roles and Features Wizard dialog box, click **Add Features.**

33. On the Select server roles screen, click **Next.**

34. On the Select features screen, click **Next.**

35. On the Active Directory Domain Services screen, read the information and click **Next.**

36. On the Confirm installation selections screen, click **Install.**

37. Wait for installation to complete and click **Close.**

38. In Server Manager, click **Notifications** and click **Promote this server to a domain controller.**

39. In the Active Directory Domain Services Configuration Wizard, on the Deployment Configuration screen, click **Add a new forest.**

40. In the Root domain name, type **ad.GiganticLife.com** and click **Next.** Note: If your environment is coexisting with other students, obtain a unique name from your instructor.

41. On the Domain Controller Options screen, in the Password and Confirm password boxes, type **Passw0rd** and click **Next.**

42. On the DNS Options screen, click **Next.**

43. On the Additional Options screen, click **Next.** Note: If your environment is coexisting with other students, obtain a unique name from your instructor.

44. On the Paths screen, click **Next.**

45. On the Review Options screen, read the information and click **Next.**

46. Wait for the prerequisite check to complete and click **Install.**

47. After the reboot, sign in as **AD\Administrator** with a password of **Passw0rd.**

13

The remaining steps in this activity are optional and only required if multiple students need to authenticate to the same server. If you are not sharing a server with other students, the activity is complete.

48. In Server Manager, click **Manage** and click **Add Roles and Features**.

49. In the Add Roles and Features Wizard, click **Next**.

50. On the Select installation type screen, click **Remote Desktop Services installation** and click **Next**.

51. On the Select deployment type screen, click **Quick Start** and click **Next**.

52. On the Select deployment scenario screen, click **Session-based desktop deployment** and click **Next**.

53. On the Select a server screen, click **Next**.

54. On the Confirm selections screen, select the **Restart the destination server automatically if required** check box and click **Deploy**.

55. Wait for installation to complete and the server to reboot. This can take 10–15 minutes.

56. Sign in as **AD\Administrator** with a password of **Passw0rd**.

57. Wait for the installation to complete and click **Close**.

58. In Server Manager, click **Tools** and click **Group Policy Management**.

59. In Group Policy Management, expand **Forest: ad.GiganticLife.com**, expand **Domains**, expand **ad.GiganticLife.com**, expand **Domain Controllers**, and click **Default Domain Controllers Policy**.

60. In the Group Policy Management Console dialog box, select **Do not show this message again** and click **OK**.

61. Right-click **Default Domain Controllers Policy** and click **Edit**.

62. In the Group Policy Management Editor, browse to **\Computer Configuration\Administrative Templates\Windows Components\Remote Desktop Services\Remote Desktop Session Host\Connections** and double-click **Restrict Remote Desktop Services users to a single Remote Desktop Services session**.

63. In the Restrict Remote Desktop Services users to a single Remote Desktop Services session window, click **Disable** and click **OK**. This setting allows multiple users to sign in remotely as the administrator account at the same time.

64. Close all open windows.

Active Directory Partitions

Active Directory is not a single monolithic database with all of the information about the network. To make Active Directory more manageable, it is divided into the domain partition, configuration partition, and schema partition:

- The **domain partition** holds the user accounts, computer accounts, and other domain-specific information. This partition is replicated only to domain controllers in the same domain.

- The **configuration partition** holds general information about the Active Directory forest. Also, applications such as Exchange Server use the configuration partition to store application-specific information. This partition is replicated to all domain controllers in the Active Directory forest.

- The **schema partition** holds the definitions of all objects and object attributes for the forest. This partition is replicated to all domain controllers in the Active Directory forest.

 Active Directory also contains application partitions, but they are outside the scope of this text.

One special case for replication of information in the domain partition is global catalog servers. A **global catalog server** is a domain controller that holds a subset of the information in all domain partitions. For example, a global catalog has information about all users in the entire Active Directory forest, but only some of the information that is available about the users in each domain. Global catalog servers are used to hold the membership of universal groups and by applications such as Microsoft Exchange Server. Exchange Server uses global catalog servers to perform address book lookups and locate user mailboxes.

Active Directory Sites and Replication

Active Directory uses multimaster replication. This means that Active Directory information can be changed on any domain controller and those changes will be replicated to other domain controllers. This process ensures that all domain controllers have the same information. However, replication is not immediate, and the amount of time required to replicate data depends on whether domain controllers are in the same site or different sites.

An **Active Directory site** represents a physical location in your network. However, Active Directory is not aware of physical locations and sites are defined by IP subnets. As administrator, you create sites and define the IP subnets in each site. In most cases, you should create an Active Directory site for each physical location in your network. However, if you have fast (10 Mbps) and reliable WAN links, you can consider making separate physical locations part of the same site.

Within a site, Active Directory replication is uncontrolled. The replication process is completely automatic. When a change is made to an Active Directory object, the change begins replication to all domain controllers in the site after 15 seconds.

Between sites, Active Directory replication is controlled by site links. By default, all replication is controlled by a single site link that allows replication to occur every 180 minutes, but can be shortened to 15 minutes.

Active Directory and DNS

One of the most common configuration problems in Active Directory networks is incorrect DNS configuration on servers and workstations. Proper configuration of DNS is essential for Active Directory. Active Directory stores information about domain controllers and other services in DNS. Workstations use the information in DNS to find domain controllers in their local site and sign in.

Incorrect DNS configuration can result in:

- Slow user sign-ins

- Inability to apply group policies

- Failed replication between domain controllers

In most cases, all workstations and servers should be configured to use an internal DNS server. This ensures that all domain controllers register their information in the correct location and that all workstations have access to domain controller information. The internal DNS server can resolve Internet DNS records on behalf of clients as well. An external DNS server that is provided by an Internet service provider is typically unable to accept dynamic registration of DNS records, which is required for Active Directory.

Activity 13-2: Viewing Active Directory DNS Records

Time Required: 10 minutes
Objective: View the DNS records for Active Directory

Description: Active Directory DNS records are used to locate domain controllers and other domain services. In this activity, you use the DNS management tool console to view the DNS records registered by a domain controller.

 If you are sharing a server, use Remote Desktop Connection to sign in to the domain controller from your Windows 10 computer.

1. Sign in to the DC as **AD\Administrator** with a password of **Passw0rd**.
2. If necessary, click the **Start** button and click **Server Manager**.
3. In Server Manager, click **Tools** and click **DNS**.
4. In the left pane, expand **DC**, expand **Forward Lookup Zones**, and then click **_msdcs. ad.GiganticLife.com**. This is the domain that holds DNS records for Active Directory.
5. Expand **_msdcs. .ad.GiganticLife.com**, expand **dc**, and then click **_tcp**. Notice that DC.ad. GiganticLife.com is listed for the _kerberos and _ldap services. These records are used by clients to find a domain controller for sign-in.
6. Expand **Sites**, expand **Default-First-Site-Name**, and then click **_tcp**. Notice that DC.ad. GiganticLife.com is listed for the _kerberos and _ldap services in this Active Directory site.
7. Close all open windows.

Joining a Domain

When a workstation joins a domain, it is integrated into the security structure for the domain. Administration of the workstation can be performed centrally by using Group Policy. Also, domain administrators are automatically given the ability to manage the workstation.

The following security changes occur when a workstation joins a domain:

- The Domain Admins group becomes a member of the local Administrators group.
- The Domain Users group becomes a member of the local Users group.
- The Domain Guests group becomes a member of the local Guests group.

The process of joining a workstation to a domain creates a computer account. It is this computer account that allows the workstation to integrate with Active Directory. If the computer account is removed, the workstation can no longer be used to access domain resources by users with domain-based accounts.

After a workstation is joined to the domain, it synchronizes time with domain controllers in the domain. This is necessary because the authentication process used by domain controllers is time sensitive. If the clock on a workstation is more than 5 minutes off from the domain controller, users on the workstation cannot be authenticated.

By default, a computer account changes its password in the domain every 30 days. This happens in the background automatically. If the computer operating system is restored, the password that is restored might be an old password, which prevents the computer from authenticating. At this point, Windows 10 might present a message indicating that the trust relationship with the domain has been lost. One way to fix this is to put the computer back in a workgroup and rejoin the domain.

You can also use the Test-ComputerSecureChannel PowerShell cmdlet. The Test-Computer-SecureChannel cmdlet reports the status of the trust relationship with the domain. If the trust relationship is broken, you can use the -Repair parameter to fix it.

 ### Activity 13-3: Joining a Domain

Time Required: 15 minutes
Objective: Join Windows 10 to an Active Directory domain

Description: Joining a domain integrates Windows 10 into the security system for Active Directory. In this activity, you join a Windows 10 workstation to an Active Directory domain and view the security changes.

 This activity can be performed with a physical computer or a virtual machine with Windows 10 installed. The computer must be on the same IPv4 network as the domain controller and must be using the domain controller for the DNS server.

1. If necessary, start your computer and sign in.

2. Click the **Start** button and click **Settings**.

3. In the Settings window, click **System** and click **About**.

4. In the SYSTEM window, click **Join a domain**.

5. In the Join a domain window, in the Domain name box, type **ad.GiganticLife.com** and click **Next**.

6. Sign in as **Administrator** with a password of **Passw0rd**.

7. On the Add an account screen, click **Skip**. This screen provided you the opportunity to give a domain user account administrator permissions if required.

8. Click **Restart now**.

9. Sign in to your computer as **AD\Administrator** with a password of **Passw0rd**.

10. Right-click the **Start** button and click **Computer Management**.

11. In Computer Management, expand Local Users and Groups, **click Groups**, and then double-click **Administrators**.

12. In the Administrator Properties window, verify that AD\Domain Users has been added to the Administrators group and click **OK**.

13. Double-click **Users**, verify that **AD\Domain Users** has been added to the Users group, and then click **OK**.

14. Close Computer Management.

15. Click the **Start** button, type **power**, right-click **Windows PowerShell**, and then click **Run as administrator**. You are not prompted by UAC because you are signed in as the domain administrator account.

16. At the Windows PowerShell prompt, type **Test-ComputerSecureChannel** and press **Enter**. That status of True indicates that the trust relationship with the domain is working properly.

17. Close the Windows PowerShell prompt.

Group Policy

Group Policy is a feature integrated with Active Directory that can be used to centrally manage the configuration of a Windows 10 computer. There are thousands of Group Policy settings that you can use to control almost any aspect of Windows 10.

The Group Policy settings used by Windows 10 are contained in a **Group Policy Object (GPO)**. A GPO is a collection of registry settings applied to the Windows 10 computer. To apply GPO settings, the GPO is linked to an OU, Active Directory site, or domain. A GPO can also be applied locally to a single computer. Configuration of Group Policy Objects is performed with the Group Policy Management Console, as shown in Figure 13-3.

13

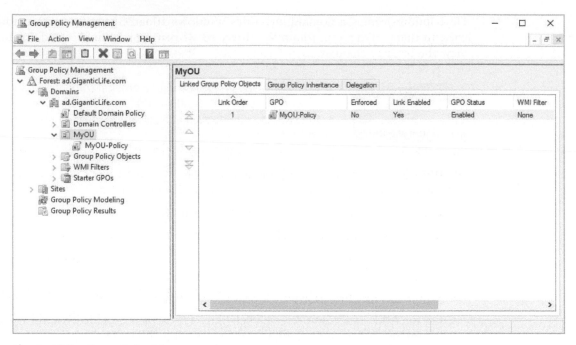

Figure 13-3 Group Policy Management

The settings in a GPO are divided into user settings and computer settings. The user settings are applied to any user accounts in the OU to which the GPO is linked. Computer settings in the GPO are applied to any computer accounts in the OU to which the GPO is linked. In Figure 13-4, if Bob signs in to WS1, the user settings from the GPO linked to the Marketing OU and the computer settings from the GPO linked to the Head Office OU are applied.

ad.GiganticLife.com

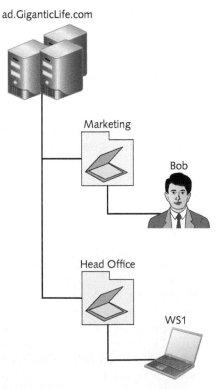

Figure 13-4 Group Policy application

Windows workstations and member servers download Group Policy settings during startup and approximately every 90 minutes thereafter. If you are testing GPO settings, you can use the *gpupdate* utility to trigger faster Group Policy Object downloads. Domain controllers download Group Policy settings every 5 minutes.

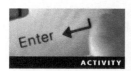

Activity 13-4: Creating a GPO

Time Required: 15 minutes
Objective: Create and apply a Group Policy Object (GPO)

Description: You can create GPOs to control users and their workstations. In this activity, you create a GPO and verify that it is applied to your Windows 10 computer.

1. If necessary, start DC and sign in as **AD\Administrator** with a password of **Passw0rd**.
2. In Server Manager, click **Tools** and click **Active Directory Users and Computers**.
3. In Active Directory Users and Computers, expand **ad.GiganticLife.com** and click **ad.GiganticLife.com**.
4. Right-click **ad.GiganticLife.com**, point to **New**, and then click **Organizational Unit**.
5. In the New Object - Organizational Unit window, in the Name box, type **MyOU** and click **OK**. If you are sharing the domain with other students, get a unique name for your OU from your instructor.
6. Right-click **MyOU**, point to **New**, and then click **User**.
7. In the New Object - User window, in the First name box, type **Samantha**.
8. In the Last name box, type **Lopez**.
9. In the User logon name box, type **SLopez** and click **Next**. If you are sharing the domain with other students, get a unique sign-in name from your instructor.
10. In the Password and Confirm password boxes, type **Passw0rd**.
11. Deselect the **User must change password at next logon** check box and click **Next**.
12. Click **Finish** and click **Active Directory Users and Computers**.
13. In Server Manager, click **Tools** and click **Group Policy Management**.
14. In Group Policy Management, click **MyOU**, right-click **MyOU**, and then click **Create GPO in this domain, and Link it here**.
15. In the New GPO window, in the Name box, type **MyOU-Policy** and click **OK**. If you are sharing the domain with other students, get a unique GPO name from your instructor.
16. In Group Policy Management, expand **MyOU**, right-click **MyOU-Policy**, and then click **Edit**.
17. In the Group Policy Management Editor, browse to **\User Configuration\Policies\Administrative Templates\System\Ctrl+Alt+Del Options**.
18. Double-click **Remove Task Manager**, click **Enabled**, and then click **OK**.
19. Close all open windows.
20. On your Windows 10 computer, sign in as **AD\Administrator** with a password of **Passw0rd**.
21. Right-click the **Start** button and click **Command Prompt (Admin)**.
22. If necessary, in the User Account Control dialog box, click **Yes**.
23. At the command prompt, type **gpupdate** and press **Enter**.
24. Sign out and sign in as **AD\SLopez** with a password of **Passw0rd**.
25. After the profile is ready, press **Ctrl+Alt+Delete**.
26. Verify that Task Manager is not available and click **Sign out**.

13

27. Sign in as **AD\Administrator** with a password of **Passw0rd**.

28. Press **Ctrl+Alt+Delete**, verify that Task Manager is an option, and then click **Cancel**.

Group Policy Inheritance

Group Policy Objects can be linked to the Active Directory domains, OUs, and Active Directory sites. In addition, each Windows 10 computer can have local Group Policy Objects. It is essential to understand the precedence given to each of these policies. For example, when a local policy configures the home page for Microsoft Edge as *http://www.microsoft.com* and a domain policy configures the home page for Microsoft Edge as *http://intranet*, which one is effective? The precedence determines what settings apply when there are conflicting settings between policies.

When a Windows computer starts, GPOs are applied in the following order:

1. Local computer

2. Site

3. Domain

4. Parent OU

5. Child OU

All of the individual GPO settings are inherited by default. For example, a Group Policy setting on a parent OU is also applied to child OUs and to all users and computers in the child OUs. One computer or user can process many policies during startup and sign-in.

At each level, more than one GPO can be applied to a user or computer. If there is more than one GPO per container, the policies are applied in the order specified by the administrator. The following steps are used to determine which policy settings to apply:

1. If there is no conflict, the settings for all policies are applied.

2. If there is a conflict, later settings overwrite earlier settings. For example, the setting from a domain policy overrides the setting from a local policy. This means that a child OU would be applied last and have the greatest priority by default.

3. If the settings in a computer policy and user policy conflict, the settings from the computer policy are applied.

When you are troubleshooting Group Policy application, it can be difficult to track down which policies are being applied. You can generate an HTML report to identify which Group Policy Objects are being applied. Use *gpresult /h report.html* to generate the report.

Activity 13-5: Generating a Report for GPO Troubleshooting

Time Required: 5 minutes
Objective: Generate and view a report for GPO troubleshooting

Description: When Group Policy settings are not being applied as you think they should be, it can be difficult to identify why. Gpresult.exe can be used to generate a report that shows which GPOs and specific settings are being applied. In this activity, you use gpresult.exe to generate a report and then view the contents of the report.

1. Sign in to your Windows 10 computer as **AD\SLopez** with a password of **Passw0rd**.

2. Right-click the **Start** button and click **Command Prompt**.

3. At the command prompt, type **gpresult /h report.html** and press **Enter**.

4. Type **report.html** and press **Enter**.

5. In the How do you want to open this file dialog box, click **Microsoft Edge** and click **OK**.

6. Review the contents of the report. Notice that MyOU-Policy was applied. Also notice that no computer settings are reported because SLopez is not a local administrator and does not have the necessary permissions to view information about the computer.

7. Close all open windows.

Group Policy Preferences

A typical Group Policy setting is applied to a computer and cannot be changed by the user, even if the user has full administrative privileges to the computer. A **Group Policy Preference** is pushed down to the computer as part of the same process as Group Policy settings; however, a Group Policy Preference can be changed by the user. For example, you can use Group Policy Preferences to configure power options such as configuring the computer to sleep after 10 minutes of inactivity. The user can manually change this. However, the next time the computer is restarted, the Group Policy Preference is reapplied.

Group Policy Preferences provide a way to configure a number of Windows 10 features that might have been done with scripting in the past. Many organizations have replaced logon scripts with Group Policy Preferences. Some of the things you can configure with Group Policy Preferences include:

- ODBC data sources
- Enable and disable devices
- Printers
- Drive mappings
- Scheduled tasks
- Service configuration
- VPN and dial-up connections
- Registry keys

One of the unique features of Group Policy Preferences is the ability to target them. By using targeting, you can have a single Group Policy Object that provides different settings for different users. For example, you can configure a drive mapping that is only applied if you are a member of the Sales group.

Activity 13-6: Configuring Group Policy Preferences

Time Required: 15 minutes
Objective: Configure and test Group Policy Preferences

Description: One of the common tasks performed by sign-in scripts is creating drive mappings. Management of drive mappings can be simplified by using Group Policy Preferences to apply the drive mappings. In this activity, you create a file share and then create a drive mapping to that file share that is distributed by using Group Policy Preferences.

1. If necessary, sign in to **DC** as **AD\Administrator** with a password of **Passw0rd**.

2. In Server Manager, click **Tools** and click **Computer Management**.

3. In Computer Management, expand **Shared Folders** and click **Shares**.

4. Right-click **Shares** and click **New Share**.

5. In the Create A Shared Folder Wizard, click **Next**.

6. In the Folder path box, type **C:\MyFolder** and click **Next**. If you are sharing the domain with other students, obtain a unique folder name from your instructor.

7. Click **Yes** in the dialog box to create the folder.

8. On the Name, Description, and Settings screen, click **Next** to accept the default settings. Notice the Share path.

9. On the Shared Folder Permissions screen, click **Customize permissions** and click **Custom**.

10. In the Customize Permissions window, with **Everyone** selected, select the **Allow Change** check box and click **OK**.

11. Click **Finish** and then click **Finish** again.

12. On the taskbar, click **File Explorer** and browse to **C:**.

13. Right-click **MyFolder** and click **Properties**.

14. In the MyFolder Properties window, click the **Security** tab and click **Edit**.

15. In the Permissions for MyFolder window, click **Users (AD\Users)**, select the **Allow Modify** check box, and then click **OK** twice.

16. Close File Explorer.

17. In Server Manager, click **Tools** and click **Group Policy Management**.

18. In Group Policy Management, right-click **MyOU-Policy** and click **Edit**.

19. In the Group Policy Management Editor, under **User Configuration**, expand **Preferences**, expand **Windows Settings**, and then click **Drive Maps**.

20. Right-click **Drive Maps**, point to **New**, and then click **Mapped Drive**.

21. In the New Drive Properties window, in the Location box, type **\\DC\MyFolder**.

22. In the Drive Letter area, click **Use** and select **S** in the drop-down list.

23. Click the **Common** tab and review the options. Item-level targeting is the option used to apply preferences to specific groups of users.

24. Click **OK**.

25. Close all open windows.

26. On your Windows 10 computer, sign in as **AD\SLopez** with a password of **Passw0rd**.

27. Click the **Start** button, type **gpupdate**, and then click **gpupdate**.

28. On the taskbar, click **File Explorer** and browse to **This PC**. Notice that the S: drive is listed. If the S: drive is not listed, sign out and sign in again.

29. Close File Explorer.

Multiple Local Policies

In a nondomain environment, it can be useful to have different Group Policy settings applied to administrative and nonadministrative users. Typically, this functionality is useful when you are trying to set up a public computer that is locked down when signed in with a public account, but unlocked when signed in with an administrative user.

You can create a local GPO for any local group or local user. You cannot create a local GPO directly for domain users. However, a domain user can be a member of a local group, which has a local GPO. You select who a local GPO applies to in the Microsoft Management Console (MMC) when you are adding the Group Policy Object Editor snap-in, as shown in Figure 13-5.

Controlling Device Installation

In a security-conscious organization, there are often concerns about users having the ability to remove organizational data by using a USB drive. One of the ways you can mitigate that risk is by controlling device installation. You can use Group Policy to define specific device types that are allowed or not allowed on the computer.

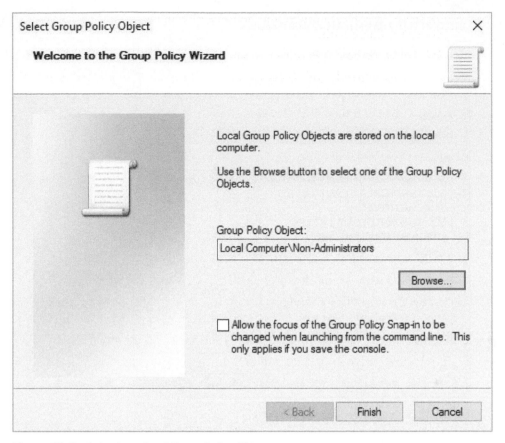

Figure 13-5   Selecting a local Group Policy Object

 By default, the restrictions on device installation by using Group Policy described in this section do not apply to users with local administrator permissions.

Identifying Devices   When a new device is installed into a Windows 10 computer, the operating system uses a device identification string and device setup class to properly install the new device. The **device identification string** is used to find an appropriate driver for the device. The **device setup class** controls how the device driver software is installed. Both the device identification string and the device setup class can be used when controlling the installation of devices.

A device often reports multiple device identification strings when queried by the operating system. A hardware ID is the most specific device identification string. When multiple hardware IDs are reported, there is typically one very specific hardware ID that includes make, model, and revision, then other less-specific hardware IDs, such as make and model. Figure 13-6 shows the hardware IDs for a hard disk.

Including multiple hardware IDs in a device allows the best available driver to be installed from those that are available. From a device installation control perspective, you can use the more generic hardware IDs to control installation rather than the very specific ones.

Device setup classes are used during the installation process for a new device to describe how the installation should be performed. The device setup class identifies a generic type of device rather than a specific make or model. Each device setup class is identified by a globally unique identifier (GUID).

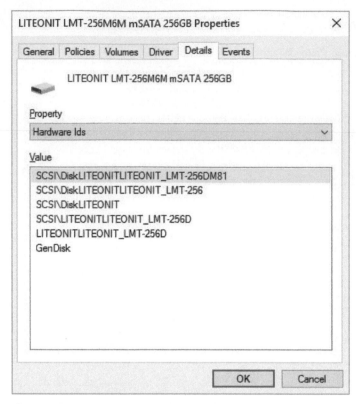

Figure 13-6   Hardware IDs for a hard disk

Some devices have multiple GUIDs defined if they are multifunction devices such as scanner/fax/printer devices. The parent device (overall device) has one GUID, and other functions (scanner, fax, printer) each have their own GUID.

Device Installation Group Policy Settings   Windows 10 includes Group Policy settings specifically to control device installation, as shown in Figure 13-7. They control which

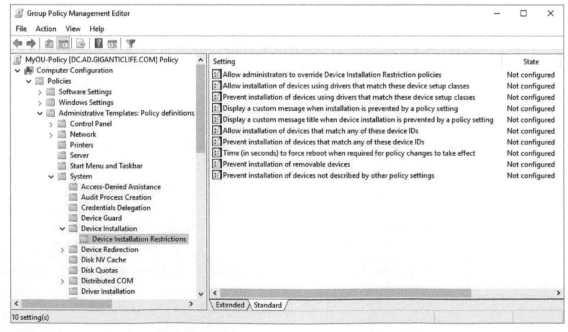

Figure 13-7   Device installation Group Policy settings

devices can and cannot be installed. Also, you can define a default option for whether users are allowed to install new devices. All of these settings are located in Computer Configuration\Policy\Administrative Templates\System\Device Installation\Device Installation Restrictions.

Removable Storage Group Policy Settings   Because access to removable storage is a concern for many organizations, there are additional Group Policy settings, as shown in Figure 13-8, which can be used to control access to different types of removable storage, rather than preventing installation. With these policy settings, you can deny read or write access to specific removable storage types. All of these settings are located in Computer Configuration\Policy\Administrative Templates\System\Removable Storage Access and User Configuration\Policy\Administrative Templates\System\Removable Storage Access.

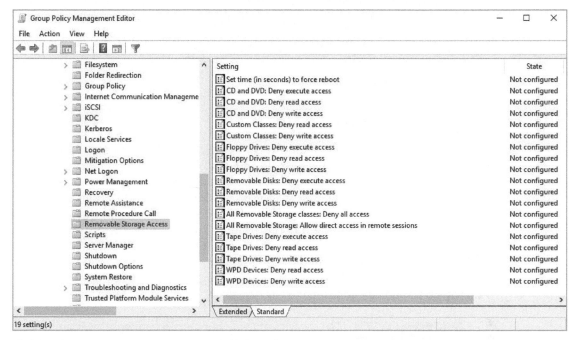

Figure 13-8   Removable storage Group Policy settings

In some cases, a reboot is required to enforce removable storage Group Policy settings. This is normally a problem only when a device is in use. In such a case, you can define how long the system waits to apply the changes before rebooting the system. Rebooting the system allows the policy changes to be applied.

Activity 13-7: Controlling Device Installation

Time Required: 15 minutes
Objective: Use Group Policy settings to control device installation

Description: Windows 10 includes a number of Group Policy settings to control the installation of devices and access to removable storage. In this activity, you use Group Policy settings to prevent the installation of any new disks, including portable storage devices such as USB drives.

1. On your Windows 10 computer, sign in as **AD\Administrator** with a password of **Passw0rd**.

2. Right-click the **Start** button and click **Device Manager**.

3. In Device Manager, expand **Disk drives**, right-click a disk installed in your system, and then click **Properties**.

4. In the disk Properties window, click the **Details** tab, and in the Properties box, select **Hardware Ids**. This displays the hardware IDs reported by your disk. Notice that the lowest value in the list is GenDisk. This is the least specific reference to your disk.

5. Close all open windows.

6. On DC, sign in as **AD\Administrator** with a password of **Passw0rd**.

7. In Server Manager, click **Tools** and click **Group Policy Management**.

8. In Group Policy Management, right-click **MyOU-Policy** and click **Edit**.

9. In the Group Policy Management Editor, browse to **Computer Configuration\Policies\Administrative Templates\System\Device Installation\Device Installation Restrictions**.

10. Select each Group Policy setting and read the description.

11. Double-click **Prevent installation of devices using drivers that match these device setup classes**.

12. In the Prevent installation of devices using drivers that match these device setup classes window, click **Enabled** and click **Show**.

13. In the Value box, type **GenDisk** and click **OK**.

14. In the Prevent installation of devices using drivers that match these device setup classes window, click **OK**.

15. Close all open windows.

Enterprise Deployment Tools

In smaller organizations, Windows 10 is often introduced as new systems are purchased. This means that there is often a mix of old and new operating systems. In larger organizations, there is a greater need for standardization. Typically, the change to a new operating system is a large project with a formal planning process. This is essential in larger organizations to keep support costs down.

To deploy Windows 10 quickly, it is not reasonable to use manual deployment methods such as using an installation DVD. You need to automate the deployment process. Chapter 2, Installing Windows 10, discussed some tools that can be used to automate deployment such as Sysprep, Windows System Image Manager (Windows SIM), Deployment Imaging Servicing and Management (DISM), and Windows Imaging and Configuration Designer (Windows ICD). However, there are additional tools that many large organizations use.

 The specifics of configuring these enterprise tools are out of scope for most desktop support professionals. However, it is important to be aware of the tools that are available and their capabilities. It makes you a more valuable part of your organization.

User State Migration Tool

You can use the **User State Migration Tool (USMT)** to migrate user settings, documents, and application configuration settings from the previous operating system to Windows 10. This allows users to keep a consistent work environment from the old operating system to Windows 10.

 Before using USMT to migrate user profiles, you need to consider whether user profile migration is really necessary. Many of the user settings in a profile are not compatible from an older operating system and applications to Windows 10 with the latest version of Microsoft Office. A simpler process that only captures essential information such as browser bookmarks might be more effective.

USMT has only a command-line interface and is designed for scripting. All configuration for USMT is done by using .xml files with the necessary information. The .xml files used to control USMT are:

- *MigApp.xml*—Used to include or exclude the setting for specific applications.

- *MigUser.xml*—Used to control which file types, user folders, and desktop settings are included in the migration.

- *MigSys.xml*—Used only when migrating operating system and browser settings to a Windows XP computer.

- *Config.xml*—Used to allow you to control the migration process in detail. For example, this custom configuration file can control which operating system component settings or which specific applications settings are migrated.

USMT Migration Process   The migration process performed to move settings from the old operating system to Windows 10 is the same regardless of whether a new computer is being used or an older computer is having a clean install performed. Figure 13-9 shows the USMT migration process.

Figure 13-9   USMT migration process

When ScanState is used to collect settings and files, they are stored in an intermediate location such as a network server. The settings and files cannot be transferred directly to an existing Windows 10 computer.

All applications should be installed on the destination computer before LoadState is used. This ensures that the installation of the application does not overwrite any of the imported configuration settings. Using LoadState before the necessary applications are installed can have unpredictable results.

Using Config.xml   Config.xml does not exist by default. It is generated by running ScanState.exe with the /genconfig option. This option captures all of the settings that are being migrated. You can then edit this file to control which of the settings are actually migrated when ScanState.exe is run.

To create a single Config.xml file that includes all possible application settings, install a workstation explicitly for this purpose. On this workstation, install each application used in your organization for which you want to migrate the settings. Then, after all applications are installed, you can create the Config.xml file based on this workstation. This single Config.xml file can be used to migrate settings and applications for all computers in the organization, rather than maintaining separate Config.xml files for computers with a specific set of applications.

You can use multiple Config.xml files to control the migration process in different ways for users with different needs. For each component listed in the Config.xml file, you can specify yes or no to migrating the component.

Windows Deployment Services

Windows Deployment Services (WDS) is a server role included with Windows Server 2008 and newer. You can use WDS to deploy operating system images, including Windows 10, over the network. With a gigabit network, this means you can deploy an image in only a few minutes. WDS can be managed by using the WdsMgmt administrative tool or the *wdsutil* command-line tool.

The following are required for successful installation and use of WDS:

- *Active Directory*—The WDS server must be a member server or domain controller in an Active Directory domain.

- *DHCP*—DHCP is used by client computers to obtain an IP address and communicate with the WDS server.

13

- *DNS*—DNS is used by client computers to resolve the host name of the WDS server.
- *An NTFS partition on the WDS server*—The images must be stored on an NTFS-formatted volume on the WDS server.

WDS Images   WDS uses different image types to accomplish different tasks in the deployment process. The four types of images are:

- *Install image*—These are WIM images that include the operating system and may include applications that are deployed to workstations. You can use an unattend.xml file to modify the operating system as part of the deployment process.
- *Boot image*—These are WIM images that include Windows PE. They are used to deploy install images. The default boot image (boot.wim) displays a menu that allows you to select which install image to deploy.
- *Capture image*—These images are used to automate the collection of a deployment image from a computer that has been configured as a reference image. Sysprep is run on the computer before the image is captured. The capture image uses Windows PE as an operating system and runs imaging software to collect the image.
- *Discover image*—These images are used to deploy the deployment images on computers that do not support PXE. Discover images are ISO files that can be stored on removable media, such as DVD or USB drive. At the client, you can boot from removable media to connect to the WDS server and download images.

WDS Deployment Process   WDS uses a combination of technologies to load an image onto a workstation. Some of the most important technologies are PXE and DHCP. Figure 13-10 shows the WDS deployment process.

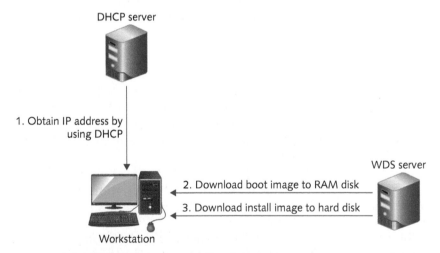

Figure 13-10   WDS deployment process

When deploying an image by using WDS, the following process is used:

1. Enable PXE in the client computer and configure it to boot from the network first.
2. Reboot the workstation and press F12 to perform a PXE boot.
3. The workstation obtains an IP address from a DHCP server and contacts the WDS server.
4. Select a PXE boot image if required. You may create additional boot images to support network drivers not available in the default Windows PE configuration.
5. The boot image is downloaded to a RAM disk on the client computer and Windows PE is booted.

6. Select an install image to deploy from the menu.

7. The install image is copied to the computer.

By using customized boot images and answer files, the installation process can be controlled to minimize user intervention. Also, additional tasks such as disk partitioning can be performed.

For more information about WDS, visit the Microsoft TechNet website (*http://www.microsoft.com/technet*) and search for Windows Deployment Services.

System Center Configuration Manager

System Center Configuration Manager is a solution from Microsoft to control the configuration of Windows computers. The main tasks you can accomplish with Configuration Manager are:

• Inventory

• Standardized configuration

• Software deployment

• Operating system deployment

• Software updates

When you use Configuration Manager to deploy operating systems, you can completely automate system deployment to the point where you do not need to physically touch the computer. After you deploy the operating system, you can also push out any required applications. It is a complete desktop management solution.

Microsoft Deployment Toolkit

The **Microsoft Deployment Toolkit (MDT)** is a solution that helps you configure scripted installations of operating systems and applications. You can use MDT with Configuration Manager and WDS or on its own. If you use MDT with Configuration Manager, you can perform zero-touch installations that are completely scripted. If you do not use Configuration Manager, MDT can configure light-touch installations.

A light-touch installation requires someone to start the remote computer from a boot image. However, after the boot image is started, the entire installation process for the operating system and applications can be automated.

In addition to tools that configure scripted installations of Windows 10 and applications, the MDT includes a wide range of documentation about the deployment of Windows 10. This guidance on best practices for deployment is as valuable as the scripted installations.

You can learn more about using MDT to deploy Windows 10 at *https://technet.microsoft.com/en-us/itpro/windows/deploy/deploy-windows-10-with-the-microsoft-deployment-toolkit.*

Boot to VHD

A typical installation of Windows 10 is located on a hard drive partition. In most scenarios, this is the best way to install Windows 10. However, Windows 10 allows the operating system to be installed to and booted from a virtual hard disk (VHD) file instead of a disk partition. When the boot process begins, the VHD file is mounted and used just like a physical disk.

After a VHD is copied to the computer, you need to configure the computer to use the VHD during the boot process. The *BCDboot* command-line tool is used to configure the boot process to load Windows 10 from the VHD.

Large enterprises with a virtualized desktop environment might find the ability to perform a VHD boot useful for power users. In a virtualized desktop environment, Windows 10 is run as a virtual machine (VM) on centralized servers. Each user has a VM on the centralized servers. Each VM shares the resources available on the centralized servers. Some power users may need an instance of Windows 10 with more resources than can be provided by the centralized servers. In such a case, the standardized VHD file used in the virtualized environment can be copied to a physical computer and configured to boot.

VHD boot can also be used to simplify dual-booting. Normally, dual-booting a computer requires a separate disk partition for each operating system. When VHD boot is used, there can be a single disk partition with multiple VHD files. However, only Windows 7 or newer can be used with VHD boot. You can use dual-booting for testing hardware drivers.

For more information about boot to VHD, visit the Microsoft TechNet website (*http://www.microsoft.com/technet*) and search for Boot to VHD.

Enterprise Management Tools

Larger organizations need automated tools to simplify management of their desktop computers. Some tools included with Windows Server can be used for this purpose. Microsoft also provides the Microsoft Desktop Optimization Pack (MDOP) for customers who have purchased software assurance. In MDOP, **Microsoft BitLocker Administration and Monitoring (MBAM)** and **User Experience Virtualization (UE-V)** are two tools that are useful for desktop management.

Windows Server Update Services

You can use **Windows Server Update Services (WSUS)** to manage the deployment of Windows updates to desktop computers and servers. WSUS contacts Microsoft Update and downloads updates rather than each client computer downloading updates. This is very efficient for network utilization because each update is downloaded only once and stored on the WSUS server. You can even organize multiple WSUS servers in a hierarchy so that WSUS servers can obtain updates from another WSUS server.

Client computers are configured to contact a WSUS server for updates rather than contacting the Microsoft update service directly. This can be configured by editing the registry or by using a Group Policy Object.

WSUS is significantly more flexible than automatic updates downloaded directly from Microsoft. You can organize computers into groups to control the update process and generate reports to view which computers have been updated and which have not. The ability to test updates before they are generally applied to workstations significantly reduces the risk of an update causing system downtime. You can also use WSUS to remove updates that have already been installed. The WSUS update process is shown in Figure 13-11.

The WSUS update process still relies on the client computers to trigger the installation of updates. After updates are approved for a specific computer, the update is downloaded by that computer from the WSUS server the next time Automatic Updates is triggered.

You can configure rules on the WSUS server to automatically approve some updates for specific computers. For example, you might want to automatically approve all updates for your test computers to reduce administrative work.

The updates downloaded automatically from Microsoft can be controlled by product, product family, update classification, and language. For example, you can choose to download only English updates or only critical updates. You can manually specify to download any updates that are not configured to download automatically.

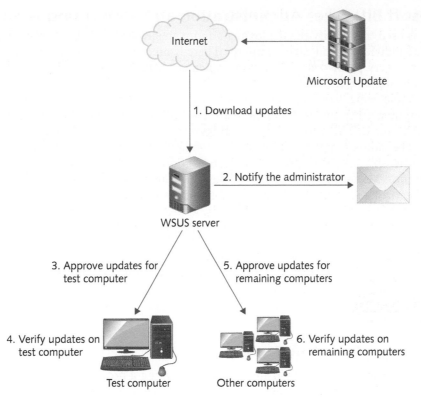

Figure 13-11   WSUS update process

Activity 13-8: Configuring Clients for WSUS

Time Required: 10 minutes
Objective: Use Group Policy settings to configure clients to use WSUS

Description: After installing and configuring a WSUS server, you need to configure clients to use the WSUS server. In this activity, you use Group Policy settings to configure clients to use a WSUS server.

This activity only performs the client configuration necessary to use WSUS because WSUS server configuration is outside the scope of this text.

1. On your Windows 10 computer, sign in as **AD\Administrator** with a password of **Passw0rd**.
2. In Server Manager, click **Tools** and click **Group Policy Management**.
3. In Group Policy Management, right-click **MyOU-Policy** and click **Edit**.
4. In the Group Policy Management Editor, browse to **Computer Configuration\Policies\ Administrative Templates\Windows Components\Windows Update**.
5. Select each of the Group Policy settings and read the description.
6. Double-click **Specify intranet Microsoft update service location**.
7. In the Specify intranet Microsoft update service location window, click **Enabled**.
8. In the Set the intranet update service for detecting updates and Set the intranet statistics server boxes, type **http://wsus.ad.GiganticLife.com** and click **OK**. This step assumes that you have a Windows server with WSUS installed with the name wsus.ad.GiganticLife.com.
9. Close all open windows.

13

Microsoft BitLocker Administration and Monitoring

MBAM is used to simplify the deployment and management of BitLocker. By default, BitLocker is enabled individually on each computer. There is no centralized management of BitLocker except for recovery passwords. When you implement MBAM, you enable centralized deployment and monitoring of BitLocker.

To enable centralized management of BitLocker, you need to install the MBAM agent on each computer. Once this is done, there are Group Policy settings that are read and applied by the MBAM agent. The Group Policy settings are part of a new .admx template that is part of MBAM. The .admx template allows you to configure the new Group Policy settings in a GPO.

For organizations that use Configuration Manager, MBAM can be integrated as part of Configuration Manager. Management of the TPM can be performed by Configuration Manager. MBAM reporting is also integrated into Configuration Manager reporting.

To simplify recovery of encrypted drives, MBAM includes a self-service web portal to look up recovery keys. In some cases, this means that users will be able to perform their own recovery without needing to call support.

For more information about MBAM, visit the Microsoft TechNet website (*http://www.microsoft.com/technet*) and search for MBAM.

User Experience Virtualization

UE-V provides user state virtualization similar to roaming profiles. When users sign in to different domain-joined computers, their settings follow them from computer to computer. However, UE-V provides more advanced functionality that is not provided by roaming profiles:

- Synchronization is based on templates for fine-grained control of specific application settings.
- Synchronization can be performed between multiple operating systems where user profiles would not be compatible.
- Settings are synchronized while the user is signed in rather than at sign-in or sign-out.

To implement UE-V, you need to install the UE-V agent on all of the computers you want to allow synchronization on. Then, you configure Group Policy settings to configure the client. There are two important settings:

- *Setting storage location*—This location is a file share where the settings for users are stored by the agent.
- *Settings template catalog location*—This location is a file share where settings location templates that describe how to synchronize settings for specific applications are stored. The agent reads the settings location templates.

You do not need to create settings location templates for all apps for which you want to synchronize settings. UE-V includes the ability to synchronize settings for Microsoft Office and many Windows settings. Settings location templates typically need to be created for custom apps and non-Microsoft apps.

For more information about UE-V, visit the Microsoft TechNet website (*http://www.microsoft.com/technet*) and search for UE-V.

Enterprise File Services

The file-sharing functionality in Windows provides a high level of control for security, but can be difficult to use in a large organization with multiple locations. In particular, if there are locations connected by slow WAN links, opening files over those links is very slow. Distributed File System (DFS) and BranchCache help to mitigate this issue.

Distributed File System

Distributed File System (DFS) is composed of DFS replication and DFS namespaces. DFS replication is used to synchronize data between files shares. DFS namespaces are used to virtualize access to shared folders and hide the true location of the shared folder. When you implement DFS, you can have multiple replicated copies of data and provide highly available access to that data. Figure 13-12 shows how DFS replication and DFS namespaces work together.

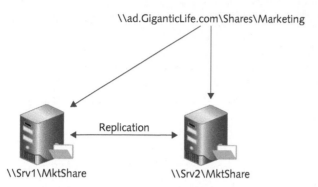

\\ad.GiganticLife.com\Shares\Marketing

Replication

\\Srv1\MktShare   \\Srv2\MktShare

Figure 13-12   DFS folder with multiple targets

Some scenarios for using DFS are:

- *High availability in a single location*—In this scenario, file shares are replicated between two servers in the same site. The namespaces point at both servers. If one server goes down, clients continue using the other server.

- *Close data access between locations*—In this scenario, file shares are replicated between two servers in different locations. The namespaces point at both servers. When users roam between the two sites, they automatically use the file share in the local location.

- *Data backup off-site*—In this scenario, file shares are replicated between two locations. The namespaces point at both servers. The file shares for remote users are backed up in the central location.

DFS replication is very efficient between locations. When a file is changed, only the changes to that file are replicated between the two servers.

Windows 10 includes DFS client software for accessing DFS namespaces. A DFS namespace appears to be a single, large file structure, but can really be composed of shared folders on multiple servers. This allows administrators to change the location of file shares without impacting client computers. When the DFS namespace is updated, clients automatically begin using the new location.

You can customize the connection process, but by default, when a DFS namespace refers to multiple file shares (targets), the client is directed to a file share in the local Active Directory site. If there are multiple file shares in the local Active Directory site, one file share is randomly selected. If connectivity to the first file share fails, the client connects to another available file share identified by the namespace.

The list of targets provided by a DFS namespace is known as a referral list. The order of targets in the referral list determines the order in which the client attempts to access the targets. If the target being used by a client becomes unavailable, the client switches over to another target almost immediately.

When changes are made to the list of targets, clients are not updated immediately. By default, clients cache the folder referral list for 30 minutes before refreshing it. If you remove a target from a folder, clients continue to use it until the cache for that folder is updated. Similarly, if you add a new target for a folder, the clients might not be informed for up to 30 minutes. You can change the cache time in the properties of a folder, but it is seldom required because changes to DFS namespaces are typically well planned and can be implemented over the span of a few hours or days. Figure 13-13 shows the properties of a folder in DFS Management.

13

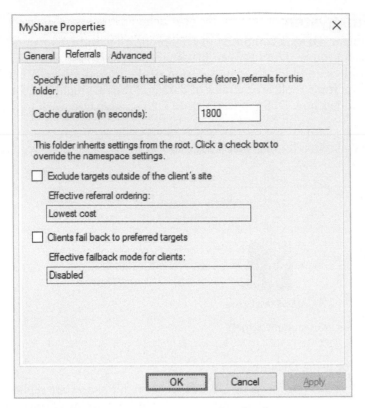

Figure 13-13   DFS folder Properties, Referrals tab

If Windows 10 connects to a nonoptimal target in a remote site due to a short-term error, Windows 10 remains connected to the nonoptimal target unless the *Clients fail back to preferred targets* option has been enabled on the folder. If this option is enabled, Windows 10 fails back to the preferred target at the next refresh. If the option is not enabled, you can cause clients to fail back by restarting, sleeping, or hibernating. As part of the startup process, the cache is cleared.

There is no interface for managing the DFS client in Windows 10. The settings are configured in DFS Management on the server. For trouble-shooting, you can use *dfsutil.exe* from the Remote Server Administrative Tools for Windows 10.

BranchCache

BranchCache is a file-caching technology for domain-joined computers in remote locations with slow WAN links. Files are stored in a file share in a central location, but are cached at the remote site to make it faster to open the files. In addition to files in file shares, BranchCache can also cache data from web servers and application servers using Background Intelligent Transfer Service (BITS).

BranchCache has two modes:

- *Distributed cache mode*—In this mode, each computer maintains a cache and the computers in a single site share cache data. If a computer with cached data is turned off, other clients must obtain the data from the file share over the slow WAN link.

- *Hosted cache mode*—In this mode, a Windows server is used as a central cache by all computers in the remote site. This maximizes the availability of cached data because the server will always be on.

When you open a file that has been cached, BranchCache verifies with the server hosting the file share that the file has not been modified since it has been cached. If the file has not been modified, it is opened from the cache. If the file has been modified, it is opened from the file share over the WAN link. This process ensures that an out-of-date file is never used, but it also means that if the WAN link is down, cached data cannot be accessed. Saving a file is always done back to the file share and the cache.

In most cases, you enable BranchCache on clients by using a GPO. However, it is possible to manually enable BranchCache and view BranchCache configuration by using *netsh* and Windows PowerShell cmdlets. To view the Windows PowerShell cmdlets available for managing BranchCache, run Get-Command *-BC*.

BranchCache is available only in the Enterprise and Education editions of Windows 10.

For more information about BranchCache, visit the Microsoft TechNet website (*http://www.microsoft.com/technet*) and search for BranchCache.

Activity 13-9: Configuring Clients for BranchCache

Time Required: 10 minutes

Objective: Use Group Policy settings to configure clients to use BranchCache

Description: To use BranchCache, it needs to be enabled on the client and the server hosting the data. To enable clients to use BranchCache, you use Group Policy settings. In this activity, you enable clients to use BranchCache in distributed cache mode.

This activity does not configure the server for BranchCache because it is outside the scope of this text.

1. On your Windows 10 computer, sign in as **AD\Administrator** with a password of **Passw0rd**.
2. In Server Manager, click **Tools** and click **Group Policy Management**.
3. In Group Policy Management, right-click **MyOU-Policy** and click **Edit**.
4. In the Group Policy Management Editor, browse to **Computer Configuration\Policies\ Administrative Templates\Network\BranchCache**.
5. Click each setting and read the description.
6. Double-click **Turn on BranchCache**, click **Enabled**, and then click **OK**.
7. Double-click **Set BranchCache Distributed Cache mode**, click **Enabled**, and then click **OK**.
8. Close all open windows.

Chapter Summary

- Active Directory is a database of network information about users, computers, and applications. A network based on Active Directory is far more scalable than workgroup-based networks. The components of Active Directory are domains, OUs, trees, and forests.

- Servers in an Active Directory domain can be either domain members or domain controllers. A domain member is integrated into the security structure of the domain. A domain controller holds a copy of the Active Directory information for the domain.

- Active Directory is composed of a domain partition, configuration partition, and schema partition. The replication of the information in each partition is controlled by Active Directory sites.

- Clients use DNS to locate domain controllers. If DNS is not configured properly, client performance suffers and group policies may not be applied.

- Group Policy is used to configure and control workstations. Group Policy settings are stored in Group Policy Objects. The order of application for Group Policy Objects is: local, site, domain, parent OU, and child OU. If there is a conflict, the last applied policy has the highest priority. Multiple local policies can be created.

- You can use Group Policy settings to control device installation and the use of removable storage devices. Both of these enhance the ability of organizations to control data leaving the organization.

- Enterprise environments need tools to help automate and standardize Windows 10 deployment. The User State Migration Tool (USMT) is used to transfer settings from old computers to new computers. Windows Deployment Services (WDS) can image computers over the network. Configuration Manager can perform zero-touch installations and deploy software. The Microsoft Deployment Toolkit (MDT) can help configure light-touch deployments or zero-touch deployments in conjunction with Configuration Manager.

- Enterprise environments need tools to help manage Windows 10 computers. Windows Server Update Services (WSUS) centrally manage the approval and deployment of Windows updates. Microsoft BitLocker Administration and Monitoring (MBAM) is used to centrally deploy and monitor BitLocker. User Experience Virtualization (UE-V) is used to provide advanced roaming of user settings between computers.

- Enterprise environments often used advanced file services functionality. Distributed File System (DFS) is used to replicate file shares and virtualize access to the file shares with namespaces. BranchCache is used to speed up file access in remote locations.

Key Terms

Active Directory   A directory of network information about users, computers, and applications that links multiple domains together.

Active Directory site   A set of IP subnets representing a physical location that is used by Active Directory to control replication.

BranchCache   A feature in Windows 10 that speeds up access to files over slow connections by caching files. It operates in distributed cache mode or hosted cache mode.

configuration partition   The Active Directory partition that holds general information about the Active Directory forest and application configuration information. It is replicated to all domain controllers in the Active Directory forest.

device identification string   One or more identifiers included in a hardware device that is used by Windows 10 to locate and install an appropriate driver for a hardware device.

device setup class   An identifier included with a hardware device driver that describes how the device driver is to be installed.

Distributed File System (DFS)   A server role in Windows Server that includes replication of shared folders and virtualization of paths providing access to the shared folders.

domain   A logical grouping of computers and users in Active Directory.

domain controller   A server that holds a copy of Active Directory information.

domain partition   The Active Directory partition that holds domain-specific information, such as user and computer accounts, that is replicated only between domain controllers within the domain.

forest   Multiple Active Directory trees with automatic trust relationships between them.

global catalog server   A domain controller that holds a subset of the information in all domain partitions for the entire Active Directory forest.

Group Policy A feature integrated with Active Directory that can be used to centrally manage the configuration of Windows 2000 and newer Windows computers, including Windows 10.

Group Policy Object (GPO) A collection of Group Policy settings that can be applied to client computers.

Group Policy Preferences Part of a Group Policy Object that is typically used to configure the user environment. Preferences can be changed by the user, but are reset again at next sign-in.

Microsoft BitLocker Administration and Monitoring A tool included in the Microsoft Desktop Optimization Pack that is used to centrally deploy, manage, and monitor BitLocker.

Microsoft Deployment Toolkit (MDT) A set of best practices, scripts, and tools to help automate the deployment of Windows operating systems.

organizational unit (OU) A container within a domain that is used to create a hierarchy that can be used to organize user and computer accounts and apply group policies.

schema partition The Active Directory partition that holds the definition of all Active Directory objects and their attributes. It is replicated to all domain controllers in the Active Directory forest.

System Center Configuration Manager A software package that can perform inventory, implement a standardized configuration, deploy software, deploy operating systems, and deploy software updates.

tree A group of Active Directory domains that share the same naming context and have automatic trust relationships among them.

User Experience Virtualization (UE-V) A tool included in the Microsoft Desktop Optimization Pack that is used to synchronize operating system and application settings for a user between computers.

User State Migration Tool (USMT) A utility with both a command-line and graphical interface that is used to migrate user settings, files, and application configuration from a source computer to a destination computer.

Windows Deployment Services (WDS) A Windows Server service that is used to simplify the process of applying images to computers.

Windows Server Update Services (WSUS) A Windows Server application that is used to control the process of downloading and applying updates to Windows servers and Windows clients.

Review Questions

13

1. Which type of server is used to sign in clients that are joined to an Active Directory domain?

   a. domain controller

   b. member server

   c. global catalog server

   d. RADIUS server

2. Which type of server holds some of the domain information for all domains in the forest?

   a. domain controller

   b. member server

   c. global catalog server

   d. RADIUS server

3. Which Active Directory partitions are replicated to all domain controllers in the Active Directory forest? (Choose all that apply.)

   a. domain partition

   b. configuration partition

   c. schema partition

   d. application partition

4. The _____ partition contains the definition of the objects and their attributes that can exist in Active Directory.

5. Which network service is used by workstations to find domain controllers?

    a.   Active Directory

    b.   DHCP

    c.   DNS

    d.   NetBIOS

6. Group Policy can be used to distribute software to a Windows 10 computer. True or False?

7. Approximately how often does a Windows 10 computer download Group Policy Objects?

    a.   every 5 minutes

    b.   every 90 minutes

    c.   only at shutdown

    d.   only at startup

8. Which Group Policy setting location has the lowest priority and will always be overridden by other GPOs when there is a conflict?

    a.   Local

    b.   Site

    c.   Domain

    d.   Parent OU

    e.   Child OU

9. Which configuration file for USMT does not exist by default and must be created by running ScanState with the /genconfig option?

    a.   MigApp.xml

    b.   MigUser.xml

    c.   MigSys.xml

    d.   Config.xml

10. Which utility or software package can completely automate the deployment of Windows operating systems with no interaction?

    a.   Configuration Manager

    b.   WDS

    c.   USMT

    d.   MDT

    e.   WSUS

11. Which WDS image type is used by workstations to connect to the WDS server and select an image to install?

    a.   install image

    b.   boot image

    c.   capture image

    d.   discover image

12. Which Windows technologies require an agent to be installed? (Choose all that apply.)

    a.   DFS

    b.   BitLocker

    c.   MBAM

    d.   BranchCache

    e.   UE-V

13. A DFS folder can have a maximum of two targets. True or False?

14. Which of the following is true about UE-V?

    a. UE-V synchronizes only Microsoft Office settings.

    b. UE-V cannot synchronize data files.

    c. UE-V can be used by workgroup members.

    d. UE-V is a free download.

15. Which command-line utility can you use to configure Windows 10 to boot to VHD?

    a. vhdconfig

    b. bootconfig

    c. bcdboot

    d. systemconfig

    e. bootmon

16. Group Policy Preferences can be overridden by users. True or False?

17. By default, how long do DFS clients cache the referral list for a folder?

    a. 30 seconds

    b. 5 minutes

    c. 15 minutes

    d. 30 minutes

    e. 90 minutes

18. Which program integrates with Configuration Manager to provide zero-touch installations?

    a. MDT

    b. WSUS

    c. USMT

    d. Windows ICD

    e. Windows SIM

19. Which methods can you use to fix a Windows 10 computer that has a broken trust relationship with the domain? (Choose all that apply.)

    a. Move the workstation to a workgroup and then rejoin the domain.

    b. Run Repair-ComputerTrust.

    c. Run dism /rejoin.

    d. Synchronize the time with the domain controller.

    e. Run Test-ComputerSecureChannel-Repair.

20. After a computer has been joined to a domain, all domain users can sign in to that computer. True or False?

13

Case Projects

Case 13-1: Enterprise Group Policy Application

Gigantic Life Insurance is planning to implement Group Policy to control user desktops. Some of the desired settings are to be implemented for the entire organization, while other settings apply only to particular regions or departments.

Gigantic Life Insurance is organized as a single domain. The network manager is concerned that dividing into multiple domains to apply individual group policies will be a lot of work and disrupt users. Explain why this is not a concern.

Case 13-2: Small-Office Group Policy Application

Buddy's Machine Shop has a kiosk computer located in the lobby for customers to use. The kiosk computer has recently been updated to Windows 10 from Windows 7 and is not part of a domain. The local computer policy created for Windows 7 has been applied to Windows 10. This policy severely restricts the use of the computer, so that customers can only use the web browser.

Occasionally, an administrator needs to sign in to the kiosk computer to perform maintenance and update software. However, this is awkward because the administrator needs to disable settings in the local policy before performing any task. Then, when the tasks are complete, the administrator needs to re-enable the settings in the local policy. Explain how this system can be improved upon.

Case 13-3: Controlling Software Updates

Currently, all computers at Enormous Financial Corporation download updates directly from Microsoft. You have heard that many other companies use WSUS to download and apply updates. You would like to use WSUS in your organization. To justify implementing WSUS, describe the benefits of using WSUS and your plan for implementing it.

chapter 14

Remote Access and Client Support

After reading this chapter and completing the exercises, you will be able to:

- Describe remote data access options
- Configure clients for virtual private networks
- Configure and troubleshoot DirectAccess clients
- Configure Remote Desktop and Remote Assistance
- Describe and configure data synchronization options

User expectations for mobile support keep growing and IT organizations need to provide support for accessing data and applications from remote locations. There is also demand to use personal devices that might not be domain joined. You need to understand the options for supporting these users.

In this chapter, you learn about the options available for remote access, remote control, and data synchronization. You also learn about the various virtual private network protocols and how to configure clients. DirectAccess, a new variation of a virtual private network, is also covered. You learn how Remote Desktop and Remote Assistance are used to provide connectivity to Windows 10 computers. Finally, you learn about the data synchronization options that allow data to be used even if there is no network connectivity.

Overview of Remote Data Access

Mobile and remote users do not have direct access to the network resources, such as data and applications, that are located at the main office. The lack of a direct network connection is a barrier to accessing those resources. Public networks allow traveling users to obtain a remote network connection, but the security of that connection is suspect and a threat to the safety of the resources being accessed by mobile workers. To address these issues, Microsoft provides remote access, remote control, and data synchronization technologies. All of these support mobile and remote users in different ways.

Remote Access

Remote access consists of a dedicated computer acting as a remote access server and clients connecting to that server. Once clients are connected to the remote access server, the clients have access to resources on the network where the remote access server is located. For example, remote access clients can open and save files on a file server back in the main office, as shown in Figure 14-1. In fact, the client gets an IP address for the organizational network.

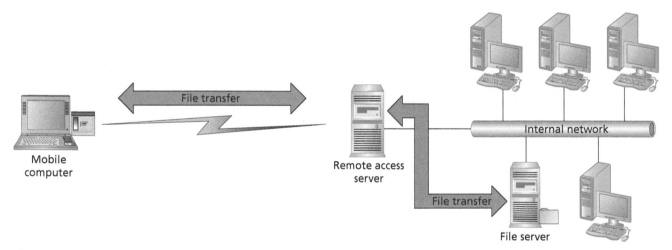

Figure 14-1 Remote access

The oldest technology for remote access is dial-up networking. Dial-up networking clients have a modem and connect to the remote access server over telephone lines. This technology is seldom used now because it is very slow when compared with Internet connectivity. Dial-up connectivity is limited to approximately 56 Kbps (kilobits per second). A 4G data plan on most mobile phones is over 1000 times faster.

It is much more common for remote access to be done over a **virtual private network (VPN)**. A VPN creates an encrypted connection between the VPN clients and the remote access server over a public network such as the Internet. Because the connection is encrypted, anyone between the VPN client and the remote access server is prevented from viewing the data in transit.

A VPN is much faster than dial-up because it operates at almost the same speed as the Internet connection. However, latency is still much higher over a VPN than on a local area network (LAN). Therefore, even with a fast connection, accessing data is slower over a VPN than it is locally. Opening and saving files such as Word documents is a noticeably slower process over a VPN, but might be tolerable. For many apps that use a central database for data storage, a VPN is not practical because the app running on the client generates many small requests and each request has high latency, which delays processing in the app.

Remote Control

Remote control technologies improve on remote access technologies by reducing the amount of data that needs to be sent between the client and the server. All resource access and data processing is performed on a server that is remote controlled, as shown in Figure 14-2. The remote client uses remote control software to send keyboard and mouse commands to the computer being remotely controlled. These commands are processed on the remote-controlled computer, not on the remote client computer. The remote client is sent a visual update of the screen from the remotely controlled computer.

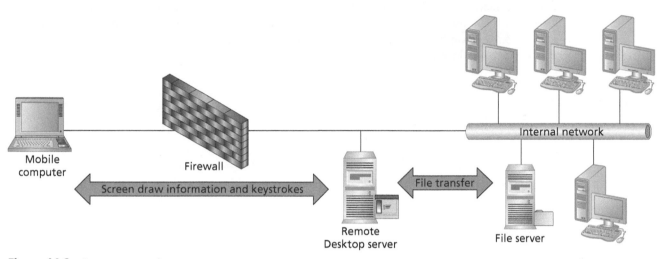

Figure 14-2   Remote control

This solution requires much less bandwidth between the remote client and server than remote access does. Remote control technologies perform well over slower networks such as the Internet and are generally preferred to remote access technologies.

 In Chapter 9, Windows 10 Application Support, Remote Desktop Services and RemoteApp were discussed for application deployment. Both of those technologies are remote control technologies.

Data Synchronization

The main weakness for both remote access technologies and remote control technologies is that they require connectivity. There are scenarios where no network connectivity is available or is of poor quality. Sometimes clients do not provide guest Wi-Fi access and hotels are notorious for having poor quality Wi-Fi that sometimes does not even allow remote control technologies to work well.

When there is either no connectivity or poor connectivity, **data synchronization** can be a solution. Data synchronization copies files locally to mobile computers. Then, users can work with the files whether they are connected to a network or not. At some point, the changed files are copied back (uploaded) to the server. The timing of the synchronization varies depending on the technology used for data synchronization.

One key consideration for data synchronization is shared application data. Users cannot access shared app data by using data synchronization unless the app performs its own offline data synchronization process. So, generally, data synchronization is good for personal files, but not as useful for shared data.

Configuring VPN Clients

One of the main concerns when you allow remote access to resources is security. A VPN encrypts communication between the VPN clients and the remote access server, as shown in Figure 14-3. On the internal network, the remote access server sends the data as unencrypted cleartext just as if the client were located on the internal network. When you evaluate VPN security, you need to be aware of the different protocols and authentication methods that can be used.

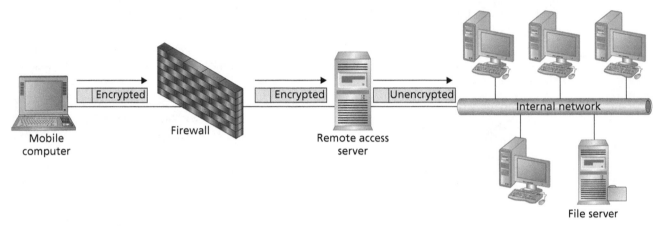

Figure 14-3   VPN design

Windows Server 2016 can be configured as a remote access server by installing the Routing and Remote Access server role. When you use Windows Server as a remote access server, the required protocols for connectivity with Windows 10 are included in Windows 10. There is no additional software to deploy on the clients.

Many organizations use a non-Microsoft solution for their VPN. Often, these solutions are provided by network equipment vendors, such as Cisco, Juniper, Palo Alto, SonicWALL, Fortinet, and WatchGuard. Most of the non-Microsoft solutions require you to install a VPN client that is specific to their solution.

VPN Protocols

The VPN protocols that are supported by Windows 10 are the protocols supported when you use Windows Server as a remote access server. When you are planning a VPN deployment, you decide which protocols will be offered based on your analysis of how secure they are and how easy they are to use. When you configure the VPN clients, you need to select a protocol that is already configured on the server.

PPTP   Point-to-Point Tunneling Protocol (PPTP) is one of the easiest protocols to use for a VPN. Authentication for PPTP is typically based on a user name and password, which is easy for users to work with. It is possible to configure certificate-based authentication, which is more secure, but this is seldom done.

Most remote locations, such as hotels, allow PPTP packets to pass through their firewalls. PPTP is widely supported because it is an older protocol that has been available since the 1990s. However, PPTP is also one of the most insecure protocols. A determined hacker who has captured authentication traffic for PPTP can easily determine the user name and password. Despite the security concerns, PPTP is still used for some networks with low security requirements.

The PPTP protocol is initiated by the VPN client communicating with the remote access server on TCP port 1723. At this point, a Generic Routing Encapsulation (GRE) tunnel is created. The GRE packets are IP protocol type 47 and need to be allowed through any firewalls. The GRE packets have a source and destination IP address, but they are not TCP (6) or UDP (17) packets. This is why they require special consideration.

L2TP   Layer 2 Tunneling Protocol (L2TP) is only an authentication protocol. When you create an L2TP VPN connection, IPsec is used with L2TP to provide data encryption. The authentication provided by L2TP is based on user credentials. IPsec includes authentication for the VPN client and remote access server. The combination of the two authentication levels increases security, but also makes it more difficult to manage L2TP VPN connections. As a consequence, L2TP has never become very popular.

The authentication for IPsec can be based on:

- *Pre-shared key*—This is a password that needs to be configured on both the VPN client and the remote access server. A pre-shared key is relatively easy to implement, but, because a single password is shared by all clients and the remote access server, this is not very secure.

- *Certificates*—If the VPN client and the remote access server have both been configured with certificates that are trusted, certificate authentication can be used. This is more secure than a pre-shared key, but it can be awkward to deploy certificates to all of the VPN clients.

- *Kerberos*—Windows-based networks use Kerberos to authenticate users and computers. This same protocol can be used by IPsec. Using IPsec is only possible if the VPN client computer and the remote access server are members of the same Active Directory forest.

To allow L2TP connectivity through a firewall, you need to allow UDP port 500, UDP port 4500, and IP protocol type 50. IP protocol type 50 is Encapsulating Security Payload (ESP) that is used by IPsec.

SSTP   To simplify firewall configuration and ensure the best compatibility with remote locations, many VPNs are now based on Secure Sockets Layer (SSL). An SSL VPN uses TCP port 443, which is also used by secure websites. All public networks allow connectivity using TCP port 443. Microsoft has implemented **Secure Socket Tunneling Protocol (SSTP)** as an SSL VPN.

An SSTP connection is authenticated by a user name and password to make it easier for users. In addition, the remote access server is authenticated because the certificate used for SSL must be trusted.

When SSTP was originally introduced in Windows 2008, lack of support in Windows XP prevented many organizations from using this protocol. However, SSTP can be used by any Windows Vista SP1 or newer Microsoft client operating system. Consequently, due to ease of implementation and the use of modern encryption protocols, SSTP is preferred over L2TP and PPTP.

IKEv2 Tunneling Protocol   Internet Key Exchange v2 Tunneling Protocol (IKEv2) is a newer VPN protocol that allows IPsec to be used for data encryption. This protocol is available for Windows 7 and newer clients. Unlike L2TP, authentication for an IKEv2 VPN connection does not require that IPsec authentication be configured separately. You can use authentication based only on a user name and password.

The main benefit of IKEv2 is better support for poor network connections. Microsoft refers to this feature as **VPN Reconnect**. Unlike a typical VPN connection, which may lose connectivity when there is a network interruption, IKEv2 can reconnect automatically when network connectivity is restored. In some cases, users might not notice that the VPN was ever disconnected.

Firewall configuration for IKEv2 is the same as for L2TP. You need to allow UDP port 500, UDP port 4500, and IP protocol type 50.

Creating a VPN Connection

In most cases, a typical user will have only one VPN connection back to the main office to access data. However, a support technician with multiple clients may have a VPN connection for each client. Your specific scenario determines which method for creating VPN connections will work best for you.

Individual Windows 10 users can create a VPN connection from Settings, as shown in Figure 14-4. You can also create a new connection from Network and Sharing Center by selecting *Set up a new connection or network*. When users configure a VPN connection manually, you will need to provide instructions on how to create the VPN connection, including any settings that are necessary. Even with instructions, the process tends to be error-prone because users make mistakes in the configuration.

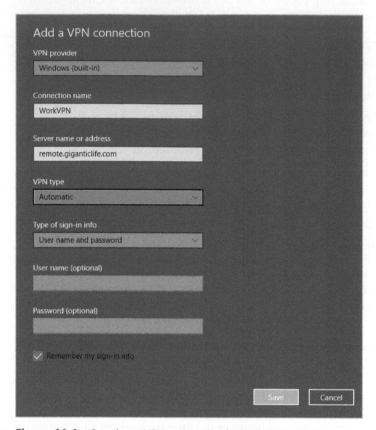

Figure 14-4 Creating a VPN connection in Settings

When you configure a VPN from Settings, you need to provide the following information:

- *VPN provider*—The VPN provider is the software that creates and controls the VPN connection. Windows 10 includes the Windows VPN provider, but other vendors can make providers available to support their specific type of VPN. Other VPN providers need to be installed as additional software because they are not included in Windows 10.

- *Connection name*—Each VPN connection needs a name to identify it. This should be named something that relates to its purpose.

- *Server name or address*—This is the FQDN or IP address of the remote access server that the VPN client connects to.

- *VPN type*—The default value for VPN type is Automatic, which attempts to detect the type of VPN automatically. This avoids the need for the user to know the specific VPN type. If the type of VPN is not detected properly, you can select a specific VPN type, such as PPTP or SSTP, as defined on the remote access server.

- *Type of sign-in info*—Many organizations allow users to sign in by using a user name and password. However, you can enhance sign-in security by using smart cards, one-time passwords, or certificates.

There is an option to enter and save credentials (user name and password) when you create the VPN connection. If you save the credentials, any user who gains access to your computer could remotely access over the VPN. This is less of a risk if BitLocker is being used to protect the hard drive.

Activity 14-1: Creating a VPN Connection

Time Required: 5 minutes
Objective: Create a VPN connection that connects to a remote access server

Description: You want to connect to the remote access server at your office to access files securely over the Internet. In this activity, you configure a VPN connection.

1. If necessary, start your computer and sign in.
2. Click the **Start** button and click **Settings**.
3. In the Settings window, click **Network & Internet** and click **VPN**.
4. Under the VPN heading, click **Add a VPN connection**.
5. In the Add a VPN connection window, in the VPN provider box, select **Windows (built-in)**.
6. In the Connection name box, type **WorkVPN**.
7. In the Server name or IP address box, type **vpnserver.giganticlife.com**.
8. In the VPN type box, select **Automatic**.
9. In the Type of sign-in info box, select **User name and password** and click **Save**.
10. In the Settings window, click **WorkVPN** and click **Advanced options**.
11. Review the list of options and close all open windows.

Automated Deployment   Automating the deployment of VPN connections is generally preferred to manually creating VPN connections. Automating deployment of VPN connections removes the chance of user error during configuration. There are several methods for deploying VPN connections automatically. These methods are listed in Table 14-1.

Table 14-1 Methods to deploy VPN connections

Deployment method	Description
Group Policy Preferences	You can distribute VPN connections by using Group Policy Preferences. For domain-joined computers, this is the simplest way to configure VPN connections automatically. This method cannot be used for computers that are not domain joined.
Connection Manager Administration Kit (CMAK)	**Connection Manager Administration Kit (CMAK)** is a feature that can be installed on Windows 10 or Windows Server. You use CMAK to create VPN connections that are packaged as an executable file. Users can run the executable file to create VPN connections on their computer. Computers do not need to be domain joined.
Windows PowerShell	Although it is possible to create and manage VPN connections by using Windows PowerShell cmdlets, it is beyond the scope of this book to identify the cmdlet details for occasional use. However, you could create a script that creates VPN connections as an alternative to distributing an executable created with CMAK. Computers do not need to be domain joined, but users need to be knowledgeable enough to run the Windows PowerShell script.

14

Activity 14-2: Using CMAK

Time Required: 15 minutes
Objective: Use CMAK to create a deployment package for a VPN connection

Description: You would like to create a deployment package for a VPN connection that can be used by Windows 10 computers that are domain joined or not domain joined. In this activity, you install CMAK and create a deployment package for a VPN connection.

1. If necessary, start your computer and sign in.

2. Click the **Start** button, type **features**, and then click **Turn Windows features on or off**. If necessary, in the User Account Control dialog box, click **Yes**.

3. In the Windows Features window, scroll down, select the **RAS Connection Manager Administration Kit (CMAK)** check box, and then click **OK**.

4. When installation is complete, click **Close**.

5. Click the **Start** button, type **admin**, and then click **Administrative Tools**.

6. In the Administrative Tools window, double-click **Connection Manager Administration Kit**.

7. In the User Account Control dialog box, click **Yes**.

8. In the Connection Manager Administration Kit Wizard window, click **Next**.

9. On the Select the Target Operating System screen, click **Windows Vista or above** and click **Next**.

10. On the Create or Modify a Connection Manager profile screen, click **New profile** and click **Next**.

11. On the Specify the Service Name and the File Name screen, in the Service name box, type **GiganticLifeVPN**.

12. In the File name box, type **GLvpn** and click **Next**.

13. On the Specify a realm name screen, click **Do not add a realm name to the user name** and click **Next**.

14. On the Merge Information from Other Profiles screen, click **Next**.

15. On the Add Support for VPN Connections screen, select the **Phone book from this profile** check box.

16. In the VPN server name or IP address area, click **Always use the same VPN server**, type **remote.giganticlife.com**, and then click **Next**.

17. On the Create or Modify a VPN Entry screen, click **GiganticLifeVPN Tunnel <Default>** and click **Edit**.

18. In the Edit VPN Entry window, click the **Security** tab.

19. In the VPN Strategy box, select **Try Secure Socket Tunneling Protocol First**.

20. In the Logon security area, click **Use Extensible Authentication Protocol (EAP)**, select **Microsoft: Protected EAP (PEAP) (encryption enabled)**, and then click **OK**.

21. On the Create or Modify a VPN Entry screen, click **Next**.

22. On the Add a Custom Phone Book screen, clear the **Automatically download phone book updates** check box and click **Next**.

23. On the Configure Dial-up Networking Entries screen, click **Next**.

24. On the Specify Routing Table Updates screen, click **Next**.

25. On the Configure Proxy Settings for Internet Explorer screen, click **Next**.

26. On the Add Custom Actions screen, click **Next**.

27. On the Display a Custom Logon Bitmap screen, click **Next**.

28. On the Display a Custom Phone Book Bitmap screen, click **Next**.

29. On the Display Custom Icons screen, click **Next**.

30. On the Include a Custom Help File screen, click **Next**.

31. On the Display Custom Support Information screen, click **Next**.

32. On the Display a Custom License Agreement screen, click **Next**.

33. On the Install Additional Files with the Connection Manager profile screen, click **Next**.

34. On the Build the Connection Manager Profile and Its Installation Program screen, click **Next**.

35. On the Your Connection Manager Profile is Complete and Ready to Distribute screen, verify the location of the .exe file and click **Finish**.

Activity 14-3: Using Windows PowerShell to View VPN Connections

Time Required: 5 minutes
Objective: Use Windows PowerShell to view the VPN connections on a computer

Description: As an administrator, you want a quick way to see the VPN connections that have been created on a computer. In this activity, you use Windows PowerShell to view the VPN connections on a computer.

1. If necessary, start your computer and sign in.
2. Click the **Start** button, type **powershell**, right-click **Windows PowerShell**, and then click **Run as administrator**.
3. In the User Account Control dialog box, click **Yes**.
4. At the Windows PowerShell prompt, type **Get-Command *vpn*** and press **Enter**.
5. Type **Get-VpnConnection** and press **Enter**.
6. Close all open windows.

Authentication Protocols When you create a VPN connection in Settings, you are required to specify the type of sign-in info. This setting defines the options that are used for authentication, as shown in Figure 14-5. In most cases, you should configure the type of sign-in info through Settings rather than modifying the authentication settings directly.

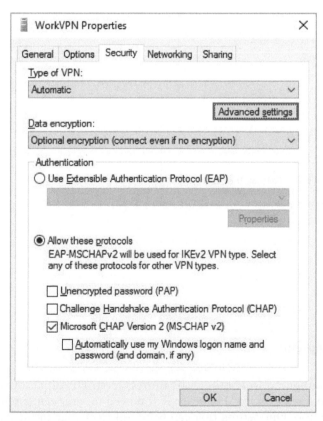

Figure 14-5 VPN security settings

For the purpose of understanding documentation and using other tools, such as Windows PowerShell, for VPN management, it is useful to understand the authentication protocols.

Extensible Authentication Protocol (EAP) is a framework that allows multiple authentication methods to be integrated with the sign-in process. There are multiple authentication methods included with Windows 10 and more can be added by vendors. EAP can be used by the newer VPN protocols. IKEv2 requires the use of EAP.

Windows 10 includes Password Authentication Protocol (PAP) and Challenge Handshake Authentication Protocol (CHAP). Both of these protocols should be used only if there is no other choice. PAP transmits unencrypted credentials during authentication and CHAP has serious security flaws that make it easy to obtain the credentials. **Microsoft CHAP version 2 (MS-CHAP v2)** provides significantly better security than PAP and CHAP, but it is also known to be vulnerable with minimal effort and should be avoided whenever possible.

PAP, CHAP, and MS-CHAP v2 are used with PPTP VPNs. A preferred alternative is to use another VPN type for better security. If that is not possible, evaluate the possibility of using PEAP-MS-CHAP v2 with PPTP. This authentication method uses MS-CHAP v2 within **Protected EAP**. Protected EAP uses SSL to protect the authentication process and make it secure.

Network Settings   A VPN connection has network settings just like an Ethernet or Wi-Fi connection, as shown in Figure 14-6. The Client for Microsoft Networks and File and Printer Sharing for Microsoft Networks can be disabled, but there are no configuration settings. IPv4 and IPv6 have configuration options similar to a standard network adapter.

Figure 14-6   VPN networking settings

By default, IPv4 is configured to obtain an IP address from DHCP automatically. In most cases, this is the preferred configuration. However, if you need to, you can configure a static address for the VPN connection. One setting that can be useful to change in the Advanced TCP/IP Settings is for the default gateway, as shown in the next activity.

The setting *Use default gateway on remote network* is selected by default. When this setting is enabled, all network access is done through the VPN. This is on by default to ensure that VPN clients can access resources on remote networks where the remote access server is located. However, this also means that all Internet access goes through the VPN, which might make Internet access slow. In some cases, the remote access server can be configured to provide static routes to the VPN clients for internal resources and then allow VPN clients to continue using their normal default gateway.

Activity 14-4: Disabling the VPN as Default Gateway

Time Required: 5 minutes

Objective: Disable a VPN from being used as a default gateway

Description: You want to optimize Internet connectivity for a VPN client. The VPN server provides static routes for all of the internal networks and the VPN clients use the local Internet connection as a default gateway. In this activity, you disable the use of the VPN as a default gateway.

1. If necessary, start your computer and sign in.

2. Click the **Start** button, type **Network**, and then click **Network and Sharing Center**.

3. In the Network and Sharing Center window, click **Change adapter settings**.

4. In the Network Connections window, right-click **WorkVPN** and click **Properties**.

5. In the WorkVPN Properties window, click the **Networking** tab, click **Internet Protocol Version 4 (TCP/IPv4)**, and then click **Properties**.

6. In the Internet Protocol Version 4 (TCP/IPv4) Properties window, click **Advanced**.

7. In the Advanced TCP/IP Settings window, on the IP Settings tab, clear the **Use default gateway on the remote network** check box and click **OK**.

8. In the Internet Protocol Version 4 (TCP/IPv4) Properties window, click **OK**.

9. In the WorkVPN Properties window, click **OK**.

10. Close all open windows.

Configuring DirectAccess

DirectAccess is a new technology that behaves like an always-on VPN connection. Microsoft documentation explicitly states that DirectAccess is not a VPN because it does not require you to turn on a connection. However, like a VPN, DirectAccess provides secure connectivity for clients that are outside of the organization over public networks.

Because DirectAccess is always on, it provides some benefits:

- *Easier for users*—Users do not need to do anything for DirectAccess to work. Access to all resources can be maintained with the only difference being slower access.

- *Clients are manageable*—Because DirectAccess is always on, the clients are manageable even when they are on the road. Group Policy Objects (GPOs) can still be applied and software deployment technologies still work. Generally, with a VPN, clients are not considered to be manageable.

How DirectAccess Works

With DirectAccess, users are never prompted for authentication. Instead, authentication is performed automatically in the background whenever there is connectivity between the roaming client and the DirectAccess server. The initial release of DirectAccess for Windows 7 required certificates to be issued for authentication, but Windows 10 does not require certificates. Instead, a Kerberos proxy can be used for Windows 10 if some advanced features such as high availability are not required.

As part of DirectAccess configuration, a Network Location Server is configured. The Network Location Server is a website that DirectAccess clients use to identify whether they are on the internal network or not. If clients can connect to the Network Location Server, they do

14

not use DirectAccess. If clients cannot connect to the Network Location Server, this indicates that they are roaming and the DirectAccess client is connected.

DirectAccess relies on IPv6 for connectivity. However, because most DirectAccess clients do not have IPv6 connectivity directly to the DirectAccess server, Teredo is used to tunnel IPv6 packets over the IPv4 Internet back to the DirectAccess server. If Teredo fails to make a connection, IP-HTTPS is used. IP-HTTPS tunnels IPv6 packets in HTTPS packets.

The initial release of DirectAccess in Windows Server 2008 R2 required all resources accessible through DirectAccess to use IPv6. In current configurations of DirectAccess that use Windows Server 2012 or newer as the DirectAccess server, the resources can be using IPv4.

Configuring DirectAccess

Windows 10 is configured for DirectAccess by using GPOs. The GPOs are created on the server side during the DirectAccess configuration process. So, there is no manual configuration required on the Windows 10 clients. In the vast majority of cases, once DirectAccess is properly configured on the server, there is nothing to do on the client side. However, you might still be required to do troubleshooting if there is a connectivity issue.

The GPOs for DirectAccess are applied to a specific Active Directory group that is selected during configuration. For DirectAccess GPOs to apply to computers, the computer accounts need to be added to that group.

The first DirectAccess troubleshooting tool you have is in Settings. New in Windows 10, the status of DirectAccess is displayed. In earlier Windows clients, you needed to use a tool to view connection status. To view connection status, go to Settings, Network & Internet, DirectAccess. The DirectAccess tab is visible only if DirectAccess has been configured.

You can also view connectivity information and DirectAccess configuration by using GroupPolicy. The Get-DAConnectionStatus PowerShell cmdlet shows the connection status for DirectAccess. The Get-CAClientExperienceConfiguration cmdlet shows the configuration information for DirectAccess.

The most common DirectAccess issues are network connectivity and Group Policy application. If a client has never had DirectAccess working, verify that the computer account is in the proper group for Group Policy application. You can use *gpresult.exe* to help identify why the GPO is not being applied. If DirectAccess was previously working, verify that there is Internet connectivity for the client before moving on to more advanced troubleshooting.

DirectAccess is supported only for the Enterprise and Education editions of Windows 10. Windows 10 Pro does not include DirectAccess.

Configuring Remote Desktop and Remote Assistance

In Chapter 9, Windows 10 Application Support, using Remote Desktop Services (RDS) and RemoteApp were discussed for providing applications to roaming users. To use these services, clients connect to a Remote Desktop Web Access (RD Web Access) server and select a desktop or a RemoteApp to use. The client computer downloads an .rdp file from the RD Web Access server that includes all of the necessary configuration information for connecting to the desktop or RemoteApp. The .rdp file is used by **Remote Desktop Connection**.

Administrators sometimes need to provide remote control connectivity to servers and computers that are not configured for RDS. You can enable **Remote Desktop** on any individual Windows 10 computer. When Remote Desktop is enabled, as shown in Figure 14-7, local administrators and members of the local Remote Desktop Users group have permission to connect. There are no members of the Remote Desktop Users by default. To give standard users access to connect, they must be members of this group.

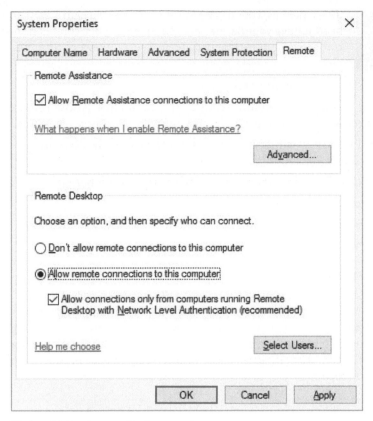

Figure 14-7   Remote Desktop settings

Remote Desktop listens on TCP port 3389. When you enable Remote Desktop, Windows Firewall is automatically configured to allow connectivity on port 3389. It is possible to change the port used by Remote Desktop by editing the registry, but this is seldom required. If you change the port for Remote Desktop, you need to manually create a firewall rule to allow it.

By default, Remote Desktop uses Network Level Authentication. When Network Level Authentication is enabled, Remote Desktop Connection obtains sign-in information from users before connecting to the remote computer. This prevents users from connecting until the connection is authenticated. If Network Level Authentication is not used, you can connect to a computer and see the sign-in screen before you authenticate. This is a security risk because that screen might display the last signed-in user.

You cannot sign in to Remote Desktop by using a Microsoft account and Network Level Authentication. You must use a local or domain account with a user name and password.

Unlike RDS, where multiple users can connect to a single server at once, Remote Desktop for Windows 10 is not multiuser. When you connect to a remote computer by using Remote Desktop, a local user cannot be signed in and using the computer at the same time.

Activity 14-5: Enabling Remote Desktop

Time Required: 5 minutes
Objective: Enable Remote Desktop for a computer

Description: You want to be able to connect to a Windows 10 computer remotely by using Remote Desktop Connection. In this activity, you enable Remote Desktop.

If time permits, consider testing Remote Desktop with a partner. You will need to give your partner the IP address of your computer. Also, both computers must be able to communicate on the network.

1. If necessary, start your computer and sign in.

2. Click the **Start** button, type **enable remote**, and then click **Allow remote access to your computer**. If necessary, in the User Account Control dialog box, click **Yes**.

3. In the System Properties window, on the Remote tab, in the Remote Desktop area, click **Allow remote connections to this computer**.

4. If necessary, click **OK** to close the warning about sleep and hibernation.

5. Click **Select Users**.

6. Read the information in the Remote Desktop Users window and click **OK**.

7. In the System Properties window, click **OK**.

Remote Desktop Connection

Remote Desktop Connection, shown in Figure 14-8, is the Remote Desktop Protocol (RDP) client that you use to connect to a remote desktop. There are many different settings that you can configure in Remote Desktop Connection and you might want these settings to be different when connecting to different computers. To simplify using different settings, you can save settings, including the remote computer name, in .rdp files. Then, you can double-click the .rdp file to initiate the connection.

Figure 14-8   Remote Desktop Connection

The Display tab in Remote Desktop Connection lets you select the screen resolution and color depth for the remote session. The larger both of the values are, the more data will be sent back and forth between the two computers. If you select *Use all my monitors for the remote session*, you can have a multimonitor connection to the remote computer.

The Local Resources tab in Remote Desktop Connection controls which resources in the local computer are available for the session. These settings provide better integration between the local and remote computers to provide a better experience. Some of the things you can configure are:

- Enable playback of sound from the remote computer on the local computer.
- Allow printers from the local computer to be used in the remote session.
- Allow copying of Clipboard data between the local and remote computers.
- Allow hard drives from the local computer to be accessed in the remote session.
- Allow smart cards on the local computer to be used in the remote session.

The Experience tab in Remote Desktop Connection allows you to enable and disable various display-related settings that can impact the amount of data sent between the local and remote computers. On slower network connections, you can disable some of these settings to reduce delays in seeing results after you click items or move them around. By default, Remote Desktop Connection detects the connection quality automatically and adjusts the features as necessary. Automatic configuration works well in most cases, but for very slow connections, you might find the experience better if you manually disable most of the features.

On the Advanced tab in Remote Desktop Connection, you can configure server authentication settings and Remote Desktop Gateway (RD Gateway) settings. The server authentication settings control how Remote Desktop Connection behaves when the certificate used by the server does not match the name you use when connecting. By default, a warning is displayed. To increase security, you can prevent mismatched names from being allowed, but this means that you will not be able to connect directly by IP address.

An RD Gateway server is used to secure access to Remote Desktop from public networks, such as the Internet. When Remote Desktop Connection is configured to use an RD Gateway, RDP traffic is tunneled in HTTPS packets to the RD Gateway server. The RD Gateway server sends the RDP packets on to the internal network. Effectively, this is like an SSL VPN that is specifically designed for Remote Desktop and RDS. Figure 14-9 shows the settings for RD Gateway in Remote Desktop Connection.

Figure 14-9 RD Gateway settings

Most of the time, you will start Remote Desktop Connection from the Start button. However, you can start Remote Desktop Connection from a command prompt by running *mstsc.exe*. You can view all of the options available by running *mstsc.exe /?*. Table 14-2 lists some configuration options that are available at the command prompt but not in the graphical interface.

Table 14-2   Mstsc.exe options

Option	Description
/admin	Connects to the console of a remote computer rather than an RDP session. This can be useful in some cases when you are troubleshooting and a typical RDP is not working properly.
/public	Prevents Remote Desktop Connection from saving information to the local computer. For example, credentials and the name of the remote computer are not cached for later use.
/restrictedAdmin	Prevents the remote computer from accessing your credentials. The session uses the local computer account for permissions instead, which might not allow you to access network resources. This is useful when a remote system may have been compromised.
/remoteGuard	Prevents the remote computer from accessing your credentials similarly to /restrictedAdmin. However, this mode allows connectivity to network resources by routing requests back through Remote Desktop Connection.
/shadow	Allows you to connect to an existing session and view what another user is doing.
/control	Allows someone else to control your session if that person is viewing it with you.
/noConsentPrompt	Allows someone to shadow your session without prompting you for consent.

For more information about Restricted Admin mode, see *https://blogs. technet.microsoft.com/kfalde/2013/08/14/restricted-admin-mode-for- rdp-in-windows-8-1-2012-r2/*.

Activity 14-6: Customizing Settings for Remote Desktop Connection

Time Required: 10 minutes
Objective: Customize settings for Remote Desktop Connection

Description: You want to create a set of customized settings for connecting to a specific remote desktop. In this activity, you configure settings in Remote Desktop Connection and save them as an .rdp file for later use.

1. If necessary, start your computer and sign in.
2. Click the **Start** button, type **mstsc**, and then click **Remote Desktop Connection**.
3. In Remote Desktop Connection, in the Computer box, type **w10-45.giganticlife.com** and click **Show Options**.
4. Click the **Display** tab and in the Display configuration area, select **1024 by 768 pixels**.
5. Click the **Local Resources** tab and clear the **Printers** check box.
6. Click the **Experience** tab and in the Choose your connection speed to optimize performance box, select **Low-speed broadband (256 kbps – 2 Mbps)**.
7. Click the **Advanced** tab and in the Connect from anywhere area, click **Settings**.
8. In the RD Gateway Server Settings window, click **Use these RD Gateway server settings**.
9. In the Server name box, type **RD-Gateway.giganticlife.com** and click **OK**.
10. In Remote Desktop Connection, click the **General** tab and click **Save As**.
11. In the Save As window, in the File name box, type **w10-45** and click **Save**.
12. Close Remote Desktop Connection.

Remote Assistance

Remote Desktop allows you to connect to a remote computer for troubleshooting. However, for the best results when troubleshooting, it is often useful to have users show you the problem they are experiencing, which is not possible with Remote Desktop. You can use **Remote Assistance**, shown in Figure 14-10, to view what a user is doing and even take control to resolve the issue.

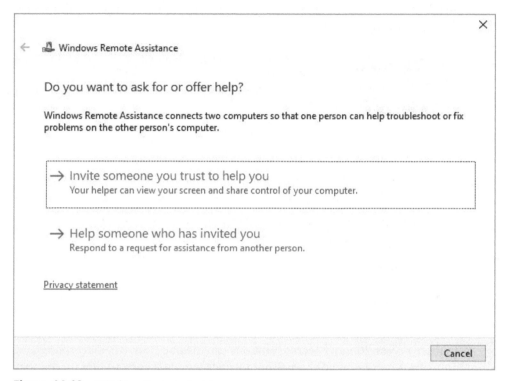

Figure 14-10   Windows Remote Assistance

Remote Assistance can be initiated in the following ways:

- *Invitation file*—Users can create an invitation file that they send to a helper. When the helper opens the file, remote assistance starts. This method does not work over routers that perform Network Address Translation (NAT) because the IP address information in the invitation file is the internal IP address of the computer that is not accessible over the Internet.

- *Easy Connect*—When users select Easy Connect instead of an invitation, the user is provided with a password that needs to be sent to the helper. The helper enters that password to be connected. This type of connection works over the Internet and through NAT. Easy Connect tunnels IPv6 packets over IPv4 networks.

- *Administrator initiated*—As a helper, you can offer remote assistance to users if you know the IP address or computer name. After the connection to the computer is established, the user is prompted to allow the connection.

   You can start Windows Remote Assistance by running *msra.exe*.

After an invitation has been created or Easy Connect has been initiated, the user needs to leave Windows Remote Assistance open. If the Windows Remote Assistance window is closed, the helper cannot connect.

Activity 14-7: Creating a Remote Assistance Request

Time Required: 5 minutes
Objective: Create a Remote Assistance request

Description: You want to create a Remote Assistance request so that you can send it to a colleague to work through a problem together on your computer. In this activity, you create a Remote Assistance request.

 If there is time, consider working with a partner to test Remote Assistance. You will need to give your partner the invitation file created in the lab. Also, both computers must be able to communicate with each other on the network.

1. If necessary, start your computer and sign in.
2. Click the **Start** button, type **msra**, and then click **msra**.
3. In the Windows Remote Assistance window, click **Invite someone you trust to help you**.
4. On the How do you want to invite your trusted helper screen, click **Save this invitation as a file**.
5. In the Save As dialog box, note the location and file name and click **Save**.
6. Note the password that is displayed that must also be given to your helper.
7. Close Windows Remote Assistance.

Synchronizing Data

When you are in a location without network connectivity, you cannot use a VPN or other forms of remote access. Remote access solutions can also be slow when accessing and saving files. Synchronizing data can avoid these issues by maintaining a copy of files on the roaming computer in addition to the initial source location.

OneDrive

OneDrive is an example of how file synchronization can be used. Multiple computers can access the same OneDrive account and all of the computers can synchronize the files locally. When you edit files, it is from a local copy, which is faster than accessing the file remotely. When you modify a file, the changes are synchronized back up to OneDrive. If you are offline when you modify a file, the changes are synchronized the next time you have an Internet connection.

In addition to the consumer version of OneDrive that was covered in Chapter 8, User Productivity Tools, there is also a version that is included as part of Office 365. The version of OneDrive in Office 365 has approximately the same functionality as the consumer version, but is part of SharePoint Online in Office 365. In Office 365, you can also synchronize files from libraries in SharePoint Online.

Offline Files

Offline files is a Windows 10 feature that synchronizes files from a shared folder to a Windows 10 computer. Synchronization happens when the computer has connectivity to the server sharing the files. So, files are typically synchronized while in the office, used and modified offline while on the road, and then synchronized again when the computer is back in the office.

Offline files need to be enabled on both the Windows 10 computer and on the file share. If offline files are enabled in both locations, the default behavior is for the user to manually select any files or folders that will be cached (available offline). It is possible to configure a share to automatically make files available offline, but that is not recommended.

After files have been cached, they are available even when not connected to a network. Users access offline files using the exact same path as was used when the files were cached. If a user enables a folder on a mapped drive letter, such as H:\Important, to be offline, the files are accessible through H:\Important when disconnected from the network.

Typically, the offline files feature is not used for shared data, only personal data such as a home folder. This minimizes the risk of conflicts where a cached copy of the file has been modified and the original source also has been modified. There is no automated mechanism to resolve such conflicts; the user needs to look at both files and merge the changes together if necessary. Some apps provide functionality to merge changes between two files, but sometimes it must be done manually.

To review any synchronization errors, you can use Sync Center, as shown in Figure 14-11. Sync Center shows any replication conflicts. Sync Center lists the locations being synchronized.

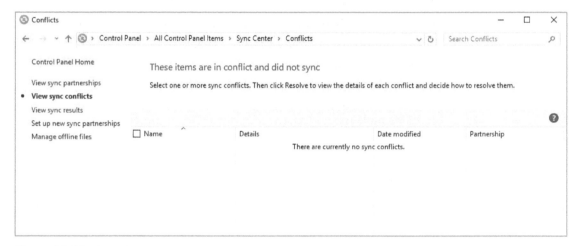

Figure 14-11   Sync Center

Activity 14-8: Enabling Offline Files

Time Required: 5 minutes
Objective: Enable offline files

Description: You want to use offline files to store the contents of your home folder on your laptop. In this activity, you enable offline files on your computer.

1. If necessary, start your computer and sign in.
2. Click the **Start** button, type **Control,** and then click **Control Panel.**
3. In the Control Panel window, in the **Search Control Panel** box, type **sync** and click **Sync Center.**
4. In Sync Center, click **Manage offline files.**
5. In the Offline Files window, click **Enable offline files** and click **OK.**
6. Close all open windows.

Work Folders

When you implement **Work Folders,** each user is given a unique folder for file storage that can be synchronized across multiple devices. The folder for each user is stored on a file server. So, it is possible to access the folder through a file share and also to synchronize the

14

folder contents by using the Work Folders client. The Work Folders client is available for Windows 7 and newer client operating systems. You can also obtain a Work Folders client for iOS and Android devices.

 Work Folders is similar to running a private version of OneDrive.

When Work Folders is configured on the server(s), a URL is identified for accessing Work Folders. Clients need to be configured to use that URL. There are several methods that can be used to configure the clients, but automatic discovery is preferred because it supports devices that are not domain joined.

Automatic discovery of the Work Folders URL is based on the email address of the user. If the user's email address is *susan@giganticlife.com*, the Work Folders client attempts to connect to *https://workfolders.giganticlife.com*. In a single-server deployment of Work Folders, this directs all users directly to the server hosting their Work Folder.

If there are multiple Work Folder servers, you can still use automatic discovery, but you also need to configure each user object in Active Directory with the appropriate Work Folders URL. When *susan@giganticlife.com* contacts *https://workfolders.giganticlife.com*, she is redirected to the Work Folders URL configured in her user object. The URL is stored in the *msDS-SyncServer-Url* attribute of the user object.

Another simple method that works when devices are not domain joined is manually entering the Work Folders URL. This is provided as an option in the Work Folders configuration screen, as shown in Figure 14-12. When allowing users to enter the URL, there is always a risk of the URL being incorrectly entered.

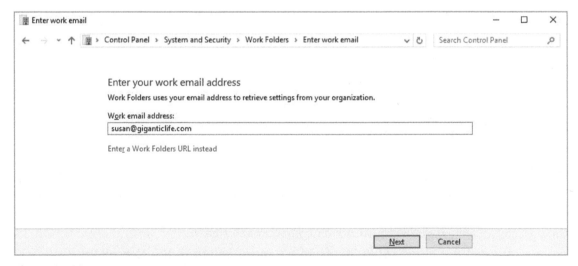

Figure 14-12   Work Folders configuration

For domain-joined computers, you can use Group Policy to configure the Work Folders URL. You can also use Group Policy to force the Work Folders client to be enabled instead of waiting for the user to start configuration.

Chapter Summary

- Remote data access can be performed by using remote access, remote control, or data synchronization. Remote access can be performed by dial-up or VPN. Remote control is used for Remote Desktop Services (RDS), Remote Desktop, and Remote

Assistance. Data synchronization can be provided by OneDrive, offline files, or Work Folders.

- VPNs can use various protocols such as PPTP, L2TP, SSTP, or IKEv2. PPTP is an older protocol that is considered insecure. L2TP is more secure but also more difficult to configure. SSTP is an SSL VPN. IKEv2 allows you to enable VPN Reconnect for a better user experience on poor-quality networks.

- DirectAccess provides remote access to data similar to a VPN, but it is always on, which increases opportunities for remote management of mobile users. All configuration is done on the server side, but you can perform some troubleshooting tasks on the client.

- Remote Desktop uses the RDP protocol when using Remote Desktop Connection to remote control a Windows 10 computer. Remote Desktop is disabled by default and must be enabled.

- Remote Assistance is used to shadow what users are doing on their computers. You can also request control and resolve issues for users.

- OneDrive synchronizes files with a cloud-based service as long as there is an Internet connection. The offline files feature synchronizes files from a file share when the computer is connected to the file server. Work Folders synchronizes a user-specific folder across devices from a file server as long as there is an Internet connection.

Key Terms

Connection Manager Administration Kit (CMAK)   A feature that can be installed on Windows clients or servers to create VPN deployment packages.

data synchronization   A system that synchronizes files between multiple devices. This allows data to be accessed when offline.

DirectAccess   An always-on replacement for on-demand VPN connections. All configuration is done on the server side to allow domain-joined clients to connect. Always-on connectivity allows for additional management options.

Extensible Authentication Protocol (EAP)   A framework that allows multiple authentication protocols to be integrated with the VPN sign-in process.

Internet Key Exchange v2 Tunneling Protocol (IKEv2)   A newer VPN protocol that uses IPsec to secure data, but can authenticate by using a user name and password. This protocol supports VPN Reconnect.

Layer 2 Tunneling Protocol (L2TP)   An authentication-only VPN protocol that is combined with IPsec to provide data encryption. It is seldom used because it is difficult to configure.

Microsoft CHAP v2 (MS-CHAP v2)   An older authentication protocol commonly used with PPTP VPNs that is now considered insecure.

offline files   A feature that Windows 10 clients can use to synchronize files from a file share to the local computer for offline use.

Point-to-Point Tunneling Protocol (PPTP)   An older VPN protocol that authenticates based on user name and password. It is generally considered insecure, but is easy to configure.

Protected EAP   An enhanced variation of EAP that secures authentication by using SSL. For PPTP VPN connections, it can secure MS-CHAP v2 authentication.

remote access   A system that allows dial-up or VPN clients to remotely retrieve and save data as though they are on the local network, but with much slower performance.

Remote Assistance   A feature in Windows 10 that allows a helper to connect to a Windows 10 computer and view the screen or remotely control the computer.

remote control   A system for remote data or application access where only screen draw commands and keystrokes are sent between the client and computer being remote controlled. Typically, remote control provides better performance than remote access.

14

Remote Desktop   The feature in Windows 10 that you can enable to allow remote control of the computer by using RDP on port 3389.

Remote Desktop Connection   The client software included in Windows 10 that uses RDP to connect to Remote Desktop and RDS. It can be started at a command line with additional options by running *mstsc.exe*.

Secure Socket Tunneling Protocol (SSTP)   A VPN protocol that uses SSL to secure authentication credentials and data.

virtual private network (VPN)   An encrypted connection from a client to a remote access server over a public network.

VPN Reconnect   A feature of IKEv2 VPN connections that automatically reconnects after a network interruption.

Work Folders   A system that allows users to synchronize a single folder on a file server between multiple devices. The Work Folders client is included in Windows 10.

Review Questions

1. Which type of remote data access provides the best performance for applications accessing databases?
   a. dial-up
   b. VPN
   c. RDS
   d. Remote Assistance
   e. Work Folders

2. Which type of remote data access is best suited to watching users remotely while they demonstrate a process that is causing an issue?
   a. dial-up
   b. VPN
   c. Remote Desktop
   d. Remote Assistance
   e. Work Folders

3. You want to connect to a user desktop to review Windows 10 configuration settings when the user is not present. Which technology should you use?
   a. VPN
   b. Remote Desktop
   c. RDS
   d. Remote Assistance
   e. offline files

4. Which of the following technologies allows you to access files from a Windows 10 computer that is not currently connected to a network (wired or wireless)? (Choose all that apply.)
   a. VPN
   b. Work Folders
   c. OneDrive
   d. Remote Desktop
   e. offline files

5. PPTP is the preferred VPN protocol. True or False?

6. Which of the following are authentication methods that can be used by IPsec? (Choose all that apply.)

   a. pre-shared key

   b. hash value

   c. certificates

   d. Kerberos

   e. NTLM

7. Which port numbers and packet types are relevant for allowing L2TP/IPsec through a firewall? (Choose all that apply.)

   a. TCP port 1723

   b. UDP port 4500

   c. TCP port 443

   d. IP protocol type 47 (GRE)

   e. IP protocol type 50 (ESP)

8. Which port numbers and packet types are relevant for allowing SSTP through a firewall?

   a. TCP port 1723

   b. UDP port 4500

   c. TCP port 443

   d. IP protocol type 47 (GRE)

   e. IP protocol type 50 (ESP)

9. Which VPN protocol supports the VPN Reconnect feature?

   a. PPTP

   b. L2TP/IPsec

   c. SSTP

   d. IKEv2

   e. DirectAccess

10. Which remote connectivity type automatically connects clients to the main office when they are roaming?

    a. PPTP

    b. L2TP/IPsec

    c. SSTP

    d. IKEv2

    e. DirectAccess

11. Selecting a VPN type of Automatic is suitable for most VPN deployments. True or False?

12. Which automated method for VPN connection deployment would work best for users who are not domain joined?

    a. CMAK

    b. Group Policy Preferences

    c. VBScript

    d. Windows PowerShell

13. EAP is a framework for implementing authentication protocols rather than an authentication protocol. True or False?

14. Which VPN authentication protocol uses SSL?

    a. PAP

    b. CHAP

    c. MS-CHAP v2

    d. EAP

    e. Protected EAP

15. When you configure a VPN connection, the VPN must be used as the default gateway. True or False?

16. How does a DirectAccess client determine whether it is on the internal network or external network?

    a. If the client can resolve *enterpriseregistration.domain.com*, it is internal.

    b. If the client can resolve *enterpriseregistration.domain.com*, it is external.

    c. If the client can connect to the Network Location Server, it is internal.

    d. If the client can connect to the Network Location Server, it is external.

    e. If latency to the Network Location Server is above 40 milliseconds, it is external.

17. Which option for *mtsc.exe* prevents connection information from being cached on the local computer?

    a. /admin

    b. /shadow

    c. /restrictedAdmin

    d. /remoteGuard

    e. /public

18. Remote Desktop in Windows 10 allows multiple users to connect to one computer at the same time. True or False?

19. Which of the following operating systems can use Work Folders? (Choose all that apply.)

    a. Windows 10

    b. iOS

    c. Android

    d. Windows 8

    e. Windows 7

20. Automatic configuration for Work Folders is based on the email address of the user. True or False?

Case Projects

Case Project 14-1: Data for Traveling Users

Hyperactive Media Sales needs to provide a remote access solution for its traveling salespeople. They have a server running Windows Server 2012 R2 that can be configured as a remote access server for VPN connectivity. You have been reviewing the VPN protocols that are available and need to decide on the best protocol. The traveling salespeople often stay in hotels, so firewall compatibility is a serious concern. Which VPN protocol has the best compatibility with firewalls?

Case Project 14-2: Managing Mobile Computers

Big Bob's Construction has many construction sites where computers are located. At the remote sites, Internet connectivity can be of poor quality and intermittent. Because the computers are onsite and have poor connectivity to the main office, they are not currently domain joined. However, they could be domain joined if required.

You want to be able to manage the computers at the construction sites. Which technology can allow you to do this and not force users to reconnect constantly?

14

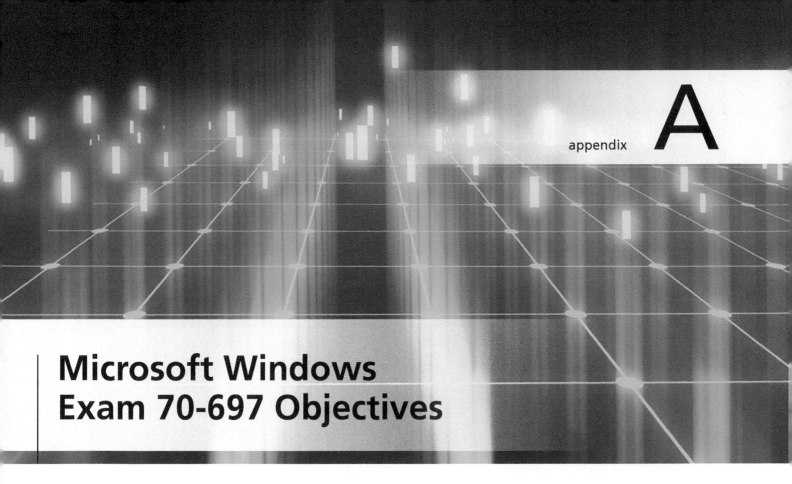

Microsoft Windows
Exam 70-697 Objectives

This appendix correlates the objectives for Microsoft Windows Exam 70-697 (Configuring Windows Devices) to the chapters and sections where they are covered in this book. For the most current version of these objectives, check *https://www.microsoft.com/en-us/learning/exam-70-697.aspx*.

1: Manage identity (10–15%)

Objective 1.1   Support Windows Store and cloud apps

Objective	Chapter & Section
Install and manage software by using Office 365 and Windows Store apps	Chapter 9, Installing Apps
Sideload apps by using Microsoft Intune	Chapter 11, Managing Apps Using Microsoft Intune
Sideload apps into online and offline images	Chapter 9, Installing Apps
Deep link apps by using Microsoft Intune	Chapter 11, App Management
Integrate Microsoft account and personalization settings	Chapter 5, User Accounts

Objective 1.2   Support authentication and authorization

Objective	Chapter & Section
Support user authentication, including multi-factor authentication, certificates, Microsoft Passport, virtual smart cards, picture passwords, and biometrics	Chapter 5, Advanced Authentication Methods
Support workgroup, homegroup, and domain membership, including Secure Channel, account policies, credential caching, and Credential Manager	Chapter 1, HomeGroups Chapter 1, Networking Models Chapter 5, Network Integration Chapter 6, Windows 10 Security Policies Chapter 13, Active Directory
Know when to use a local account versus a Microsoft account	Chapter 5, User Accounts
Configure Windows Hello	Chapter 5, Advanced Authentication Methods

2: Plan desktop and device deployment (10–15%)

Objective 2.1 Migrate and configure user data

Objective	Chapter & Section
Configure user profiles including profile version, local, roaming, and mandatory	Chapter 5, Managing User Profiles
Configure folder location	Chapter 5, Managing User Profiles
Migrate user profiles	Chapter 2, Migrating User Settings and Files Chapter 13, Enterprise Deployment Tools

Objective 2.2 Configure Hyper-V

Objective	Chapter & Section
Create and configure virtual machines including integration services	Chapter 12, Creating Virtual Machines Chapter 12, Virtual Memory Chapter 12, Virtual Processors Chapter 12, Virtual Networking
Create and manage checkpoints	Chapter 12, Managing Virtual Machines
Create and configure virtual switches	Chapter 12, Creating Virtual Machines
Create and configure virtual disks	Chapter 12, Virtual Hard Disks
Move virtual machine storage	Chapter 12, Managing Virtual Machines

Objective 2.3 Configure mobility options

Objective	Chapter & Section
Configure offline file policies	Chapter 14, Synchronizing Data
Configure power policies	Chapter 3, Power Management
Configure Windows To Go	Chapter 2, Windows To Go
Configure sync options including Sync Center	Chapter 14, Synchronizing Data
Configure Wi-Fi direct	Chapter 7, Wireless Networking
Configure powercfg	Chapter 3, Power Management

Objective 2.4 Configure security for mobile devices

Objective	Chapter & Section
Configure BitLocker	Chapter 6, Data Security
Configure startup key storage	Chapter 6, Data Security

3: Plan and implement a Microsoft Intune device management solution (10–15%)

Objective 3.1 Support mobile devices

Objective	Chapter & Section
Support mobile access and data synchronization, including Work Folders and Sync Center	Chapter 14, Synchronizing Data
Support broadband connectivity including broadband tethering and metered networks	Chapter 7, Internet Connectivity
Support Mobile Device Management by using Microsoft Intune, including Windows Phone, iOS, and Android	Chapter 11, Supporting Mobile Devices
Support mobile device policies including security policies, remote access, and remote wipe	Chapter 11, Managing Devices with Microsoft Intune

Objective 3.2   Deploy software updates by using Microsoft Intune

Objective	Chapter & Section
Use reports and In-Console Monitoring to identify required updates	Chapter 11, Deploying Software Updates Using Microsoft Intune
Approve or decline updates	Chapter 11, Deploying Software Updates Using Microsoft Intune
Configure automatic approval settings	Chapter 11, Deploying Software Updates Using Microsoft Intune
Configure deadlines for update installations	Chapter 11, Deploying Software Updates Using Microsoft Intune
Deploy third-party updates	Chapter 11, Deploying Software Updates Using Microsoft Intune

Objective 3.3   Manage devices with Microsoft Intune

Objective	Chapter & Section
Provision user accounts	Chapter 11, Microsoft Intune Overview
Enroll devices	Chapter 11, Supporting Mobile Devices
View and manage all managed devices	Chapter 11, Managing Devices with Microsoft Intune
Configure Microsoft Intune subscriptions	Chapter 11, Microsoft Intune Overview
Configure the Microsoft Intune connector site system role	Chapter 11, Microsoft Intune Overview
Manage user and computer groups	Chapter 11, Managing Devices with Microsoft Intune
Configure monitoring and alerts	Chapter 11, Managing Devices with Microsoft Intune
Manage policies	Chapter 11, Managing Devices with Microsoft Intune
Manage remote computers	Chapter 11, Managing Devices with Microsoft Intune

4: Configure networking (10–15%)

Objective 4.1   Configure IP settings

Objective	Chapter & Section
Connect to a network	Chapter 7, Networking Overview
Configure name resolution	Chapter 7, IP Version 4
Configure network locations	Chapter 7, Networking Overview

Objective 4.2   Configure networking settings

Objective	Chapter & Section
Connect to a wireless network	Chapter 7, Wireless Networking
Manage preferred wireless networks	Chapter 7, Wireless Networking
Configure network adapters	Chapter 7, Networking Overview

Objective 4.3   Configure and maintain network security

Objective	Chapter & Section
Configure Windows Firewall	Chapter 7, Windows Firewall
Configure Windows Firewall with Advanced Security	Chapter 7, Windows Firewall
Configure connection security rules (IPsec)	Chapter 7, Windows Firewall
Configure authentication exceptions	Chapter 7, Windows Firewall
Configure network discovery	Chapter 7, Windows Firewall

5: Configure storage (10–15%)

Objective 5.1   Support data storage

Objective	Chapter & Section
Support the DFS client including caching settings	Chapter 13, Enterprise File Services
Support Storage Spaces including capacity and fault tolerance	Chapter 4, Types of Disks Chapter 4, Managing Physical Disks Chapter 4, Managing Storage Spaces
Support OneDrive	Chapter 14, Synchronizing Data

Objective 5.2   Support data security

Objective	Chapter & Section
Manage permissions including share, NTFS, and Dynamic Access Control (DAC)	Chapter 4, File and Folder Permissions
Support Encrypting File System (EFS) including Data Recovery Agent	Chapter 6, Data Security
Control access to removable media	Chapter 13, Group Policy
Support BitLocker and BitLocker To Go including Data Recovery Agent, and Microsoft BitLocker Administration and Monitoring (MBAM)	Chapter 6, Data Security Chapter 13, Enterprise Management Tools

6: Manage data access and protection (10–15%)

Objective 6.1   Configure shared resources

Objective	Chapter & Section
Configure HomeGroup settings	Chapter 7, HomeGroup Networks
Configure libraries	Chapter 8, File Explorer
Configure shared folder permissions	Chapter 7, File Sharing
Configure shared printers	Chapter 8, Printing
Configure OneDrive	Chapter 8, OneDrive

Objective 6.2   Configure file and folder access

Objective	Chapter & Section
Encrypt files and folders by using EFS	Chapter 6, Data Security
Configure NTFS permissions	Chapter 4, File Systems Chapter 4, File and Folder Permissions
Configure disk quotas	Chapter 4, File Systems
Configure file access auditing	Chapter 6, Auditing
Configure authentication and authorization	Chapter 5, User Accounts Chapter 5, Advanced Authentication Methods

7: Manage remote access (10–15%)

Objective 7.1   Configure remote connections

Objective	Chapter & Section
Configure remote authentication	Chapter 14, Configuring VPN Clients
Configure VPN connections and authentication	Chapter 14, Configuring VPN Clients
Configure Remote Desktop settings	Chapter 14, Configuring Remote Desktop and Remote Assistance
Enable VPN reconnect	Chapter 14, Configuring VPN Clients
Configure broadband tethering	Chapter 7, Internet Connectivity

Objective 7.2   Configure mobility options

Objective	Chapter & Section
Configure offline file policies	Chapter 14, Synchronizing Data
Configure power policies	Chapter 3, Power Management
Configure Windows To Go	Chapter 2, Windows To Go
Configure sync options	Chapter 14, Synchronizing Data
Configure Wi-Fi direct	Chapter 7, Wireless Networking

8: Manage apps (10–15%)

Objective 8.1   Deploy and manage Azure RemoteApp

Objective	Chapter & Section
Configure RemoteApp and Desktop Connections settings	Chapter 9, Remote Desktop Services
Configure Group Policy Objects (GPOs) for signed packages	Chapter 9, Remote Desktop Services
Subscribe to the Azure RemoteApp and Desktop Connections feeds	Chapter 9, Remote Desktop Services
Export and import Azure RemoteApp configurations	Chapter 9, Remote Desktop Services
Support iOS and Android	Chapter 9, Remote Desktop Services
Configure remote desktop web access for Azure RemoteApp distribution	Chapter 9, Remote Desktop Services

Objective 8.2   Support desktop apps

Objective	Chapter & Section
Support desktop app compatibility by using Application Compatibility Toolkit (ACT) including shims and compatibility database	Chapter 9, App Compatibility
Support desktop application co-existence using Hyper-V, Azure RemoteApp, and App-V	Chapter 9, App Compatibility
Install and configure User Experience Virtualization (UE-V)	Chapter 13, Enterprise Management Tools
Deploy desktop apps by using Microsoft Intune	Chapter 11, Managing Apps Using Microsoft Intune

9: Manage updates and recovery (10–15%)

Objective 9.1 Configure system recovery

Objective	Chapter & Section
Configure a recovery drive	Chapter 10, System Recovery
Configure system restore	Chapter 10, System Recovery
Perform a refresh or recycle	Chapter 10, System Recovery
Perform a driver rollback	Chapter 10, System Recovery
Configure restore points	Chapter 10, System Recovery

Objective 9.2 Configure file recovery

Objective	Chapter & Section
Configure File History	Chapter 10, File Recovery and Backup
Restore previous versions of files and folders	Chapter 10, File Recovery and Backup
Recover files from OneDrive	Chapter 8, OneDrive

Objective 9.3 Configure and manage updates

Objective	Chapter & Section
Configure update settings	Chapter 6, Windows Update
Configure Windows Update policies	Chapter 6, Windows Update
Manage update history	Chapter 6, Windows Update
Roll back updates	Chapter 6, Windows Update
Update Windows Store apps	Chapter 6, Windows Update

Preparing for Certification Exams

This book and the course provided by your instructor are excellent resources to begin preparing for the 70-697: Configuring Windows Devices certification exam for Microsoft Specialist in Windows 10. However, most students (the authors of this book included) need to go beyond any one book or course to be successful in passing certification exams.

Studying for the Exam

The questions for Microsoft certification exams are generated by a team of subject matter experts using the same exam objectives listed in this book. Review the exam objectives (listed in Appendix A) and make sure that you understand each one. If you are not sure you understand an objective, put a little more time into studying that area.

The activities in this book are a good start for learning to use Windows 10 and becoming comfortable with its features, but you should do more. Create some activities of your own to try out different features. The process of creating the activities helps you understand how they could be used.

Use additional resources for learning. Microsoft provides extensive documentation for its products. If you want to learn more about how BranchCache works, go read about it. Even though the 70-697 exam is testing on Windows 10, sometimes understanding the server part of the configuration helps you to understand the entire process better.

Another great resource for understanding newer features in Windows 10 is Microsoft's Channel 9, where you can find thousands of videos from conferences that are available for free. You can use them to get an overview of some features and more in-depth information about others. Channel 9 is found at *https://channel9.msdn.com/*. Even though it is found on MSDN, it is not just for developers.

Taking the Exam

The questions on certification exams are not designed to be tricky. The developers of the exam questions put a lot of time into trying to create questions that have only a single correct answer. If you think that you have found a tricky question, take another look; you might be overthinking it.

For some questions, being able to identify incorrect options is as important as identifying the correct options. When you can identify incorrect options quickly, it reduces the amount of information you need to consider to find the correct answer.

There will be some questions that you do not know the answer to. It's important that you do not dwell for an extended period of time on a single question. Answer the questions you know and mark some for later review if you would like to spend more time on them. And if you truly do not know the answer to a question, eliminate the obviously incorrect options and make a guess. You might get lucky!

Glossary

.appx file A file for installing a Windows Store app.

.msi file An app packaged for installation by the Windows Installer service.

.NET Framework A commonly required application environment for Windows apps. It is available in multiple versions.

802.11 A group of IEEE standards that define how to transfer data over wireless networks.

802.1x An IEEE standard designed to enhance security of wireless networks by authenticating a user to a central authority.

access control entry (ACE) A specific entry in a file or folder's ACL that uniquely identifies a user or group by its security identifier and the action it is allowed or denied to take on that file or folder.

access control list (ACL) For those file systems that support ACLs for files and folders, such as NTFS, the ACL is a property of every file and folder in that file system. It holds a collection (that is, list) of ACE items that explicitly defines what actions are allowed to be taken on the file or folder to which it is attached.

account lockout policy A collection of settings, such as lockout duration, that control account lockouts.

Action Center A place where you can review and resolve system messages.

Active Directory (AD) A domain security database of user and computer information that is stored on domain controllers and referenced by domain member computers. This database is stored on multimaster replicating domain controllers running Windows Server 2000 or newer..

Active Directory site A set of IP subnets representing a physical location that is used by Active Directory to control replication.

address prefix The network portion of an IPv6 address.

Administrative Tools A group of MMC consoles that are used to manage Windows 10. Computer Management, Event Viewer, and Services are the most commonly used.

Administrator account The built-in Windows 10 account that is created during installation and has full rights to the system. This account cannot be deleted or locked out.

Advanced Configuration and Power Interface (ACPI) The current standard for power management that is implemented in Windows 10 and by computer manufacturers.

alert An event that is triggered when a count value is above or below the specified threshold value.

alternate IP configuration A set of static IP configuration information that is used instead of APIPA when a computer is unable to contact a DHCP server.

Android An open source operating system currently developed by Google used for smartphones and tablet computers.

answer file An XML file used during an unattended setup to provide configuration to Setup.exe. Windows 10 answer files are created by using Windows (SIM).

anycast An IPv6 unicast address that has been assigned to multiple devices. Only one closest device responds to requests on this address.

Apple Push Notification service (APNs) A service created by Apple that allows external apps to send notification data to apps installed on Apple devices.

Application Compatibility Toolkit (ACT) A collection of tools to identify and resolve app compatibility issues and help organizations run legacy software. It is included in the Windows 10 ADK.

application environment subsystem A software layer that exists between apps and the operating system to simplify app development.

application manifest An XML file that describes the structure of an application, including required DLL files and privilege requirements.

application programming interface (API) An interface used by a program to request services from the application environment, which in turn interfaces with the operating system to provide those services.

Application Virtualization (App-V) A technology that deploys applications by streaming and isolates them in a virtual environment.

AppLocker A feature in Windows 10 that is used to define which programs are allowed to run. This is a replacement for the software restriction policies found in Windows XP and Windows Vista, but it is not available in Windows 10 Pro.

arp A command-line utility that can be used to display and manage the ARP table.

assigned access A sign-in option that you can configure for a single local user account that restricts the user to using only an assigned Windows Store app; often used to configure Windows 10 as a kiosk.

asymmetric encryption algorithm An encryption algorithm that uses two keys to encrypt and decrypt data. Data encrypted with one key is decrypted by the other key.

attended installation An installation when a network administrator must be present to answer configuration questions presented during Windows 10 installation.

audit policy The settings that define which operating system events are audited.

auditing The security process that records the occurrence of specific operating system events in the Security log.

auditSystem configuration pass This configuration pass is performed *before* user sign-in when Sysprep triggers Windows 10 into audit mode.

auditUser configuration pass This configuration pass is performed *after* user sign-in when Sysprep triggers Windows 10 into audit mode.

Automatic Private IP Addressing (APIPA) A system used to automatically assign an IP address on the 169.254.x.x network to a computer that is unable to communicate with a DHCP server.

autounattend.xml An answer file that is automatically searched for during the windowsPE, offlineServicing, and specialize configuration passes.

Away Mode An instant-on, power-saving mode that keeps the system in the S0 state.

Azure AD Otherwise known as Azure Active Directory; an identity and access management cloud solution that provides the ability to manage users and groups. It provides identity information for secure access to on-premises and cloud apps, including Office 365, Azure, and Intune.

Azure AD join Connects Windows 10 computers with a domain hosted in Windows Azure AD instead of an on-premises domain.

Azure AD Premium A paid-for and enhanced version of Azure AD that includes enterprise features, such as self-service identity and access management and self-service password reset for on-premises users.

Backup and Restore (Windows 7) The legacy backup utility that is included to provide access to backups from Windows 7.

baseline A set of performance indicators gathered when system performance is acceptable.

basic disk An older, IBM-originated method used to organize disk space for x86 computers into primary, extended, and logical partitions. Basic disk technology is supported by many legacy operating systems and may be required in certain multiboot configurations.

biometric authentication Authentication that is based on physical characteristics of the user, such as a fingerprint or facial recognition.

BitLocker Drive Encryption A feature in Windows 10 that can encrypt the operating system partition of a hard drive and protect system files from modification. Other partitions can also be encrypted.

BitLocker To Go A new feature in Windows 10 that allows you to encrypt removable storage.

bottleneck The component in a process that prevents the overall process from completing faster.

Branch Office Direct Printing A feature that allows Windows 10 computers to print directly to a printer shared from a printer server rather than sending the print job through the print server.

BranchCache A feature in Windows 10 that speeds up access to files over slow connections by caching files. It operates in distributed cache mode or hosted cache mode.

Bring Your Own Device (BYOD) Allowing employees to bring their own computers, smartphones, and tablets to work and use them to access corporate resources.

broadcast address An address that indicates the destination for that packet is all available computers.

built-in local groups Groups that are automatically created for each Windows 10 computer and stored in the SAM database.

cached credentials Credentials that are stored in Windows 10 after a user has signed in to a domain or Microsoft account. Cached credentials can be used to sign in when a domain controller cannot be contacted or when there is no network connectivity.

catalog file A file used by Windows SIM to read the configurable settings and their current status for a WIM image.

central processing unit (CPU) A device responsible for the actual execution of instructions stored in applications and operating system code. Windows 10 supports 32- and 64-bit CPUs.

checkpoint A saved state of a virtual machine that you can revert to.

Choose Your Own Device (CYOD) Allowing employees to choose a computer, smartphone, or tablet from a corporate-owned pool of devices and use them to access corporate resources.

classless interdomain routing (CIDR) A notation technique that summarizes the number of binary bits in an IP address that identify the network an IP address belongs to, counted starting from the left-hand side of the IP address as written in binary form. The number of bits is written at the end of the IP address with a slash "/" symbol separating the two values (e.g., 192.168.1.0/24 or FE80::/64).

clean installation An installation that is performed on a new computer, or does not retain the user settings or applications of an existing computer.

Click-to-Run A new streaming installation technology that is used to deploy Office 365 ProPlus.

client A client allows you to communicate with a particular service running on a remote computer.

Client for Microsoft Networks The client that allows Windows 10 to access files and printers shared on other Windows computers by using the SMB protocol.

Client Hyper-V A feature in Windows 10 that allows you to run virtual machines.

cmdlet A Windows PowerShell command in verb-noun format. Most cmdlets have parameters that can be used to pass options to the cmdlet.

Compatibility View A feature in Internet Explorer 11 that provides backward compatibility for websites and applications that were targeted for previous versions of Internet Explorer.

Computer Management One of the most commonly used administrative tools. This MMC console contains the snap-ins to manage most Windows 10 components.

configuration partition The Active Directory partition that holds general information about the Active Directory forest and application configuration information. It is replicated to all domain controllers in the Active Directory forest.

configuration set The subset of files from a distribution share that are required for a particular answer file. A configuration set is more compact than a distribution share.

Connection Manager Administration Kit (CMAK) A feature that can be installed on Windows clients or servers to create VPN deployment packages.

Continuum The Windows 10 feature that automatically adjusts Windows 10 between desktop mode and tablet mode as the device state changes.

Continuum for phone The feature for Windows 10 phones that allows external peripherals, such as mouse, keyboard, monitor, or projectors, to be used.

Control Panel An alternative location to configure Windows 10 settings. Used when advanced settings are not available in Settings.

Cortana A personalized virtual search assistant. Cortana can use voice recognition to accept commands from the user.

counters The performance indicators that can be recorded in Performance Monitor.

Data Collector Set A grouping of counters that you can use to log system data and generate reports.

Data Execution Prevention (DEP) A feature designed to prevent the installation of malware by monitoring processes to ensure that they do not access unauthorized memory spaces.

Data Manager The Performance Monitor component that is used to automatically manage performance logs.

data synchronization A system that synchronizes files between multiple devices. This allows data to be accessed when offline.

default gateway A router on the local network that is used to deliver packets to remote networks.

default profile The profile that is copied when new user profiles are created.

Defragment and Optimize Drives An administrative tool that moves file blocks around in the disk to make individual files contiguous and faster to access.

Deployment Image Servicing and Management (DISM) A command-line tool that can be used to service Windows 10 images offline or online and perform imaging operations.

desktop mode The traditional configuration for a Windows 10 computer that is optimized for use with a mouse and keyboard.

device driver Software that manages the communication between Windows 10 and a particular hardware component.

device driver signing A system that ensures that a device driver is from a known publisher and that the device driver has not been modified since it was signed.

device identification string One or more identifiers included in a hardware device that is used by Windows 10 to locate and install an appropriate driver for a hardware device.

Device Manager An MMC snap-in that is used to manage hardware components and their device drivers.

device setup class An identifier included with a hardware device driver that describes how the device driver is to be installed.

differencing disk A type of virtual hard disk that tracks changes that would have been made to a parent disk.

DirectAccess An always-on replacement for on-demand VPN connections. All configuration is done on the server side to allow domain-joined clients to connect. Always-on connectivity allows for additional management options.

DirSync A Microsoft tool for synchronizing copies of local identity information into Azure AD. Many administrators still use this name for newer versions of the synchronization software such as Azure AD Connect.

Disk Cleanup An administrative tool that identifies temporary files that are no longer required and provides an option to remove them.

Disk Management console An MMC console snap-in used to administer hard disks in Windows 10.

disk quota A system of tracking owners for file data within an NTFS-formatted partition or volume and the total disk space consumed by each owner. Limits or warning can be established to restrict disk space usage.

DiskPart A command-line tool for managing disks. You can perform advanced operations with DiskPart that are not available in Disk Management.

Distributed File System (DFS) A server role in Windows Server that includes replication of shared folders and virtualization of paths providing access to the shared folders.

distribution share A share configured through Windows SIM to hold drivers and packages that can be added to Windows 10 during installation.

distribution share installation An installation of Windows 10 that is started by running Setup.exe over the network from a distribution share.

domain A logical grouping of computers and users in Active Directory.

domain controller (DC) A server responsible for holding a copy of Active Directory, the domain security database that contains a list of user and computer account security data.

Domain Name System (DNS) A standard service in the TCP/IP protocol used to define how computer names are translated into IP addresses.

domain network The location type that is used when a computer joined to a domain is on the domain network, for example, a corporate office.

domain partition The Active Directory partition that holds domain-specific information, such as user and computer accounts, that is replicated only between domain controllers within the domain.

domain-based network A network where security information is stored centrally in Active Directory.

driver store A central location in Windows 10 where drivers are located before they are installed. A large set of drivers is included with Windows 10.

DVD boot installation An installation of Windows 10 that is started by booting from DVD to run Setup.exe.

dynamic disk A method for organizing disks introduced in Windows 2000 as a replacement for basic disks, but was never very popular. Dynamic disks can have a large number of volumes and also support some fault-tolerant disk configurations.

Dynamic Host Configuration Protocol (DHCP) An automated mechanism to assign IP addresses and IP configuration information over the network.

Dynamic Link Library (DLL) A file that holds application code modules. These modules are shared among applications, so the file is also called a library. DLL files can be replaced to update an application without having to replace the entire application.

Dynamic Memory A feature of Hyper-V that allows the memory allocated to a virtual machine to be increased and decreased based on demand in the virtual machine while it is running.

dynamically expanding disk A virtual hard disk that only uses the physical disk space required to store its contents. The disk file expands and shrinks as data is moved in and out of it.

Ease of Access A collection of settings to make Windows 10 easier to use for those who have physical, visual, or hearing impairment.

Easy Upgrade A simple upgrade process that can be used to upgrade Windows 10 Home to Windows 10 Professional. An Easy Upgrade is purchased through the Windows Store.

Encrypting File System (EFS) An encryption technology for individual files and folders that can be enabled by users. Files encrypted with EFS are not readable without the correct digital identification.

enhanced session mode A type of connectivity between Virtual Machine Connection and the virtual machine based on the RDP protocol, which allows movement of data between the virtual machine and the Hyper-V host.

Enterprise Mobility Suite (EMS) A license suite available for purchase from Microsoft that includes Azure AD Premium, Microsoft Intune, and Azure Rights Management Services.

Enterprise Mode A feature in Internet Explorer and Microsoft Edge that automatically configures various compatibility modes for websites.

Event Viewer An MMC console that is used to view messages generated and logged by Windows 10, applications, and services.

Extensible Authentication Protocol (EAP) A framework that allows multiple authentication protocols to be integrated with the VPN sign-in process.

external network A virtual network that is bound to a physical network adapter and provides access to the physical network.

fast user switching Allows multiple users to have applications running at the same time. However, only one user can be using the console at a time.

File Allocation Table (FAT) A file system used to organize files and folders in a partition or volume. The common versions of FAT supported by Windows 10 include FAT, FAT32, and exFAT.

File and Printer Sharing for Microsoft Networks The service that allows Windows 10 to share files and printers by using the SMB protocol.

File History A feature that is used to back up user files to an external hard drive or file share.

File Signature Verification utility A utility (sigverif. exe) that verifies the digital signature on operating system files and device drivers.

fixed-size disk A type of virtual hard disk that takes the same physical space on disk as the volume of data that it can store.

folder redirection A feature that redirects profile folders from the local computer to a network location.

forest Multiple Active Directory trees with automatic trust relationships between them.

Full Volume Encryption Key (FVEK) The key used to encrypt the Volume Master Key (VMK) when BitLocker Drive Encryption is enabled.

fully qualified domain name (FQDN) The full name of a host on the network, including its host and domain name. For example, the FQDN *www.microsoft.com* includes the host name *www* and the domain name *microsoft.com*.

generalization A process performed by Sysprep to prepare a computer running Windows 10 for imaging. The computer SID, computer name, and hardware information are removed during generalization.

generalize configuration pass This configuration pass is performed when Sysprep is run to generalize Windows 10.

Generation 1 virtual machine A virtual machine that is compatible with older Microsoft virtualization technologies and supports older hardware standards like BIOS and IDE.

Generation 2 virtual machine A virtual machine that is compatible only with newer versions of Hyper-V and supports only newer hardware types such as UEFI. Only more recent operating systems such as Windows 8 or newer can be used.

getmac A command-line utility that can be used to display the MAC address for network adapters on a system.

global catalog server A domain controller that holds a subset of the information in all domain partitions for the entire Active Directory forest.

Group Policy A feature integrated with Active Directory that can be used to centrally manage the configuration of Windows 2000 and newer Windows computers, including Windows 10.

Group Policy Object (GPO) A collection of Group Policy settings that can be applied to client computers.

Group Policy Preferences Part of a Group Policy Object that is typically used to configure the user environment. Preferences can be changed by the user, but are reset again at next sign-in.

Guest account A built-in Windows 10 account with minimal privileges intended to give very limited access to Windows 10. This account is disabled by default.

Hardware Abstraction Layer (HAL) A low-level system driver in Windows 10 that controls communication between Windows 10 and the computer hardware.

hashing algorithm A one-way encryption algorithm that creates a unique identifier that can be used to determine whether data has been changed.

hibernate See S4 state.

hive A discrete body of registry keys and values stored in files as part of the operating system.

homegroup network A feature that allows file sharing between computers on a private network without a complicated setup process.

hostname A command-line utility that can be used to identify the name of the computer.

hybrid sleep The sleep method used by Windows 10 that combines the S3 state and S4 state. When the computer moves to the S3 state, it also saves the memory file required for the S4 state.

hyperthreading A technique used in certain Intel processors to improve their overall performance by working on more than one thread at a time.

Hyper-V Manager The graphical administrative tool for managing virtual machines.

hypervisor The software layer that controls access to hardware after virtualization is enabled.

IEEE (Institute of Electrical and Electronics Engineers) A professional society that promotes and nurtures the development of standards used in the application of electronic technology.

image A collection of files captured using DISM and stored in an image file.

image file A file that stores one or more images (typically operating system installations). The size of an image file is minimized through the use of single-instance storage when a file exists in multiple images.

image-based installation An image-based installation uses DISM to apply an image of an operating system to a computer. The image can include applications as well as the operating system.

initial account The account with administrative privileges created during the installation of Windows 10.

InPrivate Browsing An Internet Explorer 11 and Microsoft Edge feature that prevents caching of web content and logging of web activity in Internet Explorer.

integration services A set of drivers that allows operating systems to use virtualized hardware in a virtual machine. There are also services that facilitate communication between the Hyper-V host and the operating system in the virtual machine.

internal network A virtual network that can be accessed by virtual machines and the Hyper-V host.

Internet Connection Sharing (ICS) A Windows 10 feature that allows multiple computers to share an Internet connection by performing NAT.

Internet Key Exchange v2 Tunneling Protocol (IKEv2) A newer VPN protocol that uses IPsec to secure data, but can authenticate by using a user name and password. This protocol supports VPN Reconnect.

Internet Protocol Version 4 (TCP/IPv4) The standard protocol used on corporate networks and the Internet.

Internet Protocol Version 6 (TCP/IPv6) An updated version of TCP/IPv4 with a much larger address space.

iOS An operating system used for mobile devices that are manufactured by Apple.

IP address The unique address used by computers on an IPv4 or IPv6 network. An IPv4 address is commonly displayed in dotted decimal notation. For example, 10.10.0.50.

ipconfig A command-line utility that can be used to display and manage IP address settings for network interfaces on a computer.

IPsec A protocol that is used to secure and authenticate an IPv4 connection.

iSCSI A protocol for transferring files between a computer and external disk storage over an Ethernet network.

Layer 2 Tunneling Protocol (L2TP) An authentication-only VPN protocol that is combined with IPsec to provide data encryption. It is seldom used because it is difficult to configure.

libraries Virtual folders in File Explorer that combine content from multiple locations to simplify file access.

Link-Local Multicast Name Resolution (LLMNR) A protocol that defines methods for name resolution of local neighboring computers without using DNS, WINS, or NetBIOS name resolution services. LLMNR can operate on IPv4 and IPv6 networks with the use of specially crafted multicast addresses to query client names on other computers.

local security policy A set of security configuration options in Windows 10. These options are used to control user rights, auditing, password settings, and more.

local user account A user account that is defined in the SAM database of a Windows 10 computer. Local user accounts are valid only for the local computer.

Local Users and Groups MMC snap-in An MMC snap-in that is used to manage users and groups.

location type Describes the type of network: public, private, or domain. Different configuration settings are applied based on the location type.

Long Term Servicing Branch (LTSB) An update process to Windows 10 that allows devices to run a feature-stable version of Windows 10 where the operating system is not expected to change configuration frequently. The time between feature releases for LTSB versions are designed to be supported in the long term and change as infrequently as one to three years, able to run without upgrade requirements for up to 10 years.

loopback address The IP address 127.0.0.1 that is used to represent the local computer itself on the network. Traffic sent to the loopback address does not get passed over an actual network; it is processed within the operating system without using an actual network connection.

malware Malicious software designed to perform unauthorized acts on your computer. Malware includes viruses, worms, and spyware.

Manage Add-ons A tool in Internet Explorer 11 that makes it easier to identify, disable, and remove unwanted add-ons.

mandatory profile A profile that cannot be changed by users. Ntuser.dat is renamed to Ntuser.man.

Master Boot Record (MBR) The Master Boot Record exists at the very first sector of an IBM-formatted hard disk. It contains code to start the load process for an operating system from a partition or volume on the disk, a partition table to indicate what space has been reserved as partitions, and a signature sequence of bytes used to identify the disk to the operating system.

metadata Information or properties for a file or other object. Windows 10 allows you to include tags as additional metadata for files.

Microsoft account An account that is stored online by Microsoft. You can use it to authenticate to multiple Microsoft cloud services and Windows 10.

Microsoft BitLocker Administration and Monitoring A tool included in the Microsoft Desktop Optimization Pack that is use to centrally deploy, manage, and monitor BitLocker.

Microsoft CHAP v2 (MS-CHAP v2) An older authentication protocol commonly used with PPTP VPNs that is now considered insecure.

Microsoft Deployment Toolkit (MDT) A set of best practices, scripts, and tools to help automate the deployment of Windows operating systems.

Microsoft Edge The new web browser in Windows 10 that replaces Internet Explorer. It is completely redesigned to avoid the legacy support issues encountered with Internet Explorer and to have better support for web standards such as HTML5.

Microsoft Management Console (MMC) A graphical interface shell that provides a structured environment to build management utilities.

Microsoft Passport A multifactor authentication system in Windows 10 that enhances security by avoiding the use of a user name and password. Biometric authentication on the client allows access to the remote system.

Microsoft Store for Business A customizable online store for businesses to organize Windows Store apps for their users.

MMC console A collection of one or more snap-ins that are saved as an .msc file for later use.

MMC snap-in A small software component that can be added to an MMC console to provide functionality. An MMC snap-in typically manages some part of Windows.

Mobile Application Management (MAM) Software and services responsible for provisioning and controlling access to mobile apps that are used in a business environment, on both BYOD and corporate-assigned devices.

Mobile Device Management (MDM) An administrative system that allows corporate administrators to deploy, secure, monitor, and integrate mobile devices such as laptops, tablets, and smartphones into the corporate ecosystem, using various mobile service providers and mobile operating systems.

Modern Standby A new instant-on sleep mode in Windows 10. The computer remains in the S0 state but powers down as much hardware as possible.

mount point An empty folder in an NTFS-formatted file system that is used to point to another FAT, FAT32, or NTFS partition.

multicast A type of address that is shared by multiple computers or devices. All hosts in the multicast group listen for communication on the shared address and all can respond.

multifactor authentication (MFA) A security system that requires more than one method of proving someone or something is who or what it is declared to be. Different methods are used to independently verify the user's identity for a transaction or sign-in attempt, such as a password plus a fingerprint. Each layer increases the difficulty an attacker faces trying to breach the security of a target.

multimaster replication When a domain has multiple domain controllers, all domain controllers are capable of making changes to the security domain database they share. The changes are replicated from one domain controller to another.

multiple desktops A new feature in Windows 10 that allows you to switch between multiple desktops on a single monitor. Each desktop can have different applications.

multiple monitors Attaching two or more displays to a single computer. The information can be exactly the same on each display, or each display can be used independently by using extended mode.

multiprocessor A term used to refer to a computer with more than one CPU.

multitasking A term used to describe the appearance of more than one application sharing the CPU of the computer. To the user, the applications all seem to be running at the same time.

multitouch A method of input on a touch screen or a touch pad that allows two or more points of contact on a high-precision touch device. This enables precision gestures to interact with the Windows 10 environment.

nbtstat A command-line utility that can be used to display protocol statistics and current TCP/IP connections using NetBIOS over TCP/IP.

nested virtualization A new Hyper-V feature in Windows 10 that allows you to enable Hyper-V in a virtual machine, which can then host its own virtual machines.

netsh A command-line utility that can be used to display, change, add, and delete network configuration settings on a computer, including basic and advanced settings.

netstat A command-line utility that can be used to display protocol statistics and current TCP/IP network connections.

Network Address Translation (NAT) A system that allows multiple computers to share a single IP address when connecting to the Internet.

Network and Sharing Center A central location to view network status and configure network settings.

network discovery A setting that controls how your computer views other computers on the network and advertises its presence on the network.

network driver The software responsible for enabling communication between Windows 10 and the network device in your computer.

network location awareness The ability for Windows 10 to detect when it is connected to a different network and perform actions based on the change.

New Technology File System (NTFS) A file system introduced with Windows NT. NTFS supports advanced features to add reliability, security, and flexibility that file systems such as FAT and FAT32 do not have.

nslookup A command-line utility that can be used to view or debug the data returned from a DNS server in response to a DNS name resolution query.

NT File System (NTFS) A standard for organizing files and folders on a hard disk partition. This standard is more complex than FAT but adds more management features. This is the preferred standard for storing files on a hard disk.

Ntuser.dat The file containing user-specific registry entries in a user profile.

offline files A feature that Windows 10 clients can use to synchronize files from a file share to the local computer for offline use.

offline update An offline update is applied to Windows 10 during installation before Windows 10 is started. The packages used for offline updates are supplied by Microsoft.

offlineServicing configuration pass The second configuration pass that is performed after the Windows image has been copied to the local hard drive. This configuration pass applies packages such as security updates, language packs, and device drivers before Windows 10 is started.

OneDrive Cloud-based storage that is provided when you create a Microsoft account. You can access files in OneDrive through File Explorer or a web browser.

oobeSystem configuration pass The final configuration pass before installation is complete, applied during the user out-of-box experience (OOBE). This configuration pass is typically used in conjunction with Sysprep and DISM.

Open Database Connectivity (ODBC) A standard mechanism for applications to access databases.

organizational unit (OU) A container within a domain that is used to create a hierarchy that can be used to organize user and computer accounts and apply group policies.

page description language A language that defines the layout of content for a print job.

partition table A data structure contained in the MBR that is used to identify reserved areas of disk space for hard disks formatted for x86 computers. The partition table holds a maximum of four entries originally tasked to point to a maximum of four primary partitions, or three primary and one extended partitions.

pass-through authentication Automatic authentication to a remote resource when the local computer passes the local credentials to the remote computer.

password policy A collection of settings to control password characteristics such as length and complexity.

pathping A command-line utility that can be used to test IP communications between the computer running the utility and a remote target. In addition to the basic IP communication test, the *pathping* utility will trace the routers involved in establishing the IP communication path.

peer-to-peer network A network where all computers store their own security information and share data.

Performance Monitor A tool within the Microsoft Management Console (MMC) that allows you to visually display the data generated by counters and troubleshoot the performance of your computer.

performance tuning The process for collecting system performance data, analyzing system performance data, and implementing system performance improvements.

picture password authentication An authentication method where you trace gestures on a picture.

PIN A personal identification number that allows users to identify themselves during the authentication or sign-in process.

PIN authentication An authentication method where you enter a device-specific PIN rather than a user name and password.

ping A command-line utility that can be used to test IP communications between the computer running the utility and a remote target.

pixel A single dot on a display.

Plug and Play technology A general term used to describe hardware that can be plugged in to the computer system and removed at any time. The computer will recognize the hardware dynamically, load a device driver for it, and make it available to the user in a short period of time.

Point-to-Point Protocol over Ethernet (PPPoE) A protocol used to secure connections over most DSL lines.

Point-to-Point Tunneling Protocol (PPTP) An older VPN protocol that authenticates based on user name and password. It is generally considered insecure, but is easy to configure.

Pop-up Blocker An Internet Explorer and Microsoft Edge feature that prevents most pop-up advertising from being displayed while you browse websites.

Portable Document Format (PDF) A popular document format that is also supported as a page description language by some printers.

PostScript A common page description language used by printers to describe how a page is printed.

power plan A set of configuration options for power management. The Balanced, Power saver, and High performance power plans are created by default.

powercfg.exe A command-line utility for configuring power management.

preemptive multitasking A method for applications to share a CPU and appear that they are all running at the same time. This method adds time limits and priority levels to determine how long an application can use the processor and which application gets to go next. An application can also be preempted by another application if it has a higher priority level.

Previous Versions The tab available to restore files and folders that have been backed up by File History or Backup and Restore (Windows 7).

Print Management snap-in A printer management tool in Windows 10 that allows you to manage local and remote printers.

Printer Command Language (PCL) A common language used by printers to describe how a page is printed.

printer driver Software used by Windows 10 to properly communicate with a specific make and model of printer.

printer driver package An enhanced printer driver that can contain additional software.

printer driver store A location in Windows 10 that caches printer drivers and is capable of storing multiple versions of a printer driver.

private network (1) The location type in Windows 10 that is used for trusted networks where limited security is required, for example, a small office. (2) In Client Hyper-V, a virtual network that can be accessed only by virtual machines.

process A term used to describe the files, memory, and application code that combine together to form a single running application. Each application running on a multitasking system is referenced by a single process.

processor affinity A standard in which a process that starts in a computer with more than one CPU is usually assigned to that CPU again the next time it runs.

product activation A process put in place by Microsoft to reduce piracy. Unique information about your computer is sent to Microsoft to ensure that the package of Windows 10 purchased is installed on only a single computer.

Protected EAP An enhanced variation of EAP that secures authentication by using SSL. For PPTP VPN connections, it can secure MS-CHAP v2 authentication.

Protected Mode A feature in Internet Explorer 11 that isolates any code that runs within Internet Explorer to prevent malware infection.

protocol A standard set of rules that defines how different components of a system operate together.

provisioning A new configuration process for Windows 10 that modifies the configuration of an already installed Windows 10 operating system to match corporate standards.

Windows ICD creates provisioning packages that perform that configuration.

public network The location type that is used for untrusted networks where high security is required, for example, a public wireless hotspot.

public profile A profile that is merged with all other user profiles. The public profile does not contain an Ntuser.dat file.

quantum The amount of time allocated to a program running in a preemptive multitasking environment. Once a program's quantum has expired, it must wait for the next available quantum.

recovery drive An optional drive that you can create with a system image from your currently installed operating system and apps.

registry A central store for application and operating system configuration information in Windows 10.

Registry Editor The graphical tool included in Windows 10 to edit the registry. Commonly known as regedit.

registry key A section within a hive that can contain other registry keys and values.

Reliability Monitor A utility that rates the system stability of Windows 10 over time and correlates system events with changes in system stability.

remote access A system that allows dial-up or VPN clients to remotely retrieve and save data as though they are on the local network, but with much slower performance.

Remote Assistance A feature in Windows 10 that allows a helper to connect to a Windows 10 computer and view the screen or remotely control the computer.

remote control A system for remote data or application access where only screen draw commands and keystrokes are sent between the client and computer being remote controlled. Typically, remote control provides better performance than remote access.

Remote Desktop The feature in Windows 10 that you can enable to allow remote control of the computer by using RDP on port 3389.

Remote Desktop Connection The client software included in Windows 10 that uses RDP to connect to Remote Desktop and RDS. It can be started at a command line with additional options by running *mstsc.exe*.

Remote Desktop Services A server role for Windows Server that is used to provide virtual desktops and Remote-App programs to users.

RemoteApp A feature in Remote Desktop Services that presents clients with a single app in a window.

Reports Reports created in Performance Monitor that use XML-based rules to analyze logged data and display meaningful results.

Resilient File System (ReFS) A file system introduced with Windows Server 2012 that supports basic NTFS-like features and self-healing technology for resilient bulk file storage when used together with Storage Spaces technology.

Resource Monitor A utility launched from Performance Monitor that provides real-time monitoring of the most common system performance indicators.

restore point A snapshot of operating system and program files at a specific point in time that can be restored to roll back to a point in time when the operating system or apps were stable.

roaming profile A user profile that is stored in a network location and is accessible from multiple computers. Roaming profiles move with users from computer to computer.

route A command-line utility that can be used to display and manage the routing table.

routing table A data table that is used by Windows 10 to select the next IP address data must be delivered to, to ultimately deliver data to a given target address.

S0 state An ACPI power-saving mode that disables power to specific devices as requested by the operating system, but keeps the overall system running.'

S3 state An ACPI power-saving mode that disables power to all devices except RAM.

S4 state An ACPI power-saving mode that saves the contents of RAM to disk and then disables power to all devices including RAM.

schema partition Holds the definition of all Active Directory objects and their attributes. It is replicated to all domain controllers in the Active Directory forest.

screen resolution The number of pixels that are displayed on your display.

Secedit A command-line tool that is used to apply, export, or analyze security templates.

secure sign-in Adds the requirement to press Ctrl+Alt+Delete before signing in.

Secure Socket Tunneling Protocol (SSTP) A VPN protocol that uses SSL to secure authentication credentials and data.

Security Accounts Manager (SAM) database The database used by Windows 10 to store local user and group information.

Security Configuration and Analysis tool An MMC snap-in that is used to apply, export, or analyze security templates.

Security Identifier (SID) A user- or group-specific number that is added to the access control list of a resource when a user or group is assigned access.

Security Set Identifier (SSID) A unique ID that identifies a wireless access point to the wireless networking clients that send data to it.

security template An .inf file that contains security settings that can be applied to a computer or analyzed against a computer's existing configuration.

Server Message Block (SMB) The protocol used for Windows-based file and printer sharing.

service (1) A Windows application that runs in the background without user interaction. (2) Functionality provided to remote clients over the network.

Services An MMC console used to manage Windows services.

Settings A central interface for managing common Windows 10 settings. It is available from the Start menu.

smart card A physical card containing a certificate that can be used as an authentication method.

SmartScreen Filter An Internet Explorer and Microsoft Edge feature that warns you about websites known to install malicious software or used in phishing attacks.

Software Assurance (SA) An option when purchasing Microsoft software that allows you to automatically receive the latest version of a product. For example, if you purchased Windows 8 with Software Assurance, you would automatically be able to upgrade to Windows 10.

specialize configuration pass The configuration pass that is performed after hardware has been detected. This is the most common configuration pass to apply settings.

standard user account A type of user account that does not have privileges to modify settings for other users. This type of account is a member of the Users local group.

stateful automatic address configuration In IPv6, this is automatic address configuration by using DHCPv6.

stateless automatic address configuration In IPv6, this is automatic address configuration obtained from the network routers.

Steps Recorder A tool that can be used to record the steps required to generate a problem and store the steps and screenshots in a file.

storage pool A logical collection of disks that have been allocated to Storage Spaces. Disks must be assigned to a storage pool before Storage Spaces can use them.

storage space A virtual disk created from the space made available by a storage pool in Storage Spaces.

Storage Spaces The Microsoft software-based disk pooling technology that allows for different levels of resiliency to disk failure and provides virtualized volume storage within the disk pool.

subnet mask A number that defines which part of an IP address is the network ID and which part is the host ID.

symmetric encryption algorithm An encryption algorithm that uses the same key to encrypt and decrypt data.

Sysprep A tool that is used to generalize Windows 10 and prepare computers for imaging.

System Audit Mode cleanup action An option in Sysprep that triggers the computer to enter audit mode and run the auditSystem and auditUser configuration passes on reboot.

System Center 2012 Configuration Manager (SCCM) Management software developed by Microsoft to manage large groups of computers, primarily deployed on-premises.

System Center Configuration Manager A software package that can perform inventory, implement a standardized configuration, deploy software, deploy operating systems, and deploy software updates.

System Configuration The administrative tool that gives you access to control the boot configuration, service startup, application startup, and system tools.

System on a Chip (SoC) A hardware platform that combines multiple devices that would normally be found as discrete components inside a computer, but instead are combined into a single, silicon chip. The SoC design allows for the creation of computers with a small physical form factor, power savings, and simplified device construction.

System Out-of-Box Experience cleanup action An option in Sysprep that triggers the computer to run the oobeSystem configuration pass and start Windows Welcome on reboot.

System Restore The feature that uses system protection to create and restore system restore points.

Systems Management Server An earlier version of SCCM.

tablet mode The configuration for Windows 10 that is optimized for use with a touch screen.

Task Manager A utility that allows you to view overall system information and manipulate processes.

Task Scheduler A utility that allows you to schedule tasks to run at a particular time or based on specific events occurring.

Teredo A system to tunnel IPv6 addressed packets over an IPv4 network, even if NAT is used on the IPv4 network.

thread A piece of code that performs a specific, single task. An application is written as one or more threads, each of which performs a specific task within the application. The thread is typically seen as a unit of work for the CPU to perform.

Thunderbolt A trade name for a high-speed, hardware-based interface to connect external devices to a computer, co-developed by Apple and Intel.

tracert A command-line utility that can be used to trace the routers involved in establishing an IP communication path between the computer running the command and a target address.

tree A group of Active Directory domains that share the same naming context and have automatic trust relationships among them.

trusted platform module (TPM) A chip on the motherboard of a computer that is designed to securely store encryption keys and certificates.

unattend.xml An answer file that is automatically searched for during the generalize, auditSystem, auditUser, and oobeSystem configuration passes.

unattended installation An installation that does not require any user input because all necessary configuration information is provided by an answer file.

unicast A type of network address that is assigned to a single computer or device.

universal apps A developer platform strategy to enable the development of applications that can run on every Windows device, including phones, tablets, laptops, desktops, and Xbox gaming centers.

Universal Naming Convention (UNC) A naming system used by Windows computers to locate network file shares and network printers. The format is \\servername\sharename.

Universal Windows Platform (UWP) A common application platform available on every device that runs Windows 10. The UWP provides a guaranteed core programming interface across devices. The developer can create a single application package that can be installed onto a wide range of devices and unlock the unique capabilities of each device.

upgrade installation An installation that migrates all of the settings from a preexisting Windows operating system to Windows 10.

user account Required account used for authentication to prove the identity of a person signing in to Windows 10.

User Account Control (UAC) A feature in Windows 10 that elevates user privileges only when required.

User Accounts applet A legacy interface for user management in Control Panel.

User Experience Virtualization (UE-V) A tool included in the Microsoft Desktop Optimization Pack that is used to synchronize operating system and application settings for a user between computers.

User Principal Name (UPN) The name that uniquely identifies a user within an identity directory such as Active Directory or Azure Active Directory. It looks similar to an email address, with a user name followed by the @ symbol, and then a domain associated with that user. The domain name is formatted to appear like a DNS name. A sample UPN would be *Bob.Smith@example.com*. No other user in the directory could share this UPN.

user profile A collection of desktop and environment configurations for a specific user or group of users. By default, each user has a separate profile stored in C:\Users.

User State Migration Tool (USMT) A set of scriptable command-line utilities that are used to migrate user settings and files from a source computer to a destination computer.

USMT is typically used by large organizations during deployments of desktop operating systems.'

VHD Set A type of virtual hard disk that is designed to be shared between multiple virtual machines.

Virtual Desktop A new feature in Windows 10 that allows users to create multiple desktops with different applications and switch between them on a single monitor.

virtual hard disk (VHD) A file that is internally structured to store data like a file system. A VHD can be attached in Windows 10 and the contents accessed like a hard disk. VHDs can be fixed size or dynamically expanding. For Windows 10, they can also be VHD or VHDX format.

virtual machine A set of hardware resources that has been allocated for virtualization to run an operating system.

Virtual Machine Connection The graphical tool that is used to connect to virtual machines and interact with them.

virtual memory The combination of physical memory and the paging file.

virtual private network (VPN) An encrypted connection from a client to a remote access server over a public network.

virtual smart card An authentication method similar to a smart card, but the certificate is stored in a TPM on the motherboard rather than on a physical card.

virtual switch A virtual component that allows you to create virtual networks that virtual machines can use.

virtualization Allows the hardware of a single computer to be shared by multiple operating systems running at the same time.

volume A term used to refer to a region of disk space reserved to store file data. The term is used to generically refer to both dynamic disk volumes and basic disk partitions.

Volume Activation Management Tool (VAMT) A tool that can be installed to provide volume activation with KMS activation keys used with volume licensing. It is equivalent to the Volume Activation Service in Windows Server 2012 R2 and Windows Server 2016.

Volume Master Key (VMK) The key used to encrypt hard drive data when BitLocker Drive Encryption is enabled.

VPN Reconnect A feature of IKEv2 VPN connections that automatically reconnects after a network interruption.

Win32 Applications designed to run in a Windows 32-bit instruction environment.

Win64 Applications designed to run in a Windows 64-bit instruction environment.

Windows 10 Assessment and Deployment Kit (ADK) A collection of utilities and documentation for automating the deployment of Windows 10.

Windows as a Service (WaaS) An update process for Windows 10 in which new features are continuously published and installed to existing Windows 10 installations.

Windows Azure RemoteApp A cloud-based environment hosted by Microsoft that allows you to provide your own applications through RemoteApp.

Windows Backup and Restore (Windows 7) The legacy backup utility that is included to provide access to backups from Windows 7.

Windows Defender Anti-malware software included with Windows 10.

Windows Deployment Services (WDS) A Windows Server service that is used to simplify the process of applying images to computers.

Windows Firewall A host-based firewall included with Windows 10 that can perform inbound and outbound packet filtering.

Windows Firewall and Advanced Security utility A utility that is used to configure Windows Firewall and IPsec rules.

Windows Hello Biometric authentication functionality in Windows 10. At release, Windows Hello supports fingerprints, facial recognition, and iris scanning.

Windows Imaging and Configuration Designer (ICD) A utility that is used to create provisioning packages for Windows 10. Windows ICD can also create bootable media that includes a Windows 10 installation image and a provisioning package.

Windows Imaging Format (WIM) A file-based image format developed by Microsoft to store multiple images in a single file.

Windows Internet Naming Service (WINS) A system used to resolve computer NetBIOS names to IP addresses.

Windows Memory Diagnostics Tool A utility used to perform tests on the physical memory of a computer.

Windows on Windows 64 (WOW64) A system in Windows that allows 32-bit Windows apps to run on a 64-bit operating system.

Windows PE A limited version of Windows that can be used to perform recovery tasks and install Windows 10.

Windows Peer-to-Peer Networking A networking technology included in Windows Vista and later operating systems that allows clients to use IPv6 to communicate with each other over LANs or the Internet.

Windows PowerShell An enhanced command-line interface that can be used to perform administrative tasks.

Windows PowerShell Direct A new feature in Windows 10 that allows you to perform PowerShell remoting from the Hyper-V host directly to the virtual machine without using a virtual network.

Windows PowerShell ISE An integrated scripting environment for Windows PowersShell that includes color coding as you type and debugging functionality.

Windows Server Update Services (WSUS) A Windows Server application that is used to control the process of downloading and applying updates to Windows servers and Windows clients.

Windows Store apps The newest application environment that is designed to be cross-platform with phones, tablets, and desktop computers.

Windows System Image Manager (SIM) A utility that is used to create answer files for Windows 10 unattended installations. Windows SIM can also create distribution shares and configuration sets.

Windows To Go A portable version of Windows 10 that can be created on a USB drive.

windowsPE configuration pass The first configuration pass performed during Setup, which can be used to perform tasks such as disk partitioning and entering the product key.

wireless access point (WAP) A device that allows wireless devices to connect through it to a wired network.

Work Folders A system that allows users to synchronize a single folder on a file server between multiple devices. The Work Folders client is included in Windows 10.

WPA2-Enterprise A modern security type for wireless networks that uses 802.1x authentication.

WPA2-Personal A modern security type for wireless networks that uses a pre-shared key for authentication.

XML Paper Specification (XPS) A document format that describes how a page should be displayed. XPS is similar to Adobe Portable Document Format (PDF).

Index